Nursing Ethics
Across the Curriculum and Into Practice

Second Edition

Janie B. Butts, DSN, RN
The University of Southern Mississippi
School of Nursing
Hattiesburg, Mississippi

Karen L. Rich, MN, PhD, RN
The University of Southern Mississippi
School of Nursing
Long Beach, Mississippi

JONES AND BARTLETT PUBLISHERS
Sudbury, Massachusetts
BOSTON   TORONTO   LONDON   SINGAPORE

World Headquarters
Jones and Bartlett Publishers
40 Tall Pine Drive
Sudbury, MA 01776
978-443-5000
info@jbpub.com
www.jbpub.com

Jones and Bartlett Publishers
Canada
6339 Ormindale Way
Mississauga, Ontario L5V 1J2
CANADA

Jones and Bartlett Publishers
International
Barb House, Barb Mews
London W6 7PA
UK

Jones and Bartlett's books and products are available through most bookstores and online booksellers. To contact Jones and Bartlett Publishers directly, call 800-832-0034, fax 978-443-8000, or visit our website, www.jbpub.com.

Substantial discounts on bulk quantities of Jones and Bartlett's publications are available to corporations, professional associations, and other qualified organizations. For details and specific discount information, contact the special sales department at Jones and Bartlett via the above contact information or send an email to specialsales@jbpub.com.

Library of Congress Cataloging-in-Publication Data
Butts, Janie B.
Nursing ethics : across the curriculum and into practice / Janie E. Butts and Karen L. Rich. — 2nd ed.
  p. ; cm.
 Includes bibliographical references and index.
 ISBN-13: 978-0-7637-4898-2 (alk. paper)
 ISBN-10: 0-7637-4898-6 (alk. paper)
 1. Nursing ethics. I. Rich, Karen, MN. II. Title.
 [DNLM: 1. Ethics, Nursing. WY 85 B988n 2008]
 RT85.B78 2008
 174.2—dc22
                          2007023655
6048

Production Credits
Executive Editor: Kevin Sullivan
Acquisitions Editor: Emily Ekle
Associate Editor: Amy Sibley
Production Director: Amy Rose
Editorial Assistant: Patricia Donnelly
Associate Production Editor: Amanda Clerkin
Senior Marketing Manager: Katrina Gosek
Associate Marketing Manager: Rebecca Wasley
Manufacturing and Inventory Supervisor: Amy Bacus
Composition: Paw Print Media
Cover Design: Kristin E. Ohlin
Cover Image and Interior Icon Credit: © Bortel Pavel/ShutterStock, Inc.
Printing and Binding: Malloy, Inc
Cover Printing: Malloy, Inc.

Printed in the United States of America
12 11 10 09 08   10 9 8 7 6 5 4 3

Acknowledgments

To Ronnie—Forever my husband, lover, greatest friend, and eternal soul mate!

To our family—David and Annie who continue to be most passionate about life and who co-wrote the lyrics "Questions Make Me Free."

Denny and Valerie who are realizing their dreams together and are saturating themselves with love, work, and fun.

Dylan Blake, David's son and our grandchild, who was fearlessly and wonderfully made, and the "I Ching" for our abode! You "guys" kindle our lives, and put the song, the passion, and joy in our hearts!

To our fabulous dachshunds—Copper, Savannah, and Bridget

You are my wonderful crew who has been at my side for every word that I have written and every step I have taken.

I love you all.

—Janie B.

To Patsy, my family, and my students. You all have taught me so much.

—Karen

Special Acknowledgments

We want to express our sincere appreciation to the staff at Jones and Bartlett Publishers, especially Kevin, Tricia, and Amanda for their continued encouragement, assistance, and support during the writing process and publication of our book.

We also want to express our thanks to Dr. Beverly Kopala, Associate Professor, Marcella Niehoff School of Nursing, Loyola University Chicago for her encouragement and suggestions for the 2nd edition of our book.

Contents

Chapter 9 • Psychiatric/Mental Health Nursing Ethics   311

Karen L. Rich

Chapter 10 • Ethics and the Nursing Care of Elders   353

Karen L. Rich

Preface

Like poppies, nurses must learn to thrive in disturbed soil.

We believe that this is a very exciting time in the history of nursing. Although nurses continue to experience many difficult areas in their terrain of practice, nurses have more autonomy than ever before. With autonomy comes responsibility. Nurses face many day-to-day ethical issues that they must be prepared to handle. Nurses need to develop a firm sense of practical wisdom and to think critically about the ethics of their practice. Practical wisdom and moral ways of being do not just happen. They must be developed with careful education and thought and intelligent habits of practice.

We chose the poppy flower as our theme for the second edition of *Nursing Ethics: Across the Curriculum and Into Practice.* We believe that there are several ways that poppies can be used as a metaphor for nursing ethics. Poppies thrive well in conditions of drought. They grow and produce beautiful blooms even when their seeds are not planted deep into the soil. Though they are individually gorgeous, poppies often look best when they are mixed among other flowers. Lastly, poppies are used to pictorially describe a form of mistreatment and jealousy among professional colleagues with the metaphor of "the tall poppy syndrome." This syndrome is discussed in Chapter 2 of the book.

Nurses must learn to flourish in work environments that are not always ideal. Often, nurses, like poppy seeds, are thrown into situations in which they must flourish when they do not feel that they are planted deeply. Nurses help patients the most when they work collaboratively with other members of the healthcare community. It is unfortunate that current evidence has shown that nurses often treat one another badly. The tall poppy syndrome is something that nurses need to acknowledge but work to eliminate within the nursing community. Nurses, like a variety of poppy flower colors, differ from one another; however, all ethical nurses are valued members of the one group. White poppies are a symbol of peace and harmonious relationships. We believe that harmonious relationships are at the heart of nursing ethics.

Special Notes to Educators, Students, and Practicing Nurses

NLNAC and AACN Recommendations

Accrediting agencies have recommended that nursing educators include ethics and ethical decision-making strategies in their nursing curricula (American Association of Colleges of Nursing [AACN], 2003; National League of Nursing Accrediting Commission [NLNAC], 2006). The NLNAC competencies for the 21st century for nurses were adapted based on the Pew Health Commission Competencies for 2005. Specifically, the following excerpt contains the core competency and strategies for nurses practicing ethical behaviors:

NLNAC Core Competency: *Exhibit Ethical Behaviors in all Professional Activities*

- Embrace a personal ethic of social responsibility and service
- Provide counseling for patients in situations where ethical issues arise
- Participate in discussion of ethical issues in health care as they affect communities, society, and health professions (NLNAC, Interpretive Guidelines, 2006, p. 86)

In the draft of the revised document, as well as the existing document, titled *The Essentials of Baccalaureate Nursing Education* by AACN (2007), members emphasized that nursing students and professional nurses must be able to meet the challenges of today by seeking continued higher education. Nursing educators need to incorporate ethical principles and concepts of ethical decision making in nursing curricula for nursing students. The essential component of ethical reasoning is emphasized by AACN in this document.

AACN Essentials: *Integrative Strategy for Ethics*

- Involvement in activities to promote ethical reasoning, advocacy, collaboration, and social justice (p. 5)

AACN Essentials: *End-of-Program Competency*

- Engage in ethical reasoning and actions to promote social justice, advocacy, collaboration, and understanding across cultures (p. 3)

Before we began writing our book, we evaluated the significance of the NLNAC and AACN documents. Some of the moral issues that nurses encounter on a daily basis leave nurses on uncertain ethical ground. Whether practicing nurses become bogged down in ethical situations about death, abortion, or saving premature infants, nurses will most likely experience moral suffering when they begin to question the meaning and issues of life and death. Nurses must be prepared to attach their own meanings to life and death, and nursing students and practicing nurse clinicians need to acquire foundational knowledge about ethics, ethical reasoning, and decision-making strategies to prepare them for the ethical issues that they encounter daily. Included in this book are decision-making approaches and models, rationale for decisions, and various topics about ethical patient care.

NCLEX-RN®️ Test Plan for 2007

The National Council of State Boards of Nursing's new *NCLEX-RN®️ Test Plan* (2007) has as its goal for nursing care in any setting, "preventing illness; alleviating suffering; protecting, promoting, and restoring health; and promoting dignity in dying" (p. 1).

   NCLEX-RN®️ Test Plan: Safe and Effective Care Environment—Management of Care

- Ethical practice

   NCLEX-RN®️ Test Plan: Psychosocial Integrity

- End-of-life care
- Grief and loss
- Religious and spiritual influences on health

   NCLEX-RN®️ Test Plan: Physiological Integrity—Basic Care and Comfort

- Palliative/comfort care

Purposes and Readership

We have four purposes for this book. First, we wanted to provide a nursing ethics book that includes an exploration of a wide array of ethical issues in nursing. We wanted to include bioethical issues that nurses encounter every day—the ones that Fry and Veatch (2000) stated were the "flesh and blood" issues (p. 1)—but we wanted to cover the issues from a humanistic perspective. In the body of the text, we have included the most current scholarly literature, related news briefs, and research and legal findings regarding ethical issues. The content of our book is also based on theoretical foundations, clinical evidence, and case study analysis for students and nurse clinicians in practice.

Second, a prominent feature of this book is its "across the curriculum" format for undergraduate nursing students. The book can be used as a supplementary textbook when students use it in each nursing course. We strongly believe that if ethical concepts and bioethical issues are integrated in the beginning of nursing programs and throughout curricula, students will become more mindful of the myriad of ethical challenges that they will face in practice and then become habituated to resolving moral conflicts. Ultimately, we believe nurses will want to find ways to participate in the large-scale bioethical deliberations and decision making regarding their patients' and families' life and death issues.

As a third purpose, the book also is intended for RN to BSN students and their curricula, especially in ethics courses, professional development courses, or leadership courses. Even though RN to BSN students bring a wealth of real flesh-and-blood experiences with them to share in the classroom, they often return to school without substantial exposure to ethics classes or ethical content.

The last part of the book's title, "into practice," is related to the book's fourth purpose. Nurses' work is nursing ethics. The content of the book will stimulate the moral imagination of practicing nurses so that they can integrate ethical principles, theories, and decision-making skills into their everyday practice.

Pedagogical Features

We have presented in this second edition a more comprehensive view of the concepts that we presented in the first edition of the book. We focused more on the philosophical and theoretical aspects of ethical issues and dilemmas so that the foundation for practical application is sound. The pedagogical features highlighted in our second edition are designed to stimulate critical thinking and reflective, moral reasoning for students and nurse clinicians. We have provided Web links to healthcare and nursing information related to everyday ethics for students and nurse clinicians. The features of the book include:

- Quotes at the beginning of each chapter and some throughout the book
- Key terms at the begnning of each chapter and bolded throughout the text with definitions throughout the body of the text
- Content objectives at the beginning of each chapter
- Numerous critical thinking activities entitled "Ethical Reflections" at the end of many topical discussions
- Critical thinking and reflection boxes entitled "Highlights from the Field" throughout each chapter

- "Web Ethics" boxes in each chapter
- Summary of concepts at the end of each chapter
- A case study at the end of most chapters with critical thinking questions
- Multiple choice questions at the end of every chapter
- ANA *Code of Ethics for Nurses with Interpretive Statements* (2001) in full text as Appendix A and references to the *Code of Ethics for Nurses* throughout this text and a boxed reference within most chapters
- *ICN Code of Ethics for Nurses* (2006) in full text as Appendix B and references to this *Code of Ethics for Nurses* throughout the text
- American Hospital Association's *A Patient's Bill of Rights* as Appendix C
- The *Mississippi Advance Health-Care Directive* along with sample forms as Appendix D

Key Content

Chapter 1: Introduction to Ethical Philosophy, Theories, and Approaches
- Introduction to the meaning of ethics and morality
- Types of ethical inquiry
- Values and a history of moral reasoning
- Overview of ethical theories and approaches

Chapter 2: Introduction to Bioethics, Nursing Ethics, and Ethical Decision Making
- Introduction to bioethics
- Ethical principles
- Social justice
- Definition of ethical dilemmas
- Introduction to nursing ethics
- Critical thinking and ethical decision making
- The Moral Ground Model of ethical decision making
- Nurses as members of the health care team
- The Four Topics Approach to ethical decision making

Chapter 3: Ethics in Professional Nursing Practice
- History of ANA's and ICN's codes of ethics in nursing
- Overview and explanation of the codes of ethics
- Professional boundaries
- Explicit and implied concepts of professional nursing practice

Chapter 4: Ethics in Organizations and Leadership
- Organizational culture
- Organizational trust and other ethical issues
- Unethical and illegal behaviors in organizations, including a highlight of healthcare fraud and conflicts of interest
- Compliance and ethics programs
- Exemplary obligations for healthcare organizations
- Elements of ethical leadership

Chapter 5: Reproductive Issues and Nursing Ethics
- Central ethical dilemmas of abortion and reproductive technology
- Women's reproductive rights
- Moral standing of the fetus and of the mother
- Management of care for women of child-bearing age based on Bergum's (2004) "relational ethics" of environment, embodiment, mutual respect, and engagement

Chapter 6: Infant and Child Nursing Ethics
- Mothering
- Newborn genetic screening
- Universal vaccination
- Children underserved by the United States healthcare system
- Global problems of poverty and infectious diseases
- Child abuse
- Surrogate decision making
- Refusal of treatment
- Withholding and withdrawing treatment

Chapter 7: Adolescent Nursing Ethics
- Health risk behaviors and life-threatening behaviors
- Health risk messages as fear appeals
- Ethical dilemmas involving prevention education: abstinence-only and comprehensive sex education prevention programs
- Management of care for adolescents based on the virtues of trustworthiness, genuineness, compassion, and honesty

Chapter 8: Adult Health Nursing Ethics
- Moral integrity and honesty in nursing
- A reflection on telling the truth by an exemplary nurse from the play *W;t*
- Medicalization and compliance

- Ethical nursing care for patients with chronic illness
- Organ transplantation: the newest recommendations
- Dead donor rule, donors, and recipients
- Ethical nursing care for organ donors and families

Chapter 9: Psychiatric/Mental Health Nursing Ethics
- Characteristics of psychiatric nursing
- Ethical implications of diagnoses
- Stigma
- Boundaries
- Privacy, confidentiality, and privileged communication
- Decisional capacity
- Psychiatric advance directives
- Humanistic approaches and theories

Chapter 10: Ethics and the Nursing Care of Elders
- Ageism
- Elders' search for meaning
- Decisional capacity
- Vulnerability
- Quality of life
- Elder abuse
- Social justice
- Humanistic nursing care

Chapter 11: Community/Public Health Nursing Ethics
- Moral communities
- Principles and approaches to the ethical practice of public health
- Ethics and environmental health
- Communitarian ethics
- Social justice and health disparities
- The virtue of *just generosity*
- Communicable diseases
- Terrorism and disasters
- Genomics
- Servant leadership

Chapter 12: Ethical Issues in End-of-Life Nursing Care
- The ideal death, the history of death, and euthanasia

- The concept of human suffering as it relates to death and dying
- Types of advance directives, surrogates, and end-of-life issues
- Landmark legal cases, such as the Schiavo case
- Physical, emotional, and spiritual care of dying patients and their families

Instructor's Resources

Instructor's Resources are provided on the catalog page for our book at the Jones and Bartlett Publishers Web site (www.jbpub.com/nursing). Instructor's Resources will include PowerPoint slides for each chapter, chapter overviews and objectives, student activities, and chapter test questions.

Comments and Feedback

We are dedicated to making this nursing ethics book the one that will meet your needs for the future. We are interested in your comments about the book. Please email us at jbondbutts@comcast.net or karenrich@cableone.net with feedback or questions concerning the book, questions about ethics, or any questions that you may have regarding the case studies or multiple choice questions in the book. We appreciate your support!

References

American Association of Colleges of Nursing [AACN]. (2007). Draft: Revision of *The essentials of baccalaureate nursing education*. Retrieved August 13, 2007, from http://www.aacn.nche.edu/Education/pdf/BEdraft8-1-07.pdf

Fry, S. T., & Veatch, R. M. (2000). *Case studies in nursing ethics* (2nd ed.). Sudbury, MA: Jones & Bartlett Publishers.

National Council of State Boards of Nursing. (2007, April). *NCLEX-RN test plan*. Retrieved August 13, 2007, from https://www.ncsbn.org/RN_Test_Plan_2007_Web.pdf

National League of Nursing Accrediting Commission. (2006). *Accreditation manual with interpretive guidelines by program type: Core competencies for practicing nurses*. Retrieved August 13, 2007, from http://www.nlnac.org/manuals/NLNACManual2006.pdf

Part I • Theory and Concepts

Introduction to Ethical Philosophy, Theories, and Approaches

Karen L. Rich

A seed will only become a flower if it gets sun and water.

—Louis Gottschalk

OBJECTIVES

After reading this chapter, the reader should be able to:

1. Define the terms *ethics* and *morals* and *philosophical uses of these terms.*
2. Discuss systems of moral reasoning as they have been used throughout history.
3. Use a variety of ethical approaches and theories in personal and professional relationships.

KEY TERMS

Ethics	Ethical relativism	Virtue ethics
Utilitarianism	Ethic of justice	Morals
Ethical subjectivism	Virtues	Narrative ethics
Normative ethics	Cultural relativism	Natural law theory
Casuistry	Common morality	Ethical objectivism
Deontology	Critical theory	Meta-ethics
Values	Kantian deontology	Feminist ethics
Descriptive ethics	Moral reasoning	Categorical imperative
Ethic of care		

Introduction to Ethics

In today's world, "we are in the throes of a giant ethical leap that is essentially embracing all of humankind" (Donahue, 1996, p. 484). Scientific and technological advances, economic realities, pluralistic world views, and global communication make it impossible for nurses to ignore the important ethical issues in the world community, their individual lives, and their work. As controversial and sensitive ethical issues continue to challenge nurses and other health care professionals, many professionals have begun to develop an appreciation for personal philosophies of ethics and the diverse viewpoints of others.

Ethical directives sometimes are not clearly evident and people often disagree about what is right and wrong. These factors lead some people to believe that ethics can be based merely on personal opinions. However, if nurses are to enter into the global dialogue about ethics, they must do more than practice ethics based simply on their personal opinions, their intuition, or the unexamined beliefs that are proposed by other people. It is important for nurses to have a basic understanding of the various concepts, principles, approaches, and theories used in ethics throughout history and to identify and analyze ethical issues and dilemmas that are relevant to nurses in the 21st century. Mature ethical sensitivities are critical to ethical practice, and as Hope (2004) proposed, "we need to develop our hearts as well as our minds" (p. 6).

Know the past to relate it to the present

The Meaning of Ethics and Morality

Ethics, a branch of philosophy, means different things to different people. When the term is narrowly defined according to its original use, ethics is the study of ideal human behavior and ideal ways of being. The approaches to ethics and the meanings of ethically related concepts have varied over time among philosophers and ethicists. For example, Aristotle believed that ideal behaviors are practices that lead to the end goal of *eudaimonia*, which is synonymous with a high level of happiness or human well-being; whereas Immanuel Kant, an 18th-century philosopher and ethicist, believed that ideal behavior is acting in accordance with one's duty. Human well-being for Kant is having the freedom to exercise autonomy (self-determination) and the capability to think rationally.

ethics

As a philosophical discipline of study, ethics is a systematic approach to understanding, analyzing, and distinguishing matters of right and wrong, good and bad, and admirable and deplorable as they exist along a continuum and as they relate to the well-being of and the relationships among sentient beings. Ethical determinations are applied through the use of formal theories, approaches, and codes of conduct, such as codes that are developed for professions and religions. Ethics is an active process rather than a static condition. Therefore, the concept of *doing ethics* is used by some ethicists. When people are doing ethics, they need to support their beliefs and assertions with sound reasoning. In other words, even if people believe that ethics is totally subjective, they must be able to justify their positions through logical, theoretically based arguments.

As contrasted with *ethics*, **morals** are specific beliefs, behaviors, and ways of being derived from doing ethics. One's morals are judged to be good or bad through systematic ethical analysis. A negative form of the term *morality* is *immorality*, which means that a person's behavior is in opposition to accepted societal, religious, cultural, or professional ethical standards and principles. Examples of immorality include dishonesty, fraud, murder, and sexually abusive acts. *Amoral* is a term that people use to refer to actions that are done with a lack of concern for morally good behavior. For example, murder is immoral; but if a person commits murder with absolutely no sense of remorse or maybe even a sense of pleasure, the person is acting in an amoral way. Acts are considered to be *nonmoral* if moral standards essentially do not apply to the acts; for example, choosing between cereal and toast and jam for breakfast is a nonmoral decision.

When people consider matters of ethics, they are usually considering matters about freedom in regard to personal choices, one's obligations to other sentient beings, or judgments about human character. The term *unethical* is used to describe ethics in its negative form when, for instance, a person's character or behavior is contrary to admirable traits or the code of conduct that has been endorsed by one's society, community, or profession. Because the word *ethics* is used when one may literally be referring to a situation of morals, the process-related conception of ethics is sometimes overlooked today. People often use the word *ethics* when referring to a collection of actual beliefs and behaviors, thereby using the terms *ethics* and *morals* in essentially synonymous ways. In this book some effort has been made to distinguish the words *ethics* and *morals* based on their literal meanings; however, because of common uses, the terms have generally been used interchangeably.

Billington (2003) delineated some important features about the terms *morals* and *ethics*:

- Probably the most important feature about ethics and morals is that no one can avoid making moral or ethical decisions because the social connection with others necessitates that people must consider moral and ethical actions.
- Other people are always involved with one's moral and ethical decisions. Private morality does not exist.

■ Moral decisions matter because every decision affects someone else's life, self-esteem, or happiness level.
■ Definite conclusions or resolutions will never be reached in ethical debates.
■ In the area of morals and ethics, people cannot exercise moral judgment without being given a choice; in other words, a necessity for making a sound moral judgment is being able to choose an option from among a group of choices.
■ People use moral reasoning to make moral judgments, or to come to discover right actions.

Types of Ethical Inquiry

Ethics is categorized according to three types of inquiry or study: normative ethics, meta-ethics, and descriptive ethics. The first approach, **normative ethics**, is an attempt to decide or prescribe values, behaviors, and ways of being that are right or wrong, good or bad, and admirable or deplorable. When using the method of normative ethics, inquiries are made about how humans *should* behave, what *ought* to be done in certain situations, or what type of character one *should* have or how one *should* be.

Outcomes of normative ethics are the prescriptions derived from asking normative questions. These prescriptions include accepted moral standards and codes. One such accepted moral standard is **common morality**. Common morality consists of normative beliefs and behaviors that the members of society generally agree about and that are familiar to most human beings. For example, the belief that robbing a bank is wrong is part of common morality in the United States, whereas because of the many, varying positions about the rightness or wrongness of abortion, abortion is not a part of our common morality. A normative belief in the nursing profession is that nurses ought to be compassionate, that is, nurses should work to relieve suffering. This claim is supported by the *Code of Ethics for Nurses with Interpretive Statements* (American Nurses Association [ANA], 2001) and *The International Council of Nurses Code of Ethics for Nurses* (International Council of Nurses [ICN], 2006).

The focus of ***meta-ethics***, which means "about ethics," is not an inquiry about what ought to be done or what behaviors should be prescribed. Meta-ethics is concerned with understanding the language of morality through an analysis of the meaning of ethically related concepts and theories, such as the meaning of *good*, *happiness*, and *virtuous character*. For example, a nurse who is actively engaging in a meta-ethical analysis might try to determine the meaning of a *good* nurse-patient relationship.

Descriptive ethics often is referred to as a scientific rather than a philosophical ethical inquiry. It is an approach used when researchers or ethicists want to describe what people think about morality or when they want to describe how people actually behave, that is, their morals. Professional moral values and behaviors can be described through nursing research. An example of descriptive ethics is research that identifies nurses' attitudes regarding telling patients the truth about their terminal illnesses.

Ethical Perspectives

Ethical thinking, valuing, and reasoning fall somewhere along a continuum between two opposing views: (1) ethical relativism and (2) ethical objectivism.

Ethical Relativism

Ethical relativism is the belief that it is acceptable for ethics and morality to differ among persons or societies. There are two types of ethical relativism—ethical subjectivism and cultural relativism (Brannigan & Boss, 2001). People who subscribe to a belief in **ethical subjectivism** believe "that individuals create their own morality [and that] there are no objective moral truths—only individual opinions" (p. 7). People's beliefs about actions being right or wrong or good or bad depend on how people *feel* about actions rather than on reason or systematic ethical analysis. What is believed by one person to be wrong might not be viewed as wrong by one's neighbor depending on variations in opinions and feelings.

Ethical subjectivism has been distinguished from cultural relativism. Pence (2000) defined **cultural relativism** as "the ethical theory that moral evaluation is rooted in and cannot be separated from the experience, beliefs and behaviors of a particular culture, and hence, that what is wrong in one culture may not be so in another" (p. 12). People opposed to cultural relativism argue that when it is practiced according to its extreme or literal meaning, this type of thinking can be dangerous, because it may theoretically support relativists' exploitative or hurtful actions (Brannigan & Boss, 2001). An example of cultural relativism is the belief that the act of female circumcision, which is sometimes called female genital mutilation, is a moral practice. Though not considered to be a religious ritual, this act is considered ethically acceptable by some groups in countries that have a Muslim or an Egyptian Pharaonic heritage. In most countries and cultures, however, it is considered to be a grave violation of human rights in accordance with the United Nations' Declaration of Human Rights.

Ethical Reflections

- Throughout history, wars have been fought because groups of people differ in regard to beliefs about good or bad behaviors and ways of being. Discuss examples of cultural relativism that have caused conflict among groups of people with cultural differences.
- Conduct a literature search about cultural relativism and nursing. How does cultural relativism impact nursing in the United States and around the world?

Ethical Objectivism

Ethical objectivism is the position that universal or objective moral principles exist. This view is held, at least to some degree, by many philosophers and health care ethicists because they adhere to a specific approach in determining what is good. Examples of objectivist ethical theories and approaches are deontology, utilitarianism, and natural law theory, which are discussed later in this chapter. Though some ethicists believe that these different theories or approaches are mutually exclusive, theories and approaches often, in fact, overlap when used in practice. "Moral judgment is a whole into which we must fit principles, character and intentions, cultural values, circumstances, and consequences" (Brannigan & Boss, 2001, p. 23).

Ethical Reflections

- Where does your worldview fall on the continuum between ethical relativism and ethical objectivism? Support your personal worldview and provide examples.

Values and Moral Reasoning

Because ethics falls within the abstract discipline of philosophy, ethics involves many different perspectives of what people value as meaningful and good in their lives. A **value** is something of worth or something that is highly regarded. Values refer to one's *e-valu-ative* judgments about what one believes is good or what makes something desirable. The things that people esteem as good influence how personal character develops and how people think and subsequently behave. Professional values are outlined in professional codes. A fundamental position in the ANA's (2001) *Code of Ethics for Nurses with Interpretive Statements* is that professional values and personal values must be integrated. Values and moral reasoning in nursing fall under the domain of normative ethics, that is, professional values contained in the *Code of Ethics* guide nurses in how they ought to be and behave.

Reasoning is the use of abstract thought processes to think creatively, to answer questions, to solve problems, and to formulate strategies for one's actions and desired ways of being. When people participate in reasoning, they do not merely accept the unexamined beliefs and ideas of other people. Reasoning involves thinking for oneself to determine if one's conclusions are based on good, or logical, foundations. More specifically, **moral reasoning** pertains to reasoning focused on moral or ethical issues. Moral reasoning for nurses usually occurs in the context of day-to-day relationships between nurses and the recipients of their care and between nurses and their co-workers.

Moral Reasoning throughout Western History

Different values, worldviews, and ways of moral reasoning have evolved throughout history and have different points of emphasis in varying historical periods. In regard to some approaches to reasoning about moral issues, "what was old becomes new again," as in the case of the renewed popularity of virtue ethics, that is, reasoning about the sort of person one wants to be.

Ancient Greece

In Western history, much of what is known about formal moral reasoning generally began with the ancient Greeks, especially with the philosophers Socrates (c. 469–399 B.C.E.), Plato (c. 429–347 B.C.E.), and Aristotle (384–322 B.C.E.). Though there are no primary texts of the teachings of Socrates (his teachings were recorded by Plato), it is known that Socrates was an avid promoter of moral reasoning and critical thinking among the citizens of Athens. Socrates is credited with the statement that "the unexamined life is not worth living," and he developed a method of reasoning called the Socratic Method that is still used today (see Box 1.1).

Socrates had many friends and allies who believed in his philosophy and teachings. In fact, Socrates was such a successful and well-known teacher of philosophy and moral reasoning in Athens that he was put to death for upsetting the sociopolitical status quo. Socrates was accused of corrupting the youth of Athens who, under his tutelage, had begun to question their parents' wisdom and religious beliefs. These accusations of corruption were based on Socrates' encouraging people to think independently and to question dogma generated by the ruling class. Though he was sentenced to death by the powerful, elite men within his society, Socrates refused to

BOX 1.1: HIGHLIGHTS FROM THE FIELD: THE SOCRATIC METHOD

Socrates raised challenging questions, and he would then ask another question about the answers that he received. An example of his method of questioning might be as follows:

Socrates: "Why should nurses study ethics?"
Nurse: "To be good nurses."
Socrates: "What is a *good nurse*?"
Nurse: "It means that my patients are well taken care of."
Socrates: "How do you know that your patients are well taken care of?"

And the questioning goes on until the concepts stemming from the original question are thoroughly explored. Socratic questioning does not mean that one ends up with a *final* answer; however, this form of discussion leads people to think critically and reflectively.

apologize for his beliefs and teachings. He ultimately chose to die by drinking poisonous hemlock rather than to deny his values.

Ethical Reflections

- Begin a Socratic dialogue with classmates or colleagues. Develop your own questions or use one of the following examples:
  ○ What does *lying* to a patient mean?
  ○ What does *caring* mean in nursing?
  ○ How are *competence* and *ethics* related in nursing?

Socrates' student, Plato, is believed by some people to have been the most outstanding philosopher to have ever lived. Plato's reasoning was based on his belief that there are two realms of reality. The first is the realm of Forms, which transcends time and space. According to Plato, an eternal, perfect, and unchanging ideal copy (form) of all phenomena exists in the realm of Forms that is beyond everyday human access. Plato believed that the realm of Forms contained the essence of concepts and objects, and even the essence of objects' properties. Essences that existed in the realm of Forms included, for example, a perfect Form of *good*, *redness* (the color red), and a *horse*. In the realm of Forms, the essence of *good* existed as ideal Truth and *redness* (a particular property of some objects such as an apple) existed as the color red in its most perfect state. A horse in the realm of Forms was the perfect specimen of the animal that is a horse. This perfect horse contained the "horseness" factors that, for example, distinguish a horse from a cow. Plato considered the world of Forms to be the real world, though humans did not live in that world.

The second realm is the world of Appearances, which is the everyday world of imperfect, decaying, and changing phenomena; the world in which humans live. The underlying purpose or goal of imperfect phenomena in the world of Appearances is to emulate their associated essences and perfect Forms. For example, a horse's purpose in life is to strive toward becoming identical to the perfect specimen of a horse that exists in the world of Forms.

Plato also proposed that humans have a tripartite soul. The three parts of the soul consisted of the Faculty of Reason associated with thought and Truth, which is located in one's head; the Faculty of Spirit that expresses love, beauty, and the desire for eternal life, which is located in one's chest; and the Faculty of Appetite that is an expression of human desires and emotions, which is located in one's gut. Plato believed that influences of these three parts of the soul exist in greater to lesser degrees in each person. Therefore, one person may be more disposed to intellectual pursuits as compared to another person who is more interested in physical pleasures. Plato based other associations, such as one's best-suited occupation, on the degree of influence of the three parts of the soul. The founder of modern nursing, Florence Nightingale, was a passionate student of ancient Greek philosophy. It is believed that Nightingale may have aligned the function of nurses with the Faculty of Spirit (see Box 1.2).

Ethical Reflections

- Discuss how and when nurses *are* and *are not* the guardians of their patients.
- How are nurses and physicians different in their roles as guardians? How are they similar?

One of Plato's most famous stories about reasoning is his allegory of the cave. In this story, a group of people lived their lives chained to the floor of a cave. Behind them burned a fire that cast shadows of people moving on the wall in front of the people who are chained. The chained prisoners believe that the shadows are actually real people. When one of the prisoners is freed from his chains, he leaves the cave. First, he

BOX 1.2: HIGHLIGHTS FROM THE FIELD: NURSES AS GUARDIANS

Plato associated the tripartite soul with three classes in Greek society. Persons were believed to have an individual aptitude that particularly suited them to their purpose in society.

1. Philosopher Kings were associated with the Faculty of Reason and wisdom.
2. Societal guardians were associated with the Faculty of Spirit and protecting others.
3. Artisans and craftsmen were associated with the Faculty of Appetite and technical work.

Because of her education in classical Greek literature and culture and her views about nursing, it has been proposed that Nightingale might have compared her purpose as a nurse with the role of a societal guardian. In contrast, early physicians, whose profession developed through apprenticeship guilds that emphasized technical practices, might best be compared to the artisan class.

LeVasseur, J. (1998). Plato, Nightingale, and contemporary nursing. *Image: Journal of Nursing Scholarship, 30*(3), 281–285.

is blinded by the brightness of the sun. After his sight adjusts to the light, he sees objects that he realizes are more real than the shadows within the cave. The freed person returns to the cave to encourage the other prisoners to break their chains and to enter the more expansive world of reality. The meaning of this story has been interpreted in many different ways. Whatever Plato's intended meaning, the story does prompt people to think about the problems that result when they remain chained by their closed minds and flawed reasoning.

Ethical Reflections

- Compare Plato's allegory of the cave to critical thinking in nursing.
- Discuss examples of how and when nurses are "chained in the cave and see shadows as reality."

- Discuss examples of how and when nurses are like the escaped prisoner and see the world clearly.
- Think of a few personal examples of when you have been "chained in the cave." What were the circumstances? What were the outcomes? What made a difference in your thinking?

Plato's student, Aristotle, developed science, logic, and ethics to world-altering proportions. Though he was influenced by his teacher, Plato, Aristotle took a more practical approach to reasoning than believing in an "other worldly" realm of ideal Forms. He was guided in his reasoning by his belief in the importance of empirical inquiry and the belief that all things have a purpose or end goal. In *Nichomachean Ethics*, Aristotle (trans. 2002) discussed practical wisdom (*phronesis*) as being necessary for deliberation about what is good and advantageous if people want to move toward their human purpose or desired end goal of *eudaimonia* (happiness or well-being). Aristotle believed that a person needs education to cultivate *phronesis*, which is intellectual excellence.

Aristotle's conception of *phronesis* is similar to Plato's conception of the virtue of prudence. Wisdom is focused on the good achieved from being wise, which means that one knows how to act in a particular situation, deliberates well, and has a disposition that embodies excellence of character. Therefore, in ancient Greece, prudence involved more than having good intentions or meaning well. It was knowing what to do and how to be, but it also involved transforming that knowledge into well-reasoned actions. Aristotle believed that people are social beings whose reasoning should lead them to be a good citizen and a good friend, and to act in moderate ways.

The Middle Ages

After the Roman Empire was divided by barbarians (c. 476 C.E.), the golden age of intellectualism and cultural progress in Western Europe ended. The next historical period was the Middle or Dark Ages, which lasted until about 1500 C.E. In the gap left by the failed political system of Rome, Christianity became the dominant religion in Western Europe as the Catholic Church took on the powerful role of educating the European people. Christianity is a monotheistic (one God), revelatory religion, whereas ancient Greek philosophy was based on the use of reason and polytheism (many gods). Because Greek philosophy was believed to be heretical, its examination was discouraged during the Church-dominated Middle Ages. However, it is interesting that two Catholic saints, Augustine and Aquinas, provided the major influence in terms of ethics during the Middle Ages, and both men were influenced by the ancient Greeks.

St. Augustine (354–430 C.E.) is often considered to be the "Plato of the Middle Ages." Though Augustine was a Christian and Plato was a non-Christian, Augustine's belief in a heavenly place of unchanging moral Truths is similar to Plato's belief in the realm of ideal Forms. Augustine believed that these Truths are imprinted by God on the soul of each human being. According to Augustine, one has a duty to love God, and moral reasoning should direct one's senses in accordance with that duty. Being subject to this obligation is what leads to moral perfection. Generally, St. Augustine believed only in the existence of *good*, similar to how the essence of good would exist if it was an ideal Form. Therefore, evil is present only when good is missing or has in some way been perverted from its existence as an ideal Truth.

Augustine was 56 years old when the Roman Empire fell. In one of his most famous writings, *The City of God*, Augustine used the fall of the Roman Empire to explain a philosophy that is sometimes compared to Plato's conception of the worlds of Forms and Appearances. People who live according to the spirit live in the City of God (world of perfection/Forms). People who live according to the flesh live in the City of Man (world of imperfection/Appearances). To move away from evil, one must have the grace of God. Humans were viewed as finite beings that must have the divine aid of grace in order to bridge the gap required to have a relationship with the infinite Being of God.

The Crusades influenced Europe's exodus from the Dark Ages. When Christians entered Islamic lands, such as Spain, Portugal, and North Africa, they were reintroduced to intellectualism, including texts of the ancient Greeks, especially Aristotle. The moral teachings of St. Thomas Aquinas (1224–1274) are sometimes viewed as a Christianized version of Aristotle's ethical teachings. Aquinas tried to reconcile Aristotle's teachings with the teachings of the Catholic Church. Like Aristotle, Aquinas believed that people have a desirable end goal or purpose and that practicing excellences of character (virtues) leads to human happiness and good moral reasoning. Aristotle's non-Christian moral philosophy was based on humans moving toward an end goal or dynamic state of *eudaimonia* (happiness or well-being) through the cultivation of excellent intellect and excellent moral character.

Aquinas expanded Aristotle's conception of the end goal of perfect happiness and grounded the requirements for happiness as existing only in the knowledge and love of God and Christian virtues (excellences). Aquinas replaced Aristotle's emphasis on the virtue of pride with an emphasis on the virtue of humility. Aristotle believed that pride is an important characteristic of independent, personally strong men. In contrast, Aquinas valued the characteristic of humility because it represented one's need to depend on the benevolence of God. In addition to virtue ethics, Aquinas is strongly associated with a belief in reasoning according to the natural law theory of ethics. Both of these ethical approaches are covered later in this chapter.

Modern Philosophy and the Age of Enlightenment

The period of modern philosophy began with two changes in the outlook of people within European societies that differed from the practices and beliefs of people who lived during the Middle Ages. The Catholic Church began to have a diminishing influence within society, while the influence of science began to increase. The scientific revolution began in 1543 with the Copernican theory but did not rapidly advance until the 17th century when Kepler and Galileo moved scientific debates to the forefront of society.

With these changes came a new freedom in human moral reasoning, which was based on people being autonomous, rational thinking creatures rather than being primarily influenced and controlled by Church dogma and rules. During the 18th-century Enlightenment era, humans believed that they were coming out of the darkness of the Middle (Dark) Ages into the light of true knowledge.

Some scientists and philosophers were bold enough to believe that humans could ultimately be perfected and that all knowledge could be discovered. As the belief in empirical science grew, a new way of thinking was ushered in that compared both the universe and people to machines. Many scientists and philosophers believed that the world, along with its inhabitants, could be reduced through analyses into their component parts. These *reductionists* hoped that after most or all knowledge was discovered, the universe and human behavior could be predicted and controlled. People still identify evidence of this way of thinking in health care today when *cure* is highly valued over *care*, and uncertainty is considered to be something that can be, or needs to be, eliminated in regard to diseases. A mechanistic approach is one that focuses on fixing problems as if one is fixing a machine, as contrasted to a humanistic or holistic approach in which one readily acknowledges that well-being and health occurs along a complex continuum and that some situations and health problems cannot be fixed or cured.

Ethical Reflections

- Identify examples of mechanistic practices in health care.
- Identify examples of holistic practices in health care.
- Are all mechanistic health care practices "bad"? Why or why not?
- Are all holistic health care practices "good"? Why or why not?

During the 18th century, an important belief about moral reasoning was proposed by David Hume (1711–1776). Hume argued that there is a distinction between facts and values when moral reasoning is considered. This fact/value distinction also has been called the "is/ought gap." A skeptic, Hume suggested that a person cannot acknowledge a fact and then make a value judgment based on that fact. One logically cannot take a fact of what *is* and then determine an ethical judgment of what *ought to be*. If Hume's position is accepted as valid, people should not make assumptions such as: (a) if all dogs have fleas (assuming that this is a known fact), and (b) Sara is a dog (a fact), therefore, (c) Sara *ought not* be allowed to sleep on the sofa because having fleas on the sofa is a bad thing (a value statement). According to people who believe in the truth of the fact/value distinction, the chance of Sara spreading her fleas to the sofa might be a fact if she sleeps on it, but determining that having fleas on the sofa is a bad thing is based only on one's feelings.

Postmodern Era

After the scientific hegemony of the Enlightenment Era, people began to question whether a single-minded allegiance to science was creating problems for human societies. Postmodernism often is considered to have begun about 1950 after the end of World War II. However, some people trace its beginning back to the German philosopher Friedrich Nietzsche in the late 1800s. Pence (2000) defined postmodernism as "a modern movement in philosophy and the humanities that rejects the optimistic view that science and reason will improve humanity; it rejects the notion of sustained progress through reason and the scientific method" (p. 43). The postmodern mind is one that is formed by a pluralistic view or a diversity of intellectual and cultural influences. People who live according to a postmodern philosophy acknowledge that reality is constantly changing and that scientific investigations cannot provide one grand theory or correct view of absolute Truth that can guide human behavior, relationships, and life. Human knowledge is thought instead to be shaped by multiple factors with storytelling and narrative analysis being viewed as core components of knowledge development.

——————————— Ethical Reflections ———————————

- Conduct a literature search about postmodernism. Do you have a postmodern worldview? Support your answer.

Care-Based Versus Justice-Based Reasoning

A *care* approach to moral reasoning is often associated with a feminine way of thinking, and a *cure* approach is usually associated with a masculine Enlightenment-era way of thinking. In 1981 Lawrence Kohlberg, a psychologist, reported his landmark research about moral reasoning based on 84 boys that he had studied for over 20 years. Based on the work of Piaget, Kohlberg defined six stages of moral development ranging from childhood to adulthood. Interestingly, Kohlberg did not include any women in his research, but he expected that his six-stage scale could be used to measure moral development in both males and females.

When the scale was applied to women, they seemed to score only at the third stage of the sequence, a stage in which Kohlberg described morality in terms of interpersonal relationships and helping others. Kohlberg viewed this third stage of development as somewhat deficient in regard to mature moral reasoning. Because of Kohlberg's exclusion of females in his research and his negative view of this third stage, one of Kohlberg's associates, Carol Gilligan, raised the concern of gender bias. Gilligan, in turn, published an influential book in 1982, *In a Different Voice*, in which she argued that women's moral reasoning *is* different, but it is not deficient. The distinction that is usually made between moral reasoning as it is suggested by Kohlberg and Gilligan is that Kohlberg's is a male-oriented ethic of justice and Gilligan's is a more feminine ethic of care (covered later in this chapter).

Learning from History

Often, it is only in hindsight that people are able to analyze a historical era in which there is a converging of norms and beliefs that are held in high esteem or valued by large groups within a society. Like the overlapping approaches used by some ethical objectivists, the influences of historical eras also build upon each other and are often hard to separate. Christians still base much of their ethical reasoning on the philosophy generated during the Middle Ages. At the same time, it is evident that individualistic ways of thinking that were popular during the Enlightenment era remain popular in Western societies today because autonomy (self-direction) is so highly valued. The varied historical influences that have affected moral reasoning, consequently, have formed a pattern of rich and interesting values, perspectives, and practices that are evident in the globally connected world that people live in today.

Ethical Theories and Approaches

Normative ethical theories and approaches function as moral guides to answer the questions "What ought I to do or not do?" and "How should I be?" A theory can provide individuals with guidance in moral thinking and reasoning, as well as providing justification for moral actions. The following theories and approaches are not all-inclusive nor do they necessarily include all variations of those theories and approaches that are discussed.

Western Ethics

Virtue Ethics

Watch your thoughts; they become words.
Watch your words; they become actions.
Watch your actions; they become habits.
Watch your habits; they become character.
Watch your character; it becomes your destiny.

—FRANK OUTLAW

Rather than centering on what is right or wrong in terms of one's duties or the consequences of one's actions, the excellence of one's character and considerations of what sort of person one wants to be is emphasized in **virtue ethics**. Since the time of Plato and Aristotle, **virtues**, *arête* in Greek, have referred to excellences in regard to persons or objects being the best that they can be in accordance with their purpose. Even an inanimate object can have virtue as the concept was conceived by the ancient Greeks. For example, the purpose of a knife is to cut. *Arête* in regard to a knife means that the knife has a sharp edge that cuts very well. If one needs the services of a knife, it is probably safe to assume that a knife that exhibits excellence in cutting would be the type of knife that one would want to use. Most people would want to use a knife that accomplishes its purpose in the best way possible.

For humans, virtue ethics addresses the question "What sort of person must I be to be an excellent person?" rather than "What is my duty?" Virtues for humans are habitual, excellent traits that are intentionally developed throughout one's life. A person of virtue, consistent with Aristotle's way of thinking, is a person who is an excellent friend to other people, an excellent critical thinker, and an excellent citizen of a community.

Aristotle's (trans. 2002) approach to virtue ethics is grounded in two categories of excellence. One category contains intellectual virtues and the other contains character or moral virtues. According to Aristotle, "the intellectual sort [of virtue] mostly . . . comes into existence and increases as a result of teaching (which is why it requires experience and time), whereas excellence of character results from habituation" (p. 111). Though Aristotle divided virtues into two sorts—those of the intellect and those of character—the two categories of virtues cannot be distinctly separated. Aristotle made this point by proposing that "it is not possible to possess excellence in the primary sense [that is, having excellence of character] without wisdom, nor to be wise without excellence of character" (p. 189).

Aristotle realized that good things taken to an extreme could become bad. He therefore proposed that there is a "Golden Mean" in terms of ways of being. Most virtues are considered to exist as a moderate way of being between two kinds of vices or faults, which are consistent with the extremes of excess and deficiency. For instance, Aristotle named *courage* as a virtue, but the extremes of *rashness* at one end of a continuum and *cowardice* at the other end of the same continuum are its related vices. The virtue of *truthfulness* is the mean between *boastfulness* and *self-deprecation*. The mean for each virtue is unique for each type of virtue and situation; in other words, the mean is not a mathematical average.

Other examples of virtues include benevolence, compassion, fidelity, generosity, and patience. Plato designated the four virtues of prudence (wisdom), fortitude (courage), temperance (moderation), and justice as cardinal virtues, meaning that all other virtues hinge on these primary four. Prudence corresponds to Plato's idea of the Faculty of Reason, fortitude corresponds to the Faculty of Spirit, and temperance corresponds to the Faculty of Appetite. The virtue of justice is an umbrella virtue that encompasses the other three.

The ancient Greeks are most frequently associated with virtue ethics, but other philosophers and ethicists also have proposed views about virtues. Though they are by no means the only other approaches to virtue ethics, two philosophies that differ from the Greeks were proposed by the Scottish philosopher David Hume and the German philosopher Frederick Nietzsche (1844–1900).

Hume, whose approach is used by some feminist philosophers, believed that virtues flow from a natural human tendency to be sympathetic or benevolent toward other people. Virtues are human character traits that are admired by most people and are judged to be generally pleasing. Virtues are traits of character that benefit or are useful to other people, are useful to oneself, or are useful to both other people and to oneself. Because of Hume's focus on the usefulness of virtues, his approach to ethics also is associated with utilitarianism, which is discussed later in this chapter. Hume's philosophy of ethics is based on emotion as the primary human motivator for admirable behavior rather than motivation by reason. However, Hume did not propose that ethics is based merely on personal opinion. Virtuous behavior is validated by the consensus of members of communities according to what is useful for a whole community's well-being.

A different and more radical view of virtue ethics is based on the philosophy of Nietzsche. Rather than viewing people as caring, sympathetic beings, Nietzsche proposed that the best character for people to cultivate is based on a "will to power." Nietzsche believed that the "will to power" rightly should motivate people to achieve dominance in the world. Strength was praised as virtuous whereas "feminine" virtues, such as caring and kindness, were considered by Nietzsche to be signs of weakness. This means that, according to Nietzsche, virtue is consistent with hierarchical power or power over other people, which makes the Christian virtue of humility a vice. It is believed that another German, Adolph Hitler, adopted the philosophy of Nietzsche as his worldview. Though Nietzsche is a well-known and important person in the history of philosophy, Nietzsche's approach to virtue ethics has little place in nursing ethics.

Although virtue ethics is again popular today, over the years this ethical approach experienced a significant decline in interest among Western philosophers and nurses (MacIntyre, 1984; Tschudin, 2003). Many Western philosophers lost interest in the virtues when the philosophers became entrenched in the schools of thought popularized during the Enlightenment era that emphasize individualism and autonomy (MacIntyre).

Over time, nurses concluded that it was unfashionable to follow the tradition of Florence Nightingale because Nightingale's view of virtues in nursing included a virtue of obedience (Sellman, 1997). However, Nightingale's valuing of obedience needs to be viewed within the context of the time in which she lived. Also, Nightingale's liberal education in Greek philosophy may have influenced her use of the virtue of obedience to reflect her belief in the value of practical wisdom as conceived by Aristotle (LeVasseur, 1998; Sellman). In connecting obedience to practical wisdom, some nurses now understand that Nightingale's conception was one that approached something akin to intelligent obedience rather than a blind allegiance of nurses to physicians.

Ethical Reflections

- Do you believe that a specific set of virtues can be identified as being essential for the nursing profession?
- If so, what are the virtues contained in the set? Why did you select them? Why are other virtues excluded?
- If you do not believe that a specific set of virtues is identifiable, defend your position.

- Partner with a colleague and list several real life examples that are related to each line of Frank Outlaw's quotation at the beginning of the virtue ethics section.
- What do you believe might be legitimate criticisms of virtue ethics?

Natural Law Theory

Most modern versions of natural law theory have their basis in the philosophy of St. Thomas Aquinas. People who use **natural law theory** believe that the rightness of actions is self-evident because morality is determined by inherent human nature, not by customs and preferences. According to this theory, the law of reason is implanted in the order of nature (usually thought to be implanted by God), and this law provides the rules or commands for human actions. Consequently, natural law theory is often associated with rule-based Judeo-Christian ethics. Natural law theory is the basis of religious prohibitions against acts that some people consider unnatural, such as homosexuality and the use of birth control.

─────────────── **Ethical Reflections** ───────────────

- What do you believe might be legitimate criticisms of a natural law approach to ethics?

Deontology

Deontology, literally the "study of duty," is an approach to ethics that is focused on duties and rules. The most influential philosopher associated with the deontological way of thinking was the German Immanuel Kant (1724–1804). Kant defined a person as a rational, autonomous (self-directed) being with the ability to know universal, objective moral laws and the freedom to decide to act morally. **Kantian deontology** prescribes that each rational being is ethically bound to act only from a sense of duty. When deciding how to act, the consequences of one's actions are considered to be irrelevant.

According to Kant, it is only through dutiful actions that people have moral worth. Even when individuals do not want to act from duty, Kant believed that they are ethically required to do so. In fact, having one's actions motivated by duty is superior to acting from a motivation of love. Because rational choice is within one's control as compared to one's tenuous control over personal emotions, only reason and not emotion is sufficient to lead a person to moral actions.

Kant believed that people are ends in themselves and should be treated accordingly. Each autonomous, self-directed person has dignity and is due respect. One should never act in ways that involve using other people as a means to one's personal ends. In fact, when people use others as a means to ends, even if they believe that they are using persons to reach ethical goals, Kant believed that people could be harmed. An example of this would be a failure to obtain informed consent from a research participant even though the researcher steadfastly believes that the research will be beneficial to the participant.

Kant identified rules to guide people in thinking about their obligations. He drew a distinction between two types of duties or obligations: the hypothetical imperative and the categorical imperative. Hypothetical imperatives are optional duties or rules that people ought to observe or follow if certain ends are to be achieved. Hypothetical imperatives are sometimes called "*if-then*" imperatives, which means that they involve conditional or optional actions; for instance, "*if* I want to eat tonight, *then* I should go to the grocery store today."

However, where moral actions are concerned, Kant believed that duties and laws are absolute and unconditional. Kant proposed that people ought to follow a universal, unconditional framework of maxims, or rules, as a guide to know the rightness of actions and one's moral duties. He called these absolute and unconditional duties **categorical imperatives**. When deciding about matters of ethics and acting according to a categorical imperative, one needs to ask the question: "If I perform this action, could I will that it should become a universal law for everyone to act in the same way?" No action can ever be judged as right, according to Kant, if it is not reasonable that the action has the potential to become a binding, ethical law for all people. For example, Kant's ethics imposes the categorical imperative that one should never tell a lie, because a person cannot rationally wish that all people should be able to pick and choose when they have permission not to be truthful. Another example of a categorical imperative is that suicide is never acceptable. A person, when committing suicide, cannot rationally wish that all people should feel free to commit suicide or the world would become chaotic.

Ethical Reflections

- Are there categorical imperatives (absolute duties) that nurses must follow to be ethical professionals? If so, identify examples. If not, defend your answer.
- Answer the following question and provide philosophical support for your answer: Is it more important for a nurse to have a virtuous character or to be dutiful?

- Review the ANA's *Code of Ethics* in the appendix. Is the *Code* based on a deontological approach to nursing? Is it based on a virtue ethics approach? Discuss specific examples in the *Code* that support your answers.
- What do you believe might be legitimate criticisms of deontological ethics?

Consequentialism

Consequentialists, as distinguished from deontologists, do consider consequences to be an importance indication of the moral value of one's actions. Utilitarianism is the most well-known consequentialist theory of ethics. **Utilitarianism** means that actions are judged by their utility, that is, they are evaluated according to the usefulness of their consequences. When people use the theory of utilitarianism as the basis for ethical behavior, they attempt to promote the greatest good (happiness or pleasure) and to inflict the least amount of harm (suffering or pain) that is possible in a situation. In other words, utilitarians believe that it is useful to society to achieve "the greatest good for the greatest number" of people who may be affected by a rule or action. People who use a utilitarian approach to ethics place great emphasis on what is best for collective groups, not individual people, though each individual's happiness is worthy of equal consideration as compared to every other individual in a group.

The British philosopher Jeremy Bentham (1748–1832) was an early promoter of the principle of utilitarianism. During Bentham's life, British society functioned according to aristocratic privilege. Poor people were mistreated by people in the upper classes and were given no choice other than to work long hours in deplorable conditions. Bentham tried to develop a theory that could be used to achieve a fair distribution of pleasure among all British citizens. He went as far as to develop a systematic decision-making method of using mathematical calculations. Bentham's method was designed to determine ways to allocate pleasure and to diminish pain by using the measures of intensity and duration. Bentham's approach to utilitarianism has been criticized because he equated all types of pleasure as being equal.

Another Englishman, John Stuart Mill (1806–1873), challenged Bentham's views when he clearly pointed out that particular experiences of pleasure and happiness do have different qualities and that different situations do not necessarily produce equal consequences. For example, Mill stated that the higher intellectual pleasures may be differentiated from lower physical pleasures. The higher pleasures, such as enjoying a work of art or a scholarly book, are considered to be better because only human beings, not other animals, possess the mental faculties to enjoy this higher level of happiness.

According to Mill, happiness and pleasure are measured by quality and not quantity (duration or intensity). In making these distinctions between higher and lower levels of happiness and pleasure, Mill's philosophy is focused on ethics and morally right acts that produce the most good in terms of the most happiness.

Mill believed that communities usually agree about what is good and about the things that best promote the well-being of the most people. An example of an application of Mill's utilitarianism is the use of mandatory vaccination laws. Individual liberties are limited so that the larger society is protected from diseases. The consequence is that people generally are happier because they are free of diseases. People using Mill's form of utilitarian theory often can use widely supported traditions to guide them in deciding about rules and behaviors that probably will produce the best consequences for the most people, such as the maxim that stealing is wrong. Through experience, humans have generally identified many behaviors that will produce the most happiness or unhappiness for society as a whole.

Ethical Reflections

- Working for the greatest good for the greatest number of people is an essential principle of public health nursing. Can you identify examples of utilitarian ethics in the ANA's *Code of Ethics for Nurses with Interpretive Statements* (2001) in the appendix? Explain.
- Identify specific situations in which nurses need to use a utilitarian approach to nursing care.
- If the deontological approach is based on considering one's duty but not the consequences of one's actions, and the utilitarian approach is based on the goodness of the consequences of one's actions, can nurses use both approaches in their practice? Can nurses legitimately consider themselves to be both deontologists and utilitarians? Why or why not?
- Discuss ethical objectivism in relation to the questions in the above bullet.
- What do you believe might be legitimate criticisms of utilitarian or consequentialist ethics?

Casuistry

Casuistry is another approach to ethics that is based in Judeo-Christian history. When people use **casuistry**, they make decisions inductively based on individual cases. The analysis and evaluation of strongly similar or outstanding cases (i.e., paradigm cases) provides guidance in ethical decision making. When people use casuistry, their ethical decision making begins as a bottom-up approach by considering the details of specific cases rather than beginning from the top down by applying absolute rules and principles. Long ago, Jewish people often tried to sort out the relevance of sacred laws in specific situations in ways that were practical and case based rather than absolute and inflexibly rule based. In Catholic history, the practice of persons individually confessing their sins to priests to receive absolution reflects the use of casuistry. Based on the confessor's specific case (i.e., the circumstances surrounding the occasion of sinning) a person receives a personal penance from the priest that is required for absolution.

Today, casuistry is often the method used by health care ethics committees to analyze the ethical issues surrounding specific patient cases. The Four Topics Method of ethical decision making that is discussed in Chapter 2 is based on a casuistry approach.

--- **Ethical Reflections** ---

- Conduct an Internet search for landmark cases in health care ethics.
- Identify three important cases.
- How have these three cases affected subsequent health care ethics decisions and debates?
- What do you believe might be legitimate criticisms of casuistry as an approach to ethics?

Narrative Ethics

There are stories and stories. There are the songs, also, that are taught.. Some are whimsical. Some are very intense. Some are documentary. Everything I have known is through teachings, by word of mouth, either by song or by legends.
—TERRANCE HONVANTEWA, HOPI, (AS CITED IN CLEARY, 1996,
NATIVE AMERICAN WISDOM, P. 40)

Because it is a story-based approach, **narrative ethics** has obvious similarities to casuistry. Also, according to one of the foremost modern-day virtue ethicists, Alasdair MacIntyre (1984), narrative thinking and virtue ethics are closely connected. Both narrative ethics and virtue ethics are firmly embedded in human relationships. MacIntyre proposed that a human is "essentially a story-telling animal"; a person is "a teller of stories that aspire to truth" (p. 216). Narratives, such as novels and literary stories, change us in remarkable ways (Murray, 1997). Most people from childhood obtain moral education about character development from stories, such as fairy tales. When using a narrative approach to ethics, nurses remain open to learning from a storied, nuanced view of life; that is, they are sensitive to how personal and community stories evolve, are constructed, and can be changed. Narratives are stories that are being lived, read, watched, heard, discussed, analyzed, or compared.

Narratives are very context or situation bound. For people to decide what they should do in particular circumstances, they may first identify how their moral character and actions fit within the greater stories of their culture. People are situated within their personal life narratives and their stories intersect with and are interwoven into the narratives of other people with whom they interact. Nurses who use narrative ethics are aware that there is much more to a patient's story than is usually known or discussed among health care providers. People are not solitary creatures, and as they interact with other people and their environment, they must make choices about what they believe and how they will act.

When using a narrative approach to ethics, nurses realize that individual human stories are being constantly constructed in relation to the stories of a greater community of people. In nursing, a good example of narrative ethics involves nurses encountering each patient's unfolding life story in everyday practice with sensitive awareness. These nurses also know that their actions while caring for patients influence the unfolding stories of those patients in both large and small ways. A "narrative approach to bioethics focuses on the patients themselves: these are the moral agents who enact choices" (Charon & Montello, 2002, p. xi). In narrative ethics, patients' *and* nurses' stories matter; however, no one story should be accepted without critical reflection.

Ethical Reflections

- Discuss specific stories in books and movies that have affected your moral views.
- Obtain a copy of one or all of the following children's books:
  - *The Three Questions* by Jon J. Muth
  - *Stone Soup* "retold" by Jon J. Muth
  - An original edition of *The Little Engine that Could* by Watty Piper
  - *Old Turtle* by Douglas Wood
    - Identify themes and symbolism in the story.
    - Apply the themes and symbolism to nursing, including the nursing meta-paradigm of person, health, environment, and nursing.
    - As much as possible, apply the information in Chapter 1 to these stories.
- What do you believe might be legitimate criticisms of a narrative approach to ethics?

Critical Theory

Critical theory, sometimes referred to as critical social theory, is a broad term that identifies theories and worldviews that address the domination perpetrated by specific powerful groups of people and the resulting oppression of other specific groups of people. There are a number of different critical theories that are included under the one broad heading. In citing the group of German philosophers who originated the concept of critical theory, Bohman (2005) stated that critical theories can be distinguished from traditional theories because the purpose of critical theories is to promote human emancipation. Specifically, the purpose of using critical theories is "to liberate human beings from the circumstances that enslave them" (Horkheimer, 1982, p. 244, as cited in Bohman, 2005, para. 1). According to Brookfield (2005), there are three core assumptions in critical theory that explain how the world is organized. Critical theory purports:

1. That apparently open, Western democracies are actually highly unequal societies in which economic inequity, racism, and class discrimination are empirical realities.
2. That the way this state of affairs is reproduced and seems to be normal, natural, and inevitable (thereby heading off potential challenges to the system) is through the dissemination of dominant ideology.
3. That critical theory attempts to understand this state of affairs as a necessary prelude to changing it. (p. viii)

One critical theory that is widely used by nurses is a feminist approach to ethics. Under this broad feminist approach is the ethic of care that originated from the Kohlberg-Gilligan debate that was discussed earlier in this chapter.

Feminist Ethics

According to Tong (1997) "to a greater or lesser degree, all feminist approaches to ethics are filtered through the lens of gender" (p. 37). This means that **feminist ethics** is specifically focused on evaluating ethically related situations in terms of how these situations affect women. The concept of feminist ethics tends to have a political connotation and addresses the patterns of women's oppression as this oppression is perpetrated by dominant social groups, especially socially powerful men.

An **ethic of care** is grounded in the moral experiences of women and feminist ethics. It evolved into an approach to ethics that gained popularity because of the Gilligan-Kohlberg debate about the differences in women's and men's approaches to moral reasoning. Rather than being based on duty, fairness, impartiality, or objective principles (**ethic of justice**) similar to the values that were popularized during the Enlightenment era, an ethic of care emphasizes the importance of traditionally feminine traits such as love, compassion, sympathy, and concern about the well-being of other people. The natural partiality in how people care more about some people as compared to others is acknowledged in an ethic of care. Also, the role of emotions in moral reasoning and behavior is accepted as being a necessary and natural compliment to rational thinking. This position distinguishes an ethic of care from an ethic of justice and duty-based ethics that emphasize the preeminence of reason and minimize the importance of emotion in guiding moral reasoning and the moral nature of one's relationships.

Ethical Reflections

- Conduct an Internet search regarding critical theory. What are other specific examples of this type of theory?
- Discuss why critical theory is related to ethical behavior.
- In what areas of nursing can critical theory be applied?
- What do you believe might be legitimate criticisms of using a critical theory approach to ethics?
- Do you believe that *caring* is a virtue? Support your answer.

Principlism

Principles are rule-based criteria for conduct that naturally flow from the identification of obligations or duties. Consequently, the theory of deontology discussed earlier in this chapter is a forerunner of the approach of principlism. Principles are usually reducible to concepts or statements, such as the principle of beneficence or the respect for persons' autonomy. Principles often are used as the basis for ethically related documents, such as documents that reflect positions about human rights. Examples of principle-based documents include the American Hospital Association's Patient's Bill of Rights and the Universal Declaration of Human Rights formulated by the United Nations. Because principlism is so popular in the field of bioethics, this approach will be discussed in Chapter 2.

Eastern Ethics

Ethics in Asian societies has similarities to and important differences from Western ethics. In both cultures, ethics is often intertwined with spiritual or religious thinking, but ethics in Eastern societies is usually indistinguishable from general Eastern philosophies. Both Eastern and Western philosophies of ethics examine human nature and what is needed for people to move toward well-being. However, some of the differences in the two cultural systems are quite interesting and distinct.

Whereas the goal of Western ethics is generally for people to achieve self-direction and to understand themselves personally, the goal of Eastern ethics often is to understand universal interconnections (see Box 1.3), to be liberated from the self, or to understand that people really do not consist of a self at all (Zeuschner, 2001). Ethics viewed from Christian or other theological perspectives tends to be based on a belief in human flaws that require an intermediary (God) to transcend these imperfections. Eastern ethical systems usually are focused on individuals' innate but unrecognized perfection and the ability to transcend earthly suffering and dissatisfaction through one's own abilities. Therefore, Eastern ethics is not imposed from outside of a person but is instead imposed from within oneself. Eastern ethics tends to be a discipline of training the mind, and unethical behavior leads to karmic results (i.e., the quality of one's actions results in fair consequences according to the universal law of cause and effect). The four largest Eastern ethical systems, which contain myriad variations and now exist in a number of different countries, are Indian ethics (Hinduism and Buddhism) and Chinese ethics (Taoism and Confucianism).

Ethical Reflections

- How is the story about the Net of Indra in Box 1.3 related to ethics?

BOX 1.3: HIGHLIGHTS FROM THE FIELD: THE NET OF INDRA

The Buddhist *Avatamsaka Sutra* contains a story about how all perceiving, thinking beings are connected in a way that is similar to a universal community. The story is about the heavenly net of the god Indra. "In the heaven of Indra, there is said to be a network of pearls, so arranged that if you look at one you see all the others reflected in it. In the same way each object in the world is not merely itself but involves every other object and in fact *is* everything else. In every particle of dust there is present Buddhas without number."

Sir Charles Eliot, as cited in Capra, F. (1999). *The Tao of Physics*, (4th ed.), Boston: Shambhala, p. 296.

Indian Ethics

Hinduism

Hinduism is an ancient ethical system. It originated with writings called the Vedas (c. 2000 to 1000 B.C.E.) that include magical, religious, and philosophical teachings, which existed long before the well-known ethical philosophy of the ancient Greeks. The main emphasis in Hindu ethics is cosmic unity. Because of reincarnation, people are believed to be stuck in *maya*, an illusory, everyday, impermanent experience. The quality of one's past actions, *karma*, influences one's present existence and future incarnations or rebirths. Therefore, people need to improve the goodness of their actions, which will subsequently improve their karma. Liberation, *moksha*, means that the soul of each person is no longer reincarnated but becomes one with the desirable cosmic or universal self, *atman,* and the absolute reality of *Brahman.*

Buddhism

The historical Buddha, Siddhartha Gautama (6th century B.C.E.) was a Hindu prince. Because Siddhartha's father wanted to prevent the fulfillment of a prophecy that Siddhartha might become a spiritual teacher, he tried to shield his son from the world outside of his palace. However, Siddhartha left the confinement of his palace and saw in his fellow human beings the suffering associated with sickness, old age, and death. He decided to devote his life to understanding and ending suffering.

The Buddha's core teachings, the teachings that all Buddhist sects profess, are called the Four Noble Truths. The First Noble Truth is that unsatisfactoriness or suffering (*dukkha*) exists as a part of all forms of existence. This suffering is different from the common Western notion of physical or mental misery. Suffering in a Buddhist sense, for example, arises when people are ego-centered and cling to their impermanent existence and impermanent things. Suffering is emphasized in Buddhism, not to suggest a negative outlook toward life but instead as a realistic assessment of the human condition. The Second and Third Noble Truths suggest that the cause of suffering is attachment (clinging or craving) to impermanent things and that suffering can be transcended (enlightenment). The Fourth Noble Truth contains the path for transforming suffering into enlightenment or liberation. This path is called the Eight-fold Path, and it is composed of eight right practices: Right View, Right Thinking, Right Mindfulness, Right Speech, Right Action, Right Diligence, Right Concentration, and Right Livelihood. (See the Moral Ground Model in Chapter 2.)

Because of the central place of virtues in Buddhist philosophy, one interpretation of Buddhist ethics is to identify Buddhism as an ethic of virtue. There are four virtues that are singled out by Buddhists as being immeasurable because when these virtues are cultivated, it is believed that they will grow in a way that can encompass and transform the whole world. The Four Immeasurable Virtues are compassion (*karuna*), loving-kindness (*metta*), sympathetic joy (*mudita*), and equanimity (*upekkha*). Each of these virtues is included in the Moral Ground Model, which is discussed in Chapter 2.

Chinese Ethics

The two most influential Chinese ethical systems were developed between 600 and 200 B.C.E. during a time of social chaos in China. The two systems are Taoism and Confucianism.

Taoism

The beginning of Taoism is attributed to Lao-tzu (c. 571 B.C.E.) who wrote the Taoist guide to life, the *Tao Te Ching*. The word *Tao* is translated in English as the *Way* or *Path*, meaning the natural order or harmony of all things. Like Buddhists, Taoists do not believe in a creator God. Instead, Taoists have a very simple perspective toward reality—the underlying purpose of humans and the underlying purpose of nature cannot be separated. Based on the cyclic nature of life observed by ancient Chinese farmers, Taoist philosophy underscores the flux and balance of nature through yin (dark) and yang (light) elements. Living well or living ethically is living authentically, simply, and unselfishly in harmony and oneness with nature.

Confucianism

K'ung Fu-tzu (551 to 479 B.C.E.), who was later called Confucius by Christians visiting China, originated the Confucian ethical system. The teachings of Confucian ethics are generally contained in the moral maxims and sayings attributed to K'ung Fu-tzu along with the later writings of his followers. Confucian ethics is described through the concepts of *li* and *yi* (Zeuschner, 2001). *Li* provides guidance in regard to social order and how humans should relate to one another, including rules of etiquette such as proper greetings and social rituals. *Yi* emphasizes the importance of one's motivations toward achieving rightness rather than emphasizing consequences. Sincerity, teamwork, and balance are critically important to ethical behavior. The primary virtue of Confucian ethics is *jen*, which is translated in English as benevolence or human goodness. Overall, Confucianism is a communitarian ethical system in which social goals, the good of society, and the importance of human relationships are valued.

---------------------- **Ethical Reflections** ----------------------

- From your limited reading of Eastern philosophy contained in this chapter, does it make sense to you that general Eastern philosophical worldviews are ethics related? Why or why not?
- What is your reaction to these readings about Eastern philosophies and ethics?
- Compare and contrast Eastern and Western ethical approaches as they may relate to holism, reductionism, and the nursing meta-paradigm.

Summary

In the world today, discussions about ethical issues in health care are complex. If nurses are to be able to intelligently participate in a dialogue about health care ethics across populations and disciplines, nurses need to have a broad philosophical basis and rationale for their ethics-related positions and decisions. Therefore, nurses need to have an understanding of historical perspectives of moral reasoning and ethical theories and approaches, many of which are still useful in the 21st century.

Key Points

- Ethics usually refers to the analysis of matters of right and wrong, whereas morals refer to actual beliefs and behaviors. However, the terms are often used synonymously.
- Values refer to judgments about what one believes is good or what makes something desirable. Values influence how a person's character is developed and how people think and subsequently behave.
- Normative ethics is an attempt to decide or prescribe values, behaviors, and ways of being that are right or wrong, good or bad, and admirable or deplorable. When doing normative ethics, people ask questions such as "How ought humans to behave?", "What should I do?", and "What sort of person should I be?"
- Ethical thinking, valuing, and reasoning generally fall along a continuum between ethical relativism and ethical objectivism.
- Virtue ethics emphasizes the excellence of one's character.

- Deontological ethics emphasizes one's duty rather than the consequences of one's actions.
- Utilitarian ethics emphasizes the consequences of one's actions in regard to achieving the most good for the most people that may be affected by a rule or action.
- Eastern philosophies and systems of ethics often are inseparable.
- The study of values and ways of moral reasoning throughout history can be useful for people living in the 21st century. Specific values and ways of moral reasoning tend to overlap and converge over time.

Web Ethics

Philosophers and their work: http://www.iep.utm.edu

Online guide to ethics and moral philosophy: http://caae.phil.cmu.edu/Cavalier/80130/

Ethics links: http://www.hopkinsmedicine.org/bioethics/links.html

References

American Nurses Association. (2001). *Code of ethics with interpretive statements.* Silver Spring, MD: Author.

Aristotle. (2002). *Nicomachean ethics* (C. Rowe, Trans., S. Broadie, Intro. & Commentary). New York: Oxford University Press.

Billington, R. (2003). *Living philosophy: An introduction to moral thought* (3rd ed.). London, UK: Routledge—Taylor & Francis Group.

Bohman, J. (2005). Critical theory. In E. N. Zalta (Ed.). *The Stanford encyclopedia of philosophy.* Retrieved June 28, 2007 from http://plato.stanford.edu/archives/spr2005/entries/critical-theory/

Brannigan, M. C., & Boss, J. A. (2001). *Healthcare ethics in a diverse society.* Mountain View, CA: Mayfield.

Brookfield, S. D. (2005). *The power of critical theory: Liberating adult learning and teaching.* San Francisco: Jossey-Bass.

Capra, F. (1999). *The Tao of physics* (4th ed.). Boston: Shambhala.

Charon, R., & Montello, M. (2002). Introduction: The practice of narrative ethics. In R. Charon & M. Montello (Eds.), *Stories matter* (pp. ix–xii). New York: Routledge.

Cleary, K.M. (1996). *Native American wisdom.* New York: Barnes & Noble Books.

Donahue, M. P. (1996). *Nursing the finest art: An illustrated history* (2nd ed.). St. Louis: Mosby.

Gilligan, C. (1982). *In a different voice: Psychological theory and women's development.* Cambridge, MA: Harvard University Press.

Hope, T. (2004). *Medical ethics: A very short introduction.* New York: Oxford University Press.

International Council of Nurses. (2006). *The ICN code of ethics for nurses.* Geneva: Author.

LeVasseur, J. (1998). Plato, Nightingale, and contemporary nursing. *Image: Journal of Nursing Scholarship, 30*(3), 281–285.

MacIntyre, A. (1984). *After virtue: A study of moral theory* (2nd ed.). Notre Dame, IN: University of Notre Dame Press.

Murray, T. H. (1997). What do we mean by "narrative ethics"? *Medical Humanities Review, 11*(2), 44–57.

Pence, G. (2000). *A dictionary of common philosophical terms.* New York: McGraw-Hill

Sellman, D. (1997). The virtues in the moral education of nurses: Florence Nightingale revisited. *Nursing Ethics, 4*(1), 3–11.

Tong, R. (1997). *Feminist approaches to bioethics: Theoretical reflections and practical applications.* Boulder, CO: Westview Press.

Tschudin, V. (2003). Introductory paragraph of Scott, P. A. (2003). *Virtue, nursing and the moral domain of practice.* In V. Tschudin (Ed.), *Approaches to ethics: Nursing beyond boundaries* (pp. 25–32). Edinburgh, UK: Butterworth-Heinemann.

Zeuschner, R. B. (2001). *Classical ethics East and West: Ethics from a comparative perspective.* Boston: McGraw-Hill.

CHAPTER 1 QUESTIONS

1. As a branch of philosophy, ethics is
   a. a process or an analysis.
   b. a set of moral Truths.
   c. easily distinguished from morals.
   d. a relatively new discipline.

2. The position that "my beliefs about ethics and your beliefs about ethics, though they are different, are equally valid" describes
   a. ethical objectivism.
   b. cultural objectivism.
   c. ethical relativism.
   d. philosophical relativism.

3. If one uses a deontological approach to ethics, a person believes that behavior should be guided by
   a. one's character.
   b. achieving good consequences.
   c. one's duty.
   d. individual cases.

4. The best descriptor of virtue is
   a. excellence of character.
   b. knowing one's duty.
   c. achieving the best consequences.
   d. achieving the greatest good for the greatest number.

5. Feminist ethics can be classified as a
   a. utilitarian approach.
   b. deontological approach.
   c. virtue ethics approach.
   d. critical theory approach.

6. One common element in Eastern ethics and Western ethics is
   a. both ethical systems tend to be based on the belief that human flaws require an intermediary, such as a creator God, to transcend imperfections.
   b. both ethical systems tend to be a discipline of training the mind and unethical behavior influences one's future existence.
   c. both ethical systems are imposed from within oneself and not outside the person.
   d. both ethical systems examine human nature and what is needed for people to move toward well-being.

7. Aristotle's conception of the Golden Mean is best described as
   a. an injunction to "do unto others as you would have them do unto you."
   b. a belief that virtues are moderate ways of being that exist between two extremes of excess and deficiency.
   c. a belief that virtues are an exact average between two types of vices.
   d. a reactionary response to Plato's conception of the four cardinal virtues.

8. Narrative ethics includes an emphasis on
   a. one's duty in each life story.
   b. consequences identified through stories.
   c. the context of situations.
   d. identifying bioethical principles in stories.

9. The belief that reality is constantly changing and that scientific investigations cannot provide people with one absolute Truth best characterizes the world view of
   a. Ancient Greece.
   b. the Enlightenment.
   c. Modernism.
   d. Postmodernism.

10. A well-known utilitarian ethicist is
    a. John Stuart Mill.
    b. Aristotle.
    c. Immanuel Kant.
    d. Lawrence Kohlberg.

CHAPTER 1 ANSWERS

Question 1: The correct answer is A.
Ethics is not a static condition; ethics is an active analysis of matters of right and wrong and good and bad.
Choices B, C, and D are incorrect because there is no one set of absolute moral Truths; the words *ethics* and *morals* are often used interchangeably; historically, ethics is a very old discipline

Question 2: The correct answer is C.
Ethical relativism is the position that it is acceptable for conceptions of right and wrong to differ among persons or societies.
Choices A, B, and D are incorrect because objectivism means that people have definite beliefs about what is right and wrong and believe that ethics should not vary among people and societies; the term philosophical relativism is too broad

Question 3: The correct answer is C.
Deontology, primarily associated with the philosophy of Immanuel Kant, is based on good behavior motivated by one's sense of duty.
Choices A, B, and D are incorrect because virtue ethics is based on the excellence of one's character; utilitarianism is focused on the consequences of actions and achieving the greatest good for the greatest number of people; a focus on individual cases is not relevant

Question 4: The correct answer is A.
Virtue represents excellence, usually associated with excellence of character when one is referring to virtue ethics
Choices B, C, and D: see question 3.

Question 5: The correct answer is D.
Feminist ethics focuses on how ethically related issues are viewed from the unique position of women; a feminist approach to ethics has a political connotation that considers issues of women's oppression by dominant groups.

Choices A, B, and C: see question 3.

Question 6: The correct answer is D.
Ethical systems across cultures are focused on human well-being.

Choices A, B, and C are incorrect because Eastern ethics generally does not involve a creator God; training the mind is not emphasized in Western ethics; some Western ethical systems are based on being imposed from outside of oneself

Question 7: The correct answer is B.
Aristotle's Golden Mean is not an exact average but a middle ground that varies among situations and virtues.

Choices A, C, and D are incorrect because these answers do not describe the Golden Mean; the Golden Mean cannot be defined as an exact average

Question 8: The correct answer is C.
Narrative ethics is story and context focused; the nuances of situations are valued.

Choices A, B, and D are incorrect because narrative ethics is not focused on one's duty, consequences, or acting according to ethical principles

Question 9: The correct answer is D.
The statement in the stem of question 9 describes the world view of postmodernism.

Choices A, B, and C are incorrect because the world views represented by these eras are not commonly identified with philosophical pluralism.

Question 10: The correct answer is A.
John Stuart Mill is considered to be one of the "fathers" of utilitarianism.

Choices B, C, and D are incorrect because these men are not associated with utilitarianism. Aristotle is associated with virtue ethics; Kant is associated with deontology; Kohlberg is associated with moral reasoning, specifically justice-focused reasoning.

Introduction to Bioethics, Nursing Ethics, and Ethical Decision-Making

Karen L. Rich

The tiniest hair casts a shadow.
—JOHANN WOLFGANG VON GOETHE (1749–1832) GERMAN POET AND DRAMATIST

OBJECTIVES

After reading this chapter, the reader should be able to:

1. Compare and contrast the disciplines of bioethics and nursing ethics.
2. Use the approach of ethical principlism in nursing practice.
3. Identify criteria that define an ethical dilemma.
4. Analyze ethical issues in nursing relationships.
5. Consider how critical thinking is used in ethical nursing practice.
6. Use selected models of reflection and decision making in ethical nursing practice.

KEY TERMS

Bioethics
Beneficence
Paternalism
Justice
Social justice
Nonmaleficence
Nursing ethics

Unavoidable trust
Human dignity
Patient advocacy
Critical thinking
Moral imagination
Ethical dilemma
Slippery slope argument

Ethical principlism
Autonomy
Informed consent
Patient Self-Determination
  Act (PSDA)
Ethics committee
Moral suffering

Introduction to Bioethics

The terms *bioethics* and *health care ethics* sometimes are used interchangeably. **Bioethics**, born out of the rapidly expanding technical environment of the 20th century, is a specific domain of ethics that is focused on moral issues in the field of health care. During World War II, President Franklin D. Roosevelt assembled a committee to improve medical scientists' coordination in addressing the medical needs of the military (Jonsen, 2000). As often happens with wartime research and advancements, the work aimed at addressing military needs also affected civilian sectors, such as the field of medicine.

Between 1945 and 1965, antibiotic, antihypertensive, antipsychotic, and cancer drugs came into common medical use; surgery entered the heart and the brain; organ transplantation was initiated; and life-sustaining mechanical devices, the dialysis machine, the pacemaker, and the ventilator were invented. (Jonsen, 2000, p. 99)

However, with these advances also came increased responsibility and distress among health care professionals. Patients who would have died in the past began to have a lingering, suffering existence. Health care professionals were faced with trying to decide how to allocate newly developed scarce medical resources. During the 1950s, scientists and medical professionals began meeting to discuss these confusing problems. Eventually, health care policies and laws were enacted to address questions of "Who lives? Who dies? and Who decides?" A new field of study was developed that was called *bioethics*, a term that first appeared in the literature in 1969 (Jonsen, 1998, 2000, 2005). Key events in the early days of bioethics are listed in Box 2.1.

Ethical Principles

Because shocking information surfaced about serious ethical lapses, such as the heinous World War II Nazi medical experiments in Europe and the unethical Tuskegee research in the United States, societies around the world became very conscious of the possible ethical pitfalls in conducting biomedical and behavioral research. In the United States, the National Research Act became law in 1974, and a commission was created to outline the underlying principles that must be supported during research involving human subjects (National Institutes of Health, 1979). In 1976, to carry out their charge, the commission held an intensive 4-day meeting at the Bel-

BOX 2.1: HIGHLIGHTS FROM THE FIELD: EARLY EVENTS IN BIOETHICS

August 19, 1947: The Nuremberg trials of Nazi doctors who conducted heinous medical experiments during WWII begin.

April 25, 1953: Watson and Crick publish a one-page paper about DNA.

December 23, 1954: First renal transplant.

March 9, 1960: First use of chronic hemodialysis.

December 3, 1967: First heart transplant by Dr. Christiaan Barnard.

August 5, 1968: Definition of brain death developed by an ad hoc committee at Harvard Medical School.

July 26, 1972: Revelations appear about the unethical Tuskegee syphilis research.

January 22, 1973: *Roe v. Wade.*

April 14, 1975: A comatose Karen Ann Quinlan was brought to Newton Memorial Hospital; she becomes the basis of a landmark legal case about the removal of life support.

July 25, 1978: Baby Louise Brown was born; the first "test tube baby."

Spring 1982: Baby Doe becomes the basis of a landmark case that resulted in legal and ethical directives about the treatment of impaired neonates.

December 1982: The first artificial heart was implanted into the body of Barney Clark who, thereafter, lived 112 days.

April 11, 1983: *Newsweek* publishes the story that a mysterious disease called AIDS is at epidemic levels.

Jonsen, A. R. (2000). *A short history of medical ethics* (pp. 99–114). New York: Oxford University Press.

mont Conference Center at the Smithsonian Institute. Thereafter, discussions continued until 1978 when the commission released its report, called the Belmont Report.

The report outlined three basic principles for all human subjects research: *respect for persons, beneficence,* and *justice* (National Institutes of Health, 1979). The principle of beneficence, as set forth in the Belmont Report, included the rule to do good. However, the description of beneficence also included the rule that is now commonly attributed to the principle of nonmaleficence, that is, to do no harm.

The report contained guidelines regarding how to apply the principles in research through informed consent, the assessment of risks and benefits to research participants, and the selection of research participants.

In 1979, as an outgrowth of the Belmont Report, Beauchamp and Childress published the first edition of their book, *Principles of Biomedical Ethics*, which featured four bioethical principles—autonomy, nonmaleficence, beneficence, and justice. Currently, the book is in its fifth edition. In the current edition of the book, the principle of autonomy is now described as *respect for autonomy*.

Doing ethics based on the use of principles, the approach of **ethical principlism,** does not involve the use of a theory or a formal decision-making model; rather, ethical principlism provides guidelines that can be used to make justified moral decisions and to evaluate the morality of actions. Ideally, when using the approach of principlism, no one principle should automatically be assumed to be superior to the other principles.

Some people have criticized the use of ethical principlism because they believe that it is a top-down approach that does not include allowances for the context of individual cases and stories. Critics contend that simply applying principles when making ethical determinations results in what might be described as a linear way of doing ethics, that is, the fine nuances present in all relationship-based determinations will not be adequately respected. Nevertheless, the approach of ethical principlism using the four principles outlined by Beauchamp and Childress (2001) has become one of the most popular tools used today for analyzing and resolving bioethical problems.

Autonomy

Autonomy is the freedom and ability to act in a self-determined manner. It denotes the right of a rational person to generate personal decisions independent of outside interference. It can be argued that autonomy occupies a central place in health care ethics because of the popularity of the Enlightenment era philosophy of Immanuel Kant (see Chapter 1). However, it is noteworthy that autonomy is not emphasized in an ethic of care and virtue ethics, and these also are popular approaches to ethics today.

The principle of autonomy sometimes is described as *respect* for autonomy (Beauchamp & Childress, 2001). In the domain of health care, respecting a patient's autonomy includes obtaining informed consent for treatment; facilitating and supporting patients' choices regarding treatment options; allowing patients to refuse treatments; disclosing comprehensive and truthful information, diagnoses, and treatment options to patients; and maintaining privacy and confidentiality. Respecting autonomy also is important in less obvious situations, such as allowing home care patients to choose a tub bath versus a shower when it is safe to do so. Restrictions on an individual's autonomy may occur in cases where a person presents a potential for harm to others, such as exposing other people to communicable diseases or acts of violence. People generally lose the right to exercise autonomy or self-determination in such instances.

Informed Consent

Informed consent in regard to a patient's treatment is a legal as well as an ethical issue of autonomy. At the heart of **informed consent** is respecting a person's autonomy to make personal choices based on the appropriate appraisal of information about the actual and/or potential circumstances of a situation. There are three basic elements necessary for informed consent to occur (Dempski, 2006):

1. *Receipt of information:* Description of, risks and benefits of, and reasonable alternatives to the treatment; information should be specifically tailored to a person's personal circumstances.
2. *Consent for the treatment must be voluntary:* Depending on the circumstances, consent may be verbalized, written, or implied by behavior.
3. Persons must be competent: Persons must be able to communicate consent and to understand the information provided to them.

It is not ethical or legal for a nurse to be responsible for obtaining informed consent for procedures that are performed by a physician (Dempski, 2006). Nurses may need to display the virtue of courage if physicians attempt to delegate this responsibility to them. Though both nurses and physicians in some circumstances may believe that nurses are well versed in assuring that the three elements of informed consent are met for medical or surgical procedures to be performed by a physician, nurses must refrain from this responsibility. On the other hand, it is certainly within a nurse's domain of responsibility to notify appropriate parties if the nurse knows that a patient has not given an informed consent for a procedure. In fact, it is ethically incumbent upon nurses to facilitate patients' opportunities to give informed consent. Nurses also may be legally liable if they know or should have known that informed consent was not obtained, and nurses do not appropriately notify physicians or supervisors about this deficiency.

Patient Self-Determination Act

The **Patient Self-Determination Act (PSDA)** passed by the U.S. Congress in 1990 is the first federal statute designed to facilitate a patient's autonomy through the knowledge and use of advance directives. Health care providers and organizations must provide written information to adult patients regarding state laws covering the right to make health care decisions, to refuse or withdraw treatments, and to write advance directives. One of the underlying aims of the PSDA is to increase meaningful dialogue about patients' rights to make autonomous choices about receiving or not receiving health care.

It is important that dialogue about end-of-life decisions and options not be lost in organizational admission processes, paperwork, and other ways. Nurses provide the vital communication link between the patient's wishes, the paperwork, and the provider. When the opportunity arises, nurses need to take an active role in increasing their dialogue with patients in regard to patients' rights and end-of-life decisions. In addition to responding to the direct questions that patients and families ask about advance directives and end-of-life options, nurses would do well to "listen" for patients' subtle cues that signal their anxiety and uncertainty about end-of-life care. A good example of compassionate care is when nurses actively listen to patients and try to alleviate patients' uncertainty and fears in regard to end-of-life decision making.

Ethical Reflections

- Other than issues of informed consent and advance directives, identify one specific example of upholding and one specific example of violating the principle of autonomy in the nursing care of patients.
- Discuss the condition of vulnerability in relation to the respect for autonomy.
- In addition to the examples previously mentioned, might respecting autonomy ever be a harmful process? Provide a rationale for your answer and situational examples.

Nonmaleficence

Nonmaleficence is the principle used to communicate the obligation to "do no harm." Emphasizing the importance of this principle is as old as organized medical practice. Health care professionals have historically been encouraged to do good (beneficence), but if for some reason they cannot do good, they generally are required to at least do no harm. Because of the "two sides of the same coin" connotation between these two principles, some people consider them to be essentially one and the same. However, Beauchamp and Childress (2001) do make a distinction between the two of them.

Nonmaleficence is the maxim or norm that "one ought not to inflict evil or harm" (Beauchamp & Childress, 2001, p. 115), whereas beneficence includes the following three norms: "one ought to prevent evil or harm, one ought to remove evil or harm, [and] one ought to do or promote good" (p. 115). As evidenced by these maxims, beneficence involves action to help someone and nonmaleficence requires "*intentionally refraining* from actions that cause harm" (p. 115). In addition to violating the maxim not to intentionally harm another person, some of the issues and concepts listed by Beauchamp and Childress as frequently involving or requiring the obligation of nonmaleficence are included in Box 2.2.

Best practice and due-care standards are adopted by regulatory agencies to minimize harm to patients. This is done through oversight procedures to ensure that health care providers maintain the competency and skills needed to properly care for patients. Nonmaleficence has a wide scope of implications in health care that includes the need to avoid negligent care, the need to avoid harm when deciding to withhold or withdraw a patient's treatment, and considering extraordinary or heroic treatment.

The distinctions included in number 3 of Box 2.2 are usually associated with end-of-life care, which is discussed in Chapter 12. Particularly, the first three distinctions may involve issues of medical futility. Though it is sometimes difficult to accurately predict the outcomes of all interventions, futile treatments are those treatments that a health care provider, when using good judgment, does not believe will provide a beneficial outcome for a patient. Consequently, these treatments may instead cause harm

Box 2.2: Highlights from the Field: Issues and Concepts Surrounding the Principle of Nonmaleficence

1. Negligence: untended harm; "the absence of due care" (p. 118)
2. Standard of due care: "not imposing *risks* of harm" (p. 117)
3. Distinctions of and decisions about:
   a. Withholding and withdrawing life-sustaining treatment
   b. Extraordinary (or heroic) and ordinary treatment
   c. Artificial feeding and life-sustaining medical technologies
   d. Intended effects and merely foreseen effects (p. 119)

Beauchamp, T. L., & Childress, J. F. (2001). *Principles of biomedical ethics* (5th ed.). New York: Oxford University Press.

to a patient, such as a patient having to endure a slow and painful death that may have otherwise occurred in a quicker and more natural or humane manner. The Rule of Double Effect, described in Chapter 12, is a good example of actions that must be gauged according to the intended effects as compared to merely foreseen effects (as delineated in Box 2.2, number 3d).

Slippery Slope Argument

Often a **slippery slope argument** is a metaphor that is used as a "beware the Ides of March" warning with no justification or formal, logical evidence to back it up (Ryan, 1998, p. 341). A slippery slope situation is one that may be morally acceptable when the primary event is currently being discussed or practiced but one that could hypothetically slip toward a morally unacceptable situation. A slippery slope situation is somewhat like a runaway horse that cannot be stopped once the barn door is left open. People proposing a slippery slope argument often believe the old saying that when people are given an inch, they may eventually take a mile. Because it is argued that harm may be inflicted if the restraints on a particular practice are removed, the concept of the slippery slope is sometimes considered to fall under the domain of nonmaleficence.

Slippery slope arguments may move toward illogical extremes. Therefore, people who are afraid of a dangerous slide to the bottom of the slope on certain issues need to find evidence that justifies their arguments rather than trying to form public opinions and policies based only on alarmist comparisons. One example of a slippery slope argument is focused on the legalization of physician-assisted suicide (PAS). Proponents of the slippery slope argument say that allowing PAS, which involves a patient's voluntary decision and self-administration of lethal drugs in well-defined circumstances, may or may not in itself be morally wrong. However, slippery slope proponents argue that the widespread legalization of PAS may lead to the eventual legalization of nonvoluntary practices of euthanasia (see Chapter 12 for more explanation on euthanasia). Opponents of slippery slope arguments often believe that people proposing this type of argument mistrust people's abilities to make definitive distinctions between moral and immoral issues and to exercise appropriate societal controls.

Ethical Reflections

- Nurses are not directly responsible for decisions such as the withholding and withdrawing of patients' life support. However, because of their relationships with patients and their families, nurses often are involved in more than a peripheral way with these events.

- ○ Discuss one specific example of upholding the principle of nonmaleficence in the nursing care of a terminally ill patient.
- ○ Discuss one specific example of a possible violation of the principle of nonmaleficence in the nursing care of a terminally ill patient.
- Identify one specific example of upholding and one specific example of violating the principle of nonmaleficence that is not related to the end-of-life nursing care of a patient.
- Identify current bioethical issues that are or can be argued as slippery slope issues. Analyze both sides of the argument for one of these issues. Take a position and defend it.
- Do you believe that most people can be trusted to make their decisions based on the overall good of human beings? Explain.

Beneficence

The principle of **beneficence** consists of deeds of "mercy, kindness, and charity" (Beauchamp & Childress, 2001, p. 166). Beneficence means that people take actions to benefit and to promote the welfare of other people. Whereas people are obligated to act in a nonmaleficent manner toward all people, that is, not to harm anyone, there are limits to beneficence or to the benefits that people are expected to bestow on other people. Generally, people act more beneficently toward people whom they personally know or love rather than toward people not personally known to them, though this is certainly not always the case.

Sometimes there are limits to the good that nurses can do, but nurses are directed in the *Code of Ethics for Nurses with Interpretive Statements* (American Nurses Association [ANA], 2001) to always place their patients' interests and well-being as their primary concern. Therefore, nurses have a more stringent obligation to act according to the principle of beneficence than does the general public. Doing good toward and facilitating the well-being of one's patients is an integral part of being a moral nurse.

Paternalism

Occasionally, health care professionals may experience ethical conflicts when confronted with having to make a choice between respecting a patient's right to self-determination (autonomy) and doing what is good for a patient's well-being (beneficence). Sometimes nurses or other health care professionals believe that they, not their patients, know what is in a patient's best interest. In these situations, health care professionals may be tempted to act in ways that they believe promote a patient's well-being (beneficence) when the actions actually are a violation of a patient's right to exercise self-determination (autonomy). The deliberate overriding of a patient's opportunity to exercise autonomy because of a perceived obligation of beneficence is called **paternalism**.

An example of paternalism is when a nurse avoids telling a patient that her blood pressure reading is elevated when the patient questions the nurse, because the nurse believes that this information will upset the patient and consequently further elevate her blood pressure. A more ethical approach is to unexcitedly give the patient truthful information while helping her to remain calm and facilitating successful ways to manage her blood pressure. Though the practice of paternalism is usually discouraged today, it once was a common practice among health care professionals. Paternalism is still a common practice among people of some cultures who, for example, do not believe that patients should be given bad news such as a terminal diagnosis.

--- **Ethical Reflections** ---

- Identify one specific example of upholding and one specific example of violating the principle of beneficence in the nursing care of patients.
- Have you ever practiced paternalism with your patients? If so, discuss the circumstances and your rationale for this practice. Evaluate the ethics of this action using the approach of principlism.
- How might the issue of paternalism be related to virtue ethics? Deontology? Utilitarianism?
- Have you witnessed a nurse colleague or physician practicing paternalism? Evaluate the ethics of the circumstance and how you responded to the other person's actions.
- If you have not witnessed paternalism being practiced by another health care professional, provide an imagined example of witnessing the behavior and outline a plan of how you would respond.
- Do you believe that paternalism is ever justified? Defend your position.

Justice

Justice as a principle in health care ethics refers to fairness, treating people equally and without prejudice, and the equitable distribution of benefits and burdens. Most of the time, difficult health care resource allocation decisions are based on attempts to answer questions regarding who has a right to health care and who will pay for health care costs. Remember, however, that justice, as it was discussed in Chapter 1, also is one of Plato's cardinal virtues. This means that justice is a broad concept in the field of ethics.

Social Justice

Social justice is usually thought of in terms of how benefits and burdens should be distributed fairly among members of a society, or ideally, how all people in a society should have the same rights, benefits, and opportunities. The mission to define and attain some measure of social justice is an ongoing and difficult activity for the world community. One only needs to think about the obligations of beneficence to identify how these two principles are related. For example, what are the limits of the obligation that people have to "do good" in distributing their assets to help others?

An analysis of social justice mostly has been used to evaluate the powers of competing social systems and the application of regulatory principles on an impartial basis. Theories of social justice differ to some extent, but most of the theories are based on the notion that justice is related to fair treatment and that similar cases should be treated in similar ways. People who take a communitarian approach to social justice will seek the common good of the community rather than individual freedoms. If people think beyond borders in promoting social justice, they must consider how basic health care for all people can be provided and what can be done to prevent social injustice worldwide, such as trying to alleviate poverty and hunger.

In his book, *A Theory of Justice*, Rawls (1971) proposed that fairness and equality be evaluated under a "veil of ignorance." This concept means that if people had a veil to shield them from their own or others' economic, social, and class standing, each person would be likely to make justice-based decisions from a position that is free from biases. Consequently, each person would view the distribution of resources in impartial ways. Under the veil, people would view social conditions neutrally because they would not know what their own position might be at the time the veil is lifted. This "not knowing" or ignorance of persons about their own position means that they cannot gain any type of advantage for themselves by their choices. Rawls advocated two principles of equality and justice: (1) everyone should be given equal liberty regardless of their adversities, and (2) differences among people should be recognized by making sure that the least advantaged people are given opportunities for improvements.

In 1974, Robert Nozick presented the idea of an entitlement system in his book, *Anarchy, State, and Utopia*. He proposed that individuals should be entitled to health care and the benefits of insurance only if they are able to pay for these benefits. Nozick emphasized a system of libertarianism meaning that justice and fairness are consistent with rewarding only those people who contribute to the system. People who cannot afford health insurance are disadvantaged if Nozick's entitlement theory is used as a philosophy of social justice.

Later, in his book, *Just Health Care*, Daniels (1985) used the basis of Rawls's concept of justice and suggested a liberty principle. Daniels advocated national health care reform and proposed that every person should have equal access to health care and reasonable access to health care services. Daniels suggested that there should be critical standards for a fair and equitable health care system, and he provided points of reference, or benchmarks, for this application of fairness in the implementation and development of national health reform.

Distributing and allocating health care resources continues to be a major problem in the United States. As of 2005, 46.6 million people did not have health insurance (U.S. Census Bureau, 2005). This number reflects an increase in 1.3 million uninsured people from 2004. No matter what theory is applied, there needs to be a standard by which health care and other resources are distributed. Ethicists have contended that some version of the following standards needs to be applied or considered when distributions are made (Brannigan & Boss, 2001):

- Distribute according to market, that is, to those who can afford to pay
- Distribute according to social merit
- Distribute according to medical need
- Distribute according to age
- Distribute according to queuing, or first-come, first-served
- Distribute according to random selection (p. 619)

——————————————— **Ethical Reflections** ———————————————

- Discuss personal experiences with justice in your work with patients. Provide one specific example of upholding and one specific example of violating the principle of justice that you have encountered in the nursing care of patients.
- Of the standards listed in the bullet points above the Ethical Reflections box, which one(s) best fit(s) your beliefs and value system? Justify your choice(s).
- Discuss your views about the limits of social justice. What do you believe people "owe" one another? Defend your answers.

Ethical Dilemmas

An **ethical dilemma** is a situation in which an individual is compelled to choose between two actions that will affect the welfare of a sentient being, and both actions are reasonably justified as being good, neither action is readily justified as being good, or the goodness of the actions is uncertain. One action must be chosen, thereby generating a quandary for the person or group who is burdened with the choice.

Kidder (1995) focused on one characteristic of an ethical dilemma when he described the heart of an ethical dilemma as "the ethics of right versus right" (p. 13). Though the best choice about two right actions is not always self-evident, according to Kidder, "right versus right" choices clearly can be distinguished from "right versus wrong" choices. Right versus right choices bring us closer to common societal and personal values whereas the closer one analyzes right versus wrong choices, "the more they begin to smell" (p. 17). He proposed that people generally can judge *wrong* choices according to three criteria: violation of the law, departure from the truth, and deviation from moral rectitude. Of course, the selection and meaning of these three criteria can be a matter of debate among many people.

Ethical Reflections

- Review the concepts of ethical relativism and ethical subjectivism in Chapter 1. How are these concepts related to ethical dilemmas in health care?
- What criteria would you suggest to identify unethical or "wrong" choices in your life? Were your criteria developed subjectively or objectively? Defend the ethics of your criteria.
- Describe an ethical dilemma that you have personally encountered during your work as a nurse or student nurse.
  ○ Explain why your example fits the criteria of an ethical dilemma.
  ○ What were your thoughts and feelings during the experience?
  ○ Describe the process that you used to make a decision in the situation.
  ○ What was the outcome of the situation?
- Describe an ethical dilemma that you have personally witnessed during your work as a nurse or student nurse but you were not responsible for making the necessary decision (for example, a decision made by a physician or supervisor).
  ○ Explain why this example fits the criteria of an ethical dilemma.
  ○ What were your thoughts and feelings during the experience?
  ○ Critique the process (as you understand it) that was used to make a decision in the situation.
  ○ What was the outcome of the situation?
- Identify an ethical dilemma that may occur in everyday life that is not related to health care.

Introduction to Nursing Ethics

All of the bioethical issues discussed in the previous sections of this chapter are applicable in some way to ethics in nurses' work. However, nurses usually are not the direct decision makers in the types of bioethical decisions that capture the attention of the news media. Nevertheless, the profession of nursing now has matured to the point that many nurse ethicists believe that the nursing profession has a distinct category of ethics that is unique. Because **nursing ethics** falls within the philosophy and science of health care, nursing ethics, like medical ethics, is a subcategory of bioethics.

Varcoe et al. (2004) emphasized that the field of nursing ethics now must be focused on the experiences and needs of practicing nurses, the exploration of the meaning of nursing ethics, and ethical practice in terms of nurses' perceptions. Johnstone (1999) defined nursing ethics as: "the examination of all kinds of ethical and bioethical issues from the perspective of nursing theory and practice . . ." (p. 46). The key point here is that issues of nursing ethics are viewed from a *nursing* perspective. Nursing ethics is relationship based and specifically refers to ethical issues as they directly relate to and affect nurses and their patients (individuals, families, communities, or populations) in nurses' daily work, whatever that work may be. However, it is most important for nurses to understand that to practice nursing ethically, nurses must be sensitive enough to recognize when they are facing seemingly obscure ethical issues in their day-to-day work.

Relationships

To a disciple who was constantly complaining about others the Master said, "If it is peace you want, seek to change yourself, not other people. It is easier to protect your feet with slippers than to carpet the whole earth."

—ANTHONY DE MELLO, *ONE MINUTE WISDOM*, 1985, P. 38

The ANA's (2001) *Code of Ethics for Nurses with Interpretive Statements* places patients in the position of the central focus of nursing and nursing relationships. However, the quality of patient care rendered by nurses often depends on the existence of harmonious relationships between nurses and physicians, other nurses, and other health care workers. Nurses who are interested in providing compassionate care to patients must be concerned about their relationships with colleagues as well as with their direct relationships with patients. If nurses view life as a web of interrelationships, all of a nurse's relationships potentially can affect the well-being of patients.

Moral Suffering in Nursing

Many times nurses experience a disquieting feeling of anguish, uneasiness, or angst that can be called **moral suffering**. Suffering in a moral sense has similarities to the Buddhist concept of *dukkha*, a Sanskrit word that is translated as suffering. *Dukkha* "includes the idea that life is impermanent and is experienced as unsatisfactory and imperfect" (Sheng-yen, 1999, p. 37). The concept of *dukkha* evolved from the historical Buddha's beliefs that the human conditions of birth, sickness, old age, and death involve suffering and *are* suffering. Nurses confront these human conditions every day. Not recognizing and struggling against the reality that impermanence, or the changing and passing away of all things, is inherent to human life, the world, and all objects is a cause of suffering.

Moral suffering can be experienced when nurses attempt to sort out their emotions when they find themselves in imperfect situations that are morally unsatisfactory or when forces beyond their control prevent them from positively influencing or changing unsatisfactory moral situations. Suffering occurs because nurses believe that situations must be changed or fixed in order to bring well-being to themselves and others or to alleviate the suffering of themselves and others.

Moral suffering may arise, for example, from disagreements with imperfect institutional policies, such as an on-call policy or work schedule that the nurse believes does not allow adequate time for the nurse's psychological well-being. Nurses also may disagree with physicians' orders that the nurses believe are not in patients' best interests, or they may disagree with the way a family treats a patient or makes patient care decisions. Moral suffering can result when a nurse's compassion is aroused when caring for a severely impaired neonate or an elder who is suffering and life-sustaining care is either prolonged or withdrawn. These are but a few examples of the many types of encounters that nurses may have with moral suffering.

Another important, but often unacknowledged, source of moral suffering may occur when nurses freely choose to act in ways that they, themselves, would not defend as morally commendable if the actions were honestly analyzed. For example, a difficult situation that may cause moral suffering for a nurse would be "covering up" a patient care error made by a valued nurse best friend. On the other hand, nurses may experience moral suffering when they act virtuously by doing what they believe is morally right despite anticipated disturbing consequences. Sometimes, doing the right thing or acting as a virtuous person would act is hard, and it is incumbent upon nurses to habitually act in virtuous ways, that is, to exhibit habits of excellent character.

The Dalai Lama (1999) proposed that how people are affected by suffering is often a matter of *choice* or personal perspective. Some people view suffering as something to accept and to transform, if possible. Causes may lead toward certain effects, and nurses are often able to change the circumstances or conditions of events so that positive effects occur. Nurses can try to choose and cultivate their perspectives, attitudes, and emotions in ways that lead toward happiness and well-being rather than toward suffering.

The Buddha was reported to have stated, "Because the world is sick, I am sick. Because people suffer, I have to suffer" (Thich Nhat Hanh, 1998, p. 3). However, in the Four Noble Truths the Buddha postulated that the cessation of suffering can be a reality through the Eightfold Path of eight *right* ways of thinking, acting, and being, sometimes grouped under the three general categories of wisdom, morality, and meditation. In other words, suffering can be transformed. When nurses or others react to situations with fear, bitterness, and anxiety, it is important to remember that wisdom and inner strength are often most increased during times of the greatest difficulty. Thich Nhat Hanh (1998) wisely stated, "without suffering, you cannot grow" (p. 5). Therefore, nurses must learn to take their disquieting experiences of moral anguish and uneasiness, that is, moral suffering, and transform them into experiences that lead to more flourishing moral ground.

Ethical Reflections

- Have you experienced moral suffering during your work as a nurse or student nurse? Explain.

Nurse-Patient-Family Relationships

Unavoidable Trust

When patients enter the health care system, they are usually entering a foreign and forbidding environment (Chambliss, 1996; Zaner, 1991). Intimate conversations and activities, such as touching and probing, that normally do not occur between strangers are commonplace between patients and health care professionals. Patients are frequently stripped of their clothes, subjected to sitting alone in cold and barren rooms, and made to wait anxiously for frightening news regarding the continuation of their very being. When patients are in need of help from nurses, they frequently feel a sense of vulnerability and uncertainty. The tension that patients feel when accessing health care is heightened by the need for what Zaner, in primarily discussing patient-physician relationships, called **unavoidable trust**. Zaner's concept also can be applied in other patient–health care professional relationships. Patients, in most cases, have no option but to trust nurses and other health care professionals when the patient is at the point of needing care.

This unavoidable trust creates an asymmetrical, or uneven, power structure in professional-patient and family relationships (Zaner, 1991). Nurses' responsiveness to this trust needs to include the promise to be the most excellent nurses that they can be. According to Zaner, health care professionals must promise "not only to take care of, but to care for the patient and family—to be candid, sensitive, attentive, and never to abandon them" (p. 54). It is paradoxical that trust is necessary *before* health care is rendered, but it can be evaluated only in terms of whether or not the trust was warranted *after* care is rendered. Nurses must never take for granted the fragility of patients' trust.

Ethical Reflections

- Explain how a nurse might assess if a patient is experiencing uncomfortable feelings associated with unavoidable trust.
- Suggest nursing actions that may help decrease patients' uncomfortable feelings when they are experiencing unavoidable trust.
- Why is unavoidable trust an ethical issue?

Human Dignity

In the first provision of the *Code of Ethics for Nurses with Interpretive Statements*, the ANA (2001) included the standard that a nurse must have "respect for **human dignity**" (p. 7). However, Shotton and Seedhouse (1998) proposed that the term *dignity* has been used in vague ways. They characterized dignity as persons being in a position to use their capabilities. In general terms, a person has dignity "if he or she is in a situation where his or her capabilities can be effectively applied" (p. 249). For example, a nurse can enhance dignity when caring for an elderly person by assessing the elder's priorities and determining what the elder has been capable of in the past and what the person is capable of in the present.

A lack of or loss of capability is frequently an issue when caring for patients such as children, elders, and the physically and mentally disabled. Having absent or diminished capabilities is consistent with what MacIntyre (1999) was referring to in his discussion of human vulnerability. According to MacIntyre, people generally progress from a point of vulnerability in infancy to achieving varying levels of independent practical reasoning as they mature. However, all people, including nurses, would do well to realize that all persons have been or will be vulnerable at some point in their lives. Taking a "there but for the grace of God go I" stance may prompt nurses to develop what MacIntyre called the virtues of acknowledged dependence. These virtues include *just generosity, misericordia,* and *truthfulness* and are exercised in communities of giving and receiving. *Just generosity* is a form of giving generously without "keeping score" of who gives or receives the most, *misericordia* is a Latin word that signifies giving based on urgent need without prejudice, and *truthfulness* involves not withholding information from others that is needed for their own good. Nurses who cultivate these three virtues can move toward preserving patients' dignity and toward working for the common good of a community.

Patient Advocacy

Nurses acting from a point of **patient advocacy** try to identify unmet patient needs and then follow up to address the needs appropriately (Jameton, 1984). Advocacy, as opposed to advice, involves the nurse's moving from the patient to the health care system rather than moving from the nurse's values to the patient. The concept of advocacy has been a part of the International Council of Nurses' (ICN) code and the ANA code since the 1970s (Winslow, 1988). In the *Code of Ethics for Nurses with Interpretive Statements,* the ANA (2001) continues to support patient advocacy in elaborating on the "primacy of the patient's interest" (p. 9) and requiring nurses to work collaboratively with others to attain the goal of addressing the health care needs of patients and the public. Nurses are called upon to assure that all appropriate parties are involved in patient care decisions, that patients are provided with the information needed to make informed decisions, and that collaboration is used to increase the accessibility and availability of health care to all patients who need it. The ICN (2006), in the *Code of Ethics,* affirms that the nurse must share "with society the responsibility for initiating and supporting action to meet the health and social needs of the public, in particular those of vulnerable populations" (p. 2).

Nurse-Physician Relationships

Relations between nurses and physicians have had a long and sometimes uneasy history. In their pamphlet, *Witches, Midwives, and Nurses: A History of Women Healers,* Ehrenreich and English (1973) provided a history of the male domination of women who were doing healing work. This interesting pamphlet details the burning at the stake of women healers from the 14th to the 17th centuries. These accused "witches" were some of the first empiricists in the field of health care who endured many centuries of oppression from male-dominated hierarchies, such as religious institutions. Finally, when efforts were made to transform medical men from a group receiving very little respect to a preeminent profession of great status, women and people of color were almost driven out of autonomous roles in health care in the United States. By the early 1900s, Florence Nightingale's work had drawn respect for the role of nurses, but Ehrenreich and English contended that nursing and other mostly female "occupations were presented as simple extensions of women's 'natural' domestic role" (p. 38). Nurses, to varying degrees, have been working ever since this time to overcome this perception.

In 1967, Stein, a physician, wrote an article characterizing a type of relationship between physicians and nurses that he called "the doctor-nurse game" (Stein, Watts, & Howell, 1990). The game is based on a hierarchical relationship with doctors being in the position of the superior. The hallmark of the game is that open disagreement between the disciplines is to be avoided. Avoidance of conflict is achieved when an experienced nurse, who is able to provide helpful suggestions to a doctor regarding patient care, cautiously offers the suggestions in a way that the physician does not directly perceive that consultative advice is coming from a nurse. In the past, student nurses were educated about the rules of "the game" while attending nursing school. Over the years, others have given credence to the historical accuracy of Stein's characterization of doctor-nurse relationships (Fry & Johnstone, 2002; Jameton, 1984; Kelly, 2000).

Stein, along with two other physicians, wrote an article revisiting the doctor-nurse game in 1990, 23 years after the phrase was first coined (Stein et al., 1990). They proposed that nurses unilaterally had decided to stop playing the game. Some of the reasons for this change and some of the ways the change was accomplished have involved nurses' increased use of dialogue rather than gamesmanship, the profession's goal of equal partnership status with other health care professionals, the alignment of nurses with the civil rights and women's movements, the increased percentage of nurses who are receiving higher education, and the joint demonstration projects on collaboration between nurses and physicians. In conjunction with the dismantling of the doctor-nurse game, many nurses have taken a less than communitarian stance with physicians. Some nurses believe that they need to continue an adversarial fight for freedom to establish nursing as an autonomous profession.

However, rather than generating an environment of competition with physicians, the nursing profession might be better served if nurses take a communitarian approach with physicians. It is within communities that morality in general, and bioethics in particular, receive their meanings (Engelhardt, 1996; see the section on Communitarian Ethics in Chapter 11). Communities work toward a common good and are held together by moral traditions. Nurses and physicians, as members of the health care community, must work together for the health and well-being of patients, whether those patients are individuals, families, groups, communities, or populations. When overt or covert turf battles are waged between nurses and physicians, moral problems arise and patients may be the losers. Some ethicists have contended that the best approach for healing involves actually bringing patients into the community of health care providers (Hester, 2001). If nurses and physicians do not see themselves as members of a common community, the best interests of patients may not be served.

Ethical Reflections

- What have been your overall experiences in working as a respected professional along with physicians?
  - Identify a specific plan of action for individual nurses to work with physicians in a communitarian manner.
  - Identify a plan for the whole nursing profession.

Nurse-Nurse Relationships

As in the case of nurse-physician relationships, nurse-nurse relationships can be thought of as relationships within a community. Nurses in a nursing community might be what Engelhardt (1996) called moral friends. According to Wildes (2000), moral friends exist together within communities and use similar moral language. They "share a moral narrative and commitments [and] common understandings of the foundations of morality, moral reason, and justification" (p. 137). Communities are strongest when moral friends share "common moral traditions, practices, and [a] vision of the good life" (p. 137). In placing patients first in nurses' priorities, nurses in a community work together for a common good, using professional traditions to guide the communal narrative of nursing.

Unfortunately, nurses often treat other nurses in hurtful ways through what some people have called lateral or horizontal violence (Kelly, 2000; McKenna, Smith, Poole, & Coverdale, 2003). Lateral or horizontal violence involves interpersonal conflict, harassment, intimidation, harsh criticism, sabotage, and abuse among nurses, and may occur because nurses feel oppressed by other dominant groups such as physicians or institutional administrators. Kelly reported that some nurses have characterized the violence perpetrated by nurses against other nurses who excel and succeed as the "tall poppy syndrome." Nurses who succeed are ostracized, thereby creating a culture among nurses that discourages success.

Lateral violence in nursing is very counterproductive for the profession. A more productive path to moral ground for nurses might be to cultivate the virtue that Buddhists call *sympathetic joy* that is included in the Moral Ground Model (see Figure 2.2 and Table 2.1 later in the chapter). Sympathetic joy means that one is joyful about other persons' experiences of happiness and the good things received by others. The nursing community does not benefit from lateral violence, but nurses who cultivate the virtue of sympathetic joy can strengthen a sense of community among nurses. Nurses need to support other nurses' successes rather than treating colleagues as "tall poppies" that must be cut down.

However, there are occasions when unpleasant but nonmalicious action must be taken in regard to nursing colleagues. In addition to directly advocating for patients' unmet needs, nurses are advocates when they take appropriate action to protect patients from the unethical, incompetent, or impaired practice of other nurses (ANA, 2001). When nurses are aware of these situations, they need to be compassionate toward offending co-workers while assuring that patients receive safe, quality care. Concerns need to be expressed to the offending nurse when personal safety and patient safety are not jeopardized in doing so, and appropriate guidance must be obtained from supervisory personnel and institutional policies. Though action needs to be taken to safeguard patients' care, the manner in which a nurse handles situations involving unethical, incompetent, or impaired colleagues must not be a matter of gossip, condescension, or unproductive derogatory talk.

Introduction to Critical Thinking and Ethical Decision-Making

In health care and nursing practice, ethical dilemmas and moral matters are so ever-present that nurses often do not even realize that they are making minute-to-minute moral decisions (Chambliss, 1996; Kelly, 2000). It is vitally important that nurses have the analytical thinking ability and skills to respond to many of the everyday decisions that must be made. Listening attentively to other people, including patients, and not developing hasty conclusions are essential skills for nurses to conduct reasoned, ethical analyses. Personal values, professional values and competencies, ethical principles, and ethical theories and approaches are variables that must be considered when a moral decision is made. Pondering the questions: "What is the right thing to do?" and "What ought I to do in this circumstance?" are ever-present normative considerations in nursing.

Critical Thinking

The words **critical thinking** are used quite liberally today in nursing. Many nurses probably have a general idea about the meaning of the concept, but they may not be able to clearly articulate answers to questions about its meaning. Examples of such questions include: Specifically, what is critical thinking? Are critical thinking and problem solving interchangeable concepts? If not, what distinguishes them? Can critical thinking skills be learned or does critical thinking either occur naturally or not at all? If the skill can be learned, how does one become a critical thinker?

Socrates' method of teaching and questioning (see Chapter 1) is one of the oldest systems of critical thinking. In modern times, a preeminent U.S. philosopher, John Dewey (1859–1952), is considered to be one of the early proponents of critical thinking. In his book, *How We Think*, Dewey (1910/1997) summarized reflective thought as

active, persistent, and careful consideration of any belief or supposed form of knowledge in light of the grounds that support it, and the further conclusions to which it tends. . . . [Dewey continued by saying that] once begun it is a conscious and voluntary effort to establish belief upon a firm basis of reasons. (p. 6)

Paul and Elder (2006), directors of the Foundation for Critical Thinking, defined critical thinking as "the art of analyzing and evaluating thinking with a view to improving it" (p. 4). They proposed that critical thinkers have certain characteristics. Critical thinkers:

- Ask clear, pertinent questions and identify key problems.
- Analyze and interpret relevant information by using abstract thinking.
- Are able to generate reasonable conclusions and solutions that are tested according to sensible criteria and standards.
- Remain open minded; they consider alternative thought systems.
- Solve complex problems by effectively communicating with other people.

Critical thinking is summarized by Paul and Elder (2006) as "self-directed, self-disciplined, self-monitored, and self-corrective thinking [that] requires rigorous standards of excellence and mindful command of their use" (p. 4). Fisher (2001) described the basic way to develop critical thinking skills as simply "thinking about one's thinking" (p. 5).

Ethical Reflections

- Search the Internet and nursing literature and gather additional information about the meaning and elements of critical thinking. One good Web site to explore is http://www.criticalthinking.org.
- Perform a written self-analysis of your critical thinking skills. What are your strengths? In what ways do you need to improve?
- Explain why asking intelligent questions is essential to good nursing practice. What type of questions do you routinely ask of yourself during your work? What type of questions do you routinely ask of other people during your work?
- Provide a personal example of a good question that you asked about an important issue that arose during your work. Provide a personal example of a time when you should have asked a question but did not do so. Analyze the different circumstances of these situations.
- Assuming that you want to be a critical thinker in your nursing practice, provide the following:
  - A list of the personal characteristics that you need.
  - An outline of a specific plan to develop critical thinking skills. What actions are necessary?
  - A specific description of how you would think and act if you were a critical thinker.
- Consider definitions of the terms *problem* and *problem solving*. Compare and contrast critical thinking and problem solving. Can the terms be correctly used interchangeably? Provide a rationale for your answer.
- From what you have learned about ethics and critical thinking, discuss why critical thinking is an important element of doing ethics.

Moral Imagination

[Persons], to be greatly good, must imagine intensely and comprehensively; [they] must put [themselves] in the place of another and of many others. . . . The great instrument of moral good is the imagination.

—Percy Bysshe Shelley, *Defense of Poetry*

The foundation underlying the concept of **moral imagination**, an artistic or aesthetic approach to ethics, is based on the philosophy of the American philosopher John Dewey. Imagination, as Dewey proposed it, is "the capacity to concretely perceive what is before us in light of what could be" (Fesmire, 2003, p. 65). Dewey (1934) stated that imagination "is a *way* of seeing and feeling things as they compose an integral whole" (p. 267). Moral imagination is moral decision making through reflection that involves "empathetic projection" and "creatively tapping a situation's possibilities" (Fesmire, p. 65). It involves moral awareness and decision making that goes beyond the mere application of standardized ethical meanings, decision-making models, and bioethical principles to real life situations.

The use of empathetic projection helps nurses be responsive to patients' feelings, attitudes, and values. To creatively reflect on a situation's possibilities helps prevent nurses from becoming stuck in their daily routines and instead encourages them to look for new and different possibilities in problem solving and decision making that go beyond mere habitual behaviors. Although Aristotle taught that habit is the way that people cultivate moral virtues, Dewey (1922/1988) cautioned that mindless habits can be "blinders that confine the eyes of mind to the road ahead" (p. 121). Dewey proposed that habit should be combined with intellectual impulse. He stated:

Habits by themselves are too organized, too insistent and determinate to need to indulge in inquiry or imagination. And impulses are too chaotic, tumultuous and confused to be able to know even if they wanted to. . . . A certain delicate combination of habit and impulse is requisite for observation, memory and judgment. (p. 124)

Dewey (1910/1997) provided an example of a physician trying to identify a patient's diagnosis without proper reflection:

Imagine a doctor being called in to prescribe for a patient. The patient tells him some things that are wrong; his experienced eye, at a glance, takes in other signs of a certain disease. But if he permits the suggestion of this special disease to take possession prematurely of his mind, to become an accepted conclusion, his scientific thinking is by that much cut short. A large part of his technique, as a skilled practitioner, is to prevent the acceptance of the first suggestions that arise; even, indeed, to postpone the occurrence of any very definite suggestions till the trouble—the nature of the problem—has been thoroughly explored. In the case of a physician this proceeding is known as a diagnosis, but a similar inspection is required in every novel and complicated situation to prevent rushing to a conclusion. (p. 74)

Although Dewey's example is about an individual patient-physician clinical relationship, the example also is applicable for illustrating the dangers of rushing to conclusions in the moral practice of the art and science of nursing with individuals, families, communities, and populations. The following story provides an example of a nurse not using moral imagination. A young public health nurse moves from a large city to a small country town and begins working as the occupational health nurse at a local factory. The nurse has noticed that a large number of workers at the factory have developed lung cancer. He immediately assumes that the workers have been exposed to some type of environmental pollution at the factory and that the factory owners are morally irresponsible people. The nurse discusses his assessment with his immediate supervisor and an official at the local health department. Upon further assessment, the nurse finds data showing that the factory's environmental pollution is unusually low. However, the nurse does learn that radon levels are particularly high in homes in the area.

In the following example, a home health nurse uses moral imagination. The nurse visits a homebound, elderly African American patient diagnosed with congestive heart failure. The patient tells the nurse that she has difficulty affording her medications and that she does not buy low-sodium foods that the nurse recommends because the fresh foods are too expensive. However, the patient has a new television that she is usually watching when the nurse visits. The home health aide that visits the patient tells the nurse "No wonder Mrs. S. can't afford her medications . . . she spent her money on a TV." Rather than judging the patient, the nurse uses her moral imagination to try to empathetically envision what it must be like to be Mrs. S.—homebound, consistently short of breath, and usually alone. The nurse decides that Mrs. S.'s TV may have been money well spent in terms of the patient's quality of life. With Mrs. S's physician and social worker, the nurse explores ways to help the patient obtain her medications. The nurse also works patiently with Mrs. S. to try to develop a healthy meal plan.

Dewey (1910/1997) seemed to be trying to make the point that critical thinking and moral imagination require suspended judgment until problems and situations are fully explored and reflected upon. Moral imagination includes engaging in frequent considerations of "What if?" with regard to day-to-day life events as well as novel situations. In a public interview on July 22, 2004, immediately after the U.S. Congress released its 9/11 Commission Report, former New Jersey Governor and the September 11 Commission's chairman, Thomas Kean, made a statement with regard to the findings about the probable causes of the failure to prevent the terrorist attacks on September 11, 2001 (Mondics, 2004). The commission concluded that, above all, there was a "failure of imagination" (p. A4).

An important role for nurses is to provide leadership and to help create healthy communities through individual, family, and population-based assessments, program planning, program implementation, and evaluation. When assuming this key leadership role, nurses must continually make choices and decisions that may affect the well-being of both individuals and populations of people. Opinions must not be hastily formed, nor should actions be taken without nurses cultivating and using their moral imaginations.

The High Hard Ground and Swampy Low Ground

It is generally agreed that nursing is based on the dual elements of art and science. According to the ANA's (2004) booklet, *Nursing: Scope and Standards of Practice*, the nursing process is a scientific, critical thinking framework used for clinical decision making and evidence-based practice. The ANA described the art of nursing as being based on intangible elements that affect human beings. Caring and respect are the hallmarks of nursing art.

However, Schön (1987) has postulated that professional dilemmas sometimes arise when there is tension between how to attend to knowledge based on technical, scientific foundations and indeterminate issues that lie beyond scientific laws. Schön described this tension as follows:

In the varied topography of professional practice, there is a high, hard ground overlooking a swamp. On the high ground, manageable problems lend themselves to solution though the application of research-based theory and technique. In the swampy lowland, messy, confusing problems defy technical solutions. The irony of this situation is that the problems of the high ground tend to be relatively unimportant to individuals or society at large, however great their technical interest may be, while in the swamp lie the problems of greatest human concern. The practitioner must choose. (p. 3)

Gordon and Nelson (2006) have argued that nursing has suffered by not emphasizing the profession's scientific basis and the specialized skills that are required for nursing practice. These authors proposed that the professional advancement of nursing has been hurt by nurses and others (including the general members of society) focusing too much on the virtues of nurses and the caring nature of the profession, essentially the art of nursing. According to Gordon and Nelson,

although much has changed for professional women in the twentieth century, nurses continue to rely on religious, moral, and sentimental symbols and rhetoric—images of hearts, angels, touching hands, and appeals based on diffuse references to closeness, intimacy, and making a difference. . . . When repeated in recruitment brochures and campaigns, appeals to virtue are unlikely to help people understand what nurses really do and how much knowledge and skill they need to do it. (pp. 26–27)

───────────────── **Ethical Reflections** ─────────────────

- Nurses might ask: Should we firmly stay on the high, hard ground founded on rigid scientific standards or is it equally and sometimes more important to descend into the swampy low ground full of important problems that are relatively unnoticed by people who are not directly affected? Discuss.
- Are nurses really faced with choosing "either/or" in terms of nursing science and art? Explain.
- Discuss your views about the state of the "profession" of nursing. Does a focus on the virtues and caring ways of nurses help or hinder the advancement of nursing as a profession?
- Is there a "Golden Mean" in describing nursing as a caring profession and one that requires specialized knowledge and skills? If so, how would you define the mean? Debate this issue with your colleagues.

Reflection in Nursing Practice

Schön (1987) distinguished reflection *on* action from reflection *in* action. Reflecting on action involves a looking back on one's actions whereas reflection in action involves stopping to think about what one is choosing and doing before and during one's actions. In considering the value of reflection in action, Schön stated "in an *action present*—a period of time, variable with the context, during which we can still make a difference to the situation at hand—our thinking serves to reshape what we are doing while we are doing it" (p. 26). Mindful reflection while we are still able to make choices about our behaviors is preferable to looking backwards. However, as the saying goes, hindsight is 20/20, so there is certainly learning that can occur from hindsight.

Since ethics is an active process of doing, reflection in any form is crucial to the practice of ethics. Making justified ethical decisions requires nurses to know themselves and their motives, to ask good questions, to challenge the status quo, and to be continual learners. There is no one model of reflection and decision making that can provide nurses with a cookie cutter approach to ethical practice. However, there are a number of models that nurses can use to improve their skills of reflection and decision making during their practice. Figure 2.1 includes an example of a model that is helpful for reflection *on* action. Another model, the Moral Ground Model, discussed in the following section, can be useful for developing the skills needed for reflection *in* action.

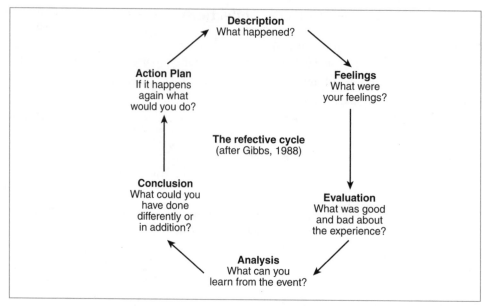

Figure 2.1 Gibbs's Reflective Cycle

Retrieved March 15, 2007 from http://www.nursesnetwork.co.uk/images/reflectivecycle.gif

Original out of print publication: Gibbs, G. (1988) *Learning by doing: A guide to teaching and learning methods.* Oxford, UK: Oxford Polytechnic.

Ethical Reflections

- Use Gibbs's Reflective Cycle to reflect on a challenging, personal ethical situation that occurred during your nursing practice.

The Moral Ground Model: A Virtue-Based Nursing Model

The Moral Ground Model has its foundation in Aristotle's approach to virtue ethics with a proposed path to moral ground adapted from the Eightfold Path and the Four Immeasurable Virtues of Buddhism. (For a review of these ethical approaches, refer to Chapter 1.) According to Keown (2001a) Buddhist ethics and health care ethics have a common focus—the alleviation of human suffering. The ethics of both Aristotle and Buddhism are arguably what can be called teleological philosophies, meaning that they both focus human morality on moving toward a final purpose or goal (Keown,

2001b). For Aristotle, the goal for humans was *eudaimonia* or happiness. For the Buddha, the goal was *nirvana* or enlightenment. This Buddhist-Aristotelian connection is illustrated in the virtue-based Moral Ground Model (see Figure 2.2).

The model implies that nurses may start at a groundless, uneducated state of moral functioning. The path from a groundless, untutored moral state to flourishing moral ground, though modeled in stages, is not linear but occurs in a dynamic, itera-

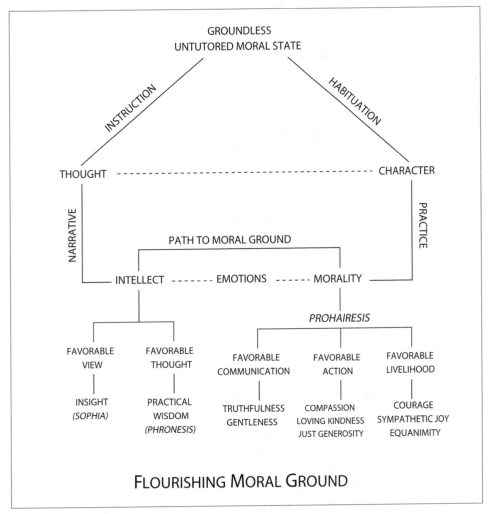

Figure 2.2   Moral Ground Model

tive pattern. The groundless, untutored moral state is one embedded in day-to-day activities in which the nurse is unaware of or unconcerned about the profound moral nature of nurses' daily work or when the nurse is immersed in unsatisfactoriness. Moral suffering is the norm. However, the nurse can move toward flourishing moral ground by traveling along a path of intellectual and moral virtues (see Table 2.1). The stages of the path are called favorable because they support and facilitate the embodiment of the virtues rather than obstructing movement along the path toward flourishing moral ground.

Mindfulness about narratives and personal experiences can educate nurses about intellectual virtues that provide insight into the nature of reality and how to achieve practical wisdom. Insight (*sophia*), a penetrating discernment about the unchangeable truths of reality, is the intellectual virtue that results from a favorable view. Included in these truths is the understanding that all things are impermanent or passing away, that moral suffering is an inherent condition between the groundless untutored moral state and the state of flourishing moral ground, and that life is characterized by interbeing (a pervasive holism or interconnection of all things). Critical elements of this insight include an awareness of the moral nature of nurses' day-to-day work and the belief that moral suffering can be transcended. Favorable thought involves using one's insight of reality in deliberative reasoning and applying the intellectual virtue of practical wisdom (*phronesis*) in directing one's actions. It includes knowing how a person

TABLE 2.1   Moral Ground Model Virtues

Intellectual Virtues	
Insight:	awareness and knowledge of the moral nature of nurses' day-to-day work and that moral suffering can be transformed.
Practical wisdom:	using deliberative reason to direct actions.

Moral Virtues	
Truthfulness:	refraining from deception through false communication; refraining from self-deception.
Gentleness:	mildness in verbal and nonverbal communication.
Compassion:	the desire to separate others from suffering.
Lovingkindness:	the desire to bring happiness and well-being to oneself and others.
Just Generosity:	giving and receiving based on need.
Courage:	putting fear aside in difficult circumstances to act for a purpose that is more important than one's fear.
Sympathetic Joy:	rejoicing in others' happiness.
Equanimity:	an evenness and calmness of being.

of virtue habitually chooses to act. Emotions regulate insight, knowledge, and the impulse to action.

Morality is achieved through choice (*prohairesis*) facilitated by insight, practical wisdom, and evenness of emotional states. Moral virtues and the excellence of the nurse's disposition, or character, are cultivated through habitual practice. The favorable paths leading to the moral virtues include favorable communication—verbal, nonverbal, and written communication that moves nurses toward flourishing moral ground; favorable action—"the compassionate protection of all [human] beings" (Mizuno, 1987, p. 132); and favorable livelihood that is consistent with being a member of the community of the nursing profession and working to alleviate the suffering and to enhance the well-being of other people.

Ultimately, developing and practicing intellectual and moral virtues minute-to-minute leads to flourishing moral ground that is likened to the desired goal or telos of a nurse. It embodies personal and professional excellence in nursing. This state is characterized by an active happiness and well-being that is consistent with an enlightened awareness of the causes of and the means of transcending moral suffering and an awareness of the importance of the day-to-day moral nature of nurses' work.

The Nurse as Part of a Health Care Team

When patients and families are experiencing extreme pain and suffering, it is often during times when decisions need to be made about end-of-life care. Family members may want medical treatment for their loved one while physicians and nurses may be explaining to the family that to continue treatment most likely would be nonbeneficial or futile for the patient. When patients are weakened by disease and illness and family members are reacting to their loved one's pain and suffering, decisions regarding care and treatment become challenging for everyone concerned. Members of the health care team may question the decision-making capacity of the patient or family, and the patient's or family's decisions may conflict with the physician's or health care team's recommendations regarding treatment. When caring for particular patients and interacting with their families, nurses sometimes find themselves caught in the middle of these conflicts.

Though nurses frequently make ethical decisions independently, they also act as an integral part of the larger team of decision makers. Many problematic bioethical decisions will not be made unilaterally—not by physicians, nurses, or any other person. By participating in reflective dialogues with other professionals and health care personnel, nurses are often part of a larger team approach to ethical analysis. This team is called an **ethics committee**. An organization's ethics committee usually consists of physicians, nurses, an on-staff chaplain, a social worker, a representative of the organization's administrative staff, possibly a legal representative and community representatives, and others drafted by the team. Also, the involved patient, the patient's family, or a surrogate decision maker may meet with one or more committee members.

At times, nurses do not agree with physicians', family members', or surrogates' decisions regarding treatment and subsequently may experience intense moral uncertainty and anxiety. When passionate ethical disputes arise between nurses and physicians or when nurses are seriously concerned about the action of patients' decision-making representatives, nurses are the ones who often seek an ethics consultation. It is within the right and duty of nurses to seek help and advice from other professionals when nurses experience moral uncertainty or witness unethical conduct in their work setting.

The Four Topics Approach to Ethical Decision Making

Jonsen, Siegler, and Winslade's (2006) Four Topics Method for ethical analysis is a practical approach for nurses and other health care professionals. The nurse or team begins with relevant facts about a particular case and moves toward a resolution through a structured analysis. In health care settings, ethics committees often resolve ethical dilemmas by using a case-based, or bottom-up, inductive, casuistry approach. (See Chapter 1 for a discussion of casuistry.) The Four Topics Method, sometimes called the Four-Box Approach (see Table 2.2) was first published in 1982 in the book, *Clinical Ethics: A Practical Approach to Ethical Decisions in Clinical Medicine*. The book is now in its sixth edition.

This case-based approach allows nurses and other health care professionals to construct the facts of a case in a structured format that facilitates critical thinking about ethical problems. Cases are analyzed according to four topics: "medical indications, patient preferences, quality of life, and contextual features" (Jonsen et al., 2006, p. 2). Nurses and other health care professionals on the team gather information in an attempt to answer the questions in each of the four boxes. The Four Topics Method facilitates dialogue between the patient-family/surrogate dyad and members of the health care ethics team or committee. By following the outline of the questions, nurses or other health care providers are able to inspect and evaluate the full scope of the patient's situation, as well as the central ethical conflict. Once the nurse or an ethics team has gathered the facts of a case, an analysis is conducted. Each case is unique and should be considered as such, but the subject matter of particular situations often involves common threads with other ethically and legally accepted precedents, such as

TABLE 2.2 Four Topics Method for Analysis of Clinical Ethics Cases

Medical Indications	*Patient Preferences*
The Principles of Beneficence and Nonmaleficence 1. What is the patient's medical problem? history? diagnosis? prognosis? 2. Is the problem acute? chronic? critical? emergent? reversible? 3. What are the goals of treatment? 4. What are the probabilities of success? 5. What are the plans in case of therapeutic failure? 6. In sum, how can this patient be benefited by medical and nursing care, and how can harm be avoided?	**The Principle of Respect for Autonomy** 1. Is the patient mentally capable and legally competent? Is there evidence of incapacity? 2. If competent, what is the patient stating about preferences for treatment? 3. Has the patient been informed of benefits and risks, understood this information, and given consent? 4. If incapacitated, who is the appropriate surrogate? Is the surrogate using appropriate standards for decision making? 5. Has the patient expressed prior preferences, e.g. Advance Directives? 6. Is the patient unwilling or unable to cooperate with medical treatment? If so, why? 7. In sum, is the patient's right to choose being respected to the extent possible in ethics and law.
Quality of Life	*Contextual Features*
The Principles of Beneficence and Nonmaleficence and Respect for Autonomy 1. What are the prospects, with or without treatment, for a return to normal life? 2. What physical, mental, and social deficits is the patient likely to experience if treatment succeeds? 3. Are there biases that might prejudice the provider's evaluation of the patient's quality of life? 4. Is the patient's present or future condition such that his or her continued life might be judged undesirable? 5. Is there any plan and rationale to forgo treatment? 6. Are there plans for comfort and palliative care?	**The Principles of Loyalty and Fairness** 1. Are there family issues that might influence treatment decisions? 2. Are there provider (physicians and nurses) issues that might influence treatment decisions? 3. Are there financial and economic factors? 4. Are there religious and cultural factors? 5. Are there limits on confidentiality? 6. Are there problems of allocation of resources? 7. How does the law affect treatment decisions? 8. Is clinical research or teaching involved? 9. Is there any conflict of interest on the part of the providers or the institution?

From Jonsen, A. R., Siegler, M., & Winslade, W.J. (2006). *Clinical ethics: A practical approach to ethical decisions in clinical medicine* (6th ed.). New York: McGraw-Hill.

landmark cases that involved withdrawing or withholding treatment. Though each case analysis begins with facts, the four fundamental principles—autonomy, beneficence, nonmaleficence, and justice—along with the Four Topics Method are considered together as the process and resolution take place (Jonsen et al., 2006). In Table 2.2, each box includes principles appropriate for each of the four topics. *Fairness* and *loyalty* are included in the contextual features box. To see an analysis of a specific case, go to http://depts.washington.edu/bioethx/tools/cecase.html

Frustration, anger, and other intense emotional conflicts may occur among health care professionals or between health care professionals and the patient or the patient's surrogates. Regretful verbal exchanges and hurt feelings can result. Openness and sensitivity toward other health care professionals, patients, and family members are essential behaviors for nurses during these times. As information is exchanged and conversations take place, nurses need to maintain an attitude of respect as a top priority. If respect and sensitivity are maintained, lines of communication more likely will remain open.

Ethical Reflections

- Gather information about the case of Terri Schiavo from Chapter 12, other literature, and the Internet. Use information about her case along with other information throughout this book to complete the following:
  - Summarize key information and events in the case of Terri Schiavo. Think about the information that would be needed by an ethics committee reviewing this case.
  - Clearly identify (list) the specific ethical issues involved in her case.
  - Imagine that you are a member of an ethics committee that has been consulted for an opinion about whether or not Schiavo's feeding tube should be removed
  - As a member of the ethics committee, complete the questions of the Four Box Method shown in Table 2.2. Some of the questions will require more discussion than other questions because of the direct relationship to Schiavo's case. If you don't have "inside information" to answer some of the questions, discuss the question(s) based on the information that you know is indicated related to a particular question. Just do your best to answer the questions comprehensively.
  - Summarize "the committee's" specific determination(s) based on the answers to the Four Box questions and your research of the case.
  - Speak for the committee to recommend removal of the feeding tube or not to remove the feeding tube and provide your rationale.

CASE STUDY: JILL BECOMES DISHEARTENED

Jill is a 28-year-old attractive, intelligent, and technically competent R.N. who has worked for 5 years on a medical-surgical unit of a small hospital. She has generally been well liked by her professional colleagues, and she habitually makes concerted attempts to deliver compassionate care to her patients. Recently, she left her job and began working in the busy surgical intensive care unit (ICU) at a local county hospital. Jill changed her job because she wanted to gain more varied nursing experience. She was very excited and enthusiastic about her new job. Shortly after Jill began working in the ICU, she began to question her career decision. The more experienced nurses in the ICU are what Jill describes as "abrupt" and "exasperated" when she asks for help in learning ICU patient care and procedures. Jill states that the ICU nurses seem to be "testing my resolve to stick it out" and seem to want her to fail at learning how to work in the ICU. Many of the surgeons who regularly have patients in the ICU are described as being demanding and impatient with the ICU nursing staff. In addition to being intimidated by the ICU nursing staff, Jill says that she also is very intimidated by the physicians and was chastised by one of them for asking what he called "a stupid question." There is an "air of dissatisfaction" among all of the nurses throughout the hospital. Jill says working at this hospital is like no other situation that she has been involved with since becoming a nurse.

1. What do you believe might be some of the underlying causes of the ICU nurses' treatment of Jill? Do you believe that it is likely that Jill's treatment has anything to do with her personal characteristics?
2. What could Jill do to try to improve her situation?
3. What are the possible implications for Jill's delivery of patient care that could arise because of the treatment that she is experiencing?
4. Do you believe that the "air of unhappiness" among all of the nursing staff at the hospital might be directly or indirectly affecting the treatment that Jill is receiving? Might it be affecting patient care hospital-wide? Please explain.
5. If Jill wants to make positive changes at the hospital what can she do?
6. Review the virtues listed in Table 2.1. Which virtues might the ICU nurses benefit by cultivating? Which virtues would be helpful for Jill to cultivate? Why?

Summary

The virtue of the candle lies not in the wax that leaves its trace, but in its light.
—ANTOINE DE SAINT-EXUPÉRY, *THE WISDOM OF THE SANDS*

During the 20th century, there was an explosive growth in the field of ethics in health care and medical research. Because of the many changes that have occurred since that time, both bioethics and nursing ethics were born. Though nurses must be competent to navigate technically related care and decisions in the area that Schön (1987) called the "high hard ground," nurses must not neglect the daily ethical decisions that need to be made in what Schön called the "swampy low ground." Nurses are responsible for preparing themselves to recognize and manage ethical situations in their everyday practice that are very important to the recipients of their care—their patients. Patients trust nurses to care *for* them and *about* them, and nurses must never betray this trust.

Key Points

- Bioethics was born out of the rapidly expanding technical environment of the 20th century.
- Nursing ethics is a unique subcategory of bioethics. Nursing ethics is relationship based and involves issues viewed from nurses' particular standpoint.
- The four most well-known and frequently used bioethical principles are: (1) autonomy, (2) beneficence, (3) nonmaleficence, and (4) justice.
- Paternalism involves an overriding of autonomy in favor of the principle of beneficence.
- Social justice emphasizes the fairness of how the benefits and burdens of society are distributed among people.
- Ethical dilemmas involve unclear choices, not clear matters of right versus wrong.
- Nurses often experience a disquieting feeling of anguish, uneasiness, or angst in their work that is consistent with what might be called moral suffering.
- It is paradoxical that patients often must trust health care providers to care for them before the providers show evidence that the trust is warranted.
- When acting as patient advocates, nurses try to identify patients' unmet needs and help to address these needs.
- Nurses often treat other nurses badly. This is sometimes called horizontal violence or the tall poppy syndrome.
- Nurses may develop good critical thinking skills by "thinking about their thinking."

References

American Nurses Association. (2001). *Code of ethics for nurses with interpretive statements.* Silver Spring, MD: Author.

American Nurses Association. (2004). *Nursing: Scope and standards of practice.* Silver Spring, MD: Author.

Beauchamp, T. L., & Childress, J. F. (2001). *Principles of biomedical ethics* (5th ed.). New York: Oxford University Press.

Brannigan, M. C., & Boss, J. A. (2001). *Healthcare ethics in a diverse society.* Mountain View, CA: Mayfield.

Chambliss, D. F. (1996). *Beyond caring: Hospitals, nurses, and the social organization of ethics.* Chicago: The University of Chicago Press.

Dalai Lama. (1999). *Ethics for the new millennium.* New York: Riverhead Books.

Daniels, N. (1985). *Just health care.* New York: Cambridge University Press.

Dempski, K. M. (2006). Informed consent—part I. In S.W. Killion & K. M. Dempski (Eds.). *Quick look nursing: Legal and ethical issues* (pp. 42–43). Sudbury, MA: Jones and Bartlett.

Dewey, J. (1934). *Art as experience.* New York: Perigee Books.

Dewey, J. (1988). *Human nature and conduct: The middle works, 1899–1924* (Vol. 14) (J. A. Boydston & P. Baysinger, Eds.). Carbondale: Southern Illinois University Press. (Original work published 1922)

Dewey, J. (1997). *How we think.* Mineola, NY: Dover Publications. (Original work published 1910)

Ehrenreich, B., & English, D. (1973). *Witches, midwives, and nurses: A history of women healers.* New York: The Feminist Press.

Engelhardt, H. T. (1996). *The foundations of bioethics* (2nd ed.). New York: Oxford University Press.

Fesmire, S. (2003). *John Dewey and moral imagination: Pragmatics in ethics.* Bloomington: Indiana University Press.

Fisher, A. (2001). *Critical thinking: An introduction.* Cambridge, UK: Cambridge University Press.

Fry, S., & Johnstone, M. J. (2002). *Ethics in nursing practice: A guide to ethical decision making* (2nd ed.). Oxford, UK: Blackwell Science.

Gibbs, G. (1988). *Learning by doing: A guide to teaching and learning methods.* Oxford, UK: Oxford Polytechnic.

Gordon, S., & Nelson, S. (2006). Moving beyond the virtue script in nursing. In S. Nelson & S. Gordon (Eds.), *The complexities of care: Nursing reconsidered* (pp. 13–29). New York: Cornell University Press.

Hanh, T. N. (1998). *The heart of the Buddha's teaching: Transforming suffering into peace, joy, and liberation.* New York: Broadway Books.

Hester, D. M. (2001). *Community as healing: Pragmatist ethics in medical encounters.* Lanham, MD: Rowan & Littlefield.

International Council of Nurses. (2006). *The ICN code of ethics for nurses.* Geneva, Switzerland: Author. Retrieved July 10, 2007, from http://www.icn.ch/icncode.pdf

Jameton, A. (1984). *Nursing practice: The ethical issues.* Englewood Cliffs, NJ: Prentice-Hall.

Johnstone, M. J. (1999). *Bioethics: A nursing perspective* (3rd ed.). Sydney, Australia: Harcourt Saunders.

Jonsen, A. R. (1998). *The birth of bioethics.* New York: Oxford University Press.

Jonsen, A. R. (2000). *A short history of medical ethics.* New York: Oxford University Press.

Jonsen, A. R. (2005). *Bioethics beyond the headlines: Who lives? Who dies? Who decides?* Lanham, MD: Rowman & Littlefield.

Jonsen, A. R., Siegler, M., & Winslade, W. J. (2006). *Clinical ethics: A practical approach to ethical decisions in clinical medicine* (6th ed.). New York: McGraw-Hill.

Kelly, C. (2000). *Nurses' moral practice: Investing and discounting self.* Indianapolis: Sigma Theta Tau International Center Nursing Press.

Keown, D. (2001a). *Buddhism and bioethics.* New York: Palgrave.

Keown, D. (2001b). *The nature of Buddhist ethics.* New York: Palgrave.

Kidder, R. M. (1995). *How good people make tough choices: Resolving the dilemmas of ethical living.* New York: Quill.

MacIntyre. A. (1999). *Dependent rational animals: Why human beings need the virtues.* Chicago, IL: Open Court.

McKenna, B. G., Smith, N. A., Poole, S. J., & Coverdale, J. H. (2003). Horizontal violence: Experiences of registered nurses in their first year of practice. *Journal of Advanced Nursing, 42*(1), 90–96.

Mizuno, K. (1987). *Basic Buddhist concepts* (C.S. Terry & R.L. Gage, Trans.). Tokyo: Kosei Publishing Co.

Mondics, C. (2004, July 23). 9/11 report details failure. *The Sun Herald*, pp. A1, A4.

National Institutes of Health. (1979). The Belmont Report. Retrieved July 10, 2007, from http://ohsr.od.nih.gov/guidelines/belmont.html

Nozick, R. (1974). *Anarchy, state, and utopia.* New York: Basic Books.

Paul, R., & Elder, L. (2006). *The miniature guide to critical thinking concepts and tools* (4th ed.). Dillon Beach, CA: Foundation for Critical Thinking.

Rawls, J. (1971). *A theory of justice.* Cambridge, MA: Harvard University Press.

Ryan, C. J. (1998). Pulling up the runaway: The effect of new evidence on euthanasia's slippery slope. *Journal of Medical Ethics, 24,* 341–344.

Schön, D. A. (1987). *Educating the reflective practitioner.* San Francisco: Jossey-Bass.

Sheng-yen, M. (1999). *Subtle wisdom: Understanding suffering, cultivating compassion through Ch'an Buddhism.* New York: Doubleday.

Shotton, L., & Seedhouse, D. (1998). Practical dignity in caring. *Nursing Ethics, 5*(3), 246–255.

Stein, L. I., Watts, D. T., & Howell, T. (1990). The doctor-nurse game revisited. *Nursing Outlook, 38*(6), 264–268.

U.S. Census Bureau. (2005). Income, poverty, and health insurance coverage in the United States: 2005. Retrieved July 10, 2007, from http://www.census.gov/prod/2006pubs/p60-231.pdf

U.S. Congress. (1990). Patient Self-Determination Act. 42 U.S.C. §§ 1395–1396.

Varcoe, C., Doane, G., Pauly, B., Rodney, P., Storch, J. L., Mahoney, K., et al. (2004). Ethical practice in nursing: Working the in-betweens. *Journal of Advanced Nursing, 45*(3), 316–325.

Wildes, K. W. (2000). *Moral acquaintances: Methodology in bioethics.* Notre Dame, IN: University of Notre Dame Press.

Winslow, G. (1988). From loyalty to advocacy: A new metaphor for nursing. In J. C. Callahan (Ed.), *Ethical Issues in Professional Life* (pp. 95–105). New York: Oxford University Press.

Zaner, R. M. (1991). The phenomenon of trust and the patient-physician relationship. In E. D. Pellegrino, R. M. Veatch, & J. P. Langan (Eds.), *Ethics, trust, and the professions: Philosophical and cultural aspects* (pp. 45–67). Washington, DC: Georgetown University Press.

CHAPTER 2 QUESTIONS

1. Obtaining informed consent from a patient is an example of adhering to the principle of
   a. autonomy.
   b. beneficence.
   c. nonmaleficence.
   d. justice.

2. A nurse being paternalistic by deciding that she should not tell a patient her lab results because the patient may become too upset is a conflict between the principles of
   a. nonmaleficence and beneficence.
   b. justice and autonomy.
   c. autonomy and beneficence.
   d. beneficence and justice.

3. During a period of extreme short staffing, a nurse needs to decide how to allocate her time. She has a dying patient who is receiving palliative care. The patient's family is very distraught. Also, the nurse has several critically ill patients. This is an example of
   a. a slippery slope.
   b. implications of the doctor-nurse game.
   c. an ethical dilemma.
   d. horizontal violence to patients.

4. Which of the following best describes how bioethics and nursing ethics are distinguished?
   a. Bioethics is focused on biological conditions and nursing ethics is focused on nursing diagnoses.
   b. Bioethics is focused on every health care discipline except nursing and nurses generally believe that bioethics does not describe nursing problems.
   c. There is no distinguishing feature; the terms are used interchangeably.
   d. Bioethics is a general term for health care ethics and nursing ethics focuses on the particular standpoint of nurses.

5. The problem of worldwide poverty is best described as a matter of
   a. social justice.
   b. slippery slope issues.
   c. deontology.
   d. ethical principlism.

6. Patients often do not personally know their health care providers before they are cared for by them. This is a matter of
   a. moral imagination.
   b. reflection-in-action.
   c. unavoidable trust.
   d. standard of due care.

7. Violating the principle of nonmaleficence is most closely associated with which of the following?
   a. Overriding patients' choices
   b. Being negligent
   c. Being unfair in distributing resources
   d. Not doing good for others

8. The meaning of the statement "nurses often treat other nurses like tall poppies" can best be described by which of the following?
   a. Nurses treat one another like beautiful flowers.
   b. Nurse educators and nurse researchers get along well.
   c. Nurses generally do not like one another.
   d. Nurses often disparage the successes of their colleagues.

9. Which of the following best represents Rawls's conception of the "veil of ignorance"?
   a. Making unbiased decisions
   b. Making decisions without a college degree
   c. Making decisions to combat unavoidable trust
   d. Making decisions to improve cultural sensitivity

10. Generally, ethical issues in nursing can best be described as occurring
    a. through the use of lateral violence.
    b. in the swampy low ground.
    c. within the context of the doctor-nurse game.
    d. in situations involving technical treatments.

CHAPTER 2 ANSWERS

Question 1: The correct answer is A.
Autonomy means that patients are given sufficient information to make self-directed decisions.

Choices B, C, and D are incorrect because the other three principles are not directly related to supporting a patient's self-direction.

Question 2: The correct answer is C.
Paternalism is a conflict between supporting patients' self-directed decisions and trying to do good for patients. Paternalism specifically refers to health care professionals believing that they know what is best for patients.

Choices A, B, and D are incorrect because a conflict between each of the principles listed does not accurately convey the meaning of paternalism.

Question 3: The correct answer is C.
The situation reflects an ethical dilemma. To give preference to either action is not an easy choice; both actions are good but both actions cannot be given equal priority.

Choices A, B, and D are incorrect because they do not describe the concept of an ethical dilemma; relationships between doctors and nurses do not directly affect decision making as needed in this situation; a slippery slope situation may have a relationship to ethical dilemmas but not in the situation described; horizontal violence is a term used to describe nurse-nurse not nurse-patient relationships.

Question 4: The correct answer is D.
Bioethics is an umbrella concept, and nursing ethics falls under this broad concept.

Choices A, B, and C are not correct because these choices are not true.

Question 5: The correct answer is A.
Social justice specifically addresses the ethics of fairly distributing the benefits and burdens among members of societies.

Choices B, C, and D are incorrect because the issue described is not related to a slippery slope situation; people may believe that they have a duty to take action regarding worldwide poverty, but deontology does not best describe the matter; as an ethical principle, justice is related to distribution of resources, but the concept of social justice better describes matters of worldwide poverty.

Question 6: The correct answer is C.

Unavoidable trust is a term used to describe the paradoxical situation of patients' need to trust health care providers before providers have demonstrated that they are trustworthy.

Choices A, B, and D are incorrect because they do not correctly represent the matter described in the question stem.

Question 7: The correct answer is B.

Nonmaleficence means that one tries not to harm other people. Failure to exercise due care may lead to harmful outcomes that are considered to be negligent.

Choices A, C, and D are incorrect because they are related to the principles of autonomy, justice, and beneficence, respectively.

Question 8: The correct answer is D.

One definition of what it means to treat a person like a "tall poppy" is that someone tries to figuratively "cut down" a successful person to minimize the person's accomplishments.

Choices A, B, and C are incorrect because the other statements are generally not relevant or are not appropriate definitions in this instance.

Question 9: The correct answer is A.

Rawls suggested the veil of ignorance as a way to approach justice-based decision making so that the decision maker is not influenced by preferences for oneself or particular others. This method is intended to lead to fairness in distributing resources.

Choices B, C, and D are incorrect because they are not directly related to Rawls's conception of the veil of ignorance.

Question 10: The correct answer is B.

Ethical issues in nursing usually occur in nurses' day-to-day work. Nurses generally are not directly involved in making major bioethical decisions that are discussed in the news media. Schön described the swampy low ground as having important day-to-day problems that are not easy to navigate.

Choices A, C, and D are incorrect because although these choices are related to nursing ethics, the day-to-day "messy" issues in nursing often cause nurses the most suffering.

Ethics in Professional Nursing Practice

Janie B. Butts

But nurses are still reaching out towards ideals which we trust may be realized in the fullness of time.

—Isabel Hampon Robb, 1900

Objectives

After reading this chapter, the reader should be able to:

1. Delineate key historical events or activities that led to the development of the ANA *Code of Ethics for Nurses with Interpretive Statements* (2001) as it is known today.
2. Formulate implications for nursing practice based on the language changes in the 2001 ANA *Code of Ethics for Nurses with Interpretive Statements*.
3. Explore the significance of concepts that are interwoven in the 2001 ANA *Code of Ethics for Nurses with Interpretive Statements* to nursing practice (see also Appendix A).
4. Compare and contrast the six professionalism and boundary concepts of nursing practice in terms of the deontology and utilitarian frameworks.
5. Investigate the eight concepts of the eHealth Code of Ethics as they relate to the fundamental principle of respect for persons.
6. Discuss the Internet Healthcare Coalition's tips for nurses to help patients and themselves in evaluating the quality of health information on the Internet.
7. Analyze potential human ethical violations that place the basic fundamental ethical principles of autonomy, beneficence, and nonmaleficence at stake.

KEY TERMS

Ethical codes	Basic dignity	Personal dignity
Giving respect	Maintaining confidentiality	Having moral courage
Culture	Giving culturally sensitive care	ASK
Power	Using power	Being a good citizen of the world
Telehealth		

Professional Codes of Ethics in Nursing

The beginning of professional nursing can be traced to 19th-century England to the school that was founded by Florence Nightingale, where profession-shaping ethical precepts and values were communicated (Kuhse & Singer, 2001). Nightingale's achievement was a landmark in nursing even though graduates of her school performed below desired expectations in the early days. For the first 30 to 40 years in Nightingale's school, the prospective nurses were trained by male physicians because there were not enough educated nurses to teach nursing. Because of the strong medical influence, early nursing educators focused on technical training rather than on the art and science of nursing, as Nightingale would have preferred.

By the end of the 19th century, modern nursing had been established, and ethics in nursing was seriously being discussed. The presence of the Nightingale Pledge, first developed in 1893 and written under the chairmanship of Detroit nursing school principal Lystra Gretter, helped establish nursing as an art and a science (as cited in Dossey, 2000). The International Council of Nurses (ICN), which has been a pioneer in developing a code of nursing ethics, was established in 1899. By 1900, the first book on nursing ethics, *Nursing Ethics: For Hospital and Private Use*, had been written by the American nursing leader Isabel Hampton Robb.

Historically, a primary value consideration in nursing ethics has been the determination of the focus of nurses' work. It is interesting to note that in Isabel Hampton Robb's nursing ethics book of 1900, the titles of the chapters were descriptive of the times, such as Chapter 4: The Probationer, Chapter 7: Uniform, Chapter 8: Night-Duty, and Chapter 12: The Care of the Patient (nurse-physician, nurse-nurse, nurse-public relationships). Refer to Box 3.1 for excerpts from Robb's book representing nursing's environment in 1900.

Until the 1960s, the focus in the nursing codes was on the physician, which is not surprising, based on the fact that over the years most nurses have been women and most doctors have been men. The focus on nurses' obedience to physicians remained

Box 3.1: Highlights from the Field

Excerpts from Nursing Ethics by Isabel Hampton Robb: The Physician-Nurse Relationship in 1900

- Unfortunately, here and there we find a nurse who through *ignorance*—but far more often from the gradual growth in her of self-conceit and an exaggerated idea of her own importance—may overstep the boundary limit . . . [*italics* added for emphasis]. (pp. 249–250)
- Moreover, if in prescribing the procedures to be employed the physician goes into minute details as to the way in which certain of them are to be carried out, *his wishes are to be law to the nurse.* The question whether she agrees perfectly with his recommendations, or believes that her own methods are better, has no bearing upon the case. Apart from the fact that she may be quite wrong in her opinions, *her sole duty is to obey orders*, and so long as she does this, *she is not to be held responsible for untoward results* [*italics* added for emphasis]. (p. 250)

Quoted from Robb, I. H. (1916). The care of the patient: Relation of the nurse to the physician. *Nursing ethics: For hospital and private use.* Cleveland, OH: E. C. Koeckert. [Original publication 1900]

at the forefront of nursing responsibilities into the 1960s, and this assumption was still reflected in the ICN *Code of Ethics for Nurses* as late as 1965. By 1973, however, the focus of the ICN code reflected a shift in nursing responsibility from the physician to the patient, where it remains to this day.

Ethical codes are systematic guidelines for shaping ethical behavior that answer the normative questions of what beliefs and values should be morally accepted. However, it must be noted that no code can provide absolute or complete rules that are free of conflict and ambiguity. Because codes are unable to provide exact directives for moral reasoning and action in all situations, some people have stated that virtue ethics provides a better approach to ethics because the emphasis is on a person's character rather than on rules, principles, and laws (Beauchamp & Childress, 2001). Proponents of virtue ethics consider that if a nurse's character is not virtuous, the nurse cannot be depended on to act in good or moral ways even with a professional code as a guide. Professional codes, however, do serve a useful purpose in providing direction to health care professionals although, ultimately, one must remember that codes do not eliminate moral dilemmas and are of no use without professionals who are motivated to act morally. For the code to have more meaning, Benner contended when speaking of the nurse's role in working for social justice, "each of us and each nursing organization" must "breathe life into the code by taking individual and collective action" (Fowler & Benner, 2001, p. 437).

American Nurses Association Code of Ethics for Nurses

"A Suggested Code" was published in the *American Journal of Nursing (AJN)* in 1926 by the American Nurses Association (ANA) but was never adopted; in 1940 "A Tentative Code" was published in *AJN*, but again was never adopted. The ANA adopted its first official code in 1950 (Daly, 2002). Three more code revisions occurred before the creation of the interpretative statements in 1976. Although it has always been implied that the code reflects ethical provisions, the word "ethics" was not added to the title until the 1985 code was replaced with its sixth and latest revision in 2001. The ANA (2001) code contains general moral provisions and standards for nurses to follow, but specific guidelines for clinical practice, education, research, and administration are found in the accompanying interpretive statements (see Appendix A for the ANA *Code of Ethics for Nurses with Interpretive Statements*).

The code is nonnegotiable with regard to nursing practice. Significant positions and changes in the 2001 ANA code included a(n): (1) return to the word "patient" rather than client; (2) application of ethical guidelines to nurses in all roles, not just clinical roles; (3) concession that research is one but not the only method contributing to nursing professional development; (4) reaffirmation against the participation of nurses in euthanasia; (5) emphasis that nurses owe the same obligations to themselves as they do to others; and (6) recommendation that members who represent nursing associations are responsible for expressing nursing values, maintaining professional integrity, and participating in public policy development (see Appendix A).

Fowler (Fowler & Benner, 2001) and Daly (2002), nursing leaders involved in revising the 2001 code, have proposed that the new code is clearly patient focused whether the patient is considered to be "an individual, family, group, or community" (Daly, p. 98). The nurse's loyalty must be first and foremost to the patient, even though institutional politics is a force in today's nursing environment. With the expanding role of nurse administrators and advanced practice nurses, each nurse must be cognizant of conflicts of interest that could potentially have a negative effect on relationships with patients and patient care. Nursing has often overlooked the responsibility to the patient held by nurses who are not in clinical roles. It is worth noting that nurse researchers, administrators, and educators are indirectly but still involved in supporting patient care. According to Fowler (Fowler & Benner, 2001), "it is not the possession of nursing credentials, degrees, and position that makes a nurse a nurse, rather it is this very commitment to the patient" (p. 435). Therefore, the code applies to all nurses regardless of their role.

One issue that created a vigorous debate during the 2001 revision of the code involved the ethical implications of collective bargaining in nursing (Daly, 2002). Ultimately, those nurses who formulated the revisions underscored the importance for the code to contain provisions supporting nurses who work to assure that the environment in which they work is conducive to quality patient care and that nurses are able to fulfill their moral requirements. Collective bargaining was determined to be an appropriate avenue for more than just negotiating for better salaries and benefits. Today nurses consider collective bargaining as a way to improve the moral level of the environment where nurses work.

Values and virtues are emphasized in the ANA (2001) *Code of Ethics for Nurses with Interpretive Statements*. Values in nursing encompass an appreciation of what is important for the nurse personally as well as what is important for patients. The ANA emphasized the magnitude of moral respect for all human beings, including the respect of nurses for themselves. Self-respect can be thought of as personal regard. Personal regard involves nurses extending attention and care to their own requisite needs. Nurses who do not regard themselves as worthy of care usually cannot fully care for others.

The ANA (2001) included statements in the code about wholeness of character, which pertains to knowing the values of the nursing profession and one's own authentic moral values, integrating these two belief systems, and then expressing them appropriately. Integrity is an important feature of wholeness of character. In a health care system often burdened with constraints, politics, self-serving groups, and organizations, threats to integrity can be a serious pitfall for nurses. According to the code, maintaining integrity involves acting consistently with personal values and the values of the profession. When nurses are asked or pressured to do something that conflicts with their values, such as to falsify records, deceive patients, or accept verbal abuse from others, emotional and moral suffering may occur (see moral integrity in Chapter 8). A nurse's beliefs, grounded in good moral reasoning, must guide actions even when other people challenge the nurse's beliefs. When compromise is necessary, the compromise must not be such that it compromises personal or professional values.

Recognizing the essential dignity of oneself and of each patient is another value that is basic to nursing, and it is given priority in moral reasoning. Pullman (1999) described two conceptions of dignity. One type, termed **basic dignity**, is intrinsic or inherent and dwells within all humans, with all humans being ascribed this moral worth. The other type, called **personal dignity**, often mistakenly equated with autonomy, is an evaluative type, such as judging others and describing behaviors as dignified or undignified. Personal dignity is a socially constructed concept that fluctuates in value from community to community, as well as globally. Most often, however, personal dignity is highly valued. (Refer to the nurse-patient-family relationships section in Chapter 2 for more information on personal dignity.)

ICN Code of Ethics for Nurses

In 1953 the ICN adopted its first code of ethics for nurses. (See Appendix B for the 2006 ICN *Code of Ethics for Nurses*.) The code had been revised and reaffirmed many times. The four principal elements contained in the ICN code involve standards related to nurses and people, practice, the profession, and co-workers. These elements in the ICN code form a framework to guide nursing conduct along with practice applications for practitioners, managers, educators, researchers, and national nurses' associations.

A Common Theme in the ANA and ICN Codes

A theme common to the ANA (2001) and ICN (2006) codes is a focus on the importance of compassionate patient care aimed at alleviating suffering. This emphasis is threaded throughout the codes but begins from the focal point of patients being the central focus of nurses' work. Nurses are to support patients in self-determination and are to protect the moral environment where patients receive care. The interests of various nursing associations and health care institutions must not be placed above those of patients. Although opportunities for nurses to exhibit compassion in the health care environment are not unique, nurses must always uphold the moral agreement that they make with patients and communities when they join the nursing profession. Nursing care includes the primary responsibilities of promoting health and preventing illness, but the heart of nursing care has always involved caring for patients who are experiencing varying degrees of physical, psychological, and spiritual suffering.

———————— Ethical Reflections ————————

- The ANA *Code of Ethics for Nurses with Interpretive Statements* currently includes the word "patient" instead of the word "client" in referring to the recipients of nursing care. Do you agree with this change? Please explain your rationale for your answer.

- Take a minute to review the ANA *Code of Ethics for Nurses with Interpretive Statements* (2001) in Appendix A. Would you add any provisions? Would you remove any provisions? Please explain your rationale for your answers.
- After reviewing the interpretive statements in the code, discuss random examples or scenarios of how nurses can justify their actions to the following approaches or frameworks: the Beauchamp and Childress principles of autonomy, beneficence, nonmaleficence, and justice; Kant's categorical imperatives based on deontology; a utilitarian framework; a virtue ethics approach; and an ethic of care approach.

Professionalism and Boundaries

In the 30th anniversary issue in 2006 of the *Journal of Advanced Nursing*, the editors reprinted and revisited the 1996 article by Esterhuizen titled, "Is the Professional Code Still the Cornerstone of Clinical Nursing Practice?," and solicited three up-to-date responses to Esterhuizen's philosophical inquiry. Verena Tschudin, one of the three respondents and editor of *Nursing Ethics*, agreed with Esterhuizen that nursing has changed only minimally, if any, regarding the lack of opportunity for personal responsibility and autonomy in moral decision making. There is plenty of fertile ground for nurses to engage in moral decisions, but they still do not have the opportunity to participate.

Tschudin (2006) reflected how article topics nowadays in *Nursing Ethics* seldom consist of codes of ethics topics as compared to years ago, but rather today reflect relationships in nursing. Nursing has moved somewhat from ethical codes of nursing to relationships in nursing because the narrative, virtue, and feminist approaches leave room for nurses to question codes of ethics, especially in the Western world. As Tschudin suggested, nurses wonder about the benefit of codes of ethics in light of today's postmodernism ambiance that leaves nurses feeling uncertain about any type of prescriptive or directive practice such as codes of nursing. One point of Tschudin's message, as evidenced by the following quote, is that nurses who have autonomy and accountability in practice do not need a code of ethics to guide them. As mentioned in the previous section of this chapter, nurses who practice with a virtue ethics approach do not need a code of ethics to guide them, and Tschudin illuminated this thought by saying:

Nurses who have been educated to the level of safe practice are able to account for their own practice, and they are more likely to do this based on conscience; the relationship with a patient; or the need to express this professionalism (as a virtue): "I am a professional nurse, therefore what I do is professional." (p. 113)

Not practicing with this degree of autonomy can only lead to further moral suffering, and although codes of ethics can serve nurses well in many cases, hospitals and other agencies are not embracing the codes to the point of relevancy in nursing practice (Tschudin, 2006). An increased integration of codes of ethics at all levels of practice is necessary for a meaningful application to practice.

Even with the focus of nursing practice shifting to evidence-based nursing practice and nursing independence, codes of ethics serve as mandates for accountability in practice. The 2001 ANA and 2006 ICN codes of ethics have multiple professional boundary issues throughout the texts. Refer to Box 3.2 for examples of the ANA (2001) boundary topics and moral obligations. All seasoned and novice nurses need to become comfortable with decision-making processes that involve ethical issues, relationships, and moral judgments. The codes provide excellent guidelines for self-development in these areas, and they serve as guides for nurses whether they are clinicians, practitioners, educators, researchers, or administrators.

Embedded in nursing boundaries and moral obligations of professionalism and practice are the explicit or implied concepts of respect, confidentiality, moral courage, cultural sensitivity, power, and just being a good citizen of the world. These concepts overlap with each other and do not serve as an exhaustive list of concepts for nursing professionalism and practice. Habitually practicing nursing ethics and using codes of ethics as guides help nurses to develop moral grounding by which to function. Because nursing is concerned with the nurturing of the whole person, these concepts penetrate every aspect of care, including the uniqueness of nursing in its promotion of care. The Web Ethics box at the end of the chapter contains some helpful Internet sites for nurses.

Giving Respect

Giving respect to patients, families, peers, and others is a major concept in relationships, decision-making processes, and boundary issues faced by nurses on a minute-by-minute basis. Rushton (2007) defined **giving respect** as "the act of esteeming another, an act that demands we ourselves have a sense of authenticity, integrity, and self-knowledge. It demands that we honor the wholeness, the essence, and the uniqueness of the other" (p. 149).

Box 3.2: Highlights from the Field

Professional Boundaries and Moral Obligations for Nurses as Specified by the ANA *Code of Ethics for Nurses with Interpretive Statements* (2001)

- *Clinical Practice Boundaries*
  - Respecting patients' dignity
  - Right to self-determination
  - Delegating tasks appropriately
  - Practicing good judgment
  - Accepting accountability in practice
  - Alleviating suffering
  - Being attentive to patients' interests
  - Working within the nurse practice acts and nursing standards of practice

- *Professional Practice Boundaries*
  - Maintaining authenticity in all relationships with others such as nurse-to-nurse relationships, nurse-physician relationships, nurse-to-patient relationships, and multidisciplinary collaboration
  - Addressing and evaluating issues of impaired practice; fraternizing inappropriately with patients or others; accepting inappropriate gifts from patients and families; confidentiality and privacy violations; and unhealthy, unsafe, illegal, or unethical environments

- *Self-Care and Self-Development Boundaries and Obligations*
  - Participating in self-care activities to maintain and promote moral self-respect, professional growth and competence, wholeness of character in nurses' actions and in relationships with others, and preservation of integrity
  - Advancing knowledge and research through professionalism, practice, education, and administrative contributions
  - Collaborating with other health care professionals and the public to promote community, national, and international efforts
  - Promoting healthy practices in the community through political activism or professional organizations by addressing unsafe, unethical, or illegal health practices that have the potential to harm the community

Respect is a foundational ethical principle in critical care and the hallmark of excellence in critical care practice, as Rushton pointed out, but respect for others crosses all specialties and roles in nursing. Nurses need to distinguish giving respect to people just because they are human beings from giving respect to people for their position, title, role, and political correctness. Suggestions for demonstrating respect in clinical practice and professional relationships are delineated as (1) attending to the whole person, (2) engaging authentically with patients in decision-making processes, (3) fully appreciating patients and their choices, (4) communicating effectively, and (5) remaining free of judgments, or exhibiting neutrality in communication and actions. Violations can occur when these five areas are not honored and maintained by nurses, and nurses are vulnerable to violations of respect toward patients, families, and health care professionals on an everyday basis. Potential violations include: (1) withholding information or not telling the full truth of a situation with patients, families, and professionals; (2) acting paternalistically instead of respecting another's decision; (3) giving judgment-laden nursing care and advice; and (4) not attending to the whole person or giving fragmented care.

Maintaining Confidentiality

Maintaining confidentiality means that a nurse, by legal and ethical standards, keeps information private that patients or families have disclosed unless the information falls under a limit of confidentiality (see Chapters 7 and 9 for the limits of confidentiality). Confidentiality is at the core of nurses establishing trusting relationships with other nurses, patients, families, and others. Nurses could be tempted to violate the trust that patients or professionals have established with them because of vulnerable situations *other than* for limits of confidentiality. Potential violations that lead nurses to feeling enticed to tell something secret or private include but are not restricted to:

- When nurse A is tempted to disclose a secret to nurse B about nurse C, who is planning to resign but does not yet want others to know
- Withholding information from a patient as directed by the family or physician although the nurse thinks the information should be revealed
- Patient information that is private and should only be shared within the nursing report on the unit
- A secret the nurse was told by administration to keep private

Having Moral Courage

Finding ways to establish and enhance a culture of moral courage is one of the noblest goals of humanity.

—R. Kidder & M. Bracy, Institute for Global Ethics

Having moral courage means that a nurse overcomes fear by confronting an issue head on, especially when the issue is a conflict of the nurse's core values and beliefs. Moral courage is having the will to speak out and do the right thing even when constraints or forces to do otherwise are present. Lachman (2007) emphasized that moral courage turns principles into actions. Even though physical harm could be a potential threat, other more likely threats are "humiliation, rejection, ridicule, unemployment, and loss of social standing" (p. 131). When nurses have the moral courage to do what they believe to be the right thing in a particular situation, they make a personal sacrifice by possibly standing alone, but at the same time will feel a sense of peace in their decision. If danger is a potential risk, the nurse will need to have moral courage to commit to core values, beliefs, or a moral conscience. Nurses experience apprehension and fear because of the uncertainty in outcomes even when they have a high degree of certitude that they are doing the right thing.

Lachman (2007) created a clever acronym to help nurses remember to have moral courage in situations and to remind nurses of the code of ethics for nurses. The acronym is CODE, which means:

C   Courage to be moral requires:
O   Obligations to honor (What is the right thing to do?)
D   Danger to manage (What do I need to handle my fear?)
E   Expression and action (What action do I need to take to maintain my integrity?) (p. 132)

Having the moral courage to admit to wrongdoing, whether the misconduct is by the nurse, a peer, or someone else, helps to rectify a situation and prevents or arrests pain and suffering associated with the moral suffering that a nurse could experience because of the wrongdoing. A few examples of moral courage are (1) confronting or reporting a peer who is stealing and using drugs at work, (2) confronting a physician who ordered questionable treatments that are not within the standard of care, (3) confronting an administrator regarding unsafe practices or staffing patterns, and (4) standing against peers who are planning an emotionally hurtful action toward another peer.

Lachman (2007) offered two strategies to help nurses to exhibit moral courage in dangerous situations. Nurses would probably regret any careless and hasty reactions, or even non-reaction or silence, on their part, so they must first try to soothe their inner feelings of fear that would trigger these behaviors. Self-talk, relaxation techniques, and an analytical method of processing information, while pushing out negative thoughts, are ways for nurses to keep calm in the face of a confrontation involving moral courage. Second, nurses must assess the whole scenario while identifying the risks and benefits involved in standing alone.

Giving Culturally Sensitive Care

If a person could actually see cultural diversity in America from a far off place, it would look like a tapestry of beautifully woven fabrics. America as a tapestry of diversity is labeled "the melting pot," but more recently one teen immigrant, when referring to cultural differences causing violence and confrontations, said that Americans have more of an appearance akin to "a salad bowl with lots of little chunks in it" (In the Mix, 2007). The analogy that this teen made is an excellent portrayal of Americans today.

Nurses must be ethically and culturally sensitive to caring for culturally diverse patients within the health care system in the United States. **Culture** refers to "integrated patterns of human behavior that include the language, thoughts, communications, actions, customs, beliefs, values, and/or institutions of racial, ethnic, religious, and/or social groups" (Lipson & Dibble, 2005, p. xi). **Giving culturally sensitive care**, based on nurses applying ethical components of a trusting, respectful, and responsible relationship with others, means that nurses possess, according to Spector (2004), "basic knowledge of and constructive attitudes toward the health traditions observed among the diverse cultural groups found in the setting in which they are practicing" (p. 8).

Without some degree of cultural knowledge, nurses cannot possibly provide ethical care; for instance, relationships with others will not develop into a trusting, respectful exchange. Lipson and Dibble's (2005) trademark name, **ASK**, serves as an acronym that nurses can use when approaching patients of various cultures; it refers to awareness, sensitivity, and knowledge. Because patients know themselves best, nurses need to implement ASK when approaching their patients. There are many views in the United States, based on each culture's belief system, regarding health, illness, pain, suffering, birth, parenting, death, dying, health care, communication, truth, and many other issues that nurses must attempt to comprehend.

Lipson and Dibble (2005) emphasized that nurses should use the term *ASK* instead of the term *competence* because they believe that competence signifies an expert, mastery level that is an unreachable goal for most nurses working in a setting with many cultures of people. Good cultural assessments are known to take multiple hours in duration, time that nurses do not have, so a basic set of questions needs to be asked of patients upon admission to a facility. Lipson and Dibble's (2005) basic cultural assessment questions were adapted from Lipson and Meleis (1985), and are:

1. What is the patient's ethnic affiliation?
2. Who are the patient's major support persons and where do they live?
3. With whom should we speak about the patient's health or illness?
4. What are the patient's primary and secondary languages, and speaking and reading abilities?
5. What is the patient's economic situation? Is income adequate to meet the patient's and family's need? (p. xiii)

Refer to Box 3.3 for communication variations that are critical to nurses providing ethical care. Verbal and nonverbal variables can limit the communication process. Some languages, such as Spanish, have numerous dialects, making the communication process difficult.

America is indeed little chunks in a big bowl of salad! To exhibit professionalism through ethically competent care, nurses must be attentive to the many variations. The *Code of Ethics for Nurses with Interpretive Statements* (2001) contains explicit guidelines for giving care to individuals regardless of social or economic status, personal attributes, or nature of health problems. Giving care based on the code includes giving care with cultural sensitivity.

Communication is integral for a correct understanding and comprehension of health care treatments, directives, and other exchanges. The U.S. Department of Health and Human Services Office of Minority Health (1997) set forth 14 standards for cultural care titled *National Standards on Culturally and Linguistically Appropriate Services* (CLAS standards). The standards are supposed to be integrated into all facets of care in organizations, institutions, and agencies (see Box 3.4 for the CLAS standards). CLAS standards are organized by themes: Standards 1 to 3: culturally competent care; Standards 4 to 7: language access services; and Standards 8 to 14: organizational supports for cultural competence.

The Office of Minority Health has suggested that the Joint Commission apply Standards 1, 2, 3, 8, 9, 10, 11, 12, and 13 for the areas of ethics, rights, and responsibilities; provision of care, treatment, and services; leadership; managing the environment of care;

BOX 3.3: HIGHLIGHTS FROM THE FIELD

Lipson and Dibble's (2005) *Cultural Variations in Communication*

Conversational Style and Pacing
- Silence can be significant and indicate respect or acknowledgement of the speaker.
- Words such as "no" can be rude if spoken aloud.
- Conversations vary from abruptness to indirect styles or from loudness to softness.
- People of some cultures will tell whole stories to communicate a point.
  Examples:
  ○ Italians tend to be volatile, passionate, and loud.
  ○ American Indians can be soft spoken, clear, and direct, and view loudness as being rude.
  ○ Russians can be direct and tend to say exactly what they think so that no one misunderstands them.

Eye Contact
- Variations in eyes include intense, direct eye contact and fleeting, roving eyes.
- People of some cultures believe that avoiding direct eye contact is necessary to convey respect, not to invade privacy, or to convey gender exchange.
  Examples:
  ○ Vietnamese often do not make eye contact with someone of unequal status, age, or opposite gender.
  ○ Iranians often find that direct eye contact is acceptable, especially for those of equal status.
  ○ African Americans generally make direct eye contact, but eye contact may vary among the generations.

Personal Space
- Variations in personal space occur.
- Standing away or backing away from someone means that the person wants distance.
- Standing too close to a person can signal aggressiveness.

(continued)

BOX 3.3: HIGHLIGHTS FROM THE FIELD
(CONTINUED)

Examples:
- ◦ The Chinese often require a comfort zone of 4 to 5 feet, but have a preference of side to side rather than face to face communication.
- ◦ The Polish tend to prefer close proximity with family members and friends but a little more distance with strangers (which includes health care professionals).
- ◦ Gypsies tend to prefer extremely close proximity to others, even more so than the U.S. dominant culture.

Touch

- Touch differs in each culture from complete touching to no touching.
- People of some cultures believe that touching is taboo for certain areas of the body.
- People of some cultures believe that touching is more appropriate for those of the same gender whereas touching of unrelated people or the opposite gender is taboo.
- People of some cultures believe that receiving health care from the opposite gender, especially when care involves genital handling such as Foley catheter insertion, is taboo.

Examples:
- ◦ Mexicans often like touching close friends and family members but experience discomfort when touched by strangers (which includes health care professionals).
- ◦ Pakistanis, specifically Muslim Pakistanis, try to avoid touching the opposite gender from puberty and beyond if they are not married or are not blood kin.
- ◦ Hawaiians often prefer permission before being touched, and then only handshakes or touching of the shoulder are acceptable.

Time Orientation

- Time orientation with some cultures is very significant, such as in the U.S. dominant culture.

(*continued*)

BOX 3.3: HIGHLIGHTS FROM THE FIELD (CONTINUED)

- People of some cultures do not place enormous value on time orientation but would rather complete an interaction and discussion with someone they have encountered.
  Examples:
  ○ Jamaicans and Central Americans tend to view being on time as less important as compared to other aspects of living.
  ○ Filipinos are generally oriented to past and present time, but future time commitments are based on a *bahala na* (Filipino for leave it to God) approach to time commitments.
  ○ Germans are generally extremely punctual, even setting their clocks ahead to avoid a rush to a deadline, and they display intolerance to others' tardiness.

and managing information. As of May 2007, the Joint Commission has incorporated these standards into accreditation requirements for hospitals. Regarding the ethics, rights, and responsibilities area, The Joint Commission (2007) stated:

> [Patients/residents/clients] deserve care, treatment, and services that safeguard their personal dignity and respect their cultural, psychosocial, and spiritual values. These values often influence the [patient/resident/client]'s perceptions and needs. By understanding and respecting these values, providers can meet care, treatment, and service needs and preferences. (p. 2)

Using Power

The nurse-patient relationship has infinite untold and unrealized power.

—JANIE B. BUTTS

"Without power, there is no action" (Hakesley-Brown & Malone, 2007, Section 2, Para. 1). **Power**, by definition, means that a group or person has influence over others in an effective way. The author of this chapter has defined **using power**, as surmised from various aspects of the literature including Manojlovich (2007), as the ability of nurses to influence persons, groups, or communities by controlling the con-

Box 3.4: Highlights from the Field

The CLAS Standards

Standard 1

Health care organizations should ensure that patients/consumers receive from all staff members effective, understandable, and respectful care that is provided in a manner compatible with their cultural health beliefs and practices and preferred language.

Standard 2

Health care organizations should implement strategies to recruit, retain, and promote at all levels of the organization a diverse staff and leadership that are representative of the demographic characteristics of the service area.

Standard 3

Health care organizations should ensure that staff at all levels and across all disciplines receive ongoing education and training in culturally and linguistically appropriate service delivery.

Standard 4

Health care organizations must offer and provide language assistance services, including bilingual staff and interpreter services, at no cost to each patient/consumer with limited English proficiency at all points of contact, in a timely manner during all hours of operation.

Standard 5

Health care organizations must provide to patients/consumers in their preferred language both verbal offers and written notices informing them of their right to receive language assistance services.

Standard 6

Health care organizations must assure the competence of language assistance provided to limited English proficient patients/consumers by interpreters and bilingual staff. Family and friends should not be used to provide interpretation services (except on request by the patient/consumer).

(continued)

Box 3.4: Highlights from the Field
(continued)

Standard 7

Health care organizations must make available easily understood patient-related materials and post signage in the languages of the commonly encountered groups and/or groups represented in the service area.

Standard 8

Health care organizations should develop, implement, and promote a written strategic plan that outlines clear goals, policies, operational plans, and management accountability/oversight mechanisms to provide culturally and linguistically appropriate services.

Standard 9

Health care organizations should conduct initial and ongoing organizational self-assessments of CLAS-related activities and are encouraged to integrate cultural and linguistic competence-related measures into their internal audits, performance improvement programs, patient satisfaction assessments, and outcomes-based evaluations.

Standard 10

Health care organizations should ensure that data on the individual patient's/consumer's race, ethnicity, and spoken and written language are collected in health records, integrated into the organization's management information systems, and periodically updated.

Standard 11

Health care organizations should maintain a current demographic, cultural, and epidemiological profile of the community as well as a needs assessment to accurately plan for and implement services that respond to the cultural and linguistic characteristics of the service area.

Standard 12

Health care organizations should develop participatory, collaborative partnerships with communities and utilize a variety of formal and informal mechanisms to facilitate community and patient/consumer involvement in designing and implementing CLAS-related activities.

(continued)

Box 3.4: Highlights from the Field (Continued)

Standard 13
Health care organizations should ensure that conflict and grievance resolution processes are culturally and linguistically sensitive and capable of identifying, preventing, and resolving cross-cultural conflicts or complaints by patients/consumers.

Standard 14
Health care organizations are encouraged to regularly make available to the public information about their progress and successful innovations in implementing the CLAS standards and to provide public notice in their communities about the availability of this information.

Quoted from U.S. Department of Health and Human Services Office of Minority Health. (1997). National standards on culturally and linguistically appropriate services (CLAS). Retrieved April 20, 2007, from http://www.omhrc.gov/templates/browse.aspx?lvl=2&lvlID=15

tent of their practice, the context of their practice, and their competence in practice. These domains of control—content, context, and competence—have become critically important in light of magnet recognition and evidence-based practice in nursing. As Manojlovich stated, "All of the magnet hospital [reported] studies have . . . consistently demonstrated positive benefits for nursing and patients when nurses control both the content and context of their practice" (Control Over the Context of Nursing Practice Section, Para. 2). However, Manojlovich conveyed a fear that these three domains are not enough to help nurses realize their power, mainly because nurses possibly do not understand how power can develop from relationships. Nurses need to increase their understanding of sources of power in the practice arena, to expand their view of empowerment with the idea that empowerment serves as a motivating factor, and to foster and nurture relationships that contribute to nursing power.

The nurse-patient relationship is a powerful force to be reckoned with for the future. The public and health care professionals will come to see the vision of power for nurses as a reality of infinite possibilities. Quality of care dictates all facets of health care. Hakesley-Brown and Malone (2007) explored nurses and patients as being an all powerful entity that has evolved over time because of clinical, political, and organizational power paradigm shifts. Nurses have facilitated patients' emancipation from a previous paternalistic form of care to today's autonomous decision makers seeking quality care. With nurses being directly involved in quality of care, nurses are in a prime position to use power to benefit not only patients, but also the professional practice of nursing.

In fact, the nurse-patient relationship has infinite untold and unrealized power. Perceptions are more powerful than just facts. Duffy and Duffy (1998) so characteristically emphasized this fact by words from the title of their article, "Power Perceived Is Power Achieved." These authors believe that even though changing perceptions is a difficult task, nurses have the power to be powerful through the hard work of effectively communicating the service provided to customers and others, talking the customer's language, building alliances, being competitive in a healthy environment, and listening to their customers.

The author of this chapter found one study most interesting—qualitative interviews by Ponte, Glazer, Dann, and colleagues (2007), who were developing a fast-track BSN-to-PhD nursing program and wanted to explore the concept of power in nursing. The development of this program was a large collaborative effort among several organizations. They interviewed nursing leaders from six organizations to understand, from the leaders' perspectives on the concept of power, ways that nurses can acquire power and ways that these leaders demonstrate power in their practice and work. From the beginning of the fast-track development, Ponte et al. wanted to incorporate characteristics associated with power into the program so that students in the program could learn how to attain positions of power. What they found was extremely valuable material, especially the mentoring component between PhD students and nursing leaders from academia and health care organizations.

According to these leaders, power lies within each nurse who engages in patient care, administrative leadership, teaching, and research. These interviewed nursing leaders emphasized the power of individual nurses through patient care, families, organizations, colleagues, and the nursing profession as a whole. As nurses develop knowledge and expertise in practice from multiple domains, these experts integrate and use their power in a "collaborative, interdisciplinary effort focused solely on the patients and families that the nurse and care team serve and with whom they partner" (Ponte et al., 2007, Characteristics of Nursing Power section, Para. 1). From these interviews, the authors extrapolated eight properties of a powerful professional practice, which could serve as a basis for current and future power in nursing. Refer to Box 3.5 for the properties of power.

Box 3.5: Highlights from the Field

Ponte et al.'s Properties of a Powerful Professional Nursing Practice

Nurses who have developed a powerful nursing practice...
- Acknowledge their unique role in the provision of patient- and family-centered care.
- Commit to continuous learning through education, skill development, and evidence-based practice.
- Demonstrate professional comportment [manner in which one conducts self] and recognize the critical nature of presence.
- Value collaboration and partner effectively with colleagues in nursing and other disciplines.
- Actively position themselves to influence decisions and resource allocation.
- Strive to develop an impeccable character; to be inspirational, compassionate, and have a credible, sought-after perspective (the antithesis of power as a coercive strategy).
- Recognize that the role of a nurse leader is to pave the way for nurses' voices to be heard and to help novice nurses develop into powerful professionals.
- Evaluate the power of nursing and the nursing department in organizations they enter by assessing the organization's mission and values and its commitment to enhancing the power of diverse perspectives.

Quoted from Ponte et al. (2007). The power of professional nursing practice—An essential element of patient and family centered care. *The Online Journal of Issues in Nursing, 12*(1) [Manuscript #3]. Retrieved April 20, 2007, from http://www.nursingworld.org/ojin/topic32/tpc32_3.htm

Ethical Reflections

There are a variety of ways that power can be abusive, coercive, or not used at all. Nurses who do not use their power for the good of a situation are ineffective. There are two examples of power presented here, one on a small scale and one on a large scale.

- This first scenario is an example of the nurse-patient relationship on a smaller scale. Ms. Gomez, whose diagnosis is inoperable and incurable cancer of the liver, is unaware of her diagnosis but realizes that she is experiencing abdominal pain that she described as 8 on a 10-point scale. Ms. Gomez is located on the cancer unit of the hospital. Everyone involved in her care is aware of her diagnosis except for her. She senses something is terribly wrong and begins to panic when physicians gather in her room and begin to discuss her "case" in front of her. Ms. Gomez could have had a better patient outcome if the nurse would have persuaded the physicians to leave her room to discuss her case and/or for them to tell her the truth about her diagnosis and prognosis. Had the nurse exerted a noncoercive power over this situation, Ms. Gomez would not have panicked. *What specific actions could this nurse have taken on a small-scale or unit level in terms of unit policies regarding clinical rounds or disclosure to patients?*

- This second scenario is an example of the nurse-patient relationship on a larger scale. Nurse Mary is a hospice nurse located in a coastal region and has six patients in her care. She saw and heard on television the national weather center forecast of several life-threatening hurricanes hitting her region during the coming hurricane season. Most of her patients are financially challenged. The nurse has choices to make: (1) she could do nothing and let nature take its course; (2) she could educate her patients and families on ways to prepare for disaster; or (3) she could educate her patients and families on disaster preparedness as well as use her power by helping poor, homebound patients—not just her patients—in her community to prepare for disaster. One way to help on a large scale could be to have a fundraiser and supply drive in her community, and once the drive is over, to recruit community or nurse volunteers, through efforts of the American Red Cross or in other ways, to distribute the supplies, hand out disaster preparedness information, and verbally educate the families. *What are other ways that this nurse or other nurses could implement to influence the community to help these patients?*

Being a Good Citizen of the World

Being a good citizen of the world, as defined by Crigger, Brannigan, and Baird (2006), means that nursing professionals "think reflectively about themselves and others, understand others' point of view, and promote social justice" (p. 23). Being a good citizen of the world entails a certain degree of cultural sensitivity in practice and in relationships. However, cultural knowledge is not the only criterion; it also involves being a compassionate professional nurse, which according to Crigger et al. is currently in the process of being defined. Part of the developing definition of being a compassionate professional nurse involves embracing a high level of social justice commitment in health care for all people and nations. (See more on social justice in Chapter 2.)

Professional nurses need to actively engage in seeking better health for the world at large. One particular entity that Crigger et al. (2006) related was the 10/90 rule of research, meaning that 10% of the world's population receives 90% of the research grants, leaving a wide disparity between the rich and poor countries. Politically working to equalize research funding distribution can be an essential part of being a good citizen of the world. Partnering through global collaborative and multidisciplinary research efforts to prevent and combat serious diseases and to decrease poverty is a primary target for nurse researchers. Curricula in schools of nursing at the graduate and undergraduate levels should consist of concepts of social justice and strategies for commitment to global health. Nursing's global mission is to support and work toward a common good. The vision of Sigma Theta Tau International Honor Society (2007) is "to create a global community of nurses who lead in nursing knowledge, scholarship, service and learning to improve the health of the world's people."

Ethical Reflections

After reading this section on professionalism and boundaries, you have learned about some of the concepts that help to make up a nurse's ethical professional composition, which include but are not limited to respect, confidentiality, moral courage, culturally sensitive care, power, and good global citizenship. The concepts overlap with each other. Habitually practicing nursing ethics and using codes of ethics as guides help nurses to develop moral grounding by which to function regarding professionalism.

Test your personal moral grounding! List the professional concepts from this section on a piece of paper and write down how they could relate to your professional nursing practice by briefly summarizing an example of an ethical situation or conflict that could arise with each concept and possible resolutions for each example:

- Giving respect
- Maintaining confidentiality
- Having moral courage
- Giving culturally sensitive care
- Using power
- Being a good citizen of the world

Codes of Ethics for Internet Use and Telehealth

The Internet has become an unprecedented phenomenon. Almost 1 billion people have connected to this global electronic community. Of the 6.6 billion people in the world early in 2007, there were 1.114 billion Internet users in all countries (Miniwatts Marketing Group, 2007). The makeup of these 1.114 billion users, in order, is Asia 36%, Europe 29%, North America 21%, Latin America 8%, Africa 3%, Middle East 2%, and Oceania-Australia 1%. As nurses and nursing students take advantage of the infinite possibilities of the Internet, they need to know standards of ethical conduct when accessing information on the Internet.

Another critical aspect for nurses and nursing students is the broad and virtual world of **telehealth**, which includes virtual patient teaching, nursing information, information technology, videoconferencing, and health education. Nurses must be able to evaluate the credibility of specific Web sources and the health information for use in patient teaching. They also need to teach patients how to evaluate the credibility of Web sites and health information.

Practical Strategies for Internet Ethics

Many people who use the Internet have already experienced, to some degree, the consequences of unethical computer behavior, such as being the target of someone else's devious acts. Because of the potential for unethical and criminal behaviors, it is imperative that nurses and nursing students understand and practice ethics on the Internet. Respect for one another on the Web and a serious commitment to Web ethics must occur as existing users continue to connect and new users continue to sign on in record numbers each year.

Johnson (2003) identified three reasons for learning ethical behavior on the Internet:

1. Adults who attended school before the integration of computers and networks may not understand the virtual world and learning ethical behavior will promote good practice.
2. The virtual world requires the application of new ethical considerations because many people see their actions in the virtual world as intangible, and even if the actions are unethical, they do not perceive these actions to be nearly as unethical as they could be in the real world.
3. The virtual world and advanced technology have served as a gateway for misuse, and thus many people view their use as low-risk, game-like challenges, rather than misuse.

Point 3 is one that needs a little explanation. Some people who use the Internet frequently or for long durations have the potential to view the virtual world as a fictional place where their activities sometimes appear to them as unreal games. Misuse at that point begins to seem like a play-like challenge and not at all like actual misuse. Therefore, the people who slide into misuse as a game sometimes see nothing wrong with their Internet behaviors. A continuous and consistent exposure to best ethical practices on the Internet will keep reality at the forefront.

Although many people view computer and virtual world behaviors as intangible or not really existing, the behaviors and actions really do exist and cause many problems and concerns. All people who search and use the Internet leave their footprints or traceable evidence, such as nonerasable histories of their searches and frequented addresses on the Internet. For instance, stealing copyrighted materials, then saving them to one's personal files, will reveal evidence of the original author of these materials in Properties. Police detectives can trace all transactions, cite visits, and other types of activities, such as in pedophile pornographic cases or the purcahse of illegal drugs on the Internet, even when a person has attempted to erase all files or completely recover the system. A few behaviors viewed as unethical or criminal include:

- Stealing copyrighted material and credit for intellectual property
- Intercepting private e-mail
- Displaying [pornographic] material
- Deliberately providing public misinformation
- Misusing research material
- Improper commercial/personal use of the Internet
- Stealing credit information (Security Issues on the Internet, 2005, Para. 4)

Rinaldi (1998) developed a highly regarded set of Internet guidelines, *The Net: User Guidelines and Netiquette*, that includes helpful ethical strategies for users. These strategies are everyday manners that form the foundation of respect on the Internet. Nine of the 21 strategic behaviors that Rinaldi delineated for electronic communications, such as e-mails, are:

- Capitalize only the words you would normally capitalize because capitalizing whole words or sentences gives the appearance of shouting.
- Keep e-mails as short and concise as possible.
- Limit line length to 65 to 70 characters if possible.
- Place asterisks around words that need to be emphasized.
- Habitually use signatures at the end of the message.
- Avoid sending chain letters.

- Maintain professionalism when e-mailing others.
- Cite all quotes and be respectful of all copyrighted or licensed information.
- Because the emotional aspect of e-mail content is difficult to detect, use emoticons to express feelings, such as **:)** *or* **:-)** to express humor and **:(** *or* **:-(** to express sadness, and try to be very careful about how and when you express sarcasm, if ever at all.

Johnson (2003) developed the Three Ps of Technology Ethics, which are respecting people's Privacy, protecting and respecting people's Property and using technology aPpropriately and constructively and not breaking the rules of the government, school, religion, or family. Another code of conduct for usage is the ever-popular Ten Commandments by the Computer Ethics Institute (1992).

1. Thou shalt not use a computer to harm other people.
2. Thou shalt not interfere with other people's computer work.
3. Thou shalt not snoop around in other people's computer files.
4. Thou shalt not use a computer to steal.
5. Thou shalt not use a computer to bear false witness.
6. Thou shalt not copy or use proprietary software for which you have not paid.
7. Thou shalt not use other people's computer resources without authorization or proper compensation.
8. Thou shalt not appropriate other people's intellectual output.
9. Thou shalt think about the social consequences of the program you are writing or the system you are designing.
10. Thou shalt always use a computer in ways that insure consideration and respect for your fellow humans.

Dozens of ethical codes of conduct exist for users of the Internet. However, no matter how many codes exist or what population they serve, the codes are of no use if they are not practiced. Nurses and nursing students need to remember the foremost principal of "respect one another" when accessing the Internet. Refer to Box 3.6 for a discussion of a nursing student's buying an APA paper on the Internet.

Nurses and Telehealth

There is an overabundance of information on the Internet regarding best health practices and treatment options, but when nurses use the information as a resource for patient teaching, they need to have a certain degree of confidence and trust that the information is credible. Nurses also need to teach their patients how to evaluate Web sites and their content as to soundness and validity.

The power of electronic information has changed the way people are obtaining health information, products, and services. The popularity of electronic health information is astounding. As of 2006, 80% of American Internet users had searched for at least 1 of 17 major health topics on the Internet, making surfing for health information

Box 3.6: Highlights from the Field

Should I Buy This APA Paper?

Megan's Paper Assignment

Megan, a nursing student, found a Web site with advertisements from a company that for a fee would customize a nursing school APA paper on any topic of choice. She needed an APA paper on the concept of compassion in nursing practice and realized that she was overloaded with assignments from school. She contemplated whether she should buy the paper and asked herself "Should I buy this APA paper?" Without further thought, however, she completed the form and ordered the paper. The company sent the paper to her within 3 days and Megan, in turn, submitted the paper electronically to the professor as her own work.

1. Who do you think is the rightful owner of the paper?
2. Do you think the action is unethical, illegal, or both? Please explain your rationale.
3. Is this action cheating, plagiarism, or both, by common university or college standards on academic honesty? Please explain your rationale.
4. What are some values and ethical implications that Megan needed to consider before buying the paper?
5. Integrate Kant's deontology framework to develop what would have been an alternative action for Megan.
6. What is a creative strategy that Megan's teacher could have used for this assignment to reduce the chance of Megan and possibly others buying an APA paper on the Net?
7. What are some examples of other similar Web incidents considered illegal or unethical?

(continued)

BOX 3.6: HIGHLIGHTS FROM THE FIELD (CONTINUED)

The story continues...

The professor required that electronic versions of the paper be submitted. What Megan did not realize was that the professor opened each document to review what name appeared in the Properties of the document. When the professor opened Megan's paper, the property name on the document was "National Nursing Papers." Much to Megan's shock and dismay, the professor questioned her regarding the name in the Properties of the document. Megan did not realize that a property name even existed or that the property name does not change on the document when saving the file to her computer. She could not give an adequate explanation for the existing name. After thinking of various options, she finally admitted to buying the paper and therefore failed the course. Megan did not receive a note dismissing her from the program for this one infraction, but the dean and professor gave her a one-time warning that if she cheated or plagiarized in any form in the future, as instructed in the university's handbook, she would be dismissed from the school of nursing and the university. Megan signed the warning document. She had no other choice if she wanted to remain in the nursing program.

8. Do you believe, based on your analysis of the deontology framework, that Megan deserved another opportunity to remain in the nursing program? Please explain your rationale.

---

one of the most popular pursuits for Internet users (Pew Internet and American Life Project, 2006). Other interesting findings from the report included:

- People want to be educated electronically so they search for new information or they review information for several reasons: to prepare for physician appointments or surgery, to share information with others, and to seek support.
- Women under age 65, college graduates, and home broadband users are the primary seekers of Web health information.
- Web users find support in Web groups and e-mail.
- People who seek health information and services on the Web find that their relationships with their health care providers change.

According to Crigger (2002):

Trust is a fundamental concern in ehealth. Indeed, it is fundamental to health care. To receive the care they need, patients must share private information and be willing to take medications, use medical devices, or often accept interventions that intrude on their bodies. They rely on health care providers to keep their personal information confidential, to provide accurate and appropriate information about their conditions and possible treatments, and to recommend the therapy they believe to be in the patient's interest. (Para. 2)

Health information encompasses a vast range of information on staying healthy, preventing disease, managing disease, and making health care decisions regarding products and services. Health products may include everything from medications to vitamins and nutritional supplements to medical devices. Internet users can access health care plans, health care providers, insurers, and health care facilities.

The Internet Healthcare Coalition members published their eHealth Code of Ethics with the goal of creating "a trustworthy environment for all users, whether they are patients, health care professionals, website sponsors, people who develop health applications and content on the web, or individuals who turn to the Internet to help them stay well" (as cited in Crigger, 2002, Para. 5). Many people cannot evaluate Web sites and information adequately. Therefore, coalition members issued this code of conduct for marketers, health professionals, and creators of Web sites in an attempt to enhance a trustworthy environment for consumers of health information, products, and services. Fundamental values of the eHealth Code of Ethics (as cited in Crigger, 2002) include the following eight concepts based on the ethical principle of *respect for persons*:

- *Candor:* Disclose beneficial information on the Web site.
- *Honesty:* Be truthful.
- *Quality:* Provide accurate and clear health information and provide information that will help consumers judge the credibility of your information, products, and services.
- *Informed consent:* Respect consumers' rights and how personal data may be collected, used, or shared.
- *Privacy:* Respect and protect the privacy of others.
- *Professionalism in online health care:* Respect ethical obligations to patients and consumers and educate patients and consumers about the potential limitations of electronic health information.
- *Responsible partnering:* Evaluate organizations and sites for their trustworthiness.

■ *Accountability:* Provide ways for consumers to give feedback and evaluate the site, and inquire through specific evaluative questions the extent to which the creators of the site complied with the eHealth Code of Ethics.

Numerous medical universities have Web sites with dependable and sound health information for health care professionals and the general public. Nurses need to follow the eHealth Code of Ethics as well as teach these same guidelines to patients. Every person shares in a responsibility to help assure the integrity and soundness of Internet health information. People can accomplish the task by evaluating information on the sites and providing meaningful feedback to the site creators and marketers. In hospitals and other health care institutions, nurses should post basic guidelines on bulletin boards by the computers regarding how to evaluate health information on the Internet. Refer to Box 3.7 for the Internet Healthcare Coalition's (2002) tips for nurses to help patients and themselves in evaluating the quality of health information on the Internet.

Nurses must adhere to the conduct set forth in the ANA *Code of Ethics for Nurses with Interpretive Statements* (2001) in every aspect of their nursing practice including Internet usage and the uploading and downloading of telehealth information. Patients and the general public depend highly on nurses as being trustworthy sources of reference and information. Therefore, nurses cannot risk placing themselves in jeopardy of violating that trust because of Internet and telehealth unethical practices, even if they do not realize when the information could be inappropriate or incorrect information. Given this predicament, nurses need to become savvy about evaluating Web sites for accuracy, readability, and validity before sharing the information with patients. Nurses must be Internet savvy and maintain the highest of ethical standards when evaluating health-related Web sites, else they could be placed at risk for violations in privacy, confidentiality, and trust. Based on this information, there are three ethical principles at stake:

■ *Respect for other persons—autonomy:* Trust, privacy, confidentiality, and human dignity
■ *Doing good—beneficence:* Promoting health and well-being of people by way of patient information and prevention of disease and illness
■ *Do no harm—nonmaleficence:* To patients, families, groups, and communities

Nurses need to justify or evaluate ethical behaviors on their Internet use just as they would any type of clinical practice. Frequently reflecting on and evaluating their own practice, whether on the Internet or at the bedside, for the degree to which their behaviors are morally consistent is an essential activity. By using the Gibbs Reflective Cycle delineated in Chapter 2, nurses must justify their practice behaviors and answer the following questions:

BOX 3.7: HIGHLIGHTS FROM THE FIELD

Tips for Patients and Nurses: Evaluating Quality Health Information on the Internet

- Choosing an online health information resource is like choosing your doctor. . . . A good rule of thumb is to find a Web site that has a person, institution, or organization in which you already have confidence.
- Trust what you see or read on the Internet only if you can validate the source of the information. Authors and contributors should always be identified, along with their affiliations and financial interests, if any, in the content.
- Question Web sites that credit themselves as the sole source of information on a topic as well as sites that disrespect other sources of knowledge.
- Don't be fooled by a comprehensive list of links. Any Web site can link to another and this in no way implies endorsement from either site.
- Find out if the site is professionally managed and reviewed by an editorial board of experts to ensure that the material is both credible and reliable.
- Medical knowledge is continually evolving. Make sure that all clinical content includes the date of publication or modification.
- Any and all sponsorship, advertising, underwriting, commercial funding arrangements, or potential conflicts should be clearly stated and separated from the editorial content. A good question to ask is: [Does the author or do the authors] have anything to gain from proposing one particular point of view over another?
- Avoid any online physician who proposes to diagnose or treat you without a proper physical examination and consultation regarding your medical history.
- Read the Web site's privacy statement and make certain that any personal medical or other information you supply will be kept absolutely confidential.
- Most important, use your common sense! Shop around, always get more than one opinion, be suspicious of miracle cures, and always read the fine print.

Quoted parts from Internet Healthcare Coalition. Tips for healthy surfing online: Finding quality information on the Internet. Retrieved April 20, 2007, from http://www.ihealthcoalition.org/content/tips.html

- What happened?
- What were your feelings?
- What was good and bad about the experience?
- What can you learn from the event?
- What could you have done differently or in addition?
- If it happens again what would you do?

Nurses need to apply one of the ethical frameworks at the beginning of the evaluation phase of the cycle and then move through the cycle with the ethical framework. The major frameworks include the utilitarian-consequential theory, the deontological theory, a virtue ethics approach, or an ethic of care approach. (See Chapter 1 for ethical theories and approaches.) The following Web Ethics box contains some helpful Internet sites for nurses, patients, and families.

Web Ethics

Web Sites for Nurses

American Nurses Association: Center for Ethics and Human Rights
   http://www.nursingworld.org/ethics/
   Brochure: http://www.hhs.state.ne.us/omh/docs/CLASBrochure.pdf
   Web site: http://www.omhrc.gov

Center for Social Justice
   http://centerforsocialjustice.org

International Council of Nurses—Nursing Networks, Geneva, Switzerland
   http://www.icn.ch/networks.htm

Medical Library Association, MLANET: A User's Guide to Finding and Evaluating Health
   http://www.mlanet.org/resources/userguide.html

Nursing Power.Net
   http://www.nursingpower.net/sitemap.html

University of Delaware Library: Internet Resources for Nursing
   http://www2.lib.udel.edu/subj/nurs/internet.htm

U.S. Department of Health and Human Service: HIPAA, Privacy, and Confidentiality
   http://www.hhs.gov/ocr/hipaa/

USDHHS, Office of Minority Health
   http://www.omhrc.gov

WalkupsWay.com—Owned and Managed by Louise Walkup, Ethics Teacher
   http://walkupsway.com

WordPress.Com: Nursing Power
   http://wordpress.com/tag/nursing-power/

Summary

This author has focused on what professionalism means to nurses and their practice or role. The author addressed three topics:

- In the first major section, professional codes of ethics in nursing, the author presented a history of the development of the ICN and ANA codes of ethics for nurses. Several significant events led to an ongoing refinement of the nursing codes. One particular activity was Nightingale's continued emphasis, both verbally and in writing, on ethical precepts and values. By the end of the 19th century, modern nursing was born, and in 1893 Lystra Gretter chaired a committee to create the Nightingale Pledge. In 1900, America's Isabel Hampton Robb wrote the first nursing ethics book, titled *Nursing Ethics: For Hospital and Private Use*. The first ANA code was adopted in 1950 and since then has evolved to the latest edition of 2001. In 1953, the ICN published its first code of ethics for nurses. ICN's code has undergone many revisions, the latest being in 2006. A common theme between the ANA and ICN codes is the significance of giving compassionate care aimed at alleviating the suffering of patients.

- The second major section, professionalism and boundaries, consisted of content on professional boundaries and moral obligations for nurses as specified by the ANA *Code of Ethics for Nurses with Interpretive Statements* (2001). The author presented three major areas of the code: (1) clinical practice boundaries, (2) professional practice boundaries, and (3) self-care and self-development boundaries and obligations. The author extrapolated six particular concepts, explicit or implied, that are embedded in the nursing boundaries and moral obligations: (1) giving respect, (2) maintaining confidentiality, (3) having moral courage, (4) giving culturally sensitive care, (5) using power, and (6) being a good citizen of the world. Throughout these sections are ethical reflections and examples of boundary violations. The CLAS standards are also included in this section.

- The third major section, codes of ethics for Internet use and telehealth, consisted of a section on practical strategies for Internet users and a section on nurses and telehealth. Practical strategies for Internet users include a list of unethical or criminal Internet behaviors, 9 of 21 best practices for netiquette by Rinaldi, and the Ten Commandments by the Computer Ethics Institute. Included in nurses and telehealth are highlights from the Pew Internet and American Life Project research of 2006, the eHealth Code of Ethics by the Internet Healthcare Coalition, and tips for patients and nurses for evaluating the quality of health information by the Internet

Healthcare Coalition. The principle of respect serves as the basis of the eHealth Code of Ethics. When misuse occurs and when inappropriate or incorrect health information is found, three major ethical principles are at stake: (1) respect for other persons—autonomy, (2) doing good—beneficence, and (3) doing no harm—non-maleficence. Nurses must learn to be good evaluators of health information on the Internet for the sake of their patients, families, the community, and themselves.

References

American Nurses Association. (2001). *Code of ethics for nurses with interpretive statements.* Silver Spring, MD: Author.

Beauchamp, T. L., & Childress, J. F. (2001). *Principles of biomedical ethics* (5th ed.). New York: Oxford University Press.

Computer Ethics Institute. (1992). The ten commandments of computer ethics. Retrieved April 20, 2007, from http://www.brook.edu/its/cei/overview/Ten_Commanments_of_Computer_Ethics.htm

Crigger, B. J. (2002). Foundations of the eHealth code of ethics. Internet Healthcare Coalition. Retrieved April 20, 2007, from http://www.ihealthcoalition.org/ethics/code-foundations.html

Crigger, N. J., Brannigan, M., & Baird, M. (2006). Compassionate nursing professionals as good citizens of the world. *Advances in Nursing Science, 29*(1), 15–26.

Daly, B. J. (2002). Moving forward: A new code of ethics. *Nursing Outlook, 50,* 97–99.

Dossey, B. M. (2000). *Florence Nightingale: Mystic, visionary, healer.* Springhouse, PA: Springhouse.

Duffy, W., & Duffy, M. C. (1998). Power perceived is power achieved. *Association of Operating Room Nurses Journal, 68*(1), 89–92.

Esterhuizen, P. (2006). 30th anniversary issue: Is the professional code still the cornerstone of clinical nursing practice? *Journal of Advanced Nursing, 53*(1), 104–113. [Original publication, 1996, *Journal of Advanced Nursing, 23,* 25–31]

Fowler, M. D., & Benner, P. (2001). Implementing the new code of ethics for nurses: An interview with Marsha Fowler. *American Journal of Critical Care, 10*(6), 434–437.

Hakesley-Brown, R., & Malone, B. (2007). Patients and nurses: A powerful force. *The Online Journal of Issues in Nursing, 12*(1) [Manuscript #4]. Retrieved on April 20, 2007, from http://www.nursingworld.org/ojin/topic32/tpc32_4.htm

In the Mix. (2007). *Teen immigrants: Five American stories* [DVD]. Harriman, NY: Castleworks.

International Council of Nurses. (2006). *The ICN code of ethics for nurses.* Geneva: Author.

Internet Healthcare Coalition. (2002). Tips for healthy surfing online: Finding quality health information on the Internet. Retrieved April 20, 2007, from http://www.ihealthcoalition.org/content/tips.html

Johnson, D. (2003). *Learning right from wrong in the digital age: An ethics guide for parents, teachers, librarians, and others who care about computer-using young people.* Worthington, OH: Linworth.

The Joint Commission Division of Standards and Survey Methods. (2007, May). The Joint Commission 2007 requirements related to the provision of culturally and linguistically appropriate health care. Retrieved April 20, 2007, from http://www.jointcommission.org/NR/rdonlyres/1401C2EF-62F0-4715-B28A-7CE7F0F20E2D/0/hlc_jc_stds.pdf

Kidder, R. M., & Bracy, M. (2001). Moral courage: A white paper. Institute for Global Ethics. Retrieved on April 20, 2007, from http://www.moral-courage.org/pdfs/moral_courage_11-03-2001.pdf

Kuhse, H., & Singer, P. (2001). What is bioethics? A historical approach. In H. Kuhse & P. Singer (Eds.), *A companion to bioethics* (pp. 3–11). Oxford, UK: Blackwell.

Lachman, V. D. (2007). Moral courage: A virtue in need of development? *MedSurg Nursing, 16*(2), 131–133.

Lipson, J. G., & Dibble, S. L. (2005). Introduction: Providing culturally appropriate health care. In J. G. Lipson & S. L. Dibble (Eds.), *Cultural and clinical care* (pp. xi–xviii). San Francisco: University of California, San Francisco Nursing Press.

Lipson, J. G., & Meleis, A. I. (1985). Culturally appropriate care: The case of immigrants. *Topics in Clinical Nursing, 7,* 48–56.

Manojlovich, M. (2007). Power and empowerment in nursing: Looking backward to inform the future. *The Online Journal of Issues in Nursing, 12*(1) [Manuscript #1]. Retrieved on April 20, 2007, from http://www.nursingworld.org/ojin/topic32/tpc32_1.htm

Miniwatts Marketing Group. (2007). Internet usage statistics: The big picture. Retrieved April 20, 2007, from http://www.internetworldstats.com/stats.htm

Pew Internet and American Life Project. (2006, October 29). Online health search 2006. Retrieved April 20, 2007, from http://www.pewinternet.org/pdfs/PIP_Online_Health_2006.pdf

Ponte, P. R., Glazer, G., Dann, E., McCollum, K, Gross, A. et al. (2007). The power of professional nursing practice—An essential element of patient and family centered care. *The Online Journal of Issues in Nursing, 12*(1) [Manuscript #3]. Retrieved April 20, 2007, from http://nursing-world.org//ojin/topic32/tpc32_3.htm

Pullman, D. (1999). The ethics of autonomy and dignity in long-term care. *Canadian Journal on Aging, 18*(1), 26–46.

Rinaldi, A. (1998). The Net: User guidelines and netiquette. Retrieved April 20, 2007, from http://www.cs.biu.ac.il/home/leagal/netguide/index.html

Robb, I. H. (1916). *Nursing ethics: For hospital and private use.* Cleveland, OH: E. C. Koeckert. [Original publication 1900]

Rushton, C. H. (2007). Respect in critical care: A foundational ethical principle. *AACN Advanced Critical Care, 18*(2), 149–156.

Security Issues on the Internet. (2005). Ethics on the web. Retrieved April 20, 2007, from http://www.echonyc.com/~ysue/ethics.html

Sigma Theta Tau International Honor Society in Nursing. (2007). Fact sheet: Vision. Retrieved April 20, 2007, from http://www.nursingsociety.org/media/factsheet.html

Spector, R. E. (2004). *Cultural diversity in health and illness* (6th ed.). Upper Saddle River, NJ: Pearson-Prentice Hall.

Tschudin, V. (2006). 30th anniversary commentary on Esterhuizen P. (1996): Is the professional code still the cornerstone of clinical nursing practice? Journal of Advanced Nursing 23, 25–31. *Journal of Advanced Nursing, 53*(1), 113.

U.S. Department of Health and Human Services Office of Minority Health. (1997). National standards on culturally and linguistically appropriate services (CLAS). Retrieved April 20, 2007, from http://www.omhrc.gov/templates/browse.aspx?lvl=2&lvlID=15

CHAPTER 3 QUESTIONS

1. A key event that led to the development of the ANA *Code of Ethics for Nurses with Interpretive Statements* (2001) as nurses know it today was
   a. the first formal training school of nursing created by Florence Nightingale in 19th-century England.
   b. the Nightingale Pledge of 1893 written under the chairmanship of Lystra Gretter at the Detroit school of nursing.
   c. the nursing paradigm shift in the 1970s from obedience to physicians to nurses' responsibility toward the care of their patients.
   d. Isabel Hampton Robb's focus on nurses' work in her book of 1900, *Nursing Ethics: For Hospital and Private Use*, which was the first published nursing ethics book.

2. Which one of the following responses best describes the essence of the ANA *Code of Ethics for Nurses* today?
   a. The patient-centered code serves as a guideline for nurses' ethical actions in all areas of clinical practice as well as in other nursing roles.
   b. The patient-centered code serves as a clinical guideline for nursing actions in all areas of practice as well as in other nursing roles.
   c. The code's focus is on the patient rather than the client for nursing actions in all areas of clinical practice as well as in other nursing roles.
   d. The code serves as a guideline for nurses' ethical and legal actions in all areas of clinical practice as well as in other nursing roles.

3. A best practice when caring for a patient and family who do not share your own cultural heritage is first to
   a. consult the agency's language translator.
   b. ask the patient and family to complete a questionnaire that contains a comprehensive set of questions regarding their cultural beliefs and values.
   c. conduct a basic 5-question cultural assessment by approaching the patient and family with a keen awareness, complete cultural sensitivity, and with knowledge.
   d. try to understand the patient's culture by conducting trial-and-error tests such as an acceptance level of touch, eye contact, and personal space.

4. An instance of exemplary moral courage that you could demonstrate in clinical practice is to
    a. break a promise that you made to another nurse about a secret that could negatively affect the daily staffing pattern on your unit.
    b. take a verbal stand against a physician in front of the patient's family by refusing to administer an ordered medication.
    c. lead a unit-wide plan of action against the nurse manger because of a disciplinary action that was enforced against a well-liked nurse co-worker who was caught leaving work and returning without punching in or out on the time clock.
    d. confront a peer who you observed placing a vial of Demerol in a jacket pocket.

5. There are three ethical principles that nurses could violate insofar as sharing telehealth information with patients. Nurse Judy was later concerned that she had violated the nonmaleficence principle when
    a. Judy called the Web Nurse Shandra and shared her patient Pam's full name, contact information, and diagnosis with Shandra for a future company marketing and sales contact.
    b. Judy retrieved information about her patient Pam's prognosis from a reputable Web site and shared this information with Pam but later found that she had retrieved inaccurate information on the prognosis.
    c. after the patient Pam requested some Web site information about the disease process, Judy did nothing to provide that information to Pam.
    d. after the patient Pam requested some Web site information about her disease process, Judy decided that the "best action" for Pam was to ask Pam's physician to come and speak with her about her disease.

CHAPTER 3 ANSWER KEY TO QUESTIONS

1. c
2. a
3. c
4. d
5. b

Ethics in Organizations and Leadership

Janie B. Butts

Ethics must begin at the top of an organization. It is a leadership issue and the chief executive must set the example.

—FORMER CHIEF JUSTICE EDWARD HENNESSEY, MASSACHUSETTS SUPREME JUDICIAL COURT

OBJECTIVES

After reading this chapter, the reader should be able to:

1. Discuss the significance of an open system for health care organizations.
2. Explore the ethical dimensions that shape the culture of an organization.
3. Compare the similarities and differences between the traditional cultures of an organization and Daft's unique list of cultures.
4. Explore the rationale for the two principles necessary for trust to exist between the community at large and the organization.
5. Specify the elements that help to explain the rationale for the critical nature of trust in nurses and organizations.
6. Delineate the common unethical and illegal behaviors that people sometimes exhibit in organizations.
7. Briefly explore the history of the adoption of compliance programs and officers in health care organizations.
8. Identify the reasons for health care fraud occurrences in the year 2006.
9. Examine Pearson et al.'s characteristics of an exemplary ethical organization.

10. Discuss prevention strategies for health care fraud and other unethical or illegal behaviors in organizations.

11. After thinking of a person that you have labeled as an ideal leader in your personal life, compare and contrast your ideal leader's characteristics with the characteristics of an exemplary leader listed in the book.

12. Analyze your level of morality about a situation involving a possible conflict of interest by taking the 8-item test of rightness or wrongness.

KEY TERMS

Organization	Organizational culture	Adaptability culture
Mission culture	Clan culture	Bureaucratic culture
Organizational trust	Fiduciary relationships	Organizational ethics
Compliance programs	Corporate fraud	Health care fraud
Billing for services not rendered	Upcoding of services	Upcoding of items
Duplicate claims	Unbundling	Excessive services
Medically unnecessary services	Kickbacks	*Qui tam* lawsuits
Conflict of interest	Ethical leadership	Ethical communication
Ethical quality	Ethical collaboration	Ethical succession
Ethical tenure		planning

Ethical Organizations

An **organization** is defined as a group, in number from two people to tens of thousands, that intentionally strives to accomplish a shared common goal or set of goals. Organizations are systems, meaning that an organization consists of highly integrated parts or groups to accomplish shared goals. An organizational system is composed of inputs (resources—monetary and human), processes (how the organization moves to achieve goals), outputs (products or services), and outcomes (end results or benefits to consumers).

An open system, such as a health care organization, focuses on external relationships, which places the organization in a larger context or environment (Boyle, DuBose, Ellingson, Guinn, & McCurdy, 2001). An open system consists of relations with suppliers, regulatory bodies, customers, allies, and competitors. These external influencers help to guide the internal processes of the organization. An example of an external influence is the Joint Commission (JCAHO) accrediting agency. For the accreditation and review process, administrators develop an internal structure and create roles to assist and coordinate, such as the role of a compliance officer. Because of the open system relationships, ethical issues emerge at a new level.

Organizational culture refers to an organization's beliefs, values, attitudes, ideologies, practices, customs, and language. Even when the beliefs of the organization stem from the chief executive officer or the board of trustees, managers and employees need to be loyal and committed to the organization's goals for a culture to be shaped. Dimensions that shape an organizational culture are highlighted in Box 4.1. How administrators and people answer the questions in Box 4.1 will determine the ethical environment of the organization.

Researchers (e.g., Cartwright & Cooper, 1993; Zammuto & Krakower, 1991; as cited in Boyle et al., 2001) have indicated that four definitive characteristics can make up cultures in organizations. The traditional view of organizational cultures identified by these researchers is:

1. *Power:* This culture's descriptors include centralization; individual power and decision making; autocratic, patriarchal power; fear of punishment; and implicit rules. The values are control, stability, and loyalty.

2. *Bureaucracy:* This culture's descriptors include a hierarchical structure, emphasis on formal procedures and rules, clearly defined role requirements and boundaries of authority, minimized risks, an impersonal and predictable work environment, employees as cogs or slots, and positions more important than people. The values include efficiency, predictability, production, and control.

3. *Achievement and innovation:* This culture's descriptors include an emphasis on the team, a strong belief in the mission of the organization, organized work of task requirements, worker autonomy and flexibility, decision making pushed to lower ranks, and the promotion of cross-functional knowledge and skills. The values include creativity, adaptability, risk taking, and teamwork.

4. *Support:* This culture's descriptors include egalitarianism, nurturance of personal growth and development, usually nonprofit organizations, a safe environment, and a nonpolitical workplace. The values include commitment, consensus, and growth.

Several authors or researchers have labeled these four organizational cultures differently but with similar meanings. Daft (2004) labeled one such set of organizational cultures, and each culture has the potential to be successful. The four cultures identified by Daft are highlighted in Box 4.2.

BOX 4.1: HIGHLIGHTS FROM THE FIELD: DIMENSIONS THAT SHAPE AN ORGANIZATIONAL CULTURE

As Defined by E. H. Schein

Relationship to the environment	Is the organization's relationship to its environment dominant, submissive, or harmonious?
The nature of reality and truth	What is fact and what is truth? How is truth determined in this organization? The nature of human nature. Is human nature evil, good, or neutral? Do humans have the potential to be perfect?
The nature of human activity	What is the right thing for humans to do regarding the stated assumptions about reality, the environment, and human nature? Should humans be active, passive, self-developmental, or fatalistic?
The nature of human relationships	What is the right way for humans to interact with each other and to distribute power and resources? Should humans be cooperative, individualistic, collaborative, or communal? Do humans follow a traditional line of authority or should they be participatory? Does the organization value diversity or homogeneity? How is conflict resolved? How are decisions made?

Largely quoted and adapted from: Schien, E. H. (1991). *Organizational culture and leadership* (2nd ed.), pp. 95–96. San Francisco: Jossey-Bass/John Wiley & Sons.

BOX 4.2: HIGHLIGHTS FROM THE FIELD: DAFT'S TYPES OF ORGANIZATIONAL CULTURES (2004)

1. *Adaptability culture:* The focus is on the external environment where innovation, creativity, risk taking, flexibility, and change are the key elements for success. This type of organization creates change in a proactive way in an effort to anticipate responses and problems. Examples that Daft gave are the e-commerce companies such as Amazon.com and Buy.com. These companies are required to change quickly in anticipation of customer needs.

2. *Mission culture:* The vision and goals are clearly focused on a high level of competitiveness and profit-making strategies. In this type of culture, executives and managers strongly communicate a strategic plan for the organization's employees and expect high productivity, performance goals, and fringe benefits for goal attainment. An example of a mission culture that Daft gave was PepsiCo.

3. *Clan culture:* The focus is on employee needs and the strategies in which employees can engage for high performance. Key values in this culture consist of leaders taking care of their employees and making sure they have appropriate avenues to satisfaction and productivity. Responsibility and ownership are other key values in this type of culture. Rapid change occurs in this environment because of changing expectations from the external environment. One example that Daft gave is the MTW Corporation, which sells Web-based software and provides consultation to state governments and the insurance industry.

4. *Bureaucratic culture:* The focus is primarily on the internal environment where stability is a mainstay. Leaders develop and carry out scrupulous and detailed plans in a cautious and stable environment with slow-paced change. In this environment, personal engagement and involvement is lower in exchange for a high level of consistency, conformity, efficiency, and integration. Because of the inflexibility of this type of culture, many organizations are forced to change to a different, more flexible culture. However, one successful organization that Daft offered as an example is the Pacific Edge Software company run by a husband and wife team that thrives on order, discipline, and control.

Adapted from: Daft, R. L. (2004). *Organizational theory and design* (8th ed., pp. 367–370). Mason, OH: South-Western.

No matter which culture is promoted by organizational leaders, the point is that the organizational culture needs to fit with the organization's strategy and environment. For a healthy organizational culture to flourish, elements of key values must be in place and practiced. These values begin with trust as an underlying and integrated premise.

A Matter of Trust

Trust is a multi-faceted virtue that serves as an umbrella over the key values in organizations. Shore (2007) stated that **organizational trust** is the essential ingredient, what he labeled as the lubricant, facilitating everyday business and interactions. People can trust other people to follow through with their work and commitments just as people in the community can depend on organizations to uphold their words and promises to them. **Fiduciary relationships** hold a high value in organizations because these relationships represent a formal duty to another or others imposed by loyalty, commitment, and organizational structure, meaning that others have placed trust in persons to carry out activities with morally good judgment related to a position.

Williams (2006) emphasized that only when the key element of fairness exists can trust thrive in organizations. Creating a culture of justice with a focus on trust is essential for an organization to flourish. Practicing the virtue of justice promotes fair distribution among individuals in the community while trust is the "adhesive that binds its members" (Para 1). According to Gutmann (1995; as cited in Williams, 2006), there are two principles that an organization must maintain so that the community of individuals it serves can have a sense of fairness: (1) nondiscrimination in the moral standing of each person, and (2) nonrepression so that each person has a deliberate voice if so chosen. Without those principles, an organization cannot be trustworthy or just.

Although the key virtues of fairness, honesty, integrity, respect for others, promise keeping, and prudence are the typical values seen in organizations, the vision and mission will often determine the differential values within each organization (Boyle et al., 2001; Kovanic & Johnson, 2004). Some of these differential values are teamwork, community, achievement, competence, knowledge, creativity, innovation, agility, having fun, leading by example, valuing diversity, encouraging others, and encouraging risk-taking. Organizations need to define their values operationally through their philosophy and mission; likewise, organizations must define their ethical practices in writing and in verbal communication. Jack Welch, past chairman and CEO of General Electric, once said: "Good business leaders create a vision, articulate the vision, passionately own the vision, and relentlessly drive it to completion" (as cited in Kovanic & Johnson, p. 101).

Trust in organizations has been eroding for years to the point of a current all-time low level of trust (Shore, 2007). Health care organizations are no different. The rapid transformation in health care organizations has been a contributing factor in the erosion of trust. As organizations must rapidly change to comply with regulatory standards, the demands of the internal and external stakeholders, and the needs of the population they serve, a greater complexity of ethical questions has emerged that are more difficult to resolve, given that organizations even want to resolve them. Executives abusing power and making self-serving corporate decisions lead to unethical behaviors in organizations (Morrison, 2006).

Trust in organizations is an obscure concept that consists of a web of convoluted relationships. A violation of trust in organizations will prompt verbalization such as angry and sarcastic remarks by personnel, especially if trust has been previously entrenched throughout the organizational levels (Williams, 2006). A violation of trust in organizations is less forgiving than in a relationship where trust historically exists between two people. Researchers have found that trust critically matters in organizations for nurses and others because

- Trust promotes economic value within organizations.
- Trust increases strategic alliances, teamwork, and productivity.
- Nurses experience a more positive practice environment as a result of trust.
- Nurses experience increased empowerment, autonomy, and overall job satisfaction because of organizational trust. (Kramer & Schmalenberg, 2002; Laschinger, Shamian, & Thomson, 2001; Williams, 2005; as cited in Williams, 2006)

Other Ethical Issues in Organizations

Organizations are sometimes compared to people in that an organization functions as a moral agent that can be held accountable for its actions; however, organizational ethics "focuses on the choices of the individual *and* the organization" (Boyle et al., 2001, p. 16). The term **organizational ethics** is a broad concept that includes not only culture and trust, but also the processes, outcomes, and character and denotes "a way of acting, not a code of principles. . . . [and] is at the heart, pumping blood that perfuses the entire organization with a common sense of purpose and a shared set of values" (Pearson, Sabin, & Emanuel, 2003, p. 42). The ethic of an organization refers to an organization's attempt to define its mission and values, recognize values that could cause tension, seek best solutions to these tensions, and manage the operations to maintain its values. The ethics process serves as a mechanism for organizations to address ethical issues regarding financial, business, management, and relationship decisions.

Even though organizational ethics often refers to an organization's image, people who work in the organizations are the ones to behave unethically or illegally and therefore are what shape the ambiance and character of the organization. Refer to Box 4.3 for a list of ethical and legal behaviors that one will observe or that one could engage in within organizations. The list is not exhaustive, but consists of the more common behaviors. Many unethical behaviors of organizations are also illegal, so the lines between ethical and legal are blurred.

Compliance and Ethics Programs

Compliance programs, "designed to prevent unlawful conduct and to promote conformity with externally imposed regulations, provide a second component of background for organizational ethics" (Pearson et al., 2003, p. 28). During the 1980s, compliance programs became popular as a way for organizations to satisfy the mandate for addressing ethical and legal issues, primarily Medicare and Medicaid fraud at that time. These programs were enormously amplified in 1991 when officials in the U.S. Department of Justice (USDOJ) created the U.S. Sentencing Guidelines (USSG) to create consistency of the sentencing in federal courts (Pearson et al.). The guidelines allowed for a reduction in penalties if a corporation had previously implemented the seven standards of compliance before the organization incurred a federal violation. In 2004 the federal government expanded the 7 guidelines to 11, which included ethical responsibilities for senior management personnel of corporations (Verschoor, 2007). Refer to the 11 guidelines in Box 4.4.

Ethically, the principles of autonomy, beneficence, nonmaleficence, and justice are at risk for violation in relation to patients, health care professionals, and the general public. When corporate schemes have the potential to harm patients without their knowing it, autonomy is violated, as is the law, in the form of the Patient Self Determination Act of 1990. Hurting or injuring someone because of illegal schemes violates beneficence, nonmaleficence, and justice.

Compliance programs are not synonymous with ethics programs, yet organizations tend to use compliance programs as a way of addressing ethical issues (Pearson et al., 2003). These two programs, compliance and ethics, are needed and can complement each other if appropriately structured. Ethics programs focus on the values of an organization, pursuing virtue, and delivering ethical patient care, whereas compliance programs focus on obedience to legal and required details of performance and have enforcement capability. Today compliance programs are mandatory, not optional. Some leaders of organizations, however, see compliance programs more as a vehicle for protecting themselves rather than as a means to instill important ethical values.

BOX 4.3: HIGHLIGHTS FROM THE FIELD: TYPICAL UNETHICAL OR ILLEGAL BEHAVIORS IN ORGANIZATIONS

- Corporate fraud
- Health care fraud
- Greediness
- Engaging in covert operations
- Producing misleading services
- Reneging or cheating on negotiated terms
- Creating unclear or inappropriate policies that can cause others to lie to get the job done
- Showing overconfidence in self-judgment
- Disloyalty
- Exhibiting poor quality in performance and apathy in goal attainment
- Engaging in humiliating and stereotyping tactics
- Engaging in bigotry, sexism, or racism
- Showing favoritism
- Suppressing rights such as freedom of speech and choice
- Obeying authority in a mindless routine
- Promoting people who are destructive go-getters yet they seem to outrun mistakes
- Price fixing as the standard regardless of the real cost
- Failing to speak up when unethical practices become evident
- Stepping on others to climb the promotion ladder
- Sacrificing innocent people to get jobs done, such as blaming subordinates
- Knowingly exaggerating the advantages of a plan to garner support
- Failing to cooperate with others
- Lying for the sake of business
- Failing to take responsibility for injurious practices
- Abusing corporate perks
- Corrupting the public process through legal means
- Obstructing or stalling actions and processes
- Dithering
- Inefficiency

Largely quoted from: Boyle et al. (2001). *Organizational ethics in health care: Principles, cases, and practical solutions* (pp. 19–20). San Francisco: Jossey-Bass/John Wiley & Sons.

BOX 4.4: HIGHLIGHTS FROM THE FIELD: U.S. SENTENCING GUIDELINES AS OF 2004

1. Develop compliance standards and procedures tailored to the company's business needs.
2. Designate high-level personnel to oversee compliance.
3. Avoid delegating substantial discretionary authority to employees with a propensity for illegal conduct.
4. Educate employees in the company's standards and procedures through publications and training.
5. Design a compliance system that includes auditing and monitoring procedures and mechanisms that encourage employees to report potential violations.
6. Enforce standards through appropriate and consistent discipline.
7. Report all violations, and take appropriate steps to improve the program.

2004 Additions

Senior management and the board of directors' responsibilities include:

8. Being knowledgeable about and exercising reasonable oversight of the program.
9. Ensuring the senior-level compliance and ethics officer has adequate resources, credibility, and access to the board of directors.
10. Exercising independent review by directors.
11. Being sufficiently informed so directors can exercise independent judgment.

Quoted from: Verschoor, C. C. (2007). How good is your ethics and compliance program? *Strategic Finance, 88*(10), 19–20.

The following sections briefly reflect corporate fraud but comprehensively discuss health care fraud. Another section presented is conflicts of interest. The topics for discussion are not an all-inclusive list; rather, the author has decided to choose some of the most critical issues for organizations.

Corporate Fraud

Corporate fraud occurs when a corporation deceives someone or the public to gain some sort of advantage to which it is not entitled. Corporate fraud has been a major priority with the Federal Bureau of Investigation (FBI) for a number of years. In 2006 alone, the FBI pursued 490 cases, and 19 of these cases cost investors $1 billion. Of the 490 cases, there were 171 indictments and 124 convictions. Besides the $1 billion loss to investors, the costs were $1 billion in restitutions, $4 billion in recoveries, and $62 million in seizures.

Health Care Fraud

Health care fraud occurs when a person steals money or services, which then become services unavailable for people who need these services. In the USSG 2004 revisions, the USDOJ mandated that organizations continuously improve their ethics and compliance programs by intermittently assessing for the risk of criminal conduct and taking steps to alleviate the violations. The USDOJ and the U.S. Department of Health and Human Services (USDHHS) began investigating and prosecuting abuse and fraud cases in health care organizations in significantly greater numbers in the 1990s (Boyle et al., 2001). The criminality in health care organizations, especially defrauding federal government programs such as Medicare, became apparent as the percentage of cases continually increased each year throughout the 1990s.

The FBI currently oversees and investigates all health care fraud for federal, state, and local levels of government and for private insurance and other programs. A recent significant trend that has concerned the FBI is the willingness for medical professionals to commit schemes risking patients' health and causing potential patient harm, some of which include unnecessary and harmful surgeries, prescriptions for dangerous drugs, and substandard care practices. The FBI (2006) believes the upsurge in incidence is because of high technology and computers. The damage that can occur from these crimes is an act of malfeasance in terms of personal injury, wrongful death, and possibly class action suits for the involved patients, not to mention the illegal corporate fraud acts.

The FBI reported in 2006 that health care fraud continues to rise dramatically each year despite the government's attempts to prevent it. In 2006 alone, there were 2,423 FBI health fraud cases, which resulted in 588 indictments and 534 convictions, plus there are numerous other cases pending. Of these cases, there were a total of $373 million in restitutions, $1.6 billion in recoveries, $172.9 million in fines, and $24.3 million in seizures.

As the U.S. population grows older more Medicare services are needed, thus more health care services are needed. The augmentation of Medicare use in light of the growth of the older population serves as a temptation for an increased incidence of corporate-driven schemes and systematic abuse. Health care fraud events in 2006 occurred throughout all segments of the health care system by means of various schemes. Refer to Box 4.5 for a highlight of 2006 schemes.

BOX 4.5: HIGHLIGHTS FROM THE FIELD: FBI FINANCIAL CRIME REPORT OF 2006— HEALTH CARE FRAUD

- **Billing for services not rendered:** The provider bills even when no medical service of any kind was rendered, the service was not rendered as described in the claim for payment, or the service was previously billed and the claim had been paid.
- **Upcoding of services:** The provider submits a bill using a procedure code that yields a higher payment than the code for the actual service rendered. Cases of upcoding include a routine follow-up doctor's office visit being billed instead as an initial or comprehensive office visit, group therapy being billed as individual therapy, unilateral procedures being billed as bilateral procedures, and 30-minute sessions being billed as 50 minutes or more.
- **Upcoding of items:** The provider delivers basic equipment to a patient, such as a manually propelled wheelchair, but instead bills for the more expensive motorized version of the wheelchair.
- **Duplicate claims:** The provider files two claims on the same service or item, but usually changes the date or some other portion of the claim on the second claim.
- **Unbundling:** The provider submits bills in a fragmented fashion to maximize the reimbursement for various tests or procedures required to be billed together at a reduced cost. For example, clinical laboratory tests are ordered individually or in a panel (e.g., lipid profile), but the provider will bill within each panel as if the tests had been done separately on different days.
- **Excessive services:** The provider bills for excessive services beyond the patient's actual needs, such as a medical care supplier billing for 30 wound care kits per week for a nursing home patient who only requires a dressing change once a day, or a provider billing for daily medical office visits when only monthly visits are needed.
- **Medically unnecessary services:** The provider bills for services not needed or unjustified based on the patient's medical condition, diagnosis, or progress, such as a provider who bills for an EKG for a patient with no signs or symptoms that justify the test.

BOX 4.5: HIGHLIGHTS FROM THE FIELD: FBI FINANCIAL CRIME REPORT OF 2006— HEALTH CARE FRAUD REPORT (CONTINUED)

- **Kickbacks:** The provider or other staff in the system engages in a scheme to receive an illegal kickback, such as when money or gifts are accepted in exchange for the referral of a patient for health care services paid by Medicare or Medicaid. Gifts can include everything from money to jewelry to free paid vacations.

Largely quoted and adapted from: Federal Bureau of Investigations. (2006). FBI 2006 financial crime report: Health care fraud. Retrieved June 10, 2007, from http://www.fbi.gov/publications/financial/fcs_report2006/financial_crime_2006.htm

Nurses may be involved in schemes unknowingly, but in these type of situations innocence would be difficult to prove in a court of law given that nurses were assisting with keeping the records where providers or others were operating secret fraudulent schemes. One such incident where nurses could be involved is in the billing and maintenance of fraudulent records on ambulance transfers of patients. A true story of ambulance fraud is highlighted in Box 4.6, except in this case Tracie Gieger, a licensed practical nurse and the wife of Jeffery Gieger, was knowingly and actively involved in the billing fraud. After reviewing her case, the Mississippi Board of Nursing revoked her license in October 1998 based on her felony conviction.

Sometimes nurse practitioners or other providers are unaware of their own acts of corporate fraud. One particular instance is when they accept gifts or possibly money from pharmaceutical companies in exchange for prescribing the company's medications. Medical suppliers and other vendors can place nurses in similar situations.

Hospital health care fraud is a tremendous problem in the United States. Two cases of hospital health care fraud are highlighted in Box 4.7. One case occurred in 2005 at HealthSouth Corporation, whose central office is located in Birmingham, Alabama, but is the largest provider of integrated health care services in numerous locations across the United States. The other case was in 2005 at Eisenhower Medical Center in Rancho Mirage, California. Readers need to keep in mind that these two cases and the Gieger case are just a few examples of the scores of cases that occur each year throughout the United States.

To reduce or prevent fraudulent schemes, Pearson et al. (2003) offered an exemplary list of broad normative ethical obligations for organizations. Although these

Box 4.6: Highlights from the Field: Example of Billing Fraud Found by the FBI: U.S. v. Gieger

Tracie and Jeffery Gieger, Laurel, Mississippi, 1998

On February 27, 1998, in the Southern District of Mississippi, the owners of Gieger Transfer Services, an ambulance company, were sentenced to 80 months in prison and ordered to pay restitution of $228,917 and a $12,500 fine [and 3 years of supervised release after the prison sentence was complete]. The defendants [Tracie & Jeffery Gieger] billed Medicare $400 per ambulance trip, claiming that patients taken on non-emergency ambulance trips were "bed confined" when, in fact, many could walk and had no need for ambulance transportation. A substantial portion of the money paid to the United States under the agreement is derived from the forced sale of beachfront properties purchased by the owners following the sale of their company in September 1997. The forced sale of the properties resulted from a $2.25 million civil settlement with the owners and the company formerly owned by them.

The Giegers were electronically billing the cases. While she was still an LPN, the Giegers founded the Gieger Transfer Service, Inc./Gieger Ambulance Service (GAS) and began transporting emergency and non-emergency patients. The company expanded quickly and by 1997 GAS operated more than 40 ambulances in 12 counties in rural southeastern Mississippi.

A large number of their ambulance transfers were elders on Medicare. After they founded GAS, the Giegers began billing Medicare by filing all of their non-emergency transfers as "bed-confined" patients, a misrepresentation that sparked the 1996 FBI investigation. They directed their paramedics and emergency medical technicians not to use the word "ambulatory" on the patient transfer report. The Giegers were indicted on 57 counts, which included charges of Medicare fraud, conspiracy to submit false claims, money laundering, transmitting money instruments or funds derived from specified unlawful activities, and a number of other similar charges. In 1997, the Giegers were tried on 46 of the 57 counts of the indictment. The jury returned a guilty verdict on Count 1—a conspiracy to submit false claims to Medicare. However, the sentencing of the Giegers was

(continues)

Box 4.6: Highlights from the Field: Example of Billing Fraud Found by the FBI: U.S. v. Gieger (continued)

increased because they abused a position of trust and the conspiracy involved vulnerable victims (related to the patients' age).

On September 24, 1999, the Giegers filed an appeal but the appellant court upheld the convictions with the exception of the enhancement of the "vulnerable victim" provision. The Giegers' prison term was completed in 2004.

Above quote from: U.S. Department of Justice. (1998). Deputy attorney general: Health care fraud report—Fiscal year 1998. Selected cases. Retrieved on June 10, 2007, from http://www.usdoj.gov/dag/pubdoc/health98.htm

From: Mississippi State Board of Nursing. (1998, October). Disciplinary actions (by date). Retrieved on June 10, 2007, from http://www.msbn.state.ms.us/disactions.htm; *and* FindLaw. (1999). United States Court of Appeals for the Fifth Circuit [No. 98-60137]. *USA versus Jeffery W. Gieger & Tracie L. Gieger.* Retrieved June 10, 2007, from http://caselaw.lp.findlaw.com/scripts/printer_friendly.pl?page=5th/9860137cr0.html

Box 4.7: Highlights from the Field: Health Care Fraud and Abuse Control Program

HealthSouth Corporation, Birmingham, Alabama, 2005

This corporation paid the U.S. government $327 million to settle the allegations of fraud against Medicare and other federally insured health care programs. The government alleged that the rehabilitative services of HealthSouth engaged in three health care fraud schemes to cheat the government. The first scheme, requiring a $170 million settlement, involved alleged false claims for outpatient physical therapy services that were not properly supported by certified plans of care, were not administered by licensed physical therapists, or were not for one-on-one therapy as the corporation represented in the billing. The second scheme, requiring a $65 million settlement, involved alleged accounting fraud

(continues)

Box 4.7: Highlights from the Field: Health Care Fraud and Abuse Control Program (continued)

that resulted in overbilling Medicare on hospital cost reports and home office cost statements. The third scheme, requiring a $92 million settlement, involved allegedly billing Medicare for a range of unallowable costs, such as luxury entertainment and travel expenses for annual administrators' meeting at Disney World, among many other incurred expenses. The remaining $76 million settlement involved four *qui tam* **lawsuits**, also known as whistleblowing lawsuits. (The term *qui tam* is an abbreviation of a Latin phrase that means "he who sues for the king as well as for himself.") *Qui tam* lawsuits are filed by private citizens who sue on behalf of the federal government by alleging fraud against those organizations who received government funding. The private citizen who filed the lawsuit receives a portion of the recovery money if the case is successful, and the government receives the major portion of recovered funds.

Eisenhower Medical Center, Rancho Mirage, California, 2005

This corporation paid the U.S. government $8 million to settle allegations of overbilling federal health insurance programs. A former employee also filed a *qui tam* lawsuit. The allegation was that the health care financial advisors helped the hospital to seek reimbursement for unallowable costs, and specifically that the advisors prepared two cost reports—an inflated one submitted to Medicare and one designed for internal use only that reflected accurately the amount of reimbursement the hospital should have received.

Largely quoted from: U.S. Department of Health and Human Services and the Department of Justice. (2006, August). Health care fraud and abuse control program annual report for FY 2005. Retrieved June 10, 2007, from http://www.usdoj.gov/dag/pubdoc/hcfacreport2005.pdf

obligations refer to organizations and not the leaders in them, providers of care and corporate leaders must make an effort to uphold these ethical obligations. Refer to Box 4.8 for a list of Pearson et al.'s exemplary obligations.

Prevention strategies are the most effective and efficient ways to deter financial loss through fraud. There is a supportive Web site by Blue Cross Blue Shield where people can access information regarding facts, statistics, and types of fraud (http://www.bcbs.com/antifraud); the site is also listed in the Web Ethics box at the

BOX 4.8: HIGHLIGHTS FROM THE FIELD: PEARSON ET AL.'S (2003) EXEMPLARY ETHICAL OBLIGATIONS FOR ORGANIZATIONS

An exemplary ethical organization must:

1. Hold deeply a set of values emphasizing care of the sick and the promotion of health.
2. Involve key stakeholders in identifying its values and in managing value conflicts.
3. State clearly and forcefully those values it commits itself to and guides itself by.
4. Disseminate understanding of its values to its entire staff.
5. Recognize that the full range of its activities influences the ethical quality of patient care.
6. Cultivate skill at identifying threats to and conflicts among its values.
7. Deliberate about value conflicts in light of what it has done and learned in previous similar conflict situations.
8. Ensure that it acts on its values: It "walks the walk" as well as "talks the talk."
9. Partner only with others who live by compatible values.

Quoted from: Pearson, S. D., Sabin, J. E., & Emanuel, E. J. (2003). *No margin, no mission: Health-care organizations and the quest for ethical excellence* (p. 33). Oxford, UK: Oxford University Press.

end of this chapter. Nurses or others who suspect health care fraud or corporate fraud of any kind should call 1-877-327-2583 to report their observations. According to the Association of Certified Fraud Examiners (2004; as cited in Adams, Campbell, Campbell, & Rose, 2006), most defrauded companies will never recover their monetary losses. If organizations do not put prevention measures in place, they could be out of business literally in days. Adams et al. suggested for organizations to create a fraud prevention program. To do so, administrators or outside consultants need to assess the state of affairs within the organization. Strategies in the assessment phase include:

- The chief executive or executive board members need to consider hiring an external consultant to conduct the assessment and administer an assessment survey.
- Answer the question "What are the current fraud risks?"
- Interviews with stakeholders such as board members, key executives including the compliance officer, and other management personnel will usually reveal the organization's risks for fraud.

- An independent agent or party needs to perform an internal audit.
- Set benchmarks for measuring best anti-fraud practices.

Adams et al. (2006) included a sample questionnaire for assessing risks of fraud in organizations. The questions will yield quantitative and qualitative data. The chief executive, nurse executive, or consultant could adapt the following questions for their organization's survey and have employees and key people complete it:

- How frequently does management review key performance indicators (e.g., weekly, monthly, quarterly, or yearly)?
- Have the board and members of the management team delineated specific responsibilities relating to the oversight and management of fraud risks with the organization?
- What is the fraud risk management budget in dollars? In full-time equivalent resources?
- How frequently is the fraud risk management strategy updated (e.g., every 6, 12, 24, or 36 months)?
- How frequently are organizational charts reviewed to ensure proper segregation of duties (e.g., every 6, 12, 24, or 36 months)?
- Is an anonymous process available at any time for employees to use in reporting improprieties or breaches of ethics?
- Is the anonymous reporting process also available to customers and suppliers?
- Do you have a formal code of ethics or conduct for the board or senior management?
- Please list what you think are the top three fraud business risks that your organization faces. How would you assess your risk of exposure to each of these? (p. 58)

Evaluating responses to these questions and logically organizing the findings and levels of risks are invaluable ways to gather good information. For instance, if the organization already has an anonymous hotline for reporting fraud, the consultant needs to assess the types of fraud assertions reported by sorting the reports by levels or degrees of wrongdoing. Additionally, benchmarking is critically important for future measures against fraud.

After the assessment phase, the organization needs a plan for developing key components, policies, responsibilities, audits, reviews, and communication strategies. Programs that need to be developed include an ethics program and a code of ethical conduct, educational and training programs at all employee levels on ethical behaviors and processes of fraud prevention, and a hotline program. Once the fraud prevention program is in place, ongoing monitoring and training are necessary.

The FBI has put into place significant measures, though largely unsuccessful at this point in time, to try to prevent health care fraud and corporate fraud. Nurses could serve in key positions to spot or report health care fraud and corporate fraud schemes in hospitals, clinics, or other places. Nurses need to remember that any illegal or unethical behavior by them, other nurses, or any licensed person could result in a suspension or revocation of their license.

--- **Ethical Reflections** ---

These three cases involve the Giegers and the two hospital cases that were highlighted in the boxes earlier in the chapter. Please review them and then refer to Pearson et al.'s (2003) exemplary ethical obligations for organizations highlighted in Box 4.8 and prevention of fraud strategies.

The Gieger Case
- Based on the jury's rationale for sentencing, make a list of the exemplary ethical obligations that the Giegers, paramedics, and EMTs did not uphold.
- Do you believe that as a paramedic working for the Giegers, your role would be to see that unethical practice was not committed? Why or why not? Give your rationale based on an ethical framework—a theory, approach, or principle.
- If you had been a paramedic working for the Giegers, jot down ways that you could have acted to alleviate or arrest these problems. Keep your ethical framework in mind as you compose your strategies.

The Two Hospitals' Cases
- Describe the feelings you might experience if you were working as a registered nurse in some area of either of these two provider organizations when the lawsuits were filed and became public knowledge to everyone in the community and the United States. Be specific with the description of your feelings.
- Make a list of the exemplary ethical obligations that these two hospitals did not uphold.
- What actions, if any, would you take in light of the charges against your place of employment? Give your rationale based on one ethical framework—a theory, approach, or principle.

Conflict of Interest

Conflicts of interest can occur on various levels from the individual to the organization, or between the internal organization and the external community. In the end, executives or board members engaging in a conflict of interest must have used their position to benefit themselves in some way at the expense of the organization. Cooper (2006) defined a conflict of interest legally as:

... situations where our personal interests are at odds with our obligations as a public official of our professional values. There may be combinations of conflicting roles and tensions between sources of authority, but more typically these occasions simply present us with an opportunity to use our public office for the sake of our private gain of our friends or relatives. (p. 129)

These types of activities present conflicts between the person's position of authority in an organization and self-interest and/or between a person's objective accountability toward an organization and personal or monetary gain or advantage. Conflicts of interest from the standpoint of ethics are broader than the legal definition because the decision to engage in a conflict of interest involves loyalties, concerns, and emotions in relationships that collide with the organizational and public interests. The main ethical issue involved in conflicts of interest is a breach of trust to the public. Whatever an executive or board member engages in also affects the organization's image by the public. The following Ethical Reflections provides an example of a moderate-sized legal conflict of interest by the chief nursing officer of a hospital.

─────────── **Ethical Reflections** ───────────

Betty, the chief nursing officer, had to make a decision about buying 120 new hospital beds for patient rooms. After she interviewed nurse mangers at the units where the beds were going to be placed, Betty compiled her findings and decided to contact a well-known equipment company to obtain prices and contracts. The equipment company's executive salesperson, Jim, discussed options at length with her and invited her and her significant other to an upcoming all-expenses-paid lavish retreat at a five-star hotel in Hawaii to see demonstrations of the beds and to hear a comprehensive sales pitch. Betty thought to herself, "We badly need some relaxation and stress relief. Hawaii would be so much fun. Would it be wrong for us to go?"

- If you were Betty, what should you do? Give your rationale. Justify your answer with an ethical framework—a theory, approach, or principle.
- What ethical principles are at stake? What breaches?
- Do you consider this situation a conflict of interest? Why or why not? Give your rationale.
- How would Betty handle this case if she believed she needed to seek advice from someone in a higher authority? With whom would she discuss this issue?
- What policies should be in place regarding a scenario such as this one?

There are various ways that conflicts of interest can occur that are not illegal but may be an ethical violation of the organization. Ritvo, Ohlsen, and Holland (2004) emphasized the difficulty for people in authoritative positions to live active and ethical lives while facing challenging decisions. Often the person's ethical obligations to fulfill job commitments can interfere with the person spending time with family or others. For example, how could an executive inform a higher-authority executive that a daughter's piano recital comes before a critical meeting with the executive board members?

Morrison (2006) mentioned other types of ethical conflicts of interest. One is when an individual's personal behavior conflicts with the organization's ethics, such as over-indulgence of alcohol or a public use of other drugs. Because patient safety and competent care are critical to the viability of a health care organization, personal behavior outside the organization is extremely important, as is personal behavior inside the organization. Nurses, in particular, are open to scrutiny by the public and by hospital officials because of their nursing license and direct care of patients. The following Ethical Reflections reveals a scenario that could be more common than people would like to admit.

─────────────── **Ethical Reflections** ───────────────

Savannah, a registered nurse in charge of direct patient care, attended a party the night before a scheduled 12-hour work day, over-indulged in cocktails, got to bed around 3 a.m., and came to work the next morning at 6:45 a.m. with a hangover and alcohol still on her breath. This situation placed Savannah in ethical violation of the organization's values and the *Code of Ethics for Nurses*, as well as a legal violation of the state board of nursing, because if alcohol is smelled on her breath, it is still in the bloodstream, which could alter her judgment. Savannah's altered judgment could result in unsafe patient care and treatments.

- Discuss the ethical implications of Savannah's partying before work. Do you believe that Savannah engaged in an ethical conflict of interest? Why or why not? Please explain your rationale.
- What ethical violations existed in Savannah's case regarding her personal behavior, the hospital's ethics and values, patient safety, the ANA Code of Ethics, and the state board of nursing?
- What other options could Savannah have considered other than going to work in an altered state of mind? Make a list of the pros and cons of at least two other alternatives Savannah could have chosen.
- Describe and justify how you would have handled this situation had you been Savannah. Justify your strategies by using an ethical framework—a theory, approach, or principle.
- What are the risks of Savannah attending work after drinking so much at the party? Explain your answers.
- Do you believe that the nursing supervisor should take action against Savannah? Why or why not? If you believe that the supervisor should take action against Savannah, describe

the specific options for disciplinary action based on your general knowledge of institutional and state board of nursing disciplinary protocol. For this particular answer, you could consider searching the internet for general institutional disciplinary protocol and your state board of nursing's disciplinary actions if you need more knowledge on this topic. Explain your rationale.

- Do you believe that the supervisor should report Savannah's behavior to the state board of nursing? Why or why not? Explain your rationale.

Compliance officers need to develop clear policies regarding conflicts of interest and conduct formal reviews of actions and transactions as well as order audits. Maintaining a sharp perception of behaviors within and outside the organization helps to spot impending conflicts of interest. Just like in fraud situations, employees and the public need to have an avenue for safe reporting of potential or alleged conflicts of interest. Conflicts of interest can occur on broad scales as well, such as massive legal violations of the organization as a whole.

Important to business activities by executives or other decision-makers is to fully disclose all material facts and arrangements of any proposed transaction to the board or other executive of higher authority (Cooper, 2006). When a board of trustees becomes aware that an executive's proposed transactions are not fully disclosed or the materials seem vague or fuzzy, the board should confront the person and allow for an explanation through deliberation. The board should then take disciplinary action toward the person if there was not a satisfactory explanation. If a board member is the one who has breached that trust, the other board members should exclude that member from meetings and deliberations until a time comes for confrontation. If money or luxury gifts are a source of the breach of trust, the state of affairs then becomes complicated. These type of breaches are difficult to prove and sometimes fall into a category of grayness. If board members cannot find solid evidence of a breach on their own, they must determine if legal fees and time are worth the effort of a trial that may never result in a conviction for that board member.

Ethical Leadership

The respect that leadership must have requires that one's ethics be without question. A leader not only stays above the line between right and wrong, he stays well clear of the "gray areas."
—G. ALAN BERNARD

For many years, philosophers and spiritualists have guided people on ethical ways to live and work. Even in light of the availability of this rich information and knowledge, there are untold numbers of temptations and acts of unethical and illegal behaviors within organizations, as evidenced by daily news media and government reports. Human beings often have a tendency to depart from the path that they know is right. It is a well known fact that power can corrupt a person in authority, and leadership is a power relationship. (See more about power in Chapter 3.) Having power opens the door for the person with power to capitalize on personal gain in certain situations. Motivations that spark wrong-doing are greed, envy, anger, fear, and even jealousy. In a letter to Mandell Creighton on April 5, 1887, Lord Acton stated, "Power tends to corrupt and absolute power corrupts absolutely." Lord Acton, an Englishman whose life work was studying the history of liberty, was one of the greatest history magistrates of the 19th century. As a magistrate, he interpreted liberty history for the application to his day and time and became a moral judge as he held the best known men to a historical standard or precedence. He quickly learned about the corruptness of powerful men. Some say that he was one of the most learned persons of his time in the world (Acton Institute, n.d.).

Organizations that do not participate in prevention and training programs or ethics programs place themselves at high risk for a substantial amount of unethical and illegal acts. Kovanic and Johnson (2004) stated, "individual behavior does not exist within a vacuum" (p. 12) and emphasized the importance of each person's role to act ethically in an organization. One person doing something unethical can perpetuate a chain of unethical actions in an organization. People within an organization need to decide how much influence they want to have on the system and in turn how much influence an organization or other individuals will have upon them.

Ethical leadership is essential in an organization because leaders who strive for ethical conduct motivate others to act in ethical ways. Ethical leadership has a structural component and a substantive character component. Substantively, leaders can use their power in a positive way to influence people through role modeling, which is the reason that many researchers have emphasized strong character for ethical leadership, thus using a virtue ethics approach (Knights & O'Leary, 2006; see virtue ethics in Chapter 1). With the crisis facing leaders today, a strong character is needed to survive within an organization. Thomas Aquinas (as cited in Knights & O'Leary) suggested that virtue ethics was more important than any of the ethical theories because he believed that all moral questions will lead to a virtue analysis, leading back to character.

Structurally, ethical leadership involves a strategic planning process so that policies, decision-making processes, consultation, accountability and ethical standards, and ongoing assessment and monitoring are in place to ensure ethical practice by the leader and the followers. Leadership is a neutral word, and therefore leaders can be extremely strong but may not be ethical, as evidenced by Hitler, Stalin, and Mussolini. Many leaders, even in organizations, abuse their power by acting immorally (Workforce Management Online, 2003).

How is ethical leadership measured? The best measure is the organization's sustainable achievements over the long term. Workforce Management Online (2003) presented five necessary elements of ethical leadership structure that the author of this chapter believes sum up leading in an ethical way. The elements are communication, quality, collaboration, succession planning, and tenure.

Ethical Communication

Ethical communication refers to a high standard of truth set by an ethical leader. Leading by example with truthful communication is excellent, but the organization also needs to adopt truth as a primary value in a top-down approach, from board members to staff people. Leaders need to conduct investigations and review allegations of lies or wrongdoing without first blaming others. The crux of the problem may be poor leadership or a malfunction of the system, and attaching blame to someone may be harming the organization more than helping it. Truthful communication is hard to come by these days, but the best executives place a high level of importance on this type of communication. The ANA *Code of Ethics for Nurses with Interpretive Statements* (2001) emphasized the need for a virtuous wholeness of character, which would include truthful communication.

Ethical Quality

Ethical quality means that a leader will initiate quality throughout the organization. Three factors are important to a flourishing competitive organization: "a quality product, quality customer service, and quality delivery" (Workforce Management Online, 2003, Para 7). The organization's leaders are responsible for implementing quality throughout every process of the organization. Leaders who are ethical know that they have an ethical obligation to the organization and community at large to (1) focus on quality at all levels, (2) use benchmarking to denote successes and failures, (3) use innovations to heighten quality, and (4) set standards and ways to measure every entity in each department. Six Sigma and the American Nurses Credentialing Center's Magnet Status Recognition are ways that health care organizations can improve their image, but there is another way to ensure quality—leaders must use common sense judgments about ensuring quality and cutting wastes by saving organizational time and money. The ANA *Code of Ethics for Nurses with Interpretive Statements* (2001) clearly indicates the need for nursing leaders and all nurses to be responsible and accountable in maintaining standards of care, which includes quality care.

Ethical Collaboration

For ethical leaders to implement **ethical collaboration** means that they collaborate to reduce risks at every level and ensure best practices, solve the many problems, and focus on the issues that their organization is facing. To do so, they must seek knowledgeable, trustworthy, astute, and ethical advisors within and outside their own organization as well as keep the advisors, not as a closed circle, but as an open and fluid circle. Leaders who collaborate regarding ethical practice usually make better and more ethical decisions for the good of the organization. With an ethical and clever group of advisors, ethical leaders will usually decide upon implementing plausible solutions with worthwhile and practical actions and procedures. Nursing leaders also have the ANA *Code of Ethics for Nurses with Interpretive Statements* (2001) as a guideline for ethical collaboration. The code emphasizes the importance of collaboration to ensure the best possible patient care and outcomes. Administration decisions, as well as ethical collaboration, affect patient care and outcomes.

Ethical Succession Planning

Ethical succession planning is a way for leaders to allow and enable other leaders to surface within an organization so that successors have an opportunity to develop their leadership skills and exercise them. Once these leaders emerge, the existing leaders need to mentor them for future succession without fear of territorial loss. Ethical leaders realize the critical nature of having leaders in the making; that is, to have a strong leadership succession program for the overall long-term success of the organization. The ANA *Code of Ethics for Nurses with Interpretive Statements* (2001) emphasized that nurse administrators have a responsibility to ensure an ethical environment for personnel to carry out standards of practice. These strategies imply that leaders must make and mentor other future leaders.

Ethical Tenure

Good ethical leaders are hard to find, but when an organization finds that leader, it must invest in that leader for the sake of the organization. The **ethical tenure** translates to the "shelf life" of a leader and the length of time of success in relationship to the person's leadership, which will depend on the ethical conduct of that leader. People sometimes rate leaders more on their trustworthiness than on their talents and skills at leadership, and on their level of commitment to serve the institution and not themselves. Leaders who can subdue their ego in order to build a successful organization will have a longer tenure within that organization.

Ethical leadership has become an essential part of organizational leadership, largely because of the leadership failure that has occurred in big business throughout the world, which has led to character-driven leadership styles. The five components just discussed are the ways to the future for ethical leadership. CoachThee (n.d.) presents an excellent test of the rightness or wrongness for ethical actions. The test consists of asking oneself and answering the following eight questions:

1. Is it legal?
2. Does it comply with my/our rules and guidelines?
3. It is in sync with my personal and our organizational values?

Box 4.9: Highlights from the Field: Essential Aspects from the Code of Ethics for Nurses with Interpretive Statement for Cultivating Ethical Leadership

- All nurses, regardless of role, have a responsibility to create, maintain, and contribute to environments of practice that support nurses fulfilling their ethical obligations (6.2, p. 21).
- Organizational structures, role descriptions,...[and] all contribute to environments that can either present barriers or foster ethical practice and professional fulfillment (6.2, p. 21).
- Nurse administrators have a particular responsibility to assure that employees are treated fairly... (6.3, p. 21).
- Nurses should not remain employed in facilities that routinely violate patient rights or require nurses to severely and repeatedly compromise standards of practice or personal morality (6.3, p. 21).
- Organizational changes are difficult to accomplish and may require persistent efforts over time (6.3, p. 21).
- The nurse as administrator or manager must establish, maintain, and promote conditions of employment that enable nurses within that organization or community setting to practice in accord with accepted standards of nursing practice... (7.1, pp. 22–23).

4. Will I be comfortable and guilt-free if I do it?
5. Does it match my commitments and promised guarantees?
6. Would I do it to my family or friends?
7. Would I be perfectly okay with someone doing it to me?
8. Would the most ethical person I know do it? (Para 6)

These questions are excellent for leaders to use in their daily practice to test their potential actions. The author of this chapter suggests that leaders, educators, staff nurses, and students keep a list of these questions with them at all times and continually monitor their actions or potential actions on a regular basis. Please refer to Box 4.9 for essential aspects of the ANA *Code of Ethics for Nurses with Interpretive Statements* (2001) that relate to cultivating ethical leadership.

Web Ethics

Federal Bureau of Investigations
    http://www.fbi.gov
U.S. Department of Justice Publications
    http://www.usdoj.gov/05publications/05_3_a.html
Blue Cross Blue Shield Information Site on Health Care Fraud
    http://www.bcbs.com/antifraud
Ethics Resource Center—Organization Ethics Links: Government
    http://www.ethics.org/resources/articles-organizational-ethics.asp?aid=1008
Ethics and Culture Management Services
    http://www.ethicsquality.com/about.htm
American Hospital Association
    http://www.aha.org
American College of Healthcare Executives
    http://www.ache.org
The CPA Journal Online (a wealth of full-text articles on organizational ethics)
    http://www.cpajournal.com
Medicare and Medicaid Agency
    http://cms.hhs.gov
Vanderbilt University, Center for Ethics
    http://www.vanderbilt.edu/CenterforEthics/resources.html#business
The University of Texas at Austin, Center for Ethical Leadership
    http://www.utexas.edu/lbj/research/leadership
Association of Certified Fraud Examiners
    http://www.acfe.com

Summary

In Chapter 4, the author presented two major sections: (1) ethical organizations and (2) ethical leadership. Organizational culture, a matter of trust, corporate fraud, health care fraud, and conflicts of interest were presented in the section on ethical organizations. Strategies for ethical leaders were presented in the section on ethical leadership. Important concepts in these two sections are:

- An organization's relationship to its environment and the organization's interpretation of reality, truth, human nature, and human relationships are the ethical dimensions that shape the organizational culture.
- Each organizational culture—adaptability, mission, clan, and bureaucratic—has the potential to be successful if the strategic plans that relate to the desired culture are accomplished and maintained.
- Trust is the multi-faceted, essential ingredient that serves as a lubricant for all operations and values in organizations. Without trust in organizations and among people, organizational values and relationships erode and crumble. The community at large will see the organization and the people in it as untrustworthy.
- Unethical and illegal behaviors committed by people ultimately shape the ambiance and character of the organization. Some of those behaviors include fraud; greediness; corruption; engaging in covert operations, humiliating tactics, bigotry, sexism, racism, cheating, reneging, and sacrificing people to get jobs done; abusing corporate perks, power, and the rights of others; and many others.
- Regulators of organizations and the government mandated the development of compliance programs to prevent unlawful behaviors and to promote conformity to regulations involving legal actions.
- In 2006 alone, the FBI investigations into corporate fraud resulted in uncovering billions of dollars of loss with 171 indictments and 124 convictions.
- In 2006, health care fraud, an entity reported separately from corporate fraud, increased dramatically. The FBI uncovered billions of dollars of loss with a total of 588 indictments and 534 convictions, and many other cases are still pending.
- Nurses are at an increased risk of participating, knowingly or unknowingly, in health care fraud cases. They need to develop a sharp perception of acts of fraud in their workplace and report their suspicions to the fraud hotline. Nurses remaining current on knowledge regarding the ANA *Code of Ethics for Nurses* and the state board of nursing rules and regulations is integral to understanding their role regarding fraud and other types of misuse.

■ The five characteristics of an ideal ethical leader are (1) ethical communication, (2) ethical quality, (3) ethical collaboration, (4) ethical succession planning, and (5) ethical tenure.

References

Acton Institute for the Study of Religion & Liberty. (n.d.) .About Lord Acton. Retrieved June 10 , 2007, from http://www.acton.org/about/lordacton/

Adams, G. W., Campbell, D. R., Campbell, M., & Rose, M. P. (2006, January). Fraud prevention: An investment no one can afford to forego. *The CPA Journal*, pp. 56–59. Retrieved June 10, 2007, from http://www.nysscpa.org/cpajournal/2006/106/essentials/p56.htm

American Nurses Association. (2001). *Code of ethics for nurses with interpretive statements*. Silver Spring, MD: Author.

Association of Certified Fraud Examiners. (2004). 2004 report to the nation on occupational fraud and abuse. Retrieved July 10, 2007, from http://www.acfe.com/documents/2004RttN.pdf

Boyle, P. J., DuBose, E. R., Ellingson, S. J., Guinn, D. E., & McCurdy, D. B. (2001). *Organizational ethics in health care: Principles, cases, and practical solutions*. San Francisco: Jossey-Bass/John Wiley & Sons.

Cartwright, S., & Cooper, C. L. (1993). The role of culture compatibility in successful organizational marriage. *Academy of Management Executive, 7*(2), 62.

CoachThee. (n.d.). Business ethics: Effective leaders. Retrieved June 10, 2007, from http://home.att.net/~coachthee/archives/businessethics.html

Cooper, T. L. (2006). *The responsible administrator: An approach to ethics for the administrative role* (5th ed.). San Francisco: Jossey-Bass/John Wiley & Sons.

Daft, R. L. (2004). *Organizational theory and design* (8th ed.). Mason, OH: South-Western.

Federal Bureau of Investigations. (2006). FBI 2006 financial crime report: Health care fraud. Retrieved June 10, 2007, from http://www.fbi.gov/publications/financial/fcs_report2006/financial_crime_2006.htm.

FindLaw. (1999). United States Court of Appeals for the Fifth Circuit [No. 98-60137]. *USA v. Jeffery W. Gieger & Tracie L. Gieger*. Retrieved June 10, 2007, from http://caselaw.lp.findlaw.com/scripts/printer_friendly.pl?page=5th/9860137cr0.html

Gutmann, A. (1995). The virtues of democratic self-constraint. In A. Etzioni (Ed.), *New communitarian thinking: Persons, virtues, institutions, and communities* (pp. 154-169). Charlottesville: University of Virginia Press.

Knights, D., & O'Leary, M. (2006). Leadership, ethics and responsibility to the other. *Journal of Business Ethics, 67*, 125–137.

Kovanic, N., & Johnson, K. D. (2004). *Lies and truths: Leadership ethics in the 21st century*. Terre Haute, IN: Rule of Thumb.

Kramer, M., & Schmalenberg, C. (2002). Staff nurses identify essentials of magnetism. In M. McClure & A. Hinshaw (Eds.), *Magnet hospitals revisited* (pp. 25–59). Washington, DC: American Nurses.

Laschinger, H., Shamian, J., & Thomson, D. (2001). Impact of magnet hospital characteristics on nurses' perceptions of trust, burnout, quality of care and work satisfaction. *Nursing Economics, 19*, 209–219.

CASE STUDY

The Infection Control Nurse Coordinator, Thomas, reported to Joyce, the Chief Nursing Officer (CNO), that blood culture contamination rates in the blood test tubes had drastically increased in the last 6 months with increasing increments on each of the 6 months. At this acute-care hospital, RNs at all units and laboratory department technicians drew blood culture samples for testing. Thomas informed her that he had strong suspicions that the briefly-trained lab technicians were the ones contaminating the tubes of blood. However, after he investigated the problem on his own and separated the RN blood culture samples from the lab technician samples, he found just the opposite to be the case. In fact, the blood culture samples that RNs drew were twice as likely to be contaminated as the samples drawn by the lab technicians. Joyce was so concerned about this problem that she met with Leon, a non-nurse Compliance Officer, for help with the situation. Together they planned a mandatory progressive and incremental long-term education and return demonstration program for the 156 patient-care RNs at the hospital. Every 2 months, the infection control team presented 30-minute education programs followed by their demonstration of the method of drawing blood culture samples and then a return demonstration by every RN. After 6 months, contamination rates of the blood culture samples began to decrease and at the end of 1 year, contamination rates were almost non-existent with the RNs. After Leon realized the value of this program, he wanted Joyce to implement quickly and aggressively three other programs, specifically on medication errors, patient falls, and wound infections, with all RNs, but Joyce was strongly against implementing these programs so quickly and aggressively after the blood sampling program.

- If you were Joyce, give your rationale for not wanting to implement the other programs so aggressively at that time. Justify your answer with a framework that is theoretical, principle-based, or another approach.
- Based on your knowledge of the work schedules of these 156 RNs and their demanding physical and mental work, plan a reasonable timeline for implementation of these three programs for the RNs. Give your rationale for your decision based on a framework that is theoretical, principle-based, of another approach.
- Determine the ethical leadership characteristics that Joyce and Thomas displayed in this scenario along with your rationale for choosing those characteristics.
- Do you think that Joyce should consider implementing a long-term certification program for the blood culture sampling and the other three programs? Why or Why not? Give your rationale.

Mississippi State Board of Nursing. (1998, October). Disciplinary actions (by date). Retrieved June 10, 2007, from http://www.msbn.state.ms.us/disactions.htm

Morrison, E. E. (2006). *Ethics in health administration: A practical approach for decision makers.* Sudbury, MA: Jones & Bartlett.

Pearson, S. D., Sabin, J. E., & Emanuel, E. J. (2003). *No margin, no mission: Health-care organizations and the quest for ethical excellence.* Oxford, UK: Oxford University Press.

Ritvo, R. A., Ohlsen, J. D., & Holland, T. P. (2004). *Ethical governance in health care: A board leadership guide for building an ethical culture.* Chicago: Health Forum.

Schein, E. H. (1991). *Organizational culture and leadership* (2nd ed.). San Francisco: Jossey-Bass/John Wiley & Sons.

Shore, D. A. (2007). The (sorry) state of trust in the American healthcare enterprise. In D. A. Shore (Ed.), *The trust crisis in healthcare: Causes, consequences, and cures* (pp. 3-20). Oxford, UK: Oxford University Press.

U.S. Department of Health and Human Services and the Department of Justice. (2006, August). Health care fraud and abuse control program annual report for fiscal year 2005. Retrieved June 10, 2007, from http://www.usdoj.gov/dag/pubdoc/hcfacreport2005.pdf

U.S. Department of Justice. (1998). Deputy attorney general: Health care fraud report—Fiscal year 1998. Selected cases. Retrieved June 10, 2007, from http://www.usdoj.gov/dag/pubdoc/health98.htm

Verschoor, C. C. (2007). How good is your ethics and compliance program? *Strategic Finance, 88*(10), 19–20.

Williams, L. (2005). Impact of nurses' job satisfaction on organizational trust. *Health Care Management Review, 30*(3), 203–211.

Williams, L. L. (2006). The fair factor in matters of trust. *Nursing Administration Quarterly, 30*(1), 30–37.

Workforce Management Online. (2003, November). HR management: Editor's choice—Five standards of excellence practiced by ethical leaders. Retrieved June 10, 2007, from http://www.workforce.com/section/09/article/23/55/60.html

Zammuto, R. F., & Krakower, J. Y. (1991). Quantitative and qualitative studies of organizational culture. *Research in Organizational Change and Development* (vol. 5, p. 86). Greenwich, CT: JAI Press.

Chapter 4 Questions

Please choose the most right answer!

1. You discovered that your co-worker and best friend, Nurse Practitioner Sandra, was accepting expensive gifts, such as a diamond watch, from a pharmaceutical company in exchange for prescribing that company's new anti-hypertensive drug to her patients with high blood pressure. Your best initial action will be to:

    a. call the health care fraud hotline and file a detailed report.

    b. confront Sandra and inform her that you are required by the state board of nursing to report her.

    c. consider this conflict of interest none of your business and do nothing.

    d. approach Sandra in a friend-to-friend manner by first allowing her to explain her rationale and then helping her to realize that what she is doing is a conflict of interest that is unethical and possibly illegal.

2. As a new RN, you are considering taking a position at the local hospital because of its geographical proximity to your home but you are hearing many negative remarks from your friends and neighbors about the hospital and its RNs, such as poor patient care, incompetency, and RN medication errors. Based on the ANA *Code of Ethics for Nurses with Interpretive Statements*, your initial action would be to:
   a. disregard the gossip, take the position, and evaluate the conditions for yourself once you begin working.
   b. verify that the stories are true before you accept the position because ANA informs nurses not to work in organizations where conditions are poor and care is incompetent.
   c. report the stories to the state-level hospital association and let them know why there is an RN shortage at that facility.
   d. confront the CNO of the hospital on Sunday when you see her at church and inform her that you cannot risk your license by taking a position at the hospital because of its negative image in the community.

3. Which one of the following statements is correct regarding organizational trust and trust violations?
   a. Nurses generally do not feel as scrutinized, questioned, or monitored in environments where trust exists.
   b. A violation of hospital-wide trust is more pardonable than a violation of trust between two best friends.
   c. Executives know that trust is the adhesive that binds its employees, so all executives work hard to ensure a high level of trust in their organizations.
   d. Trust is not an important element in the bureaucratic organizational culture.

4. What is most important in reducing or preventing illegal and unethical behaviors, such as fraud or conflicts of interest, in organizations?
   a. The organization should hire a consultant to assess and diagnose the organization's state of affairs.
   b. Each person within the organization must have a sense of right and wrong before the organization can expect people not to commit unscrupulous acts.

    c. The organization should create and develop an official compliance program with a compliance officer overseeing the state of affairs, as well as form an ethics committee to address ethical issues.

    d. The organization should have an accountant to conduct an internal audit and report the results of the audit to the board of trustees.

5. Which one of the following statements is true regarding ethical leaders and leadership?
    a. An ethical leader is also a strong leader, and vice versa.
    b. Ethical leaders will have future leaders in the making.
    c. Of the five ethical leadership characteristics, the least important one is ethical succession planning.
    d. The public and organizational personnel always judge leaders according to their level of trustworthiness rather than their talents and skills at leadership.

Chapter 4 Answers

1. d
2. b
3. a
4. c
5. b

Part II • Nursing Ethics Across the Lifespan

Reproductive Issues and Nursing Ethics

Janie B. Butts

You and I are persons. More specifically, we are human persons—persons who are members of the species Homo sapiens. But what does it mean to say that someone is a person? And what is the significance of being human?

—DAVID DEGRAZIA, *HUMAN IDENTITY AND BIOETHICS,* 2005

Sexual intercourse, reproduction, family planning, abortion, sexually transmitted infections, and sexual and reproductive rights are all topics deemed unsuitable for polite conversation at social gatherings; all generate strong opinion that is often founded in privilege, misinformation, or lack of evidence.

—DOROTHY SHAW, *LANCET, 368,* 2006

OBJECTIVES

After reading this chapter, the reader should be able to:

1. Explore the maternal-fetal conflict as it relates to rights, autonomy, nursing, health care, and medical treatment.
2. Explain ways in which the Federal Abortion Ban and the Unborn Victims of Violence Act of 2004 laws could affect the maternal-fetal relationship.
3. Discuss the views of full moral status of an embryo or fetus.
4. Contrast the issues of abortion from both sides of the debate—pro-choice groups and pro-life groups.
5. Compare the ethical issues for each of the three major types of assisted reproductive technology.

6. Discuss the importance for couples to make informed choices about pregnancy and types of assisted reproductive technology in terms of genetic screening, testing, and counseling.
7. Explore the 2006 revised guidelines for universally screening pregnant women for HIV and the implications for breastfeeding by women with HIV.
8. Discuss the ethical considerations for maternal substance abuse.
9. Integrate Bergum's relational ethics into the essential interpretational aspects of the ANA *Code of Ethics for Nurses with Interpretive Statements* (2001) for the care of childbearing women.

KEY TERMS

Maternal-fetal conflict	Partial-birth abortion
Late-term abortion	Moral rights
Liberty rights	Claim rights
Full moral status	*Roe v. Wade*
Abortion	Disenfranchised grief
Infertility	Assisted reproductive technology (ART)
In vitro fertilization (IVF)	Gamete intrafallopian transfer (GIFT)
Zygote intrafallopian transfer (ZIFT)	Surrogacy
Gestational surrogacy	Traditional surrogacy
Egg donation	Embryo donation
Surplus reproductive products	Sperm sorting/gender selection
Preimplantation genetic diagnosis (PGD)	Inheritable genetic modification (IGM)
4D ultrasound	Genetic screening
Prenatal genetic diagnosis	

Maternal-Fetal Conflict

The relationship between a woman and her fetus has created an enormous public moral and political debate in the last few decades. **Maternal-fetal conflict** encompasses "the ways that law, social policies and medical practices sometimes treat a pregnant woman's interests in opposition to those of the fetus" (Moffett, 2003, p. 1). A departure from the dyadic link such as this one can cause a restraint of maternal autonomy and rights that can advance a confrontation between a mother and fetus. A maternal-fetal conflict can occur when a pregnant woman's treatment is hazardous to the fetus or when a pregnant woman does not comply with a physician's recommendations that are traditionally believed to nurture the fetus's growth and development.

Adding to the maternal-fetal conflict has been the fact that physicians and nurses now consider care and treatment to be for two persons—woman and fetus—instead of just one (Ludwig, 1998). This ethical issue is concerned with each person's right to life versus the possibility of bringing harm to one person when treating the other of the two biologically connected persons. In years past, when physicians and nurses cared for a pregnant woman, they considered the mother and fetus as one patient unit with intricate detail. Everything about the care and treatment of the whole patient was weighed according to the perceived benefits of the whole compared with perceived combined burdens.

Today physicians and nurses give dual care; that is, they are supposed to consider the best care and medical treatment possible for each person separately and distinctly. With this dual care frame of mind, however, several ethical dilemmas surrounding a person's rights arise. Ludwig (1998) posed these questions:

- What happens when medical therapy is indicated for one patient yet contraindicated for the other?
- When does a fetus or a newborn become a person?
- People have rights. Does a fetus have rights?
- What if maternal decisions seem to be based on unusual beliefs? (Para. 1–5)

Laws Affecting the Maternal-Fetal Relationship

The National Right to Life Committee (NRLC) and other pro-life groups (also known as anti-choice groups) have campaigned for years for equal rights and protection of the unborn fetus, based on the viewpoint that the fetus is a human life, one that, if not a person yet, has the potential to be a person. President George W. Bush has signed two acts into law: the Partial-Birth Abortion Ban Act of 2003, also known as the Federal Abortion Ban, and the Unborn Victims of Violence Act of 2004, also known as Laci and Conner's Law.

Federal Abortion Ban

According to the NRLC (2003), the Federal Abortion Ban, also initially known as the Partial Birth Abortion Ban Act of 2003, was placed into law to prohibit physicians from performing partial-birth abortions and thereby "killing fetuses." **Partial-birth abortion** is a nonmedical term that refers to late-term or third-trimester abortions by way of a procedure called intact dilation and extraction (abbreviated as intact D & E).

In other words, a **late-term abortion** consists of physicians delivering a live fetus vaginally yet only partially for the sole purpose of terminating a pregnancy by way of an intact D & E. The term *partially* means that for head presentation, the entire head must be outside the mother's vagina before the fetus can be terminated. For breech presentation, any part of the fetus's trunk past its navel must be outside the mother's vagina before the fetus can be terminated.

Several states have agreed with the American Civil Liberties Union (ACLU, 2006) by striking down the federal partial-birth abortion ban, ruling it unconstitutional, whereas other states are pushing for the abortion ban as early as 12 to 13 weeks gestation, a push that is viewed by the ACLU as deceptive. The time line of 12 to 13 weeks bleeds into the first trimester of pregnancy, meaning that no longer could the term *partial-birth abortion* be used; rather, the term *abortion* must be applied.

Not long after the Federal Abortion Ban was signed by President George W. Bush in 2003, agencies filed three lawsuits in the federal courts, one lawsuit each by the ACLU, the Center for Reproductive Rights (CRR), and Planned Parenthood Federation of America (PPFA) against the ban. In 2005 the judges in all three cases ruled that the abortion ban was unconstitutional on the basis that, first, there was no health exception for pregnant women and, second, the ban implications were so broad that, if the ban passed, abortion could be illegal as early as 12 weeks of gestation (PPFA, 2006b). The three lawsuits were based on two major statements: that "women and their doctors need to be able to make medical decisions free from interference of politicians" and that the ban prevents physicians from performing several abortion procedures in the second trimester of pregnancy (ACLU, 2004, Para. 1).

The U.S. Supreme Court reviewed the Federal Abortion Ban because of the strike downs by several states, even though some states are continuing to support the ban, which leaves unresolved issues, anger, and moral fanaticism on each side of the argument. The public anxiously awaited the final decision, and on April 18, 2007, under the direction of chief justice John Roberts, the U.S. Supreme Court announced a 5 to 4 decision to uphold the Federal Abortion Ban (as cited in ACLU, 2007). Upholding the ban undermines the core tenet of Roe v. Wade that a woman's health must remain unrivaled. No health exception for women was written in the law. The ACLU (2007) emphasized:

Writing for the majority, Justice Kennedy evoked antiquated notions of women's place in society and called into question their decision-making ability. Furthermore, the Court held that in the face of "medical uncertainty" lawmakers could overrule a doctor's medical judgment. In other words, the Court sanctioned placing medical decisions in the hands of politicians, not doctors. (Para. 3)

In a written dissent, Justice Ginsburg made a strong criticism by warning the majority justices that they are placing women's health in danger and undermining women's battle for equality. Justice Ginsburg stated, "the Act, and the Court's defense of it, cannot be understood as anything other than an effort to chip away at a right declared again and again by the Court—and with increasing comprehension of its centrality to women's lives" (as cited in ACLU, 2007, para. 5). For a state to have the power to overrule a women's choice to protect her own health and human right sets a precedent that places women's health in danger.

Unborn Victims of Violence Act of 2004

The Unborn Victims of Violence Act of 2004 allows any child in utero who has been killed or injured to be recognized as a legal victim of a federal crime of violence, such as interstate stalking, kidnapping, or bombing (NRLC, 2004). At any stage of development the fetus in utero is considered a legal member of the *Homo sapiens* species. The murders of Laci Peterson and her unborn son, Conner, were the force behind Laci's family to speak in strong support for this bill; thus, the bill has been informally named Laci and Conner's Law. The language in this law recognizes the unborn fetus as a "legal person" in the United States.

The language "fetus as a legal person," not the Unborn Victims Act itself, is disturbing based on the perception of the pro-choice groups because of the future implications that a pregnant woman's rights could be violated or overturned in favor of a fetus being recognized as a legal person with equal rights. In the view of pro-choice groups, the language of "fetus as a legal person" in this particular act could lead to an undermining of maternal rights in other legal decisions not related to the Unborn Victims Act, such as a sliding or application of this act's implications to other decisions. The overall issue for pro-choice groups is that this act does nothing to prevent or reduce violence against pregnant women or any women, and the implications from this act could further curtail women's rights.

Other Issues Relating to the Maternal-Fetal Conflict

Historical records have indicated that multiple and complex ethical, legal, and political issues have occurred including criminalization of pregnant women. Courts have ordered physician-sanctioned cesarean deliveries for the sake of the fetus against the mother's wishes; pregnant women have been prosecuted for their abuse of alcohol and other drugs; and courts have ordered pregnant women to receive blood transfusions in life-threatening or other conditions even when the women were refusing blood transfusions for religious beliefs (ACLU, 1997; Chandis & Williams, 2006). Issues of abortion and forced treatments tap into questions of whether the fetus is viewed as a person, has a right to life, or is viewed as having equal moral status to the mother versus a pregnant woman's right to bodily integrity and right to privacy, dignity, and choice.

It is important at this point in the discussion for the reader to view the ACLU's opinion of government officials tampering with women's rights during pregnancy. In a 1997 article titled *Coercive and Punitive Governmental Responses to Women's Conduct during Pregnancy*, the ACLU created strong statements, as highlighted in the two quoted passages in Box 5.1.

Since the latter part of the 20th century, there have been astounding advances in reproductive technologies, so much so that the technologies have sparked public ethical and political scrutiny concerning a woman's private choice (autonomy) versus public regulation and law (Harris & Holm, 2000). The ethical issues are deep and complex with regard to maternal and fetal rights, thus the moral debate continues with no agreements forthcoming concerning the mystery of procreation, technology, abortion, and maternal-fetal conflict.

Nurses sometimes feel as if they are caught in the middle and do not know how to manage the care related to the maternal-fetal conflict. In Provisions 1, 2, and 5 of the *Code of Ethics for Nurses with Interpretive Statements,* the ANA (2001) has clarified nurses' roles in regard to appropriate ethical behavior and action toward patients. (See Appendix A for the ANA *Code of Ethics* and Box 5.6 at the end of this chapter.) Included in these three provisions are concepts to which nurses are ethically bound such as the respect for human dignity, the patient's right to self-determination, a commitment to the patient's interest, the respect of privacy and confidentiality, and the protection of the patient's rights. Individual nurses need to make certain that they follow these ethical guidelines in a nonjudgmental and caring way. Protecting the woman's rights and decisions and maintaining dialogue of the highest quality among the woman, her family, and other health care professionals are most critical because of the deeply sensitive issues that women face in reproduction, procreation, or abortion. The manner in which nurses interact and intervene with these patients often will affect their own health and emotional outcomes.

Reproductive Rights

Women's decisions to have a baby, not to have a baby, or to have an abortion are among the most critical decisions she will make in her life. Although a woman may

Box 5.1: Highlights from the Field

American Civil Liberties Union

Women's Reproductive Rights Violated

A decade ago [meaning the 1980s], we saw a rash of cases in which government officials zealously embraced a misguided mission to protect fetuses by attempting to control the conduct of pregnant women. . . . Inevitably, such actions backfire: women who fear the government's "pregnancy police" will avoid prenatal care altogether, and both they and their fetuses will suffer as a result.

The ACLU . . . defended many of the women who were subject to coercive or punitive state actions. We won case after case, and attempts to bully and punish pregnant women eventually diminished.

Recently, however, we have seen this dangerous trend revive. (Introduction)

Coercive and punitive treatment of pregnant women violates the civil liberties of individual women and fosters distrust of health care providers. . . . An influential 1988 Illinois Supreme Court decision, *Stallman v. Youngquist*, warned courts not to make "mother and child . . . legal adversaries from the moment of conception until birth." Rejecting a child's claim of damages from its mother, the court wrote:

Holding a mother liable for the unintentional infliction of prenatal injuries subjects to State scrutiny all the decisions a woman must make in attempting to carry a pregnancy to term, and infringes on her right to privacy and bodily autonomy.

Although we may not always approve of a woman's conduct during pregnancy, we must insist that women be offered educational, social, and medical services that can persuade them to make the wisest and healthiest choices. Coercion is both a counterproductive and an illegal alternative. (Section 4)

Quoted from American Civil Liberties Union. (1997). Coercive and punitive governmental responses to women's conduct during pregnancy. Retrieved January 17, 2007, from http://www.aclu.org/reproductiverights/gen/16529res19970930.html

involve significant others, this type of decision is intensely personal and is one that she will hope to make on her own without coercion or mandates from health care professionals or federal or state governments.

One of the ethical questions for the reader is, "Does a woman have a right to have a child?" Infertility, for instance, is not a life-threatening disorder but causes undue suffering and shame to millions of women and couples. Brannigan and Boss (2001) posed a question: "If there is a right to reproduce, should it include the right to use expensive and scarce medical resources in exercising this right?" (p. 276). When considering these questions, bioethicists and health care professionals need to anticipate and attempt to resolve the question of how society should strike a balance among the various options of procreation, reproduction, testing, and maternal rights.

Many times legal rights and moral rights overlap because of the policies that are legislated to laws enforcing certain rights. **Moral rights** include liberty rights and claim rights (Mahoney, 2007). **Liberty rights**, sometimes called negative rights, are those rights a person can impose on others without a fear of someone or some group preventing those rights from being exercised. Liberty rights include freedom of speech, autonomy, privacy, and others as stated in the first 10 amendments of the U.S. Constitution. Health care in the United States is a liberty right.

Claim rights, sometimes called positive or welfare rights, are those rights owed to people through active and positive steps taken by others or groups to ensure the claim is met. There are two population exceptions in the U.S. to health care liberty rights— poor people and elders—and they fall under claim rights. Social federal and state programs help to ensure that claim rights are fulfilled and preserved.

Brannigan and Boss (2001) further pondered the issue of rights and reproductive health care. If there is a right to reproduction, is it a liberty right, a claim right, or both? In addition, does an unborn fetus or child have health care rights? Answers to these questions remain unclear, but most experts agree that all health care rights are of critical importance to everyone. Reproductive rights are about human rights, quality health care, choice, liberation from enforced sexual pleasures and abuse, and population growth and distribution (Cook, Dickens, & Fathalla, 2003).

Moral Standings of Humans

Whatever factor signals the end of full moral standing would seem to be relevant as a marker of when full moral standing begins. . . . The moral problems with manipulation of sperm and egg cells are often believed to be less troublesome than those arising from manipulating a late-term fetus or postnatal infant. It is important to know why this is so. It must be that, no matter how we attribute moral status to sperm and egg cells, we view them as having a moral standing that is different from the late-term fetus or postnatal infant. If we can identify what it is that is responsible for this perceived shift in moral status, perhaps we can understand better when full moral standing accrues.

—Robert Veatch, 2003, p. 40

When the phrase "moral standing of humans" is mentioned, what comes to mind? In Veatch's (2003) quote he has suggested that whatever it is that causes moral standing to end is what makes it begin. On this topic, he pondered a general question: Could any of the physiological or neurological criteria be the signals of the beginning and ending of moral standing in humans, such as the criteria used for higher brain death, whole-brain death, or the cardiac definition of death? There is no specific way for people to determine which, if any, criterion is *the one* that determines when full moral standing begins and ends. The question of when full moral standing begins and ends requires complex considerations.

Full moral status has been recognized as a person having person privileges, meaning that the term *person* does not refer to human beings but rather to those "beings that have the capacity to reason, make autonomous decisions and consider themselves as the unique subjects of their own varied experiences" (Bortolotti, 2006, Section 2, Para. 1). Having moral status means that persons consciously consider their interests and welfare as moral agents.

However, there are numerous other views as to when full moral status occurs. These views include, but are not limited to:

- Full moral status begins at conception—a fundamentalist or strong right to life view of potentiality or Future-Like-Ours Argument. (See definition of FLOA in the next paragraph).
- Full moral status begins when humans come into existence, or become sentient beings—a biological view.
- Full moral status is acquired when the being becomes a person, or when personhood can be established—a person essentialism view
- Full moral status is based on the amount of accrued possession of interests, which was detailed by Feinberg (1974) as the interest principle, what is now known as the Time-Relative Interest Account.

In 2004, the President's Council on Bioethics (PCB) issued a report titled *Monitoring Stem Cell Research*. Based on the report, President Bush took a strong fundamentalist stance that is based on two underlying assumptions: each person originates as a single cell zygote at the time of conception, and full moral status is acquired at origination. Based on this stance, many people believe that the single cell zygote has full moral status because it has the "potential" to become a sentient being. A stronger argument that stems from potentiality is the Future-Like-Ours Argument (FLOA), which was developed in detail by Marquis (1989). The FLOA is used as a strong contention against abortion because pro-life groups argue that a fetus has the potential to become a person who has a future like other living human beings experiencing life and the possibility of its fullest actualization, lifespan, and the possibility of rational decision-making abilities. This argument includes the potential for a fetus in the future to experience having a spouse, children, other family members, friends, successful careers, and all that life has to offer.

The Biological Approach to Determining Moral Status

The biological stance is a reasonable, scientific-based approach for determination of moral status. Many philosophers and bioethicists (e.g., DeGrazia, 2006; Steinbock, 1992) have contended that the sentience of the fetus is integral to determination of moral status. To have sentience requires the fetus to have the capacity of feelings.

With the biological view, there is evidence that the single zygote cell is derived from the sperm and ovum but the cell has not come into existence or being yet, meaning that beings originate as nonsentient entities. The single zygote cell does not come into being or existence until the cell has completed the division process, at which time the entity becomes a uniquely individuated human organism (DeGrazia, 2006). During the 2-week division process after the formation of the single cell zygote, there is a potential through various biological processes for the embryo to develop into twins, either by fraternal or identical twinning (or multi-embryos) or through a unique occurrence called fusion when two embryos can actually fuse into one embryo. Based on this scientific information, the single cell zygote cannot be uniquely individuated until the division process is completed, and "if not uniquely individuated, the zygote is not yet a unique member of our basic kind (according to the biological view): human organism" (DeGrazia, p. 51).

Interest Approach to Moral Status

The possession of interests is a requirement for moral status according to Feinberg (1974), who approached the interest argument from the function of rights, or having interests at stake. If the sentient being has interests at stake, those interests must be considered when there is moral deliberation about that being. If no interests have been incurred, interests cannot be considered in a moral deliberation. Without interests, rights cannot be assumed. Steinbock (2006) suggested that Feinberg was making a conceptual link between a being's interests and consciousness. In other words, only conscious beings can have a stake in something. Nonconscious beings do not have any interests of their own. Steinbock stated:

> Embryos are not mere things. They are alive and have the potential to become beings with interests—indeed to become people, like you and me. But their potential to become persons does not give them the moral status or the rights of actual persons. Early embryos, indeed early-gestation fetuses, have no consciousness, no awareness, no experiences of any kind, even the most rudimentary. . . . Within even the precursor of a nervous system . . . or without consciousness, they cannot have desires; without desires, they cannot have interests. (p. 29)

However full moral standing is defined, these perplexing issues will not be resolved because of the profound level of disagreements to the following questions: When do we come into existence, or sentience? Does life begin at conception? Do sentience and full moral standing occur simultaneously? How does personhood fit with the full moral standing conception? Is there a supreme entity in charge of society?

Abortion

Science cannot resolve moral conflicts, but it can help to more accurately frame the debates about those conflicts.
—HEINZ R. PAGELS, *THE DREAMS OF REASON*, 1988

Because pro-choice and pro-life (also known as anti-choice) debaters justify their claims and arguments on each side, the dilemma is deadlocked with no hope in the future of resolution. These diametrically opposed sides have ethical, political, legal, and religious implications. Opposition even occurs regarding the use of labeling groups. The opposing groups have historically been labeled as *pro-choice* and *pro-life*. As both sides tightened their reigns on their beliefs and values, the pro-choice groups began labeling pro-life groups as *anti-choice*. The rationale behind this decision was that pro-life groups were making claims that pro-choice groups did not value life. The pro-choice groups strongly believe that if the term pro-life was replaced by the term anti-choice, the insinuations and accusations made by pro-life groups that pro-choice groups did not believe in the value of life itself would be diminished. The current status of this controversy is unchanged. Pro-life groups refer to themselves as pro-life, and pro-choice groups refer to pro-life groups as anti-choice. The author of this chapter takes the stance that this argument of labels is largely irresolvable and therefore will use the terms pro-choice and pro-life because of the widespread use of these terms in media venues. Abortion, especially in the first trimester, is legal in many countries, including the United States. However, intense moral and political scrutiny, even legal action, has continued to surface since the *Roe v. Wade* decision of January 22, 1973 (see the Maternal-Fetal Conflict section earlier in this chapter). In **Roe v. Wade**, the U.S. Supreme Court ruled that states could not make any laws that banned abortions in the first or second trimester, except for certain reasons in the second trimester (as cited in Devettere, 2000; *Roe v. Wade*, 1973). For an abortion to occur in the second trimester, the woman must have health risks. In the third trimester, states can make laws banning abortions. Unless a third trimester abortion is critical to a woman's survival, the woman is required to follow her state law.

In 1971, 2 years before the *Roe v. Wade* decision, Judith Jarvis Thomson (1971), a philosopher, wrote a classic and well-known article titled *A Defense of Abortion*, which has served as a foundation for the abortion debate. She agreed that every person has a right to life and that this right is extended to fetuses. To make her argument, she stated that she was *pretending* that a fetus is a person because it in fact becomes a human person at some time before birth. However, her conclusive premise was that, even assuming that the fetus has a right to life, the fetus could not morally infringe on the mother's own right to control her own body or use her body to stay alive.

The definition of **abortion** includes two meanings: to give premature birth before the fetus is capable of sustaining life, as in a miscarriage or spontaneous abortion, or a woman's intentional termination of a pregnancy. The latter definition is the core of the pro-choice and pro-life debate. The debaters argue with political fervor and bitterness, sometimes resulting in violence about the legality, rightness, or wrongness of a woman's choosing to terminate her pregnancy, but in the pro-choice view, abortion is almost always permissible and can be justified.

Almost 1 billion registered abortions were completed worldwide during the last several decades of the 20th century and through December 2006 (Johnston, 2007). In the United States alone, from 1923 to December 2006, more than 47 million registered abortions were performed. The self-reported reasons for abortion in the United States have included rape, incest, physical life of mother, physical health of mother, fetal health, mental health of mother, and personal choice (Johnston, 2006). Personal choices included too young, not ready for responsibility, too immature, economic, to avoid adjusting life, mother single or in poor relationship, and enough children already.

The Central Ethical Dilemma

The central ethical dilemma of the abortion debate is about rights: the right to life of the fetus or the woman's right to control her own body by choosing whether or not to carry a pregnancy to term, have a baby, and parent it. The fetus (or embryo) as person or nonperson and a fetus (or an embryo) with or without moral status remain at the center of most of the pro-choice and pro-life rights debates. (See the sections on Maternal-Fetal Conflict, Reproductive Rights, and Moral Standing of Humans in this chapter.)

Pro-Choice View

In the pro-choice view, a common argument is that abortion is legally permissible, regardless of the morality involved. A woman has a basic right to make up her own mind about choices of pregnancy or abortion, and her right always prevails over any other right, including any fetal rights. At the core of the pro-choice stance is the right of privacy based on the U.S. Constitution, U.S. Declaration of Independence, and the worldwide Universal Declaration of Human Rights (ACLU, 2004). Sentience, moral status, and personhood are among the various arguments used in the pro-choice view.

There are also pro-choice debaters who believe that abortion is morally as well as legally permissible. Many people contend that a fetus that cannot survive outside a woman's body is not considered viable. Therefore, a fetus cannot override the woman's right to choose an abortion when the fetus is not viable outside the womb. With this pro-choice view, there are various opinions on the beginning of life, two of which are the fetus does not have human life until the mother is in the 17th week of gestation, or the fetus with sentience and moral status has human life at the 7th month of gestation when its nervous system has fully developed.

Pro-choice believers find the two types of morning-after pills acceptable. One type is RU486, or mifepristone. This Food and Drug Administration (FDA)-approved drug is available by prescription as an alternative to a surgical abortion procedure and can be administered up to 50 days from conception. Mifepristone must be followed by another drug within 48 hours (U.S. FDA, 2006b). With mifepristone, the fetus and other tissues are aborted. The other morning-after pill is the FDA-approved emergency contraceptive called Plan B (U.S. FDA, 2006a).

In August 2006, the FDA approved the over-the-counter sale of Plan B only for women ages 18 and over. However, for ages 17 and under Plan B must be prescribed by a primary care provider. Plan B has been a popular drug among adolescents because the drug can actually prevent implantation of a fertilized egg if taken within 72 hours of intercourse. Major companies such as Walmart, Walgreens, and Kroger have at times refused to stock the drug since the FDA first approved over-the-counter sale. Even though the drug is over the counter, the person seeking it is required to ask for the drug from the pharmacist and show proof of age. To combat the problem of intentional non-access of the drug in many areas, the Planned Parenthood Federation of America

(PPFA, 2006a) announced that a "pill patrol" campaign is underway by its grassroots supporters to make sure that every neighborhood pharmacy in the United States has Plan B stocked and readily available for over-the-counter or prescription use.

Pro-choice groups believe that if a woman and fetus are warranted as having equal moral standing, a strong belief held by pro-life groups, a woman's rights are weakened, causing the woman and the fetus to be at odds with each other. Some pro-life groups argue that, in special circumstances, the woman may have an abortion, such as in cases of incest or rape or if the infant is severely deformed. Allowing circumstances to influence the pro-life groups' opinion seems to be a double standard, meaning abortion is accepted when the procedure is subjectively needed.

Even today, the argument continues as to when a fetus becomes a person—whether it is at conception, when the heartbeat develops, when the nervous system develops, when it is considered viable outside the womb, or when the baby begins the process of thinking. John Locke (1995/1690) emphasized that a person stands for "a thinking intelligent being, that has reason and reflection, and can consider itself as itself, the same thinking thing, in different times and places; which it does only by that consciousness which is inseparable from thinking, and as it seems to me, essential to it" (Chap. 27, Section 9, Para. 1). From the personhood perspective, people should have rational thinking and possess the highest possible moral importance.

Pro-Life View

No matter how you feel about it, you will always be your mother's child—or your child's mother. This relationship—fraught with emotion, expectation, joy and unconditional love—is one of the most fundamental and complex of all human relationships.

—Unknown

On the side of pro-life debaters, the view on personhood stems from a fundamental understanding that the embryo or fetus is a person. Most pro-life groups argue that life and full moral status begin at conception and that abortion is immoral and murderous and should be illegal. (See the sections on Maternal-Fetal Conflict, Reproductive Rights, and Moral Status of the Fetus in this chapter.) According to this view, the embryo, from the time of conception and throughout the development of the fetus, has the same right to life that is due each person living and outside of the womb. Historically unless a mother's life was threatened, the embryo (or fetus) was protected because it is worthy of respect yet vulnerable to murder and harm from the time of conception, but especially in the second and third trimesters. However, the Supreme Court upheld the Federal Abortion Ban of 2007, and the written language by the major justices has now opened a door for states to override a mother's health for the sake of the fetus.

Most pro-life groups believe that life begins at conception as a single cell zygote, and moral status is acquired at conception; though not biologically and scientifically possible, the belief is taken based on faith, values, and cultural origins. However, some pro-life groups have differing opinions as to when personhood begins in lieu of conception. Among the times given are:

- After the ovum splits into two cells a few hours after conception
- 12 days after conception when the fertilized ovum has attached itself to the uterine lining
- 2 weeks from conception when the yellow streak develops, which is the neural tube that protects the backbone and prevents splitting into two embryos (before the yellow streak develops, the embryo may split into identical twins)
- 3 weeks from conception as the fetus begins to develop body parts
- 4 weeks from conception when the heartbeat begins (it should be noted that when 3D and 4D ultrasounds, the HDI 3000 and HDI 4000 systems, are performed in high-risk pregnancies, heartbeats are detected very early)
- 6 weeks from conception as the first brain waves are sensed
- 2 months and again at 3 months from conception when the fetus begins to resemble a human being (again, the detailed 3D and 4D ultrasounds produce very clear pictures of fetal development such as thumb-sucking and smiling [General Electric Medical Systems, 2002])
- 4 months from conception when the fetus has its own characteristics that could be differentiated from other fetuses
- 24 weeks from conception when the fetus is said to become viable
- 26 weeks from conception when the fetus's higher brain begins to function
- At birth, only after delivery and breathing is separate from the woman's body

There are several passages in the Bible that are used by pro-life believers, but the Catholic Church's position about abortion is a little more complicated (Harris & Holm, 2003). According to the Catholic Church, the whole issue regarding the morality of abortion stems from the greater question of when the fetus receives a soul. Because there are many interpretations of the Bible, there is great uncertainty. Therefore, the Catholic Church has taken a general stance on this moral issue, as Harris and Holm stated: "because killing is such a grave moral wrong, one should act cautiously and presume that there may be ensoulment from conception. . . . Abortion and the destruction of embryos should therefore be treated as the killing of an ensouled being" (p. 122).

Speaking Out

The legal and moral debates about abortion and women's reproductive rights continue. Nancy Keenan, President of the National Abortion and Reproductive Rights Action League (NARAL) Pro-Choice America, challenged President Bush and his allies in February 2006 "to stop attacking a woman's right to choose and join the organization in supporting efforts to prevent unintended pregnancies through medically accurate sex education, birth control, including the 'morning-after' pill, and improved family-planning services" (NARAL, 2007, Para. 4).

BOX 5.2: HIGHLIGHTS FROM THE FIELD

Pro-Choice Views of Abortion

Alyssa's Story

I am a mom, in my mid thirties, with two wonderful teenage boys. My husband and I love our boys tremendously. Every free moment is spent coaching, supporting, and generally enjoying either one son or the other. I absolutely adore babies and have dedicated my life to children. That said, my husband and I are also looking forward to a time when the boys are independent and we can spend more time with each other.

So, I find myself pregnant, first at 33, then again at 35. Adding a baby to the mix at this point would not be the best choice for my two older children or for my husband and I. Adoption was never really considered, because I don't want my sons internalizing the fact that I am willing to give up their brother or sister. When they are adults and faced with difficult decisions I may share my abortion story with them. It's not something I'm ashamed of, just something they're not ready to hear yet.

I made a choice to end two pregnancies. I made a choice to continue to give my two sons the time and attention that they deserve. I made a choice to not burden our family financially. I made a choice to spend more time with my husband and to help our relationship, as not only parents, but as lifetime partners, flourish. I don't regret my decisions and I'm not sorry.

Quoted from Alyssa's Story. *I'm Not Sorry.* Retrieved on January 17, 2007, from http://www.imnotsorry.net/alyssa.htm

BOX 5.3: HIGHLIGHTS FROM THE FIELD

Pro-Choice Views of Abortion

Anti-Abortion Violence

Our members often work in a hostile environment with challenges that few other medical professionals face. They are often targeted for aggressive harassment from anti-abortion protestors, and many have experienced acts of violence carried out by extremists. NAF offers abortion providers the professional support they need to help them deal with security threats and the isolation they often experience in their field of medicine. In order to help protect patients and providers, NAF tirelessly advocated for the passage of the Freedom of Access to Clinic Entrances (FACE) Act. FACE helps ensure that women are able to access reproductive health care services and providers are able to offer these services without the threat of violence and clinic blockades. NAF also successfully advocated for the creation of the Department of Justice's National Task Force on Violence Against Reproductive Health Care Providers in 1998. Our work with the Task Force has resulted in improved law enforcement response, which has led to a significant decrease in extreme forms of violence against abortion providers.

Many times, women who are pro-choice and believe in women's reproductive rights receive abortions but do not necessarily want the procedure. They may find themselves in situations of unintended pregnancy where they must have an abortion for reasons already described in this section. Refer to Box 5.2 for Alyssa's story (*I'm Not Sorry*, 2007) regarding her abortions and Box 5.3 for a person's view of violent protestors against abortions (National Abortion Federation [NAF], 2007).

Just because a woman believes in her right to choose does not mean that her intentional decision to have an abortion and lose her fetus will not be emotionally traumatizing to her (Burke with Reardon, 2002). It should be noted that many women do not grieve their abortion, but some inevitably will experience grief and suffering. Hornstra (1998) spoke of a poem that circulated on the Internet about an aborted fetus that was speaking to its mother from the dead. Toward the end of the poem, the fetus forgave its mother for the abortion. Hornstra stated: "I think all women who have abortions hope this is how our couldn't-be babies feel" (Para. 6).

Sometimes women feel restricted from expressing their grief because they fear that no one wants to hear about it. They may believe that they cannot discuss the abortion or loss of their fetus with anyone because it needs to be kept a deep dark secret. Some women may believe that they do not have permission to grieve for the loss of their fetus, and therefore they experience extreme sorrow, which is a type of grief called **disenfranchised grief** (see Box 5.4). When one is not allowed to grieve or must hide it, the grief process is prolonged and far worse. "Such 'impacted' [disenfranchised] grief can even become integrated into one's personality and touch every aspect of one's life" (Burke with Reardon, 2002, p. 51).

BOX 5.4: HIGHLIGHTS FROM THE FIELD

Disenfranchised Grief: Forbidding the Grief of Abortion

From the words of Tina...

If you regret an abortion, nobody wants to hear about it. After all, there's nothing anyone can do to fix the problem. So you have to tell yourself what happened was good—and everyone around you tells you the same thing. After that, I knew I would never bring up the subject again. (p. 55)

From the words of Kathy...

Dear Mom, I'm sorry I never told you the truth about my abortion for so long. I told you I was having minor surgery—female problems. Remember? . . . And what really kills me the most is that you and Daddy came to see me that night in the hospital . . . I was so scared—scared you'd find out what really happened that day. Man, I was hurting inside. And there you two were standing at the foot of my bed extending your love and concern. Mom, didn't you notice I couldn't even look you in the eyes? And over the years the times I turned from you whenever the abortion issue was raised? I can still see your face the moment I finally told you. Eight years later . . . You never looked up at me . . . [and] you sat quietly and gently spoke to me. Just as long as I kept my shameful secret, you were willing to keep it too. . . . Oh how I wish you had been able to talk about it . . . to cry with me, to help me get through that horrible time. You knew it all . . . but we never talked. I was so desperately alone. (pp. 55–56)

Quoted from Burke, T., with Reardon, D. (2002). *Forbidden grief: The unspoken pain of abortion* (pp. 55–56). Springfield, IL: Acorn.

--- **Ethical Reflections** ---

- If almost all abortions during the first trimester are considered legally permissible, how should one view a woman's taking a prescribed dose of mifepristone (RU486) to abort a fetus? Would you view this drug as morally or legally permissible? Both? Neither? Explain your answer.
- After reading all the arguments on rights and human life in this section, what do you believe about abortion? Address your views to the following points and use an ethical framework (theory, approach, or principle) to justify your answers:
  - Your moral and legal views on abortion
  - When you think a human life begins
  - When you think a human life becomes a person
- Please describe these points clearly so that you will clarify your own beliefs and values regarding these issues. Remember that there is no one right answer. These views are your opinions based on your values, an ethical theory, and the readings in this book and other sources.
- If you are giving nursing care to a woman who just received a partial-birth abortion by way of an intact D & E, first describe your own beliefs concerning partial-birth abortion, and then identify nursing strategies that you would use in caring for this patient.

Reproductive Technology

On July 25, 1978, Louise Joy Brown, the world's first successful "test-tube" baby was born in Great Britain. Though the technology that made her conception possible was heralded as a triumph in medicine and science, it also caused many to consider the possibilities of future ill-use. . . . The most important question was whether this baby was going to be healthy. Had being outside the womb, even for just a couple of days, harmed the egg? . . . Today [26 years later], the process of "in vitro" fertilization is considered commonplace and utilized by infertile couples around the world.

—JENNIFER ROSENBERG, 2007

The Browns tried to conceive for 9 years before they tried in vitro fertilization. Lesley Brown's fallopian tubes were blocked. Reproductive failure can be emotionally and financially devastating to couples. Because of infertility, since 1978 more than 1 million babies have been born worldwide with assisted reproductive technology

(ART) (Gosden, Trasler, Lucifero, & Faddy, 2003). Currently, in many Western countries, ART accounts for 1% to 3% of annual births.

Infertility can be defined as a woman's not being able to become pregnant after the couple has tried for 1 year (CDC, 2007). The term **assisted reproductive technology (ART)** refers to the handling and management of sperm and eggs and every kind of fertility treatment or drug used only for the purpose of retrieving eggs to be used in the treatment. Treatments not included under the ART umbrella include those in which only sperm are managed, such as artificial insemination; surgical procedures on women or men; or drugs that involve infertility when eggs are not going to be retrieved.

The three types of ART are:

- *In vitro fertilization (IVF):* Extracting the woman's eggs, fertilizing them with sperm, and then transferring the embryo through the cervix into the uterus
- *Gamete intrafallopian transfer (GIFT):* Transferring unfertilized eggs and sperm into the woman's fallopian tubes via a very small abdominal incision
- *Zygote intrafallopian transfer (ZIFT):* Fertilizing eggs in the laboratory with sperm, and then transferring the zygote into the fallopian tubes

Embryos resulting from IVF can be frozen until the time comes that one or more of them are needed. The embryo is then unfrozen and implanted without significant risks to the fetus.

Wachbroit and Wasserman (2003) stated, "Genetic technologies seem to promise an ever-increasing control over the creation of children, altering the nature of reproduction in a fundamental way" (p. 139). The concerns over the future of human life and family structure, human cloning, the low success rate of ART, and the cost of reproductive technology give society enough reason to ask a most basic ethical question: Should reproductive technology be used at all (Munson, 2004)? The cost of reproductive technology is one that is a global concern because of scarce medical and health care resources.

As stated previously in the section on reproductive rights, reproductive health in the United States is currently a liberty right, one that a couple may pursue without interference from any governmental agency, provided there are no laws against what is being pursued. However, how do private insurance companies and other reimbursement agencies weigh the priorities of health care resource allocation and distribution for those who are dying and critically ill against those who believe they have an autonomous right to a child? Most reimbursement agencies do not pay for many of these expensive reproductive medical procedures. But what does the future hold for autonomy and rights to reproductive services? How will distributive justice be managed?

Then there are specific ethical issues about reproductive technologies other than the broad ones already mentioned. These issues are divided into five groups: (1) the risks resulting from technology; (2) surrogacy (for donor eggs, embryo donation, or carrying fetuses); (3) the handling of surplus reproductive products, such as eggs or embryos that will not be used; (4) the implications of sperm sorting or gender selection; and (5) genetic modification and enhancement (Frankel, 2003; Wachbroit & Wasserman, 2003).

The first group of ethical issues involves risks created as a result of technology. Examples include ART and freezing embryos. Recent studies have found that a congenital abnormality named Beckwith-Wiedemann syndrome occurs at a 4.2-fold increase in ART babies compared with babies who are born naturally (as cited in Gosden et al., 2003). However, other studies do not make a significant link, and Gosden et al. recommended that widespread investigations be conducted. The ethical principles here include beneficence and nonmaleficence, or promoting human good for the couple who strongly desire a baby and doing no harm to the fetus in the process. The ethical question for consideration is: Could there be an acceptable level of risk for fetuses born by the use of the ART procedure?

The second group of ethical issues involves third-party involvement through donor eggs and embryos and carrying fetuses through surrogacy. **Surrogacy** is particularly a good example, such as when a man can fertilize the woman's egg but the woman cannot carry the fetus to term for some reason. In this case, the couple may ask a surrogate woman to carry the fetus to term, a process called **gestational surrogacy**. Other types of surrogacy include **traditional surrogacy**, in which the surrogate uses her own eggs and is artificially inseminated with semen from the prospective father and carries the fetus to birth; **egg donation**, in which a woman donates her eggs for in vitro fertilization with specific semen; and **embryo donation**, when a couple with a history of past successful pregnancy and delivery donates embryos to prospective couples seeking parenthood by way of in vitro fertilization and implantation.

The ethical issues regarding surrogacy are many. Who "owns" the infant once it is delivered by the surrogate? Who is the mother—the woman who produced the egg or the one who carried the fetus to term and delivered it? Is the meaning of family integrity or biological relationships at stake, or does it matter? Other concerns are legal issues: finding a way to legally pay the surrogate woman for her time and effort because the selling of children is illegal, avoiding treating babies as commodities, and avoiding exploitation of financially needy women (Munson, 2004; Wachbroit & Wasserman, 2003). As the population increases so will surrogacy. The principles involved are autonomy and nonmaleficence. These principles involve the issues of a couple's feelings about the right to choose, the surrogate's right to choose to be a surrogate, and doing no harm to the outcome of the child, the family biological structure, and individual freedoms.

The third group of ethical issues consists of **surplus reproductive products** resulting from technology. For example, because the success rate is low for in vitro fertilization, a woman may have stored many frozen eggs in an attempt for a successful pregnancy. Once the woman is pregnant, what happens to the remaining eggs? Many of the eggs are fertilized, but only a very few are implanted. What happens to these embryos? For people who believe that life begins at conception, is destroying the remainder of the fertilized eggs (embryos) considered murder? Beliefs about the right to life, the point at which life and full moral standing begin, and the question of whether destroying embryos is murder are at the center of this debate as well as the principles are autonomy and nonmaleficence.

The fourth group of ethical issues is called **sperm sorting** or **gender selection**, which is advanced technology enabling persons to create the kind of child they want to have or avoid having, to balance the family, or to prevent X-chromosome-linked or other genetic diseases (Genetics & IVF Institute, 2007; Harris & Holm, 2003). The medical procedure through which sperm sorting is accomplished is called **preimplantation genetic diagnosis (PGD)**. Family balancing, or evening out gender representation in children, is a concept used to help justify and promote the use of gender selection prior to implantation. The principles to be considered in sperm sorting, family balancing, and gender selection include autonomy, beneficence, nonmaleficence, and justice.

Occurring in 1 of every 1,000 live births overall, more than 500 X-linked chromosome diseases have now been identified, including hemophilia, Duchenne muscular dystrophy, and X-linked mental retardation. Other genetic diseases that can be identified through PGD include Fanconi's anemia, thalassemia, sickle cell disease, neurofibromatosis, and many others (University of Minnesota Cancer Center, 2007). Sperm sorting highly increases a couple's chance of having an unaffected child. In Box 5.5, Adam and Molly Nash and their parents' decision to use PGD are highlighted.

The last ethical issue, the fifth group, is **inheritable genetic modification (IGM)**, which is a procedure used to modify genes along the germ lines that are transmitted to offspring (Frankel, 2003). Stem cell research could help prevent genetic diseases from ever occurring in families through the generations by modifying the germ

BOX 5.5: HIGHLIGHTS FROM THE FIELD

A Reflection on Molly and Adam Nash

Adam Nash was born in Colorado on August 29, 2000. He had been an embryo that was sorted, screened, and selected from at least 12 embryos from the Nash couple, Lisa and Jack, for the purpose of tissue matching for the critically ill daughter, Molly.

Molly Nash was born to the Nash parents on July 4, 1994, with Fanconi's anemia, a fatal autosomal recessive bone marrow failure (aplastic anemia), which is only treatable with a bone marrow transplant from a sibling's umbilical cord blood. At that time, the success rate of a bone marrow transplant from an unrelated donor was only 42%, but from a sibling, the success rate increased to 85%.

The Nash parents, with support of physicians, made the decision to have preimplantation genetic testing on their embryos in the hopes of saving their only child. In the process, 12 of Lisa's eggs were fertilized by Jack's sperm via in vitro fertilization; 2 of the embryos had Fanconi's anemia and were discarded. Of the remaining 10 embryos, only one matched Molly's tissue. This one became Adam Nash.

From Grady, D. (2000, Oct. 4). Baby conceived to provide cell transplant for his dying sister. *New York Times*, p. 24.

---

lines of the embryos. Genetic traits in the embryo can be enhanced with IGM. What if researchers could help a couple create the perfect baby? In 1932, Aldous Huxley suggested in his book *Brave New World* that genetics and reproductive technology would be society's worst nightmare because of the government's involvement in these activities (as cited in Frankel, 2003).

Consider the following ethical questions regarding the Nash case:

■ Were the Nashes justified in creating Adam for the purpose of helping Molly get well? In other words, should humans be used as a means to an end? Explore the connection of Kant's deontology theory and the Nashes' situation.

■ What could have potentially happened to the nine remaining embryos?

■ How was it justified to discard the two embryos that had Fanconi's anemia and keep the one that became Adam? Consider your beliefs regarding when life begins and the moral equality of each life.

What is the future of genetic modification? No one knows exactly, but Huxley's 1932 perception for the future of genetic technology is strikingly different from Frankel's forecast. Frankel (2003) stated:

But as we begin the twenty-first century, the greater danger, I believe, is a highly individualized marketplace fueled by an entrepreneurial spirit and the free choice of large numbers of parents that could lead us down a path, albeit incrementally, toward a society that abandons the lottery of evolution in favor of intentional genetic modification. The discoveries of genetics will not be imposed on us. Rather, they will be sold to us by the market as something we cannot live without. (p. 32)

When these genetic issues are mentioned, emotions flare between people divided in their opinions. One side's view is of how great society's future will be with the new developments. The other side's view is that science should not be interfering with nature or God's work. Not only do these genetic issues spark extreme emotions, they also are the most complex of all the ethical issues that people in society face today. The prospect of designing, altering, enhancing, or ending the life of fetuses or embryos is challenging.

In her 1818 book titled *Frankenstein*, Mary Shelley told the frightening story of science gone awry when Victor Frankenstein tried to create a master race but botched the experiment. Although Shelley's story of the superhuman creature did not include today's genetic technology, there is a remarkable nonscientific similarity that may leave one feeling on shaky or fearful moral ground.

The standard principles of autonomy, beneficence, nonmaleficence, and justice should be addressed in the ethics involved with all PGD and other genetic manipulations such as IGM. However, the issues seem much more complex than just principle-driven or even theory-driven justifications. Genetic manipulation is essentially an unexplored territory that leaves nurses and other health care professionals with deep moral suffering. (See Chapter 2 for more on moral suffering.) Frankel's (2003) statement with regard to IGM, which could be applied to all genetic manipulation, is "whether we will shape it or be shaped by it" (p. 36).

––––––––––––––––––––––––––– **Ethical Reflections** –––––––––––––––––––––––––––

- Do you believe that destroying a fetus or embryo is murder?
- Ben and Lynn want to select the gender of their next baby. They currently have a girl, and this time they want a boy to balance the family. Do you think the destruction of their remaining embryos would be for an inconsequential reason—family balancing? Explain your thoughts based on an ethical framework—theory, approach, or principle.
- Do you think that family balancing and the prevention of genetic diseases are reasons that should be considered equal in moral weight in a sperm sorting procedure with resultant destruction of extra embryos?
- Explore your own feelings regarding sperm sorting that involves PGD and genetic modification that involves IGM. Write down your feelings about these two procedures.
- What are ethical strategies that you as a nurse might use if you were caring for two couples using gender selection (sperm sorting), one seeking family balancing and one preventing X-linked mental retardation? Be specific when listing these strategies.

Issues of Other Reproductive Services

The 4D and 3D ultrasound systems used today have outstanding qualities that contribute to a physician's diagnostic competency (Koninklijke Philips Electronics, 2007). With high definition imaging, the **4D ultrasound** provides almost magazine-quality pictures of fetuses at every stage of development. This high-technology ultrasound has contributed to the debaters' argument about human life. But more important than the debate itself, women who see their babies so clearly in 4D ultrasounds and see them smiling or thumb sucking are personalizing the fetal face and taking action. They are seeking better prenatal care, thus preventing harm and saving lives. Some women are even changing their minds about having abortions because of seeing the fetal face so vividly. One woman said, "I didn't realize that's something inside of you. . . . That's when I decided I was not going to have an abortion. I could see the hands and the feet, and I could hear the heartbeat. It sounded like horses galloping—da-dum-da-dum-da-dum" (Stricherz, 2002, Para. 6).

The woman laughed as she was describing the heartbeat. However, the most important concept to be learned from this quote is whether the pregnant woman will care for herself better during her pregnancy as a result of seeing her fetus. Prenatal care is critical to the future health of the child. There are numerous prenatal health issues, but only the critical ethical issues of genetic counseling and testing, HIV testing, and maternal substance abuse are included in this section.

Genetic Screening and Testing

To date, more than 5,000 genetic diseases have been discovered, and that number increases every day (Munson, 2004). Genes that are causally linked to biochemical, cellular, and physiological defects are responsible for these genetic diseases. DNA testing can identify some of these diseases in the fetus, and many new technologies are available. For example, today, Down syndrome can be detected at 16 to 18 weeks of gestation in a blood sample from the pregnant woman or by the older method of amniocentesis. Diseases such as sickle cell, phenylketonuria (PKU), and Tay-Sachs, as well as many others, can be screened with high accuracy. One example is sickle cell disease, which is autosomal recessive. If one parent has the disease and the other is not affected, all four children will be carriers. However, if both parents are carriers, there is a chance that one in four children will have the disease, which makes for a 25% chance overall.

Genetic screening involves professionals counseling individuals or couples about their risk for genetically linked diseases (Munson, 2004). Genetic screening can be useful for couples with a background of genetic disease such as sickle cell anemia because of its inheritance pattern. As Munson pointed out, however, once couples have this information, they often have no idea what to do with it. Should couples decide not to have children at all based on this 25% chance? Should couples take their chances and get pregnant anyway with the 25% risk and, if so, should the woman be allowed to have a prenatal genetic test with only a 25% risk involved? Furthermore, if she found out that her fetus had a recessive disease, would she need to consider an abortion? If she would not consider having an abortion, what would be her next step? Last, should there perhaps have been no reason for the prenatal genetic test in the first place?

Couples need to consider these questions before wandering down the path of expensive prenatal testing. There is the possibility that a woman can have embryo selection, sometimes called sperm sorting, via in vitro fertilization before implantation of the embryo. (See the previous section on reproductive technology). As previously discussed, however, embryo selection means that the remaining embryos will be discarded, diseased or not, unless the couple donates them to other couples or for research purposes. Even when used for research, the embryos are destroyed after they are used.

There are a variety of prenatal tests that allow for a close inspection of tissue and bone, including ultrasound, radiography, and fiber optics. **Prenatal genetic diagnosis** is accomplished through an examination of the fetal DNA. Prenatal genetic diagnosis is commonly performed through amniocentesis at 15 weeks of pregnancy or later or by chorionic villus sampling (CVS) which is performed between 10 and 12 weeks of pregnancy (American Academy of Family Physicians, 2004). CVS carries an average 0.05% risk for fetal foot or toe deformities; with amniocentesis, the risk is that 1 in 200 women will have a miscarriage (Munson, 2004). The most common test used for prenatal genetic diagnosis is a blood test for alpha fetoprotein. It is performed 15 to 20 weeks after conception and predicts spina bifida or anencephaly with high accuracy.

Knowing when to test and when not to test could be an ethical difficulty for health care professionals. Many women want to know prior to delivery that everything is all right, and oftentimes they believe that genetic testing will provide a certain degree of control and comfort for them. Should women have prenatal tests performed for what would seem like trivial reasons to other people? Will the woman's insurance company pay for these tests? What if she has no insurance but still wants these? Does she have an autonomous right to testing just because the technology is available?

Many experts hold two basic views: (1) that prenatal testing should be done if the woman strongly believes in her right to have the procedure and wants it performed, and (2) that the costs of the prenatal testing are very small compared to the costs of raising a child with a genetic disease or debilitating disorder (Munson, 2004). These decisions reach to the very core of family values and biological structure.

Stem cell research offers considerable hope for correction of genetic diseases, but until the time comes for its full use, couples must make their decisions based on the technology available to them. Williams, Alderson, and Farsides (2002) conducted a study of when prenatal screening and testing should be conducted. They concluded from the study that testing is appropriate when a couple can depend on accurate information, make an informed choice and decision, and live with the outcome once the decision about prenatal testing is made.

Ethical Reflections

- Do you think that a couple has a right to have a child with a prenatally diagnosed disabling genetic disease? Explain your thoughts.
- Do you think that physicians and nurses should inform couples that are thinking about having a baby about all the genetic tests that are available to them? Why or why not? Explain your thoughts.
- Do you think a mother has a right to know the results of her prenatal genetic tests, whether positive or negative? Explore both sides based on the literature and then justify your answer based on an ethical framework—theory, approach, or principle.

- What approaches would you take as a nurse caring for a pregnant mother carrying a fetus with Down syndrome? Consider all the options.

HIV Testing

In 2003, there were 5 million new HIV infections and 3 million deaths worldwide from AIDS (World Health Organization [WHO], 2004). Women account for half and children account for 2.5 million of the 40 million HIV infections in the world. In 2003 alone, 700,000 children worldwide became infected with HIV, most of them through vertical transmission in utero, after delivery, and through breast milk. In the United States, as of December 2004, an estimated 944,306 people had received a diagnosis of full blown AIDS, and of that number, 529,113 had died (Branson et al., 2006).

Because 40% of all pregnancies are unplanned (but not necessarily unexpected), many times women who are infected with HIV do not receive any HIV counseling and testing until after they discover that they are pregnant. A major ethical dilemma has been whether HIV testing should be mandatory for women upon the diagnosis of pregnancy and for newborns once they are delivered. The other major ethical dilemma has been whether the mother should breastfeed her infant when failure to do so may result in severe physical risk to the infant, especially in developing countries. The principles involved are autonomy, based on privacy, confidentiality, and basic rights; beneficence, based on doing good or acting in the best interest of the mother and fetus; and nonmaleficence, based on doing no harm to either the mother or the fetus.

In the past, the U.S. Public Health Service and the ACLU have opposed mandatory HIV testing of pregnant women and newborns based on the U.S. constitutional right to privacy and based on the belief that HIV testing must be voluntary. Both agencies agreed that women should have the right to refuse testing and should not be tested without their knowledge, but emphasized that testing and counseling should be made available universally. According to WHO (2004), HIV testing and counseling may occur very late in pregnancy or even during labor.

Revised recommendations for HIV testing of pregnant women in the United States were published in the *Morbidity and Mortality Weekly Report* (*MMWR*; Branson et al., 2006) because past evidence has indicated that perinatal transmission of HIV can be reduced to less than 2% with universal screening in combination with receiving antiretroviral therapy, having a scheduled cesarean delivery when necessary, and avoiding breastfeeding. The following were the revised guidelines from the *MMWR*:

■ HIV screening should be included in the routine panel of prenatal screening tests for all pregnant women.

■ HIV screening is recommended after the patient is notified that testing will be performed unless the patient declines (opt-out screening).

■ Separate written consent for HIV testing should not be required; general consent for medical care should be considered sufficient to encompass consent for HIV testing.

■ Repeat screening in the third trimester is recommended in certain jurisdictions with elevated rates of HIV infection among pregnant women.

Regarding the issue of breast milk, there are countless infants who would face health risks if their mothers did not feed them by way of the breasts. They either do not have enough money or do not have access to baby formula or milk. Although research findings are inconclusive concerning antiretroviral therapy for breastfeeding women, WHO (2004) recommended that women should continue their treatment during breastfeeding. Even still, the United Nations group has remained firm on its recommendations that women with HIV should avoid initiating breastfeeding if at all possible (as cited in WHO, 2004).

Practical considerations for nurses caring for women during the perinatal period include promoting the availability of HIV testing and counseling services and encouraging pregnant women to be tested while avoiding coercion in any way. In the United States, pregnant women can decline the test by opting out. If women wish to be pregnant but are also HIV-infected, nurses need to be sensitive to their wishes and know that they have an enormous decision to make—whether or not to become pregnant in light of their HIV diagnosis.

A woman needs to consider all statistics available, the social contexts, and the medical futures of herself and her child (Kirshenbaum et al., 2004). What is most important for nurses to remember is that women need to have adequate information and not personal opinions from nurses. Whatever a woman decides, nurses can be supporters of reproductive rights by not interfering with a woman's freedom to make independent decisions about her reproductive choices.

Ethical Reflections

• Discuss confidentiality and issues that are relevant to HIV testing, counseling, and a positive diagnosis of HIV in pregnant women.

• An HIV-infected woman is inclined to breastfeed her newborn, and you are providing nursing care to her. Do you give advice, teach, give options, or listen to her reasons for wanting to breastfeed? Discuss therapeutic communication and identify nursing strategies that you consider important for the woman, her baby, and this nurse-patient relationship.

Maternal Substance Abuse

Maternal substance abuse is detrimental to a fetus or newborn. However according to research, some pregnant women who abuse drugs do not seem to understand the potential harm that they are inflicting on their unborn children (Perry, Jones, Tuten, & Svikas, 2003). As one would expect, the women who are unaware of the danger that they are posing to their unborn children are those women who are abusing drugs but who do not seek help. This same group of women also was found to be more likely to believe that having a small baby is a positive occurrence. The results of this research underscore the need for wide-scale community education programs about maternal drug abuse. Nurses can be a valuable resource in this effort.

Maternal drug screening is not performed routinely, and testing a woman or an infant without informed consent is considered to be a violation of a patient's right to privacy (Keenan, 2006). If health care providers perform maternal or newborn testing without the mother's consent and the test results are positive, any decision to restrict or remove parental rights would be based on illegally obtained evidence.

The handling and treatment of maternal drug abuse varies from state to state, but at the same time it is important to remember violations of women's rights (liberty rights) that have occurred in some states (See the Reproductive Rights section in this chapter). Possible violations may include:

- Prosecution of a pregnant woman who abuses drugs
- Charging a pregnant woman with drug possession if she is arrested for drug abuse prior to fetal viability
- Charging a pregnant woman with distribution of drugs to a minor if she is arrested for drug abuse after the fetus is considered viable
- Reduction of parental rights

Nurses have an ethical responsibility to recognize maternal substance abuse. Although nurses might personally find a pregnant woman's substance abuse morally objectionable, compassion is warranted. A family rather than an individual person is wounded by the woman's abusive behavior. Action is sometimes taken based on state laws to protect a fetus or child who is at risk from maternal substance abuse but nurses must consider that a woman's decision or desire to seek treatment might result in a violation of the woman's rights. A woman's decision to obtain help often involves limited trust toward health care providers.

––––––––––––––––––– **Ethical Reflections** –––––––––––––––––––

- If you were a maternal-child nurse, after considering the ACLU's statement regarding women's rights, what action would you take if you suspected that a pregnant patient at the clinic where you work was abusing drugs? What information would you need to guide your actions?
- What would you do if you suspected that the woman might avoid the clinic in the future if you address the abuse issue?

Cultivating Nursing Care

Ethical and legal issues in reproductive health are incredibly complex and challenging, but at the same time they encourage us with the promise of correcting genetic diseases. Sometimes the possibilities inherent in new genetic technologies, including human cloning, cause people to become apprehensive or fearful. First, nurses caring for child-bearing women must be educated and remain current with reproductive ethics. Nurses need to understand and respect the beliefs and practices about pregnancy and childbearing of various cultures. Refer to Box 5.6 for a highlight of three cultures on their reproductive beliefs. In the Ethical Reflections presented throughout this chapter, opportunities have been given for nurses to apply the chapter content to reflective questions. The following Web Ethics box provides Web sites that will benefit nurses and Web sites for child-bearing women.

Nursing management for child-bearing women is focused on the ethical relationship between the nurse and the woman. Refer to Box 5.7 regarding the essential aspects of the 2001 ANA *Code of Ethics for Nurses with Interpretative Statements*. Related to the *Code of Ethics for Nurses* is the relational care that is exquisitely explained by Bergum (2004), who emphasized that the nurse should always ask, "What is the 'right thing to do' for oneself and others" (p. 485). The nurse-patient relationship, as Bergum has experienced it, is a moral entity. Relational ethics is an action ethic that is created within the moral space of a relationship (Jopling, 2000; as

BOX 5.6: HIGHLIGHTS FROM THE FIELD

Reproductive Beliefs and Practices Among Three Cultures—African American, Appalachian, and Mexican Heritages

African American Heritage

- Many people do not accept the practice of abortion because of religious, moral, or Afrocentric beliefs and therefore will delay making a decision until they know that abortion is unsafe.
- Families urge pregnant women to eat clay or earth, known as geophagia, when they have this natural craving because eating the clay or earth helps to supply minerals that the fetus needs. As a special note, however, geophagia can lead to potassium deficiency, constipation, and anemia.
- The pregnant woman should eat foods craved to prevent birthmarks that have an appearance similar to the craved food.
- To initiate labor, pregnant women should ingest castor oil or a heavy meal, ride over bumpy roads, or sniff pepper.
- Having a picture taken (of pregnant woman) can cause stillbirth.
- If the baby is born with a "veil" (the amniotic sac) over its head or face, the baby will have special powers.

Appalachian Heritage

- Birth control pills, condoms, tubal ligation and other anticontraceptive methods are an individual choice.
- Abortion is an individual choice, and taking laxatives enhances abortion.
- Pregnant women carry girl fetuses higher than boy fetuses.
- Having a picture taken (of pregnant woman) can cause stillbirth.
- If the pregnant woman reaches her arm over her head, the cord will wrap around the fetus's neck and strangle it.
- If a pregnant woman craves certain foods, she should eat those foods, or else the baby will have a birthmark that appears similar to the craved food; also eating strawberries, citrus fruits, or being frightened by a snake can cause birthmarks.

(continued)

Box 5.6: Highlights from the Field (continued)

- If the pregnant woman experiences a tragedy, the baby could have a congenital defect.
- Harm could come to the fetus if the woman wears an opal ring during pregnancy.

Mexican Heritage

- Most of the fertility practices are linked with religious beliefs, primarily the Catholic Church. Condoms, for instance, will promote promiscuity. To prevent unwanted pregnancies, however, natural practices such as the rhythm method are acceptable and do not go against the church.
- Abortion is wrong but a few people view contraceptive practices such as sterilization and birth control pills as acceptable.
- A great amount of care of the pregnant woman comes from family members, which sometimes leads to a deficit of prenatal care.
- Walking in the moonlight during pregnancy could cause birth defects. Pregnant women should wear safety pins, metal keys, or other metal amulets to prevent birth deformities and defects.
- If the pregnant woman raises one arm over her head, the cord will wrap around the fetus's neck and strangle it.
- The baby's father or other men, with the exception of the physician or nurses, should not be present during delivery, or else harm can come to the baby.

Largely quoted from Purnell, L. D., & Paulanka, B. J. (2005). *Guide to Culturally Competent Health Care* (pp. 28, 53, 343-345). Philadelphia, PA: Davis.

cited in Bergum, 2004). A moral space is where the relationship is created, where nurses display responsibility, and where they respond to others. Nurses must be morally responsible to the child-bearing women for whom they care, whether they are caring for them clinically, educating them, or overseeing their care. In so doing, nurses need to remember the dual care framework for pregnant women: woman and fetus.

Bergum (2004) has identified four themes to define relational ethics: environment, embodiment, mutual respect, and engagement. No matter what ethical issue is of concern, nurses need to focus on the quality of the moral relationship between the nurse and patient. In relational ethics, the first theme, environment, is a living system. It is important to understand how the whole environment is affected by actions that each person takes. The living environment is in every nurse, and every action that is taken by nurses affects the outcome of the health care system as a whole. For example, the goal of a health care agency for a woman who had a partial-birth abortion could be to discharge her after 1 day. The patient and agency depend on the responsible and competent actions of nurses and others to meet the goal of a 1-day discharge.

Embodiment is the second theme, and is defined as one's having a scientific knowledge, a compassion for human life, and experiencing feeling and emotion for another person. For example, if after a prenatal genetic test a 16-week-pregnant woman has just been told that her fetus has Down syndrome, the nurse would understand the science behind the test and know the aftercare procedure. Also, the nurse would have a mindful reality of the woman's pain and suffering and therefore have compassion for her.

Mutual respect is the third theme in relational ethics. Mutual respect is a way for people to exist together and have equal worth and dignity. Mutual respect is difficult to attain often, but it is the central theme of relational ethics. In the example of the woman and her fetus with Down syndrome, mutual respect could be initiated by the nurse's regard for the woman's feelings, values, beliefs, and attitudes. The word *mutual* means to have a reciprocal and interactive focus. Based on this concept, the woman would need to reciprocate that respect toward the nurse.

The fourth theme, relational engagement, is when the nurse and patient can find a few minutes to interact about something that is important to them. The nurse needs to understand the patient's circumstances and vulnerability. An example of engagement for the woman and her fetus with Down syndrome can be accomplished by the nurse's engaging in a conversation with the woman about her feelings concerning the diagnosis and options for her and her fetus.

Dialogue is in the center of the moral space, at the focus of relational ethics, and is the venue for the four themes to emerge. Depersonalization and coldness often surround the health care systems that women use. Nurses must give personalization to child-bearing women by practicing relational ethics. On relational ethics and the moral life, Bergum (2004) stated

With relational space as the location of enacting morality, we need to consider ethics in every situation, every encounter, and with every patient. If all relationships are the focus of understanding and examining moral life, then it is important to attend to the quality of relationships in all nursing practices, whether with patients and their families, with other nurses, with other health care professionals, or with administrators and politicians. (p. 485)

BOX 5.7: HIGHLIGHTS FROM THE FIELD

Essential Aspects from the *Code of Ethics for Nurses with Interpretive Statements* for Cultivating Care for Childbearing Women

- The need for health care is universal, transcending all individual differences (1.1, p. 7).
- Respect for human dignity requires the recognition of specific patient rights, particularly the right of self-determination (1.4, p. 8).
- Each nurse has an obligation to be knowledgeable about the moral and legal rights of all patients to self-determination. The nurse preserves, protects, and supports those interests by assessing the patient's comprehension of both the information presented and the implications of decisions (1.4, p. 8).
- Nurses must examine the conflicts arising between their own personal and professional values, the values and interest of others who are also responsible for patient care and health care decisions, as well as those of patients (2.2, p. 10).
- In situations where the patient requires a personal opinion from the nurse, the nurse is generally free to express an informed personal opinion as long as this preserves the voluntariness of the patient and maintains appropriate professional and moral boundaries (5.3, p. 19).
- It is essential to be aware of the potential for undue influence attached to the nurse's professional role (5.3, p. 19).

Web Ethics

Organizations to Help Child-Bearing Women and Their Families

Center for Reproductive Rights
http://www.reproductiverights.org

NARAL Pro Choice America
http://www.naral.org

National Women's Health Information Center
http://www.4woman.gov

National Right to Life Committee
http://www.nrlc.org

CASE STUDY: PARTIAL-BIRTH ABORTION (INTACT D & E)

Ms. Brown, age 34 and 19 weeks into her pregnancy, received a prenatal genetic diagnosis of Huntington's disease for her fetus via amniocentesis. The day after the diagnosis, the physician explained two options to Ms. Brown: carrying the fetus to term or having a late-term abortion to terminate the pregnancy. The physician explained how the procedure would be performed. Mr. and Ms. Brown were devastated and needed a few days to process the information. When they returned to the clinic, the Browns informed the physician and nurse that they had decided to have the partial-birth abortion. They made a decision not to have any more children, even after the physician had explained the possibility of embryo selection (sperm sorting) for future children.

1. The day that the physician explains the options to Ms. Brown, you try to establish a genuine ethical relationship with her so that the two of you can have a deeper understanding of the situation. As a nurse, what specific approaches will you use for this relationship?

2. Based on the reading, what ethical issues are at stake? Explain.

3. You are in the room with the physician on the day that the Browns return with their decision to have the abortion. As a nurse, what approaches will you take with the Browns on this day? Consider your own values and beliefs about abortion, especially partial-birth abortion, in light of the fetus's having Huntington's disease.

4. If they had chosen to have this baby, the Browns would need to think about who would care for their impaired child in the case of their deaths. A person with Huntington's disease is not usually afflicted with symptoms until his or her mid-30s. Financial demands would also be a problem. Explore the ramifications of a decision to keep the fetus and raise the child, especially with the Browns knowing that the outcome would be severe impairment in the child's middle 30s.

5. How can the Browns justify having an abortion when Huntington's disease does not usually affect a person until the middle 30s, well after the child has reached maturity?

6. Explain how each principle—autonomy, beneficence, nonmaleficence, and justice—can guide or be applied in this case. How can you justify each principle?

Planned Parenthood of America
    http://www.ppfa.org
Women's Institute for Fertility, Endocrinology & Menopause
    http://www.womensinstitute.org

Organizations for Nurses

CDC's Women's Reproductive Health
    http://www.cdc.gov/reproductivehealth/wh_women.htm

Summary

In this chapter, the author presented an explanation of maternal-fetal conflict, which can lead to a constraint of maternal autonomy as perceived by many organizations, including the ACLU, Planned Parenthood of America, and pro-choice groups. There has been a perceived shift in the last few years in the way that providers sometimes view care and treatment for the mother and fetus, meaning that attention is given to each entity as having equal moral standing. New laws have the potential to negatively impact a woman's right to self-determination—the Partial-Birth Abortion Ban of 2003 and the Unborn Victims of Violence Act of 2004. Other key points in this chapter are:

- There are different variations of how organizations and people view the moral standing of the fetus. Generally, the degree to which moral standing is placed on the fetus influences maternal rights—the greater the degree of moral standing of the fetus, the more restraint of maternal rights. The central ethical dilemma regarding abortion is about rights—the right to life of the fetus or the woman's right to control her own body. The U.S. Supreme Court justices upheld the Federal Abortion Ban on April 18, 2007 (ACLU, 2007). This ban initially was known as the Partial-Birth Abortion Ban of 2003.
- Most women who have abortions agree that they could not have a baby, carry a fetus, or raise a family for personal or health reasons. Some women, though they may strongly believe in maternal rights, experience disenfranchised grief because they believe that they do not have permission to grieve the loss of their fetus, thus they experience extreme sorrow.
- Assisted reproductive technology (ART) has been a miracle and a relief for women or couples who experience infertility. There are three types of ART: in vitro fertilization (IVF), gamete intrafallopian transfer (GIFT), and zygote intrafallopian transfer (ZIFT). Ethical issues regarding ART include the risks resulting from technology; surrogacy

(donor eggs, embryo donation, or carrying fetuses); the handling of surplus embryos and fetuses; implications of sperm sorting, gender selection, and family balancing; and genetic modification and enhancement—the dream of creating a perfect child.

■ Preimplantation genetic diagnosis (PGD) is a procedure that allows implantation of a selected gender or a perfect or near perfect embryo. Many genetic diseases can be detected though gene technology, screening, and genetic diagnosis. Knowing when to test and when not to test could be an ethical difficulty for all people concerned with the issue. Maternal rights should be respected, but weighing maternal rights against burdens of costs may be a hard choice for couples and providers of care.

■ There are new 2006 guidelines from the CDC regarding HIV screening in pregnant women: (1) HIV screening should be included in the panel of tests for pregnant women; (2) pregnant women may decline the HIV test by opting out; (3) no written consent is required for HIV screening; and (4) HIV screening should be repeated in the third trimester where in certain geographic areas HIV infection rates are particularly elevated. Breastfeeding is not recommended for mothers who are HIV positive.

■ Maternal substance abuse, including alcohol and other drugs, can be detrimental to the fetus or newborn infant. There tends to be lack of education from providers of care or a deficit of pregnant women in comprehending the adverse effects of substance abuse. Maternal and infant drug screening is not performed on a routine basis and may not be done without express informed consent. Nurses have a moral responsibility to educate their patients and recognize maternal substance abuse. However, a woman's decision to obtain help is her decision, and that decision is dependent upon the degree of trust that she has developed with her providers of care.

■ Nurses should incorporate and apply essential concepts from the ANA *Code of Ethics for Nurses with Interpretive Statements* (2001) and Bergum's (2004) relational ethics. Bergum's themes of relational ethics are environment, embodiment, mutual respect, and engagement. Dialogue is in the center of the moral space, and serves as the venue in which Bergum's four themes can emerge.

References

American Academy of Family Physicians. (2004). Prenatal diagnosis: Amniocentesis and CVS. Retrieved July 28, 2004, from http://familydoctor.org/144.xml

American Civil Liberties Union. (1997). Coercive and punitive governmental responses to women's conduct during pregnancy. Retrieved January 17, 2007, from http://www.aclu.org/reproductiverights/gen/16529res19970930.html

American Civil Liberties Union. (2004). Reproductive rights. Retrieved July 17, 2004, from http://www.aclu.org/ReproductiveRights/ReproductiveRightsMain.cfm

American Civil Liberties Union. (2006). U.S. Supreme Court to hear argument in federal abortion ban challenges. Retrieved January 17, 2007, from http://www.aclu.org/reproductiverights/abortionbans/27305prs20061108.html

American Civil Liberties Union. (2007). U.S. Supreme Court upholds Federal Ban on Abortion methods: Ruling undermines women's health and equality. Retrieved June 8, 2007, from http://www.aclu.org/reproductiverights/abortionbans/29778res20070518.html

American Nurses Association. (2001). *Code of ethics for nurses with interpretive statements.* Washington, DC: Author.

Bergum, V. (2004). Relational ethics in nursing. In J. L. Storch, P. Rodney, & R. Starzomski (Eds.), *Toward a moral horizon: Nursing ethics for leadership and practice* (pp. 485–502). Toronto, Canada: Pearson-Prentice Hall.

Bortolotti, L. (2006). Disputes over moral status: Philosophy and science in the future of bioethics. *Health Care Analysis* [DOI 10.1007/s10728-006-0031-7]. Retrieved January 17, 2007, from http://www.philosophy.bham.ac.uk/pdf/Bortolotti/hca2.pdf

Brannigan, M. C., & Boss, J. A. (2001). *Healthcare ethics in a diverse society.* Mountain View, CA: Mayfield.

Branson, B. M., Handsfield, H. H., Lampe, M. A., Janssen, R. S., Taylor, A. W., Lyss, S. B. et al. (2006). Revised recommendations for HIV testing of adults, adolescents, and pregnant women in health-care settings [Electronic version]. *Morbidity & Mortality Weekly Report, 55*(RR-14), 1–17. Retrieved January 17, 2007, from http://www.cdc.gov/mmwr/preview/mmwrhtml/rr5514a1.htm

Burke, T., with Reardon, D. C. (2002). *Forbidden grief: The unspoken pain of abortion.* Springfield, IL: Acorn.

Centers for Disease Control and Prevention. (2007). Assisted reproductive technology. Retrieved February 15, 2007, from http://www.cdc.gov/ART/index.htm

Chandis, V., & Williams, T. (2006). The patient, the doctor, the fetus, and the court-compelled cesarean: Why courts should address the question through a bioethical lens. *Medicine and Law, 25,* 729–746.

Cook, R. J., Dickens, B. M., & Fathalla, M. F. (2003). *Reproductive health and human rights: Integrating medicine, ethics, & law.* Oxford, UK: Clarendon.

DeGrazia, D. (2006). Moral status, human identity, and early embryos: A critique of the President's approach. *Journal of Law, Medicine, & Ethics, 34*(1), 49–57.

Devettere, R. J. (2000). *Practical decision making in health care ethics: Cases and concepts* (2nd ed.). Washington, DC: Georgetown University.

Feinberg, J. (1974). The rights of animals and unborn generations. In W. T. Blackstone (Ed.), *Philosophy & environmental crisis* (pp. 43–68). Athens, GA: University of Georgia Press.

Frankel, M. S. (2003). Inheritable genetic modification and a brave new world: Did Huxley have it wrong? *Hastings Center Report, 33*(2), 31–36.

General Electric Medical Systems. (2002). Ultrasound: Then and now. Retrieved July 18, 2004, from http://www.gehealthcare.com/rad/us/4d/thennow.html

Genetics and IVF Institute. (2007). In vitro fertilization (IVF) program. Retrieved January 17, 2007, from http://www.givf.com/fertility/ivf.cfm

Gosden, R., Trasler, J., Lucifero, D., & Faddy, M. (2003). Rare congenital disorders, imprinted genes, and assisted reproductive technology. *Lancet, 361,* 1975–1977.

Grady, D. (2000, Oct. 4). Baby conceived to provide cell transplant for his dying sister. *New York Times,* p. 24.

Harris, J., & Holm, S. (2000). Introduction. In J. Harris & S. Holm (Eds.), *The future of human reproduction: Ethics, choice, & regulation* (pp. 1–37). Oxford, UK: Clarendon.

Harris, J., & Holm, S. (2003). Abortion. In H. LaFollette (Ed.), *The Oxford handbook of practical ethics* (pp. 112-111). Oxford, UK: Oxford University.

Hornstra, D. (1998). A realistic approach to maternal-fetal conflict. *Hastings Center Report, 28*(5), 7–12.

I'm Not Sorry. (2007). Alyssa's Story. Retrieved January 17, 2007, from http://www.imnotsorry.net/alyssa.htm

Johnston, W. R. (2006). Reasons given for having abortions in the United States. Retrieved March 15, 2007, from http://www.johnstonsarchive.net/policy/abortion/abreasons.html

Johnston, W. R. (2007). Summary of abortions worldwide, through December 2006. Retrieved March 15, 2007, from http://www.johnstonsarchive.net/policy/abortion/wrjp338sd.html

Jopling, D. A. (2000). *Self-knowledge and the self.* New York: Routledge.

Keenan, C. (2006). Maternal versus fetal rights: Part 1. In S. W. Killion & K. Dempski (Eds.), *Quick look nursing: Legal and ethical issues* (pp. 144–145). Boston: Jones & Bartlett.

Kirshenbaum, A., Hirky, A. E., Correale, J., Goldsteim, R. B. Johnson, M. O., Rotheran-Borus, M. J. et al. (2004). "Throwing the dice": Pregnancy decision-making among HIV-positive women in four U.S. cities. *Perspectives on Sexual and Reproductive Health, 36*(3), 206–213.

Koninklijke Philips Electronics N.V. (2007). Breakthrough 3D and 4D imaging. Retrieved January 4, 2007, from http://www.medical.philips.com/main/products/ultrasound/general/hdi4000/live_3d.html

Locke, J. (1995). Book II: Of ideas—Of identity and diversity: Personal identity (Chap. 27, Sec. 9). In *An essay concerning human understanding* (6th ed.). New York: Institute for Learning Technologies Digital Classics, Columbia University. Retrieved January 4, 2007, from http://www.ilt.columbia.edu/publications/locke_understanding.html

Ludwig, M. J. (1998). Ethics in medicine: Maternal-fetal conflict. University of Washington School of Medicine. Retrieved January 10, 2007, from http://depts.washington.edu/bioethx/topics/matern.html

Mahoney, J. (2007). *The challenge of human rights: Origin, development, and significance.* Oxford, UK: Blackwell.

Marquis, D. (1989). Why abortion is immoral. *Journal of Philosophy, 86*, 183–202.

Moffett, J. (2003). Conflict of interest: Maternal-fetal conflict and the politics of conservation. *Different Takes, 23*, 1–4.

Munson, R. (2004). *Intervention and reflection: Basic issues in medical ethics* (7th ed.). Belmont, CA: Wadsworth-Thomson Learning.

National Abortion and Reproductive Rights Action League Pro Choice America. (2007). Meet our president—Nancy Keenan. Retrieved January 17, 2007, from http://www.prochoiceamerica.org/about-us/meet-nancy/

National Abortion Federation. (2007). Anti-abortion violence. Retrieved January 17, 2007, from http://www.prochoice.org/about_naf/history.html

National Right to Life Committee. (2003). Final language Partial-Birth Abortion Act as approved by both houses of Congress. Retrieved January 17, 2007, from http://www.nrlc.org/abortion/pba/partial_birth_abortion_Ban_act_final_language.htm

National Right to Life Committee. (2004). Key facts on the Unborn Victims of Violence Act ("Laci and Conner's Law") (H.R. 1997). Retrieved June 7, 2007, from http://www.nrlc.org/Unborn_Victims/keypointsuvva.html

Perry, B. L., Jones, H., Tuten, M., & Svikas, D. S. (2003). Assessing maternal perceptions of harmful effects of drug use during pregnancy. *Journal of Addictive Diseases, 22*, 1–9.

Planned Parenthood Federation of America. (2006a). Emergency contraception. Retrieved January 17, 2007, from http://www.plannedparenthood.org/birth-control-pregnancy/emergency-contraception-4363%20.htm

Planned Parenthood Federation of America. (2006b). Press statements: Supreme Court agrees to review federal abortion ban. Retrieved January 17, 2007, from http://www.federalabortionban.org/press_statements/060221-court-review.asp

Planned Parenthood Federation of America. (2006c). Save Roe! Retrieved January 17, 2007, from http://www.saveroe.com

President's Council on Bioethics. (2004). *Monitoring stem cell research: A report of the President's Council on Bioethics.* Washington, DC: Author. Retrieved January 17, 2006, from http://www.bioethics.gov/reports/stemcell/index.html

Purnell, L. D., & Paulanka, B. J. (2005). *Guide to culturally competent health care* (pp. 28, 53, 343–345). Philadelphia, PA: Davis.

Roe v. Wade: The 1973 Supreme Court decision on state abortion laws. (2001). In R. M. Baird & S. E. Rosenbaum (Eds.), *The ethics of abortion*. Amherst, NY: Prometheus Books. (Reprinted from *United States Reports, 410*, 113–178.)

Rosenberg, J. (2007). First test-tube baby—Louise Brown. Your Guide to 20th Century History. Retrieved January 17, 2007, from http://history1900s.about.com/od/medicaladvancesissues/a/testtubebaby.htm

Shelley, M. (1988). *Frankenstein*. New York: Tor. (Original work published 1818)

Steinbock, B. (1992). *Life before birth: The moral and legal status of embryos and fetuses.* New York: Oxford University Press.

Steinbock, B. (2006). The morality of killing human embryos. *Journal of Law, Medicine, & Ethics, 34*(1), 26–34.

Stricherz, M. (2002). Bonding with baby: Why ultrasound is turning women against abortion. Retrieved January 17, 2007, from http://catholiceducation.org/articles/abortion/ab0066.html

Thomson, J. J. (1971). A defense of abortion. *Philosophy and Public Affairs, 1*(1), 47–66.)

University of Minnesota Cancer Center. (2007). Umbilical cord blood transplantation program. Retrieved January 17, 2007, from http://www.cancer.umn.edu/research/programs/transbioucb.html

U.S. Food and Drug Administration. (2006a). FDA approves over-the-counter access for Plan B for women 18 and older: Prescription remains required for those 17 and under [P06-118]. Retrieved January 17, 2007, from http://www.fda.gov/bbs/topics/NEWS/2006/NEW01436.html

U.S. Food and Drug Administration. (2006b). FDA: Mifeprex (mifepristone) information. Retrieved January 17, 2007, from http://www.fda.gov/cder/drug/infopage/mifepristone/

Veatch, R. (2003). *The basics of bioethics* (2nd ed.). Upper Saddle River, NJ: Prentice Hall.

Wachbroit, R., & Wasserman, D. (2003). Reproductive technology. In H. LaFollette (Ed.), *The Oxford handbook of practical ethics* (pp. 136-160). Oxford, UK: Oxford University.

Williams, C., Alderson, P., & Farsides, B. (2002). "Drawing the line" in prenatal screening and testing: Health practitioners' discussion. *Health, Risk and Society, 4*(1), 61–75.

World Health Organization. (2004). Antiretroviral drugs for treating pregnant women and preventing HIV infection in infants: Guidelines on care, treatment and support for women living with HIV/AIDS and their children in resource-constrained settings. Retrieved January 17, 2007, from http://www.who.int/hiv/pub/mtct/en/arvdrugswomenguidelinesfinal.pdf

CHAPTER 5 QUESTIONS

1. Maternal-fetal conflict can occur when
   a. providers of care tend to treat the mother and fetus as having equal moral status.
   b. a woman's treatment may be hazardous to the fetus.
   c. a pregnant women does not comply with a provider's recommendations or treatments that are believed to nurture the fetus's growth and development.
   d. All of the above

2. Which recently enacted court decision undermines a women's right to choose?
   a. Federal Abortion Ban
   b. *Roe v. Wade* decision
   c. *Holmes v. Ashbury* decision
   d. *Carthell v. Washton* decision

3. Based on the biological approach to determining moral standing of the fetus
   a. a single cell zygote is considered to have sentience and equal moral standing to the mother.
   b. sentience begins after the cell division process is completed, but moral standing of the fetus does not necessarily occur at that time.
   c. moral standing does not occur until birth, when personhood occurs.
   d. the degree of moral status is based on the fetus's interests at stake.

4. Of the five types of reproductive technology discussed in this chapter, which two involve the moral deliberation of all four principles—autonomy, beneficence, nonmaleficence, and justice?
   a. Risks related to technology and surrogacy
   b. Surplus reproductive products—embryos and fetuses
   c. PGD and IGM
   d. Traditional surrogacy and gestation surrogacy

5. The new 2006 recommendations for screening of HIV in pregnant women include that
   a. informed written consent is required for all HIV screening.
   b. pregnant women can opt out of HIV screening at their own risk.
   c. repeat screening is recommended for pregnant women in the second trimester.
   d. coercive measures can be used by the state health department officials if a pregnant woman refuses to be screened for HIV.

CHAPTER 5 ANSWERS

1. d
2. a
3. b
4. c
5. b

Infant and Child Nursing Ethics

Karen L. Rich

Heaven lies about us in our infancy.
—William Wordsworth, *Intimations of Immortality,* 1807

OBJECTIVES

After reading this chapter, the reader should be able to:

1. Discuss issues of vulnerability as they relate to the care of infants and children.
2. Analyze disparities in newborn screening and potential consequences.
3. Understand ethical issues regarding the universal vaccination of children and the nurse's role.
4. Identify issues of social justice as they apply to infants and children.
5. Evaluate ethical factors regarding refusing treatment for infants and children.
6. Discuss applications of the Baby Doe rules.
7. Understand the nurse's role as an advocate in the care of infants and children.
8. Discuss the ANA's *Code of Ethics for Nurses* in relation to nursing ethics in the care of infants and children.

KEY TERMS

Standard of best interest
Standard of substituted judgment
Baby Doe rules

Mothering

In the book *Ethics for the New Millennium*, the Dalai Lama (1999) emphasized the importance of the ethic of compassion. Empathy, one's "ability to enter into and, to some extent, share others' suffering" (p. 123), represents compassion (*nying je*) at a basic level. The Dalai Lama stated that Buddhists, and probably other people, believe that compassion can be developed that goes beyond empathy to the extent that it arises without effort and "is unconditional, undifferentiated, and universal in scope" (p. 123). Compassion is a desire to separate another being from suffering. Compassion also is a sense of intimacy toward all other feeling and perceiving beings (Dalai Lama). Persons with this well-developed level of compassion include in the scope of their compassion even those beings that may harm them. According to the Dalai Lama, this profound form of intimacy and compassion can be likened "to the love a mother has for her only child" (p. 123).

All animals are born into an initial condition of vulnerability and dependence. Human infants and children "arrive in the world in a condition of needy helplessness more or less unparalleled in any other animal species" (Nussbaum, 2001, p. 181). Historically, Western ethics generally has ignored human vulnerability and its resultant consequence of creating a need for humans to depend on one another (MacIntyre, 1999). However, some feminist philosophers, such as Virginia Held (1993) and Sara Ruddick (1995), have used the underlying premise of human dependence as the foundation for their views of ethics. In fact, feminist philosophers have proposed that the caring that occurs between a mother and her vulnerable and dependent child can be used as a model for all moral relationships. This model is similar to the model of compassion discussed by the Dalai Lama.

In considering how a feminist approach to ethics is relevant to the care of infants and children, nurses can think in terms of what Tong (1997) called a care-focused feminist ethics approach. This type of approach to ethics supports the acceptance of feminine values that often have been marginalized in male-dominated societies, including "compassion, empathy, sympathy, nurturance, and kindness" (Tong, p. 38). These values and virtues also are ones that are traditionally associated with good mothering.

There have been heated debates about the differences between the types of moral reasoning engaged in by males and females (see Care-Based Versus Justice-Based Reasoning in Chapter 1). However, Stimpson (1993) noted that "crucially, both women and men can be feminists" (p. viii). In accepting and using the feminine model of social relationships that exists between mothers and children, Stimpson stated "a moral agent, female or male, will be [what Held (1993) called] a 'mothering person'" (p. viii).

Held (1993) proposed the concept of *mothering person* as a gender-neutral term used to describe the type of mothering that would occur in a society without male domination. Held stated that there are good reasons to believe that mothering should be a practice performed by both women and men. Ruddick (1995) defined a mother as one who is capable of doing maternal work and

> a person who takes on responsibility for children's lives and for whom providing child care is a significant part of her or his working life. [She continued] I am suggesting that, whatever difference might exist between female and male mothers, there is no reason to believe that one sex rather than the other is more capable of doing maternal work. (pp. 40–41)

In considering ethics involving the care of infants and children, nurses need to be interested in supporting mothers and mothering persons, both females and males, who share in the unconditional compassion toward their children as described by the Dalai Lama.

Ethical Reflections

- Engage in a debate with your colleagues using the following positions: (1) mothering *is* an inherently female trait and (2) mothering *is not* an inherently female trait.
- What can nurses do to include fathers in the "mothering" of children?
- Discuss the Dalai Lama's statement about compassion being similar "to the love a mother has for her only child." Why do you agree or disagree with this statement?

Foundations of Trust

"A boy bathing in a river was in danger of being drowned. He called out to a passing traveler for help, but instead of holding out a helping hand, the man stood by unconcernedly and scolded the boy for his imprudence. 'Oh sir!' cried the youth, 'pray help me now and scold me afterwards.'"

—AESOP, *AESOP'S FABLES*

"Children are vulnerable, often frightened small people" (Ruddick, 1995, p. 119). An infant's development of basic trust versus basic mistrust is the first of Erik Erikson's (1950/1985) eight stages of psychosocial development. According to Ruddick, it is the responsibility of mothers to establish the feeling of trust between themselves and their children, because children's trust is ideally founded upon the nurturance and protectiveness of their mothers. Unless there are unusual circumstances, parents are entrusted with the autonomy to make decisions for their minor children. This autonomy is an endorsement of the trust that societies place in parents' ability and desire to provide care that is consistent with the best interests of their children. Although parents generally have autonomy privileges in decision making for their children, children have their own basic dignity as human beings. Kahlil Gibran (1923/2000) described an interesting perspective on the soul, or spirit, of children and parental rights (see Box 6.1).

Because most children depend on their mothering persons to be trustworthy, mothering persons must be wary when they are judging health care policies and choosing the people involved with meeting their children's health care needs. Trust becomes an even greater issue when mothering people are not able to choose their children's health care providers, including nurses. Justified maternal wariness includes a cautious trust of nurses and other health care professionals who interact with and treat one's children. However, it is natural, and often a source of comfort, for parents to believe that health care professionals have a more complete grasp of the medical

BOX 6.1: HIGHLIGHTS FROM THE FIELD: GIBRAN "ON CHILDREN"

Your children are not your children. They are the sons and daughters of Life's longing for itself. They come through you but not from you, and though they are with you yet they belong not to you. You may give them your love but not your thoughts, for they have their own thoughts. You may house their bodies but not their souls, for their souls dwell in the house of tomorrow, which you cannot visit, not even in your dreams. You may strive to be like them, but seek not to make them like you. For life goes not backward nor tarries with yesterday. You are the bows from which your children as living arrows are sent forth. The archer sees the mark upon the path of the infinite, and He bends you with His might that His arrows may go swift and far. Let your bending in the archer's hand be for gladness; for even as He loves the arrow that flies so He loves also the bow that is stable. (pp. 17–18)

Gibran, K. (2000). *The prophet.* New York: Alfred A. Knopf. (Original work published 1923)

facts and probabilities related to their child's health care than they themselves have in many instances. Consequently, parents depend on and trust health care professionals to support or guide them in making difficult health care decisions for their children. Sometimes this trust is similar to the unavoidable trust that was discussed in "Nurse-Patient-Family Relationships" in Chapter 2.

Ethical Reflections

- With your colleagues use the Socratic Method discussed in Chapter 1 to analyze the concept of nurse-family trust.
- What factors and behaviors might influence mothering persons' trust of nurses who care for their children?
- What factors and behaviors might influence nurses' trust of mothering persons?
- Discuss the different forms of paternalism (see Chapter 2 and Chapter 10) as they relate to the ethical care of children.

Newborn Genetic Screening

Because there were no consistent or national guidelines, in 2002 the American College of Medical Genetics (ACMG) was commissioned by the U.S. Health Resources and Services Administration (HRSA) and the Maternal and Child Health Bureau (MCHB) to analyze evidence-based literature regarding newborn genetic screening. The ACMG published its report in 2005 recommending that 29 conditions be targeted as a core panel for newborn screening. Twenty-five other identifiable conditions also were recommended for screening. The March of Dimes (2007) has endorsed newborn screening for these 29 treatable disorders, which are grouped under five broad categories (see Box 6.2), as well as endorsing screening for the 25 other conditions for which there are good tests but possibly no evidence-based treatments. The March of Dimes also recommends that newborns be screened for hearing loss.

Historically there have been, and continue to be, substantial variations among states regarding mandatory newborn screening. According to discussions during sessions held by the President's Council on Bioethics (2006), there is no justifiable reason for this state-to-state variability. In fact, the whole U.S. program of newborn screening was referred to by ethicists as not being a rational system. As of 2006, only 6 states mandate testing for all 29 core conditions (District of Columbia, Iowa, Maryland, Mississippi,

BOX 6.2: HIGHLIGHTS FROM THE FIELD: RECOMMENDED SCREENING CATEGORIES

- Amino acid metabolism disorders
- Organic acid metabolism disorders
- Fatty acid oxidation disorders
- Hemoglobinopathies
- Others

March of Dimes Birth Defects Foundation. (2007). Recommended newborn screening tests: 29 disorders. Retrieved from http://www.marchofdimes.com/printableArticles/14332_15455.asp

New Jersey, and Virginia), 31 states screen for more than 20 of the conditions, 12 states screen for 10–20 of the conditions, and 8 states screen for fewer than 10 of the core conditions (March of Dimes, 2006). These deficiencies in screening requirements mean that only 1 million of the 4 million infants born yearly in the United States will receive the necessary screening (ZERO to THREE Policy Network, 2006).

Although congenital conditions are rare, many of them can be detected in newborns by a simple heel-stick blood test. If detected too late, the consequences of many of these conditions can be fatal; but if they are detected early, treatment is very successful. Unfortunately, the consequences of not performing comprehensive screening of newborns has sometimes produced tragic results (see Box 6.3). Ironically, all 29 of the screening tests together usually do not cost more than $100 to perform. Nurses must become active politically in working to have more comprehensive tests mandated by each state and in educating the public about this senseless health care disparity in newborn screening among different states.

Ethical Reflections

- After his death (see Box 6.3), Ben Haygood's parents were successful in getting the Mississippi legislature to pass two laws that increased the number of mandatory newborn screening tests performed in their state. Specifically, what grassroots actions by nurses can be used to influence state officials to mandate comprehensive newborn screening tests?
- Discuss state disparities and variations in newborn screening as they relate to each of the four bioethical principles: autonomy, beneficence, nonmaleficence, and justice.

BOX 6.3: HIGHLIGHTS FROM THE FIELD: A SIMPLE $25 TEST

Before Mississippi began mandating the full scope of newborn screening tests recommended by the March of Dimes, a tragic situation happened:

Ben Haygood seemed healthy. "I treated him like a normal kid," said his mother, Robin, 37. "Because that's what I thought he was." Then . . . checking on Ben at 1:30 [one] morning, she noticed that the toddler was, "I don't know how else to say it—very floppy," she says, "and his breathing was shallow. Something wasn't right." After a desperate 911 call, Ben was helicoptered to a medical center in nearby Tupelo. By then he had stopped breathing, and despite doctors' best efforts, "they never got him back," says Robin. "He died within 12 hours of showing symptoms.' . . . A month later it became almost unbearable when the Haygoods learned that their little boy's death—from a rare but treatable hereditary disease, MCADD . . . could have been prevented with a simple $25 blood test at birth.

Schindehette, S., Atlas, D., Podesta, J. S., Stambler, L., & Duffy, T. (2004, August 2). A simple test could have saved Ben's life. *People Magazine*, pp. 107–108.

Universal Vaccination

Because of the grave threat of nonpreventable infectious diseases, people living before and during the early 20th century would have been delighted to have a wide array of available vaccines. However, due to successful public health advances in the 20th and 21st centuries, many people in the United States have not personally encountered some of the old diseases that are now vaccine preventable. Therefore, many people take the importance of available vaccines for granted. According to the National Network for Immunization Information (NNii, 2007b)

most parents today have not seen a child paralyzed by polio, or choking to death from diphtheria, or brain damaged by measles. Fear of vaccine-preventable diseases has diminished while concerns about vaccine safety have increased—even though a number of the vaccines are even safer than decades ago as a result of medical research. (Para 3)

As with mandatory newborn screening tests, states vary in regard to mandatory childhood vaccination laws, sometimes called "school laws" (Centers for Disease Control [CDC], 2007). Every state allows vaccination exemptions for medical reasons. Medical exemptions are based on documented medical information received from physicians, usually related to a child's allergy to vaccine components or an immune deficiency. If parents have sincere religious beliefs that are contrary to the acceptance of immunizations for their children, religious exemptions are allowed by all states except Mississippi and West Virginia. Fifteen states allow exemptions for parents' non-religious, philosophical objections to vaccines.

When exemptions are obtained, children can attend school without immunizations in most states, although parents or guardians may be judged liable in a civil case if, because of their child's lack of immunization, a vaccine-preventable communicable disease is transmitted to another person. Also, if parents follow the CDC's (2007) recommended guidelines to protect unvaccinated children, these unprotected children may miss months of school. The CDC recommends that unvaccinated children remain at home during vaccine-preventable disease outbreaks, which may occur in waves spanning a number of weeks.

Some parents who are opposed to a program of universal vaccination seek ways to achieve natural immunity for their children. A popular method that is sometimes used to try to achieve natural immunity for children is having children attend "exposure parties." Groups of well and previously uninfected children are brought together with a child or children that are currently believed to be infectious with a specific vaccine-preventable disease, such as chickenpox, rubella, or measles (NNii, 2007a). However, these parties are not without risks to children, including the most obvious result of having one's child endure sometimes dangerous and unnecessary illnesses.

The American Nurses Association (ANA, 1997) has published a position statement regarding childhood immunization programs. A partial list established by the ANA in regard to the role of public health nurses in the immunization of children includes

- Developing strategies to remove patient, provider, and system barriers to care
- Educating individuals and communities about the importance of immunizations
- Designing outreach activities specifically aimed at hard-to-reach populations, such as those who are geographically, culturally, and socioeconomically at risk
- Fostering data collection that supports research-based practice (Para 5)

Box 6.4 contains nonconfrontational suggestions for health care professionals to use if parents resist immunizations for their children.

BOX 6.4: HIGHLIGHTS FROM THE FIELD: OVERCOMING VACCINATION RESISTANCE

- Ascertain exactly what is bothering the parent about vaccinations.
- Clearly state your recommendation and rationale.
- Voice your respect for the parent's views.
- Develop a mutually acceptable plan.
- If possible, administer vaccines that protect against the diseases for which the child is most at risk based on the child's age and immunization history, and the prevalence of the disease in your community.
- Be sure to repeat your recommendations when you subsequently see the child and parent; parents may reconsider their decisions.

Adapted from Dias, M., & Marcuse, E. K. (2000, July). When parents resist immunization. *Contemporary Pediatrics*, 1–4. Retrieved February 16, 2007 from http://www.immunizationinfo.org/assets/files/pdfs/6_ARTICLE.pdf

---

Ethical Reflections

- Review the ethical theories and approaches in Chapters 1 and 2. Which theories and approaches are particularly relevant to ethics and immunization issues and laws?
- Research some of the reasons that parents refuse immunizations for their children and gather specific information about "exposure parties." Imagine that you are a public health nurse working at a county health department. A mother brings her newborn in for a well-baby check-up. The baby's mother tells you that she has heard that "exposure parties" are a good way to immunize children. How would you respond to the mother's comment?

Children Underserved by the U.S. Health Care System

Children are particularly vulnerable people because they must depend on other people for their life-sustaining needs, including their health and well-being. Childhood vulnerability is heightened for some children because of conditions such as poverty and unfavorable social or family situations. Evidence suggests that health care professionals often do not adequately meet the nonmedical needs of vulnerable children (Barreto, Perez, & Halfon, 2007). Providers fail to inquire about family conditions such as homelessness, social problems, substance abuse, and poverty because they are unsure about resources that are available or believe that they have no way to help families solve these problematic issues. By failing to provide interventions to improve serious nonmedical problems during childhood, health care providers unintentionally may compound these problems, such as contributing to an increased risk of developmental delays, substance and physical abuse, and emotional disorders among children and their families.

According to research commissioned by the Robert Wood Johnson Foundation (2006), 8.4 million children in the United States are uninsured, though most of these children are eligible for Medicaid or State Children's Health Insurance Program (SCHIP) services. Health care providers must begin screening underserved children who are particularly vulnerable to "the 'double jeopardy' of childhood poverty" (Barreto, Perez, & Halfon, 2007, p. 174). A two-pronged assessment needs to be conducted that focuses on "the types and impacts of higher levels of exposure to risk factors as well as assessing available levels of resources and health services (protective and health-promoting factors)" (p. 174) for children affected by poverty.

Ethical practice in the nursing care of children must include nurses' willingness to address social problems that often are very difficult to solve. Social issues such as immigration, homelessness, and poverty continue to have a major impact on the health of children in the United States.

Children of Immigrant Families

According to the Center for Health and Health Care in Schools (2005), "one in five children in the United States lives in an immigrant family" (Para 1) and "the poverty rate of children in immigrant families is 21 percent" (Para 2). Because of welfare law changes in 1996, during their first 5 years in the United States, immigrants are not eligible to receive assistance from the Temporary Assistance to Needy Families (TANF) and Medicaid programs that serve the poor. Food stamp access also is restricted among immigrant families.

Children born in the United States to non-U.S. citizen immigrant mothers automatically are granted U.S. citizenship at birth; however, some governmental officials are critics of readily providing health care benefits to these so called "anchor babies" (babies that provide a reason for noncitizen parents to remain in the United States) (*Globe* Editorial, 2006). These critics have created federal policies that involve lengthy bureaucratic red tape that often prevents these infants from rapidly receiving Medicaid coverage for health care. Although these children are "known to" the Medicaid program because the program pays the hospital bills generated from their births, the government requires additional paperwork for continued Medicaid coverage. This additional paperwork often frightens parents who fear deportation.

Consequently, many of these so called "anchor babies," who are U.S. citizens and eligible for health care programs, do not receive immunizations and other primary and secondary preventive services. Ironically, creating barriers to early health care for these children often causes more taxpayer expense because money subsequently must be spent to treat preventable diseases. The American Academy of Pediatrics (1997) proposed 10 recommendations for pediatricians to help children of immigrant families. These recommendations, which also are useful for nurses, are shown in Box 6.5.

Global Problems of Poverty and Infectious Diseases

Almost 40% of the global population is composed of vulnerable children and adolescents (World Health Organization [WHO], 2005). It is startling that the health problems of children and adolescents "account for over 50% of the gap in health equity between the world's richest and poorest people" (Para 2). Statistical data regarding the unmet needs of infants, children, and adolescents worldwide should concern all compassionate people, but especially nurses. Of special significance is the fact that most of the deaths accounted for in these statistics are the result of diseases for which there is prevention or treatment. Data provided by the WHO include the following:

- Every minute 20 children under 5 years old die, leading to over 10.6 million deaths a year.
- Over 1 million children die each year—and millions more suffer from diarrhea and acute respiratory infections—due to inappropriate breastfeeding.
- Sixty-six percent of child deaths each year are caused by diarrhea, acute respiratory infections, measles, malaria, and perinatal illnesses.
- Fifty-three percent of childhood deaths are associated with malnutrition, as a direct or indirect cause.
- AIDS now accounts for 3% of deaths in children under 5 years old worldwide— and for 6% in the WHO Africa region, where AIDS has become one of the biggest killers of young children and accounts for up to 57% of child deaths in the most affected countries. (Para 3)

BOX 6.5: HIGHLIGHTS FROM THE FIELD: RECOMMENDATIONS FOR CHILDREN OF IMMIGRANT FAMILIES

1. Oppose denying needed services to any child residing within the borders of the United States.

2. Take advantage of educational opportunities and resources to achieve a better understanding of immigrant cultures and the health care needs of immigrant children and families.

3. Tolerate and respect cultural differences in attitudes and approaches to child-rearing.

4. Be aware of the special health problems for which immigrant children are at risk, such as vaccine-preventable diseases, tuberculosis, syphilis, and parasitic diseases; poor nutritional status, delayed growth and development; poor dental health; poor mental health; and school problems.

5. Be educated about the unique stresses that immigration may place on children and families and about resources that provide services in the family's language.

6. Recognize and support the extended family in health care activities with the approval of the child's parent or legal guardian..

7. Follow up with continuing health supervision, mental health, and social services for any screening received by immigrants and refugees before they entered the United States.

8. Develop linguistically and culturally appropriate services in concert with public health, social services, and school systems in local communities.

9. Define the health care needs of immigrant children.

10. Support and participate in locally developed, community-based activities that increase access to health care for immigrant children. (pp. 155–156)

Adapted from American Academy of Pediatrics Committee on Community Health Services. (1997). Health care for children of immigrant families. *Pediatrics, 100,* 153–156.

Ethical Reflections

- Consider problems of global poverty and infectious diseases as they affect children and relate to social justice.
- What is social justice? What can nurses do to affect social justice and the world's population of children?
- Do you believe that many members of the world population avert their eyes from the health care plight of innocent children? Support your answer.
- Review critical theory in Chapter 1. Read additional literature, as needed. How can critical theory be applied to the worldwide health care disparities involving children?
- What other ethical theories and approaches discussed in Chapters 1 and 2 apply to the worldwide disparities in health care for children? Explain.

Abused Children

Child abuse, which includes physical, sexual, and emotional abuse, as well as neglect, is a form of family violence (Ramsey, 2006). Family violence is an "action by a family member with the intent to cause harm to or control another family member" (Allender & Spradley, 2005, p. 908). The most common form of child abuse falls under the category of neglect (Ramsey). Although all states have mandatory child abuse reporting laws, it is believed that abuse is significantly underreported.

The ethical responsibility of nurses in the care of children includes the responsibility to be alert to the signs of abuse and to report abuse appropriately. Nurses, along with all other health care professionals, are considered mandatory reporters of possible abuse (Ramsey, 2006). Situations that signal possible abuse include

- Conflict between the explanation of how an incident occurred and the physical findings, such as poorly explained bruises or fractures
- Age-inappropriate behaviors or behaviors that signify poor social adjustment, such as "aggressive behavior, social withdrawal, depression, lying, stealing, thumb sucking" (Ramsey, 2006, p. 59), and risk-taking (i.e., sexual promiscuity, reckless driving, etc.)
- Alcohol and other drug abuse
- Problems in school
- Suicidal ideation

The usual responsibility of handling a patient's treatment confidentially is waived in the instance of suspected child abuse, even when the person reporting the abuse is the patient (Ramsey, 2006). Abuse does not need to be confirmed as factual in order to be reportable. The identification of suspected abuse should be promptly reported to the agency designated by each state. There is legal protection in most states for professionals, including nurses, who are reporting suspected abuse in good faith. However, health care professionals may be exposed to legal sanctions if they fail to report suspected abuse to the appropriate agencies.

Surrogate Decision Making

Children are legally incompetent individuals who, in most cases, must have surrogate decision makers for important life decisions, including health care decisions. Ethicists have established standards that are accepted as being ethically appropriate for guiding health care decisions made on behalf of infants and children. The most commonly accepted ethical standard that underlies surrogate decision making for children is based on a **standard of best interest**. When using the best interest standard, surrogate decision makers base their decisions on what they believe will provide the most benefits and the least burdens for the child. The best interest standard is a quality-of-life assessment, and when using it

a surrogate decision maker must determine the highest net benefit among the available options, assigning different weights to interest the patient has in each option and discounting or subtracting inherent risks or costs. The best interest standard protects another's well-being by assessing risks and benefits of various treatments and alternatives to treatment, by considering the pain and suffering, and by evaluating restoration or loss of functioning. (Beauchamp & Childress, 2001, p. 102)

The standard of best interest is similar to the standard of substituted judgment, but the two standards are distinctly different. The aim of the **standard of substituted judgment** is for a surrogate to make decisions that abide by the previously known (either verbalized or inferred) treatment preferences that persons had when they were able to express those preferences (that is, when they were competent) at a time when persons are no longer able to express treatment preferences (that is, when they are no longer competent). Thus, some ethicists argue that only a standard of best interest is appropriate when decisions are made for children because decisions are being made for persons who have never been legally competent; consequently, there is no history of known preferences from children based on their competent thinking.

In using the best interest standard, parents must sacrifice their personal goals for their child in favor of the child's needs and interests. Parents are put in a difficult situation when they must be uncompromising in trying to attend to one child's best interest when it may conflict with the best interest of another child or children within the same family (Ross, 1998).

Refusal of Treatment

Parents sometimes refuse treatment for their children, and children themselves may, in some cases, be deemed to have decisional capacity to refuse treatment based on religious beliefs or other reasons. In general, religious and cultural beliefs are given respect in health care matters and are protected through liberties granted by the U.S. Constitution (Jonsen, Siegler, & Winslade, 2006). Serious consideration must be given to the wishes of maturing children who are judged to have good insight about the benefits and burdens of their health care treatment. The following factors should be taken into consideration and carefully weighed when evaluating the extent of autonomy to be granted to minor children in refusing health care, keeping in mind, however, that efforts need to be made not to undermine the relationship between a child and their mothering person(s) (Jonsen et al., 2002).

- The support of the child's request by the child's mothering person(s)
- The severity of the child's condition, such as a child with a terminal and irreversible condition who refuses additional painful treatment versus a situation such as meningitis in which the child's condition is acute and reversible
- The consequence of direct harm to the child that potentially could result from the child's decision and the child's realistic understanding of the possible consequences
- Fear, distress, or parental pressure as a motivation for the child's decision

Parental autonomy with regard to a child's health care treatment is usually given wide latitude (Jonsen et al., 2006; Ross, 1998); however, some parental refusals are considered to be abusive or neglectful. State laws protect children from parental health care decisions based on religious or other beliefs that can result in serious risk or harm to the child (Jonsen et al.). Nevertheless, many states do not prosecute parents for abuse or neglect if they try to refuse treatment based on religious beliefs. In general,

BOX 6.6: HIGHLIGHTS FROM THE FIELD: PROTECTION OF VULNERABLE CHILDREN

In the words of a Supreme Court decision about the authority of a Jehovah's Witness parent, "Parents may be free to become martyrs themselves, but it does not follow that they are free . . . to make martyrs of their children" (*Prince v. Massachusetts*, 1944).

Jonsen, A. R., Siegler, M., & Winslade, W. J. (2006). *Clinical ethics: A practical approach to ethical decisions in clinical medicine* (6th ed.). New York: McGraw-Hill, p. 98.

the following principles are followed in overriding parental autonomy in the treatment of children:

- The parent or parents are not given the right of parental autonomy if they are deemed to be incapacitated or incompetent because of factors such as substance abuse, certain psychiatric disorders, minimal ability to comprehend the best interest of the child, or habitual physical abuse.
- As is done when considering respect for the autonomy of a child, the severity of the child's condition and the direct harm to the child that could result from nontreatment should be evaluated. The child should be treated even against the wishes of the parents to prevent or cure serious disease or disability.
- Blood transfusions should be given to a child of a Jehovah's Witness when transfusions are needed to protect the child from the serious complications of disease or injury. Court authority need not be sought in an emergency situation; legal precedent protects the safety of the child (see Box 6.6).

When analyzing the ethical path to take in regard to refusals of treatment for children, consultation may need to be sought from mental health practitioners or an ethics committee.

Impaired and Critically Ill Children

When neonatal intensive care units (NICUs) were developed in the 1960s, the goal was to increase the likelihood that premature babies would survive. Many medical and technological advances followed, and researchers are still making great strides in neonatology today. NICUs are often complicated and scary places for parents who are grappling with the trauma of having a severely impaired or terminally ill neonate. Parents frequently must make life and death decisions about their infants within a context that would be highly stressful even in the best of circumstances. NICUs are often scary and emotionally charged places for nurses, too, as they watch the miracles of life play out before them while they also share in the experience of a family's deepest suffering.

Ethical Reflections

- Identify specific issues of social justice related to the high-technology health care provided to premature infants. What information and approaches can be used to analyze the ethics of decision making about age-based distribution of health care resources?
- How should scarce health care resources be used? For technologically advanced intensive care services for the very young? For technologically advanced intensive care services for the very old? For prevention and health promotion? Support your position(s).
- Who should decide about how scarce health care resources should be distributed? Why?

Quality of Life

In considering quality-of-life determinations for newborns and children, it is important to refer back to the ethical foundation involved with surrogate decision making for children, that is, the standard of best interest. There are at least two differences between how quality-of-life decisions are judged for infants and children as opposed to how they are judged for adults (Jonsen et al., 2006). Adults are either able to verbalize preferences that reflect their personal evaluations about the quality of their lives or other people have a general idea of those preferences when an adult becomes incapacitated. In contrast, "[i]n pediatrics, the life whose quality is being assessed is almost entirely in the future, and no expression of preferences is available" (p. 119).

Health care professionals must be aware of any tendencies they may have to judge the quality of life of pediatric patients as lower than the children, to the best of their ability, or their mothering person(s) would judge it. Nurses are not in a position to make major, ethics-laden treatment decisions in the care of infants and children. Even advanced-practice nurses, such as nurse practitioners who work in NICUs, work in collaboration with other health care professionals. However, all nurses who work with children are potentially very influential in the health care decisions made by parents and other health care providers. Practical wisdom in the tradition of Socrates, Plato, and Aristotle and the good character of nurses are essential elements in the compassionate care of children.

─────────────── **Ethical Reflections** ───────────────

- Discuss criteria and methods that health care providers can use to evaluate the motives, requests, and behaviors of mothering persons in regard to making quality-of-life decisions for their seriously impaired children. Use the story of Ashley in Box 6.7 as a Case Study. Ashley's parents asked physicians to stunt her growth so that her small size would make it easier for them to physically care for her.
  - Apply ethical theories, approaches, and decision-making models in analyzing this case.
  - Do you agree or disagree with the child receiving hormones to stop her growth? Support your answer.
  - Another parent-child ethics case that has been widely debated in the media is the case of Terri Schiavo. Research the specific events of this case.
    - Because Terri was an adult rather than a legally incompetent child, compare and contrast relevant quality-of-life determinations.
    - Evaluate the ethics-related parent-child issues involved with this case. What type of decision-making standard were Terri's parents using?
    - What is the standard that is most accepted by ethicists in a case like Terri's? Why?

Withholding and Withdrawing Treatment

A comprehensive discussion of end-of-life issues is provided in Chapter 12. This discussion generally can be used as a basis for considering decisions about withholding and withdrawing treatment for children. Infants, however, fall into a special class of persons in regard to withholding and withdrawing treatment.

Anyone seriously interested in the study of nursing and health care ethics realizes that it is difficult to separate ethics from related laws, governmental regulations, and public policies. In evaluating the ethical care of infants in terms of withholding and withdrawing treatment, it is helpful to understand the history and circumstances involved with several landmark cases. Some of these cases help to summarize and clarify the usual actions that are expected to be taken with regard to the treatment of infants, although conclusions about the ethical directions provided by these cases are by no means without dispute. The following discussion is based on public information about these cases and a history provided by Pence (2004).

**BOX 6.7: HIGHLIGHTS FROM THE FIELD:
"PILLOW ANGEL"**

The father's plea was heartfelt and most unusual. Stop the physical growth of my developmentally disabled little girl [with static encephalopathy], he asked a panel of doctors, so that we may be better able to care for her as years go by.

Strapped in a wheelchair, the daughter, a charming dark-haired 6-year-old named Ashley . . . "There's no question this little girl's world is her family," says a doctor who attended that session. "Any concerns were put to rest by watching [the parents and the child]." Which is one reason the medical staff at Seattle's Children's Hospital agreed to the father's 2004 request, deciding that it was ethical to remove Ashley's uterus and breast buds and begin hormone treatments to stop her growth.

Today Ashley is a 9-year-old girl with the mind of a baby, who will never grow into a fully developed woman. Her family . . . initially kept their decision private. But an article published in a medical journal [in October 2006] brought an outcry of public criticism about their choice. . . . For doctors, stopping Ashley's growth presented two issues: Would the novel treatment improve her life? And would it cause harm?

[As cited by Morehouse, Ashley's parents shared the following statements on their website:]

We call [Ashley] our Pillow Angel since she is so sweet and stays right where we place her—usually on a pillow. . . .

Morehouse, M. (2007, January). Girl, interrupted. *People*, 69–70.

1971 Johns Hopkins Cases

In the 1970s, two infants with Down syndrome were "allowed to die" at Johns Hopkins Hospital, based on what some people believe were the selfish motives of the parents (Pence, 2004). A third infant with Down syndrome was referred to Johns Hopkins shortly thereafter because of the hospital's reputation for allowing the other two infants to die. However, at this point the hospital staff presented a more balanced view of the infant's prognosis that resulted in a different outcome: the third baby was treated and lived.

1984 Child Abuse Prevention and Treatment Act Amendments (Baby Doe Rules)

The 1984 Child Abuse Prevention and Treatment Act Amendments, also referred to as the Baby Doe rules, are based on the case of Infant Doe who was born in Indiana in 1982. "'Baby Doe' cases arise when parents of impaired neonates or physicians charged with the care of these neonates question whether continued treatment is worthwhile and consider forgoing treatment in order to hasten death" (Pence, 2004, p. 216).

Many events happened during the short life of Infant Doe that greatly influenced the precedent that has set the direction for the treatment of impaired newborns. Infant Doe was born on April 9, 1982, and died 6 days later in Indiana (Pence, 2004). The controversy surrounding the care of Infant Doe was based on disagreements about whether treatment should be withheld because the infant had Down syndrome and a tracheo-esophageal fistula. The obstetrician who delivered Infant Doe discouraged the parents from seeking surgical correction of the fistula and indicated that the baby might become a "mere blob." Based on the obstetrician's recommendations and their own beliefs, the parents refused care for their infant. Hospital staff and administrators disagreed with this decision and appealed the decision to a county judge. No guardian ad litem was appointed for the baby, and an unrecorded, middle-of-the-night hearing was conducted by the judge at the hospital. The meeting resulted in the judge's support of the parents' decision. The hospital staff appealed the decision unsuccessfully all the way to the Indiana Supreme Court. They were in the process of taking the case to the U.S. Supreme Court when Infant Doe died.

The specific details of what followed these events are interesting but are beyond the scope of this chapter. However, the ultimate outcome was that the media attention given to the Infant Doe case precipitated action by the Reagan administration, specifically the U.S. Justice Department and the U.S. Department of Health and Human Services (DHHS) (Pence, 2004). Baby Doe rules were published by the federal government and became effective on February 12, 1984. The rules were based on Section 504 of the Rehabilitation Act of 1973, which forbids discrimination based entirely on a person's handicaps. The Baby Doe rules provide for a curtailment of federal funds to institutions that violate the regulations.

According to Pence (2004), "this interpretation by the Justice Department created a new conceptual synthesis: imperiled newborns were said to be handicapped citizens who could suffer discrimination against their civil rights" (p. 221; see Box 6.8) It is noteworthy that the federal Second Circuit Court of Appeals issued a ruling within 10 days of the Baby Doe rules that made the new rules essentially unenforceable. This ruling was based on the case of Baby Jane Doe.

BOX 6.8: HIGHLIGHTS FROM THE FIELD: THE CASE OF INFANT DOE

The U.S. Civil Rights Commission reviewed the Infant Doe case in 1989, along with other Baby Doe cases, and "the commission concluded that [the obstetrician's] evaluation was 'strikingly out of touch with the contemporary evidence on the capabilities of people with Down syndrome.'"

U.S. Commission on Civil Rights, as cited by Pence, G. 2004. *Classic cases in medical ethics* (p. 220). Boston: McGraw-Hill.

Baby Jane Doe: Kerri-Lynn

Baby Jane Doe, Kerri-Lynn A., was born in 1983 at St. Charles Hospital in Long Island, New York. She was transferred to the NICU at the University Hospital of the State University of New York (SUNY) at Stony Brook because of her complicated condition at birth. Kerri-Lynn was born with spina bifida, hydrocephalus, an impaired kidney, and microcephaly (Pence, 2004). Her parents were lower middle-class people who had been married for only 4 months when Kerri-Lynn was conceived. After Kerri-Lynn was born, there was disagreement among the medical staff and other people about whether or not she should be treated or provided with comfort measures (food, hydration, and antibiotics) and allowed to die. The parents decided in favor of withholding aggressive treatment.

The controversy resulted in legal proceedings that eventually included the involvement of the Justice Department and the DHHS. Leaders within these agencies wanted to send representatives to review Kerri-Lynn's medical records to ascertain whether the Baby Doe rules were being violated. However, the parents and the hospital objected to allowing the government representatives to review the records. Ultimately, a federal appeals court, and then the U.S. Supreme Court, ruled in favor of the parents and the hospital in the case of *Bowen v. American Hospital Association et al.* in 1986 (Pence, 2004).

This ruling essentially removed the enforcement potential from the Baby Doe rules. The rules cannot be enforced if the government has no authority to review the individual medical records of infants to determine if the rules are being violated. The Supreme Court explained that because the parents do not receive federal funds for the provision of medical care, their decisions are not bound by Section 504 of

BOX 6.9: HIGHLIGHTS FROM THE FIELD: THE CASE OF KERRI-LYNN

In 1994, B. D. Colen was Lecturer in Social Medicine at Harvard University. He provided an update on Kerri-Lynn:

Now a 10 year old . . . Baby Jane Doe is not only a self-aware little girl, who experiences and returns the love of her parents; she also attends a school for developmentally disabled children—once again proving that medicine is an art, not a science, and clinical decision making is best left in the clinic, to those who will have to live with the decision being made.

Pence, G. (2004). *Classic cases in medical ethics* (p. 226). Boston: McGraw-Hill.

the Rehabilitation Act (Pence, 2004). Baby Jane Doe's parents later allowed the recommended surgery to be performed (see Box 6.9). The attorney who had represented her parents reported in 1998 that Kerri-Lynn was 15 years old and living with her parents.

Although "in reality [the Baby Doe regulation] does not apply directly to physicians, nurses, or parents, it does get the attention of many" (Carter & Leuthner, 2003, p. 484). The 1984 Child Abuse Prevention and Treatment Act (Baby Doe rules) generally provides three reasons to withhold treatment from newborns. Confusion remains, however, about whether or not the rules are an attempt to mandate nutrition, hydration, and medications for all neonates. This confusion, in addition to the compassion that most people feel toward a dying or severely impaired child, is one reason that health care professionals experience moral uncertainty and moral suffering in relation to decisions about withholding and withdrawing treatment from neonates. The 1984 act states:

The term "withholding of medically indicated treatment" does not include the failure to provide treatment (other than *appropriate* nutrition, hydration, or medication) to an infant when, in the treating physician's . . . reasonable medical judgment:
1. the infant is chronically and irreversibly comatose,
2. the provision of such treatment would
   a) merely prolong dying,
   b) not be effective in ameliorating or correcting all of the infant's life-threatening conditions,
or
   c) otherwise be futile in terms of the survival of the infant, or

3. the provision of such treatment would be virtually futile in terms of the survival of the infant and the treatment itself under such circumstances would be inhumane. (U.S. Child Protection and Treatment Act of 1984 [italics added] as cited by Carter & Leuthner, 2003, p. 484)

According to Carter and Leuthner (2003), the language in these rules that addresses situations in which aggressive treatment of infants is not required can be interpreted to mean two different things with regard to nutrition: "(1) every infant should always be provided with medical means of nutrition [or] (2) every infant should receive nutrition appropriate for his/her medical situation" (p. 484).

Carter and Leuthner have proposed that the Baby Doe rules should not be interpreted to restrict or prevent the withdrawal of nutrition. However, interpretations of the rules with regard to withholding and withdrawing nutrition, hydration, and medications vary among health care providers and institutions, and, as mentioned previously, health care providers experience moral uncertainty regarding these rules. When situations arise that precipitate discussions about withholding and withdrawing nutrition and hydration from newborns, the involvement of an ethics committee is recommended. It also may be helpful for health care professionals serving on an ethics committee to obtain consultation from ethicists who specialize in pediatric care.

1993: In the Matter of Baby K

Although the Baby Doe rules provided a basis for the right of parents to refuse treatment for their severely disabled newborns, the ruling left the unanswered question of whether parents also have the right to insist on treatment for their newborns when medical staff believe the treatment would be futile or useless. The landmark case that provided a precedent for this type of situation involved Baby K, born with anencephaly in 1992. Baby K's mother insisted that a hospital provide maximum treatment for her child, including ventilator support. Hospital physicians disagreed with the mother's wishes and proposed that warmth, nutrition, and hydration were all that should be required in Baby K's care. The case was taken to the legal system for resolution. In reviewing this case, judges noted that medical assessments indicated that Baby K was not being subjected to care requested by her mother that would cause the baby pain or suffering. Judges serving on the U.S. Court of Appeals for the Fourth Circuit ruled in favor of the mother and ordered the hospital to provide the level of care that Baby K's mother requested (*In the Matter of Baby "K,"* 1993).

The Influence of Nurses

Those who stand for nothing, fall for anything.

—ALEXANDER HAMILTON

Advocacy

The role of nurse advocate is not age or population limited. When nurses enter the nursing profession, they are in essence agreeing to a social contract with the public that is outlined in *Nursing's Social Policy Statement* (ANA, 2003). When they become nursing professionals, nurses also need to agree to adhere to the scope and standards contained in the document *Nursing: Scope and Standards of Practice* (ANA, 2004) and the *Code of Ethics for Nurses* (ANA, 2001). Threaded throughout these ANA documents is the underlying premise that the well-being of their patients should be the primary concern of nurses. A statement contained in the ANA's *Scope and Standards* booklet that uses information taken from the *Social Policy Statement* is applicable to nursing advocacy for all patients, including the youngest among them and their families:

Patients give nurses permission to enter their lives and share their most intimate life experiences. Registered nurses remain in nursing to promote, advocate for, and strive to protect the health, safety, and rights of those patients, families, communities and populations. Registered nurses value their role as advocates in dealing with barriers encountered in obtaining health care. Similarly, society values nursing care that resolves problems or manages health-promoting behaviors. (p. 17)

Ethical Reflections

- Because, among other reasons, people normally expect that children will outlive their parents, it often is difficult for both health care professionals and parents to clearly identify when the burdens of technologically advanced treatments are outweighing benefits in the treatment of terminally ill children. Conduct a literature review about palliative care for children. Discuss as many aspects as you can about nurses' roles in regard to the following issues:
  - Talking with families about curative versus palliative care for children
  - Talking with children about their terminal illnesses
  - End-of-life decision making for children
  - Respect for the dignity of a child and family

- Nontraditional or nonmedical therapies that may enhance quality of life for children, such as music therapy, pet therapy, and the like.
- The emotions of impaired or terminally ill children and their parents, such as anger, fear, isolation, guilt, denial, despondency
- Nurses sometimes feel moral distress or suffering when they believe that they are providing care that is not beneficial to a patient, that is, medically futile care. In cases of medical futility, nurses often are advocates for patients and families and serve in an "in-between" role with families and health care providers.
  - What types of emotions and issues might result for the nurse personally when feelings of moral distress or suffering arise?
  - What types of problems might occur among a group of nurses working together who are feeling this type of distress and suffering?
  - What type of positive actions and behaviors would you suggest for nurses to manage this type of distress and suffering?

Character

The good character or virtuous behavior of nurses, other health care professionals, and parents is not the only character that is relevant to the well-being of children. A child's own character development is important, too. School nurses are in a special position to help with this, and any nurse who works with children would do well to keep in mind the importance of influencing the development of a child's good character and educating others about this development. Ryan and Bohlin (1999) suggested that children need to be engaged in "heart, mind, and head" to know "who [they] are" and "what [they] stand for" (pp. xvi–xvii).

The search for the meaning of life overshadows almost all human endeavors in people young and old. In the fast-paced world of the 21st century, parents are busy trying to provide their families with necessities and physical comforts, and children are often busy playing video games and watching television. There is scarcely time to ponder the greater mysteries of life. Ryan and Bohlin (1999) proposed that "detached from a conception of the purpose of life, virtues become merely nice ideals, empty of meaning" (p. 39). They suggested that adults should not fear stimulating children to ponder the age-old question about why they were born. All children, but particularly children who are ill, think about the meaning of life even when they do not know how to articulate their feelings. Nurses can provide these children with a kind hand and a warm heart during frightening times.

Almost any time is a good time to take the opportunity to educate children in the development of moral and intellectual virtues. As the old saying goes, "it is never too early." Stenson (1999) proposed that there are three ways to help children internalize virtuous habits and strengths of character when they are on their journey from infancy to adulthood. Those three means of internalization, and the order in which they occur, are

1. *By example:* Children learn from what they witness in the lives of parents and other adults they respect (and thus unconsciously imitate).
2. *Through directed practice:* Children learn from what they are repeatedly led to do or are made to do by parents and other respected adults.
3. *From words:* Children learn from what they hear from parents and other respected adults as explanations for what they witness and are led to do. (p. 207)

Nurses are patient advocates, but they also are role models. Nurses may never know when the example that they show to children and their mothering person(s) may influence the future of a child or may influence the future of nursing.

─────────── **Ethical Reflections** ───────────

- Box 6.10 contains examples from the ANA's (2001) *Code of Ethics for Nurses with Interpretive Statements.* How are these examples relevant to nursing ethics in the care of infants and children?
- What other provisions and statements in the ANA's *Code of Ethics for Nurses* are particularly pertinent to the nursing care of infants and children (See Appendix A)? Discuss these provisions and provide examples of how they apply to nursing practice.

Web Ethics

National Network for Immunization Information
  www.immunizationinfo.org
March of Dimes
  www.modimes.org
Newborn Screening by States
  http://www.marchofdimes.com/peristats/pdfdocs/nbs2006.pdf

Box 6.10: Highlights from the Field: *Code of Ethics for Nurses*

- Nursing care is directed toward meeting the comprehensive needs of patients and their families across the continuum of care (1.3, p. 7).
- Prior to implementation, all research should be approved by a qualified review board to ensure patient protection and the ethical integrity of the research (3.3, p. 13).
- Nurses have the duty to question and, if necessary, to report and to refuse to participate in research they deem morally objectionable (3.3, p. 13).
- Nurses are faced with decisions in the context of the increased complexity and changing patterns in the delivery of health care (4.1, p. 16).

National Newborn Screening Status Report
  http://genes-r-us.uthscsa.edu/nbsdisorders.pdf
Prevent Child Abuse America
  www.preventchildabuse.org
Character Counts
  www.charactercounts.org

Summary

In the United States and worldwide, infants and children are subjected to health care disparities and decisions about which they have little to no control. In accepting the status of professional nursing, nurses must act as advocates for infants and children. This advocacy role includes being alert to and knowledgeable about the social needs of children that affect their well-being. Because of the differences involved with the ethical care of children as compared with adults, it is incumbent upon conscientious nurses to understand these differences. Though it is generally known that many people care for and about children, children still are a vulnerable population that depend on the compassionate care of nurses.

Key Points

- The words *mother* and *mothering person* can be gender neutral.
- The best-interest standard is generally the ethical approach used in making difficult decisions about the health care treatment of children.
- Newborn genetic screening requirements vary among states, sometimes causing crucial health care disparities.
- Children and other people may be harmed when children are not immunized. Nurses must understand the best ways to interact with parents who refuse to have their children immunized.
- Ethical practice in the nursing care of children needs to include nurses' willingness to address social problems such as those resulting from immigration, homelessness, and poverty that often are very difficult to solve.
- Globally, many children become sick annually and die from preventable diseases and conditions.
- Nurses are "mandatory reporters" of child abuse. There is legal protection in most states for nurses who are reporting suspected child abuse in good faith.
- The ethics of allowing children themselves or their parents to refuse health care treatments is based on a number of factors. These factors include the severity of the potential harm to the child that may result from the refusal.
- The Child Abuse Amendments of 1984 are frequently referred to as the Baby Doe rules. Although these rules lack power in actual enforcement, they are influential in decisions regarding the withholding and withdrawing of supportive care involving infants.

CASE STUDY: TO FEED OR NOT TO FEED?

Baby S is a neonate admitted to the NICU at the county hospital where you work as the nurse manager. Mrs. S had an amniotic fluid embolus during her delivery, and Baby S experienced anoxia. Consequently, Baby S had an Apgar score of 0 at birth. The baby was "successfully" resuscitated but remains unconscious. All of the baby's organs experienced hypoxic insult. Baby S was placed on a ventilator and parenteral nutrition was later initiated. Mrs. S is physically very weak and

(continues)

CASE STUDY: TO FEED OR NOT TO FEED? (continued)

experiencing extreme grief, along with her husband, over the condition of their infant. They have two other young children, ages 2 and 5 years old. Baby S has been weaned from the ventilator but has remained unresponsive. Mr. and Mrs. S have requested that the hospital staff discontinue their infant's nutrition and hydration. The NICU medical, nursing, and social work staff have not previously experienced a situation quite like the one that is occurring with the S family.

Case Study Questions

1. You are meeting with the neonatologists, the NICU charge nurse, the infant's primary nurse, the hospital chaplain, and the social worker in the NICU. What do you contribute to the group's discussion with regard to how you believe the staff should proceed in providing the best care for Baby S and her family?

2. How do the Baby Doe rules affect this case?

3. One of the staff RNs comments, "I think the mother and father are being selfish about their request to withdraw nutrition from Baby S. I think it is because they don't want to be bothered with taking care of her at home." How do you address these comments?

4. What surrogate decision-making standard should be used in this case? What influence should the interests of Baby S's siblings have in decision making in this case?

5. Caring for Baby S and interacting with her family has caused a great deal of emotional and moral suffering for the NICU nursing staff (see "Moral Suffering in Nursing" in Chapter 2). What behaviors might you expect to observe among the nursing staff? What do you do as the nurse manager to address this situation?

6. As would be expected, Mr. and Mrs. S also are experiencing a great deal of emotional and moral suffering and grief. How would you handle your personal interactions with Mr. and Mrs. S, and what would you do to help educate your staff in working with families in a situation such as this one? What do you know about the grief that parents experience when their infant is extremely impaired or dies? How would you try to help Mr. and Mrs. S?

References

Allender, J. A., & Spradley, B. W. (2005). *Community health nursing: Promoting and protecting the public's health* (6th ed.). Philadelphia: Lippincott Williams & Wilkins.

American Academy of Pediatrics Committee on Community Health Services. (1997). Health care for children of immigrant families. *Pediatrics, 100*, 153–156. Retrieved February 18, 2007, from http://pediatrics.aappublications.org/cgi/content/full/100/1/153

American College of Medical Genetics. (2005, March 8). Newborn screening: Toward a uniform screening panel and system. Final report. Retrieved February 16, 2007 from ftp://ftp.hrsa.gov/mchb/genetics/screeningdraftforcomment.pdf

American Nurses Association. (1997). Position statement: Childhood immunizations. Retrieved July 30, 2007 from http://nursingworld.org/readroom/position/social/scimmu.htm

American Nurses Association. (2001). *Code of ethics for nurses with interpretive statements.* Silver Spring, MD: Author.

American Nurses Association. (2003). *Nursing's social policy statement* (2nd ed.). Silver Spring, MD: Author.

American Nurses Association. (2004). *Nursing: Scope and standards of practice.* Silver Spring, MD: Author.

Barreto, P., Perez, V. H., & Halfon, N. (2007). Underserved children: Preventing chronic illness and promoting health. In T. E. King & M. B. Wheeler (Eds.), *Medical management of vulnerable and underserved patients: Principles, practice, and populations* (pp. 169–178). New York: McGraw-Hill.

Beauchamp, T. L., & Childress, J. F. (2001). *Principles of biomedical ethics* (5th ed.). New York: Oxford.

Carter, B. S., & Leuthner, S. R. (2003). The ethics of withholding/withdrawing nutrition in the newborn. *Seminars in Perinatology, 27*(6), 480–487.

Center for Health and Health Care in Schools. (2005, February 25). InFocus: An in-depth analysis of emerging issues in health in schools. Retrieved February 16, 2007 from http://www.healthinschools.org/focus/2005/no1.htm

Centers for Disease Control and Prevention. (2007, February 16). National Vaccine Program Office: Immunization laws. Retrieved February 16, 2007 from http://www.hhs.gov/nvpo/law.htm

Dalai Lama. (1999). *Ethics for the new millennium.* New York: Riverhead Books.

Dias, M., & Marcuse, E. K. (2000, July). When parents resist immunization. *Contemporary Pediatrics,* 1–4. Retrieved February 16, 2007 from http://www.immunizationinfo.org/assets/files/pdfs/6_ARTICLE.pdf

Erikson, E. H. (1985). *Childhood and society* (35th ed.). New York: W. W. Norton. (Original work published 1950)

Gibran, K. (2000). *The prophet.* New York: Alfred A. Knopf. (Original work published 1923)

Globe editorial: Blaming the babies. (2006, November 11). *The Boston Globe.* Retrieved February 18, 2007 from http://www.boston.com/news/globe/editorial_opinion/editorials/articles/2006/11/11/blaming_the_babies/

Held, V. (1993). *Feminist morality: Transforming culture, society, and politics.* Chicago: University of Chicago.

In the matter of Baby "K". 832 F. Supp. 1022 (E.D. Va. 1993).

Jonsen, A. R., Siegler, M., & Winslade, W. J. (2006). *Clinical ethics: A practical approach to ethical decisions in clinical medicine* (6th ed.). New York: McGraw-Hill.

MacIntyre, A. (1999). *Dependent rational animals: Why human beings need the virtues.* Chicago: Open Court.

March of Dimes Birth Defects Foundation. (2006). Newborn screening tests by U.S. states, 2006. Retrieved July 30, 2007 from http://www.marchofdimes.com/peristats/pdfdocs/nbs2006.pdf

March of Dimes Birth Defects Foundation. (2007). Recommended newborn screening tests: 29 disorders. Retrieved February 16, 2007 from http://www.marchofdimes.com/printableArticles/14332_15455.asp

Morehouse, M. (2007, January). Girl, interrupted. *People,* 69–70.

National Network for Immunization Information. (2007a). Exposure parties. Retrieved February 16, 2007 from http://www.immunizationinfo.org/exposure_parties.cfm

National Network for Immunization Information. (2007b). Immunization issues: Vaccine misinformation. Retrieved February 16, 2007 from http://www.immunizationinfo.org/immunization_issues_detail.cfv?id=52

Nussbaum, M. C. (2001). *Upheavals of thought: The intelligence of emotions.* New York: Cambridge University.

Pence, G. E. (2004). *Classic cases in medical ethics: Accounts of cases that have shaped medical ethics, with philosophical, legal, and historical backgrounds* (4th ed.). Boston: McGraw-Hill.

President's Council on Bioethics. (2006, February 3). Session 6: Newborn screening for genetic disorders/diseases. Retrieved July 30, 2007 from http://www.bioethics.gov/transcripts/feb06/session6.html

Ramsey, S. B. (2006). Abusive situations. In S. W. Killion & K. Dempski (Eds.), *Quick look nursing: Legal and ethical issues* (pp. 58–59). Boston: Jones & Bartlett.

Robert Wood Johnson Foundation. (2006, August). *Going without: America's uninsured children.* Retrieved February 16, 2007 from http://www.rwjf.org/files/newsroom/ckfresearchreportfinal.pdf

Ross, L. F. (1998). *Children, families, and health care decision-making.* Oxford, UK: Oxford University.

Ruddick, S. (1995). *Toward a politics of peace.* Boston: Beacon Press.

Ryan, K., & Bohlin, K. E. (1999). *Building character in schools: Practical ways to bring moral instruction to life.* San Francisco: Jossey-Bass.

Schindehette, S., Atlas, D., Podesta, J. S., Stambler, L., & Duffy, T. (2004, August 2). A simple test could have saved Ben's life. *People,* 107–108.

Stenson, J. B. (1999). Appendix C: An overview of the virtues. In K. Ryan & K. E. Bohlin (Eds.), *Building character in schools: Practical ways to bring moral instruction to life* (pp. 207–211). San Francisco: Jossey-Bass.

Stimpson, C. R. (1993). Series editor's foreword. In V. Held (Ed.), *Feminist morality: Transforming culture, society, and politics* (pp. vii–ix). Chicago: University of Chicago.

Tong, R. (1997). *Feminist approaches to bioethics: Theoretical reflections and practical applications.* Boulder, CO: Westview.

World Health Organization. (2005). Child and adolescent health and development: Overview. Retrieved February 18, 2007, from http://www.who.int/child-adolescent-health/over.htm

ZERO to THREE Policy Network. (2006, August). Good health: Newborn screening. Retrieved February 16, 2007 from http://www.zerotothree.org/policy/GoodHealth.html

Chapter 6 Questions

1. Caring parents make a difficult end-of-life decision regarding the care of their young child who is in a persistent vegetative state. The standard that best supports this decision is called
   a. substituted judgment.
   b. best interest.
   c. social justice.
   d. autonomy extended.

2. Which of the following ethical approaches is often closely aligned with mother-child relationships?
   a. Deontology
   b. Utilitarianism
   c. Feminist ethics
   d. Kantianism

3. The double jeopardy of childhood poverty can best be explained as
   a. a high level of exposure to risk factors and poor access to health care.
   b. a high number of illegal immigrant parents and shorter life expectancies.
   c. a high incidence of attending exposure parties and dying from infectious diseases.
   d. a high level of lead exposure and a society that does not protect these children.

4. Considerations about withholding and withdrawing care with newborns are
   a. generally no different than considerations about older children.
   b. generally no different than considerations about older children and adults.
   c. subject to different criteria than decisions about older children and adults.
   d. purely ethical and not legal.

5. The landmark Baby Doe case resulted in an amendment to protect impaired infants that was added to an earlier law. The earlier law was passed to protect people from
   a. high medical costs.
   b. discrimination based entirely on a person's race.
   c. discrimination based entirely on a person's handicaps.
   d. unfair distribution of societal burdens.

6. Baby K was an infant with anencephaly. Baby K's mother wanted health care professionals to continue providing maximum care for Baby K even though the professionals believed that such care was futile. The courts decided
   a. in favor of Baby K's mother.
   b. in favor of the health care professionals.
   c. that the case was not resolvable.
   d. that children being provided maximum care often suffer.

7. Every state allows vaccine exemptions for
   a. religious reasons.
   b. medical reasons.
   c. philosophical objections.
   d. children that have attended exposure parties.

8. Believing that individual families must give up their right to refuse vaccines for their children in order to protect the larger community is an example of
   a. deontological ethics.
   b. virtue ethics.
   c. feminist ethics.
   d. utilitarian ethics.

9. Which of the following is true about child abuse?
   a. The most common form of abuse is physical violence.
   b. Abuse is underreported.
   c. Only doctors are mandatory reporters.
   d. Reporting possible abuse that is later not confirmed is a problem for nurses.

10. Giving a blood transfusion to a child with Jehovah's Witness parents who state that they do not want the transfusion to be given is
    a. never warranted.
    b. usually unethical.
    c. ethical and legal at times.
    d. not the concern of nurses.

Chapter 6 Answers

Question 1: The correct answer is B.
The best interest standard is used because children generally have not previously conveyed their personal wishes about end-of-life care. Decision makers must base their decisions on the child's best interest.

Choices A, C, and D are incorrect because substituted judgment and autonomy extended standards imply that surrogates make decisions based on a now incompetent person's previously verbalized or implied personal wishes about end-of-life care. Social justice is related to distribution of resources.

Question 2: The correct answer is C.
Some feminist ethicists have used mother-child relationships as a basis for articulating their views of ethics.

Choices A, B, and D are incorrect because these approaches to ethics do not use mother-child relationships as a basis.

Question 3: The correct answer is A.
Many children living in poverty are exposed to factors that increase their risk of poor health. Also, many of these children have poor access to health care.

Choices B, C, and D are incorrect because the dual parts of these choices are not consistently paired or true.

Question 4: The correct answer is C.
Newborns are protected by the Baby Doe rules, which do not apply to other patients.

Choices A, B, and D are incorrect because these choices are not true in regard to the question.

Question 5: The correct answer is C.
The rules were based on Section 504 of the Rehabilitation Act of 1973, which forbids discrimination based entirely on a person's handicaps.

Choices A, B, and D are incorrect because these choices are not true in regard to the question.

Question 6: The correct answer is A.
The courts decided in favor of Baby K's mother who was the surrogate decision maker. It was decided that the care being provided to Baby K was not causing her to suffer, so care should be continued based on the mother's wishes.

Choices B, C, and D are incorrect because these choices are not true in regard to the question.

Question 7: The correct answer is B.
Every state allows medical exemptions for vaccinations. It would be unethical to mandate that anyone receive a vaccine that is medically contraindicated.

Choices A, C, and D are incorrect because these choices are not true in regard to the question.

Question 8: The correct answer is D.
Utilitarian ethics is focused on consequences and maximizing the most good. Public health policies are often predicated on trying to achieve the greatest good for the greatest number of people.

Choices A, B, and C are incorrect because these approaches to ethics are not based on trying to achieve the best overall consequences. Deontological ethics is based on duty, virtue ethics is based on good character, and feminist ethics is based on the unique position of women.

Question 9: The correct answer is B.
Literature supports the position that child abuse is underreported.

Choices A, C, and D are incorrect because these choices are not true in regard to the question.

Question 10: The correct answer is C.
In a life-threatening emergency or a situation of critical illness, it is legal and ethical to override the wishes of Jehovah's Witness parents in favor of giving a transfusion to save the life of a child or to prevent unnecessary risks of harm.

Choices A, B, and D are incorrect because these choices are not true in regard to the question.

Adolescent Nursing Ethics

Janie B. Butts

In adolescence we are in many ways like empty but organic receptacles, fully formed though still growing waiting to be filled. And like receptacles we are capable at that stage of life of receiving with all our being, becoming one with what is within us.

—COLIN M. TURNBULL, *THE HUMAN CYCLE*

OBJECTIVES

After reading this chapter, the reader should be able to:

1. Explore the phases of development of adolescence as they relate to unhealthy and risky behaviors.
2. Delineate the major risky behaviors in which adolescents engage, and include the major causes of death of adolescents as specified by the Centers for Disease Control and Prevention.
3. Discuss the rationale for the central ethical issues of adolescents in terms of family, peers, teachers, and health care professionals, including nurses.
4. Examine the significance of appropriate and inappropriate communication for health educators teaching adolescents a prevention program with health risk messages.
5. Discuss the benefits of health educators and nurses using theory-based health risk messages with a fear appeal to deliver education programs appropriately.
6. Describe the state of the research regarding the effectiveness of abstinence-only programs versus comprehensive sexual education programs, and include the three major ethical concerns when choosing a program among the abstinence-only or comprehensive sexual education programs.

7. Compare trust, privacy, and confidentiality and their significance regarding the health care information and nursing care of adolescents and adolescent decision-making capacity.
8. Discuss the other critical health issues that trigger ethical concerns, such as depression and suicidal ideation, alcohol and other drug use, sexual abuse, and eating disorders.
9. Explore the 10 stages of grief when adolescents learn of the sudden death of a peer or family member.
10. Delineate the five stages of grief that adolescents and others experience with their own dying process.
11. Discuss the moral framework of virtues that nurses need to incorporate in the care of adolescents, and include the major concepts from the ANA *Code of Ethics for Nurses with Interpretive Statements* (2001).

KEY TERMS

Adolescent developmental process	Early adolescence
Middle adolescence	Late adolescence
Health risk behaviors	Attentive listening
Focusing	Not interrupting
Reflecting	Health risk messages
Fear appeals	Theory
Confidentiality	Privacy
Trust	Trustworthy
Limits of confidentiality	Moral self-government
Emerging capacity	Trustworthiness
Genuineness	Compassion
Hidden hut	Honesty

The Age of Adolescence

"It was the best of times, it was the worst of times, it was the age of wisdom, it was the age of foolishness . . ." is the first statement in Dickens's book, *A Tale of Two Cities* (1993/1859). This quote, which describes the turmoil leading up to the French Revolution, could easily be used as a quote concerning adolescence. It is through adolescents' best and worst times that they learn to make life decisions and move toward independence. Through these interesting times, adolescents somehow develop their identity and their sense of sexuality.

Many experts have defined adolescence as an age that occurs during the second decade of life and a period of transition that differs in length for each person (DiClemente, Hansen, & Ponton, 1996; Leffert & Petersen, 1999). Adolescence is a remarkable succession of physical, cognitive, emotional, moral, and psychosocial developmental changes.

Three separate phases, spanning 11 years, have been identified in the **adolescent developmental process** (Gullotta, Adams, & Markstrom, 2000; Leffert & Peterson, 1999). **Early adolescence** (ages 10–14) is a transitional period from childhood to middle adolescence and is usually marked by the onset of puberty. Adolescents begin puberty with experimentation and discovery. **Middle adolescence** (ages 15–17) is dominated by peer pressure, peer orientation, and stereotypical behaviors, such as following clothing trends and listening to music that is considered acceptable by peers. **Late adolescence** (ages 18–20) usually marks the transition from adolescence to adulthood. Adolescents generally begin to place more importance on their future and their life plans as they move into late adolescence.

Adolescents have a need to find out who they are and have a desire to push limits and test unknown waters. Many of the decisions that adolescents make are based on the values that they have adapted from the pressure of peer approval and the exposure to the quickly changing world around them. Mistakes and failures, but also successes, will occur along the way. Adolescents need to be encouraged to make autonomous decisions and express their values and preferences on a continuous basis so that they will evolve to maturity with a defined sense of self.

Risk-Taking Behaviors

As of 2006, there were more than 1.2 billion adolescents living in the world, the largest number of adolescents in the history of the world, and 87% of that population of adolescents were living in the developing world (United Nations Population Fund [UNFPA], 2007). More than 40 million of these young people live in the United States (Maternal & Child Health Bureau, 2003). Although risk-taking and the feeling of "it's not going to happen to me," or a feeling of invincibility, are the hallmarks of adolescence, new risks and newly discovered demands are presented every day to these young people like at no other time in history. The realities of massive social, economic, political, and cultural changes worldwide affect adolescents' development process.

Health risk behaviors include those behaviors that, according to Lindberg, Boggess, and Williams, "may threaten the well-being of teens and may prevent them from becoming fully functioning members of society" (2000, pp. 1–2). Adolescents who engage in one risky behavior have a tendency to engage in at least one or more other risky behaviors, especially paired behaviors, such as smoking cigarettes and drinking alcohol or smoking marijuana and engaging in risky sexual activities.

In a literature review on adolescents and risk-taking behaviors, McKay (2003) and Cook, Dickens, and Fathalla (2003) found that the origin of most risk-taking behaviors is social rather than medical and that these behaviors can result in injury from accidents, violence, and sexual abuse. The Web Ethics box at the end of this chapter lists helpful Web sites for nurses, adolescents, and parents seeking information on risky behaviors and ethical issues in the health care of adolescents.

Risk-taking behaviors can often lead to death in adolescents. Three critical health behaviors have been identified and connected to leading causes of death and disability among adolescents in the United States: injury due to violence (including suicide), use of alcohol and other drugs, and risky sexual activity (Centers for Disease Control [CDC], 2005). Refer to Box 7.1 for three different accounts of adolescent statistics: (1) the health risks faced by adolescents in 2007 (CDC, 2007); (2) the risky behaviors that contributed to the leading causes of death for ages 10 to 24 in 2005; and (3) the leading causes of death for ages 10 to 24 (CDC, 2005). The reader should note that data from the 2005 Youth Risk Behavior Surveillance System Survey (YRBSS) survey were taken only from U.S. high school students who were enrolled in and attending a high school.

Central Ethical Issues at a Glance

The age of adolescence brings with it overpowering family decision-making issues and health concerns, and as a result, complex health care ethical issues arise. As people in society observe the relationships between adults (or parents) and adolescents and see how these two groups seem to have moved so swiftly into disharmony through this first decade of the 21st century, they have many perplexing questions. The ethical health care issues of adolescents are focused on rights—the rights that all people expect, especially people in the Western world. Some of those rights include the right of freedom to consent to or refuse treatment, the right to confidentiality and privacy of one's medical record, and the right not to be violated or taken advantage of because of membership in a vulnerable age group. Conducting research with adolescents is a

BOX 7.1: HIGHLIGHTS FROM THE FIELD: HEALTH RISKS FACED BY ADOLESCENTS IN 2007

- More than 1 in 5 high school students in the United States are current smokers.
- Almost 80% of high school students do not eat the recommended 5 servings of fruits and vegetables a day.
- Only 1 in 3 high school students participate in daily physical education classes.
- More than 1 in 3 children and adolescents are overweight or at risk of becoming overweight.
- Every year, more than 830,000 adolescents become pregnant and more than 9 million cases of sexually transmitted diseases occur among young people ages 15–24 years.
- Nearly 5,000 cases of HIV/AIDS are reported each year among young people ages 15–24 years in areas with confidential reporting.
- Young people miss nearly 15 million school days a year because of asthma.

Centers for Disease Control and Prevention. (2007). Healthy youth: An investment in our nation's future, 2007. Retrieved January 30, 2007, from http://www.cdc.gov/HealthyYouth/about/healthyyouth.htm

Risky Behaviors that Lead to Major Causes of Death in Ages 10 to 24 Years
- Unintentional injury
- Alcohol and other drug use
- Sexual behaviors

Leading Causes of Death for Ages 10 to 24 Years
- 30% Motor vehicle crash
- 29% Other causes
- 15% Homicide
- 14% Other types of injury
- 11% Suicide
- 01% HIV infection

Centers for Disease Control and Prevention. (2005). United States—2005 youth risk behavior (YRBS) survey. Retrieved January 30, 2007, from http://www.cdc.gov/HealthyYouth/YRBS/pdf/mortality/USA.pdf

concern because of that vulnerability. Research issues are not discussed in this chapter. Nursing research books include information on the special concerns of vulnerable research subjects.

Certain central ethical themes regarding adolescents have become increasingly apparent:

- *Prevention education:* How, where, and to what extent adolescents receive information and education about prevention
  - Beneficence
  - Nonmaleficence
- *Trust, privacy, and confidentiality:* Limits of confidentiality; handling life-threatening illnesses and disorders
  - Respect for autonomy
  - Beneficence
  - Nonmaleficence
- *Consent:* Consenting to treatments without parental or guardian consent; refusal of treatment without parental or guardian consent
  - Respect for autonomy
  - Beneficence
  - Nonmaleficence
- *Research with adolescents:* A vulnerable population
  - Respect for autonomy
  - Beneficence
  - Nonmaleficence
  - Justice

Adolescent Relationships and Ethical Issues

Relationships are at the core of an adolescent's life. Because of the value that adolescents place on relationships, nurses would do well to remember that positive and negative relationship skills learned within a family continue with children into the adolescent stage. It is because of relationships that adolescents experience a complex set of patterns and feelings such as happiness, sadness, excitement, anger, fear, frustration, stress, and even loneliness (Urban Programs Resource Network, n.d.).

Adolescents want and need to be *heard* and understood; parents want to give their opinions and be heard. Adolescents want relationships of their own with each other without interference from authority figures. On the other hand, health care and other professionals want to teach adolescents to prevent harm or illness or to manage disease, and media personnel want to grab adolescents' attention by whatever means necessary. Communication is the key issue in adolescent relationships. For instance, Box 7.2 contains four quotes from the United States: one from UNICEF, one from adolescents, one from Dryfoos and Barkin (2006) on mentoring children and teens, and one from an older mother about her views on the role of communication.

One of the most common "lines" that nurses hear from adolescents is, "My parents don't listen to me!" Ironically, parents often say, "My kid won't listen to me!" When it comes to other relationships involving adolescents, similar statements are sometimes made: "My school teacher doesn't listen to my complaints," "That nurse didn't understand my problem," and so on.

Attentive listening, meaning that the nurse is paying attention to what is being said and then giving a signal to the speaker that listening is occurring, is an effective technique for nurses when working with adolescents. Attentive listening helps nurses earn the respect of young people, which is a critical factor in nurse-adolescent relationships. Ways that nurses practice attentive listening include:

- *Focusing:* Making eye contact and not allowing the eyes to wander
- *Not interrupting:* Hearing the speaker in full before commenting and acknowledging the speaker by nods, smiles, or other expressions
- *Reflecting:* Summarizing the speaker's thoughts to clarify the meaning

Ethical Dilemmas Involving Prevention Education

Listening is important, but being the "giver" of communication—how, where, and to what extent—is a critical ethical concern for adolescent relationships of all kinds, especially in professional nurse-adolescent relationships. Beneficence and nonmaleficence are the principles that underlie the ethical management of prevention and health risk message programs involving this age group. **Health risk messages** are commonly defined as **fear appeals**, which are persuasive messages that arouse by fear by, "outlining the negative consequences that occur if a certain action is not taken" (Witte, Meyer, & Martell, 2001, p. 2). Sensationalists, political campaign personnel, religious leaders and preachers, and many other groups tend to use fear appeals. The most common way that fear appeals have been used is by health educators, nurses, physicians, and other disciplines where there are health risks involved. If fear appeals are used correctly, they can be very effective by motivating the public to take care of themselves, make healthy choices, and practice safe behaviors.

Box 7.2: Highlights from the Field: Important Messages for Adolescents

Teens are greatly influenced by the messages they receive about sex in school. It's time that the government provide funding for sexual education for the positive and healthy message of abstinence-until-marriage versus that of premarital sex and contraception. In this box are important messages from adolescents, parents, teachers, and others.

Quoted from a girl, age 19

I think it's important for people to educate girls around the world about the risk of getting STDs/AIDS and getting pregnant if you don't have any forms of protection.

Quote from UNICEF, 2006. Girls: protected and empowered. *What Young People Are Saying*. Retrieved on January 30, 2007, from http://www.unicef.org/voy/news

On Mentoring Children and Adolescents

One of my mantras is "every child must be attached to a responsible adult—if not a parent, then someone else." The need for close and consistent mentoring can change over time, but particularly in the early teen years, when communication with parents may be difficult, that someone else can play a significant role. Such a someone else can be a teacher, relative, friend, friend's parent, volunteer mentor, or youth worker [or nurse], preferably with some knowledge of youth development.

Quote from Dryfoos, J. G., & Barkin, C. (2006). *Adolescence: Growing up in America today.* New York: Oxford University Press.

From an Older Parent

My daughter used to be so wonderful. Now I can barely stand her and she won't tell me anything. I feel totally shut out. How can I find out what's going on?

Wiseman, R. (2001). *Queenbees and wannabees: Helping your daughter survive cliques, gossip, boyfriends, and other realities of adolescence.* New York: Three Rivers.

However, fear appeals can be used incorrectly and can actually do more harm than good. Giving health risk messages without the integration of a theory can be time consuming and fragmented. A **theory** provides "an explanation of how two or more variables work together to produce a certain outcome(s)" (Witte et al., 2001, p. 3). If theories are used to guide the health risk messages, there is no guesswork and time is cut shorter on the development of a message. The goal of nurses for theory-based education programs or health risk messages is to teach young people the skills they need to make healthy choices and practice healthy behaviors. This aim is consistent with a beneficent approach because nurses promote human good through education. Most education programs for adolescents are theory-based health risk messages and prevention focused. Prevention programs need to be focused not only on doing "good," but also on doing no harm, or a nonmaleficent approach.

An example of an integrated beneficent and nonmaleficent approach is a harm reduction program that incorporates health risk messages and theory. In using a harm reduction program, nurses teach adolescents to live safely with certain high-risk behaviors, such as by advocating participation in a needle exchange program for those addicted to intravenous or other needle-requiring drugs.

Another example is a prevention intervention behavioral program providing theory-based health risk messages, one that the author of this chapter has used in research—*Becoming a Responsible Teen (BART)*, which was originally developed from research by St. Lawrence, Brasfield, Jefferson, Alleyne, O'Bannon, and Shirley (1995). St. Lawrence (1994) actually developed the BART training manual, an eight-session curriculum based on two theoretical frameworks: (1) Bandura's (1977) social learning and self-efficacy theory and (2) Fisher and Fisher's (1992) information-motivation-behavioral skills model (IMB model). Today the BART behavioral intervention program is evidence-based and very popular among health educators.

Nurses who are involved in prevention education need to use a theory-based curriculum and evaluate the program early in the planning phase. Questions to consider are:

- How much information is too much information?
- When and at what age will the information be presented? What types of information are appropriate?
- Where and how should the information be presented to be effective?

Nurses who give information to adolescents may potentially harm them if they choose a wrong or inappropriate prevention education program. This situation poses a critical ethical dilemma for nurses when they must choose among the many standardized and accepted programs that are available for adolescents. For example, nurses sometimes will need to choose between teaching sexual abstinence and teaching the use of safe sexual practices, or they could be asked to focus a program on religious beliefs. Choosing an age- or content-inappropriate program for a particular group or choosing information that could easily be misinterpreted could result in adolescents being misled, or an adolescent may perceive the health risk messages differently from the way the educator intended for the message to be received. Blunders could be critical to how adolescents will react to the information.

Even though alcohol and other drugs are harmful when abused or misused, a small glass of red wine is reported to actually protect the heart against disease (Gullotta et al., 2000). Messages such as this one can be quite confusing to adolescents. Another message that could be misleading is that in the United States, marijuana is an illegal drug for most people, but for others marijuana is legally used for medicinal purposes. As of 2004, 21 states had passed legislation that recognized the medicinal value of marijuana, and 10 of those states had totally legalized it for medical use (Drug Policy Analysis, 2006; Gullotta et al., 2000). Additionally, adolescents sometimes receive conflicting and incorrect information because of others seeking political or monetary gain. For example, advertisers often show groups of attractive young people socializing and drinking beer. Some companies intend to convey a subtle message that drinking beer makes one more attractive and popular. Another critical message that has caused considerable child and adolescent psychological problems such as anorexia nervosa or bulimia is the fashion industry's blatant promotion of super-thin models, conveying a message that one must be thin to be beautiful and look good.

There are hundreds of adolescent prevention programs being used in the United States. The CDC (2007) reported last year that, even though high school students continue to engage in too many risky behaviors that lead to sexually transmitted infections (STIs), HIV, injury, addiction, depression, chronic disease, and suicide, the prevention education is beginning to work. The trends reveal that adolescents are making slight progress in some areas, such as cigarette smoking and the use of alcohol and other drugs. Although overall drug use is declining very slowly, over the past several years, preteens have been inhaling, sniffing, huffing, or bagging substances to get high at drastically increased rates (McGuinness, 2006; Partnership for a Drug-Free America, 2004). For example, the use of inhalant substances increased in eighth graders from 22% to 26% and in sixth graders from 18% to 26% over 2 years. McGuinness reported that use of inhalant chemicals is a more common practice than marijuana use among adolescents ages 12 to 13 years. In fact, there are correlations between inhalant use, conduct disorder, depression, and suicidal behavior.

There seem to be huge gaps in prevention education programs. The increase in inhalant use in preteens is an alarming fact but, at the same time, the gaps could only be a symptom of problems with prevention programs that convey controversial or inadequate information. Hallfors surveyed adolescents from 104 school districts across the United States (as cited in Manisses Communications Group, 2002). Hallfors found that lack of teacher training, not enough material resources, inconsistent use of lesson plans, and failure to match lesson plans with the appropriate age were factors that could have large negative ramifications for adolescent drug prevention programs across the country.

Because many school nurses plan and implement programs, nurses must know the objectives and content and anticipate the message that *will be heard* by adolescents who participate in the program. Adolescents will usually assume that the message they hear is correct when school nurses conduct the prevention education program. If adolescents incorporate misinterpreted information into their viewpoints and behaviors, they may be in danger of contracting STIs or HIV, developing a drug habit, sustaining alcohol- or other drug-related injuries, or developing suicidal ideation.

Abstinence-Only or Comprehensive Sex Education Programs

One critical issue today is how sexual abstinence programs measure up to comprehensive sexual education programs. In recent years, there has been a much stronger religious and political focus on the teaching of sexual abstinence in schools, homes, and churches than in past years, especially before the sexual revolution movement of the 1960s. In fact, other than through fundamental religious teachings, sexual education was seldom taught in the United States before the HIV and AIDS epidemic began in the 1980s.

The overall ethical concern about sexual education is complex, but generally, nurses must evaluate at what point along the sexual abstinence–comprehensive sex education continuum the information conveyed becomes unethical, nonbeneficial, or even harmful. Adolescents need sexual education more than ever today. The risk of acquiring HIV or other STIs is very high for adolescents. According to UNFPA (2007), half of all people newly diagnosed with HIV in the world are between the ages of 15 and 24. Most other STIs occur in this age range as well. Said another way, every 14 seconds worldwide, a young person between the ages of 15 and 24 becomes infected with HIV.

Pregnancy and abortion rates among adolescents steadily declined in the 1990s. However, more than 830,000 adolescents become pregnant every year (refer to Box 7.1). In the Sexual Information and Education Council of the United States

(SIECUS) report (2002), reasons given for the declining pregnancy rate in adolescents were that adolescents are pursuing and achieving higher levels of education and that many are exposed to comprehensive sexual education programs in schools. Therefore, adolescents learn negotiation skills and effective contraceptive practices.

Three Major Ethical Concerns along the Continuum

Recent statistics worldwide reveal that adolescents continue to have unprotected sex. There are three major ethical concerns about the sexual abstinence–safe sex education continuum and adolescents. The first issue that nurses must face is that there is no clear definition of sexual abstinence today. Traditionally, adolescents have equated "having sex" with just intercourse alone. Young people have sought more creative ways, other than coital sex, to express sexual intimacy, such as mutual masturbation, even oral and anal sex, because these types of sex have not been viewed as "traditional sex" (Remez, 2000). The term *sexual abstinence* in recent years has led to dissimilar and ambiguous opinions. A clear definition must be developed for, and then be communicated to, today's adolescents. Meanwhile, parents, educators, and others who teach sexual abstinence continue to say "just say no to sex," "don't have sex before marriage," or "delay the onset of sex." What do these statements mean exactly? Does abstinence mean not having vaginal penetration? Is oral or anal sex all right just as long as one does not participate in penis-vagina intercourse? Is abstinence referring only to a male and female relationship? What about same-sex relationships? How does abstinence apply in those situations?

Based on the CDC's (1988) recommendation not to exchange any bodily fluids, including saliva in exchanges such as French kissing, and to use latex protection where indicated, adolescents are placing themselves at high risk when they have unprotected sexual relations with body fluid exposures. Could abstinence be defined these days as a person's being able to engage in any type of sexual activity just as long as the couple or group is protected with latex and does not exchange bodily fluids?

Without a clear definition, educators, parents, and others have only vague communication between themselves and adolescents about the meaning of sexual abstinence. What adolescents perceive as the definition of sexual abstinence and what adults are trying to teach as sexual abstinence most likely include a variety of different opinions. Ethically, this vagueness itself can be harmful, not beneficial, because the information may be misperceived. As a result, adolescents are left to their own interpretations. Misinterpreted information may lead to unprotected sex, which, in turn, may lead to an unwanted pregnancy, an STI, or infection with HIV.

A second issue is adolescent sexual intimacy, a reality that cannot be denied. In an in-depth study of intimacy and sexual abstinence, Hartwig (2000) contended that long-term abstinence damages individuals' development of their "capacity to love with greater depth and integrity" (p. 3). Although this depth of intimacy can be built upon by other means, Hartwig stated that intimate relationships through sex help people to move past fears and perplexities that sometimes cannot otherwise be overcome.

Early-stage adolescents, ages 13 to 15, may not be capable of managing the strong physical and emotional feelings that go with sexual relationships. Intimate relationships could be injurious to adolescents' emotional development in the short term, as well as having long-term effects. This issue is a challenge to educators and parents. Hartwig (2000) posed this question to adults: "How does one discourage premature sexual intimacy among those who intensely desire physical sexual intimacy and who often assume they are emotionally mature enough to form intimate relationships without shaming or vilifying sexual intimacy?" (p. 36).

However, according to Hartwig (2000), sometimes adolescents are restricted from learning to eliminate risks when they are exposed solely to abstinence-only programs. Adolescents need what Hartwig called a poetic approach to sexual education and sexual virtue, which complements and balances a moral approach. Poetic intimacy teachings must begin with young children. For adolescents, a process such as this one includes integrating the poetics of sexuality. Examples include exposing adolescents to narratives that highlight tenderness and sensuality and teaching them to practice the use of graceful sexual language, not bad and dirty language. If adolescents are not taught to manage sexual intimacy in a beneficial way, the ethical implication is that harm may result in their developmental and emotional processes. Developing this type of intimacy helps them come to terms with their sexual changes and feelings. Adolescents who learn graceful poetic intimacy develop ways to deepen their desire for intimacy without necessarily having sexual relationships, or they learn to make healthier choices when they decide to have sex.

A third issue is that there is controversy about whether or not abstinence-only programs seem to be working. "It's not a small matter that more and more teens will not have the comprehensive information that could literally save their lives," stated Elizabeth Toledo, the vice president at that time for communications for the Planned Parenthood Federation of America in New York City (as cited in Bowman, 2004, p. A617). Many adolescents are breaking the no-sex pledges that they make to their church leaders, school teachers, and parents. Leaders of schools and churches continue their efforts to teach abstinence-only programs.

Adults in the United States would like to see a comprehensive sexual education program implemented in schools that includes healthy choices, abstinence, and strategies to be safe. As pregnancy rates have slowly declined over the last decade for adolescents, STIs have remained alarmingly high and of deep concern to public health officials. In a January 2004 poll of 1,759 people in the United States, only 15% of adults thought that school officials should teach abstinence only and not provide information about contraception (Princeton Survey Research Associates; as cited in Bowman, 2004). According to Boonstra (2004), prevention is critical, but prevention must go beyond education. Adolescents need to be able to access health care services that provide them with family planning and STI treatment on a regular basis because many STIs are treatable and curable. Cervical cancer may follow if adolescents are not treated properly for STIs.

This third issue is one of great concern for nurses who work with adolescents. Inconsistency exists across programs. Ethically, nurses need to think about the possible harm that could be done as a result of the type of sexual education program they choose. Nurses need to evaluate the program early in the planning process by using the guidelines already mentioned in this chapter. It is important for nurses to think about the ways in which adolescents may perceive, interpret, or put into practice the content that is being presented to them. Once nurses can effectively focus on the adolescents who are receiving the message, they need to clarify the message, try to focus on what they are really saying to adolescents, and, most of all, attempt to clarify and anticipate as much as possible the message that adolescents are actually hearing. If a nurse takes time to focus on the audience and the content of the message, adolescents will realize that the nurse cares for them and is respecting them for their values and beliefs. As the nurse provides well-defined content and becomes an attentive listener, a reciprocal trusting and respectful relationship is more likely to develop.

--------- Ethical Reflections ---------

- If you were a school nurse planning a prevention education program for your rural middle school students on alcohol, other drugs, and sex, what would you need to consider before actually beginning your program?
- What is the most effective prevention program that you could use?
- What ethical considerations would you incorporate into program planning?
- What message do you think adolescents need to hear?
- What type of relationship do you hope to establish with the students?

Confidentiality, Privacy, and Trust

Confidentiality, privacy, and trust cannot be viewed as separate entities in a nurse-adolescent relationship. Confidentiality is linked with privacy and trust, and usually means that information given to someone is to be kept secret (Blustein & Moreno, 1999). Privacy used in this way means for someone to keep information secluded or secret from others. Trust means that adolescents sometimes explore their vulnerabilities with health care providers but, at the same time, believe that these providers will not take advantage of them. In other words, adolescents believe that the providers are reliable and dependable in managing their health and vulnerabilities. From an ethical standpoint, confidentiality, privacy, and trust are tightly woven with respect for autonomy, the adolescent's right to privacy, and the rights of service. Any breach of confidentiality, privacy, or trust is viewed as a violation of autonomy.

Trust is important to a healthy and respectful relationship. Once trust is broken and mistrust develops, it is very difficult for the informer (nurse) to regain trust. Adolescents will probably refuse to listen to anything that the nurse tries to convey. Trust is a basic need that must be developed in the first stage of life, according to Erik Erikson (1963). If trust is broken early in an individual's life, mistrust carries over in all of the person's relationships.

If adolescents do not trust the nurse, for example, they may not believe the nurse with regard to an informed consent (Blustein & Moreno, 1999). Adolescents may not listen to explanations. The most important way for nurses to gain the trust of adolescents is by relentlessly proving themselves: being consistent, giving correct information, keeping commitments, and showing concern and caring. These activities, combined, help indicate that nurses are trustworthy, meaning that nurses are dependable and authentic because they take responsibility for their own behavior and commit to their obligations (Gullotta et al., 2000).

The Clinton administration passed a law called the Health Insurance Portability and Accountability Act (HIPAA) of 1996, which outlined requirements for the protection and privacy of medical records and the confidential information of minors (as cited in Dailard, 2003). More specifically, under the act, if adolescents had consented to their treatment and care, they could be assured of confidentiality with all related records. The act protected adolescents seeking sensitive health services, such as for pregnancy, abortion, and oral contraceptives. The Clinton administration wanted to make sure that adolescents were allowed every possible avenue to seek the health care that they need for these sensitive issues.

However, early in the Bush administration, in April 2001, there was a proposal for critical changes to this act. In August 2002, a new law went into effect that somewhat altered adolescents' rights to privacy and confidentiality with regard to their medical records and their right to consent to health care. Under the new law, each state has a right to decide how much privacy, confidentiality, and control adolescents have over their own medical records and treatment. It should be pointed out, however, that most states keep silent on this issue and leave those decisions to health care professionals as much as possible.

Trust-Privacy-Confidentiality Dilemma

A legal, ethical, political, and practice issue surfaces when a trusting relationship may exist and the nurse is entrusted with an adolescent's confidential information. Sometimes the sensitive issue and the nature of the information is potentially harmful to the adolescent if it is not reported to proper authorities or others (University of Chicago, 2005). Adolescents are very concerned about their privacy and what others think of them, especially their parents and peers. Nurses need to ensure that adolescents are examined privately and away from their parents and peers. Many times the physical and emotional health outcomes of risky behaviors force adolescents to seek medical treatment. Because of the sensitive issues involved and a potential for these issues to cause embarrassment, adolescents want to keep the information secret, especially from their parents.

Well-established research findings in the United States reveal that the likelihood adolescents will seek health services for sensitive issues depends on how well their sensitive issues will remain confidential (Dailard, 2003). Adolescents can seek family planning services at the state level, such as counseling and contraception through the Planned Parenthood Federation of America, which is a program that is federally funded by Title X of the Public Health Service Act, and be guaranteed confidentiality (Planned Parenthood of America, 2007). Each state has a broad range of laws that stem from the federal laws concerning confidentiality and consent of adolescents. However, Title X will not provide funds for abortion for adolescents.

In the United States, the exception to adolescent autonomy over medical records involves the issue of abortion. Seventeen states require no parental involvement in an adolescent's decision to have an abortion. As of 2007, 35 states require some parental involvement in an adolescent's choice to have an abortion, with 22 states requiring parental consent, 11 states requiring only parental notification, and 2 states requiring parental consent and notification (Guttmacher Institute, 2007). Even with required parental consent, the 35 states with this requirement have sought ways to work around complete parental involvement by having a judicial bypass, meaning that adolescents may obtain approval from a court to bypass parental involvement. Six of these states also permit family members, such as an aunt or a grandparent, to be involved in the abortion decision so that adolescents can avoid informing their parents. However, most states allow for exceptions to the parental involvement law when abortions become a medical emergency or when an extraordinary situation exists, such as when the pregnancy was the result of sexual assault or incest.

Limits of Confidentiality

Nurses need to assure adolescents from the beginning of the interaction that confidentiality is an important component of the nurse–patient relationship. However, confidentiality must never be guaranteed; confidentiality can be breached in instances that place the adolescent or others at harm or danger—an exception called **limits of confidentiality** (University of Chicago, 2005). The nurse can assure the adolescent that unless harm or a potential threat to the patient or to known others is involved, confidentiality will not be breached. In cases of potential harm, an adolescent must always be given a chance to disclose sensitive or controversial information to parents, guardians, or others involved, as appropriate. If the adolescent refuses to do so, nurses and other health care professionals are obligated to report the following information to state officials according to state laws:

- Suicidal ideation
- Homicidal ideation
- Physical abuse
- Sexual abuse
- Behaviors that put one at risk of physical harm (University of Chicago, 2005, Para 2)

Nurses must hold to these standards. Even if the situation is not considered a "limit of confidentiality," the nurse should make every effort to involve the parents or guardians if the adolescent is younger than age 14. The lines of confidentiality and consent are even more vague and unclear before the age of 14.

Consent Dilemma

Adolescents under the age of 18 can give consent for their own care in a broad range of circumstances and services. The minors who can consent are those who are over a certain age, mature, legally emancipated, married, in the armed forces, living apart from their parents, high school graduates, pregnant, or already parents (University of Chicago, 2005). They may also refuse treatment. An adolescent's right to consent to treatment or to refuse treatment is more frequently honored with certain types of services. These services include:

- Emergency care
- Family planning services, such as pregnancy care and contraceptive services
- Diagnosis and treatment of STIs or any other reportable infection or communicable disease
- HIV or AIDS testing and treatment
- Treatment and counseling for alcohol and other drugs
- Treatment for sexual assault and collection of the medical evidence for sexual assault
- Inpatient mental health services
- Outpatient mental health services

Deciding whether adolescents really have autonomous decision-making capacity is a consideration tightly linked to their personal self-directedness and characteristics, what Blustein and Moreno (1999) called **moral self-government**. The goal during adolescence is development of the moral self, and most adolescents' moral self is not yet fully formed. Blustein and Moreno stated that adolescents have an emerging capacity, which means that the moral self is evolving but it is not doing so evenly or consistently. Age and the stage of cognitive, emotional, and social development are factors that influence a person's ability to make mature decisions. An adolescent's capacity for decision making does not occur before the age of 15. Some experts have said that adolescents should not take part in significant autonomous decision making before age 14 (University of Chicago, 2005).

For many years, adults in the United States have valued the right to control their medical decisions. Adolescents are no different. In most states, these decisions are left up to health care professionals. If a valid consent between a nurse and an adolescent takes place, the initial phase should be more of a dialogue and educational exchange. During the consent process, the nurse's responsibility is to evaluate the adolescent's capacity for understanding and appreciating the process, especially with anticipated treatments or interventions.

The consent process may be more than a single event in time, such as in cancer treatments. It could be that one or both parents were highly involved with the adolescent's initial treatment and consent. Later in the process, adolescents may develop considerable maturity and then have the capacity to consent or not consent to subsequent treatments. Therefore, the adolescent's level of understanding and appreciation of the content of the consent may have progressively increased. Over time, the adolescent can take on more, if not all, of the responsibility in the decision-making process, and dialogue and education continue throughout the treatment. During the treatment and consent phases, documentation of the adolescent's progress in development of the moral self is essential.

————— **Ethical Reflections** —————

- Kelly, age 16, has come to a clinic where you work as a nurse. She has stated that she is at least 12 weeks pregnant but has not told anyone, not even her parents or boyfriend. She is scared of telling her boyfriend for fear of losing him. She wants an abortion, has cash money, and does not want anyone to know about the pregnancy or the abortion. Explore the ethical issues surrounding this situation. Consider the trust-confidentiality-privacy dilemma and the consent dilemma.
- Identify specific nursing strategies that you must consider using with Kelly. The clinic is in a state that does not require direct parental involvement but does require consent by someone of legal age.

Health Issues that Trigger Ethical Concerns

Many adolescent health issues cause nurses to have genuine ethical concerns. Some topics have already been discussed in this chapter, but there are others that are also just as critical to adolescents' health and survival, such as depression and suicidal ideation, substance use and abuse, sexual abuse, and eating disorders. There are many everyday critical issues for adolescents as well, but the author will not present them in this chapter.

The same guidelines for privacy, confidentiality, and consent that were discussed in the last section apply to these critical health issues. The ethical principles involved with these issues are beneficence (doing good, such as with prevention education) and nonmaleficence (protecting adolescents from harm). The common ethical concern for nurses managing these four health problems is that they are all potentially harmful and may even lead to death if left undetected. In the majority of situations, these problems need reporting to the proper authorities or other people within the health care or school system, such as school officials, mental health counselors, or physicians. Because these conditions are harmful and fall into the category of "limits of confidentiality," nurses should never promise privacy and confidentiality to adolescents when nurses have received such information. Nurses may not promise to the adolescent that they will keep critical health information a secret or confidential, once disclosed by the adolescent. When the nurse first detects a health problem, protection and safety must come first.

Depression and Suicidal Ideation

Depression and suicide are closely linked. Because the age of adolescence is such a time of great emotions and drama, depressive behavior may be hidden in daily displays of extremes. There are risk factors for adolescent suicidal ideation and attempts, many of which include family disturbances, familial tendency, sexual orientation conflicts, and socioenvironmental problems.

Every year close to 30,000 Americans commit suicide, but more than 300,000 Americans are treated or hospitalized because of suicide attempts (Goldrick, 2005). The suicide rate has declined over the years for the overall category of suicide, but it is important to note that for adolescents ages 10 to 14 years, suicide rates have increased by greater than 100% and for adolescents ages 15 to 19 years, they have increased by 6%. Suicide remains the third leading cause of death in the United States for ages 15 to 24. Of the adolescent suicides, 90% have had a psychiatric diagnosis (Goldrick, 2005).

Obtaining treatment for depression is essential for the prevention of suicide. Nurses may be fearful of making a mistake or missing signs of changes in adolescents. If a nurse finds an adolescent who is exhibiting behaviors that look suspiciously like signs of depression or suicidal tendency, the nurse must quickly identify the problem, ascertain the intention of the adolescent, and clearly explain the process of notification while offering hope and the prospect of a treatment plan. In 80% of youth suicides, adolescents had told someone about their suicidal ideation prior to the act.

Many state educational systems have initiated a program called "Gatekeepers" to spot suicidal youth (Goldrick, 2005). In Virginia, for instance, the trainers of the Gatekeepers first educated school nurse coordinators to be trainers, who provide training to other school nurses. Gatekeepers learn to recognize risky behaviors that may indicate suicidal ideation. Refer to Box 7.3 for warning signs of adolescent suicide.

Alcohol and Other Drugs

Adolescents with a family history of abuse are at high risk for developing substance abuse problems, along with those who are depressed, have low self-esteem, and feel like outcasts or that they do not fit in with their peers. An ethical issue raised with the use and abuse of alcohol and other drugs is the dilemma of balancing adolescents' rights to autonomy, privacy, and freedom to determine their own actions against the harmful effects of irresponsible use of alcohol and other drugs. Now that drug preven-

BOX 7.3: HIGHLIGHTS FROM THE FIELD: OBSERVABLE SIGNS OF SUICIDE RISK IN ADOLESCENTS

Decreased academic performance
Skipping classes
Inattentiveness and disruptive behavior
Boredom and sleepiness
Written, artistic, or other work that reveals suicide themes
Loss of interest in activities that the teen previously loved
Giving away possessions that they had once loved
Relationship changes and withdrawing
Avoidance of touching others and not wanting to be touched
Changes in dress, appearance, weight, and sleep patterns
High-risk-taking behaviors becoming more prominent
Alcohol and other drug abuse
Mental illness characteristics, such as self-mutilation and compulsive behavior
Extreme dependency on others
Sudden happiness after prolonged depression
Unrealistic expectations of self

From American Academy of Child & Adolescent Psychiatry. Facts for families: Teen suicide, 2004. Retrieved January 30, 2007, from http://aacap.org/page.ww?name=Teen+Suicide&section=Facts+for+Families

tion programs are widespread, adolescents are talking more than ever about substance use and abuse (Banks, 1999). Dryfoos and Barkin (2006) delineated some early predictors of alcohol and drug abuse and protector (see Box 7.4).

There is a federal government prevention campaign, called the Initiative on Underage Drinking, spearheaded by the Surgeon General and the National Institute on Alcohol Abuse and Alcoholism (NIAAA, 2007). Disturbingly, 5,000 adolescents under the age of 21 die each year from underage drinking. Statistics include 1,900 deaths from motor vehicle accidents, 1,600 from homicides, 300 from suicide, and the remaining numbers from injuries such as falls, burns, and drowning. Because drinking continues to be a broad and widespread problem among adolescents, the

BOX 7.4: HIGHLIGHTS FROM THE FIELD: PREDICTORS AND PROTECTORS

Predictors of Drug Abuse

- Aggressiveness in early childhood
- Rebelliousness
- Unconventionality
- High-risk friends
- Parents who have problems or use drugs

Predictors of Alcohol Abuse

- Alcoholic parent(s)
- Restless, impulsive, aggressive behavior in early childhood
- Conduct disorder
- Depression
- Peers who drink
- Lack of parental monitoring, support, and supervision

Protectors

- Parents who talk to their teens, set expectations, and enforce consequences
- Close family ties
- Adult role models
- Participation in religious and other activities
- Positive attitudes toward school
- School achievement

Jessor, R., Van Den Bos, J., Vanderryn, J., Costa, F., & Turbin, M. (1995). Protective factors in adolescent problem behavior: Moderator effects and developmental change. *Developmental Psychology, 31,* 923–933.

Surgeon General is hoping that this program will help to reduce the amount of alcohol consumption by underage people.

There is concern by many people that the campaign could backfire and cause teens to hide and drink, or go underground to drink, especially if parents are asked not to allow their underage children to drink (Underage Drinking Debate, 2006). Underground or secret drinking can lead to major unintended consequences. Another concern raised is overmoralizing the issue. In fact, many professionals believe that moralizing should not be part of the message. Underage drinking is illegal and not necessarily an immoral act. The other issue is parenting—knowing what to teach and what not to teach. The consensus by most professionals is that parents should teach their children how to be and act responsibly and teach what is legal and illegal. There is a double standard; in other words, parents worry about their teens drinking alcohol but, at the same time, adults continue to be the largest consumers of alcohol (Dryfoos & Barkin, 2006).

School nurses need to take part in educating teens and parents on underage drinking. Striking a balance between a nurse's confidentiality regarding information learned and protecting the adolescent is a complex and difficult situation. The trust between the nurse and adolescent should not be broken unless there is evidence of impending physical harm, which is a limit of confidentiality.

Sexual Abuse

According to Banks (1999), sexual abuse is "an issue which is surrounded by apprehension and fear" (p. 157). Hundreds of thousands of minors are physically or sexually abused each year, most of the time within the family. Sexual abuse, however, may occur outside the home as well. All states have clear laws, policies, and guidelines for child protection from abuse.

Dating violence, though it always has been a problem, has come to the forefront in the last few years. Just as adults have and must solve romantic conflicts, so do adolescents. Middle to late adolescents are more apt than younger adolescents to be in a relationship involving violence that is usually related to anger, jealousy, emotional hurting, one partner's behavior, and one person trying to gain control over the other one (Wolfe, Jaffe, & Crooks, 2006). Males and females have communicated that jealousy is the main reason for aggression in a dating relationship. Other types of violence and abuse are evident within the adolescent population, such as gang violence, gay baiting and homophobic violence, bullying, harassment, and rape.

Nurses are responsible for critical event changes that are encountered during actual discussions with adolescents. Sexual abuse or other abuses are considered to fall under the limits of confidentiality. Nurses who work with adolescents must report any cases that they encounter to proper officials or health professionals. For example, a school nurse would report the abuse or violence to the principal, or a nurse in an emergency department would report sexual abuse to the physician, mental health worker, or social worker. Before explaining the severity of the situation to the adolescent, nurses should make every effort to help adolescents express their own feelings and reactions about their situation. The most effective prevention programs for risky behaviors, including violence, are those in which the content is focused on the risk factors associated with the problem area. Prevention programs must be multifaceted to be successful (Wolfe, Jaffe, & Crooks, 2006). Once the risk factors are addressed, the focus shifts to protective factors that provide adolescents with interpersonal relationship skills, conflict resolution, and decision-making skills. Interpersonal relationship skills are the focus of violence prevention programs.

Eating Disorders

Physical appearance is one of the most important aspects of self-image for all adolescents, but especially for girls. In fact, Whitlock, Williams, Gold, Smith, and Shipman (2005) reported that as many as 50% to 75% of adolescent girls in the United States continually diet, but that only 16% are actually overweight. Most girls dream and wish for beautiful lean and trim bodies, and many of them tend not to be satisfied with their own bodies. More recently, adolescent boys have begun to develop eating disorders (Harris & Cumella, 2006).

Two common eating disorders that lead to serious medical complications, and even death, if not treated correctly are anorexia nervosa and bulimia. The physical and emotional outcomes can be disastrous and deadly if these conditions are left untreated. The tragedy is that most adolescents who experience these two disorders are skilled at hiding them until medical problems become severe. Nurses who work closely with adolescents need to be highly skilled in assessing and monitoring adolescents who are at risk for these eating disorders. Refer to Box 7.5 for warning signs and symptoms that nurses need to monitor. Other than weight loss, some signs that may alert the nurse to these disorders include the need to be "perfect" or a high achiever, low self-esteem, open displays of intense guilt, signs of depression, or signs of obsession with food, calories, fat grams, or weight.

For many adolescents, obesity has become a disturbing problem. Adolescents who are obese tend to be very self-conscious of how they look to others, which may lead to a lifelong cycle of anxiety, depression, and overeating. Chronic overeating and obesity lead to severe health problems, such as heart disease, hypertension, type 2 diabetes, and respiratory problems.

The fact that these eating disorders exist in many adolescents is a warning that severe emotional hurting is present. In turn, if left undetected or untreated, the emotional distress may progress to more disturbing behavior, such as complete withdrawal, being friendless, expressions of anger and aggression, and self-harm. Psychotherapy is the treatment of choice, and nurses need to monitor for warning signs of all of these

BOX 7.5: HIGHLIGHTS FROM THE FIELD: WARNING SIGNS OF EATING DISORDERS: ANOREXIA NERVOSA AND BULIMIA

- Sudden and dramatic weight loss
- Relentless exercising
- Ritual eating—tiny bits, rearranging food on the plate
- Obsession with counting calories
- High achiever or a need to be perfect
- Frequent weighing on scales
- Common use of laxatives, diuretics, and diet suppressants
- Binge eating or purging
- Avoiding meals altogether or often eating alone
- Self-image of being and looking fat even though weight loss continues
- Interpersonal relationship problems
- Sense of helplessness that is curbed with controlling eating

disorders and talk with the adolescent and parents so that the nurse can make the appropriate referrals to a primary care provider and a psychotherapist.

Ethical Reflections

As a school nurse, you notice that you have a 15-year-old boy named Eric who keeps to himself and never talks to anyone. Lately, his behavior has become what you would note as extreme: not eating in the cafeteria, keeping his head down at all times, and never making eye contact with anyone. He has completely withdrawn from any social interaction at school. The other teens are making fun of him and his behavior and say that he is acting strange. These actions against him just seem to make him go deeper into withdrawal. You believe that he is very depressed, and from literature that you have read recently, you gather that he may be at risk for committing suicide. As a nurse, explore your moral obligations and the specific actions that you would take in this situation.

Facing Death

Adolescents facing death can be in the form of losing a loved one or can be facing their own death, and some adolescents face both forms of death. The author will present these two forms of death in the next sections.

Losing a Loved One

Losing a loved one is a catastrophic tragedy for an adolescent. Healing strategies include simple activities for the nurse, such as being present, attentive listening, and allowing adolescents to express themselves as long as they need to do so. It is important for nurses to realize that some adolescents do not want to disclose information about their feelings of losing someone, and they need to be alone. Many adolescents turn to prayer, hope, and a belief in absoluteness, or a higher being. Some adolescents heal through self-talk, memories, and dreams. It is a difficult thing for an adolescent to lose a parent. Robert, a 16-year-old boy, expressed his thoughts about the memory of his mother 3 years after her death (Markowitz & McPhee, 2002) in Box 7.6. He was only 13 years old when his mother died.

BOX 7.6: HIGHLIGHTS FROM THE FIELD: SOMETIMES I DREAM ABOUT HER

Words of an adolescent boy about the loss of his mother:
Every day I miss her, but it is just something that I've accepted that I have to deal with and can't change. One time I followed someone [in the car] until she turned, because she had the same color hair as my mom. Even though I knew it wasn't her, there was the fascination of, "What if it was . . . ?" Sometimes I dream about her, but then I wake up . . . and it knocks me back down to earth. It isn't a sad thing, because it is nice to see her again. . . . The thing that stops me in my tracks is seeing her handwriting. I still have a list of chores she'd written out—there was so much personality in her voice and in her writing, that even though it was just a chore list it is something that is so beautiful to me.

Quoted from Robert, age 16. Markowitz, A., & McPhee, S. Adolescent grief: "It never really hit me . . . until it actually happened." *Journal of the American Medical Association, 288*(21), 2741.

Although people can expect death at some point in life, most of the time people are not prepared for it, especially adolescents. In 2000, more than 20,000 school-aged children or teens, ranging in age between 5 and 18 years, died in the United States (Lazenby, 2006). When a student dies, often the teacher and school nurse will hold off on their grief and focus on the children left behind in the school. Lazenby conducted qualitative research to explore how teachers deal with the death of a student. When the researchers asked the teachers about their perception of received support, one of the informants

BOX 7.7: HIGHLIGHTS FROM THE FIELD: TEACHERS AND STUDENT DEATHS

One Teacher's Experience with the Death of Billy

It was a sunny Friday morning as the teacher stood before her fourth-grade class calling roll. She was struck by Billy's absence as he had not missed a day of school the entire year. Making comments to the effect that he was probably sick, she proceeded with the day as usual. Upon her arrival home, she received a phone call informing her that Billy had been murdered by a family member earlier that day. Her first thoughts were of denial and guilt. It was possible that she had been talking about the child at the exact moment that life left his body.

How will this teacher face her fourth-grade class on Monday after one of their beloved friends has lost his life? How will she have the strength to clear all of the items from his desk or remove his name from the roll? How many other teachers will experience the death of a student during the school year? What emotions will those teachers experience? (p. 50)

One Teacher's Irony of a Student's Final Day at School

[One teacher] recalled the irony of his student's final day of school. While sharing with his class about the statistics and dangers of drinking and driving, the student was engaged in conversation with another student. The teacher's perception was that the student was intending to do the very thing he was telling the students to avoid: drinking and driving. The teacher vividly remembered thinking, "I wish he would listen to me." That was on Friday. The student was buried on Monday as the result of a motor vehicle accident involving alcohol. (p. 54)

Quoted from Lazenby, R. B. (2006). Teachers dealing with the death of students: A qualitative analysis. *Journal of Hospice and Palliative Nursing, 8*(1), 50, 54.

stated: "'They never acknowledged to us (teachers) that maybe we needed to do something too and we were not allowed time to sit down and gather all our thoughts or listen to the counselors'" (p. 56). Refer to Box 7.7 regarding two teachers' experiences with the death of a student.

If allowed to grieve appropriately, however, in most cases adolescents will heal without permanent scarring. When death is unexpected, such as in violence or an accident, screams and loud bursts of "Oh God, why?" and "No!" from adolescents are often voiced. The death of a fellow student may shock others to a state of numbness and disbelief. When adolescents unexpectedly or expectedly lose someone they love, friend or family member, how do they say goodbye, progress through the hurting and pain, and move on?

Adolescents realize that death is a final and irreversible act. When grieving has not progressed appropriately, however, dysfunctional grieving may occur. It is normal for adolescents to live in the present and often not think in terms of consequences. Grief is a complex process for anyone, but especially for adolescents. During the grieving process, they may take more risks than usual and harm themselves. They may even seek thrills that are potentially life-threatening events.

Ethically, the nurse or school nurse must try to promote beneficence and non-maleficence by helping adolescents through the 10 stages of grief when they lose a loved one (see Box 7.8). If a long-term nurse-adolescent relationship exists, the nurse must try to help the adolescent overcome barriers to development tasks. Nurses and teachers need to be aware of dysfunctional grieving signs other than adolescents taking abnormal risks, such as: (1) symptoms of chronic depression, sleeping problems, and low self-esteem issues; (2) low academic performance or an indifference to school-related activities; and (3) relationship problems with family members and old friends. School nurses are in an ideal situation to provide support to grieving adolescents and to educate teachers on how to cope with death and dying in school settings. Lazenby (2006) emphasized that there is considerable research that has revealed a deficit of knowledge and "know-how" for teachers working with adolescents coping with death and dying of their peers and family members.

Adolescents Facing Their Own Deaths

Adolescents may be facing their own deaths if they have a terminal illness. In this case, they also may take life-threatening risks to impress their peers or others. Stillion and Papadatou (2002) poignantly stated: "Terminally ill young people find themselves struggling with major issues of identity in the face of a foreclosed future" (p. 302). They ask questions such as "Who am I now?", "Who was I?", "Who would I like to

BOX 7.8: HIGHLIGHTS FROM THE FIELD: STAGES OF GRIEF

Stages of Grief that People Experience After the Loss of a Loved One

Stage 1   Shock
Stage 2   Expression of emotion
Stage 3   Depression and loneliness
Stage 4   Physical symptoms of distress
Stage 5   Panic
Stage 6   Guilt
Stage 7   Anger and resentment
Stage 8   Resistance
Stage 9   Hope
Stage 10   Affirmation of reality

Stages of Grief for Those Who Are Personally Experiencing Death

Stage 1   Denial: It is hard to believe or accept the impending death.
Stage 2   Anger: Why me? The anger is directed at everybody.
Stage 3   Bargaining: Some people may try to bargain to put off death.
Stage 4   Depression: Depression results when a person realizes that death is happening.
Stage 5   Acceptance: The dying person accepts death and may withdraw from others.

Quote from National Education Association. (2000). Hands on assistance—Tools for educators: Crisis communications guide and toolkit. Tool 32—Children's concept of death. Retrieved from http://www.nea.org/crisis/images/crisisguide-b4.pdf

become?", "Who will I be?", and "How will I be remembered by my friends?" (p. 303). The stages of grief that people go through when they know they are dying are different from when a person is grieving for another person. In this case, grieving consists of five stages that have been widely recognized: Stage 1—Denial; Stage 2—Anger; Stage 3—Bargaining; Stage 4—Depression; and Stage 5—Acceptance (Kübler-Ross, 1970; see Box 7.8).

While struggling with whether or not to engage in intimate relationships and searching for purpose and meaning to their time-limited lives, adolescents with a terminal illness may live almost aimlessly from day to day. They may fear that they will hurt others if they die. "They [adolescents] must learn to live in two worlds—the medical world with the threat of painful treatment, relapse, and death; and the normal world of home, school, and community, with all the challenges that healthy children face" (Stillion & Papadatou, 2002, p. 303).

The central ethical principles involved in this type of nurse-adolescent relationship are beneficence, nonmaleficence, and autonomy. The same grief stages that apply to the death of a loved one are at work here as well, and nurses who are involved with dying adolescents need to first explain the stages to the adolescent. Then, nurses and family members need to be alert to problems that may arise. Extreme behaviors and risk-taking are signs that can alert nurses and family members to take measures to prevent harm (nonmaleficence). Benefiting or doing good for terminally ill adolescents includes maintaining or improving their quality of life as much as possible. Ways to improve quality of life are to allow expressions of their fears and concerns, to be sensitive to meeting cultural and spiritual needs, to have compassion and show benevolence (kindness), and to remember that they experience most of the same challenges that healthy adolescents experience. Nurses must encourage sick adolescents to engage in autonomous decision making, as appropriate, as they progress through these developmental challenges.

Cultivating the Nursing Care

In this chapter, there has already been considerable discussion about the ethical management of adolescents concerning consent, confidentiality, prevention, and illness. In addition to these issues are fundamental moral virtues that nurses need to understand and practice consistently in all areas with adolescents. The ANA *Code of Ethics for Nurses with Interpretive Statements* (2001) have essential aspects that relate to the moral integrity of nurses and their practice (see Box 7.9). Nurses who base their practice on a moral framework that includes the following virtues are more likely to be successful in developing a respectful relationship between themselves and the adolescents with whom they work.

Trustworthiness

Trustworthiness, as already defined, means that nurses are dependable and authentic because they take responsibility for their own behavior and commit to their obligations (Gullotta et al., 2000). For example, a teen girl trusts that a school nurse is going

**BOX 7.9: HIGHLIGHTS FROM THE FIELD:
ESSENTIAL ASPECTS FROM THE CODE OF ETHICS
FOR NURSES WITH INTERPRETIVE STATEMENTS
FOR CULTIVATING CARE FOR ADOLESCENTS**

- Only information pertinent to a patient's treatment and welfare is disclosed, and only to those directly involved with the patient's care. Duties of confidentiality, however, are not absolute and may need to be modified in order to protect the patient, other innocent parties, and in circumstances of mandatory disclosure for public health reasons. (3.2, p. 12)
- Nurses have a duty to remain consistent with both their personal and professional values and to accept compromise only to the degree that it remains an integrity-preserving compromise. An integrity-preserving compromise does not jeopardize the dignity or well-being of the nurse or others. (5.4, p. 19)
- Virtues are habits of character that predispose persons to meet their moral obligations; that is, to do what is right. Excellences are habits of character that predispose a person to do a particular job or task well. (6.1, p. 20).
- Virtues such as wisdom, honesty, and courage are habits or attributes of the morally good person. Excellences such as compassion, patience, and skill are habits of character of the morally good nurse. For the nurse, virtues and excellences are those habits that affirm and promote the values of human dignity, well-being, respect, health, independence, and other values central to nurses. (6.1, p. 20)

to follow through with an appointment to discuss a sensitive issue, such as the possibility of the girl's being pregnant and the choices that are available to her.

Genuineness

Adolescents are more perceptive to how genuine a person is than any other population (Gullotta et al., 2000). **Genuineness** is how credible or *real* the nurse is. For example, if the nurse puts on a facade that there is genuineness in a relationship with an adolescent because of not desiring a genuine relationship, the adolescent will perceive the disingenuousness. The pretense may be more damaging to the adolescent than the nurse's admitting the desire not to have a genuine relationship.

Compassion

Compassion means for the nurse to have an understanding of the adolescent's suffering and a desire to take action to alleviate that suffering. The display of compassion is uncommon but is a human quality that nurses need to possess. In the ANA *Code of Ethics for Nurses with Interpretive Statements* (2001) and the International Council of Nurses *ICN Code of Ethics for Nurses* (2006), compassion and alleviation of suffering are common themes.

An example of a compassionate action by a nurse is to intervene on behalf of an adolescent who has a hidden hurt. A **hidden hurt** is one that causes a great degree of mental stress, such as when family members or peers tease, make fun of, or bully a person because of a weight problem, poor grades in school, freckles, a big nose, other facial distortions, or other shortcomings (Urban Programs Resource Network, n.d.). The victimized person feels emotionally abused and belittled but, over time, a lowered sense of self-worth will occur, with a display of extremes in behaviors, such as aggression, violence, passiveness, and becoming withdrawn. An example of a compassionate school nurse is one who takes immediate measures to stop the aggressive behavior and compassionately acts by attempting to establish a trusting relationship with an adolescent who is being bullied or teased continuously. Notifying the school counselor or the principal, and talking with the adolescent's parents are important considerations.

Honesty

The old cliché of "honesty is the best policy" has proved to be good for nurse relationships. **Honesty** means being forthright, truthful, and not deceptive. According to Gullotta et al. (2000), "without honesty there can be no relationship" (p. 281). Nurses should express their feelings and emotions in relationships. For example, expressing sadness, dissatisfaction, pleasure, or displeasure about an adolescent's behavior is better than trying to cover up feelings. Hiding one's feelings can cause a barrier in the relationship—and irreparable damage.

If nurses practice the virtues of trustworthiness, genuineness, compassion, and honesty with adolescent care, a healthy and respectful relationship between the nurse and adolescent is more likely to develop. However, the adolescent must be able to perceive that the virtues are evident in the nurse's practice, otherwise a trusting relationship between the two may never evolve.

Spiritual Considerations

"One of the most important things we can do to nurture the spiritual growth of our youth is listen to their stories and share with them ours," stated Ingersoll (2000), yet "we have a spiritual emptiness in our society" (pp. A6 20, A61). Spirituality is an essential part of being human. (See the definition of spirituality in Chapter 10.) If adolescents believe in a higher being, or what some may call absoluteness, they usually voice comfort in living with this belief. For adolescents, spirituality can provide a type of healthy, nonpunitive socialization and acceptance. Nurses can facilitate an adolescent's spiritual growth by remembering the little actions that help adolescents' spirituality, such as attentive listening, being present, or keeping commitments to them. Spirituality transcends all religious beliefs; therefore, nurses could better help teens by being familiar with different religious beliefs.

Nurses can do several things to help adolescents with spiritual growth. It should be emphasized that if nurses help promote adolescents' spirituality, nurses may consciously or unconsciously begin developing their own spiritual growth. Small actions that may help to deliver huge positive consequences are showing love and showing compassion.

Love is difficult to define, but Ingersoll (2000) stated, "Many people know it when they feel it" (Para 55). Showing love, according to Scott Peck, is "the willingness to extend oneself for the purpose of nurturing one's own or another's growth" (as cited in Ingersoll, 2000, Para 55). Nurses need to maintain a perceptive eye in differentiating this type of nurturing from unethical and illegal sexual advances.

Compassion is one of the virtues already mentioned in the "Cultivating the Nursing Care" section of this chapter. However, for a nurse to promote spiritual growth by practicing compassion, several related virtues emerge:

- *Forgiveness:* Always being open to others' situations and reasons for the circumstances
- *Patience and tolerance:* Detaching from one's own agenda and outcomes and waiting on and being open to another's agenda
- *Equanimity:* Being engaged in a situation with a patient and working toward a patient's well-being without the unhealthy attachment that may cause harm to the relationship
- *Sense of responsibility:* Knowing that people are interconnected and that responsibility grows from the interconnectedness
- *Sense of harmony:* Remaining in contact with the reality of a situation and with others
- *Contentment:* An intermittent feeling of comfort that comes to a person as a result of practicing and following a spiritual direction (Ingersoll, 2000)

Many Americans have taken a renewed interest in spirituality and would prefer a label of "being spiritual" rather than religious (Ingersoll, 2000). One reason for this interest is that most people believe that spirituality is at the core of human life experience. If nurses talk with adolescents and truly listen to them, spiritual growth may occur for adolescents as well as nurses. Please refer to the Box 7.9 for essential aspects from the ANA *Code of Ethics for Nurses with Interpretive Statements* in caring for adolescents.

Web Ethics

Organizations to Help Adolescents and Parents

Parenting of Adolescents
    http://parentingteens.about.com

National Education Association: Crisis Communication Guide and Toolkit (for teachers, parents, and teens)
    http://www.nea.org/crisis/images/crisisguide-b4.pdf

Parenting Adolescents
    http://parentingadolescents.com/archivpa.html

Teen Health (for teens)
    http://www.chebucto.ns.ca/health/teenhealth/

Go Ask Alice! (for teens) Columbia University Health Services
    http://www.goaskalice.columbia.edu/

Organizations for Nurses and Teachers

Youth Risk Behavior Surveillance System Survey, CDC
    http://www.cdc.gov/HealthyYouth/yrbs/index.htm

UNFPA: United Nations Population Fund—State of the World Population
    http://www.unfpa.org

Guttmacher Institute
    http://www.guttmacher.org/index.html

Population Reference Bureau
    http://www.prb.org

National Education Association: Crisis Communication Guide and Toolkit (for teachers and nurses)
    http://www.nea.org/crisis/images/crisisguide-b4.pdf

Summary

This chapter has discussed the adolescent three-phase developmental process involving early adolescence, middle adolescence, and late adolescence. Risk-taking behaviors are at the highest rate in middle adolescence. When implementing any type of prevention intervention program for adolescents, nurses need to incorporate theory-based health risk messages along with behavioral interventions that are beneficial and nonharmful. Nurses are faced with a dilemma of choosing a program that is appropriate and healthy for a particular group. There are a variety of standardized and evidence-based programs for adolescents. Misleading, age- or content-inappropriate information, or non-theory-based information can cause more harm than good and may be a factor in an increase of unhealthy risky behaviors.

An increasingly difficult challenge exists for nurses to provide sexual education to adolescents that is ethical and acceptable, and that the information taught is actually heard *as intended*. Nurses need to know where along the sexual abstinence–comprehensive sexual education continuum that information becomes unethical, nonbeneficial, or even harmful. There are three major ethical concerns for nurses teaching along this continuum: (1) there is no clear definition of sexual abstinence today; (2) adolescent sexual intimacy is alive and well, and long-term abstinence has the potential to damage a young person's capacity to love with greater depth and integrity; and (3) there continues to be controversy as to whether abstinence-only programs are working.

Nurses must gain trust by relentlessly proving themselves to adolescents by being consistent, giving correct information, keeping commitments, and showing concern and caring. These strategies are tried and true ways to gain trust with others, especially with adolescents. A trust-privacy-confidentiality dilemma emerges when the nurse is entrusted with an adolescent's confidential health and social information. In fact, research has revealed the likelihood that adolescents will seek health services for sensitive issues depends on how well their confidential issues will be maintained. There are limits to confidentiality when potential harm to others or self are at stake. Limits of confidentiality generally include suicidal ideation, homicidal ideation, physical abuse, sexual abuse, and other behaviors that place the adolescent at risk of physical harm.

If adolescents ever really have autonomous decision-making capacity for consenting to or refusing treatments, it is closely linked to their moral self-development characteristics and how self-directed they are. Information that is gathered in a nurse-adolescent relationship must be kept private and confidential by the nurse, with the exception being limits of confidentiality.

Adolescents cope differently and sometimes worse than do adults. When a peer at school dies suddenly, reactions are usually widespread throughout the community and school. Shock and disbelief will emotionally paralyze the adolescents. Teachers and school nurses must hold off on their grief to focus on supporting and helping the grieving adolescents. The school nurse or community nurse must try to promote beneficence and nonmaleficence by helping adolescents through the 10 stages of grief when

CASE STUDY: AN ADOLESCENT COUPLE WITH HIV

Alexa was a 17-year-old senior in high school and had been an "A" student in school her whole life. Her goal was to earn a bachelor's degree in science and to one day become a physician. She had gone steady with Robert for 3 years, but he was 2 years older and was already at the local university. Robert was going to be an accountant. They were planning on marriage at some point in time. They were having unprotected sex on a regular basis but to prevent pregnancy she was on oral contraceptives. She did not worry. However, Alexa began to get sick often, such as having no appetite, losing weight, and having nausea, diarrhea, cramping, and other mysterious symptoms. She finally went to her physician. She received a diagnosis of HIV. She was shocked! She had never had sex with anyone but Robert and she never doubted Robert's faithfulness to her. After confronting him, she found out that Robert had been getting high on drugs and having unprotected group sex with his college friends of both genders since he began his studies. Although he too had been having symptoms, he was unaware that he had HIV on the night when Alexa confronted him. He later received a diagnosis of HIV.

Case Study Questions

- You are the nurse who is working the day that Alexa finds out that she has HIV. She is in the clinic for more than one hour with you while you try to counsel and console her. You have had formal HIV counseling training, so you go through the official guidelines with her. Several weeks later, after Alexa is more composed and has had time to think more about her situation, she drops by the clinic and wants to talk with you on a more personal basis. She needs comforting. What approaches are you going to take with Alexa? Please explore how to use and apply the virtues to help Alexa. Be specific with your approaches.
- You know that spiritual promotion for adolescents is an important consideration. What are methods that you would use with Alexa to promote her spirituality? Be very specific. In doing so, consider her life goals with or without her boyfriend, what might happen to her relationship with Robert, her medical future, and her future in general. Imagine what you might actually say to her and do for her. Imagine a conversation that would take place between the two of you. An option to try is role-play with your peers.

they lose a loved one or classmate. Adolescents facing their own death will experience the 5 stages of grief that were labeled by Kübler-Ross. It is likely that adolescents grieving for self or the death of classmates will engage in high-risk behaviors intermittently.

Nurses need to base their practice with adolescents on a moral framework of virtues that includes trustworthiness, genuineness, compassion, and honesty. The ANA *Code of Ethics for Nurses with Interpretive Statements* (2001) and the *ICN Code of Ethics for Nurses* (2006) emphasize moral integrity in practice. Spiritual considerations are important to adolescents in all aspects of tribulations experienced. Nurses should practice the virtues of spirituality as well as teach these virtues to adolescents.

- Listen to adolescents, their stories, and their problems.
- Remember the little things that nurses can do in times of stress and need.
- Be compassionate.
- Be forgiving and remain open to others.
- Stay engaged in a situation with adolescents as needed.
- Maintain a sense of responsibility.
- Develop a sense of harmony.
- Be content.

References

American Academy of Child and Adolescent Psychiatry. (2004). Facts for families: Teen suicide. Retrieved January 30, 2007, from http://aacap.org/page.ww?name=Teen+Suicide&section=Facts+for+Families

American Nurses Association. (2001). *Code of ethics for nurses with interpretive statements*. Silver Spring, MD: Author.

Bandura, A. (1977). *Social learning theory.* New York: General Learning Press.

Banks, S. (1999). *Ethical issues in youth work*. New York: Routledge.

Blustein, J., & Moreno, J. D. (1999). Valid consent to treatment and the unsupervised adolescent. In J. Blustein, C. Levine, & N. N. Dubler (Eds.), *The adolescent alone: Decision making in health care in the United States* (pp. 100-110). New York: Cambridge University Press.

Boonstra, H. (2004, March). Comprehensive approach needed to combat sexually transmitted infections among youth. *The Guttmacher Report on Public Policy, 7*(1), 3–4, 13. Retrieved January 30, 2007, from http://www.guttmacher.org/pubs/tgr/07/1/gr070103.html

Bowman, D. H. (2004). Cover story: Abstinence-only debate heating up. *Education Week, 23*(22), 1–2.

Centers for Disease Control and Prevention. (1988). Guidelines for effective school health education to prevent the spread of AIDS. *Morbidity & Mortality Weekly Report, 37*(S-2), 1–14. Retrieved January 30, 2007, from http://www.cdc.gov/mmwr/preview/mmwrhtml/00001751.htm

Centers for Disease Control and Prevention. (2005). United States—2005 youth risk behavior system (YRBS) survey. Retrieved January 30, 2007, from http://www.cdc.gov/HealthyYouth/YRBS/pdf/mortality/USA.pdf

Centers for Disease Control and Prevention. (2007). Healthy youth: An investment in our nation's future, 2007. Retrieved January 30, 2007, from http://www.cdc.gov/HealthyYouth/about/healthyyouth.htm

Cook, R. J., Dickens, B. M., & Fathalla, M. F. (2003). *Reproductive health and human rights: Integrating medicine, ethics, and law.* New York: Oxford University Press/Clarendon.

Dailard, C. (2003). New medical records privacy rule: The interface with teen access to confidential care. *The Guttmacher Report on Public Policy, 6* (1), 6–7. Retrieved January 30, 2007, from http://www.guttmacher.org/pubs/tgr/06/1/gr060106.html

Dickens, C. (1993). *A tale of two cities.* New York: Everyman's Library. (Original work published in 1859)

DiClemente, R. J., Hansen, W. B., & Ponton, L. E. (1996). *Handbook of adolescent health risk behavior.* New York: Plenum.

Drug Policy Analysis. (2006). Medicinal marijuana. Retrieved January 30, 2007, from http://www.drugpolicy.org/marijuana/medical/

Dryfoos, J. G., & Barkin, C. (2006). *Adolescence: Growing up in America today.* New York: Oxford University Press.

Erikson, E. (1963). *Childhood and society* (2nd ed.). New York: Norton.

Fisher, J. D., & Fisher, W. A. (1992). Changing AIDS risk behavior. *Psychological Bulletin, 111,* 455–474.

Goldrick, L. (2005). Issue brief—Youth suicide prevention: Strengthening state policies and school-based strategies. *National Governors Association Center for Best Practices.* Washington, DC: Author. Retrieved January 30, 2007, from http://www.nga.org/Files/pdf/0504suicideprevention.pdf

Gullotta, T. P., Adams, G. R., & Markstrom, C. A. (2000). *The adolescent experience.* (4th ed.). San Diego, CA: Academic.

Guttmacher Institute. (2007). State policies in brief: Parental involvement in minors' abortions. Retrieved January 30, 2007, from http://www.guttmacher.org/statecenter/spibs/spib_PIMA.pdf

Harris, M., & Cumella, E. J. (2006). Eating disorders across the life span. *Journal of Psychosocial Nursing, 44*(4), 20–26.

Hartwig, M. J. (2000). *The poetics of intimacy and the problem of sexual abstinence.* New York: Peter Lang.

Ingersoll, R. E. (2000, May). Spirituality as a counseling resource for adolescents: Reality is complex, complexity is our friend. MetroHealth presentation. Retrieved January 30, 2007, from http://www.csuohio.edu/casal/spirsyl.htm

International Council of Nurses. (2006). *ICN Code of ethics for nurses.* Geneva, Switzerland: Author. Retrieved January 30, 2007, from http://www.icn.ch/icncode.pdf

Jessor, R., Van Den Bos, J., Vanderryn, J., Costa, F., & Turbin, M. (1995). Protective factors in adolescent problem behavior: Moderator effects and developmental change. *Developmental Psychology, 31,* 923-933.

Kübler-Ross, E. (1970). *On death and dying.* New York: Macmillan.

Lazenby, R. B. (2006). CE education: Teachers dealing with the death of students: A qualitative analysis. *Journal of Hospice and Palliative Nursing, 8*(1), 50–56.

Leffert, N., & Peterson, A. C. (1999). Adolescent development: Implications for the adolescents alone. In J. Blustein, C. Levine, & N. N. Dubler (Eds.), *The adolescent alone: Decision making in health care in the United States* (pp. 31-49). New York: Cambridge University Press.

Lindberg, L. D., Boggess, S., & Williams, S. (2000). Multiple threats: The co-occurrence of teen health risk behaviors. Office of the Assistant Secretary for Planning & Evaluation [Contract No. HHS-100-95-0021]. Retrieved January 30, 2007, from http://www.urban.org/publications/410248.html

Manisses Communications Group. (2002). Study finds many school districts not using prevention programs effectively. *Alcoholism and Drug Abuse: News for Policy and Program Decision-Makers, 14*(32), 1, 4–5.

Markowitz, A. J., & McPhee, S. J. (2002). Adolescent grief: "It never really hit me until it actually happened." *Journal of the American Medical Association, 288*(21), 2741.

Maternal and Child Health Bureau. (2003). Child health USA 2003: Health status—adolescents. Retrieved January 30, 2007, from http://mchb.hrsa.gov/chusa03/pages/status_adolescents.htm

McGuinness, T. M. (2006). Nothing to sniff at: Inhalant abuse & youth. *Journal of Psychosocial Nursing, 44*(8), 15–18.

McKay, S. (2003). Adolescent risk behaviors and communication research: Current directions. *Journal of Language and Social Psychology, 22*(1), 74–82.

National Education Association. (2000). Hands on assistance—Tools for educators: Crisis communications guide and toolkit. Tool 32—Children's concept of death. Retrieved January 30, 2007, from http://www.nea.org/crisis/images/crisisguide-b4.pdf

National Institute on Alcohol Abuse and Alcoholism. (2007). The Surgeon General's call to action to prevent and reduce underage drinking—initiative on underage drinking. Retrieved January 30, 2007, from http://www.niaaa.nih.gov/AboutNIAAA/NIAAASponsoredPrograms/underage.htm

Partnership for a Drug-Free America. (2004). More pre-teens abusing inhalants. Retrieved January 30, 2007, from http://www.drugfree.org/Portal/About/NewsReleases/More_Pre-Teens_Abusing_Inhalants

Planned Parenthood of America. (2007). Title X: America's family planning program. Retrieved January 30, 2007, from http://www.plannedparenthood.org/news-articles-press/politics-policy-issues/birth-control-access-prevention/title-x-13163.htm

Remez, L. (2000). Oral sex among adolescents: Is it sex or is it abstinence? *Family Planning Perspectives, 32*(6), 298–304.

Sexual Information & Education Council of the United States. (2002). Teen pregnancy, birth and abortion. Retrieved January 30, 2007, from http://www.siecus.org

St. Lawrence, J. S. (1994). *Becoming a responsible teen [BART]: An HIV risk program for adolescents.* Jackson, MS: Jackson State University.

St. Lawrence, J. S., Brasfield T., Jefferson, K. W., Alleyne, E., O'Bannon, R. E., & Shirley, A. (1995). Cognitive-behavioral intervention to reduce African-American adolescents' risk for HIV infection. *Journal of Consulting and Clinical Psychology, 63*(2), 221–237.

Stillion, J. M., & Papadatou, D. (2002). Suffer the children: An examination of psychosocial issues in children and adolescents with terminal illness. *American Behavioral Scientist, 46*(2), 299–315.

Turnbull, C. M. (1983). *The human cycle.* New York: Simon and Schuster.

Underage drinking debate: Zero tolerance vs. teaching responsibility. (2006). *The Brown University Child and Adolescent Behavior Letter, 22*(3), 1, 6, 7.

United Nations Children's Fund. (2006). Girls: Protected and empowered. *What Young People Are Saying.* Retrieved January 30, 2007, from http://www.unicef.org/voy/news

United Nations Population Fund. (2007). State of the world population 2006. Retrieved January 30, 2007, from http://www.unfpa.org/adolescents/overview.htm

The University of Chicago, Pritzker School of Medicine. (2005). Approach to assessing adolescents on serious or sensitive issues and confidentiality. Retrieved January 30, 2007, from http://ped-clerk.bsd.uchicago.edu/confidentiality.html

Urban Programs Resource Network. (n.d.). Family works: Strategies for building stronger families. Retrieved January 30, 2007, from http://www.urbanext.uiuc.edu/familyworks/respect-03.html

Whitlock, E. P., Williams, S. B., Gold, R., Smith, P. R., & Shipman, S. A. (2005). Screening and interventions for childhood overweight: A summary of evidence for the U.S. Preventive Services Task Force. *Pediatrics, 116,* e125–e144.

Wiseman, R. (2001). *Queenbees and wannabees: Helping your daughter survive cliques, gossip, boyfriends, and other realities of adolescence.* New York: Three Rivers.

Witte, K., Meyer, G., & Martell, D. (2001). *Effective health risk messages: A step-by-step guide.* Thousand Oaks, CA: Sage.

Wolfe, D. A., Jaffe, P. G., & Crooks, C. V. (2006). *Adolescent risk behaviors: Why teens experiment and strategies to keep them safe.* New Haven, CT: Yale University Press.

Chapter 7 Questions

1. High-risk behaviors that often lead to major causes of death in adolescents include:
   a. HIV infection.
   b. smoking cigarettes.
   c. unintentional injury.
   d. drinking wine at dinner.

2. The central ethical principle for nurses regarding prevention education programs is:
   a. respect for autonomy.
   b. beneficence.
   c. justice.
   d. truthtelling.

3. The three major ethical concerns along the abstinence-only–comprehensive sexual education continuum include all of the following items *except*:
   a. Adolescent sexual intimacy is alive and well, and long-term abstinence has the potential to damage a young person's capacity to love with greater depth and integrity.
   b. There is no clear definition of sexual abstinence today.
   c. There is controversy about whether abstinence-only programs are working.
   d. Adolescents are restricted from learning to eliminate risks when they are exposed to abstinence-only programs.

4. Which one of the following items is true regarding the trust-privacy-confidentiality issue?
   a. An example of a limit of confidentiality is for an adolescent to exhibit signs of suicidal ideation.
   b. Adolescents are usually not concerned about their privacy or about what others think of them when their information regards health issues.
   c. Adolescents, from ages 14 and up, can give consent for any procedure that is required for health purposes or elective procedures without parental or guardian involvement.
   d. A school nurse is bound to confidentiality with an adolescent with an eating disorder case who has lost a drastic amount of weight, passed out at school, and exhibits signs of malnutrition.

5. All of the following characteristics are evident in adolescents who have suddenly learned of the death of their best friend *except*:
   a. Adolescents unconsciously view death as a reversible act to help them better cope with the news.
   b. Adolescents often turn to prayer, hope, and a belief in absoluteness or a higher being when they hear the news.
   c. Adolescents generally feel that they are invincible.
   d. Adolescents do not usually self-talk, dream, or think of memories of their association with the friend because the pain of remembering hurts too deeply.

Chapter 7 Answers

1. c
2. b
3. c
4. a
5. d

Adult Health Nursing Ethics

Janie B. Butts

The depth and strength of a human character are defined by its moral reserves. People reveal themselves completely only when they are thrown out of the customary conditions of their life, for only then do they have to fall back on their reserves.

—LEONARDO DA VINCI

OBJECTIVES

After reading this chapter, the reader should be able to:

1. Identify ways in which a nurse could discern whether another nurse's character fits Aristotle's description of "the truthful sort" and relate two actual or imaginary examples of nurse characters—one whose character fits the truthful sort and one whose character does not fit the truthful sort.

2. Explore ways in which a physician's exercise of therapeutic privilege not to disclose the whole truth to a patient who could be dying with cancer will affect your nursing care for that patient.

3. Discuss truth-telling in terms of three ethical frameworks: deontology, ethic of care approach, and virtue ethics approach.

4. Explore nursing care in terms of the changes that have taken place since the 1970s regarding physician predominance of medicalization.

5. Examine cultural views related to self-determination, decision making, and the American health care professionals' values of medicalization and compliance.

6. Construct nursing care interventions in accordance with the nine themes that emerged from the interviews between the Chronic Illness Alliance researchers and patients with chronic illness and disease.

7. Delineate strategies that nurses can practice to create an ethical environment for chronically ill and suffering patients.
8. Contrast the organ procurement methods of presumed consent, mandated choice, donor cards, and required response in terms of a utilitarian framework, a virtue ethics approach, and a deontology framework.
9. Evaluate the three current ethical debates regarding retrieval of a person's organs as related to the dead donor rule.
10. Imagine ways in which nursing care would change from the perspective of an expanded legal definition of death to include patients with higher-brain functioning but no lower-brain functioning.
11. Recommend nursing care strategies for families of brain dead donors during the period of uncertainty and shock, during the life-sustaining mechanical ventilation period, and during the harvesting process.

Key Terms

Moral integrity	Honesty	The truthful sort
Truthfulness	Therapeutic privilege	Medicalization
Compliance	Noncompliance	Chronic illness
Organ procurement	Presumed consent	Mandated choice
Donor cards	Required response	Dead donor rule
Non–heart-beating donor (NHBD)	Controlled NHBD	Uncontrolled NHBD

Moral Integrity

T. G. Plante (2004) stated that, although no one is mistake free, people with integrity follow a moral compass, and they do not vary by appeals to act immorally. Most of the time when people speak of a person's **moral integrity**, they are referring to the person's quality of character (Cox, La Caze, & Levine, 2005; Plante, 2004). Integrity represents a person's whole character: "integration of self . . . maintenance of identity . . . standing for something . . . [having] moral purpose . . . [and] integrity as a virtue" (Cox et al., Para 3). People with moral integrity pursue a moral purpose in life, understand their moral obligations in the community, and are committed to following through without any constraints imposed on them by their moral stance (Cox et al.).

To have moral integrity means that a person has integrated several virtues; two closely linked ones are honesty and truthfulness.

Honesty in Nursing

Honesty is more than just telling the truth. It involves a willingness to dig for truth in a rational, methodical, and diligent way and having the ability to place emphasis on resolve and action, to achieve a just society (Brannigan & Boss, 2001; Vallee, n.d.). A person with maturity in honesty will place bits of truths into perspective and prudently search for the missing truths before addressing the issue. In other words, honesty is well-thought-out behavior that reflects commitment and integrity.

In the 2006 Gallup poll survey of many professions, the nursing profession was rated as the most honest and ethical profession (Saad, 2006). Of the next five professions that topped the list, four professions were in the health or medical arena. Members of Congress, lawyers, and business professions, such as HMO administrators, ranked toward the bottom of the list. Based on the surveys of the last few years, the nursing profession continues to rank the highest every year.

There are many ways that nurses can portray honesty. For example, nurses must stay committed to their promises to patients and follow through with appropriate behaviors, such as returning to patients' hospital rooms, as promised, to help them with certain tasks. If nurses do not follow through with their commitments, trust may be broken, and patients may see nurses as dishonest or untrustworthy.

Honesty is also about being honest with oneself. For example, if a nurse was in the process of administering medications and a pill fell on the hospital floor, would the nurse be justified in wiping it off and placing it back in the cup if no one was there to see the action? Nurses might be tempted to wipe off the pill and administer it just to keep from completing a required medication form. If nurses evaluate their problems and make decisions based on the thought "be honest with myself," it is more likely that they would make rational, trustworthy decisions regarding the care of patients. (See more on honesty in Chapter 7.)

Telling the Truth in Nursing

Aristotle recognized truthfulness as the mean between imposture (excessiveness) and self-deprecation (deficiency) and as one of the 12 excellences (virtues) that he identified in his book *Nicomachean Ethics* (trans. 2002). Aristotle emphasized that people need to practice the virtues habitually with the intent of striving for an integrated moral character and the ultimate goal of happiness exhibited by a flourishing human life. Aristotle maintained that people accomplish their ultimate goal of happiness only by exercising rational and intellectual thinking, which he called wisdom or contemplation. Aristotle explained his view of a truthful person as being **the truthful sort** (refer to Box 8.1).

Truthfulness is "not only what we say but, more importantly, how we say it" (Brannigan & Boss, 2001, p. 126). Truthfulness, translated to telling the truth in the health care arena, based on the principle of veracity, means nurses are ethically obligated to tell the truth and not intentionally to deceive or mislead patients (Aiken, 2004). In the *Code of Ethics for Nurses with Interpretive Statements*, the ANA (2001) emphasized the need for the habitual practice of virtues such as wisdom, honesty, and courage because these virtues reflect a morally good person and promote the values of human dignity, well-being, respect, health, independence, and other nursing and life values.

Because of the emphasis in the Western world on patients' right to know about their personal health care, telling the truth has become the basis for relationships between health care professionals and their patients in the last few decades (Beauchamp & Childress, 2001). In the older traditional approach, disclosure or telling the truth was more of a beneficent or paternalistic approach and involved basing actions on the answers to the questions "What is best for the patient to know?" or "If I tell the truth to the patient, will it bring harm?"

Even today, health care professionals, not intentionally meaning to be paternalistic, use various levels of what one can call a beneficent type of deception. People using this type of deception avoid telling the full truth in an attempt to protect patients

BOX 8.1: HIGHLIGHTS FROM THE FIELD: ARISTOTLE—THE TRUTHFUL SORT

We are not here talking about the person who tells the truth in the context of agreements, or anything of that sort . . . but about contexts in which . . . a person is truthful both in the way he talks and in the way he lives, by virtue of being such by disposition. Someone like this would seem to be a decent person. For the lover of truth, since he also tells the truth where it makes no difference, will tell the truth even more where it does make a difference; for there he will be guarding against falsehood as something shameful, when he was already guarding against it in itself. Such a person is to be praised.

Quote from Aristotle (384–322 B.C.). (2002). *Nichomachean Ethics*. C. Rowe (Trans.). New York: Oxford University Press.

from sad and heartbreaking news or to avert damaging the professionals' own emotions. Nurses or physicians may omit certain information because they do not know the facts, or they may state what they know to be untrue about the situation rather than admit everything they know to be true. Physicians and nurses wonder if patients want them to be so brutally truthful while patients often wonder if physicians and nurses are telling them the full truth about their diagnosis, treatment, and prognosis.

The ethical question to ask is: Are there ever circumstances when nurses should be ethically excused from telling the truth to their patients? The levels of disclosure in health care and the cultural viewpoints on telling the truth create too much complexity for a clear line of distinction to be drawn between telling and not telling the truth for nurses. Nurses are obligated by the ANA *Code of Ethics for Nurses* (2001) to be honest in matters involving patients and themselves, and to express a moral point of view when they become aware of unethical practices.

Fry and Johnstone (2002) stated that in some Western cultures, such as the United States, autonomy is so valued that withholding information is unjust. Under this same autonomy principle, it is assumed that patients have a right not to know their medical history if they so desire. There are cultures, such as those in some Eastern countries, that do not cherish autonomy as other cultures do, and family members will usually decide how much and what information, if any, needs disclosing to the patient.

Brannigan and Boss (2001) stated that physicians are obligated to tell the truth to their patients unless they have substantial reason to believe that disclosing the truth would cause undue harm, such as causing a patient extreme emotional distress, which is a circumstance known as **therapeutic privilege**. Sometimes physicians and nurses become confused about this privilege because they often do not know how much truth to withhold. When physicians exercise this right, they usually base their opinion on data gathered from their interactions with the patient, family, and other health care professionals. Evidence can also come from the patient's medical record, such as documentation of a history of mental and emotional problems.

The complexity of the situation leaves physicians with a difficult decision to make and leaves nurses with moral suffering, especially when patients want to know the full truth and physicians have decided to disclose only part of the truth—or none of it—to the patient (see Moral Suffering in Chapter 2). In these circumstances, nurses must evaluate the situation carefully, as Aristotle stated that people should do, with wisdom and contemplation, before making any decision. Nurses should not go against the physician's exercise of therapeutic privilege in most situations. Mappes and DeGrazia (2001) emphasized: "When all is said and done, many arguments for individual cases of lying do not hold water. Whether or not knowing the truth is essential to the patient's health, telling the truth is essential to the health of the doctor- [and nurse-] patient relationship" (p. 92). Refer to Box 8.6 at the end of this chapter for essential aspects of the ANA *Code of Ethics for Nurses* that apply to the care of adult patients.

An excellent example of telling the truth is from the play *W;t* (pronounced "Wit") by Margaret Edson, winner of the 1998 Pulitzer Prize; the play became an HBO Home Movie in 2001 and is now available for purchase. Susie Monahan, RN, decided to tell the truth to and be forthright with a patient despite a few physicians who chose not to do so (refer to Box 8.2).

Box 8.2: Highlights from the Field: Susie Monahan, RN, W;t— Telling the Truth

Susie Monahan was a registered nurse who was caring for Vivian Bearing, a dying patient with cancer, at a large research hospital. Vivian was getting large doses of cancer chemotherapy without any success of remission. In fact, the cancer was only progressing at an alarming rate. She was near death but the research physicians wanted to challenge her body with chemotherapy for as long as possible to observe outcome effects. Everyone on the medical staff had been cold, technically minded, and no one had shown any concern for her except for Susie. Vivian had not been informed about the chemotherapy failure, her prognosis, or that she was dying. One night, Susie found Vivian crying and in a state of panic. Susie first helped to calm her, then shared a popsicle with Vivian at the bedside while she disclosed the full truth to Vivian about her chemotherapy, her prognosis, her choices about Code Blue or DNR, and her imminent death. Susie affectionately explained:

> You can be "full code," which means that if your heart stops, they'll call a Code Blue and the code team will come and resuscitate you and take you to Intensive Care until you stabilize again. Or you can be "Do Not Resuscitate," so if your heart stops we'll . . . well, we'll just let it. You'll be "DNR." You can think about it, but I wanted to present both choices . . ." (p. 67).

Susie felt an urge to be truthful and honest. By giving human respect to Vivian, Susie was showing her capacity to be human.

From Edson, M. (1999). *W;t*. New York: Faber & Faber.

--- **Ethical Reflections** ---

You are caring for a woman scheduled for a hysterectomy because of uterine cancer. Her surgeon is known to have a bad surgical record in general but especially in performing hysterectomies. The woman has heard gossip to this effect and asks you about it before her surgery because she is apprehensive about using that surgeon. You know for a fact that at least one legal suit has been filed against him—a woman with a botched hysterectomy—because you personally know the woman involved in the case. Your choices are that you could be brutally honest and truthful with your preoperative patient; you could give her part of the truth by giving her information that you know to be untrue about certain gossip or not confirming the truth about certain gossip; or you could be totally untruthful by remaining silent or by telling her that you have heard nothing. Discuss these options and any other ideas that you may have in regard to this case. As a nurse who wants to be committed to an ethical nursing practice, what would you do in this very difficult circumstance? Be as objective as possible.

- Now that you have sorted out your actions, please justify these actions by applying either Kant's deontological theory or a virtue ethics approach.
- Describe the major differences, or any similarities, between these two frameworks (deontology vs. virtue ethics).
- Other than just verbally telling the truth to patients and others, how else can you display honesty in an ethical nursing practice? Think of how you would portray honesty in different settings and situations—bedside nursing of patients, documentation, dealing with co-workers, and administration—while taking into consideration the ANA *Code of Ethics for Nurses with Interpretive Statements.*

Medicalization

Medicalization is a term used to describe an attitude and motivation for action that emphasizes cure over care, especially in physician-to-patient relationships. Patients of all ages are included in this terminology. Medicalization, a concept widely written about since the 1970s, has evolved in its meaning over time because of the changes occurring in the medical process (Conrad, 2005). Even though physicians remain the gatekeepers for medical treatment, their focus is shifting to a more subordinate role in light of three substantial market-driven interests: (1) managed care, (2) biotechnology—genetic possibilities and pharmaceutical treatments, and (3) consumers. Medical professional dominance began to change drastically to dominance by managed care organizations, causing health care systems to focus on "doing more with less" insofar as cost control and quality.

As this shift to managed care emerged, patients began to think like consumers regarding choosing the type of medical services and physicians they wanted and the type of health insurance policies they bought. During this same time period pharmaceutical companies made enormous profits, and still do, on new drug treatments, and by the 1990s the Human Genome Project shifted society's focus to new possibilities in diagnoses and treatments. As the 1990s ended, medical professional dominance in health care and treatments diminished, although physicians continue practicing with a certain degree of control. McKinlay and Marceau (2002) referred to the 1970s as the "golden age of doctoring," which was when medical professional dominance was at its peak and medicalization was a "top-down" approach.

Even with the shifting of power, some patients are still experiencing the hegemonic practices of the medical profession in health care. Beverly Hall (2003), a nurse who wrote about her own treatment for breast cancer, gave three examples of medicalization:

(a) giving useless treatments to keep the patient under medical care; (b) demeaning and undermining efforts at self-determination and self-care; and (c) keeping the patient's life suspended by continual reminders that death is just around the corner, and that all time and energy left must be devoted to ferreting out and killing the disease. (p. 53)

Hall's three examples reflect that a certain degree of paternalistic practices by physicians could still be occurring. In these instances, the goal of the nurse would be to help facilitate the patient's acceptance of and adaptation to the pain and suffering that cannot be changed. (Refer to Chapter 12 for more information about suffering.)

Compliance

The term **compliance**, which falls under the umbrella of medicalization, means that individuals or a group of individuals submit their power to the demands of another person or group. In a health care context, compliance refers to a written or nonwritten agreement between a patient and a physician's medical treatment or nurse's health care regimen that represents the patient's intentions of obeying the wishes of the provider's regimens. **Noncompliance** means that the patient exhibits behaviors that do not reveal conformity to the physician and nurse's regimens. In light of these definitions, compliance could border on coerciveness or even a paternalistic approach by physicians and nurses to "make or force" the patient to behave in a manner that reveals a submission to provider regimens.

Barofsky (1978; as cited in Berg, Evangelista, & Dunbar-Jacob, 2002) emphasized three levels on a self-care continuum of patient responses to treatments outlined by physicians and nurses: (1) compliance, (2) adherence, and (3) therapeutic alliance. In Barofsky's continuum, compliance means coercion, adherence means conformity, and self-care is a therapeutic alliance between the providers of care and the patient.

In health care today, the issue of "doing more with less" and cost containment in care are critical to providers promoting strategies that have the potential to improve a person's health. The ethical issue of promoting healthy behaviors and yet trying to respect one's rights to self-determination is a "catch-22" situation. An ethical question to answer is: How far should providers of care go in terms of respecting the self-determination of patients when some of the noncompliant behaviors cost society the enormous burdens of money and resources? For physicians and nurses to practice ethically, they must be attuned to patients' right of self-determination and attempt to be nonpaternalistic and less coercive in teaching patients' strategies to promote healthy behaviors (Berg et al., 2002). At the same time, variables must be factored in that include efficient cost containment of treatments, patient and provider risks and benefits of proposed treatments, the costs to society for patients to maintain noncompliant behaviors, and the responsibility that patients have regarding their self-care.

Cultural Views on Medicalization and Compliance

In this complex mix of variables on compliance and medicalization, providers of care must take into consideration the cultural values regarding autonomy, independence, self-care, and authoritative figures of the family. In the United States, health care professionals value and depend on their ability to teach patients self-care strategies to reduce illness and disease; they value efficiency; and they value self-control (Galanti, 2004). In so doing, some patients and families view the eagerness of providers teaching them self-care as more of a coercive tactic. Patients of various cultures do not necessarily appreciate the teaching or the upfront way that American providers of care practice, such as giving warnings of consequences with continued unhealthy behaviors or getting caught up in a procedure while not paying attention to the patient's modesty. The patient's values often conflict with the values of American providers of care.

Another cultural consideration is the manner in which the decision is made. Generally speaking, all human beings want to know how to care for themselves, but sometimes patients will value the input from their families and will not make decisions without direction from them. The decisions will come from a group "think and do" approach rather than unilateral patient decisions. Some cultures such as Asian people have the head of the family make the decisions, whereas Native Americans would prefer that grandparents make the health care decisions. U.S. health care providers' emphasis on self-control, self-care, autonomy, money, and cure over care, no matter how much money the cure costs, is evidenced in practices such as the extensive use of life support, fetal monitoring, organ transplants, and many other life-controlling and -sustaining methods.

Most people have learned how to adapt their cultural traditions in the broader environment so that they can function without much difficulty. Galanti (2004) emphasized, "When cultural conflicts occur, it is often because what is successful under one set of environmental circumstances may be less so under others" (p. 17). Galanti proposed the adaptation theory to reduce cultural conflicts; that is, people adapting to the physical and social environment where they live. Nurses specifically can promote adaptation to a point of individual comfort so that social isolation and anomie do not occur. In the *Code of Ethics for Nurses with Interpretive Statements*, the ANA (2001) emphasized that nurses are to care for patients in a respectful and an unbiased way (see Appendix A for the ANA *Code of Ethics for Nurses with Interpretive Statements*). In the Preamble of the International Council of Nurses *ICN Code of Ethics for Nurses* (2006; see Appendix B for the *ICN Code of Ethics for Nurses*), the ICN stated:

Inherent in nursing is respect for human rights, including cultural rights, the right to life and choice, to dignity and to be treated with respect. Nursing care is respectful of and unrestricted by considerations of age, colour, creed, culture, disability or illness, gender, sexual orientation, nationality, politics, race or social status. (p. 3)

Ethical Reflections

- Discuss one situation where you have experienced the effects of medicalization and a patient's compliance or noncompliance in your nursing practice as a nurse or nursing student. Describe these effects as either positive or negative but also think about the influencers—health care system, nurses and other providers of care, the hospital or agency, and the family—and how these influenced the patient outcomes with regard to the whole person.
  - In this patient situation, do you recall the context of the care? Were human dignity, privacy, respect, and other concepts a consideration? Please give your rationale for your answers.
  - In this situation, were there cultural variances that needed attention and sensitivity? Please explain.
- What ethical frameworks or principles would guide the practice of providers (nurses and physicians) in a health care facility with a major concern of "doing more with less." What conflicts might you encounter if you practice according to your moral conscience derived from the *Code of Ethics for Nurses*?

Chronic Illness

Life is full of misery, loneliness, and suffering—and it's all over much too soon.
—WOODY ALLEN

As advances in medical technology and treatment increase exponentially, the length of life of those people who have chronic illnesses also continues to increase. A powerful statement by Booth, Gordon, Carlson, and Hamilton (2000) conveys the global problem of chronicity: "Our society is at war. Although it may not be commonly publicized in this manner, make no mistake, our society, and even the world's population in general, is truly at war against a common enemy. That enemy is modern chronic disease" (p. 775). The Chronic Illness Alliance (CIA, 2007) defined **chronic illness** as "an illness that is permanent or lasts a long time. It may get slowly worse over time. It may lead to death, or it may finally go away. It may cause permanent changes to the body. It will certainly affect the person's quality of life" (Para 2). Some CIA members, who are located mainly in Australia, convened in 2002 in an attempt to define chronic illness as a result of their qualitative interviews. In the final research report by the CIA, the team could not agree on a definition, so the definition on the Web site still stands. What *is* interesting in this research, however, are the comments made by the informants about their chronic illness and how it has affected their lives. Most informants saw chronic illness as a negative term and state of being that robbed them of any hope of recovery. Box 8.3 provides a summation of the informants' comments on chronic illness.

This Australian research has significant implications globally for those who care for patients with chronic illness. Erlen (2002) proposed three fundamental ethical concerns related to chronically ill persons: "lack of control, suffering, and access to services" (p. 416). These three concerns link closely to the concept of medicalization discussed in the previous section.

Patients with chronic illnesses frequently feel as if their illnesses are controlling them, rather than feeling that they are in control of their own lives. As indicated in the CIA (2002) report, the reality of power imbalances between vulnerable-feeling patients and the persuasion of health care providers magnify negative feelings of lack of control. Unless patients have the potential to cause harm to others, health care professionals must compassionately allow rational patients to be in control of their own lives to the degree they desire.

Catherine Garrett's (2005) work on chronic illness and suffering was based on her own chronic illness experience with irritable bowel syndrome, a cluster of symptoms that include gastric pain, intestinal pain and spasms, and malfunctioning digestion.

BOX 8.3: HIGHLIGHTS FROM THE FIELD: RESEARCH BRIEF ON CHRONIC ILLNESS: INFORMANTS' VIEWS

The 43 informants of this Australian study reported 27 different chronic illnesses. Arthritis or musculoskeletal diseases topped the list followed by mental depression, multiple sclerosis, breast cancer, chronic pain, asthma, epilepsy, stroke, thyroid problems, and hypertension. Other diseases were less frequent. The researchers extrapolated 9 major themes from the 43 interviewees. The themes were:

- *The social impact of living with a chronic illness:* Included not being able to work; living with an illness that they know will lead to their dependency on someone or even death, poverty, isolation, and loneliness; and requiring many types of support in the home.
- *The relationship between the patient with a chronic illness and the medical providers:* Patients' feelings that health care providers were frustrated by their patients' chronicity, health care staff not properly trained to care for them, the medical model dominance in terms of the many treatments and medications that did not seem to help, poor medical management, and inconsistent treatments.
- *The stigma associated with chronic illness:* Patients' feelings of discrimination and stigmatization, friends and family telling the loved one to try harder, patients labeled as noncompliant by medical and nursing providers of care if they did not or could not follow the regimen, and patients labeled as difficult if they verbalized that the regimen was not working well.
- *The way that they were labeled or classified:* Patients' feelings of being labeled or classified in a certain medical language brought about negativity from the wider world perception, and terms such as *chronic, long-standing,* and *long-term* were labels that brought about discrimination against them.
- *The need for a new definition of chronic illness:* Patients' desire for a new definition with a broader perspective on chronic illness and patients' feelings for including the complexity of one's experience in chronic illness.
- *The essential features of chronic illness for patients:* Patients' beliefs that their chronic illness had the following features:
  - Ongoing and problematic
  - Quality of work compromised

(continued)

BOX 8.3: HIGHLIGHTS FROM THE FIELD: RESEARCH BRIEF ON CHRONIC ILLNESS: INFORMANTS' VIEWS (CONTINUED)

- ○ Relationships compromised
- ○ Lifelong and substantial commitment by caregiver
- ○ Elements of uncertainty
- ○ Expensive treatments and visits to providers
- ○ Incurable
- ○ Untreatable
- ○ Requires complex and ongoing management
- ○ Life threatening
- ○ Unresolved
- ○ Complex
- ○ Permeates the whole of life
- ○ Fatigue
- *The need of a "health-promoting" definition of chronic illness:* Patients' desire for a new "health-promoting" definition to help others understand their difficulties and needs.
- *Consumers' views that policies should account for chronic illness:* Patients' fears that society and the government punished them for their chronic illness.
- *Chronic illness and activism:* Patients' commitment to fight for rights.

From Chronic Illness Alliance. (2002). Developing a shared definition of chronic illness: The implications and benefits for general practice (GPEP 843: Final Report). Retrieved April 20, 2007, from http://www.chronicillness.org.au/reports.htm#shareddefinition

Garrett has lived with this pain and suffering for 40 years, and her desire in writing the book titled *Gut Feelings: Chronic Illness and the Search for Meaning* was to recount and share her story and scholarly research on sickness, disability, violence, grief, loss, confusion, and despair. These symptoms make up what she called her suffering. Garrett explained that suffering related to chronic illness is just one kind of suffering, but that people suffer in many ways.

Garrett (2005) stated that her work was a quest for the physical, emotional, intellectual, and spiritual components that connect to chronic illness and suffering. The excellent quote by Woody Allen at the beginning of this section reflects these broad perspectives on suffering. Suffering related to chronic illness is similar to the tormenting symptoms of suffering so familiar in dying patients and their families. (Refer to Chapter 12 for more on human suffering and its definition.)

Chronic illness results in a relentless, ongoing, and unhealing suffering, and if any inseparable part is suffering, the whole person will suffer. Garrett (2005) highlighted the extent of suffering to Aristotle's four inseparable parts—appetitive, vegetative, deliberative, and contemplative. (Refer to Chapter 12 on human suffering for more explanation.) Chronic conditions produce enormous demands and conflicts to which the ill person must respond. Patient suffering related to chronic illness can be a result of many entities such as unrelieved pain, the stigma of chronic illness, and disparities between the consequences of extending life and the quality of life that results from the ability to extend it.

Patients with chronic illness feel alone and miserable, as Woody Allen so stated, or put another way, the self is suffering and the signs of suffering become evident. Many chronically ill patients often struggle with trying to attach meaning to their suffering through searching their soul, through spirituality, or by just trying to find out why they are the ones having to suffer so much, no matter whether the illness is depression, alcoholism, arthritis, diabetes mellitus, or another condition.

People suffering with chronic illness have feelings of fear, anxiety, shame, guilt, anger, and depression, all of which bring them to a belief that they often cause their own suffering (Garrett, 2005). In Box 8.4, the writers of the lyrics of the song "Questions Make Me Free" were conveying the struggle and suffering that conforming to conventional lifestyles (rite) can bring to people who chronically suffer. These song lyrics are exemplary in revealing how people will hide from themselves and push their own feelings away to avoid the pain and suffering of seeing the reality of themselves.

Ethical Nursing Care for Chronically Ill Patients

How can nurses intervene or help chronically ill patients who are suffering and struggling? Erlen (2002) discussed several ways in which nurses can create an ethical environment for giving care: (1) nurses need to increase their understanding of ethics, (2) nurses need to be advocates for their chronically ill patients, and (3) nurses need to communicate effectively with their patients and with other members of the health care team. Refer to Box 8.6 at the end of this chapter for essential aspects of the ANA *Code of Ethics for Nurses* that apply to care of adult patients.

Box 8.4: Highlights from the Field: A Scenario of Suffering: "Questions Make Me Free"

Questions Make Me Free
Laying in bed
Cried to sleep.
Tried to do rite—
It failed ME!

This round world
Looks flat to ME
If **U** come inside
I know how to hide from ME!

Prayn' it makes sense
Struggling deep inside!
I can't give up now,
But my dreams are running dry!

The answer's all around
But I still can't see.
Loved U so much
Pushed U away
Didn't want U to hurt
The **Hurt** that's been Killing Me!

Not much time
Gone through hell.
No answers?
But the QUESTION:
Can't U see,
Look in the mirror.
If U find yourself,
You can just be free!
All along it's been RIGHT IN FRONT OF ME!

Lyrics by David W. Butts and Annie Brock. Copyright 2007.

The first intervention, increasing their knowledge of ethics, is essential for nurses to understand the substance and depth of human dignity, respect, autonomy (patient self-determination), beneficence (doing good for the patient), nonmaleficence (doing no harm), and justice (fair treatment). Ways that nurses can increase their knowledge and understanding of ethics is by attending ethics conferences, reading, participating in journal ethics clubs, completing online or classroom courses on ethics, and identifying a mentor who has expertise in ethics.

The second intervention involves nurses being advocates for their chronically ill patients. In the Australian research by the Chronic Illness Alliance group (2002), the predominant echo that infiltrated all of the nine major themes was the need for a clear health-promoting definition of chronic illness so that labeling and stereotyping are avoided. Another strong theme that emerged was that people with chronic illnesses require special attention and understanding at a level that other patients may not require. Building a therapeutic alliance with chronically ill patients serves as an avenue for advocacy. Relationships need to be ongoing and long term in the sense that nurses and patients develop a long, trustworthy relationship. Even though medical management is a concern and sometimes a requirement, patients with chronic illness need emotional support, gentle prodding or teaching, and most of all the security of knowing the nurse will be there for them. As Erlen (2002) emphasized, advocacy requires that nurses take a risk—a risk in the relationship, a risk in speaking out for their chronically ill patients, and a risk of being caught in the middle of a conflict between the patient and others.

Instead of nurses building a wall of self-protection to avoid personal injury, they need to see the possibilities of "what could be" in the nurse-patient relationship by sensitizing themselves toward the human side of chronically ill persons. Nurses being open to experience their patients' pain and suffering can sometimes be emotionally and physically draining, which brings this advocacy intervention back to nurses and their self-care practices. Rituals of self-care are vital for replenishing physical and emotional energy that is critically needed in ethical relationships and in being an advocate for chronically ill patients. Garrett (2005) performed ritualistic behaviors to promote self-healing, such as yoga, spiritual meditations, stress-relieving activities, reiki, storytelling, writing, and some other mystical experiences. Nurses can choose their healing ritual for their own soul, but equally important is that nurses need to encourage chronically ill and suffering patients to create some type of ritualistic behaviors for their ongoing healing process.

Communicating effectively, Erlen's (2002) third intervention, relates highly to advocacy and involves conveying the issues and concerns of chronically ill patients to ethics committees, political groups, professional organizations, and the media. Nurses must speak out about the concerns and issues of chronically ill patients. One such example would be speaking out for improved access to health care services and better individualized care instead of the Band-aid type of care that many patients experience.

—————————— **Ethical Reflections** ——————————

You have a middle-aged female patient, Ms. S., with a 23-year history of crippling rheumatoid arthritis. Ms. S. has returned to the hospital with an injury to her head because she fell. She has no complaints of pain regarding the bump on her head. However, she is suffering with extreme arthritic pain as she has a long history of relentless pain, bilateral swelling of her hands and feet, severe fatigue, intermittent fever, and general aching all over her body. Her hands and feet are crippled from years of inflammation and erosions of the joints and bones, and therefore she must rely on others for care and support. As her nurse, you see that Ms. S. is suffering to the point that her whole existence seems weakened and compromised. The suffering experience has robbed Ms. S. of joy, contentment, and enthusiasm. In your conversations with her, she related to you that her passion for living is gone and she wants to be free from her burden of suffering.

- Identify the feelings and beliefs of patients who are chronically ill and experiencing suffering.
- What ethical issues might nurses encounter when they care for chronically ill and suffering patients who are experiencing the predominance of medicalization and noncompliance issues?
- Discuss the moral imperatives that are critical for nurses to practice in the care of chronically ill and suffering patients.
- Integrate an ethic of care ethical approach in your plan of care. Discuss ways that you could care for Ms. S. based on your ethical plan.
- Explore ways that you could offer support to Ms. S. in terms of a nursing and a multidisciplinary approach.

Organ Transplantation

Every day in the United States, 77 people receive an organ transplant and another 19 people die while on the organ "wait list" (U.S. Department of Health and Human Services, 2007). In 1954, a surgeon named Joseph Murray performed the first successful kidney transplant in Boston (President's Council on Bioethics, 2003). Murray later received a Nobel Prize for Medicine in 1990. The first human heart transplant was performed in 1967 by a surgeon named Christiaan Barnard from Cape Town, South Africa (refer to Box 8.5).

Organ transplantation is more accepted in the 21st century than it was in the 1950s. The ethical questions regarding removing organs from dead donors then were just as intense and angst provoking as the ethical questions faced today regarding human cloning. One issue in the 1950s was that, for the first time in history, surgeons were forced to decide criteria for organ recipients in light of a severely sparse supply of organs; in other words, for the first time ever, surgeons were literally choosing who

BOX 8.5: HIGHLIGHTS FROM THE FIELD: WOULD YOU CHOOSE THE LION OR SWIM FROM THE CROCODILES?

The First Human Heart Transplant

A heart surgeon named Christiaan Barnard and his 19 team members pushed the medical and scientific limits in 1967 to perform the first human heart transplant. Barnard stated: "On Saturday, I was a surgeon in South Africa, very little known . . . [and] . . . On Monday, I was world renowned" (Para 4).

Barnard transplanted the heart of a 25-year-old female auto-crash victim, named Denise Darvall, into a 55-year-old South African man named Louis Washkansky who at the time was dying of heart disease. For Louis Washkansky, the choice was to live a little longer with the donated heart or die very soon with his diseased heart. Barnard stated:

> For a dying man it is not a difficult decision . . . because he knows he is at the end. If a lion chases you to the bank of a river filled with crocodiles, you will leap into the water convinced you have a chance to swim to the other side. But you would not accept such odds if there were no lion. (Para 18)

There was success with the surgery. The heart began beating during surgery. Louis Washkansky's prescribed medication for preventing rejection of his "new" heart caused failure of his immune system. He died 18 days after his surgery.

Source: One News Health. (2001, Sept. 3). Pioneer heart surgeon Barnard dies. Retrieved April 20, 2007, from http://tvnz.co.nz/view/page/425826/55309

would live and who would die. Another major issue was that many people were dying from organ rejection because of inadequate and harmful antirejection medications. It was not until 1978 that the effective immunosuppressive medication cyclosporin was available for use.

More than 50 years after the first kidney transplant of 1954, ethical issues regarding organ donation and transplantation are still passionately debated. The issues in the 21st century have shifted to a more diverse set of problems. One major issue is the societal pressure for organ harvesting resulting from the global demand for organs that far outweighs the supply. Another major issue is individuals questioning their own moral beliefs about death and the legal definition of death as it relates to organ donation.

Organ Procurement

As of April 2007, there were 96,314 candidates on the waiting list for organs in the United States (United Network for Organ Sharing [UNOS], 2007). There is evidence that people are increasingly refusing to donate their organs, which is one of the reasons for the severe imbalance in supply and demand (Kerridge, Saul, Lowe, McPhee, & Williams, 2002; Magee, 2004). The definition of **organ procurement** is the obtaining, transferring, and processing of organs for transplantation through systems, organizations, or programs. Organ donation is a delicate subject for most people. The very thought of donating an organ could lead to individuals having disturbing thoughts about their own death or loss of a body part.

To counterbalance the supply–demand crisis, the U.S. Department of Health and Human Services has implemented new programs to increase organ supply in the last 3 years. Meanwhile, people continue to die in the United States while on the waiting list for an organ. A societal ethical conflict exists between the national officials' proposals and the values of potential donors. Many program coordinators want to use a utilitarian ethical framework as a basis for setting and accomplishing the goals of increasing organ supply whereas potential donors, especially in the Western world, value and presently abide by a deontological ethical framework of respect for autonomy and human dignity. (See the Utilitarianism definition in Chapter 1.) With autonomy and decision making as a focus for individuals, utilitarian-based programs find it a challenge to increase the number of organ donors. For a utilitarian approach, some countries use a **presumed consent** approach, meaning that individuals automatically consent to donating their organs unless they specifically indicate otherwise (Brannigan & Boss, 2001). Another approach is **mandated choice**, which means that competent individuals would be required to make a choice as to whether they wanted to become an organ donor on license applications, tax returns, and other official state identification records. Once they decide to become a donor, this mandated choice binds them by way of the cards they signed; however, an advance directive or a written change of mind can reverse that decision.

In the United States, donor cards are a legal but rarely the sole document used in the organ donation process. **Donor cards** that are carried by people give permission for the use of their bodily organs in the event of death. Advance directives also are legal documents that are used to express one's desires about organ donation. (See Advance Directives in Chapter 12.) The UNOS ethics committee has requested that U.S. citizens use a method called **required response**, which means that all adults will be required to express their wishes regarding organ donation. At that time, they will be able to object or willingly agree to donate their organs in addition to having an opportunity to allow a relative to be their designated surrogate.

A financial incentives program for organ procurement in the United States is being studied with great fervor. The 2004 Joint Commission on Accreditation of Healthcare Organizations (JCAHO) committee report stated that a committee for the Centers for Medicare and Medicaid Services is proposing allowing hospital reimbursement for potential donors prior to their being declared dead. Presently, the Centers for Medicare and Medicaid Services only reimburses hospitals for potential donors after the declaration of death while the donors' bodies are maintained by mechanical ventilation and circulation methods until the organs are harvested.

Death and the Dead Donor Rule

According to the 1981 Uniform Determination of Death Act (UDDA), death is an irreversible cessation of circulatory and respiratory functions *or* irreversible cessation of all functions of the brain (President's Commission, 1981; as cited in Mappes & DeGrazia, 2001, p. 318; see a full explanation on the definition of death in Chapter 12). Rubenstein, Cohen, and Jackson (2006) posed the questions: (1) "Why does having a sound definition of death matter at all?" (2) "What are the human goods at stake in getting this question right?" and (3) "What are the moral hazards in getting it wrong?" (Intro., Para 5). The medical community has adopted two guiding moral principles, known as the **dead donor rule**, as the norm for managing potential organ donors. The principles of the dead donor rule are (1) the donor must first be dead before the retrieval of organs and (2) a person's life and care "must never be compromised in favor of potential organ recipients" (Mappes & DeGrazia, p. 325).

Three unresolved ethical debates regarding the retrieval of a person's organs in accordance with the legal definition of death are (1) the issue of properly caring for the dying person until death is pronounced, (2) the issue of the well-being of the loved ones who must say goodbye to the dying one, and (3) the issue of the good of the organ donation itself (Rubenstein et al., 2006). The first issue is the assurance of non-compromised and competent care until the person is dead. The dead donor rule, if followed, applies here. Nurses and physicians must first tend to the care of this dying patient, which could mean administering aggressive treatment or affirming that this person's treatment is medically futile.

The second ethical issue is the well-being of families and as an extraneous concern is the issue of health care professionals. When the potential donor is declared brain dead, the dead patient continues to remain on a mechanical ventilator as if still living, having warm skin, up and down chest movement, and receiving intravenous fluids. Families see this pronounced dead patient's chest moving up and down as their still living loved one. This picture leaves health care professionals and families with feelings of ambiguity.

Nurses experience moral suffering when they see these types of moral uncertainties (see Moral Suffering in Nursing in Chapter 2). Normally, once a person is declared dead, medical treatment and ventilation support are suspended. Following a declaration of death for potential organ donors, however, providers of care maintain the physical body by way of ventilation and circulatory support until the organ procurement team can harvest the organs. The procurement teams, well trained in their field, tread on morally shaky ground with families of a newly pronounced dead loved one. Approaching the grieving family at this time is difficult, even when the team just needs to confirm the patient's or family's wish of wanting to donate the organs. Sometimes the person's death will have occurred suddenly, such as in car accidents or other injuries, and families must have time to sort out or come to terms with the death of their loved one.

A point that Rubenstein et al. (2006) made was, "these final moments of life and first moments of death *belong* to the grieving at least as much as to the departed person" (Intro., Para 7), yet this same window of time also belongs to the procurement team and surgeons. The procurement team needs to act quickly to remove the organs and deliver them to the unknown beneficiary once the organs are harvested. The ethical issue involved here is the risk of causing harm to the grieving families when there has not been sufficient time given for them to grieve and process the information versus the risk of not having viable organs if the families wait too long to come to terms with the death.

The third issue involves the good of organ donation itself. From one perspective, the donation of organs can give death a certain degree of meaning, such as a last act of benevolence and selflessness. An example could be the parents' wish to donate their underaged newly brain-dead child's organs as an imagined way to carry on that child's life. From another perspective, patients preregistering their desires to be a donor helps them to have autonomy and self-determination. The procurement team often views itself as an advocate for carrying out the patient's wish after death, which actually goes beyond the principle of autonomy in health care. Even still, this view of autonomy and beneficence for the recipient, or the releasing of the dead person's organs for the good of another person, is a widely accepted utilitarianism paradigm in society.

There is an intensely debated ethical issue surrounding the dead donor rule and its legitimacy in today's society: Is the dead donor rule outdated in this postmodern society? Alan Shewmon (2004; also cited in Rubenstein et al., 2006) clarified his latest thoughts on death as an unreal and unknowing ontological (study of being or existence) event that is without significant meaning, especially when society defines a person as dead by the legal standard that humans created in the last 26 years. Shewmon stated:

"Is the patient dead?" is not only the wrong question to ask on the practical, physical level; it is not even a meaningful one when asked on a microscopic time-scale in the transition between life and death. This would be like zooming in on the prismatic spectrum midway between green and blue, and demanding that someone not only identify that point unequivocally as either "green" or "blue" but also have a convincing, logical rationale for doing so. (p. 292)

Many bioethicists are attempting to define death as an event versus death as only a process as they grapple with expanding the utilitarianism perspective to overturn the dead donor rule so that organs can be retrieved from patients who have no higher brain function. Examples include patients with lower brain (and no higher brain) function such as those in a persistent vegetative state (PVS) like Terri Schiavo and babies born with anencephaly. Patients with no higher brain function, such as patients in a PVS, have an intact brain stem and usually breathe without the assistance of mechanical ventilation.

Pronouncing dead those patients with a functioning brain stem but without higher brain functioning would be a complete ontological shift in how society views death. Overturning the dead donor rule and retrieving organs from patients who are still alive by the UDDA definition of death would be a utilitarian ethical framework when viewed from the perspective of longer-term quality of life and the number of people that could be saved. For example, one person's organs may save three or four people. For patients in a PVS, higher brain functioning does not exist. For anencephalic babies, there is usually very little, if any, higher brain function. Society must answer these questions:

1. If the dead donor rule changes so that organ teams can harvest organs in patients without higher brain function, but with lower brain function, how will the definition of death change to include these patients?

2. Do patients without higher brain function but who are not dead by the current legal definition of death have full moral standing?
3. If persons can breathe on their own, such as those in a PVS, could they ever be dead as defined by a new legal definition of death?

Society must also reckon with the utilitarian morality of a dead person's organs being good for several people versus being good for only one family. Finally, society needs to search for what death really means in terms of the moral imperative of doing good for others versus acting within moral limits and respecting *primum non nocere* (first do no harm).

Non–Heart-Beating Organ Donors

Organ donation was originally based on the principle of procuring organs from cadavers. A **non–heart-beating donor** (NHBD) is one whose heart has ceased at the time that the organ is retrieved. There are two types. **Controlled NHBDs** are donors who are maintained on mechanical ventilation until their organs are harvested; many times, these donors have advance directives. **Uncontrolled NHBDs** are donors who have a cardio-respiratory arrest outside the hospital and cannot be resuscitated but have a declaration of death prior to retrieval of their organs. There are two critical NHBD protocols that physicians must follow: There can be no discussion of organ donation or the consent process with family members before the decision has been made by everyone concerned to withdraw life support, and the physician who declares death cannot be linked with any organ recovery agency, transplant team, or recovery team (UNOS, 2007). Nurses must adhere to the first protocol.

Social Justice and Organ Transplantation

Social justice is a consideration that cannot be overlooked in the face of scarce health care resources and a scarce supply of organs (Gillett, 2000; see a full explanation of social justice in Theories of Social Justice in Chapter 2). The ethical question is twofold: How are people chosen for the organ "wait list," and how are they chosen to receive the organ? Gillett stated:

our ability to act for the benefit of any given individual must be tempered by the requirements of justice. If there is one kidney and more than one possible recipient, some basis has to be found to make the choice between recipients. It is tempting to believe that there must be some ethical way of regulating such choices. . . . The obvious way is to accept the principle of first-come first-served. (p. 249)

First-come/first-served may not be an adequate guideline for many people because this method would not address the sickest people first; rather, it is based on a fairness principle. Organ coordinators face complex decisions regarding the allocation of organs, deciding who gets the organ and then justifying that decision. The sickest patients have many more complications and suffer more. However, if they are chosen first, as they often have been in the past, their success rate with the new organ may not be as good as that of a donor chosen based on other criteria. The approach of using the sickest patients first is a medical entitlement method, similar to that of medical emergency department triage.

Trying to select organ recipients based on social worth, self-destructive behavior, and a potential for rehabilitation is difficult to justify from an ethical perspective. One example of a self-destructive behavior is chronic smoking. Suppose there is a chronic smoker who needs a lung transplant. Would the organ team determine that this smoker is not as worthy to live or to receive an organ as another potential recipient because the person smokes? Is this not a value judgment?

If potential recipients were chosen from a utilitarian-consequential perspective, they would receive an organ based on their potential for longer-term survival with a higher quality of life. Gillett (2000) stated about utilitarianism: "Every individual should count for one and nobody for more than one. . . . The more one debates the issue, the more it seems the only fair way to determine how to distribute scarce resources" (p. 249).

Ethical Reflections

- Discuss from a utilitarian framework how you think the organ supply could increase. What are the issues?
- Discuss from a virtue ethics approach how you think the organ supply could increase. What are the issues?
- Discuss from a deontology framework how you think the organ supply could increase. Explore the issues of human dignity and that persons should not be used as a means to an end.
- Explore your thoughts on the dead donor rule as it is presently defined and how the rule could be changed to include people who no longer have higher brain function but have lower brain function, such as patients in a PVS. How would changing this rule change societal values and your own values concerning life and death?

Nurses and Organ Donors

Nurses coordinate and give care to potential organ donors, recipients, and their families, and the organ procurement teams consist of nurses, surgeons, and other health care professionals. According to the *Code of Ethics for Nurses*, nurses work within a moral framework of good personal character to promote the principle of beneficence. Refer to Box 8.6 at the end of this chapter for essential aspects of the ANA *Code of Ethics for Nurses* that apply to the care of adult patients. Most of the time, nurses want to have a sense of satisfaction based on their belief that they promote human good, preserve their patients' dignity as much as possible, and maintain a caring environment. Nurses in intensive care units and on transplant teams coordinate organ donations and transplants on a daily basis. The psychosocial impact and outcome of the organ transplantation process for donors, donor families, and recipients are unique.

Pearson, Robertson-Malt, Walsh, and Fitzgerald (2001) conducted a study of the attitudes of intensive care nurses toward brain-dead organ donors. Two major themes of caring that emerged from the study were the family and the nurse.

The Family

Of central importance to the nurses in the study was meeting the needs of their patients' families. Some important considerations for nursing care of donor family members are:

- Prioritizing the family's needs
- Empathizing with the family's tragedy
- Supporting the family's decisions
- Realizing that caring for the patient shows care for the family
- Encouraging space and privacy for the family to grieve, say their goodbyes, and, hopefully, accept the situation
- Not intruding on the family's grief (p. 135)

The Nurse

A challenge for intensive care nurses is finding meaning in the case of each brain-dead patient, including the potential donors (Pearson et al., 2000). In this study, nurses stated that brain-dead patients should be treated as if they were alive because this action shows respect for the patients and their families, and they were adamant that family members must be shown respect and kindness. A compassionate way to show ultimate kindness is to give excellent care to the families' loved ones.

BOX 8.6: HIGHLIGHTS FROM THE FIELD: ESSENTIAL ASPECTS FROM THE *CODE OF ETHICS FOR NURSES WITH INTERPRETIVE STATEMENTS* FOR CULTIVATING CARE OF ADULT PATIENTS

- An individual's lifestyle, value system and religious beliefs should be considered in planning care with and for each patient. (1.2, p. 7)
- Nurses actively participate in assessing and assuring the responsible and appropriate use of interventions in order to minimize unwarranted or unwanted treatment and patient suffering. (1.3, p. 8)
- Support of autonomy in the broadest sense also includes recognition that people of some cultures place less weight on individualism and choose to defer to family or community values in decision-making. (1.4, p. 9)
- Respect not just for the specific decision but also for the patient's method of decision-making is consistent with the principle of autonomy. (1.4, p. 9)
- Nursing holds a fundamental commitment to the uniqueness of the individual patient; therefore, any plan of care must reflect that uniqueness. (2.1, p. 9)
- Moral respect accords moral worth and dignity to all human beings irrespective of their personal attributes or life situation. Such respect extends to oneself as well; the same duties that we owe to others we owe to ourselves. (5.1, p. 18)
- Integrity is an aspect of wholeness of character and is primarily a self-concern of the individual nurse. (5.4, p. 19)
- For the nurse, virtues and excellences are those habits that affirm and promote the values of human dignity, well-being, respect, health, independence, and other values central to nursing. (6.1, p. 20)
- All nurses, regardless of role, have a responsibility to create, maintain, and contribute to environments of practice that support nurses in fulfilling their ethical obligations. (6.2, p. 21)
- The nurse should affirm human dignity and show respect for the values and practices associated with different cultures and use approaches to care that reflect awareness and sensitivity. (8.2, p. 24)

In the midst of giving competent care, tending to family needs, and providing much needed emotional support, nurses tend to become emotionally drained from feeling a need to clarify the definition of brain death and other medical terms to the families. Nurses also feel emotional strain in regard to their own ambiguities about the definition of brain death. With the ever-increasing organ procurement system, nurses find themselves experiencing moral suffering because of internal moral conflicts regarding the uncertainties of life and death. If nurses take advantage of extra education on organ transplantation nursing care and grieving families, they may be better prepared for managing their own personal emotions and those of families in crisis.

Web Ethics

Web Sites for Nurses for Ethics Education

Walkup's Way (owned and managed by Louise Walkup, ethics teacher)
    http://walkupsway.com

National Institutes of Health Ethics Program
    http://ethics.od.nih.gov/default.htm

American Nurses Association Position Statements: Ethics and Human Rights
    http://www.ana.org/readroom/position/ethics/

University of Washington School of Medicine (A good overview of the case analysis approach)
    http://depts.washington.edu/bioethx/tools/cesumm.html

Organizations Related to Chronic Illness

Holistic Health Topics
    http://www.holistichealthtopics.com/HMG/default.html

Health and Wellness Web Sites: Chronic Illness
    http://www.unh.edu/health-services/library_websites.cfm?cat=Chronic%20Illness

Centers for Disease Control and Prevention: Chronic Disease Prevention
    http://www.cdc.gov/nccdphp/index.htm

Organizations Related to Organ Transplantation

Official U.S. Government Information on Organ Donation and Transplantation
    http://www.organdonor.gov

United Network for Organ Sharing
    http://www.unos.org

Organ Procurement and Transplantation Network
    http://www.optn.org

Summary

Chapter 8 contained four major sections: (1) moral integrity, (2) medicalization, (3) chronic illness, and (4) organ transplantation. The first section, moral integrity, includes several virtues that make up the moral integrity of a person, two of which are covered in this chapter: honesty and telling the truth. People with moral integrity, defined as a person's quality of character, have a moral purpose in life, understand their moral imperatives in the community, and are committed to following through with their commitments. In this moral integrity section, the author presented Aristotle's vision of "the truthful sort"; the cultural considerations on truth-telling, therapeutic privilege, nurses and truth-telling; and an excerpt about truth-telling and a registered nurse, Susie Monahan, from the Pulitzer Prize–winning play and HBO Home Movie *W;t*.

In the second section, the author explored the traditional 1970s concept of medicalization in what was known as the "golden age of doctoring," and the three market-driven forces that have caused the physician's role to shift from one of dominance in the 1970s to one today of less dominance that borders on subordinate. The three forces that contributed to this paradigm shift were managed care, biotechnology, and consumers. With the shift, patients now think like consumers as they cleverly choose types of medical services and physicians and choose the types of insurance policies they want. Under the umbrella of medicalization are the concepts of compliance and noncompliance. Compliance, as perceived by many people, reflects a negative connotation that "forces" patients to behave in a manner that reveals a submission to provider regimens. In this same section, the author related cultural views on medicalization and compliance.

Chronic illness, the topic of the third section, includes concepts such as suffering, labeling, isolation, and loneliness associated with long-standing disease. In this section, the author presented the Chronic Illness Alliance research in 2002 on developing a newly expanded definition of chronic illness, one that would include health-promoting concepts. From the research, 9 themes emerged from data of 43 interviewed patients. Nursing care for chronically ill patients involves themes from Erlen's (2002) thoughts on creating an ethical environment: (1) nurses need to increase their understanding of ethics, (2) nurses need to be advocates for their chronically ill patients, and (3) nurses need to communicate effectively with their patients and with other members of the health care team.

The fourth and last section is about organ transplantation. In the section, the author presented the methods of organ procurement, the dead donor rule, the three unresolved ethical debates regarding the retrieval of a person's organs in accordance with the legal definition of death, non–heart-beating organ donors, and social justice regarding organ transplantation. In this same section, the author presented nursing care of brain-dead organ donors with regard to families and nurses themselves.

At the end of the chapter, the author presented several online ethics sites that are helpful for nurses and adult patients, specifically Web sites for nurses on ethics education, Web sites on chronic illness, and Web sites on organ transplantation. The author

CASE STUDY: WHO WILL RECEIVE THE LIVER?

- Mr. Mann, 50 years old, has been a heavy drinker since high school and has end-stage liver disease (ESLD) due to alcoholic cirrhosis. He will soon die if he does not receive a liver. He has been unemployed for years, even before his illness, and has received state financial assistance. Mr. Mann has stated that once he receives his new liver he will try to quit drinking on a long-term basis but will make no promises. He is not drinking now because he is in the hospital and knows he must remain abstinent for a period of time before the actual organ transplant and during the recovery process. Mr. Mann is divorced, lives alone, and has two sons who are married and working. Mr. Mann and his two sons are not on good terms.
- Mrs. Bay, 37 years old, has ESLD due to hepatitis B. Mrs. Bay is a wife and a mother of two children, one who is 16 years old and the other 12. The family is well known and active in the community. The family members have a great relationship. The children have stated that they do not want to lose their mother but Mrs. Bay is very sick though not in the hospital. At this time, Mrs. Bay experiences days when she feels critically sick and cannot move from the bed. Other days are a little better. Her prognosis is grave while she waits for a liver. She is ahead of Mr. Mann on the "wait list."

Based on your knowledge of the two diseases, you know that alcoholic cirrhosis patients with new livers may have a better success rate and longer life than do those suffering from hepatitis B, despite the fact that recovering alcoholics may have a high recidivism (relapsing to old behavior) rate. Giving hepatitis B patients new livers is controversial, and the success rate is varied. Mr. Mann is at the maximum end of the age range for organ recipients (usually age 50 or more).

Case Study Questions

Explore all situations between the two organ candidates. Whom do you choose? Give a full justification for choosing your candidate for the liver. You could briefly search the Internet regarding qualification criteria for organ recipients. Then you could search for these two diseases—alcoholic cirrhosis and hepatitis B—on past success rates of organ transplantation in similar patients. Think

(continued)

CASE STUDY: WHO WILL RECEIVE THE LIVER? (continued)

about the following ranking criteria for allocating organs, some of which are discussed in this chapter:

- *The sickest patients:* Medical entitlement method
- *First-come, first-served:* Fairness principle
- *Social worth principle:* A method of placing more value on some people and not on others because of certain individual characteristics
- *Best success rate and long-term outcome:* Utilitarian-consequential perspective
- *Proximity:* Location in relation to the area of the hospital where the organ will be transplanted (immediate area, county, region). What about the United States versus another country?

also presented essential aspects from the ANA *Code of Ethics for Nurses with Interpretive Statements* on cultivating nursing care of adult patients.

Important concepts from this chapter are:

- People with integrity use it as a moral compass to guide their lives.
- Honesty is more than just telling the truth. An honest person searches for the truth in a rational, methodical way and in the process, has the ability to place emphasis on resolve and action to achieve a just society.
- In the medicalization and managed care environment today, the issue of "doing more with less" and cost containment in care are critical to providers promoting strategies that have the potential to improve a person's health. The ethical issue of promoting healthy behaviors and yet trying to respect one's rights to self-determination is a "catch-22" situation. An ethical question to answer is: How far should providers of care go in terms of respecting the self-determination of patients when some of the noncompliant behaviors cost society the enormous burdens of money and resources?
- There is a supply-and-demand crisis for organ donation. Utilitarian-based programs to increase the number of organs remain challenged, especially in Western countries where such value is placed on autonomy and respect for human dignity.
- Expert bioethicists continue to debate the pros and cons of altering the dead donor rule so that patients who have no higher brain function, but have lower brain function, can be considered potential organ donors.

References

Aiken, T. D. (2004). *Legal, ethical, & political issues in nursing* (2nd ed.). Philadelphia: F.A. Davis.

American Nurses Association. (2001). *Code of ethics for nurses with interpretive statements.* Silver Spring, MD: Author.

Aristotle. (2002). *Nicomachean ethics.* (C. Rowe, Trans.). New York: Oxford University Press.

Barofsky, L. (1978). Compliance, adherence, and the therapeutic alliance: Steps in the development of self-care. *Social Science and Medicine, 12,* 369–376.

Beauchamp, T. L., & Childress, J. F. (2001). *Principles of biomedical ethics* (5th ed.). New York: Oxford University Press.

Berg, J., Evangelista, L. S., & Dunbar-Jacob, J. M. (2002). Compliance. In I. M. Lubkin & P. D. Larsen (Eds.), *Chronic illness: Impact and interventions* (5th ed., pp. 203–232). Sudbury, MA: Jones & Bartlett.

Booth, F. W., Gordon, S. E., Carlson, C. J., & Hamilton, M. T. (2000). Waging war on modern chronic diseases: Primary prevention through exercise biology. *Journal of Applied Physiology, 88,* 774–787.

Brannigan, M. C., & Boss, J. A. (2001). *Healthcare ethics in a diverse society.* Mountain View, CA: Mayfield.

Chronic Illness Alliance. (2002). Developing a shared definition of chronic illness: The implications and benefits for general practice (GPEP 843: Final Report). Retrieved April 20, 2007, from http://www.chronicillness.org.au/reports.htm#shareddefinition

Chronic Illness Alliance. (2007). Chronic illness. Retrieved April 20, 2007, from http://www.chronicillness.org.au

Conrad, P. (2005). The shifting engines of medicalization. *Journal of Health and Social Behavior, 46*(3), 3–14.

Cox, D., La Caze, M., & Levine, M. (2005). Integrity. In E. N. Zalta (Ed.), *The Stanford Encyclopedia of Philosophy.* Retrieved April 20, 2007, from http://plato.stanford.edu/entries/integrity/

Edson. M. (1999). *W;t.* New York: Faber & Faber.

Erlen, J. A. (2002). Ethics in chronic illness. In I. M. Lubkin & P. D. Larsen (Eds.)., *Chronic illness: Impact and interventions* (5th ed., pp. 407-430). Sudbury, MA: Jones & Bartlett.

Fry, S. R., & Johnstone, M. J. (2002). *Ethics in nursing practice: A guide to ethical decision making* (2nd ed.). Oxford, UK: Blackwell Science.

Galanti, G. A. (2004). *Caring for patients from different cultures* (3rd ed.). Philadelphia: University of Pennsylvania Press.

Garrett, C. (2005). *Gut feelings: Chronic illness and the search for healing* (At the Interface/Probing the Boundaries series, Vol. 16). Amsterdam, Netherlands: Rodopi.

Gillett, G. (2000). Ethics and images in organ transplantation. In P. T. Trzepacz & A. F. DiMartini (Eds.), *The transplant patient: Biological, psychiatric, and ethical issues in organ transplantation* (pp. 239-254). Cambridge, UK: Cambridge University Press.

Hall, B. A. (2003). An essay on an authentic meaning of medicalization: The patient's perspective. *Advances in Nursing Science, 26*(1), 53–62.

International Council of Nurses. (2006). *ICN code of ethics for nurses.* Geneva, Switzerland: Author.

Joint Commission on Accreditation of Healthcare Organizations. (2004). Health care at the crossroads: Strategies for narrowing the organ donation gap and protecting patients. Retrieved April 20, 2007, from http://www.jointcommission.org/PublicPolicy/organ_donation.htm

Kerridge, I. H., Saul, P., Lowe, M., McPhee, J., &. Williams, D. (2002). Death, dying and donation: Organ transplantation and the diagnosis of death. *Journal of Medical Ethics, 28,* 89–94.

Magee, M. (2004). Organ transplantation: A supply and demand crisis. Health politics. Retrieved April 20, 2007, from http://www.healthpolitics.org/archives.asp?previous=prog_48

Mappes, T. A., & DeGrazia, D. (2001). *Biomedical ethics* (5th ed.). Boston, MA: McGraw-Hill.

McKinlay, J. B., & Marceau, L. D. (2002). The end of the golden age of doctoring. *International Journal of Health Services, 32*(2), 379–416.

One News Health. (2001, Sept. 3). Pioneer heart surgeon Barnard dies. Retrieved April 20, 2007, from http://tvnz.co.nz/view/page/425826/55309

Pearson, A., Robertson-Malt, S., Walsh, K., & Fitzgerald, M. (2001). Intensive care nurses' experiences of caring for brain dead organ donor patients. *Journal of Clinical Nursing, 10,* 132–139.

Plante, T. G. (2004). *Do the right thing: Living ethically in an unethical world.* Toronto, ON: Raincoast Books—New Harbinger Publications.

President's Commission for the Study of Ethical Problems in Medicine and Biomedical and Behavioral Research. (1981). *Defining death* (pp. 33, 73). Washington, DC: Government Printing Office.

President's Council on Bioethics. (2003, January). Organ transplantation: Ethical dilemmas and policies. Retrieved April 20, 2007, from http://bioethicsprint.bioethics.gov/background/org_transplant.html

Rubenstein, A., Cohen, E., & Jackson, E. (2006, September). *PCBE. The definition of death and the ethics of organ procurement from the deceased.* Washington, DC: PCBE. Retrieved April 20, 2007, from http://bioethicsprint.bioethics.gov/background/rubenstein.html

Saad, L. (2006, December 14). The Gallup Poll—Nurses top list of most honest and ethical professions: Integrity of most medical professionals also highly related. Retrieved April 20, 2007, from http://www.galluppoll.com/content/?ci=25888&pg=1

Shewmon, D. A. (2004). The dead donor rule: Lessons from linguistics. *Kennedy Institute of Ethics Journal, 14*(3), 277–300.

United Network for Organ Sharing. (2007). Organ donation and transplantation. Retrieved April 20, 2007, from http://www.unos.org

U.S. Department of Health and Human Services. (2007). U.S. government information on organ and tissue donation and transplantation. Retrieved April 20, 2007, from http://www.organdonor.gov

Vallee, V. (n.d.). The roots of sound rational thinking. Salt Lake City. Retrieved April 20, 2007, from http://www.plusroot.com/dbook/08Honesty.html

Chapter 8 Questions

Please choose the most correct answer to each question.

1. When a physician has exercised therapeutic privilege with a patient who is in the end stage of kidney failure, the nurse should:
   a. Never go against the physician's decision not to disclose the full truth to the patient.
   b. Tell the full truth regardless of the physician's choice not to fully disclose.
   c. Evaluate each circumstance uniquely because telling the truth is critical to the patient-nurse relationship.
   d. Evaluate each circumstance uniquely based on the nurse's personal values and beliefs about telling the truth.

2. All of the following statements about medicalization are correct *except*:
   a. Medicalization has traditionally been about dominance in the medical profession and hegemonic practices.
   b. Nurses, patients, and families need to understand the critical influence that compliance, an element of medicalization, can have on producing successful health outcomes of patients.
   c. Even as the golden age of doctoring has shifted to a managed care environment, hegemonic medical practices continue to occur.
   d. Themes of medicalization include an undermining of patient self-determination and giving useless treatments to keep the patient under medical care for a longer duration.

3. Most patients with chronic illness believe that their illness:
   a. Actually helps them to access health care quicker and better.
   b. Is a benefit for them because of political attention brought about by the special needs of people with a chronic illness.
   c. Is a source of extreme and constant pain and suffering and is life compromising.
   d. Is viewed by health professionals as not being well understood.

4. An organ donor who requires mechanical ventilation is:
   a. A patient without higher brain function but does have lower brain function.
   b. A patient with higher brain function but does not have lower brain function.
   c. A patient with no higher or lower brain functions.
   d. A patient with intermittent and brief moments of higher and lower brain functions but overall labeled as brain dead.

5. The most significant nursing intervention for potential organ donors who are brain dead is:
   a. Meet the needs of the family members by giving pristine care to the loved one.
   b. Give psychosocial support to the donor and family members.
   c. Prevent yourself as a nurse from experiencing moral suffering so that you can continue to give competent care to the donor.
   d. Set aside a daily time schedule for the family members to grieve.

Chapter 8 Answers

1. c
2. b
3. d
4. c
5. a

Psychiatric/Mental Health Nursing Ethics

Karen L. Rich

The Royal Pigeon
Nasruddin became prime minister to the king. Once, while he wandered through the palace, he saw a royal falcon. Now Nasruddin had never seen this kind of a pigeon before. So he got out a pair of scissors and trimmed the claws, the wings, and the beak of the falcon. "Now you look like a decent bird," he said. "Your keeper had evidently been neglecting you. You're different so there's something wrong with you!"
—ANTHONY DE MELLO, *THE SONG OF THE BIRD*, 1982, P. 7

OBJECTIVES

After reading this chapter, the reader should be able to:

1. Identify how personal and professional values affect psychiatric/mental health nursing.
2. Discuss the ethical implications of diagnostic labeling.
3. Examine ways that psychiatric patients are stigmatized by both health care professionals and the general public.
4. Adhere to appropriate boundaries in nurse-patient relationships.
5. Discuss the differences among privacy, confidentiality, and privileged communication as they apply to psychiatric/mental health nursing.
6. Describe psychiatric patients' rights in directing their care.
7. Use humanistic theories in psychiatric/mental health nursing practice.
8. Discuss the ANA's *Code of Ethics for Nurses* in relation to psychiatric/mental health nursing.

KEY TERMS

Stigma	Privacy	Confidentiality
Privilege	Duty to warn	Psychiatric advance directive

Characteristics of Psychiatric Nursing

Although psychiatric/mental health nursing does not have what some nurses perceive to be the excitement of other nursing specialties, such as intensive care and emergency department nursing, mental health care is extremely important. Most nurses are inspired when they realize that psychiatric/mental health nursing care is focused on the very nucleus of personal identity. However, this realization brings with it an awesome moral responsibility.

According to Radden (2002a), there are three areas that distinguish psychiatry from other medical specialties: the characteristics of the therapeutic relationship, the characteristics of psychiatric patients, and what Radden called the "therapeutic project." Keltner, Schwecke, and Bostrom (2003) proposed that psychiatric nursing can be divided into three components: "the psychotherapeutic nurse-patient relationship (words), psychopharmacology (drugs), and milieu management (environment), all of which must be supported by a sound understanding of psychopathology" (p. 14). Ethical implications involved with these different aspects of psychiatric care and special issues in mental health are addressed in this chapter.

In general, professional health care practices are made credible because of formal expert knowledge, but the nature of professional-patient relationships, the first distinguishing area of psychiatry, may be even more important in mental health care than in other health care specialties (Radden, 2002a; Sokolowski, 1991). One reason is that facilitative relationships are often the key to therapeutic effectiveness with psychiatric patients. The nurse-patient relationship in psychiatry has been characterized from the perspective of the nurse's "therapeutic use of self," which has been defined as "the ability to use one's personality consciously and in full awareness in an attempt to establish relatedness and to structure nursing intervention" (Travelbee, 1971, p. 19). Radden compared the therapeutic relationship to a "treatment tool analogous to the surgeon's scalpel" (p. 53). When nurses are using their personalities to effect changes in patients, it becomes very important that the nurses' behaviors reflect moral character.

The second distinguishing feature of psychiatry involves the characteristics of psychiatric patients. Psychiatric patients may be more vulnerable than other patients to exploitation, dependence, and inequality in relationships (Radden, 2002a). A presumed decrease in the ability to exercise judgment in psychiatric patients and the stigma associated with mental illness lead to this special vulnerability. A central issue in psychiatric ethics is vulnerability with regard to "treatment refusal, involuntary hospitalization for care and protection, responsibility in the criminal setting, and the set of issues surrounding the criterion of competence (competence to stand trial, competence to refuse and consent to treatment, competence to undertake legal contracts, for example)" (Radden, 2002b, p. 400).

The third distinguishing feature of psychiatric care proposed by Radden (2002a), the therapeutic project, is an important part of the overall relationship between ethics and mental health. The therapeutic project is a major undertaking that involves "reforming the patient's whole self or character, when these terms are understood in holistic terms as the set of a person's long-term dispositions, capabilities and social and relational attributes" (p. 54). As with the nurses' use of self, nurses have an important moral responsibility in working with psychiatric patients in regard to the therapeutic project. Radden stated that there are only a few other societal projects that compare with the impact of the therapeutic project. One is the raising of children, which also places great responsibility on the person who is in a position of power with vulnerable others.

A Value-Laden Specialty

We do not know our own souls, let alone the souls of others.
—Virginia Woolf, *On Being Ill,* 1930/2002, p. 11

The Greek philosopher Socrates said the unexamined life is not worth living. This thought underlies the aim of much of the care that patients receive from psychiatric/mental health nurses. However, one might add two supplementary statements to the famous statement made by Socrates:

1. Many people are unable to adequately examine their lives; these lives are still worth living.
2. Even for people who try to examine the content and context of their lives, understanding is often elusive.

Although personal values pervade all discussions of nursing ethics, an emphasis on values is even more relevant to psychiatric/mental health nursing because it is largely involved with subjective experiences rather than objective diseases. According to Dickenson and Fulford (2000), psychiatry is sometimes referred to as a moral discipline rather than a medical discipline. Human values are generally shared values with regard to the experiences and behaviors addressed by physical medicine. However, in psychiatry, values relating to experiences and behaviors are usually diverse. These diverse values among mental health professionals and patients focus on motivation, desire, and belief as opposed to an overall agreement about objective findings, such as an agreement that cancer and heart disease are bad conditions. Problems arise in psychiatric/mental health care when nurses do not know how to use practical wisdom in navigating through value disparities and disagreements with patients and other health care providers.

Seedhouse (2000) proposed that there is often a fundamental values difference between what nurses are traditionally taught about the goals of nursing care and the priorities of the medical model in psychiatry (see Box 9.1). According to Seedhouse, the psychiatric system often relegates nursing priorities to the rank of secondary importance. In mental health organizations, professionals other than nurses may view it as an irritation when nurses try to reinforce the personal worth of patients by trying to find meaning in the patients' behaviors and experiences. However, the acknowledgement of this problem is not intended to mean that nurses should make negative generalizations about the psychiatric health care system as a whole. Instead, nurses' knowledge of the views of other health care professionals should encourage them to be aware of the values that influence the systems in which they function.

It is important for psychiatric/mental health nurses to remember that truly knowing oneself is hard and that understanding what underlies the emotions, words, and behaviors of other people often is even more difficult. Ethical practice in psychiatry is generally consistent with a foundationally nonjudgmental attitude. This does not mean, however, that nurses should not have thoughts, values, and considered judgments or opinions. It is unrealistic to believe that nurses' values do not affect their work, that is, that the work of nurses can be completely value neutral. The key to moral care is to have moral values. Nurses are responsible for using practical wisdom in their judgments, for being truthful with themselves about their own values, and for being compassionately truthful in their work with patients (see ANA [2001] *Code of Ethics for Nurses with Interpretive Statements*, Provisions 5.3 and 5.4; also see Appendix A). Nurses need to take care that their attitude does not degenerate into one of condescension or pity. Keeping a "there but for the grace of God go I" attitude when working in a psychiatric/mental health setting often contributes to compassionate care.

BOX 9.1: HIGHLIGHTS FROM THE FIELD: POSSIBLE PRIORITY DISPARITIES

Nursing Priorities

[Nurses are] supposed to be respectful of all other people's beliefs, treat people as equals, care personally to the extent that [they enter] patients' subjective worlds, uphold their dignity, ensure their privacy, be ethical at all times, nurture all patients and—of course—work for their health (in this case work for their mental health).

Psychiatric [System] Priorities

The psychiatrist is trained to diagnose and treat mental illnesses supposedly as real and independent of the psychiatrist as [if treating] cold sores and bronchitis.

Seedhouse, D. (2000). *Practical nursing philosophy: The universal ethical code*. Chichester, UK: John Wiley & Sons, p. 138.

Ethical Reflections

- How has mental health care been shaped by the values of Western societies?
- In what ways do you believe that a nurse's values might have greater ethical implications in psychiatric nursing than in other areas of nursing?
- How can nurses reconcile disparities in care priorities among psychiatric health care professionals?

Mental Health: A Specialty in Crisis?

Some people believe that psychiatry is the one health care specialty in which 19th-century philosophies continue to exert a strong influence on today's approach to practice (Beresford, 2002). Even in the 21st century, "bad" is often equated with "mad," and many people closely associate dangerous and murderous activities with mental illness. Until the discovery of new drug therapies revolutionized the field of psychiatry, mentally ill patients were frequently warehoused in asylums, often for very long periods of time or even for a lifetime (Hobson & Leonard, 2001). Research in the 1950s and

1960s produced new psychotropic medications that ushered in a metamorphosis in psychiatry. The new medications provided a way to manage psychiatric symptoms that had been difficult or impossible to manage before, but these drugs still caused many serious side effects related to their use.

However, because of the discovery of new drugs, there was a wide-scale release of patients from mental institutions in the 1960s and 1970s, and many of these people eventually became homeless or were jailed (Hobson & Leonard, 2001; Keltner et al., 2003). When patients were released from hospitals, the doors were almost literally locked and barred behind them. The patients were assured that they would receive adequate treatment for their mental illnesses in the community, but society and the medical community did not keep their promises to these patients. Satisfactory community treatment never materialized, and access to care is still a problem in mental health today. Although health care professionals often use the term *mental health* when speaking about the specialty of psychiatry, the system of psychiatric care continues to be based on mental illness (Beresford, 2002).

After the 1970s, patients were still not well managed with the new psychotropic drugs, and psychoanalysis had started to lose favor. When in the 1980s and 1990s health maintenance organizations further constrained the care and treatment of psychiatric patients, holistic care almost fell apart (Hobson & Leonard, 2001). The payment that psychiatrists received to conduct therapy sessions with their patients was no longer an incentive to provide these services. Now, psychiatrists have been pushed in the direction of focusing on biomedical treatment while nonphysician therapists provide counseling but no prescriptions for medications. This trend in treatment began a severe fragmentation in the environment of psychiatric care. Physicians and therapists have traditionally not communicated well amongst themselves and sometimes fight turf battles that further impede the quality of patient care.

Although in recent years there have continued to be many more improvements in the psychiatric medications that are available, medications still provide, at best, a symptom-only treatment, not a cure. Generally, there continues to be a fragmentary divide between professionals who treat mental illnesses biomedically and professionals who provide psychological therapy and counseling (Hobson & Leonard, 2001). This fragmentation, or treatment gap, has ethical implications for the quality of care that patients receive. It is in filling this treatment gap that nurses can move forward from a moral perspective.

Nurses are in a crucial bridge, or in-between, position to advance the holistic care of psychiatric patients by assessing their behavior and responses to medications and by providing education and valuable psychological and spiritual care, counseling, and support.

Advanced-practice psychiatric/mental health nurse practitioners can prescribe medications as well as provide therapeutic and supportive counseling. However, one of the primary ways that all mental health nurses can affect the ethical environment of psychiatric/mental health care is to act as patient advocates within the imperfect system.

Advocacy

There is often a fragmentation in mental health care when patient treatment is separated into the biomedical sphere of psychiatrists and the psychological sphere of therapists such as psychologists and social workers. Nurses are in a unique position to act as patient advocates in bridging this fragmentary divide. Advocacy in nursing has been defined as "the active support of an important cause" (Fry & Johnstone, 2002, p. 37). According to Seedhouse (2000), "more than any other branch of nursing, mental health nursing exposes the rift between nursing's nurturing instincts and medicine's/society's insistence that aberrant behaviors are contained" (p. 153).

Nurses must try to bring to the forefront the idea that there need not be a sharp distinction between physical or biomedical health promotion and prevention and mental health promotion and prevention. This integration can be accomplished by nurse-led dialogue among the whole team of health care providers caring for psychiatric patients. Nurses must be open to listening and sensing the feelings, emotions, and goals of all members of the team, while practicing existential advocacy as described by Sally Gadow. According to Gadow (as cited in Bishop & Scudder, 2001), "the nurse as existential advocate does not merely help patients choose what they want—for example, the drug user who wants to be as 'high' as possible while in the hospital. The existential advocate is there to help patients recognize and realize their best selves, given their situation" (pp. 76–77).

Ethical Implications of Diagnosis

Although it is not always a case of such serious proportions, through the use of mental illness diagnostic categories "people may be locked up, subjected to compulsory (and health damaging) 'treatment' and have their rights restricted" (Beresford, 2002, p. 582). This issue is closely tied to considerations of the stigma that psychiatric patients face. Pipher (2003), a psychologist, acknowledged that ethical guidelines in clinical mental health practice do not address some of the important moral issues. Disagreement about the application of psychiatric diagnoses is one of these issues. In a qualitative study conducted by Watts and Priebe (2002), the psychiatric patient participants expressed that they perceived the psychiatric system and the labeling involved with psychiatric diagnoses as "an attack on their identity" (p. 446).

Corey (2005) cautioned counselors that cultural differences must be considered when patients are diagnosed with mental disorders:

Certain behaviors and personality styles may be labeled neurotic or deviant simply because they are not characteristic of the dominant culture. Thus, counselors who work with African Americans, Asian Americans, Latinos, and Native Americans may erroneously conclude that a client is repressed, inhibited, passive, and unmotivated, all of which are seen as undesirable by Western standards. (p. 45)

Because psychiatric diagnoses often represent the boundaries of what is categorized as normal versus abnormal in society, psychiatric diagnoses along with cultural, gender, and class biases can perpetuate oppressive power relationships (Crowe, 2000). Consequently, the psychiatric diagnosing of patients is a morally charged issue. Psychiatric/mental health advanced-practice nurses are in a position to assign a psychiatric diagnosis to patients, but the assigning of diagnoses is an ethical issue about which generalist nurses also must be aware. Crowe proposed that even when nurses are not responsible for assigning a diagnosis to a patient, they are collaborators in the diagnostic process when they

- Provide data and descriptions of observations to enable a diagnosis
- Integrate the nomenclature of diagnosis into the language of mental health nursing practice
- Administer medications that have been determined by psychiatric diagnosis
- Engage in service user and family education based on psychiatric diagnosis and treatment (p. 585)

In psychiatry, there often are no definitive tests that can be used to diagnose illness, which has led to arguments over the years about the subjectivity of diagnosing mental illness (Kahn, 2001). However, the third edition of the *Diagnostic and Statistical Manual of Mental Disorders (DSM-III)*, published in 1980, radically changed how psychiatric diagnoses were categorized, which began to satisfy some of the critics. The *DSM-III* was the first in a series of the *DSM* manuals to use research as a basis for categorizing diagnoses. The developers of the *DSM-IV* went even further in using biological data for diagnostic categories. Diagnosing with the *DSM-IV-TR* (4th edition, text revision) is intended to be based on observed data rather than on what is subjective or merely based on theory. Although some practitioners disagree with this assumption, many professionals believe that the DSM system is a good one. Practi-

BOX 9.2: HIGHLIGHTS FROM THE FIELD: ANTIPSYCHIATRY

Practitioners who have an antipsychiatry view want:

> to focus more on the beliefs and values of their patients and to include the spiritual, political, and socio-cultural dimensions of experience in their practice. This approach indicates that the concept of illness is far too restrictive to assist us in understanding insanity and reminds us that in order to understand mental illness some deconstruction of what constitutes mental illness is necessary.

O'Brien, O., Woods, M., & Palmer, C. (2001). The emancipation of nursing practice: Applying anti-psychiatry to the therapeutic community. *Australian and New Zealand Journal of Mental Health Nursing, 10,* 4.

tioners generally identify the same diagnoses when using the system (that is, the system is reliable), but some people contend that the DSM diagnoses are not always valid or correct. Seedhouse (2000) suggested that people who take an antipsychiatric view (see Box 9.2) believe that the *DSM-IV-* is a "house of cards" (p. 126) based on speculative assumptions. Kahn (2001) proposed that practitioners are best served if they remain openminded when using the *DSM* system for diagnosing patients. In other words, the system is useful but not infallible.

When mental health professionals are forced by insurance companies to assign a diagnosis to patients, ethical dilemmas may arise (Corey, 2005). In suggesting that there are ethical implications and problems with subjectivity in identifying the psychiatric diagnoses of patients, Pipher (2003) presented a story about a young boy with an apparent obsessive-compulsive disorder. The boy's hands were chafed from frequent handwashing, and he insisted that all of his possessions be rigidly organized. The young man might even have qualified for special services at school based on his having a specific diagnosis, but there was a question about whether the diagnosis would ultimately help or hurt the boy. How would a label affect the child's self-perception and the perception of other people who might learn about the diagnosis? In the end, Pipher decided that a diagnosis was not necessary in this boy's case. Distraction was used as a treatment, and the child's family physician was available to prescribe appropriate medications as needed.

The point of Pipher's story is that clinicians must be very careful in labeling patients because health care professionals are often unable to determine what additional problems might be triggered by a psychiatric label. According to Pipher (2003), clinicians would do well to ask the following questions before diagnosing psychiatric patients: "Why are we doing this? Will a diagnosis allow clients to get the help they need? Can the diagnosis hurt the client?" (p. 143).

Diagnoses are often generated or changed based on information gathered and reported by nurses. Staff nurses must remember that loosely applied diagnoses that the nurse might offhandedly repeat to other people, whether these people are co-workers, the patient, families, or health care insurers, can be harmful to the best interests of patients. In other words, a psychiatric diagnosis is not something to be applied without skillful and reflective consideration by professionals who are specially educated to do so. Even then, nurses must be aware that often the determination of psychiatric diagnoses is a subjective and inexact science and can sometimes be detrimental to a patient's well-being.

Ethical Reflections

- Do you believe that psychiatric nursing is more of an art or a science? Explain.
- What factors make an objective diagnosis difficult in the field of psychiatry? What are some of the moral implications related to this difficulty? How might this issue affect nursing care?

Stigma

The days of telling your patients to "pull themselves together" should be over. It is not our patients who should be pulling themselves together: we should look at ourselves.
—J. BOLTON, "REDUCING THE STIGMA OF MENTAL ILLNESS," APRIL 2003, PP. 104–105

It is common knowledge that people with psychiatric illnesses and conditions are stigmatized by a broad spectrum of society (Bolton, 2003; Green, Hayes, Dickinson, Whittaker, & Gilheany, 2003; Knight, Wykes, & Hayward, 2003; Rosen, Walter, Casey, & Hocking, 2000; Wahl, 2003). In fact, some people believe that this stigma even extends to professionals, such as nurses and physicians, who care for psychiatric patients (Bolton; Halter, 2002). Rosen et al. defined psychiatric **stigma** as "the false and unjustified association of individuals who have a mental illness, their families, friends and service providers with something shameful" (p. 19). This negative perception is perpetuated by the media and frequently results in hostility in communities and discrimination by service providers and employers. Fears are exacerbated and illnesses are left untreated.

When referring to people with mental illnesses, the U.S. Surgeon General stated: "stigma tragically deprives people of their dignity and interferes with their full participation in society" (U.S. Department of Health and Human Services [DHHS], 1999, p. viii). The National Alliance on Mental Illness (NAMI) (2006) cited a study that revealed people's reluctance to use psychiatric drugs when they are needed because people are afraid of the stigma that they will endure (see Box 9.3).

Unfortunately, even health care professionals perpetuate the stigma of mental illness (see Box 9.4). Bolton (2003), a hospital liaison psychiatrist, voiced his distress with regard to health care professionals' negative perceptions of patients with mental illnesses. He stated that professionals who refer patients to him often say things such as "we've got another nutter for you" (pp. 104-105). Bolton followed up this concern by saying that he no longer accepts this sort of language and stigmatization without tactfully educating the user of such language about its inappropriateness.

Goffman (1963), a sociologist, did landmark work about stigma contrasting the *normals* of society with stigmatized people, or people who may be called the *discreditables*. He proposed that people with a particular stigma, such as mental illness, have common experiences in terms of how they learn to view their stigma and their very conception of self. Goffman described this phenomenon as a common moral career.

BOX 9.3: HIGHLIGHTS FROM THE FIELD: A HISTORY OF STIGMA

"The Greeks . . . originated the term *stigma* to refer to bodily signs designed to expose something unusual and bad about the moral status of the signifier. The signs were cut or burnt into the body and advertised that the bearer was a . . . blemished person, ritually polluted, to be avoided, especially in public places."

Goffman, E. (1963). *Stigma: Notes on the management of spoiled identity.* New York: Simon & Schuster, p. 1.

BOX 9.4: HIGHLIGHTS FROM THE FIELD: STIGMATIZING BELIEFS

Stigmatizing Beliefs about Mental Illness

- People with mental illnesses are dangerous to others.
- Mental illness is feigned or imaginary.
- Mental illness reflects a weakness of character.
- Disorders are self-inflicted.
- Outcome is poor.
- Disorders are incurable.
- It is difficult to communicate with people with mental illness.

Bolton, J. (April 2003). Reducing the stigma of mental illness. *Student British Medical Journal, 11,* 104–105.

These common experiences, or moral careers, involve four phases that range from having an inborn stigma to developing a stigma later in life. However, regardless of the progression of the moral careers of stigmatized persons, it is a significant point in time when these persons realize that they possess the stigma and are exposed to new relationships with others who also have the same stigma. Goffman proposed that on first meeting other people who the stigmatized person must accept as "his own," there is often ambivalence, but eventually a sense of identity develops.

It is important for nurses who practice in mental health settings to understand the meaning of relationships among psychiatric patients. If nurses become sensitive to the lived experiences of psychiatric patients and the therapeutic value of these patients' relationships with other people who are mentally ill, it ultimately may help to create a more supportive environment for these patients. Psychiatric patients, who are marked with a stigma by society, their own families, and even health care professionals, often can find a sense of camaraderie with other people who have experienced similar moral careers.

Frequently, nurses find patient-to-patient camaraderie disconcerting and sometimes attempt to minimize the support that psychiatric patients develop among themselves. However, psychiatric patients often find encouragement in these relationships, as illustrated by the comments of a former psychiatric patient, Irit Shimrat (2003) (see Box 9.5). Although sound judgment on the part of nurses is essential when assessing safety factors and the therapeutic value of relationships among psychiatric patients,

Box 9.5: Highlights From the Field:
A Common Moral Career

Former psychiatric patient Irit Shimrat stated:

> What saved me was the help I got from other patients, and the fact that I was able to help them. By showing each other compassion, by listening to each other, against all odds, we were able to remember that we were still alive. . . . When I'm feeling terrified of the world, I can talk to someone else who's been terrified of the world, but who isn't right now, and they can free me from that terror. The stories we tell ourselves about the world and our place in it have a huge influence on how we feel and what we're capable of. When people who have been labeled mentally ill can talk to each other about these stories, without fear of being judged, the feedback we get, and give, can be enormously liberating.

Shimrat, I. (2003, July-August). Freedom. *Off Our Backs, 55,* p. 18.

compassionate nursing care involves being sensitive to the stigma experienced by psychiatric patients and how this stigma affects patients' perceptions of other people who have lived through similar experiences.

Reducing Stigma

With regard to stigma, Goffman (1963) proposed that people who are stigmatized often have a turning point in their lives. Sometimes this turning point is recognized when it occurs, but sometimes it is recognized only in retrospect. Goffman stated that the turning point is an

isolating, incapacitating experience, often a period of hospitalization, which comes later to be seen as the time when the individual was able to think through his problem, learn about himself, sort out his situation, and arrive at a new understanding of what is important and worth seeking in life. (p. 40)

Because nurses are unaware of when patients are ready to undergo such a significant or potentially life-changing event, nurses must constantly cultivate a humanistic environment or milieu that facilitates the personal growth of patients. Smart (2003) stated that he has realized that it is best to think of sanity as occurring along

BOX 9.6: HIGHLIGHTS FROM THE FIELD: WAYS TO REDUCE STIGMA

- Examine our own attitudes.
- Update our knowledge of mental illness.
- Listen to what our patients say about mental illness and its consequences.
- Watch out for stigmatizing language.
- Be an advocate for those with mental illness.
- Add political activism to our daily work.
- Challenge stigma in the media.

Bolton, J. (2003). Reducing the stigma of mental illness. *Student British Medical Journal, 11*, 104–105.

a continuum rather than as a them versus me event. Bolton (2003) suggested other ways that stigma can be reduced (see Box 9.6).

Ethical Reflections

- After returning from the Iraq War, soldiers have stated that they were not comfortable seeking psychiatric treatment for posttraumatic stress disorder. One soldier interviewed on National Public Radio stated that his officers pressured him to cancel his mental health counseling appointments in order to participate in scheduled military maneuvers. What might be the source of the discrimination and stigma associated with soldiers' postwar psychiatric treatment? What role do nurses have in regard to this issue?

Borderline Personality Disorder

And it seems to me you lived your life like a candle in the wind, never knowing who to cling to when the rain set in.

—ELTON JOHN AND BERNIE TAUPIN, *CANDLE IN THE WIND*

Borderline personality disorder (BPD) is probably the most stereotyped and stigmatized psychiatric disorder in North America (Nehls, 1998). Therefore, BPD warrants special consideration in terms of mental health stigma. It has been proposed that the very term, BPD, creates a prejudice and stigma that necessitate a need for changing the name of the diagnostic label (as was done in the past with the term *hysteria*). However, as Nehls proposed, merely changing the name of the disorder will not prevent the same stigma from being attached to a subsequent label.

The behaviors exhibited by persons with BPD—poor judgment, overdramatizing situations, relational inconsistency, not keeping appointments and then demanding immediate attention, and so on—tend to "engender feelings of anger, irritation, confusion, helplessness, and hopelessness in providers" (McCann & Ball, 2001, p. 194). These feelings may prompt health care professionals to exhibit nontherapeutic behaviors such as:

- Blaming the patient for lack of improvement
- Believing that the patient would be better off dead
- Failing to return phone calls
- Failing to carefully assess the ongoing risk of prescribing medications
- Labeling the patient's motivation as the cause of treatment failure
- Overzealous use of potentially addictive medications
- Arguing with patients
- Arguing with other professional staff regarding the patient (p. 194)

Nurses need to be self-aware of the personal emotions that are engendered by all psychiatric patients while being particularly cognizant of these emotions when they arise in response to interactions with persons diagnosed with BPD. Lynn Williams (1998), a woman who professed to have experienced "world-class" symptoms of BPD, but whose condition improved, wrote a poignant article intended to help health care professionals understand some of the experiences of the disorder (see Box 9.7). Remembering that patients with BPD are worthy of nurses' concern and worthy of the best nursing care is important with regard to moral psychiatric practice.

Ethical Reflections

- What words or phrases have you heard being used that are stigmatizing to people with mental illnesses? What are the ethical implications when health care professionals use stigmatizing talk?
- In what ways do you believe that the media has contributed to the stigma of mental illness? In what ways might this media influence also affect the way the public views mental health nurses?
- How can nurses help to change negative perceptions of mental illness?

Boundaries

A discussion of boundaries is particularly relevant to psychiatric/mental health nursing because of the particular vulnerability of mentally ill patients and the importance of trust in supporting therapeutic nurse-patient relationships. Boundary violations occur when a nurse or patient exceeds the therapeutic limits of the nurse-patient relationship. Professional boundaries are specifically covered in Provision 2.4 of the *Code of Ethics for Nurses with Interpretive Statements* (ANA, 2001; see Appendix A). By keeping in mind that the primary concern of nurses' care is "preventing illness, alleviating suffering, and protecting, promoting, and restoring the health of patients" (ANA, p. 11), nurses can find guidance in maintaining professional boundaries. Nurses must ask themselves if the actions that they take, the words that they say, and the behaviors that they model are in the best interest of patients. In other words, nurses must be very conscious of how their behavior might affect patients and be interpreted by them. It cannot be assumed that psychiatric patients will react the same way that other patients might react to the behaviors of the nurse.

Concepts that underlie nurse-patient boundaries include power, choice, and trust (Maes, 2003). The asymmetry of power in favor of the nurse can place nurses in a position of influencing the decisions of patients. Patients need complete information to make choices, and nurses must help patients receive the information that they need.

BOX 9.7: HIGHLIGHTS FROM THE FIELD: BORDERLINE PERSONALITY DISORDER

Someone answering to my name was once a terrified, angry person who was showing up in emergency rooms nearly every night and throwing up into a basin, or was being looked for regularly by the police when threatening suicide. . . . But that wasn't the real me. That's not who I want to be. Nor are the other people who are seen through the pathology of borderline personality disorder showing their real selves. As frustrating as these acutely ill people may be, please don't write them off. Maybe, just maybe, you'll be able to help one of them. I'm living proof that—over time—we can be helped.

Williams, L. (1998). A "classic" case of borderline personality disorder. *Psychiatric Services, 49*(2), 174.

Though psychiatric patients may try to test nurses' good judgment by pushing nurse-patient boundaries to inappropriate limits, overall, patients trust nurses to have the knowledge, prudence, and skill necessary to provide them with ethical and competent care. Nurses must be faithful to that trust.

Potential violations of nurse-patient boundaries can involve gifts, intimacy, inappropriate limits, neglect, abuse, and restraints (Maes, 2003). Gifts are often nontherapeutic in psychiatric/mental health nurse-patient relationships, and gifts given to nurses by patients need to be considered in terms of why the gift was given, its value, and whether the gift might provide therapeutic value for the patient. Gifts should not influence the type of care provided by the nurse or the quality of the nurse-patient relationship. General guidelines for the inappropriate acceptance of gifts from patients include situations in which the gift is very expensive; the patient is seeking approval by giving the gift; the gift is given early in the relationship, which may set the stage for lax boundaries; the nurse does not feel comfortable accepting the gift but does so because of not wanting to hurt the patient's feelings; or the nurse is having difficulty setting boundaries (Corey, Corey, & Callanan, 2003). Nurses should never accept money as tips or gifts.

The cultural implications of gift giving also need to be considered. For example, patients from Asian cultures may view giving an inexpensive gift as a sign of gratitude and respect, whereas nurses responding from a Western perspective may view the taking of a gift from a patient as a boundary violation. If a nurse refused an inexpensive gift from an Asian patient, the patient may be insulted (Corey et al., 2003). It is important for nurses to keep ethical boundaries in mind, but sometimes inflexibility is damaging to therapeutic relationships. Each situation must be evaluated individually and in accordance with the policies of the employing health care facility

In addition to an obvious violation of intimacy through inappropriate sexual relationships, a violation of intimacy might occur if a nurse inappropriately shares information with other people in ways that violate a patient's privacy. The nature of nurses' work with both patients and colleagues has a very personal element, but nurse-patient relationships are not to be confused with the common definition of friendship (see *Code of Ethics* Provision 2.4; also Appendix A). Nurses are not discouraged from having a caring relationship with patients, patients' families, or colleagues. However, caring and jeopardizing professional boundaries are two very distinct issues. Although carefully chosen self-disclosure is sometimes therapeutic, revealing personal information to psychiatric patients often is detrimental to patient care. Nurses are cautioned to observe limits that prevent either the nurse or the patient from becoming uncomfortable in their relationship (ANA, 2001). Psychiatric patients are best helped when they remain the focus of nursing care rather than when attention is diverted to the personal experiences of nurses.

Physically, chemically, and environmentally restraining patients, which is discussed in most psychiatric/mental health nursing textbooks, can provide a major pitfall for nurses in terms of boundary violations (ANA, 2001). Nurses are responsible for providing safe, reasonable, and compassionate care to all patients according to appropriate ethical codes, professional standards, state nurse practice acts, and organizational policies. Nurses must do everything possible to prevent or stop patient abuse in whatever form it occurs whether the abuse is perpetrated by a patient's family or a member of the health care team. The safe and appropriate use of physical, chemical, and environmental restraints is a particularly important issue about which nurses must be continuously aware during patient care. It is essential that nurses know the policies of their employer as well as the standards set by professional organizations and accrediting agencies to safeguard patients (see Box 9.8).

Ethical Reflections

- What criteria would you use to evaluate whether it would be ethical to accept a gift that a patient made in a therapy group?
- What would you say to a patient who offered you his dead mother's pearl necklace? What would you do if a co-worker told you that she accepted jewelry from a patient?

Whose Needs Are Being Served?

An issue closely tied to relationship boundaries and the restraint of patients is the ethical obligation of determining whose needs are being served in professional-patient relationships. When discussing counselor-client relationships, Corey (2005) proposed that counselors need to be aware of when they may be placing their own needs before those of their client. This type of assessment and awareness of needs is equally applicable in nurse-patient relationships. It is easy for nurses to unintentionally become absorbed in their own self-interests during day-to-day patient care. Personal needs of the nurse that may be placed before the patient's needs include:

- The need for control and power
- The need to be nurturing and helpful
- The need to change others in the direction of our own values
- The need to persuade

BOX 9.8: HIGHLIGHTS FROM THE FIELD: RESTRAINT RECOMMENDATIONS FROM THE APNA

The American Psychiatric Nurses Association (APNA) recognizes that the ultimate responsibility for maintaining the safety of those in the treatment environment and for maintaining standards of care in the day-to-day treatment of these clients rests with nursing and the hospital or behavioral health care organization that supports the unit.

- Clients have the right to be treated with respect and dignity and in a safe, humane, culturally sensitive and developmentally appropriate manner that respects client choice and maximizes self-determination.
- Seclusion or restraint must never be used for staff convenience or to punish or coerce patients.
- Seclusion or restraint must be used for the minimal amount of time necessary and only to ensure the physical safety of the individual, other patients or staff members and when less restrictive measures have proven ineffective.
- Clients who are restrained must be afforded maximum freedom of movement while assuring the physical safety of the client and others. The least number of restraint points must be utilized and the client must be continuously observed.
- Seclusion and restraint reduction requires preventative interventions at both the individual and milieu management levels using evidence based practice.

Approved by the American Psychiatric Nurses Association Board of Directors, May 15, 2000. Retrieved from http://www.apna.org/i4a/pages/index.cfm?pageid=3346 on September 20, 2007.

- The need for feeling adequate, particularly when it becomes overly important that the client confirm our competence
- The need to be respected and appreciated (Corey, 2005, p. 38)

Nurses may have to take special care to keep in mind that patients' needs are to be placed first. As is stated in the second provision of the ANA (2001) *Code of Ethics with Interpretive Statements*, "the nurse's primary commitment is to the patient, whether an individual, family, group or community" (p. 9). Because of the psychological nature of their conditions, psychiatric/mental health patients may be particularly vulnerable to nurses placing them in dependent positions.

Psychotropic drugs sometimes make patients more manageable for nurses, which raises the question of whose needs are being served: the nurse's or the patient's? Similar to the point made with regard to nurses' complicity in the diagnostic labeling of patients, nurses have a very important role in determining the type and amount of medications that are ordered for and administered to psychiatric patients, particularly in hospital settings. Nurses are the professionals who spend the most time with hospitalized psychiatric patients, and physicians often base treatment decisions on nurses' formal or informal comments, reports, and documentation. Nurses must be very aware of whose needs are being served and must use careful reflection in determining how they choose to represent patients' behaviors and conditions to other people.

Ethical Reflections

- What questions might nurses ask to evaluate their motives before giving p.r.n. medications to psychiatric patients?
- What could a nurse do to positively influence a co-worker who tends to oversedate patients because she likes patients to be "easy to handle"?

Privacy, Confidentiality, and Privileged Communication

Although privacy, confidentiality, and privileged communication are similar concepts, there are important differences to be considered. Confidentiality and privileged communication are both issues of a patient's right to privacy; however, confidentiality is usually more associated with ethics, whereas privileged communication pertains more to the legal nature of provider-patient relationships (Corey et al., 2003).

Privacy

The concept of **privacy** began receiving attention in the 1920s when the U.S. Supreme Court addressed the liberty interest of families with regard to decision making about their children (Beauchamp & Childress, 2001). The court's rulings were designed to protect part of a person's private life from state intrusion, which incidentally was also the foundation for overturning restrictive abortion laws in 1973. However, the right to privacy cannot be reduced to a narrow context of having a right to act autonomously. In addition to autonomy, the rights that fall within the boundaries of privacy include a person's right to be protected from no more than limited physical and informational access by others.

Allen (as cited in Beauchamp & Childress, 2001) described four types of privacy that address limited personal access:

- *Informational privacy:* Communication of information
- *Physical privacy:* With regard to personal spaces
- *Decisional privacy:* With regard to personal choices
- *Proprietary privacy:* Property interests, including interests with regard to bodily tissues, one's name, etc.

The value placed on privacy varies among situations and people. Sometimes, for example, persons may feel comfortable with other people knowing that they have a psychiatric condition, but they are not comfortable with other people knowing the exact nature of the condition. Nurses need to err on the side of strictly maintaining a patient's privacy unless there is a justifiable reason for privacy to be violated, such as a duty to warn (see the following "Privileged Communication" section).

Confidentiality

In health care ethics, **confidentiality** is one of the oldest moral commitments, dating back to the Hippocratic Oath (Gillon, 2001). Confidentiality, or nondisclosure of information, involves limits on the communication of "any information a nurse obtains about a patient in the context of the nurse-patient relationship" (Killion, 2006b, p. 36). It includes limits on the communication of information related to any of the five types of privacy previously listed. The Joint Commission on Accreditation of Healthcare Organizations (1998) defined confidentiality as "an individual's right, within the law, to personal and informational privacy, including his or her health care records" (p. 139). Confidentiality is one of the most important ethical precepts in psychiatric/mental health nursing because the therapeutic nurse-patient relationship is grounded in trust.

Privileged Communication

Whereas confidentiality involves a professional duty not to disclose certain information, **privilege** provides relief from having to disclose information in court proceedings (Smith-Bell & Winslade, 2003). Patients have a legal right to believe that their communication with nurses will be kept confidential, but there are limits to confidentiality in psychiatric/mental health practice. Limits to both confidentiality and privilege would permit disclosure of information by the nurse when:

- Patients are a threat to themselves (suicide, for example) or to identifiable others
- Statutes require the disclosure of certain happenings, such as abuse, rape, incest, or other crimes
- The patient consents to release of the information
- A court mandates the release
- The information is needed for other caregivers to provide care to the patient, that is, when certain people have a "need to know" information (Corey, 2005; Killion, 2006b)

Nurses cannot disclose patient information to unidentified or unauthorized telephone callers or to relatives, significant others, or friends of the patient without the patient's consent (Killion, 2006b).

Duty to Warn

In some cases, nurses may have a **duty to warn**, which involves "a duty to disclose confidential information to protect an identifiable victim" (Killion, 2006b, p. 37). Documentation by nurses of patient threats is necessary, but this may not be enough in some cases. Nurses also may have a duty to warn appropriate authorities about threats made by patients or even to warn the specific person(s) targeted by the threats. This duty is weighed by viewing it as a dilemma between respecting a patient's privacy and respecting society's need to be informed about acts that are dangerous to citizens (Everstine et al., 2003). The duty to warn is based on the case of *Tarasoff v. Board of Regents of the University of California* (see Box 9.9).

Decisional Capacity

According to Beauchamp and Childress (2001), some people distinguish competence and capacity based on who is making the determination, that is, capacity is assessed by health care professionals, and competence is determined within the court system. Singer (2003) defined competence "as a group of capacities" (p. 152). However, some people propose that for all practical purposes, the consequences of the determination of capacity versus competence are basically the same (Grisso & Appelbaum, 1998). In psychiatric care, both capacity and competence are related to questions of whether patients have a right to consent to and refuse treatment, and are closely associated with the issue of autonomy.

Box 9.9: Highlights From the Field: Tarasoff v. Board of Regents of the University of California

In August 1969 a voluntary outpatient, Prosenjit Poddar, was being counseled at the student health center at the University of California, Berkeley campus. The patient threatened to kill a woman (Tatiana Tarasoff) who was unnamed, but who was identifiable to the therapist. The therapist warned the campus police about the threat but the police spoke with Poddar and deemed him to be "rational" and did not take action to warn Ms. Tarasoff. The therapist continued to pursue the issue, but Ms. Tarasoff was not warned of the threat and was later killed by Poddar. Her family sued the Board of Regents and the university staff for failing to warn the victim. In 1976, the California Supreme Court ruled in favor of the parents. The Court proclaimed: "The protective privilege ends where the public peril begins."

Tarasoff v. Board of Regents of the University of California, 1976, p. 347.

Corey, G., Corey, M. S., & Callanan, P. (2003). *Issues and ethics in the helping professions*. Pacific Grove, CA: Wadsworth Group-Brooks/Cole.

Statutory Authority to Treat

Involuntary commitment poses ethical as well as legal problems for psychiatric health care professionals. Based on a general social policy of deinstitutionalization, involuntary hospitalization decisions can be made only after less restrictive options have failed or have carefully been determined not to be a viable option (Corey et al., 2003). The decision is usually made based on a person being a danger to self, a danger to others, or, in some states, being gravely disabled. Each state jurisdiction has statutes that allow psychiatrists to hold persons involuntarily for psychiatric treatment, and health care professionals are responsible for following their state's particular laws and regulations (Corey et al., 2003; Jonsen, Siegler, & Winslade, 2006; Videbeck, 2006). If a patient is determined by a psychiatrist to be incompetent, state statutes can be followed for a temporary involuntary commitment. Court proceedings are then initiated to extend the involuntary treatment or commitment. This legal process is expedited while the person is being (temporarily) held involuntarily.

This process begins with a presumption of competency (Killion, 2006a). However, when it is determined by a psychiatrist that the person exhibits a lack of decision-making capacity, a petition is filed with the court to determine competency. The person receives a court-appointed guardian or legal counsel and undergoes psychological testing procedures. A hearing is scheduled, and evidence is presented with regard to the person's ability to handle personal affairs and to understand the consequences of personal decisions. Negotiations are conducted with the aim of determining the least restrictive alternative for the person's care and treatment. Outcomes of the hearing can result in a dismissal of the petition, the appointment of limited guardianship, or an appointment of complete guardianship.

These outcomes may be appealed, and a restoration hearing can be held later if the person's circumstances change and warrant a removal of guardianship. This process is often inappropriately called a "medical hold" (Jonsen et al., 2006, p. 92). The psychiatric commitment process does not automatically include an authorization to treat a patient involuntarily for medical, in addition to psychiatric, conditions. A legally authorized appointee also must be specially assigned to make medical decisions other than those that are determined to be for a life-saving emergency, in which an implied consent is sufficient.

Competence and Informed Consent

Competence and informed consent are intricately connected. Informed consent, as required by legal authorities, is impossible in situations involving incompetent patients (Singer, 2003). A patient, even when involuntarily committed, has a right to refuse treatment, such as psychotropic medications, until or unless the patient has been deemed incompetent by formal legal proceedings. In the case of *Rivers v. Katz*, the New York State Court of Appeals established that there are only limited circumstances in which a patient's right to refuse unwanted treatment can be overridden. A patient's right to refuse medications may be overridden only on the determination that a patient is a danger to self or other people. Patients may not be prevented from refusing medications based on health care professionals' desire to create a therapeutic environment, for the convenience of hospital staff, or to facilitate the process of deinstitutionalization.

There are no uniform standards that can be used to determine competence, although it is accepted that incompetence is founded on cognitive impairment (Berg, Appelbaum, & Grisso, as cited in Singer, 2003). Brody (1988) outlined general criteria of competency that also are applicable with regard to psychiatric patients. These criteria include:

- The ability to receive information from the surroundings
- The capacity to remember the information received

- The ability to make a decision and give a reason for it
- The ability to use the relevant information in making the decision
- The ability to appropriately assess the relevant information (pp. 101-102)

To this list, Singer (2003) added the capacity to participate constructively in discussions with the caregiver regarding treatment, including the "ability to engage in mutual questioning and answering" (p. 153). Singer called this supplementary capacity of communicative interchange *dialogic reciprocity* (see Box 9.10).

Psychiatric Advance Directives

The Patient Self-Determination Act (PSDA) enacted by the federal government in 1990 has drawn focused attention to patients' right to autonomy in making health care decisions. Similar to medical advance directives, the **psychiatric advance directive** (PAD) developed as an outcome of the PSDA and is legal in about 25 states. A PAD may be completed by competent psychiatric patients who want to direct their psychiatric care when and if they later lose their capacity to voice their treatment choices.

BOX 9.10: HIGHLIGHTS FROM THE FIELD: DIALOGIC RECIPROCITY

Dialogic "reciprocity . . . involves mutual respect for the autonomy and authority of all the participants in a discussion, a respect that . . . should be accorded to them as a matter of right. . . . Respecting a person's authority in this sense can be thought of as a type of empowerment: empowerment to have one's contribution to the discussion taken seriously, even if it may be subsequently rejected or overridden. . . . In the exercise of dialogic reciprocity we reflect autonomously and critically on our own judgments as well as those of the others with whom we are in dialogue. Therefore, we are open to change, even though the dialogue may result in strengthening our original position."

Singer, B. J. (2003). Mental illness: Rights, competence, and communication. In G. McGee (Ed.), *Pragmatic Bioethics* (pp. 158–159). Cambridge, MA: Massachusetts Institute of Technology.

Treatment issues that can be addressed in the PAD include choices regarding medication administration, hospital admission, and electroconvulsive therapy. There are limits to the PAD, such as directives that might conflict with laws, life-threatening needs, and professional practice standards. In addition to treatment directives, a proxy for directing one's psychiatric care can be designated in the PAD. Psychiatric patients often find having a PAD to be an important means of supporting their sense of autonomy and feelings of self-worth. Box 9.11 contains statements from psychiatric patients about their PADs.

─────────────────────── **Ethical Reflections** ───────────────────────

- Partner with a peer and develop a patient case scenario that involves the use of a PAD. Trade cases with other peers and determine the ethical issues involved. Compare answers.

Mental Illness and Children

When nurses are considering ethical issues surrounding the subject of mental illness and children, one of the primary considerations should be nurses' own sensitivity in recognizing signs of problems with a child's mental health. Mental illness, with associated impairment, occurs in one in five children and adolescents (Kalb, 2003). A study cited by the National Institute of Mental Health (NIMH, 2006b) revealed that "the number of antipsychotic medication prescriptions for children and adolescents increased six-fold from 1993 to 2002" (Para 1).

Any nurse who works with children is obliged to be educated, at the very least, regarding the basic signs and symptoms of mental illness in childhood, such as the symptoms of depression, which can manifest differently in children than in adults. Children and adolescents often have more difficulty expressing feelings that are indicative of depression and may exhibit more irritability than depressed adults (Keltner et al., 2003). In some instances, a nurse may be the primary link between preventing a child's suicide and helping the child imagine a meaningful future.

Another ethical issue involves nurses being active in helping children with mental disorders deal with stigma and the consequent development of what Goffman (1963) referred to as the stigmatized person's moral career. One childhood mental disorder that is particularly surrounded by stigma, confusion, and misinformation is attention deficit hyperactivity disorder (ADHD).

Box 9.11: Highlights From the Field: Patients Speak about PADs

We talked about what was in my PAD. The doctor didn't treat me like a "nut case" because some hospitals do. He said, "You've got rights and it's great that you know you have them—and we'll try to respect those completely." He did a lot for my health, too.

This time, with a PAD, I did not receive any treatments that I did not want. They were very respectful. I really felt like the hospital took better care of me because I had my PAD. In fact, I think it's the best care that I've ever received.

My health care agent is a real close friend and she knows about my illness. She's been around my illness for so long and basically, she knows what's going on with me. I trust her judgment.

Selected and edited statements from research interviews with participants in a study of PADs at Duke University Medical Center. Retrieved September 20, 2007, from http://www.nrc-pad.org/index.php?option=com_content&task=view&id=141&Itemid=55

ADHD

The assessment and treatment of ADHD in children is a controversial issue in the United States. Some health care professionals and people in the general public have voiced concerns about a possible trend toward the overidentification of behavioral problems being labeled and treated as ADHD. According to the National Institute of Mental Health (NIMH, 2006a), approximately 3–5% of school-aged children in the United States are affected by ADHD. When ADHD is recognized, a debate often ensues about whether the disorder should be treated with medication or behavioral therapy (Powell, Welch, Ezell, Klein, & Smith, 2003). There also is some evidence that teachers assess ADHD differently in children based on the teacher's culture and the child's gender, culture, and ethnicity (Office of University Relations, 2003). One research study revealed that teachers viewed African-American males as having the most severe symptoms of ADHD, followed equally by African-American females and Caucasian males. Caucasian females were viewed as having the fewest symptoms. Variations also were identified based on a child's cultural upbringing in regard to the child generally being expressive or quiet and how well the child's culture-based behaviors matched the cultural norms of the teacher.

Dodson (2001) listed the following possible causes for the perception by many people that ADHD may be overdiagnosed and overtreated:

- Increased awareness of the condition by the public
- Acceptance of a broader set of diagnostic criteria
- Greater appreciation of the course of the illness and its ultimate impact on adult life, which justifies lengthier and uninterrupted treatments
- Diminished concern about growth retardation, predisposition to drug use, and long-term effects of stimulant-class medications
- Increased treatment of adults (p. 304)

Nurses and other health care professionals need to keep in mind that, as with almost any mental disorder, ADHD can be over- or underdiagnosed and treated. Nurses working with children, such as nurses who work in schools, need to seek a thorough understanding regarding the appropriate assessment of ADHD, referral to other health care professionals, and treatment options. Some children who have ADHD are required to take their medication during the school day, although new long-acting medications make this situation less common. However, having to take medications at school or be monitored for a physical or psychological disorder can be a source of stigma for any child, separating the child from the so-called "normals" within the social structure of the school (see Box 9.12). The ethical responsibility of nurses and other health care professionals with regard to ADHD and all childhood mental illnesses involves an interest in the careful and individualized evaluation, treatment, and follow-up of each child as well as being alert and active in trying to minimize stigma.

BOX 9.12: HIGHLIGHTS FROM THE FIELD: ABOUT NORMAL

Right now, I don't know what Normal is anymore. That's because Normal has been changing so much, so often, lately. For a long while of lately. I'd like Normal to be okayness. Good health . . . emotional health, medical health, spiritual health. I'd like Normal to be like that. I'd like Normal to stay, like that. For now though, I know that Normal won't be normal for a little while . . . but somehow, sometime, even if things are not Normal, they'll be okay. That's because I believe in the great scheme of things and life.

Stepanek, M. J. T. (2002). *Hope through heartsongs*. New York: Hyperion.

——————————— Ethical Reflections ———————————

- What specific actions can school nurses take to reduce the stigma of children who are not among the "normals" of the school?
- What interventions can a nurse provide if a mother cries and expresses feelings of guilt with regard to her child's diagnosis of ADHD?
- How and why would the nature of these interventions be ethically related?

Humanistic Nursing Care in Psychiatric/ Mental Health Nursing

As was mentioned at the beginning of this chapter, some people say that psychiatry is a moral discipline rather than a medical discipline (Dickenson & Fulford, 2000). Ethics in nursing has been distinguished as a special area of ethics based on its grounding in relationships (Austin, Bergum, & Dossetor, 2003; Nortvedt, 1998; Scott, 2003). Humanistic care is provided from the perspective that all humans are of equal worth and deserving of respect. Yalom (1995), when discussing humanistic or person-centered therapy as advanced by Carl Rogers, said, "experienced therapists today agree that the crucial aspect of therapy, as Rogers grasped early in his career, is the therapeutic relationship" (p. ix). Psychiatric/mental health nursing is morally enriched by humanistic nurse-patient relationships that lead to human flourishing. Three humanistic approaches that were developed in the 1960s and 1970s but are still relevant to psychiatric nursing care today have been included in the discussion of humanistic nursing care.

Person-Centered Approach

The concepts of humanistic psychology and existentialism form the basis of psychologist Carl Rogers's person-centered approach (Corey, 2005). According to Rogers (1980), the development of "person" is the central goal of any person-centered relationship. For a growth-promoting environment to exist in the relationship, three conditions are necessary: (1) genuineness or realness; (2) acceptance, caring, or prizing; and (3) empathic understanding. The nurse who employs the element of genuineness or realness does not maintain a distant professional facade with the patient. The nurse truly experiences the feelings that are occurring in the relationship. The nurse who is exhibiting Rogers's second condition of a therapeutic relationship maintains an attitude of unconditional positive regard for a patient. The patient is prized in a total way and can *be* whatever feelings are occurring. Acceptance of the patient is not conditional. The last of Rogers's facilitative factors, empathic understanding, is a deep sensitivity to the patient's feelings, both those feelings on the level of awareness and those below. The professional nurse is able to sense the personal meanings of the patient's experience and communicates this understanding to the patient.

Humanistic Nursing Practice Theory

Paterson and Zderad first published their Humanistic Nursing Practice Theory in 1976 when nurses were in the midst of assertiveness training as a result of the women's movement in the United States (Moccia, 1988). Moccia proposed that the power that is supported by Paterson and Zderad's theory involves authentic dialogue with patients, students, and other health care professionals. According to Paterson and Zderad (1988), humanistic nursing emphasizes both the art and science of nursing. "Humanistic nursing embraces more than a benevolent technically competent subject-object one-way relationship guided by a nurse in behalf of another" (p. 3). Nursing, rather, involves a responsible searching for nurse-patient two-way interactions that receive their meaning from and are grounded in the nurse's and patient's existential experiences, or the experiences of living. A brief overview of Paterson and Zderad's perspectives about the domain of nursing—person, nurse (nursing), health, environment—provides some clarification of their theory, which can be used imaginatively by nurses in moral psychiatric/mental health practice.

Persons (including patients and nurses) have freedom to make choices. Persons have a personal unique view of the world; are adequate, having the capacity to hope and envision alternatives to what is immediately apparent; have the capacity for authentic presence and intersubjective relatedness; and have meaningful personal histories, although their histories do not control them.

Nursing is an art-science, meaning that nursing is derived from subjective, objective, and intersubjective experiences. Nursing is a form of unique knowledge that is developed through dialogical human processes. Finally, nursing is *being* and *doing*, which focus on being present with another and engaging in two-way dialogue.

Health does not always mean the absence of disease. The nurse's aim is to provide comfort to patients, with comfort conceptualized as being all that one can be at a particular point in time. Nurses try to promote well-being and *more-being* of others, emphasizing that persons are adequate as they are (well-being) but are free to become more than they are (more-being).

Environment, the final part of the domain, focuses on time and space, the here and now or the connectedness of past, present, and future. It also focuses on the nursing situation, which includes the whole world of people and things, a world that is more than just the patient and the nurse—the "all-at-once" or an awareness of all of the emotions, values, and experiences that work together to increase wisdom, a community of persons striving toward a common center, and a complementary synthesis or living out the tension between the objective scientific world and the subjective and intersubjective domains of nursing (O'Connor, 1993; Paterson & Zderad, 1988).

Human-to-Human Relationship Model

The human-to-human relationship model developed by Joyce Travelbee was developed from her experiences in psychiatric nursing and grounded in the philosophy of existentialism. Travelbee (1971) proposed that (1) nurses must possess a body of knowledge and know how to use it, and (2) nurses must learn to use themselves therapeutically if helping relationships are to be established. The phases that lead to the establishment of human-to-human relationships, as described by Travelbee, can be used for ethical practice in psychiatric/mental health nursing. These phases are:

1. *The phase of the original encounter:* First impressions of both the patient and nurse are perceived. The nurse must be aware of value judgments and feelings.
2. *The phase of emerging identities:* A bond is established between the nurse and the patient. There is again an emphasis on awareness by the nurse of how the patient is being perceived. Nurses must develop an awareness and a valuing of the uniqueness of others.
3. *The phase of empathy:* This is a conscious process of sharing in another person's experiences.
4. *The phase of sympathy:* In this phase, the nurse progresses further than empathy and wants to alleviate a patient's distress.
5. *The phase of rapport:* Rapport is the end goal of all nursing endeavors; it is a process, an experience, or a happening; it is the human-to-human relationship (Rangel, Hobble, Lansinger, Magers, & McKee, 1998; Travelbee, 1971).

Recognizing Inherent Human Possibilities

Rogers (1980) believed that there is an underlying movement toward inherent possibilities that all human beings exhibit. He proposed that it is a self-actualizing tendency for complete development and that life is an active process that moves toward maintaining, enhancing, and reproducing, even when conditions are not favorable. Rogers compared this view of human flourishing to a story about sprouting potatoes that he observed in his youth. He noticed that even when potatoes were stored in the basement during winter, they would produce pale (as opposed to healthy green) sprouts that twisted toward what little light they might have. Life was still trying to flourish, although conditions were not favorable. Rogers's words very eloquently compare how these potatoes can be likened to psychiatric patients, or any patients, whose lives nurses touch. Rogers said

In dealing with clients whose lives have been terribly warped, in working with men and women on the back wards of state hospitals, I often think of those potato sprouts. So unfavorable have been the conditions in which these people have developed that their lives often seem abnormal, twisted, scarcely human. Yet, the directional tendency in them can be trusted. The clue to understanding their behavior is that they are striving, in the only ways that they perceive as available to them, to move toward growth, toward becoming. To healthy persons, the results may seem bizarre and futile, but they are life's desperate attempt to become itself. (p. 119)

Ethical Reflections

- Box 9.13 contains examples from the ANA's (2001) *Code of Ethics for Nurses with Interpretive Statements*. How are these examples relevant to psychiatric/mental health nursing?
- What other provisions and statements in the ANA's *Code of Ethics for Nurses* are particularly pertinent to psychiatric/mental health nursing [see Appendix A]? Discuss these provisions and provide examples of how they apply to nursing practice.

Web Ethics

National Institute of Mental Health
   http://www.nimh.nih.gov

National Alliance on Mental Illness
   http://www.nami.org

Mental Health America
   http://www.nmha.org/index.cfm

American Psychiatric Nurses Association
   http://www.apna.org

Stigma.org
   http://www.stigma.org

National Resource Center on PADs
   http://www.nrc-pad.org

National Empowerment Center
   http://www.power2u.org/index.html

Box 9.13: Highlights from the Field: *Code of Ethics for Nurses*

- The nurse respects the worth, dignity and rights of all human beings irrespective of the nature of the health problem (1.3, p. 7).
- Each nurse has an obligation to be knowledgeable about the moral and legal rights of all patients to self-determination (1.4, p. 8).
- The nurse recognizes that there are situations in which the right to individual self-determination may be outweighed or limited by the rights, health and welfare of others. . . . (1.4, p. 9).
- When acting within one's role as a professional, the nurse recognizes and maintains boundaries that establish appropriate limits to relationships (2.4, p. 11).
- The patient's well-being could be jeopardized and the fundamental trust between patient and nurse destroyed by unnecessary access to data or by the inappropriate disclosure of identifiable patient information (3.2, p. 12).
- Duties of confidentiality are not absolute and may need to be modified in order to protect the patient, other innocent parties, and in circumstances of mandatory disclosure for public health reasons (3.2, p. 12).
- As an advocate for the patient, the nurse must be alert to and take appropriate action regarding any instances of incompetent, unethical, illegal, or impaired practice by any member of the health care team or the health care system or any action on the part of others that places the rights or best interests of the patient in jeopardy (3.5, p. 14).

Summary

Because psychiatric nursing care is focused on affecting the nature and manifestations of patients' thoughts, emotions, personalities, and behaviors through relationships as well as through biomedical means, ethics pervades good practice. Patients with mental illnesses are stigmatized by large segments of the population, and it is very unfortunate when they are further stigmatized by health care professionals. Nurses who understand and are sensitive to the experiences of psychiatric patients and the cultural implications of psychiatric labeling will be better prepared to take action to improve the public's perception of mental illness. Although mentally ill patients may relate to others in ways that are sometimes difficult to comprehend, nurses, through providing humanistic care, must steadfastly continue to pursue the goal of well-being and more-being with their psychiatric patients.

CASE STUDY: IS THERE A DUTY TO WARN?

Kendrick M. is a 25-year-old man hospitalized with a paranoid delusional disorder. When Kendrick was admitted, he was very angry and vehemently verbalized that he believed that his ex-mother-in-law had been spreading lies about him around town, and he accused her of getting him fired from his last job. When Kendrick's sister, Rose, visited him at the hospital, he gave consent for you, his nurse, and his psychiatrist to talk with her about his condition. At that time, Rose stated that Kendrick's ideas about his ex-mother-in-law were delusional thinking and that there was no basis in fact regarding his beliefs. Kendrick's condition has improved with adjustments of his psychotropic drugs (he is no longer actively exhibiting angry and paranoid behavior), and he is being discharged today. When you are talking with Kendrick today in preparation for his discharge, he tells you "I'm still not finished with my ex-mother-in-law." You ask him to explain this statement, and he is evasive but answers with cryptic statements that seem to indicate veiled threats against the woman.

Case Study Questions

1. As Kendrick's nurse, how would you evaluate the duty to warn in this situation?
2. Do you believe that Kendrick still should be discharged today? Please provide a rationale for your answer and discuss the information that would be needed to make this decision.
3. What actions would you take?
4. Discuss ethics–related principles, precedents, and concepts that are relevant to this case.

Key Points

- Psychiatry may be thought of as a moral discipline rather than a medical discipline because it is often involved with subjective experiences and relationships rather than objective tests and diseases.
- Nurses must be sensitive to the moral implications of using diagnostic labels when referring to patients, because diagnostic labels can be a source of harm and distress for patients.
- People in society often stigmatize mentally ill persons, and health care professionals sometimes perpetuate this stigma. Even those people who care for mentally ill persons are often stigmatized.

- Confidentiality and privileged communication are issues of a patient's right to privacy. Confidentiality is usually thought of in ethical terms whereas privileged communication pertains more to legal protection.
- In some situations, there are limits to a patient's right to confidentiality and privileged communication, such as when health care professionals have a duty to warn identifiable others of threats made by patients.
- The decision to involuntarily hospitalize a person is usually based on the person being a danger to self, a danger to others, or in some states, being gravely disabled.
- Humanistic nursing care is grounded in the belief that through genuine, intersubjective experiences and relationships, nurses can help patients to be free to become all that they can be.

References

American Nurses Association. (2001). *Code of ethics for nurses with interpretive statements.* Silver Spring, MD: Author.

Austin, W., Bergum, V., & Dossetor, J. (2003). Relational ethics: An action ethic as a foundation for health care. In V. Tschudin (Ed.), *Approaches to ethics: Nursing beyond boundaries* (pp. 45–52). Edinburgh: Butterworth-Heinemann-Elsevier Science.

Beauchamp, T. L., & Childress, J. F. (2001). *Principles of biomedical ethics* (5th ed.). New York: Oxford University Press.

Beresford, P. (2002). Thinking about "mental health": Towards a social model. *Journal of Mental Health, 11*(6), 581–584.

Bishop, A., & Scudder, J. (2001). *Nursing ethics: Holistic caring practice* (2nd ed.). Sudbury, MA: Jones and Bartlett.

Bolton, J. (2003). Reducing the stigma of mental illness. *Student British Medical Journal, 11,* 104–105.

Brody, B. A. (1988). *Life and death decision making.* New York: Oxford University Press.

Corey, G. (2005). *Theory and practice of counseling and psychotherapy* (7th ed.). Belmont, CA: Brooks/Cole-Thomson Learning.

Corey, G., Corey, M. S., & Callanan, P. (2003). *Issues and ethics in the helping professions.* Pacific Grove, CA: Wadsworth Group-Brooks/Cole.

Crowe, M. (2000). Psychiatric diagnosis: Some implications for mental health nurse care. *Journal of Advanced Nursing, 31*(3), 583–589.

Dickenson, D., & Fulford, K. W. M. (2000). *In two minds: A casebook of psychiatric ethics.* New York: Oxford University Press.

Dodson, W. W. (2001). Attention-deficit hyperactivity disorder. In J. L. Jacobson & A. M. Jacobson (Eds.), *Psychiatric secrets* (2nd ed., pp. 302–309). Philadelphia: Hanley & Belfus.

Everstine, L., Everstine, D. S., Heymann, G. M., True, R. H., Frey, D. H., Johnson, H. G., et al. (2003). Privacy and confidentiality in psychotherapy. In D. N. Bersoff (Ed.), *Ethical conflicts in psychology* (3rd ed., pp. 162–164). Washington, DC: American Psychological Association.

Fry, S., & Johnstone, M. J. (2002). *Ethics in nursing practice: A guide to ethical decision making* (2nd ed.). Oxford, UK: Blackwell Science.

Gillon, R. (2001). Confidentiality. In H. Kuhse & P. Singer (Eds.), *A companion to bioethics* (pp. 425–431). Oxford, UK: Blackwell.

Goffman, E. (1963). *Stigma: Notes on the management of spoiled identity*. New York: Simon & Schuster.

Green, G., Hayes, C., Dickinson, D., Whittaker, A., & Gilheany, B. (2003). A mental health service users' perspective to stigmatization. *Journal of Mental Health, 12*(3), 223–234.

Grisso, T., & Appelbaum, P. S. (1998). *Assessing competence to consent to treatment: A guide for physicians and other health care professionals*. New York: Oxford University.

Halter, M. J. (2002). Stigma in psychiatric nursing. *Perspectives in Psychiatric Care, 38*(1), 23–28.

Hobson, J. A., & Leonard, J. A. (2001). *Out of its mind: Psychiatry in crisis—A call to reform*. Cambridge, MA: Perseus.

Joint Commission on Accreditation of Healthcare Organizations. (1998). *Ethical issues and patient rights: Across the continuum of care*. Oakbrook Terrace, IL: Author.

Jonsen, A. R., Siegler, M., & Winslade, W. J. (2006). *Clinical ethics* (6th ed.). New York: McGraw-Hill.

Kahn, M. W. (2001). Introduction to DSM-IV. In J. L. Jacobson & A. M. Jacobson (Eds.), *Psychiatric secrets* (2nd ed., pp. 18-20). Philadelphia: Hanley & Belfus.

Kalb, C. (2003, September 22). Troubled souls. *Newsweek*, 68–70.

Keltner, N. L., Schwecke, L. H., & Bostrom, C. E. (2003). *Psychiatric nursing* (4th ed.). St. Louis, MO: Mosby.

Killion, S. W. (2006a). Competency and guardianship. I. In S. W. Killion & K. Dempski (Eds.), *Quick look nursing: Legal and ethical issues* (pp. 40–41). Sudbury, MA: Jones & Bartlett.

Killion, S. W. (2006b). Confidential communication-Part I. In S. W. Killion & K. Dempski (Eds.), *Quick look nursing: Legal and ethical issues* (pp. 36–37). Sudbury, MA: Jones & Bartlett.

Knight, M. T. D., Wykes, T., & Hayward, P. (2003). "People don't understand": An investigation of stigma in schizophrenia using interpretative phenomenological analysis (IPA). *Journal of Mental Health, 12*(3), 209–222.

Maes, S. (2003). How do you know when professional boundaries have been crossed? *Oncology Nursing Society News, 18*(8), 3–5.

McCann, R. A., & Ball, E. M. (2001). Borderline personality disorder. In J. L. Jacobson & A. M. Jacobson (Eds.), *Psychiatric secrets* (2nd ed., pp. 190–197). Philadelphia: Hanley & Belfus.

Moccia, P. (1988). Preface. In J. G. Paterson & L. T. Zderad, *Humanistic nursing* (pp. iii–v). New York: National League for Nursing.

National Alliance on Mental Illness. (2006). Study confirms that stigma still a barrier to psychiatric care. Retrieved December 17, 2006, from http://www.nami.org/Template.cfm?Section=20065&Template=/ContentManagement/ContentDisplay.cfm&ContentID=31897

National Institute of Mental Health. (2006a). Attention deficit hyperactivity disorder. Retrieved December 7, 2006, from http://www.nimh.nih.gov/publicat/adhd.cfm

National Institute of Mental Health. (2006b, June 19). Science update: Antipsychotic prescriptions rise sharply for children and adolescents. Retrieved December 18, 2006, from http://www.nimh.nih.gov/press/kidantipsychrx.cfm

Nehls, N. (1998). Borderline personality disorder: Gender stereotypes, stigma, and limited system of care. *Issues in Mental Health Nursing, 19*, 97–112.

Nortvedt, P. (1998). Sensitive judgment: An inquiry into the foundations of nursing ethics. *Nursing Ethics, 5*(5), 385–392.

O'Brien, O., Woods, M., & Palmer, C. (2001). The emancipation of nursing practice: Applying anti-psychiatry to the therapeutic community. *Australian and New Zealand Journal of Mental Health Nursing, 10,* 4.

O'Connor, N. (1993). *Paterson and Zderad: Humanistic nursing theory.* Newbury Park, CA: Sage.

Office of University Relations, Texas A&M University. (2003, June 23). Cultural and gender biases may influence diagnosing of ADHD in kids. *Aggie Daily.* Retrieved December 18, 2006, from http://www.tamu.edu/univrel/aggiedaily/news/stories/03/062303-3.html

Paterson, J. G., & Zderad, L. T. (1988). *Humanistic nursing.* New York: National League for Nursing.

Pipher, M. (2003). *Letters to a young therapist: Stories of hope and healing.* New York: Basic Books.

Powell, S. E., Welch, E., Ezell, D., Klein, C., & Smith, L. (2003). Should children receive medication for symptoms of attention deficit hyperactivity disorder? *Peabody Journal of Education, 72*(3), 107–115.

Radden, J. (2002a). Notes towards a professional ethics for psychiatry. *Australian and New Zealand Journal of Psychiatry, 36,* 52–59.

Radden, J. (2002b). Psychiatric ethics. *Bioethics, 16*(5), 397–411.

Rangel, S., Hobble, W. H., Lansinger, T., Magers, J. A., & McKee, N. J. (1998). Joyce Travelbee: Human-to-human relationship model. In A. M. Tomey & M. R. Alligood (Eds.), *Nursing theorists and their work* (4th ed., pp. 364–374). St. Louis, MO: Mosby.

Rogers, C. R. (1980). *A way of being.* Boston: Houghton Mifflin.

Rosen, A., Walter, G., Casey, D., & Hocking, B. (2000). Combating psychiatric stigma: An overview of contemporary initiatives. *Australasian Psychiatry, 8*(1), 19–26.

Scott, A. P. (2003). Virtue, nursing and the moral domain of practice. In V. Tschudin (Ed.), *Approaches to ethics: Nursing beyond boundaries* (pp. 25–32). Edinburgh: Butterworth-Heinemann-Elsevier Science.

Seedhouse, D. (2000). *Practical nursing philosophy: The universal ethical code.* Chichester, UK: John Wiley & Sons.

Shimrat, I. (2003, July-August). Freedom. *Off Our Backs, 55,* 18.

Singer, B. J. (2003). Mental illness: Rights, competence, and communication. In G. McGee (Ed.), *Pragmatic bioethics* (2nd ed., pp. 151–162). Cambridge, MA: Massachusetts Institute of Technology.

Smart, D. (2003, April 7). Take action now to banish mental health prejudices. *Pulse-I-Registrar.*

Smith-Bell, M., & Winslade, W. J. (2003). Privacy, confidentiality, and privilege in psychotherapeutic relationships. In D. N. Bersoff (Ed.), *Ethical conflicts in psychology* (3rd ed., pp. 157–161). Washington, DC: American Psychological Association.

Sokolowski, R. (1991). The fiduciary relationship and the nature of professions. In E. D. Pellegrino, R. M. Veatch, & J. P. Langan (Eds.), *Ethics, trust, and the professions: Philosophical and cultural aspects* (pp. 23–43). Washington, DC: Georgetown University.

Stepanek, M. J. T. (2002). *Hope through heartsongs.* New York: Hyperion.

Travelbee, J. (1971). *Interpersonal aspects of nursing.* Philadelphia: F. A. Davis.

U.S. Department of Health and Human Services. (1999). *Mental health: A report of the Surgeon General—Executive summary.* Rockville, MD: Author.

Videbeck, S. L. (2006). *Psychiatric mental health nursing* (3rd ed.). Philadelphia: Lippincott, Williams, & Wilkins.

Wahl, O. F. (2003). Depictions of mental illnesses in children's media. *Journal of Mental Health, 12*(3), 249–258.

Watts, J., & Priebe, S. (2002). A phenomenological account of users' experiences of assertive community treatment. *Bioethics, 16*(5), 439–454.

Williams, L. (1998). A "classic" case of borderline personality disorder. *Psychiatric Services, 49*(2), 173–174.

Yalom, I. D. (1995). Introduction. In C. R. Rogers (Ed.), *A way of being* (pp. vii-xiii). Boston: Houghton Mifflin.

CHAPTER 9 QUESTIONS

1. Nurses' role in diagnosing psychiatric patients is important because
   a. nursing diagnoses are critical to the process.
   b. nurses are collaborators in the diagnostic process.
   c. nurses often know more about patients than psychiatrists do.
   d. nurses are less biased than physicians.

2. Ethical problems may arise with diagnosing psychiatric patients because of
   a. subjectivity.
   b. short staffing.
   c. choosing the wrong diagnostic tests.
   d. patients' relationships with one another.

3. When talking with his nurse, a patient threatens to kill his wife. The nurse wonders if she should tell the patient's wife about this conversation. Which of the following provides overriding guidance in this situation?
   a. Health Insurance Portability and Accountability Act
   b. Patient Self-Determination Act
   c. A duty to warn
   d. Patients' Bill of Rights

4. Nurse Susie believes that it is important to be empathetic in psychiatric/mental health nursing. She is interested in identifying an approach that might be helpful to her. Which of the following theoretical approaches might she want to study?
   a. Psychoanalysis
   b. Feminist theory
   c. Postmodernism
   d. Humanism

5. Providing care to patients with borderline personality disorder is sometimes difficult for nurses. In relating to these patients, an ethical practice for the nurse is to be
   a. self-aware.
   b. a utilitarian.
   c. a clinical expert.
   d. a good diagnostician.

6. Mr. Green was admitted to a psychiatric hospital. He refuses the antipsychotic medication that the nurse tries to give to him. As his nurse, you know that Mr. Green
   a. cannot refuse this medication if he has a diagnosis of schizophrenia.
   b. can refuse this medication if he has not been deemed incompetent by formal legal proceedings.
   c. may refuse this medication only if his doctor agrees.
   d. cannot refuse this medication regardless of his diagnosis.

7. A patient presents a psychiatric advance directive (PAD) to you, her nurse. You know that the following is true of PADs:
   a. They are unique because even incompetent persons can initiate these directives.
   b. They are ethically but not legally binding.
   c. They are based on the principle of paternalism.
   d. They are legally binding in a limited number of states.

8. A nurse believes that strictly approaching mental illness according to the medical model is too limiting. The nurse tells you that health care professionals need to focus more on psychiatric patients' beliefs and values in providing care. You wonder if this nurse approaches psychiatric nursing from which of the following viewpoints?
   a. DSM-based
   b. Ethics-based
   c. Antipsychiatry based
   d. Antistigma based

9. You are a school nurse who is interested in learning more about ADHD. Your literature search reveals which of the following about ADHD and school-aged children in the United States?
   a. Approximately 3% to 5% are affected.
   b. Culture usually is not an issue in regard to identifying symptoms.

    c. Fortunately, there is little stigma associated with the disorder.

    d. Diagnosing is fairly clear to most health care professionals.

10. A. nurse caring for vulnerable psychiatric patients needs to be sensitive to which of the following boundary issues in regard to the nurse's personal motivation?

    a. Stigma sensitivity

    b. Educational level of nurse

    c. Theoretical approach

    d. Power differentials

CHAPTER 9 ANSWERS

Question 1: The correct answer is B.

Though nurses who are not advance practice nurses do not directly generate a medical diagnosis for patients, the information provided and disseminated by nurses contributes to the diagnostic process.

    Choices A, C, and D are incorrect because nursing diagnoses do not directly affect a patient's medical diagnosis; choices C and D generally cannot be assumed to be true.

Question 2: The correct answer is A.

The diagnostic process with psychiatric patients often cannot be based on objective clinical data.

    Choices B, C, and D are incorrect because short staffing and patients' relationships with one another generally do not directly relate to the diagnostic process; often there are no clinical tests to assist with identifying a diagnosis.

Question 3: The correct answer is C.

The duty to warn based on the *Tarasoff v. Board of Regents of the University of California* case provides the overriding guidance in this situation.

    Choices A, B, and D are incorrect because though the HIPAA, PSDA, and Patients' Bill of Rights are important in guiding nurse-patient interactions, the duty to warn takes precedence in this case. The nurse has a duty to protect a person from a real threat of being harmed by a patient.

Question 4: The correct answer is D.

A humanistic approach to psychiatric/mental health care is based on a health care professional's (1) genuineness or realness; (2) acceptance, caring, or prizing; and (3) empathic understanding.

Choices A, B, and C are incorrect because these approaches are not directly related to humanism; psychoanalysis is focused on understanding patients' inner experiences, such as the unconscious and defense mechanisms; feminist theory focuses on the unique standpoint of women; postmodernism focuses on pluralistic world views.

Question 5: The correct answer is A.

Nurses interacting with patients with BPD need to be self-aware in regard to how these patients may precipitate negative reactions in health care providers. Interactions with patients with BPD can be intense.

Choices B, C, and D are incorrect because these practices are nonspecific in regard to caring for a patient with BPD.

Question 6: The correct answer is B.

Patients who have not been legally deemed incompetent have the right to refuse medications.

Choices A, C, and D are incorrect because these choices, as worded, generally are not true in terms of the question.

Question 7: The correct answer is D.

At the current time, PADs are legally valid only in 25 states.

Choices A, B, and C are incorrect because incompetent people cannot initiate legally binding PADs; PADs are legally binding in some states; PADs are based on the principle of autonomy rather than paternalism.

Question 8: The correct answer is C.

Antipsychiatry describes the personal view that as a discipline, psychiatry is too focused on medical treatments and classification systems rather than on understanding persons' emotional and spiritual needs, beliefs, and values.

Choices A, B, and D are incorrect because these choices do not describe the meaning of antipsychiatry.

Question 9: The correct answer is A.

According to data from the NIMH, approximately 3-5% of school-aged children in the United States are affected by ADHD.

Choices B, C, and D are incorrect because these choices are not true in regard to ADHD and school-aged children in the United States.

Question 10: The correct answer is D.

Sometimes nurses become too centered on their power over vulnerable psychiatric patients rather than being self-aware that patients' needs must be their primary concern.

Choices A, B, and C are incorrect because these choices are not true in regard to the question.

Ethics and the Nursing Care of Elders

Karen L. Rich

At first, people wanted to help the old ones in any way they could, but the women would not allow too much assistance, for they enjoyed their newly found independence. So The People showed respect for the two women by listening to what they had to say.

— VELMA WALLIS, *TWO OLD WOMEN:*
AN ALASKA LEGEND OF BETRAYAL, COURAGE, AND SURVIVAL, 1993, P. 135

OBJECTIVES

After reading this chapter, the reader should be able to:

1. Define ageism.
2. Identify factors that influence elders' experiences of living meaningful lives.
3. Discuss the principle of autonomy as it relates to the ethical care of elders.
4. Assess the practice range of paternalism as it relates to ethical nursing practice.
5. Discriminate between different levels of moral agency.
6. Discuss different perspectives about quality of life assessments.
7. Identify the signs of elder abuse and appropriate nursing interventions.
8. Discuss the ANA's *Code of Ethics for Nurses* in relation to the nursing care of elders.

KEY TERMS

Ageism	Moral agency	Decisional capacity
Autonomy	Paternalism	Quality of life
Personal evaluation	Observer evaluation	Weak paternalism
Basic dignity	Personal dignity	Justified paternalism

Aging in America

The President's Council on Bioethics (2005) proposed that "we are on the threshold of a 'mass geriatric society,' a society of more long-lived individuals than ever before in human history" (p. xvii). People are living longer and healthier due to the technological advances that have occurred in medicine and public health during the last century. According to the U.S. Census Bureau (2006), there were approximately 35 million Americans over the age of 65 in 2005, and it is predicted that nearly 82 million Americans will be over the age of 65 by the year 2050. Life expectancy has increased from 49 years in 1900 to approximately 78 years today (Arias, 2006). Although the quantity of human life years has been extended, questions remain about how the quality of those years is threatened by chronic debilitating conditions, ageism, and limited support and resources for elders and their caregivers.

Often, chronic conditions such as cerebrovascular disease and Alzheimer's disease cause elders to lose their most crucial link with others, their voice within society. A loss of voice to express their individual feelings, desires, and needs is arguably one of the most profound causes of isolation for elders (Smith, Kotthoff-Burrell, & Post, 2002). Considerations about the loss of the voice of elderly persons and diminished societal recognition of the meaningfulness of their lives underlie many of the ethical issues discussed in this chapter. A large portion of elder-focused ethics is based on the relationships that elders have with other people in society, including their families and health care professionals. Often, the lives of elders are "set aside" from the lives of other adults in communities. It is this overall view of separateness among generations that makes it necessary to study elder-focused ethics.

Ageism, a way of thinking that was originally described by Butler (1975), has influenced some people within society to view elders as fundamentally different from others. Consequently, some people cease to identify elders as normal human beings (Agich, 2003). Just as racism and sexism describe the stereotyping of and discrimination against people because of their skin color or gender, ageism involves the same type of negative perceptions toward older adults based on age. Ageism perpetuates the idea that elders as a population are cognitively impaired, "set in their ways," and "old-fashioned" in regard to their morals and abilities (Agich; Butler).

It probably is disquieting to elders when they realize how youth oriented Western society is today. One can see that the media's target audience is most often young adults and the financially affluent young middle-aged population. Media emphasis is placed on having beautiful bodies even if expensive elective surgery is needed to do so. Pictures of beautiful and famous young people and couples are prominently displayed on magazine covers, and young athletes are revered in Western society. Older actors, and particularly actresses, lament the lack of "good roles" for them in the movie industry. It is not surprising that as people age, they often become despondent about the losses that they experience in regard to how they look and their physical abilities. The seemingly vital, active, and glamorous lives of the young people portrayed in the media serve as a stark contrast to what many elderly persons may be experiencing. Agich (2003) proposed that "a society that values productivity and material wealth above other values is understandably youth oriented; a natural consequence is that the old come to be seen, and to see themselves, as obsolete and redundant" (p. 54).

So, who are the elders in today's society? Savishinsky (1991) stated:

The class of *the elderly* includes both the rich and poor, sick and well, sane and insane; it also embraces the relatively healthy so-called *young old* between 60 and 75 and the more vulnerable *old old* who are living beyond their eighth decade. Some are intimately connected with family and community, whereas others are cut off from their kin. Some are active and ardent; others are disengaged and hopeless. (p. 2)

At the end of the 18th century and in the early 19th century, old people were encouraged to view their lives as a pilgrimage and to prepare for death while still participating in service to family and community. However, starting around the 1850s, societies began to instill the belief that thoughts about death should be avoided. The emphasis changed to a focus on valuing "the virtues of youth rather than age, the new rather than the old, self-reliance and autonomy rather than community" (Callahan, 1995, p. 39).

These views formed the foundation of the beginning of ageism in the 20th century. The realities of old age were not consistent with the new world view of the morality of self-control and autonomy; rather, the decay inherent in aging was associated with dependence and failure. Though ageism began to be a general social theme after World War II, today it may be focused more on elderly persons who are disabled (Cohen, 1988).

The lives of people of all ages are overshadowed by an awareness of their eventual aging and death, and it is during one's later years that these issues can no longer be ignored. When one actually does confront the facts of unavoidable aging and death, the mysteries involved can be startling. The feminist philosopher Simone de Beauvoir (1972) proposed that "the old are invisible because we see death with a clearer eye than old age itself" (p. 4). Agich (2003) interpreted this statement to mean that old people are set apart from the rest of society because people tend to look beyond the elderly persons themselves, who they perceive as close to death, and instead see the prospects of their own death.

Moody (1992) proposed that the modern advances in biomedical technology that have facilitated longer lives for many elderly persons have made it necessary to confront critical ethical questions that society may want to ignore. These questions involve dilemmas about death and dying, the perception of what is meant by quality of life, and judgments about the mental and physical functional capacity of old adults. Moody questioned whether the typical models and approaches to bioethics based on rights and duties fit well with considerations of ethics and aging. He asked the question, "What ethical ideals are appropriate for an aging society?" (p. 243). According to Moody, focusing on individual autonomy and justice between generations will not provide people with the desired ethical model for engaging in relationships with elders. Elder-focused ethics includes negotiation and a foundation in the virtues. Principles and rules also must be included, but principles and rules can thwart desired ends if the practical wisdom and good character of caregivers are not emphasized as a part of the overall scheme of ethics.

Ethical Reflections

- Can an ethicist or nurse simply apply the bioethical principles of autonomy, beneficence, nonmaleficence, and justice to situations involving elderly patients? Why or why not? What is a good approach to elder-focused ethics?
- How can nurses combat ageism in their local, state, and national communities?
- Do you believe that ageism is based solely on age or on the degree of an elderly person's disability? On socioeconomic level? On race? Explain the rationale for your beliefs.

Life Meaning and Significance

Once, while Mahatma Gandhi's train was pulling slowly out of the station, a European reporter ran up to his compartment window. "Do you have a message I can take back to my people?" he asked. It was Gandhi's day of silence, a vital respite from his demanding speaking schedule, so he didn't reply. Instead, he scrawled a few words on a scrap of paper and passed it to the reporter: "My life is my message."

—E. EASWARAN, *YOUR LIFE IS YOUR MESSAGE*, 1992, P. 1

The issues of autonomy, vulnerability, dependency, and good relationships are important when considering ethics and elders. However, there is another issue that is important to the moral world of elders and those with whom they relate. That issue is elderly persons' own feelings about the significance and meaning of their lives. According to Callahan (1995), underlying the strong desire by society and scientists to abolish the biology of aging is "a profound failure of meaning" (p. 39).

As people age, often they begin to realize the truth of Gandhi's words—that their life is their message—but does Western society support elders' reflecting on the meaning and significance of their lives? In earlier times, tradition was highly valued by society, and the meaning and significance of elderly persons' lives were viewed differently than they are today in our culturally and morally diverse society (Callahan, 1995). In the past, elders had an elevated status in communities because their wisdom was prized for its own sake and because their wisdom placed them in a special position of being called upon to perpetuate and interpret societal moral traditions.

The current Western culture that includes diverse moral views sometimes undermines the community-wide role of elderly persons in passing on moral traditions. Therefore, one of the traditional societal purposes for elders has diminished. Today, elderly persons are important to businesses if they are financially well off, to families if they are willing and able to provide care for grandchildren, to politicians as a voting block, and to nonprofit agencies as volunteers (Callahan, 1995). Some people believe that these roles for elders make older persons valuable within society. However, upon closer inspection one can determine that it is not age as such that is held in high regard but the accidental features of old age such as disposable income and free time.

According to Cole (1986), *meaning* is "an intuitive expression of one's overall appraisal of living. Existentially, meaning refers to lived perceptions of coherence, sense, or significance, in experiences" (p. 4). Callahan (1995) described meaning as an inner feeling supported by "some specifiable traditions, beliefs, concepts or ideas, that one's life" has purpose and is well structured in "relating the inner self and the outer world—and that even in the face of aging and death, it is a life which makes sense to oneself; that is, one can give a plausible, relatively satisfying account" (p. 33). Callahan described *significance* as "the social attribution of value to old age, that it has a sturdy and cherished place in the structure of society and politics, and provides a coherence among the generations that is understood to be important if not indispensable" (p. 33).

Nurses may question why it is relevant to nursing ethics for them to consider elderly persons' pursuit of life meaning and significance. The answer is that nursing ethics is first and foremost about relationships and alleviating patients' suffering and facilitating patients' well-being. In relation to elders, nursing ethics also is focused on helping elderly persons find and keep their voice or means of expressing their values and feelings. Finding meaning and significance alleviates suffering and promotes well-being for many elderly persons (see Box 10.1).

The Search for Meaning

The Viennese neurologist and psychiatrist, Viktor Frankl (1905–1997), wrote the influential book *Man's Search for Meaning*, which was originally published in 1959. Over 10 million copies of this book have been sold, and it was rated as one of the 10 most influential books read by respondents to a survey conducted by the Library of Congress (Greening, 1998). The book is about how Frankl found meaning in his experiences in Auschwitz and other concentration camps during World War II. In the preface to the third edition of the book, Allport (1984) stated that Frankl proposed that "to live is to suffer, to survive is to find meaning in the suffering. If there is a purpose in life at all, there must be a purpose in suffering and in dying" (p. 9).

Frankl (1959/1984) suggested that meaning is the primary motivation in the lives of humans. He determined that the last of his human freedoms in the concentration camp was to choose his attitude toward his suffering. Being in a concentration camp was an unchangeable situation for Dr. Frankl, as are the facts that aging will happen to all people who do not die young and that all people will eventually die. It is in continuing to make the choices to find meaning in the circumstances that people encounter as their life stories are created and unfold that will eventually form the fabric of a meaningful life when people are old.

Frankl (1959/1984) believed that the transitoriness or fleeting nature of life, similar to what Buddhists call impermanence, must not be denied by persons who are interested in putting the search for meaning at the center of their lives. Rather, even suffering and dying can be actualizing experiences. Though no one can supply another person's life meaning, nurses can help elderly people on their journey through life by

BOX 10.1: HIGHLIGHTS FROM THE FIELD: DISCOVERING MEANING

In the story *The Fall of Freddie the Leaf*, a leaf named Freddie questioned a wise older leaf, Daniel, about life and its meaning. When Daniel told Freddie that all of the leaves on their tree and even the tree itself would eventually die, Freddie asked: "Then what has been the reason for all of this? Why were we here at all if we only have to fall and die?"

Daniel answered. "It's been about the sun and the moon. It's been about happy times together. It's been about the shade and the old people and the children [that sat and played beneath the tree]. It's been about colors in Fall. It's been about seasons. Isn't that enough?"

Buscaglia, L. (1982). *The Fall of Freddie the Leaf.* Thorofare, NJ: Charles B. Slack, pp. 19–20.

helping them to discover meaning in their lives and to feel that they are significant members of communities.

Updating the Eriksonian Life Cycle

In exploring the moral treatment of elderly persons, Callahan (1995) proposed that the search for common meaning in aging requires a consideration of the updated theory of the life cycle as elaborated by Erik Erikson. Erikson's book, *The Life Cycle Completed*, published in 1982, emphasized that all eight stages of the Eriksonian life cycle cannot be distinctly separated but are interrelated. After Erikson's death in his early 90s, his wife Joan used her own ideas and notes written by her husband to update the book. She proposed a ninth stage of development and addressed other issues related to old-old people. Joan Erikson was in her 90s when she wrote this updated book, and she used her voice to speak for many old-old people about their experiences.

The ninth stage of the life cycle is an extension of the eighth stage, which is a time that elders develop to some degree either despair and disgust or integrity. Wisdom is the strength or virtue that some elders depend on to successfully navigate both the eighth and ninth stages of development. The ninth stage is the stage of the lived experiences of persons in their eighth or ninth decades of life. The following are some of the difficulties that occur in the ninth stage that make wisdom and integrity hard for elders to achieve (Erikson & Erikson, 1997):

- Wisdom requires the senses of sight and hearing to see, hear, and remember. Integrity is compared with tact (as in the word *intact)*, which is related to touch. In their 90s, elderly persons often lose or have impaired senses of sight, hearing, and touch.
- When persons reach the age of late 80s or enter the decade of their 90s, despair may occur because people realize that life is too short now to try to make up for missed opportunities.
- Despair may occur because the old-old person is just trying to "get through the day" because of physical limitations even without the added burdens of regrets about one's earlier life. When persons believe that their lives are not what they wished them to be, the despair is deepened.
- Persons in their 80s and 90s are likely to have experienced losses of relationships to a greater degree than at any other age. In addition to the suffering directly related to these losses, suffering is generated when the person realizes that "death's door is open and not so far away" (p. 113).

Like virtue ethicists who have drawn connections between the "good life" and being a vital member of a community (Blum, 1994; MacIntyre, 1984), Joan Erikson (1997) said that her husband, Erik, often proposed that the life cycle cannot be appropriately understood if it is not viewed within a social context or in terms of the community in which it is actually lived. The Eriksons' belief that individuals and society are interrelated and are constantly involved with the give and take of a dynamic community is a key position of communitarian ethicists today. When society lacks a sound ideal of old age, a holistic view of life is not well integrated into communities. If elders are excluded from being among the valued members of a community, they are often viewed as the embodiment of shame instead of the embodiment of wisdom.

Joan Erikson was convinced that if persons in their 80s and 90s have developed hope and trust in earlier life stages, they will be able to move further down the path to gerotranscendence, a concept she borrowed from the work of Lars Tornstam. Transcendence means "to rise above or go beyond a limit, [to] exceed, [to] excel" (Erikson & Erikson, 1997, p. 124). Erikson described the experiences of gerotranscendent individuals as:

- Feeling a cosmic union with the universal spirit
- Perceiving time as being limited to *now* or maybe only *next week*; otherwise the future is misty
- Feeling that the dimensions of space have been decreased to the perimeter of what the person's physical capabilities allow

- Feeling that death is a sustaining presence for the person and viewing death as being "the way of all living things" (p. 124)
- Having an expanded sense of self that includes "a wider range of interrelated others" (p. 124)

Erikson then activated the word *transcendence* into the word *transcendance* to associate its meaning with the arts and specifically "the dance of life [that] can transport us into all realms of making and doing with every item of body, mind, and spirit involved" (p. 127).

Ethical Reflections

- In what ways does society often perpetuate elders being viewed as the embodiment of shame?
- Joan Erikson said "to grow old is a great privilege" (Erikson & Erikson, 1997, p. 128). How can nurses help elderly persons realize this privilege?

Moral Agency

It is generally believed that elders are a vulnerable population because of the natural progression toward frailty that usually occurs with aging. Because of this vulnerability, moral agency is often a key consideration in relationships with elders. The ability to make deliberate choices and to act deliberately in regard to important life experiences that affect the suffering and well-being of sentient beings, including oneself, refers to a person's **moral agency**. Moral agency implies that people are responsible for their beliefs and actions. Arguments about moral agency generally result from debates about a person's mental capacity in regard to decision making. Referring to whether or not the person is or is not autonomous is usually at the heart of the debate.

Decisional Capacity

Decisional capacity or incapacity is the ability or inability to come to what most adults would consider to be reasonable conclusions or resolutions. Decisional capacity can generally be equated with the concept of competence, though competence has more of a legal connotation. Competence is closely tied to formal situations that legally require informed consent. Questions of decisional capacity and competence are associated most often with the three populations of "(a) mentally disabled persons, (b) cognitively impaired elderly persons, and (c) children" (Stanley, Sieber, & Melton, 2003, p. 398). Decisional capacity in regard to minor children and mentally disabled persons is discussed in Chapters 6 and 9, respectively.

There is no one set of published criteria to be used in all assessments of decisional capacity and competence. A method cited by Beauchamp and Childress (2001) is unique because it includes a range of the *inabilities* that someone who is incompetent would exhibit as opposed to being based on the person's actual *abilities*. The standards begin by describing the behaviors that persons exhibit with the least ability of competence and moves toward those standards that require higher ability. The standards are:

- Inability to express or communicate a preference or choice
- Inability to understand one's situation and its consequences
- Inability to understand relevant information
- Inability to give a reason
- Inability to give a rational reason (although some supporting reasons may be given)
- Inability to give risk/benefit-related reasons (although some rational supporting reasons may be given)
- Inability to reach a reasonable decision (as judged, for example, by a reasonable person standard) (p. 73)

Nurses must be sensitive to the fact that vulnerable and dependent elderly patients are often *assumed* to be mentally incapacitated or incompetent based on faulty impressions and ageism. When ungrounded assumptions are made based on a person's frail appearance, for example, elderly patients are often left out of the process of decision making that is important to their well-being. Elders who are physically frail may not be included in decision making ranging from deciding when they want to take their bath in a long-term care facility to health care professionals aiding family members in legally taking away the older person's decisional capacity for treatment options and the management of their financial affairs.

Though in most cases family members have ethical motives when caring for elderly family members, this is not always the case. Occasionally, family members and caregivers are more interested in their own self-serving desires than the well-being of an elder when the family or caregivers want to deem the elder as incompetent. Biased decisions, which are intentional or unintentional, may be based on a desire to gain or maintain access to an elder's money or on feelings of disgust or exasperation. Nurses must be cautiously and wisely alert when assessing patients and situations that affect determinations of elders' decisional capacity. As directed in the *Code of Ethics for Nurses* (American Nurses Association [ANA], 2001), a nurse's primary commitment is to the patient.

Autonomy and Paternalism

Autonomy in bioethics means that persons are rational and allowed to direct their own health related and life decisions. **Paternalism** occurs when a health care professional makes choices for a patient based on the health care professional's beliefs about "the best interest of the patient" or "the patient's own good." Physicians and nurses sometimes believe that patients are unable to understand the full extent of their care needs. A less justifiable reason for paternalistic behavior is based on health care professionals' belief that their profession accords them a justified place of power over patients.

Although the practice of paternalism was once an expected behavior among health care professionals and was encouraged by educators, it is not as readily accepted today by professionals or the recipients of their care. However, elders are still at a high risk for having their autonomy violated by health care professionals. This often results from incorrect assumptions about elders' decisional capacity because of their frail appearance and the influences of societal ageism. Even when elders are confused regarding the minor details of a situation, they may retain decisional capacity. In fact, elderly persons may be disoriented to time and to the names and roles of other persons and still retain the capacity to make reasonable decisions regarding their lives and treatment. For example, if an elderly patient does not remember the name of an emergency department physician when the physician comes and goes in and out of the room, this does not necessarily mean that the patient is not competent to make treatment decisions. A more important assessment would be whether the patient knows that she is in a hospital emergency department. However, even this determination may not be sufficient to determine decisional capacity in regard to treatment decisions.

When elders are confused about some of the details regarding their current situation, health care professionals are often tempted to act paternalistically. Even if an elder does not know that she is in a hospital emergency department, health care professionals should not automatically overrule the patient's refusal of treatment. Instead, the whole context of the elder's life must be evaluated in terms of the ability to understand the benefits, risks, and consequences of decisions as well as the overall consistency of the elder's conversations and expressions of wishes over time. Health care professionals need to assess whether the elder's current wishes are consistent with previously expressed desires and ways of being. People sometimes want to quickly overrule elders' decisions and requests when their autonomy should rightfully be honored.

Some ethicists believe that the excessive paternalistic behavior exhibited by physicians and nurses in the past has caused a current backlash resulting in an elevated and imbalanced interest in respecting a patient's autonomy. According to some ethicists, the pendulum has now swung too far in the direction of an overinflated interest in preserving autonomy, and this stance minimizes the importance of the give and take needed for good human relationships, a desire to cultivate a strong sense of community, and the usefulness of virtues (Agich, 2003; Callahan, 1995; Hester, 2001; MacIntyre, 1984, 1999; Moody, 1992). Therefore, behavior exhibited toward elderly patients may fall somewhere along a wide continuum from a point of unjustified paternalism to a point of rigid adherence to respecting autonomy. Hester, a communitarian ethicist, has argued that healing requires communal involvement, not an overdeveloped interest in autonomy. When autonomy becomes the consuming focus in health care, the involvement of communities and personal relationships may be sidelined.

Elderly patients often need the care of nurses not because they need someone to respect their capacity for autonomy but because they have lost mental and/or physical abilities. Rather than focusing on the use of rules and principles such as autonomy, a humanistic focus on facilitating the well-being and alleviating the suffering of elders may be the more important focal point of care. Respect for autonomy remains extremely important in bioethics and nursing ethics, but a humanistic approach is needed that puts the patient's humanity and well-being at the center of care rather than an unquestioned allegiance to rule-oriented behavior.

Also, nurses may believe that they should minimize family involvement in order to support an elderly patient's autonomy. Although healthcare providers need to support elders in maintaining self-direction, family caregivers usually should not be excluded from decision making regarding elders' care. Autonomous elderly patients are not necessarily bound by their family's decisions or recommendations, and often elders appreciate the caring concern of their family and even the appropriate decisional support provided by trusted nurses. Caregivers, including nurses who are well-known by elderly patients through repeated contacts over time, are intimates to the patient, not strangers. It is unreasonable to believe that nurses who care about the well-being of their patients would be objectively detached from actively interacting with patients regarding the patients' health care decisions. When providing decisional support to elders, nurses need to use practical wisdom in evaluating whether capricious assumptions, ageism, and prejudices are influencing the support and direction that they are providing to patients. Ultimately, wise and compassionate decisional support is a critically important part of nursing care and patient advocacy.

Vulnerability and Dependence

In addition to autonomy, vulnerability and dependence are integrally related to moral agency. In order to facilitate communities working toward the common good of their members, MacIntyre (1999) emphasized that people need to acknowledge their animal nature. When realizing that human nature is also animal nature, vulnerability and dependence are accepted as natural human conditions. Vulnerability and dependence are inherent human conditions as people move from childhood to adulthood. Barring complicating circumstances, people progress from vulnerability and dependence in childhood to being capable of independent practical reasoning as adults.

As adults, however, humans may reexperience vulnerability and dependence due to the effects of physical and cognitive changes during aging. According to MacIntyre (1999), ethicists frequently talk in terms of stronger, independent persons benevolently bestowing their virtues on people who are vulnerable and dependent. Nurses would do well to keep in mind that all people are subject to vulnerabilities and dependence, even nurses themselves. There is a vast amount of knowledge to learn from vulnerable and dependent elders if nurses are open to hearing and entering into their patients' life stories (Butts & Rich, 2004).

Dementia

Nurses, particularly nurses working in home care and long-term care settings, often provide care to patients with dementia. Kitwood (1997) suggested that our evolving culture has supported society and health care communities treating persons with dementia as the "new outcasts of society" (p. 44). According to Jenkins and Price (1996), the loss experienced by persons with dementia can be likened to a loss of personhood. Examples of personal tendencies that depersonalize other people are listed in Box 10.2.

When people become adjusted to the dwindling capacities of persons with dementia, they often begin reacting to these people as if they are less than persons (Moody, 1992). People with dementia can still be aware of their feelings even when the person they once seemed to be appears to be withering away. It is reasonable to assume that an extreme sense of vulnerability can occur as a person enters the early and middle stages of a progressive dementia. This occurs when a remainder of cognitive ability may still exist in the awareness of personhood and connectedness to the environment and to others.

Kitwood's (1997) reference to persons with dementia becoming the outcasts of society becomes very relevant when these people lose their dignity in terms of how

BOX 10.2: HIGHLIGHTS FROM THE FIELD: DEPERSONALIZING TENDENCIES TO AVOID

1. *Treachery:* Using deception to distract or manipulate
2. *Disempowerment:* Not allowing persons to use their abilities
3. *Infantalization:* Patronizing; acting as an insensitive parent would act toward a child
4. *Intimidation:* Inducing fear through physical power or threats
5. *Labeling:* Using a category, such as dementia, as the basis for interactions and explanations
6. *Stigmatization:* Treating someone as an outcast or a diseased object
7. *Outpacing:* Pressuring others to act faster than they are able; presenting information too rapidly
8. *Invalidation:* Failing to acknowledge others' subjective experiences and feelings
9. *Banishment:* Physical or psychological exclusion
10. *Objectification:* Treating others as a "lump of matter" rather than as sentient beings
11. *Ignoring:* Talking or interacting with others in the presence of a person as if he or she is not there
12. *Imposition:* Forcing a person to do something; overriding or denying the possibility of choice
13. *Withholding:* Refusing to provide asked-for attention or to meet evident needs
14. *Accusation:* Blaming for actions or failures that arise from lack of ability or misunderstanding
15. *Disruption:* Crudely intruding into a person's actions or reflections
16. *Mockery:* Humiliating; making jokes at another's expense
17. *Disparagement:* Damaging another person's self-esteem; conveying messages that someone is useless, worthless, incompetent

Kitwood, T. (1997). *Dementia reconsidered.* Buckingham, UK: Open University Press, pp. 46–47.

other people perceive them. Dignity is acknowledged or denied in the relatedness of daily interactions between people with dementia and their significant others and health care professionals. Though families and nurses may not recognize the subtle risks involved, dignity may be jeopardized when caregivers are so focused on making ethical decisions regarding the care of persons with dementia that they forget to actually *relate* to the persons themselves (Moody, 1992).

Family and paid caregivers of people with dementia often become frustrated and anxious. Nurses can serve as mentors to other caregivers by exhibiting the virtues of lovingkindness and equanimity when interacting with patients with dementia and their caregivers (see Table 2.1 in Chapter 2). Gentle communication used by nurses helps to support the overall sense of dignity surrounding the care of patients with dementia. Environmental calm is created with gentle words as opposed to an environment of fear and anxiousness that can be created when loud and harsh words are used. Inexperienced caregivers learn by observing nurses. Nurses must always be aware of their potential to ultimately help or harm patients by the example they set for others.

Virtues Needed By Elders

May (1986) asserted that aging is a mystery rather than a problem, and as a society, people must focus on how they behave toward aging rather than how to fix it. Doctors and nurses' position of power as compared to the seemingly passive beneficiary position of vulnerable patients is a frequent topic in bioethics. The behavior of health care professionals directed toward aged individuals is very important because elderly persons frequently perceive that the treatment that they receive from health care professionals is symbolic of what they can expect from the larger community.

May (1986) proposed that even when they are seemingly powerless, elderly persons remain moral agents who are personally responsible for the quality of their lives. An ethic of caregiving that is one sided on the part of nurses and physicians is not the answer to power imbalances between health care professionals and patients. Elders may experience more meaning in their lives if they remain dynamically involved in creating their own sense of well-being. Life is not static; it can be vital into old age.

The following are virtues that May (1986) proposed that elders need to cultivate in order to enhance the quality of their moral lives. These virtues articulated by May were considered valuable enough to be included by the President's Council on Bioethics (2005) in their report *Taking Care: Ethical Caregiving in Our Aging Society*. Nurses who are aware of the continued moral development that occurs in old age can support elderly patients in cultivating these virtues as elders continue their journey of moral progress.

- *Courage:* Courage is consistent with St. Thomas Aquinas's definition of "courage as a firmness of soul in the face of adversity" (May, 1986, p. 51). Elderly persons need courage when facing the certainty of death and loss in their lives.

- *Humility:* Elderly people need humility when their dignity is assaulted through seeing and feeling their bodily decay, when they interpret the looks that they receive from young people as a sign that their frailty is noticeable and possibly repugnant to others, and when they progressively lose more people and things of value in their lives. Humility is a virtue also needed by caregivers to counteract the arrogance that may arise because of their position of power in their relationships with elders. Nurses need to be receivers as well as givers in patient-professional relationships. Nurses can receive the gifts of insight and practical wisdom when they actively listen to the narratives of their elderly patients who have lived many years and experienced many joys and sufferings.

- *Patience:* Although old age sometimes stimulates the emotions of bitterness and anger, a positive conception of the virtue of patience can help combat these reactive emotions. "Patience is purposive waiting, receiving, willing . . . it requires taking control of one's spirit precisely when all else goes out of control" (May, 1986, p. 52). Patience is the virtue that can help elders bear with the frustrations of their frail bodies rather than "cursing their fate," such as becoming frustrated when they become short of breath trying to walk short distances.

- *Simplicity:* Simplicity is a virtue referred to by Benedictine monks as a moral mark of old age. Simplicity becomes the virtue of a pilgrim who "has at long last learned how to travel light" (May, 1986, p. 53). Simplicity is exhibited when elderly persons experience great joy in the small pleasures of life, such as a meal with friends, rather than in accumulating material possessions.

- *Benignity:* Benignity is another moral mark of old age according to the Benedictines. Benignity is defined "as a kind of purified benevolence" (May, 1986, p. 53). It is opposed to the vice of grasping and avarice (greed) that has been associated with some elders' attempts to hold onto life in the face of death. Benevolence provides an answer to the tightfistedness of avarice "not with the empty-handedness of death, but the openhandedness of love" (p. 53). Elders who exhibit the virtue of benignity have usually realized the meaning of their lives as well as the meaning that can be found in their deaths. They have learned to find joy in serving others.

- *Integrity:* The virtue of integrity represents "an inclusive unity of character" (May, 1986, p. 53) that summarizes all of the other virtues of character in old age. Character is a moral structure and requires an overriding virtue when character is "at one with itself" (p. 53). Integrity, or an intactness of character, is the foundation that helps elders remain kind and optimistic in terms of their transcendent connection with the universe even when loss and impermanence could easily pull them in a more negative direction.

■ *Wisdom (prudence):* Wisdom or prudence makes integrity possible through the lessons learned from the experiences of one's past. Prudence was defined by medieval moralists as consisting of three parts: *memoria, docilitus,* and *solertia. Memoria* "characterizes the person who remains open to his or her past, without retouching, falsifying, or glorifying it" (May, 1986, p. 57). *Docilitus* does not represent the passiveness of one who is merely docile but rather is "a capacity to take in the present—an alertness, an attentiveness in the moment" (p. 58). It implies a contrasting state from the need to talk excessively that sometimes serves to separate elders from others. *Solertia* is "a readiness for the unexpected" (p. 58). It provides a contrast to being inflexible with routines (see Box 10.3). However, it should be noted that some amount of ritual helps elders develop strength of character.

■ *Detachment and nonchalance:* Detachment and nonchalance are similar virtues. May (1986) proposed that detachment is a virtue linked with wisdom and is consistent with what Erikson defined as "an attitude that depends in part upon a store of experience" (May, p. 58). People who are experienced weigh and react to situations wisely, calmly, and with love. People who are inexperienced overreact and become engulfed by catastrophe. May based nonchalance on a Biblical virtue that allows one the "capacity to take in one's stride life's gifts and blows" (p. 59). For example, the virtue of detachment or nonchalance might allow elderly persons who have serious medical problems to enjoy the gifts in their lives, such as being with

Box 10.3: Highlights From the Field: Flexibility and Life

When a man is living, he is soft and supple; when he is dead he becomes hard and rigid. When a plant is living, it is soft and tender; when it is dead, it becomes withered and dry. Hence, the hard and rigid belongs to the company of the dead. The soft and supple belongs to the company of the living.

Tzu, L. (1961/1989). *Tao teh ching.* (J.C.H. Wu, Trans.). Boston: Shambhala, p. 155.

their great grandchildren, while calmly accepting the realistic assessment that they may not live to see their great grandchildren graduate from college.

- *Courtesy:* Courtesy, too, is based on a Biblical link to wisdom. Courtesy is a "capacity to deal honorably with all that is urgent, jarring, and rancorous on the social scene" (May, 1986, p. 59). (See Box 10.4.)
- *Hilarity:* A final virtue outlined by May (1986) is another virtue of old age identified by Benedictine monks. Though the risk for depression is more common in elders than at other ages because of conditions such as naturally lowered serotonin levels; anxiety over fixed incomes; physical, personal, and material losses; and disturbed sleep patterns, the monks wisely believed that hilarity is a realistic virtue of old age. *Hilaritas* is "a kind of celestial gaiety in those who have seen a lot, done a lot, grieved a lot, but now acquire that humored detachment of the fly on the ceiling looking down on the human scene" (p. 60). It involves not taking oneself too seriously.

Ethical Reflections

- How important is elders' personal responsibility for the moral nature of their lives and relationships? As a nurse, how can you affect an elder's personal views regarding this responsibility?
- How can nurses help elderly persons cultivate the virtues identified by May?
- Discuss your experiences with elders. Provide examples of situations in which you have observed elders displaying May's virtues. Provide examples of situations in which elders seemed to need the virtues but lacked them.

Quality of Life

What do people mean when they discuss the issue of **quality of life**? Often, people, including health care professionals, talk about quality of life as if it is a concept that is self-evident. But is it? According to Jonsen, Siegler, and Winslade (2006), determinations of quality of life are value judgments, and value judgments imply variations among the people who are determining value. If it is determined that a patient's quality of life is seriously diminished, justifications often are proposed to refrain from life-prolonging medical treatments. Some people find this position problematic because of their views about the sanctity of life. These people believe that because all human life is sacred, life must be preserved no matter what the quality of that life might be.

BOX 10.4: HIGHLIGHTS FROM THE FIELD: LAST ACTS OF COURTESY

Ida was a 79-year-old Alzheimer's patient seen by Dr. Muller, a psychiatrist, in the ER because she became agitated at her foster home. Ida looked younger than her years and "still had some of the light that usually leaves the face of the demented. Her score was 7 out of 30" on the Mini Mental Status Exam. "Ida gave little information during the interview, though she showed every sign of wanting to cooperate." Plans were made for Ida to be discharged back to the foster home on Haldol. When Dr. Muller went to say good-bye to Ida he found her "straightening the sheet and flattening out the pillow on the gurney where she had been placed prior to the interview. She was trying to put [styrofoam cups and food wrappers] into a trash container" but was having difficulty in doing so. Dr. Muller stated "I was struck by what was still left of this sweet lady's demented brain and mind—which did not know the year, season, month, or day—that made her want to attempt these last acts of courtesy before leaving the ER." Muller quoted the neurologist, Oliver Sacks, who stated "style, neurologically, is the deepest part of one's being, and may be preserved, almost to the last, in a dementia."

Muller, R. (2003). *Psych ER*. Hillsdale, NJ: The Analytic Press, pp. 63–65.

Many people do believe that treatment can be withheld or withdrawn based on quality of life determinations while preserving a reverence for the sanctity of life. Scales have been developed and measures of physical and psychological functions have been suggested to objectify quality of life determinations. However, people differ significantly in how they respond to scales and measurements that are supposed to quantify the quality of their own or others' lives. Studies have shown that at least one group of health care professionals, physicians, frequently rate the quality of a patient's life lower than the patient rates it (Jonsen et al., 2006).

Determining the quality of life can be divided into categories of personal evaluations and observer evaluations. According to Jonsen et al. (2006), a **personal evaluation** is "the personal satisfaction expressed or experienced by individuals in their own physical, mental, and social situation" (pp. 111–112). **Observer evaluations** refer to quality of life judgments made by someone other than the person "living the life." Observers tend to base their evaluations on some standard below which they believe that life is not desirable. It is observer evaluations that generate most ethical problems in regard to quality of life determinations, because observer evaluations can reflect incorrect assumptions, biases, prejudices, or beliefs about conditions that are not necessarily permanent, such as homelessness or family conditions.

Problems with quality of life determinations that are specifically related to elderly patients can arise due to discrimination against patients by health care professionals based on the patient's chronological age, a perception of a patient's social worth, a patient's dementia, or differences between the professional's and the patient's life goals and values (Faden & German, 1994; Jonsen et al., 2006). Decisions regarding treatment must always be made based on honest determinations of medical need and patients' current or previously communicated preferences. If a patient's wishes were not previously communicated, decisions should be based on projections of what loved ones believe that the patient would want done. Problems can easily arise when professionals try to project what a "reasonable person" would want in a particular situation. It is at this point that prejudices and biased discriminations based on ageism can enter into observer evaluations.

When acting in regard to elderly patients, special attention needs to be focused on an assumption that values and goals are different among people of different age groups (Faden & German, 1994; Jonsen et al., 2006). The values that might be consistent among young health care professionals could be expected to be very different from the values held by old-old adults. Automatic projections of values by nurses and other health care professionals are not consistent with the moral care of elderly persons. Elders may view their lives as having quality when younger persons, still in the prime of their lives, do not readily see the same quality there. In addition to nurses using moral imagination in simply stopping to *reflect* about the dangers of forming automatic assumptions, conducting a values history with elderly patients when they enter a new health care system can be invaluable in trying to assure the ethical treatment of elders. This history must be reevaluated as appropriate (see Box 10.5).

Ethical Reflections

- A decision not to attempt to resuscitate an unconscious, frail elderly person in an emergency department should not be made based solely on chronological age. What factors must be considered in such a decision?
- How might ageism affect end-of-life decisions and the elderly? What can nurses do to combat end-of-life care and decisions based solely on ageism?

BOX 10.5: HIGHLIGHTS FROM THE FIELD: CONDUCTING A VALUES HISTORY

Sample questions for conducting a values history with elders:

1. What would you like to say to someone reading [a] document about your overall attitude toward life?
2. What, for you, makes life worth living?
3. How do you feel about your health problems or disabilities? What would you like others (family, friends, doctors, nurses) to know about these feelings?
4. How do you expect friends, family, and others to support your decisions regarding medical treatment you may need now or in the future?
5. If your current physical or mental health gets worse, how would you feel?
6. How does independence or dependence affect your life?
7. What will be important to you when you are dying (e.g., physical comfort, no pain, family members present, etc.)?
8. Where would you prefer to die?
9. What general comments would you like to make about medical treatment?
10. How do your religious background or beliefs affect your feelings toward serious, chronic, or terminal illness?

Institute for Ethics, University of New Mexico. (n.d.). Values history. Retrieved December 2, 2006, from http://hsc.unm.edu/ethics/pdf/Values_History.doc, pp. 1–14.

As previously discussed, Frankl (1959/1984) maintained that "man's search for meaning is the primary motivation in his life" (p. 105). Humans embark on the search for meaning in order to alleviate and understand suffering and to move toward well-being. Frankl proposed that inner tension rather than inner equilibrium may result from the search for meaning. He believed that inner tension is a prerequisite for mental health. Valuing the need to strive toward equilibrium and homeostasis (a tension-less state) is a dangerous misconception according to Frankl. This way of thinking can be especially true when interacting with elderly persons whose whole being does not generally remain in a state of equilibrium.

An acceptance of the belief that equilibrium is not necessarily the healthiest state supports the belief that suffering should not be attacked as if it is something to eliminate at all costs. Rather, well-being often involves the relief of suffering through the *acceptance* of suffering. In discussing the often misguided goals of a modernist society, Callahan (1995) proposed that the novelist George Eliot had captured this philosophy with the word *meliorism*. The concept of meliorism describes "an ethic of action oriented toward the relief, not the acceptance, of pain and suffering" (p. 30).

An emphasis on holistic care has helped to eliminate some of the beliefs from the Enlightenment period that the human body can be compared with a machine (sometimes referred to as reductionism). Mechanics fix machines but the health care professional-patient relationship should not be viewed in a similar way. However, the health care system and health care professionals today often still perpetuate the meliorism described by Eliot. Meliorism causes doctors and nurses to work toward curing disease and relieving suffering at all costs. In working with patients of all ages, but especially in patients' later years, attempts must be made to alleviate suffering while realizing that completely relieving suffering and curing diseases is not always possible.

In these instances, the nurse's goal is to help patients accept the pain and suffering that cannot be changed and find meaning in their suffering. Amid the chaos and pain of patients' suffering, nurses can be compared to the calm person described by the Buddhist monk, Thich Nhat Hanh (see Box 10.6). Patients' suffering can lead to a profound transforming life experience for both patients and nurses.

BOX 10.6: HIGHLIGHTS FROM THE FIELD: CALM WITHIN THE STORM

In Vietnam there are many people, called boat people, who leave the country in small boats. Often the boats are caught in rough seas or storms, the people may panic, and boats can sink. But if even one person aboard can remain calm, lucid, knowing what to do and what not to do, he or she can help the boat survive. His or her expression—face, voice—communicates clarity and calmness, and people have trust in that person. They will listen to what he or she says. One such person can save the lives of many.

Thich Nhat Hanh. (2001). *Thich Nhat Hanh: Essential writings* (R. Ellsberg, Ed.). New York: Orbis Books, p. 162.

--------------- Ethical Reflections ---------------

- Health care professionals' beliefs about the proper treatment of elders falls along a continuum from discounting elders' personal quality of life judgments to believing that only curing disease and being successful in eliminating physical suffering are worthwhile goals. Provide examples of nurses' opportunities to act as patient advocates in relation to this continuum.

Assessing the Capacity to Remain at Home

Assessing elders' capacity to safely continue to live alone in their own homes is a problem often faced by nurses working with elders in the community and nurses helping to plan discharges of patients from acute care to home care. These determinations become particularly difficult when frail elders adamantly want to remain in or return to their homes and caregivers disagree with an elder's decisions. Caregivers must consider the real and perceived capacities and incapacities of elders and question the safety of their living situation. Ways to assess cognitive capacity have been covered earlier in this chapter and in Chapter 9. If it is believed that an elder is incapacitated, a consideration of respecting elders' autonomy versus supporting caregivers' beneficence may be needed. The ethical issue becomes a matter of deciding whether to act in a way that Beauchamp and Childress (2001) called weak or soft paternalism, which is a concept that was originally suggested by Feinberg.

Weak paternalism involves an intervention by a caregiver based on the principles of beneficence or nonmaleficence that is enacted "to protect persons against their own substantially nonautonomous action(s)" (Beauchamp & Childress, 2001, p. 181). Nonautonomous actions are actions that are not based on rational decision making. Persons who are the receivers of weak paternalistic actions must have some form of compromised ability for the weak paternalism to be justified. It is debatable as to whether weak paternalism actually qualifies to be labeled as paternalism. Acting in a person's best interest is not usually disputed when people must be protected from harm resulting from circumstances that are beyond their control, including a personal desire based on faulty information when a person is incapacitated. However, issues of self-harm often constitute dilemmas when elders with intact decisional capacity want to remain at home when it is not safe to do so because of the elder's physical limitations. Family caregivers and health care providers must carefully weigh when and the degree to which weak paternalism is justified in preventing self-harm.

Long-Term Care

Issues regarding moral relationships between nurses and patients in long-term care facilities are similar to other issues discussed in this chapter; that is, the relationships are often focused on issues of autonomy. However, as previously proposed, focusing too narrowly on respecting autonomy can cause nurses to miss the real day-to-day complexities that make up moral relationships with elders. In many instances, elders are in long-term care facilities because they no longer are able to exercise self-direction in safely caring for themselves. This fact sometimes makes attempts at trying to respect and preserve autonomy, in a comprehensive sense, a futile undertaking. When unrealistic goals are not acknowledged in long-term care, it often frustrates nurses and aides who work in long-term care facilities; unfortunately, these frustrations can ultimately be directed against long-term care residents.

Pullman (1998) proposed that an ethic of dignity be used as opposed to an ethic of autonomy in long-term care. With an ethic of dignity, the moral character of caregivers is the focus rather than the autonomy of the recipients of care. Of course autonomy must be respected when it is realistic to do so, but when working with long-term care residents who are no longer able to exercise their full autonomy, a communal ethic of dignity can provide a compassionate means of care. Even when elders are able to fully exercise their autonomous choices, an ethic of dignity provides an appropriate grounding framework from which to work.

Pullman (1998) divided dignity into **basic dignity**, which is the dignity inherent in all humans, and **personal dignity**, which is an evaluative type of dignity decided upon by communities but that does not have to be solely tied to a person's autonomy. Personal dignity can be viewed as a community's valuing of the interrelationship of members of the community. Acknowledging elders' basic and personal dignity, through the adoption of an ethic of dignity, includes the "confidence that caregivers will strive to serve the on-going interests of their patients to the best of their abilities" (Pullman, p. 37). If there is a belief that elderly residents of long-term care facilities need to be independent because being dependent is bad, and if the goal is to minimize the elders' need for care rather than to provide more care, then the relationships between nurses and elderly residents of long-term care facilities are in trouble from their outset.

Pullman (1998) suggested that long-term care often requires paternalistic interventions from the beginning of patient-health care provider relationships. He defined a rule of **justified paternalism** as a guide for these paternalistic interventions. That rule is: "the degree of paternalistic intervention justified or required, is inversely proportional to the degree of autonomy present" (p. 37). Nurses must be extremely sensitive and aware in assuring that they cultivate the intellectual virtue of practical wisdom so that errors in judgments are not made about respecting patients' autonomy versus practicing justified or weak paternalism in patient care.

When elders have the capacity to make choices regarding treatments and daily living activities, they must have the freedom to make personal decisions. Those options include such things as choosing to refuse medications and refusing physical therapy treatments. However, respecting elders' autonomy does not mean that compassionate nurses should not take considerable time, if needed, to calmly discuss the potential consequences of controversial choices made by elderly persons. Nurses who work from an ethic of dignity are not emotionally detached from their patients but, instead, are willing to risk feeling a personal sense of failure or loss when their elderly patients make choices that a nurse believes are not in the elder's best interest.

Ethical Reflections

- Cohen (1988) said that elders often focus all of their energy toward avoiding "the ultimate defeat, which is not death but institutionalization and which is regarded as a living death" (p. 25). How can nurses help to change the experience of residence in a long-term care facility being like a "living death"?
- When caring for elders, both chemical and physical restrictions and restraints should be limited to the least amount possible to maintain the safety of patients and caregivers. Imagine that you are working as an RN in a large long-term care facility. You are asked to help with something on your colleague's wing of the facility. As you are walking down the hall of her wing, you hear a resident crying out very loudly. You enter the resident's room and notice that the resident is tightly restrained to the bed. What would you do?
- Do you believe that nurses who work in long-term care facilities are stigmatized in any way? If so, what do you believe is the underlying cause of this stigmatization? How can this perception be changed?

Elder Abuse

Nurses are frequently the first people to recognize that patients are the victims of violence or abuse. This is especially true in regard to emergency department and home care nurses. Moral care of elders requires nurses to be interested in recognizing the signs of abuse and in taking appropriate actions. Elder abuse includes physical abuse, sexual abuse, emotional or psychological abuse, neglect, abandonment, financial or material exploitation, and self-neglect (National Center on Elder Abuse [NCEA], 2006b).

A report of the most recent survey regarding abuse of adults 60 years of age and older, which was conducted and co-authored by the National Committee for the Prevention of Elder Abuse in conjunction with the National Adult Protective Services Association (2006), revealed that there has been a significant increase in reports of elder abuse, neglect, and exploitation since the 2000 survey. Between 2000 and 2004, the reports of abuse of adults of all ages increased by 19%. The alleged abuse usually occurred in a home (89.3%), and women were much more likely to be victims of abuse than men (NCEA, 2006a). Perpetrators of elder abuse and neglect were women in 52.7% of cases reviewed in the survey. Adult children accounted for 32.6% of the total number of perpetrators, and other family members accounted for 21.5%.

Clues that abuse may be occurring include explanations about injuries that seem inconsistent with what the nurse actually sees; delays in seeking treatment for conditions and injuries; unusual behaviors such as caregivers giving extensive details about the elder's injuries, refusing to allow the elder to be interviewed or treated by the nurse without the caregiver being present, and showing an unreasonable interest in the cost of treatment (Ramsey, 2006). The conditions of elder abuse are often different from abuse involving other adults or children (Bergeron, 2000). Older males are more prone to abuse than younger males, and generally there are limited resources in terms of safe houses for males. Elderly persons who are abused tend to be less accepting of help from police and the court system than younger victims of abuse. This reluctance is particularly prevalent when the abuser is the elder's child. When an abuser is a spouse, elderly persons are more resistant to seeking a divorce or separation from the spouse than happens with younger persons. Because of limited financial resources, elderly persons usually feel more constrained by their housing and living situations and are reluctant to disrupt the status quo even when they are being abused.

The NCEA (2006a) recommended that accurate elder abuse data need to be continuously collected at both the state and national levels. Trends need to be tracked, studied, and addressed through appropriate interventions, and education about identifying and reporting elder abuse needs to be increased. Nurses can have a key role in regard to all of these recommendations. It is morally imperative that nurses be active in recognizing the abuse of elders and knowing state statutes regarding the handling of elder abuse. Nurses also have a key role in teaching other health care professionals and the community about recognizing and reporting elder abuse. The following list provides a guideline for meeting moral responsibility in reporting abuse.

Report to:

- Adult Protective Services
- Long-term care ombudsman (usually when an agency or health care provider is involved)
- State licensing board (when a health care provider is involved)
- Law enforcement (if required under statute)

When:

- Written or verbal report within 24 hours of incident (Ramsey, 2006, p. 58)

In conjunction with the 2006 World Elder Abuse Awareness Day, the Administration on Aging (U.S. Department of Health and Human Services, 2006) encouraged people "to volunteer to call or visit an isolated senior who may be at risk of elder abuse, neglect or exploitation, or to participate in activities that are intended to create awareness of elder mistreatment, such as submitting an editorial or press release to [a] local newspaper" (Para 2). State and local resources are often lacking to help elders who are abused or are at high risk for abuse. The bottom line in the moral care of abused elders is that nurses must be persistent in their efforts to obtain help for these vulnerable adults.

Age-Based Distribution of Health Care Resources

There has been a substantial debate among bioethicists and philosophers about the need for a plan to fairly distribute health care resources among different generations (Callahan, 1995; Daniels, 1988; Moody, 1992). The Alliance for Aging Research, a nonprofit group focused on improving the well-being of elders, published a report in 2003 that outlined five ways that the U.S. health care system has failed elders (see Box 10.7). According to the Alliance, the reason underlying these failures is a fundamental ageist bias among U.S. society.

Even if one concedes that there is an ageist bias among the American public, it is known that a large percentage of all U.S. health care dollars are spent on the care of elders during their last year of life. Because of the expensive health care that they often

BOX 10.7: HIGHLIGHTS FROM THE FIELD: FIVE DIMENSIONS OF AGEIST BIAS

1. Health care professionals do not receive enough training in geriatrics to properly care for many older patients.
2. Older patients are less likely than younger people to receive preventive care.
3. Older patients are less likely to be tested or screened for diseases and other health problems.
4. Proven medical interventions for older patients are often ignored, leading to inappropriate or incomplete treatment.
5. Older people are consistently excluded from clinical trials, even though they are the largest users of approved drugs.

Alliance for Aging Research. (2003). Ageism: How healthcare fails the elderly. Retrieved January 17, 2007, from http://www.agingresearch.org/brochures/ageism/ageism_booklet_final.pdf, p. 1.

receive, it is the very young (neonates) and the very old who are the focus of debates about the distribution of health care resources. Currently, no plan for fairly distributing health care dollars among different generations has received widespread acceptance in the United States.

Social justice in distributing health care resources according to age has been described as a type of rationing. Moody (1992) defined rationing as a system that is associated with crisis situations like the rationing of gasoline during oil embargoes and butter during World War II. Rationing is used when there is a scarcity of resources, but it is often only a temporary solution. Rationing usually is not a method that is appropriate to use in making decisions about the distribution of health care resources, especially in nonemergency situations. American health care practices that can be compared to acts of rationing include: "the distribution of organs for transplantation, the practice of triage in admission to hospital emergency rooms, [and] extensive queuing for health care services provided through the Veterans Administration" (p. 199).

In fact, Moody (1992) said that the United States already has an allocation scheme for making decisions regarding health care for elders in the form of the Medicare program, which was established in 1965. The Medicare program has limits in regard to the care and treatment that can be provided under the program, but these limits usually are not referred to as rationing. However, the limits of the Medicare program, unfortunately, may contribute to the ineffective system of distributing resources. For example, restrictions on payments for home care may contribute to the number of elders living in long-term care facilities.

Callahan (1995) proposed that the idea of the "natural life span" and a "tolerable death" might need to be included in considerations about distributing health care resources to elders. Callahan defined these terms as "a fitting life span followed by a death that is relatively acceptable in its timeliness within that life span" (p. 64) (see Box 10.8). Moody (1992) agreed that using considerations of a natural life span can be helpful in the rationing-allocation debate, but he added that in the real world bringing theory and practice together is very difficult and requires prudent political judgment. The debate regarding allocating health care resources among different generations is a heated one, and seems to have no immediate end in sight.

Ethical Reflections

In the United States, approximately $5,700 is spent per capita annually on health care. This figure is more than the money spent on health care per capita in any other country. However, health indicators and outcomes in the United States do not reflect this great expenditure. For example, life expectancy in the United States is below the level of other industrialized countries, and infant mortality rates in the United States are high.

- Discuss the ethics of how money is allocated for the health care provided to different aged populations in the United States. Is the allocation system justice based? Why or why not?
- Is too much money allocated to caring for people at both ends of the spectrum of life, the very young and the very old? What is the rationale for your answer to this question?
- Do you believe that the U.S. public would spend less on health care during the last year of an elder's life if more preventive care was provided to the population of elders? Explain and include examples.
- Why is the intergenerational distribution of health care resources an ethical issue of concern for nurses?

Ethics and the Humanistic Nursing Care of Elders

Travelbee (1971) described the human-to-human relationship as a "mutually significant experience" (p. 123) between a nurse and the recipient of care. According to Travelbee,

BOX 10.8: HIGHLIGHTS FROM THE FIELD: IS THERE A DUTY TO DIE?

Hardwig (2000) proposed that "death does not always come at the right time" and that death does not happen to hermits, that is, "death is a death in the family" (p. 81). In regard to his own life, Hardwig stated that he may "one day have a duty to die" because of his connections with his family. He suggested that in some situations "preserving my life can only devastate the lives of those who care about me" (p. 86).

1. Do you believe that people ever have a "duty to die"? If so, under what circumstances?
2. Defend your position.

Hardwig, J. (2000). *Is there a duty to die? and other essays in medical ethics.* New York: Routledge.

"each participant in the relationship perceives and responds to the human-ness of the other; that is, the 'patient' is perceived and responded to as a unique human being—not as 'an illness,' 'a room number,' or as a 'task to be performed'" (p. 124). Unfortunately, elders often feel dehumanized when interacting with health care professionals, which further compounds the dehumanization that they encounter in society. Travelbee made a profound statement: If just one health care professional would treat a recipient of care as a *human being*, this gesture might give the person the strength to cope with 10 other health care professionals who perceive that same person as merely a *patient*.

Nurses who are compassionate dedicate themselves to helping patients transcend or accept unavoidable suffering. It is a challenge to relate to others compassionately, to really communicate to the heart, according to Chodron (1997). "Compassion is not a relationship between the healer and the wounded. It is a relationship between equals" (Chodron, 2001, p. 50).

For many elders, the world is a lonely place. Nurses who have a sincere desire to take action to alleviate or facilitate acceptance of the suffering of this vulnerable group are widening the circle of compassion in the world. Solomon (2001) stated that research has revealed that elders have a higher response to placebo treatment than is normally expected. Solomon reported that this higher response has been attributed to the attention that elderly persons receive when they participate in research studies. He proposed that elders must be very lonely for this slight attention to provide them with such a lift.

Compassion and healing can be thought of as paired needs of elders. Capra (1982) described healing as a "complex interplay among the physical, psychological, social, and environmental aspects of the human condition" (p. 124). Capra postulated that healing has been excluded from medical science because it cannot be understood in terms of reductionism. Healing suggests a moving toward wholeness that goes beyond a single human being; it is consistent with a belief in the interconnection of all beings and the universe. Healing does not imply curing; it is a realization that not all things can be *fixed*. This idea of healing encompasses the recognition of the nature of impermanence and accepts unpredictability and the inability to strictly control events.

Nurses must establish human-to-human relationships with elderly patients and recognize the interplay of many factors that may affect the older person's state of well-being. Many factors that affect elders cannot be changed; they must be peacefully accepted and used in achieving integrity. However, there are active healing interventions that nurses can employ.

The need for physical touch is heightened at a time when elders are already experiencing significant losses in their lives—loved ones, belongings, and sensory losses. Touch is one form of healing communication that nurses can use to convey compassion to elders. Many elders perceive the nurse's touch as a comforting touch. In her experimental study, Butts (1998, 2001) found that in long-term care facilities the nurse's comforting touch significantly improved female elderly residents' perceptions of five factors: self-esteem, well-being and social status, health status, life satisfaction and self-actualization, and faith and belief—as compared to those female elders in long-term care facilities who were not touched.

Caring for elders requires dynamic interventions blending art and science. Suffering and loss are inherent in the daily lives of elders, and the reality of impermanence forms a glaring presence that is difficult for the aged to ignore. Although there are many approaches in the ethical care of elderly patients, nurses might adopt an approach to care similar to a way of being suggested by Thich Nhat Hanh (1998) based on the Buddhist *Lotus Sutra*. Thich Nhat Hanh stated that the sutra advises one "to look and listen with the eyes of compassion." He further stated that "compassionate listening brings about healing" (p. 86). Compassionate listening by nurses gives individual elders their voice in an often uncompassionate world.

Ethical Reflections

- Box 10.9 contains examples from the ANA's (2001) *Code of Ethics for Nurses with Interpretive Statements*. How are these examples relevant to the nursing care of elders?
- What other provisions and statements in the ANA's *Code of Ethics for Nurses* are particularly pertinent to the nursing care of elders [see Appendix A]? Discuss these provisions and provide examples of how they apply to nursing practice.

Web Ethics

Administration on Aging (AOA)
   http://www.aoa.gov

Alliance for Aging Research
   http://www.agingresearch.org

The Alzheimer's Association
   http://www.alz.org

Family Caregiver Alliance
   http://www.caregiver.org

National Council on Aging
   http://www.ncoa.org

National Institute on Aging
   http://www.nia.nih.gov

U.S. Department of Justice Office of Victims of Crime: Elder Abuse
   http://www.ojp.usdoj.gov/ovc/help/ea.htm

Summary

Because modern societies often value the vibrancy and independence of youth rather than the decay and dependence of old age, the voices of elders are sometimes silenced. The search for meaning is important for people of all ages, but it becomes especially important for elders. Nurses have the opportunity to take a key role in opposing ageism in health care and society and in helping elders cultivate virtues that facilitate well-being in the eighth and ninth developmental stages of the life cycle.

BOX 10.9: HIGHLIGHTS FROM THE FIELD:
CODE OF ETHICS FOR NURSES

- The worth of an individual is not affected by disease, disability, functional status, or proximity to death (1.3, p. 7).
- Nursing care aims to maximize the values that the patient has treasured in life and extends supportive care to the family and significant others (1.3, p. 7).
- The nurse preserves, protects, and supports [patients' self-determination] by assessing the patient's comprehension of both the information presented and the implications of decisions (1.4, p. 8).
- Nurses may not delegate responsibilities such as assessment and evaluation; they may delegate tasks. The nurse must not knowingly assign or delegate to any member of the nursing team a task for which that person is not prepared or qualified (4.4, p. 17).

Key Points

- Ageism, or discrimination based on chronological age, underlies many ethical issues related to elders.
- Society often neglects to notice the meaning of elders' lives as scientists work to abolish the biology of aging.
- Determinations of decisional capacity in regard to elders are sometimes made based upon prejudiced assumptions rather than facts.
- Elders may perceive the quality of their lives to be higher than health care professionals perceive it based on observational judgments.
- Weak or justified paternalism is sometimes a compassionate approach to caring for elderly persons.
- Focusing on an ethic of dignity rather than a strict ethic of autonomy may be more realistic in caring for some elders, especially in long-term care facilities when elderly persons are not completely able to exercise their autonomy.

CASE STUDY: WHOSE WISHES SHOULD BE HONORED?

Mrs. R., a frail, 85-year-old woman who lives alone, was admitted to a gero-psychiatric unit because of irritability, confusion, and increasing incontinence. Mrs. R.'s family stated that she was continually refusing assistance from her home health aides and became angry when her family and home care nurses tried to reason with her about these refusals. The patient's family had installed child gates in her home to block her entry into her bathroom, trying to force Mrs. R. to use a bedside commode. Mrs. R. began having frequent "accidents" of incontinence on the floor near the bathroom door while trying to get through the gates. During her hospital admission, Mrs. R. was hydrated with intravenous fluids and a couple of her medications were adjusted. She subsequently became calm and cooperative with the care that she received while in the hospital. When the RN and social worker talked with Mrs. R. about the safety risks of her living in her home alone, the patient stated "I am 85 years old and think that I should be able to decide how I want to live the remainder of my life. I'm willing to take my chances." Mrs. R. was often unsure about the correct day of the week when questioned, yet she knew the name of the hospital and the reason that she was admitted for treatment. She was often confused about the names of the hospital staff but was able to state her own name and the names of her children. Though Mrs. R agreed to cooperate with home care providers, her family continued to insist that Mrs. R. be admitted to a long-term care facility. Her family requested that the psychiatrist complete the paperwork so that a judge could have the patient declared incompetent. The psychiatrist did not usually seem sincerely interested in his patients, and he had spent little time with Mrs. R. This psychiatrist was usually willing to comply with most families' wishes. The RN and social worker disagreed with the decision to declare Mrs. R. to be incompetent and were in favor of allowing her to return home as she wished.

Case Study Questions

1. Based on the information provided, does it seem that Mrs. R. has decision-making capacity? What criteria can be used as a basis for your decision? What needs to be included in a complete assessment of Mrs. R.'s decision-making capacity?

(continued)

CASE STUDY: WHOSE WISHES SHOULD BE HONORED? (continued)

2. Does safety at home for Mrs. R. seem feasible? If so, how might this be accomplished? If not, why not?
3. What could the RN and social worker do to try to resolve the disagreement among the patient, her family, the doctor, and themselves?
4. Is a form of paternalism being used by any of the people involved in this case? If so, is it a form of weak or justified paternalism? Does the approach seem to be ethical? Why or why not?
5. What type of quality of life evaluation is most appropriate in this situation? Explain.
6. How is the issue of Mrs. R.'s dignity involved in this case?
7. How might the RN and social worker enter into a discussion of life meaning with Mrs. R.? With her family? With the physician?

References

Agich, G. J. (2003). *Dependence and autonomy in old age: An ethical framework for long-term care* (2nd ed., rev. ed.). Cambridge, UK: Cambridge University Press.

Alliance for Aging Research. (2003). Ageism: How healthcare fails the elderly. Retrieved January 17, 2007, from http://www.agingresearch.org/brochures/ageism/ageism_booklet_final.pdf

Allport, G. W. (1984). Preface. In V. E. Frankl, *Man's search for meaning: An introduction to logotherapy* (3rd ed., pp. 7–10). New York: Simon and Schuster.

American Nurses Association. (2001). *Code of ethics for nurses with interpretive statements.* Silver Spring, MD: Author.

Arias, E. (2006). United States life tables, 2003. *National Vital Statistics Reports, 54*(14). Retrieved November 30, 2006, from http://www.cdc.gov/nchs/data/nvsr/nvsr54/nvsr54_14.pdf

Beauchamp, T. L., & Childress, J. F. (2001). *Principles of biomedical ethics* (5th ed.). New York: Oxford University Press.

Bergeron, R. (2000, September). Servicing the needs of elder abuse victims. *Policy & Practice,* 40–45.

Blum, L. A. (1994). *Moral perception and particularity.* Cambridge, UK: Cambridge University Press.

Buscaglia, L. (1982). *The fall of Freddie the leaf: A story of life for all ages.* Thorofare, NJ: Charles B. Slack.

Butler, R. (1975). *Why survive? Being old in America.* New York: Harper & Row.

Butts, J. B. (1998). *Outcomes of comfort touch in institutionalized elderly female residents.* Unpublished doctoral dissertation, University of Alabama at Birmingham.

Butts, J. B. (2001). Outcomes of comfort touch in institutionalized elderly female residents. *Geriatric Nursing, 22*(4), 180–184.

Butts, J. B., & Rich, K. L. (2004). Acknowledging dependence: A MacIntyrean perspective on relationships involving Alzheimer's disease. *Nursing Ethics, 11*(4), 400–410.

Callahan, D. (1995). *Setting limits: Medical goals in an aging society with "a response to my critics."* Washington, DC: Georgetown University Press.

Capra, F. (1982). *The turning point: Science, society, and the rising culture.* New York: Bantam Books.

Chodron, P. (1997). *When things fall apart: Heart advice for difficult times.* Boston: Shambhala.

Chodron, P. (2001). *The places that scare you: A guide to fearlessness in difficult times.* Boston: Shambhala.

Cohen, E. S. (1988). The elderly mystique: Constraints on the autonomy of the elderly with disabilities. *Gerontologist, 28*(Suppl.), 24-31.

Cole, T. R. (1986). The tattered web of cultural meanings. In T. R. Cole & S. Gadow (Eds.), *What does it mean to grow old? Reflections from the humanities* (pp. 3–7). Durham, NC: Duke University Press.

Daniels, N. (1988). *Am I my parents' keeper?* New York: Oxford University Press.

de Beauvoir, S. (1972). *The coming of age* (P. O'Brien, Trans.). New York: Putnam.

Easwaren, E. (1992). *Your life is your message: Finding harmony with yourself, others, and the earth.* New York: Hyperion.

Erikson, E. H., & Erikson, J. M. (1997). *The life cycle completed* (extended version). New York: W.W. Norton & Company.

Faden, R., & German, P. S. (1994). Quality of life: Considerations in geriatrics. *Clinics in Geriatric Medicine, 19*(3), 541-551.

Frankl, V. E. (1984). *Man's search for meaning: An introduction to logotherapy* (3rd ed.). New York: Simon and Schuster.

Greening, T. (1998). Viktor Frankl, 1905-1997. *Journal of Humanistic Psychology, 38*(1), 10–11.

Hardwig, J. (2000). *Is there a duty to die? and other essays in medical ethics.* New York: Routledge.

Hester, D. M. (2001). *Community as healing: Pragmatist ethics in medical encounters.* Lanham, MD: Rowman & Littlefield.

Institute of Ethics, University of New Mexico. (n.d.). Values history. Retrieved December 2, 2006, from http://hsc.unm.edu/ethics/pdf/Values_History.doc

Jenkins, D., & Price, B. (1996). Dementia and personhood: A focus for care? *Journal of Advanced Nursing, 24*(1), 84–90.

Jonsen, A. R., Siegler, M., & Winslade, W. J. (2006). *Clinical ethics: A practical approach to ethical decisions in clinical medicine* (6th ed.). New York: McGraw-Hill.

Kitwood, T. (1997). *Dementia reconsidered: The person comes first.* Buckingham, UK: Open University Press.

MacIntyre, A. (1984). *After virtue.* Notre Dame, IN: University of Notre Dame Press.

MacIntyre, A. (1999). *Dependent rational animals: Why human beings need the virtues.* Chicago: Open Court.

May, W. F. (1986). The virtues and vices of the elderly. In T. R. Cole & S. Gadow (Eds.), *What does it mean to grow old? Reflections from the humanities* (pp. 43–61). Durham, NC: Duke University Press.

Moody, H. R. (1992). *Ethics in an aging society.* Baltimore: The Johns Hopkins University Press.

Muller, R. J. (2003). *Psych ER.* Hillsdale, NJ: The Analytic Press.

National Center on Elder Abuse. (2006a). Fact sheet: Abuse of adults aged 60+, 2004 survey of adult protective services. Retrieved December 1, 2006, from http://www.elderabusecenter.org/pdf/2-14-06%2060FACT%20SHEET.pdf

National Center on Elder Abuse. (2006b). The basics: Major types of elder abuse. Retrieved December 1, 2006, from http://www.elderabusecenter.org/default.cfm?p=basics.cfm

National Committee for the Prevention of Elder Abuse and National Adult Protective Services Association. (2006). The 2004 survey of state adult protective services: Abuse of adults 60 years of age and older. Retrieved December 1, 2006, from http://www.elderabusecenter.org/pdf/2-14-06%20FINAL%2060+REPORT.pdf

President's Council on Bioethics. (2005). *Taking care: Ethical caregiving in our aging society.* Washington, DC: Author.

Pullman, D. (1998). The ethics of autonomy and dignity in long-term care. *Canadian Journal on Aging, 18*(1), 26-46.

Ramsey, S. B. (2006). Abusive situations. In S. W. Killion & K. Dempski (Eds.), *Quick look nursing: Legal and ethical issues* (pp. 58-59). Sudbury, MA: Jones & Bartlett.

Savishinsky, J. S. (1991). *The ends of time: Life and work in a nursing home.* New York: Bergin & Garvey.

Smith, N. L., Kotthoff-Burrell, E., & Post, L. F. (2002). Protecting the patient's voice on team. In M. D. Mezey, C. K. Cassel, M. M. Bottrell, K. Hyer, J. L. Howe, & T. T. Fulmer (Eds.), *Ethical patient care: A casebook for geriatric health care teams* (pp. 83-101). Baltimore: The Johns Hopkins University Press.

Solomon, A. (2001). *The noonday demon: An atlas of depression.* New York: Scribner.

Stanley, B., Sieber, J. E., & Melton, G. B. (2003). Empirical studies of ethical issues in research: A research agenda. In D. N. Bersoff (Ed.), *Ethical conflicts in psychology* (3rd ed., pp. 398–402). Washington, DC: American Psychological Association.

Thich Nhat Hanh. (1998). *The heart of the Buddha's teaching: Transforming suffering into peace, joy and liberation.* New York: Broadway.

Thich Nhat Hanh. (2001). *Thich Nhat Hanh: Essential writings* (R. Ellsberg, Ed.). New York: Orbis.

Travelbee, J. (1971). *Interpersonal aspects of nursing* (2nd ed.). Philadelphia: F.A. Davis.

Tzu, L. (1989). *Tao teh ching* (J. C. H. Wu, Trans.). Boston: Shambhala. (This edition originally published 1961)

U.S. Census Bureau. (2006). Income, poverty, and health insurance coverage in the United States. Retrieved December 8, 2006, from http://www.census.gov/prod/2006pubs/p60-231.pdf

U.S. Department of Health and Human Services, Administration on Aging. (2006). Elder rights & resources: Elder abuse. Retrieved December 6, 2006, from http://www.aoa.gov/eldfam/Elder_Rights/Elder_Abuse/Elder_Abuse.asp

Wallis, V. (1993). *Two old women: An Alaska legend of betrayal, courage, and survival* (10th anniversary ed.). New York: Perennial.

CHAPTER **10** QUESTIONS

1. Moral agency implies that people are
   a. usually ethical.
   b. responsible for the care of others.
   c. responsible for their beliefs and actions.
   d. beings that want to be autonomous.

2. Determinations of quality of life are
    a. based on a person's ability to act according to ethical principles.
    b. value judgments that vary from person to person.
    c. usually consistent beliefs over one's lifetime.
    d. based on a patient's self-determination.

3. What is the focus of an ethic of dignity as proposed by Pullman?
    a. The autonomy of patients
    b. Preventing patients from feeling shamed
    c. Patients' inherent dignity
    d. The moral character of caregivers

4. The rule of justified paternalism means that
    a. it is acceptable for caregivers to override a patient's autonomy if the caregivers have the patient's best interest as their primary motive for actions.
    b. the degree of paternalistic intervention that is justified goes up according to the degree that the patient's rational capabilities are diminished.
    c. patients should be allowed to determine how much paternalism that they prefer from their nurses.
    d. ethics committees should be consulted to determine how much paternalism should be used with patients.

5. An important ethical activity for nurses in regard to elder abuse is
    a. to be persistent in trying to obtain help for vulnerable elders.
    b. to volunteer at adult protection agencies.
    c. to talk calmly to the perpetrators of elder abuse to minimize the potential for additional abuse.
    d. to know the guidelines for admission to long-term care facilities to facilitate elders having a safe place to live.

6. Which of the following words best describes ageism?
    a. Dignity
    b. Discrimination
    c. Determinism
    d. Disability

7. Health care professionals often focus on trying to minimize the effects of patients' aging. However, elders may want their caregivers to support them in the existential task of
   a. discovering their life's meaning.
   b. preparing for the costs of long-term care.
   c. communicating with baby boomer family members.
   d. deciding how much autonomy they should aspire to achieve.

8. The primary virtue or strength that elders need in order to successfully navigate the ninth stage of the Eriksonian life cycle is
   a. courtesy.
   b. temperance.
   c. justice.
   d. wisdom.

9. If elders do not successfully navigate the ninth stage of the Eriksonian life cycle, the resulting condition for the elder may be
   a. poverty.
   b. despair.
   c. poor health.
   d. dependence.

10. Which of the following choices is least associated with a correct description of decisional capacity?
   a. Clearly defined assessment criteria
   b. Needing time to consider treatment choices
   c. Asking family members for advice
   d. Asking for information to be repeated

CHAPTER 10 ANSWERS

Question 1: The correct answer is C.
Agency implies responsibility and self-directed actions. Moral agency means that people are responsible for their own beliefs, values, and actions that are associated with ethical matters.

Choices A, B, and D are incorrect because these choices do not correctly define responsibility for oneself as implied by the term *moral agency*.

Question 2: The correct answer is B.

Quality of life determinations are value judgments, which means that they are judgments based on what people believe is desirable; beliefs about what people find desirable vary from person to person.

Choices A, C, and D are incorrect because quality of life determinations are not based on people's ability to act according to ethical principles; quality of life values often change as one ages; caregivers frequently enter into discussions about a patient's quality of life, for example, when a patient is in a persistent vegetative state.

Question 3: The correct answer is D.

Pullman proposed that an ethic of dignity focuses on the moral character of caregivers rather than the autonomy of care recipients.

Choices A, B, and C are incorrect because these choices do not reflect Pullman's conception of an ethic of dignity.

Question 4: The correct answer is B.

If patients are not fully able to exercise self-direction, some degree of acting in their best interest rather than trying to support their autonomy is justified as moral care. As patients' abilities to safely be autonomous move downward, the justification for caregivers to act in their best interest without trying to maintain their autonomy moves upward.

Choices A, C, and D are incorrect because paternalism in a pervasive or general sense is considered to be ethically inappropriate. However, patients often want caregivers to help them consider their treatment options.

Question 5: The correct answer is A.

Because it often is difficult to obtain help for abused elders, nurses must be persistent in their efforts to do so. If nurses are not diligent in their role as advocate, vulnerable elders could be harmed.

Choices B, C, and D are incorrect because these actions may be needed, but they do not reflect the most important means of helping alleviate suffering because of elder abuse.

Question 6: The correct answer is B.

Ageism is discrimination or bias based on chronological age.

Choices A, C, and D are incorrect because issues of dignity and disability may be related to the experience of ageism, but these terms are not the best description of it. Determinism is not directly related to ageism.

Question 7: The correct answer is A.
Some ethicists believe that members of society devote too many resources toward trying to combat the inevitable experience of aging, because they do not recognize the importance of the existential need to find meaning in one's life.

Choices B, C, and D are incorrect because these activities may be relevant to some people, but the search for meaning is a pervasive need.

Question 8: The correct answer is D.
Wisdom is one of the high-level virtues that some virtue ethicists believe is needed for a good and happy life. Wisdom is specifically noted to be important in the Eriksonian life cycle to support integrity in old age.

Choices A, B, and C are incorrect because these virtues are important but do not provide the best answer to this question.

Question 9: The correct answer is B.
The ninth stage of the Eriksonian life cycle is an extension of the eighth stage. The struggle is to achieve integrity versus despair.

Choices A, C, and D are incorrect because although elders may confront these issues, they are not representative of the Eriksonian life cycle in the ninth stage.

Question 10: The correct answer is A.
There is no one set of criteria that is used by all professionals to identify a person's decisional capacity.

Choices B, C, and D are incorrect because these choices are not inconsistent with a person having decisional capacity.

Community/Public Health Nursing Ethics

Karen L. Rich

To be a [person] is, precisely to be responsible. It is to feel shame at the sight of what seems to be unmerited misery. . . . It is to feel, when setting one's stone, that one is contributing to the building of the world.

—ANTOINE DE SAINT-EXUPERY, *A GUIDE FOR GROWN-UPS: ESSENTIAL WISDOM FROM THE COLLECTED WORKS*

OBJECTIVES

After reading this chapter, the reader should be able to:

1. Distinguish a moral community from a population.
2. Apply different ethical approaches to specific community/public health (C/PH) nursing issues.
3. Discuss health care disparities and identify populations at risk.
4. Analyze communicable disease-related ethical issues.
5. Identify ethical issues and questions that are outcomes of the human genome project.
6. Explain what it means for a nurse to be a servant leader.
7. Discuss the ANA *Code of Ethics for Nurses with Interpretive Statements* (2001) in relation to C/PH nursing.

KEY TERMS

Moral community
Social justice
Service learning

Precautionary principle
Health disparities
Servant leadership

Communitarian ethics
Just generosity

Introduction

In their own way, community/public health (C/PH) nurses are contributors to the building of the world. Although the terms *community health nursing* (CHN) and *public health nursing* (PHN) ideally are differentiated, the terms generally have not been distinguished in this chapter. However, the greatest content emphasis in the chapter is focused on PHN. "Public health nurses integrate community involvement and knowledge about the entire population with personal, clinical understandings of the health and illness experiences of individuals and families within the population" (American Public Health Association, PHN Section, 2007, Para 1). "The practice is population-focused with the goals of promoting health and preventing disease and disability for all people through the creation of conditions in which people can be healthy" (American Nurses Association [ANA], 2007, p. 5). The following eight principles outlined in the ANA's *Public Health Nursing: Scope and Standards of Practice* distinguish PHN from other nursing specialties. Because of the nature of the content of these principles, PHN, like all types of nursing, is inherently ethical in nature.

1. *The client or* unit of care *is the population.*
2. *The primary obligation is to achieve the greatest good for the greatest number of people or the population as a whole.*
3. *The processes used by public health nurses include working with the client as an equal partner.*
4. *Primary prevention is the priority in selecting appropriate activities.*
5. *Public health nursing focuses on strategies that create healthy environmental, social, and economic conditions in which populations may thrive.*
6. *A public health nurse is obligated to actively identify and reach out to all who might benefit from a specific activity or service.*
7. *Optimal use of available resources to assure the best overall improvement in the health of the population is a key element of the practice.*
8. *Collaboration with a variety of other professions, populations, organizations, and other stakeholder groups is the most effective way to promote and protect the health of the people.* (pp. 8–9)

The fundamental purpose of C/PH nursing is consistent with the purpose articulated by the U.S. Department of Health and Human Services (DHHS, 2000) in *Healthy People 2010,* the nation's public health agenda. The purpose of this national agenda is "promoting health and preventing illness, disability, and premature death" (p. 1). The goals of C/PH nursing are likewise consistent with the goals of *Healthy*

People 2010 to "increase quality and years of healthy life" and to "eliminate health disparities" among the public (p. 2).

Population is the term used to describe the recipients of the health promotion and disease and disability prevention care that is the primary focus of C/PH nursing. In this chapter, a population is defined as a group of people who share at least one common descriptive characteristic but who do not necessarily have a collective commitment to a common good. The name used to denote a population is often related to the common characteristic(s) of the people who make up the population, such as male alcoholics or pregnant teenagers. People within populations may or may not interact or share in a collective dialogue.

The word *community* means different things to different people (see Box 11.1). A community is a group of people who have a shared interest in a common good, and members of the group have the potential to share in a collective dialogue about their common good. Membership in the community forms some part of each member's identity. The sharing in a commitment to promote the community's well-being, which transcends individual interests and goals, makes personal relationships within the community moral in nature. A **moral community** is formed by members who care about collectively alleviating the suffering and facilitating the well-being of other members of the community and who may take action in doing so. Individual persons may be active or inactive members of a moral community.

A moral community can be as large as the global community whose members are generally committed to the common good and prosperity of the inhabitants of the earth or as small as a community of senior nursing students at a university. The common good of a community of nursing students might be the collective concern of obtaining professional nursing licensure while maintaining individual physical and psychological well-being. The student community accomplishes its goals through the members' shared commitment to providing emotional support to community members and to helping one another move toward the successful completion of the National Council Licensure Examination (NCLEX). An even smaller community is a family that is committed to common goals beyond the individual personal goals of family members.

Members of a community may or may not share close geographic boundaries; however, if members of a community share some type of geographic boundaries, the primary moral connection among the members is not based solely on that geography. Nurses, patients, and other people in society are usually members of more than one community. A nurse is a member of the community of registered nurses who are collectively committed to the common good of alleviating patients' suffering and promoting

> ## BOX 11.1: HIGHLIGHTS FROM THE FIELD: COMMUNITY
>
> Community. A word of many connotations—a word overused until its meanings are so diffuse as to be almost useless. Yet the images it evokes, the deep longings and memories it can stir, represent something that human beings have created and recreated since time immemorial, out of our profound need for connection among ourselves and with Mother Earth.
>
> Forsey, H. (1993). *Circles of strength: Community alternatives to alienation.* Philadelphia: New Society, p. 1.

patients' well-being. The same nurse also may be a member of a faith community; a member of a geographic neighborhood community, which is interested in the common good and safety of the neighbors; and a member of a parent-teacher organization, which is committed to the common good of a population of children.

Ethical Approaches to Public Health

As it is with all sorts of ethical considerations regarding nurses' personal and professional beliefs and behaviors, it is difficult to limit one's philosophy to only one ethical theory or approach in public health practice. At varying times and in varying situations one of a number of important ethical approaches and theories may help guide nurses' actions and the development of public health policies.

According to the ANA (2007), public health nurses must adhere to the ethical principles outlined in the *Code of Ethics for Nurses with Interpretive Statements* (ANA, 2001), the *Principles of Ethical Practice of Public Health* (Public Health Leadership Society, 2002), and the *Environmental Health Principles and Recommendations for Public Health Nursing* (APHA, 2006) (see Boxes 11.2 and 11.3). C/PH nurses are charged with honoring "the diverse values, beliefs and cultures present in the population served" (ANA, 2007, p. 9) and providing information necessary for members of populations to discuss health care choices and make noncoerced health care decisions. Because of the scope of C/PH nursing, ethical practice is especially focused on social justice and the rights of various populations. The ANA noted that the precautionary principle is a good guide to use in supporting social justice and populations' rights.

Box 11.2: Highlights From the Field: Principles of the Ethical Practice of Public Health

1. Public health should address principally the fundamental causes of disease and requirements of health, aiming to prevent adverse health outcomes.
2. Public health should achieve community health in a way that respects the rights of individuals in the community.
3. Public health policies, programs, and priorities should be developed and evaluated through processes that ensure an opportunity for input from community members.
4. Public health should advocate and work for the empowerment of disenfranchised community members, aiming to ensure that the basic resources and conditions necessary for health are accessible to all.
5. Public health should seek the information needed to implement effective policies and programs that protect and promote health.

Public Health Leadership Society. (2002). *Principles of the ethical practice of public health*, p. 4.

For a complete list of principles go to http://www.apha.org/codeofethics/ethicsbrochure.pdf

The Precautionary Principle

The concept known as the **precautionary principle** is based on the German word, *vorsorgeprinzip*, which means the principle of forecaring. The word *forecaring* conveys more than being cautious. It means that one uses foresight and preparation, and it is aligned with the principle of "first do no harm" (nonmaleficence) and the adage "better safe than sorry" (Science & Environment Health Network [SEHN], n.d. a). In 1998, a multinational, multiprofessional group met for a conference sponsored by the SEHN at the Wingspread headquarters of the Johnson Foundation to discuss using the precautionary principle as the basis of international agreements, especially those related to the environment and health. The participants at the Wingspread conference developed a statement to guide actions by governmental and nongovernmental agencies. The group stated: "When an activity raises threats of harm to the environment or human health,

BOX 11.3: HIGHLIGHTS FROM THE FIELD:
ENVIRONMENTAL HEALTH PRINCIPLES AND
RECOMMENDATIONS FOR PHN

1. Environmental health is integral to the role and responsibilities of *all* public health nurses.
2. The *Precautionary Principle* is a fundamental tenet for all environmental health endeavors.
3. Environmental justice is a right of all populations.
4. Collaboration is essential to effectively protecting the health of all people from environmental harm.
5. Environmental health advocacy must be rooted in scientific integrity, honesty, respect for all persons, and social justice.

American Public Health Association, Public Health Nursing Section. (2006). Environmental health principles and recommendations for public health nursing, p. 5.

For a complete list of principles go to http://www.astdn.org/downloadablefiles/ Principles%20and%20Recommendations%20Document_4-06.doc

precautionary measures should be taken even if some cause and effect relationships are not fully established scientifically" (Para 1).

According to SEHN (n.d. b), "the key element of the principle is that it incites us to take anticipatory action in the absence of scientific certainty" (Para 1). Advocates of using the precautionary principle contend that we should not wait until we have "certain evidence" from traditional science to show the causal connection between various actions or toxins and their effects. Minimum standards for citing evidence of cause and effect relationships via traditional science are usually very high (SEHN, n.d. a). The type of science needed to support the precautionary principle has been called *appropriate science*, as distinguished from *traditional science* (Kriebel, Tickner, & Crumbley, 2003). Appropriate science is based on the context of the problem at hand rather than requiring that scientific pursuits be forced into a preconceived idea of necessary rigor.

People who oppose the precautionary principle contend that if science has not provided certain evidence that a particular activity or substance is harmful to humans and/or the environment, then the activity or substance is assumed to be safe until shown to be otherwise. However, proponents of using the precautionary principle answer with the argument that by the time harmful causal relationships are established as certainty, much damage already may have occurred. An example cited by proponents of the precautionary principle is the harmful connection between smoking and lung cancer. "Smoking was strongly suspected of causing lung cancer long before the link was demonstrated conclusively" (SEHN, n.d. a, Para 3). Fortunately, many smokers had stopped smoking based on precautionary measures rather than waiting on scientific certainty to confirm the harmful effects.

Today, there is evidence that the incidence of chronic illnesses, birth defects, infertility, cancer, Alzheimer's disease, and autism are increasing while certain causal links to these conditions are lacking. Advocates of using the precautionary principle strongly propose that society should limit exposure to potentially harmful substances even before those substances are shown to have direct causal links to human health problems.

For C/PH nurses to practice ethically, it is recommended in the ANA's (2007) *Public Health Nursing: Scope and Standards of Practice* that public health nurses use the precautionary principle. As a follow-up to the Wingspread conference, another community of philosophers, scientists, and environmentalists, called the Blue Mountain group, met to discuss the ethics that underlie the precautionary principle. This group's consensus was that the precautionary principle is an integration of science and ethics (Raffensperger & Myers, 2001). Whereas traditional science tries to separate evidence from values, the precautionary principle supports the integration of the two, and the precautionary principle is "an ethic of survival" (Para 8). The Blue Mountain group contended that emotions and "values such as compassion, sympathy, gratitude, and even humor are based on sound instinct" (Para 8). Societal values become societal actions. The group argued that people must live in a positive reciprocal relationship with nature as well as with one another if society is to survive.

Kantian Ethics (Deontology)

Kantian ethics emphasizes that all rational persons are autonomous, ends-in-themselves and worthy of dignity and respect. (See Chapter 1 for a more complete discussion of Kantian ethics.) Kantianism is highly valued in Western medicine because of the focus on individual rights and informed consent. In the U.S. health care system and in Western bioethics, the choices of rational individuals are generally respected. However, in public health, practitioners often must balance the rights of individuals with the rights of populations and communities. Sometimes, navigating this delicate balance can be controversial or generate dilemmas, such as considering appropriate actions when a person with a stigmatizing communicable disease may jeopardize the health of other people. This situation results in a need to balance respecting the autonomy and protecting the confidentiality of one person while trying to protect the safety of other persons.

Utilitarianism (Consequentialism)

As discussed in Chapter 1, utilitarianism is an ethical approach based on maximizing the good or moral consequences of one's decisions and actions. Although there are variations in utilitarian theories, when utilitarianism is used in health care, the goal or intended consequence generally is to produce the greatest good for the greatest number of people. Because of the emphasis on population-focused care, utilitarianism is one of the most widely used ethical approaches in public health practice. The second distinguishing element of public health nursing outlined in the ANA's (2007) *Public Health Nursing: Scope and Standards of Nursing* is that "*the primary obligation is to achieve the greatest good for the greatest number of people or the population as a whole*" (p. 8). This directive for public health nurses is a classic example of utilitarianism.

Communitarian Ethics

There is no power for change greater than a community discovering what it cares about.
—MARGARET WHEATLEY, *TURNING TO ONE ANOTHER*

Communitarian ethics is based on the position that "everything fundamental in ethics derives from communal values, the common good, social goals, traditional practices, and cooperative virtues" (Beauchamp & Childress, 2001, p. 362). Communitarian ethics is relevant to moral relationships in any community, and this ethical approach is particularly useful in the practice of PHN because of the focus on populations and communities rather than on the care of individuals.

The notion that communitarian ethics is based on the model of friendships and relationships that existed in the ancient Greek city-states described by Aristotle was popularized in modern times by the philosopher and ethicist Alasdair MacIntyre (1984) in his book, *After Virtue*. In general societal ethics and in bioethics, the valuing and consideration of community relationships has come to mean different things to different people (Beauchamp & Childress, 2001). Communitarian ethics as an ethical approach is distinguished because the epicenter of communitarian ethics is the community rather than any one individual (Wildes, 2000). Populations, in general, and moral communities, in particular, also are the starting points for C/PH nursing practice.

The value of discussing and articulating an approach to communitarian ethics lies in the benefit that can be gained through illuminating and appreciating the relationships and interconnections between people that are often overlooked in everyday life. Although personal moral goals, such as the pursuit of personal well-being, are significant, the importance of forming strong communities and identifying the moral goals of communities must not be neglected in order for both individuals and communities to flourish.

An important distinction that legitimately can be drawn between communitarian and other popular ethical approaches, such as deontological or rule-based ethics, is based on communitarian ethicists' proposal that it is natural for humans to favor the people with whom they live and have frequent interactions. Kantian deontologists base their ethics on an impartial stance toward the persons who experience the effects of their morally related actions.

However, using a communitarian ethic and valuing partiality as a way of relating to other people does not have to exclude caring about people who are personally unknown to moral agents. Although it is often easier for people to care about and have compassion for people who are relationally closest to them, it is not unrealistic to believe that people also can develop empathy or compassion toward people who are personally unknown to them. Such behavior and expectations are an integral part of Christian and Buddhist philosophies, for example. Accepting the notion that humans usually are more partial to people with whom they are most closely related, while at the same time believing that it is possible to expand the scope of their empathy and compassion to unknown others, broadens the sphere of morality in communitarian ethics.

Nussbaum (2004) suggested that people often develop an "us" versus "them" mentality, especially when violence occurs among various groups and significant ethnic and cultural differences separate them. People are able to generate sympathy, or fellow-feeling, when they hear about epidemics, disasters, and wars occurring on continents that are far away, but it is often difficult for people to sustain their sympathy for more than a short period of time after media coverage diminishes. People tend to stop and notice the needs of other people and then soon turn back to their own personal lives. According to Nussbaum, humanity will "achieve no lasting moral progress unless and until the daily unremarkable lives of people distant from us become real in the fabric of our own daily lives" (p. 958) and until people include others that they do not know personally within the important sphere of their lives (see Box 11.4). C/PH nurses

BOX 11.4: HIGHLIGHTS FROM THE FIELD: THE DELUSION OF SEPARATENESS

A human being is a part of the whole called by us universe, a part limited in time and space. He experiences himself, his thoughts and feelings as something separated from the rest, a kind of optical delusion of his consciousness. This delusion is a kind of prison for us, restricting us to our personal desires and to affection for a few persons nearest to us. Our task must be to free ourselves from this prison by widening our circle of compassion to enhance all living creatures and the whole of nature in its beauty.

Albert Einstein. (1930). *What I believe*. Retrieved August 20, 2007, from http://home.earthlink.net/~johnrpenner/Articles/Einstein3.html

must broaden their scope of concern to consistently include people affected by health care disparities, diseases, epidemics, and the impact of ethnic violence and wars all over the world, not only when issues are highlighted in the media.

"All communities have some organizing vision about the meaning of life and how one ought to conduct a good life" (Wildes, 2000, p. 129). C/PH nurses have an important role in bringing populations and communities together to work toward a common humanitarian good. Transforming a community from an "us" versus "them" mentality to one that seeks a common good is possible through education (Nussbaum, 2004). "Children [and people] at all ages must learn to recognize people in other countries as their fellows, and to sympathize with their plights. Not just their dramatic plights, in a cyclone or war, but their daily plights" (p. 959). This need for empathetic understanding also is important in one's own country, state, city, town, or neighborhood. Many people of all ages are suffering in the United States and throughout the world because they lack adequate health care, proper food, a sanitary environment, and good housing.

The education of communities often occurs through role modeling (Wildes, 2000). Members of communities learn about what is and is not accepted as moral through personal and group interactions and dialogue within their communities. Narratives are told by nurses about the lives of exemplars, such as Florence Nightingale and Lillian Wald, to illustrate moral living. By her efforts to improve social justice and health protection through environmental measures and her efforts to elevate the character of nurses, Nightingale exhibited moral concern for her local society, the nursing profession, and people remote from her local associations, such as the population of soldiers affected by the Crimean War. Likewise, Lillian Wald was an excellent role model for members of communities because of her efforts to improve social justice through her work at the Henry Street Settlement. When learning from the example of Nightingale and Wald, communitarian-minded C/PH nurses are in an excellent position to educate the public and other nurses and health care professionals about why they in many ways should assume the role of being their brothers' and sisters' keepers.

——————————— **Ethical Reflections** ———————————

- To what communities do you belong? What can be identified as the common good of each of these communities?
- Have you noticed "us" versus "them" thinking among members of the nursing community? Among members of the larger community of health care professionals? If so, what effect has this thinking had on relationships among members of the particular community?
- Can a community exist when there is "us" versus "them" thinking among the members? Why or why not?
- What patient populations might be particularly susceptible to having people approach them as "us" versus "them"? What evidence did you use for your answer? How can nurses change this type of separatist thinking?

Social Justice

As discussed in Chapter 1, **social justice** is related to the fair distribution of benefits and burdens among members of a society. However, in our U.S. society, market justice is the dominant model (Beauchamp, 1999). Market justice is based on the principle that the benefits and burdens of a society should be distributed among its members according to the members' individual efforts and abilities. In a market-justice system, money for health care tends to be invested in technology and curing diseases rather than in health promotion and disease prevention.

Major public health problems usually are concentrated among a small minority of the U.S. population. For social justice to be achieved, members of U.S. society who are not directly experiencing problems such as a lack of access to health care, poverty, poor quality of housing, and malnutrition may have to significantly reduce their share of societal benefits and increase their share of societal burdens. Therefore, public health and social justice involve important ethical decisions about how members of societies choose to distribute their resources and provide for the well-being of their fellow citizens.

Health Disparities

If we gloss over the difficulties that people face in their communities, we cannot hope to build a better world.
—HELEN FORSEY, *CIRCLES OF STRENGTH: COMMUNITY ALTERNATIVES TO ALIENATION*, P. 50

Health disparities are inequalities or differences in health care access and treatment that result in poor health outcomes for persons and populations. Health disparities occur because of some characteristic(s) of the persons or population affected. After the first goal of aiming to "increase quality and years of healthy life" (U.S. DHHS, 2000, p. 8), the second goal of *Healthy People 2010* "is to eliminate health disparities among segments of the population, including differences that occur by gender, race or ethnicity, education or income, disability, geographic location, or sexual orientation" (p. 11). Eliminating health disparities is a moral issue for C/PH nurses because social justice and communitarian ethics are based on building flourishing communities that support the common good of all community members.

According to nurse anthropologist Lundberg (2005), "social and cultural factors give context and meaning to health, illness, and injury. The experience is more than that of the patient. It also reflects the worldview of the individuals helping the person in distress" (p. 152). A major concern of bioethicists is the recognition that people's health and access to health care is adversely affected in proportion to their lack of power and privilege in a society (Sherwin, 1992). Consequently, poverty and the placement of people within the margins of society are key factors in the determination of public health. When any community members are suffering or are in need, all people in the communities are affected, even if it is in imperceptible ways. One must only think about the hypothetical Net of Indra (see Box 1.3 in Chapter 1) to imagine how this situation might be a reality.

The aim of the *Healthy People 2010* (U.S. DHHS, 2000) agenda is that "every person in every community across the Nation deserves equal access to comprehensive, culturally competent, community-based health care systems that are committed to serving the needs of the individual and promoting community health" (p. 16). Racial and ethnic minorities suffer serious health disparities in regard to access to care and health outcomes. The DHHS has selected six target areas of focus to try to minimize disparities among minorities (Centers for Disease Control [CDC], 2006a). The six areas of emphasis are infant mortality, cancer screening and management, cardiovascular disease, diabetes, HIV infections/AIDS, and immunizations. Several of the many specific examples of health disparities experienced by minorities include a black-to-white infant mortality ratio of 2.5 to 1, diabetes being 2.6 times more likely to be diagnosed in American Indians and Alaska Natives than in non-Hispanic whites, and the influenza and pneumococcal vaccine being less likely to be received by people age 65 and older who are Hispanics and African Americans than by non-Hispanic white people.

C/PH nurses need to play a role in helping members of communities to collectively accept their responsibility for their own health and to develop the capacity to help themselves in resolving problems that lead to health disparities. One coordinated plan to address public health disparities involves four phases or themes: community participation, community mobilization, commitment to social justice, and the leadership challenge (Berkowitz et al., 2001).

C/PH nurses can support members of communities by participating in the validation of suspected problems through investigation and research and by building partnerships to collaborate on policy development. C/PH nurses facilitate community mobilization by educating members of the community about health promotion and health protection measures that would be likely to improve the lives of people in the community. Teaching people in the community about how to begin grassroots political efforts to obtain needed resources is an important advocacy role of C/PH nurses. Being committed to social justice requires C/PH nurses to speak out about health disparities to other nurses and health care professionals, to a wide group of community members, and to politicians about health disparities (see Box 11.5). In helping communities to increase participation, mobilize action, and expand social justice, the leadership challenge for C/PH nurses is to "act as a resource, consultant, facilitator, educator, advocate, and role model" (Berkowitz et al., 2001, p. 53).

A widely accepted approach to organizing communities in efforts to address their health disparity and social justice problems has been based on the thought that health care professionals must appeal to the self-interest of the community and its members (Minkler & Pies, 2002). However, Minkler and Pies argued that this traditional approach often only further divides groups of people by furthering the notion of individualism and separateness that is already a divisive way of thinking in Western societies. This approach does not support a community's interest in a common good.

Minkler and Pies (2002) adapted a feminist approach to social change as an agenda for trying to eliminate disparities in the equitable distribution of community resources. Historically, feminist philosophers and activists have approached their agenda in terms of the disparities experienced by women. Therefore, a feminist approach often can be applied with other marginalized populations. This approach

Box 11.5: Highlights from the Field: Three Parts of a Legislative Meeting

During meetings with legislators, nurses can use the following guidelines:

1. **Hook**: Briefly explain who you are.
2. **Line**: Briefly explain your issue and why you care about it. Present a strong argument, a personal story, or both. Try to put a face on your issue.
3. **Sinker**: Clearly present your specific request and try to get a commitment. It is very important to stay focused on your message and to listen attentively to feedback.

Other suggestions:

- Plan for the meeting to last no more than 15 minutes.
- Arrive 10 to 15 minutes early for your appointment.
- Before the meeting, assign responsibilities among your colleagues to carry out during the meeting, such as deciding who will begin and end the meeting.
- Rehearse your talking points before the meeting.
- Exchange business cards during the meeting.
- At the end of the meeting, thank everyone who met with you or helped schedule the meeting. Send a thank you note shortly after the meeting.

Christopher Kush. (2004). *The one hour activist: The 15 most powerful actions you can take to fight for the issues and candidates you care about.* San Francisco: Jossey-Bass.

can be used to build a bridge that connects local community efforts to eliminate disparities with efforts that can be used to address more global social concerns. Nurses and other health care professionals working with community members who are involved in becoming organized to facilitate change can ask:

(1) Does [the community's organizing effort] materially improve the lives of community members and if so, which members and how many? (2) Does [participating in the organizing process] give community members a sense of power, strength and imagination as a group and help build structures for further changes? and (3) Does the struggle . . . educate community members politically, enhancing their ability to criticize and challenge the system in the future? (Minkler & Pies, pp. 132–133)

—————————— **Ethical Reflections** ——————————

- What is meant by the term *marginalized populations*? Identify populations that may be marginalized in regard to health disparities and discuss why this may be so.
- Reflect on and discuss why appeals to self-interest in addressing health disparities might divide people and communities.
- Review critical theory in Chapter 1. Why is this theory relevant to the issue of health disparities? Provide one example of how a public health nurse could use critical theory in addressing health disparities in a specific population.
- Identify issues and problems that PH nurses might address via a meeting with a state or national legislator.

Virtue Ethics: Justice and Generosity

To a [disciple] the Master said, "I fear you are doing more harm than good."
"Why?"
"Because you stress only one of the two imperatives of justice."
"Namely?"
"The poor have a right to bread."
"What's the other one?"
"The poor have a right to beauty."

—ANTHONY DE MELLO, *ONE MINUTE NONSENSE*

Pieper (1966) proposed that "the subject of justice is the 'community'" (p. 70). Justice can be viewed in terms of what rights or resources should be accorded or distributed to persons or populations or what is their due. However, there is another conception of justice that is communitarian in nature (see Moral Ground Model in Chapter 2). This approach is based on virtue ethics and emphasizes the virtue of **just generosity**, which is a conception of justice that highlights human connections and not separateness. Indebtedness is the hallmark of this type of justice, and although the concept of justice as a stand-alone virtue is important to public health ethics, the combination of the virtue of justice with the virtue of generosity expands the scope of justice.

People are accustomed to thinking of justice in limited terms, and they are accustomed to separating the individual virtues of justice and generosity. Thinking and acting in terms of the comprehensive virtue of just generosity sometimes requires the use of one's moral imagination to envision "what could be." Whereas justice involves giving others what they are due, generosity involves giving to people from a source that is somehow personal. Fusion of the single virtues of justice and generosity into a combined activated virtue is important for people in facilitating the development of flourishing communities, both communities as large as the global community and communities as small as families.

Cultivation of the virtue of just generosity is based on a person's motivation to actively participate in a community-centered network of giving and receiving. Persons, including nurses, who exhibit the virtue of just generosity do not give merely in proportion to what an individual receiver or community is perceived as being due, but instead they give to persons or communities based on the receivers' or communities' needs. The giver believes in and does more than dispassionately allocate or distribute resources. The person or group that possesses just generosity gives from resources that in some way touch the giver(s) personally, which may not necessarily involve the giving of something that is material or tangible but often involves what might be called giving from the heart.

Salamon (2003) in her book, *Rambam's Ladder*, adapted the Jewish physician and philosopher Maimonides's (1135–1204) "ladder of charity" for contemporary use. Salamon's book provides a meditation on generosity and underscores that an awareness of the need for giving has become more important than ever in a post-9/11 world. Salamon's ladder of charity starts, as did Maimonides's ladder, with the bottom rung representing the least generous motivation for giving and progresses to the top of the ladder with the top step being what Salamon proposed to be the highest form of giving. The eight steps of the ladder are as follows, beginning with the lowest:

1. Reluctance: To give begrudgingly.
2. Proportion: To give less to the poor than is proper, but to do so cheerfully.
3. Solicitation: To hand money to the poor after being asked.
4. Shame: To hand money to the poor before being asked, but risk making the recipient feel shame.
5. Boundaries: To give to someone you don't know, but allow your name to be known.
6. Corruption: To give to someone you know, but who doesn't know from whom he is receiving help. (For example, this occurs when people are concerned that the "middlemen" distributing the gifts are not trustworthy.)
7. Anonymity: To give to someone you don't know, and to do so anonymously.
8. Responsibility: At the top of the ladder is the gift of self-reliance. To hand someone a gift or a loan or to enter into a partnership with him or to find work for him so that he will never have to beg again. (Salamon, 2003, Introduction)

C/PH nurses can use the ladder of charity as a gauge of the type of giving that occurs within communities while keeping their eyes focused on aiming for the top step of the ladder. C/PH nurses do not directly give money to people and usually do not give material resources to them. Nurses' services to individuals, families, communities, and populations can be substituted for monetary or material giving in the steps of the ladder. Salamon (2003) herself recognized that monetary giving is not always the primary means of generosity. However, depending on their particular jobs, C/PH nurses are sometimes responsible for coordinating and distributing gifts and donations to populations.

Nurses might ask themselves whether or not they give begrudgingly during their work. Do they work from the motivation of a generous servant, hoping to affect the well-being of a population or community who will not know how the nurse's services have positively affected them and their health? Must individual and community recipients of the services of C/PH nurses directly ask for each of their specific needs to be met? Do nurses use their moral imaginations and anticipate needs, reflecting and acting based on the "big picture" of "what could be" that may not be readily apparent to them unless they suspend their initial judgments? When the practice of just generosity is consistent with the top step of the ladder, C/PH nurses enter into community partnerships and teach other people to be responsible for helping themselves and their communities so that community members and, ultimately, whole communities become self-reliant whenever possible.

Ethical Reflections

Discuss the following situations and apply ethical theories and approaches discussed in this section of the chapter. If needed, refer to other chapters in the book, read ahead in this chapter, or search the Internet for more information. What theories or approaches are applicable in each situation? Could more than one approach be useful? What do you believe are the most ethical actions or positions in these situations? List and discuss as many relevant issues and considerations as possible. What additional information might you need to make your decisions? Specifically, how and where would you obtain this information?

- You are a school nurse in Mississippi. A mother does not want her school-aged child immunized for chickenpox before entering the school where you work. The child was not previously immunized and has not had chickenpox.
- Your clinic patient was newly diagnosed as being HIV positive. The patient refuses to tell his diagnosis to his sexual partner. Also, the patient tells you that he does not want you to report his status to the state health department.
- Your rich friend who owns a business and has health insurance tells you that he doesn't want to pay extra taxes so that all people in the United States will have access to basic health care.

- You are the tuberculosis (TB) nurse at the county health department. You regularly make home visits for directly observed therapy (DOT) for a woman with TB. The woman is frequently not home when she knows that you are coming to her house.

- You are a nurse working at the county health department. You learn that a rich developer is planning to build low income housing on an old landfill that was used by a chemical company. The developer has stated that there is no evidence that chemicals at the landfill will harm anyone.

- You are a nurse working at a mission in Africa, and you are participating in an HIV/AIDS research study with several doctors. The research is aimed at identifying whether circumcision reduces the transmission of HIV between heterosexual couples. During the study it becomes apparent that transmission is significantly reduced when males are circumcised. However, the doctors do not want to stop their study even though they believe that participants in the control group may unnecessarily become infected during the course of the study.

- Your colleague tells you that she doesn't ever want to work with a population of elders. She states that she becomes frustrated with the physical and emotional dependency that sometimes develops in this population.

- You are an elementary school nurse. Many of the children at the school are ethnic minorities living in single-parent families. The population of children at the school has a high incidence of health-related problems as compared to the children at the private school where your nurse friend works. You frequently are frustrated because you do not see the children's mothers trying to break their cycle of poverty. You consider quitting your job.

- While working as an occupational health nurse at a local industry, you discover that your employer is willingly pushing the limits on air and water pollution standards. Your supervisor tells you that it would cost too much money to reduce the pollution.

- Your nonsmoker friend tells you that she is angry because she has to pay health care costs for tobacco users. She states that tobacco use is one of the leading causes of diseases requiring major expenditures of health care dollars and that the smoking-related expenditures cause her cost of health care to rise. She complains that smokers are "choosing their own health" and should not receive federally funded health care through Medicare and Medicaid programs. How do you respond to your friend? Do you believe that people often choose their own health? If so, what are the ethical implications? If not, explain the justification for your position.

- You are an elementary school nurse. You are informed that the school cafeteria will begin including food from cloned animals. This type of food has not been tested exhaustively by the FDA. The school superintendent does not want to publicize the addition of the new food sources at the school.

Communicable Diseases

Public health advances in the 20th century dramatically decreased morbidity and mortality from infectious diseases in the United States; because of this progress, national health officials began to lose interest in funding and promoting research directed at infectious disease treatment and control (CDC, 2003). However, people in the government, health care systems, and the general public have begun to recognize that humanity's fight against infectious diseases is never ending (Markel, 2004). In her book about the global collapse of the public health care system, Garrett (2000) stated "we now live in comfortable ignorance about the health and well-being of people in faraway places. But in truth we are never very far away from the experiences of our forebears" (p. xii).

Societies are still tormented by diseases that have affected the public's health since ancient times, while the threat of new infections looms ominously in the future. "Together, malaria, tuberculosis and AIDS killed 5.7 million people in 2004, accounting for about one-tenth of the world's deaths" (World Health Organization [WHO], 2006b, Para 1). Some people in the United States try to avert their eyes from the global scourge of malaria, tuberculosis (TB), and AIDS, but due to media coverage of communicable disease threats such as pandemic influenza, it has become more apparent that no one in the United States or elsewhere around the world should feel safe from mass casualties involving infectious diseases. C/PH nurses will be at the epicenter of the health care system if a highly contagious pandemic occurs. C/PH nurses also must take a prominent role in current epidemics such as malaria, TB, and AIDS. The words of the poet John Donne (1962) provide a good representation of how infectious diseases that affect the global community are related to ethics in nursing:

No man is an island, entire of itself; every man is a piece of the continent, a part of the main. If a clod be washed away by the sea, Europe is the less, as well as if a promontory were, as well as if a manor of thy friend's or of thine own were. Any man's death diminishes me, because I am involved in mankind; and therefore never send to know for whom the bell tolls; it tolls for thee. (p. 1107)

Paul Farmer (2001), a physician at Harvard Medical School who also travels to central Haiti to work at the Clinique Bone Sauveur, advocated that "we can no longer accept whatever we are told about 'limited resources'" (p. xxvi). Health care professionals must challenge the often repeated mantra that resources are too limited to fund programs to treat epidemics. According to Farmer, "the wealth of the world has not dried up; it has simply become unavailable to those who need it most" (p. xxvi). He proposed that people must ask to be shown the data that support the truth of statements that there are fewer resources for public health than there were when effective therapies were not available to treat many diseases. "Our challenge, therefore, is not merely to draw attention to the widening outcome gap, but also to attack it, to dissect it, and to work with all our capacity to reduce this gap" (p. xxvi). Health care professionals and the public must make it clearly known that they are not willing to idly watch when the wealth of nations is being concentrated within limited populations and programs while, on a mass scale, people in other populations die of treatable diseases.

Ethical Reflections

- Do you believe that there are enough resources to treat diseases in populations severely affected by health disparities? On what evidence do you base your position?
- What can nurses do to become more aware of people's access to health care and how health care resources are distributed in poor countries? What can nurses do to try to improve health care access for people in poor countries that are far from the nurses' own homes?
- Is being aware of the state of health care and epidemic diseases in poor countries a moral issue? Why or why not?

Malaria

Malaria, which means "bad air," has been a problem for humans for over 4,000 years (CDC, 2004). Globally, the annual human burden of malaria is very high with malaria causing 1.1 million deaths, most of which occur in children under 5 years old, and 300-500 million total malaria cases (WHO, 2002). The social and economic burden also is very high in endemic countries. "Those at greatest risk of malaria are poor people, and populations that are marginalized, such as ethnic minorities and people displaced as a result of civic unrest" (p. 1). If corrective actions are not taken, trends over the last several decades indicate that the impact of malaria will continue to worsen.

Issues contributing to the rising burden of malaria include the following:

- Inadequate ability to treat the disease because of poor drug availability and drug resistance.
- Inadequate availability of effective and affordable insecticide-treated bed nets. The WHO has now resumed recommending the use of DDT-treated bed nets. This action reversed the WHO's 30-year policy of discouraging the use of DDT in try-

ing to control malaria because of fears about DDT's impact on human and animal health. The WHO now has proposed that DDT is the most cost-effective alternative for indoor spraying to prevent malaria.

■ User ignorance in regard to effective treatment tools.

■ Poorly coordinated partnerships and approaches to epidemiological systems.

■ War, social unrest, and poverty. (British Broadcasting Corporation News, 2006; Lobe, 2006; WHO, 2002)

Partnerships among members of the global community that have resources to combat this deadly disease will be needed to help poor populations that are suffering and dying needlessly from malaria. It is morally incumbent upon C/PH nurses to understand the human and economic burden of malaria and to advocate for adequate prevention and treatment of this serious disease.

----------------------------- **Ethical Reflections** -----------------------------

• The use of DDT to prevent malaria has been controversial. Go to the Internet and locate evidence that supports and evidence that contradicts the benefits of using DDT. What is your position about this issue? Discuss the precautionary principle in relation to the use of DDT.

Tuberculosis

"TB, with AIDS, is the leading infectious cause of adult mortality in the world, causing between 1.5 and 2 million deaths per year" (WHO, 2006c, Para 2). Almost one third of the global population (2 billion persons) is living with TB infection, and the annual infection rate continues to climb. By 2020, TB is expected to remain as one of the top 10 causes of adult mortality in the world. The only other infectious disease expected to remain on this list is HIV. "One estimate suggests 171 million new [TB] cases and 60 million deaths over this period in the 'best case scenario,' and 249 million new [TB] cases and 90 million deaths in the 'worst-case scenario' (Para 3).

Tuberculosis is airborne, and this makes the treatment of TB a major public health concern in terms of infected persons' infringement on the well-being of noninfected persons. People infected with TB who lack the capacity or desire to adhere to recommended treatment are an ongoing moral problem (Beauchamp & Childress, 2001). Freedom and autonomy are, of course, to be supported whenever possible; however, when persons infected with TB do not voluntarily adhere to treatment, it is ethically and legally obligatory to mandate treatment because of health threats to others.

Directly observed therapy (DOT), in which persons are directly observed while taking their TB medications, is one means of ensuring that affected individuals adhere to their treatment regimen. The international community has responded to the problem of the spread of TB with coordinated efforts to control it through DOT. The least restrictive and least intrusive measures for reaching treatment goals should be given priority, but if measures like DOT are not effective, detention and quarantine are ethical and may be required for the public's safety (Beauchamp & Childress, 2001).

Ethical Reflections

- Search the Internet and review the case of the American attorney, Andrew Speaker, who was infected with TB.
- List and discuss the ethical issues involved with Mr. Speaker's case.
- What are the various ethical theories or approaches that can be applied to the case? Explain. Remember to consider different perspectives.
- What is your position about the ethics surrounding the case? Be sure to provide a clear position and support it. Include one or more ethical approaches as part of your justification.

HIV/AIDS

AIDS-related illnesses killed 2.9 million people in 2006 (WHO, 2006a). Unfortunately, the previously stable or declining HIV infection rates in some countries now seem to be reversing. The AIDS epidemic is continuing to grow worldwide and there is a resurgence in new HIV infection rates in some parts of the world. A 2006 update revealed that there were 4.3 million new HIV infections, and it appeared that there may have been a 50% increase in infections between 2004 and 2006 in Eastern Europe and Central Asia. Evidence shows that HIV prevention programs produce positive outcomes if the programs are focused and sustained; but in North America and Western Europe, these programs have not been sustained and new HIV infections have remained level.

Ethical Reflections

- Imagine that you are a nurse participating in a research study with a pharmaceutical company that develops drugs to treat HIV/AIDS. You and your professional colleagues discuss that the experimental drug being researched seems to be causing severe adverse reactions in a few of the patients with AIDS and even may have caused one or two deaths.

The "line" that is delivered by the primary investigator is that AIDS patients already have a shortened lifespan. He states that although the drug may cause adverse reactions in a few patients, overall he is hoping for "the greatest good for the greatest number of patients." How do you feel about this position? Is it ethical? Why or why not? What would you do if you were helping to conduct this research?

HIV Testing

In 2006, the CDC (2006b) published major revisions to its HIV testing guidelines, and the new recommendations include routine HIV testing for patients in all health care settings. Because basic screening for treatable conditions is a common public health secondary prevention tool, it is believed that early identification of HIV infections will lead to better health outcomes. Also, risk-based screening is less effective now because the mix of people becoming infected with HIV is changing to persons who are frequently unaware of their high risk status—racial and ethnic minorities, people less than 20 years of age, non-metropolitan-area dwellers, and heterosexuals.

Major revisions in the CDC's (2006b) guidelines are contained in Box 11.6. The CDC's position is unchanged in its continued advocacy for voluntary, noncoerced agreement for testing, for no testing without a patient's knowledge, and for access to clinical care and counseling for persons whose tests are positive. However, the CDC now advocates that screening should be provided in a manner similar to other diagnostic testing without special pretest prevention counseling.

However, even when it is voluntary, HIV testing carries with it certain risks and benefits. Since the emergence of HIV, the policy issue that has generated the biggest ethical concern is how to protect the public while respecting individual rights and privacy (Beauchamp & Childress, 2001). Psychological well-being and the opportunity to prevent future infection are among the benefits to people whose test results are negative. For people whose test results are positive, benefits include "closer medical follow-up, earlier use of antiretroviral agents, prophylaxis or other treatment of associated diseases, protection of loved ones, and a clearer sense of the future" (p. 298).

People who are seronegative have no significant risks from testing; however, the psychological and social risks are significant for people who are seropositive (Beauchamp & Childress, 2001). People who are HIV positive are at a high psychological risk for anxiety, depression, and suicide and are at a high social risk for "stigmatization, discrimination, and breaches of confidentiality" (p. 299). It is the ethical responsibility of health care professionals and other people in society to try to minimize

Box 11.6: Highlights From the Field: New HIV Testing Guidelines

- Screening after notifying the patient that an HIV test will be performed unless the patient declines (opt-out screening) is recommended in all health-care settings. Specific signed consent for HIV testing should not be required. General informed consent for medical care should be considered sufficient to encompass informed consent for HIV testing.
- Persons at high risk for HIV should be screened for HIV at least annually.
- HIV test results should be provided in the same manner as results of other diagnostic or screening tests.
- Prevention counseling should not be required as a part of HIV screening programs in health-care settings. Prevention counseling is strongly encouraged for persons at high risk for HIV in settings in which risk behaviors are assessed routinely (e.g., STD clinics) but should not be linked to HIV testing.
- HIV diagnostic testing or screening to detect HIV infection earlier should be considered distinct from HIV counseling and testing conducted primarily as a prevention intervention for uninfected persons at high risk.

Centers for Disease Control. (2006b). Revised recommendations for HIV testing of adults, adolescents, and pregnant women in health-care settings. *Morbidity and Mortality Weekly Report, 55*(RR14), 1–17. Retrieved from http://www.cdc.gov/mmwr/preview/mmwrhtml/rr5514a1.htm on September 20, 2007.

the risks to these individuals. Participating in counseling, community education, and social and political activism are ways that C/PH nurses can play an important role in minimizing the risk of HIV infection among populations served and in minimizing the risk of negative effects on people who undergo HIV testing.

Exceptions to voluntary consent for HIV testing include situations in which there has been significant occupational exposure (e.g., to nurses, emergency medical technicians, firefighters, etc.) and the person whose HIV status is in question refuses testing. Other exceptions are prior to organ transplant donation, when a coroner needs to determine cause of death, and when testing is needed for emergency diagnostic purposes when the patient is unable to consent and a surrogate is not available (Dempski, 2006).

Confidentiality

Confidentiality and the duty to warn were discussed in Chapter 9 and have similar applications in ethical relationships with persons infected with HIV. Persons who know or suspect that they have HIV often avoid testing or treatment because of fears about exposure of lifestyle, including sexual practices or drug use, discrimination and stigmatization, and loss of relationships (Beauchamp & Childress, 2001; Chenneville, 2003). As a general rule, a person's HIV status is confidential information (Dempski, 2006). HIV status may be disclosed when persons or their proxies provide written authorization to do so and when health care providers have a need to know, such as workers at a coroner's office or the health care staff of a correctional facility.

Statutory laws in each state must be consulted for directions regarding the duty to warn known sexual partners of individuals with HIV. Before a person's HIV status is disclosed to a known partner or partners, attempts should be made to encourage HIV-positive persons to self-disclose to other people who are at risk of infection due to their seropositive status. Newly diagnosed HIV-positive patients need to be informed that health department personnel may contact them to voluntarily discuss partner notification (CDC, 2006b). Professionals working at health departments should be available to help patients notify sexual partners and to provide HIV counseling and testing while keeping the patient's name confidential. "In the final analysis, the health professional is expected to weigh the likelihood of harm to other parties against his or her duty to keep confidentiality and act accordingly" (Fry & Veatch, 2006, p. 305).

Chenneville (2003) proposed a decision-making model that takes into consideration the premises contained within the *Tarasoff* legal case (see Duty to Warn in Chapter 9) as well as health care ethics that focuses on the best interest of the person who is seropositive. The first step in Chenneville's model is to determine whether disclosure is warranted. Assess the foreseeability of harm and the identifiability of the victim. Questions to consider when determining foreseeability are included in Box 11.7. Chenneville's second step is to refer to professional ethical guidelines, and the final step is to refer to state guidelines (pp. 199–200).

Ethical Reflections

- Identify and describe your state's laws regarding the duty to warn known sexual partners of individuals with HIV.
- Do you agree or disagree with the ethics of these laws? Explain.
- What are the ethical principles or approaches that are reflected in the laws?

**BOX 11.7: HIGHLIGHTS FROM THE FIELD:
QUESTIONS TO ASSESS FORESEEABILITY OF HARM**

- Does the client use condoms?
- Is the client impulsive? Aggressive? Submissive?
- Does the client use substances (e.g., alcohol) that decrease inhibitions?
- Is the client afraid to disclose HIV status because of fear of rejection, discrimination, and so forth?
- Is the client intentionally trying to harm others?

Chenneville, T. (2003). HIV, confidentiality, and duty to protect: A decision-making model. In D. N. Bersoff (Ed.), *Ethical conflicts in psychology* (3rd ed., pp. 198–202). Washington, DC: American Psychological Association, p. 199.

The Duty to Provide Care

In accepting their professional nursing role, nurses make a contract or covenant with the public to provide certain services (ANA, 2003). There are only a few situations in which nurses ethically would be permitted to refuse care to individuals with HIV based on the patient being a danger to the nurse. Each health care institution should have policies that nurses can refer to for guidance in determining when concerns about the risks of care are justified in allowing nurses to refuse to provide care to these patients. One commonly accepted example or justification for refusal is when a nurse is pregnant. When patients with HIV are considered to pose a significant risk to nurses because of the patients' impaired judgment or altered mental status, security should be provided for all health care workers who are at risk.

Pandemic Influenza

Pandemics of influenza are considered to be rare but consistently recurring events (WHO, 2005). During the 1900s three influenza pandemics occurred—in 1918, 1957, and 1968. The 1918 pandemic was one of the deadliest disease events that has ever occurred, with approximately 40-50 million people dying worldwide during the pandemic. When new influenza viruses emerge and spread rapidly among the global population, the human immune system is not prepared to combat the new infection. The lack of immunity to a new influenza virus may result in many deaths as it did in 1918.

When the next influenza pandemic occurs, health care professionals, including C/PH nurses, will be faced with many ethical issues and decisions. Among these issues will be decisions about how to fairly distribute vaccines and antiviral medications and how to fairly decide about restricting personal freedoms (CDC, 2007). The CDC has prepared a document outlining specific guidelines to address ethical considerations in the management of pandemic influenza (to view this document go to: http://www.cdc.gov/od/science/phec/panFlu_Ethic_Guidelines.pdf). The following guidelines are contained within this document:

- Identification of clear overall goals for pandemic influenza (p. 2): Goals are different than in interpandemic years. During a pandemic, the goal is "preserving the functioning of society" (p. 3) rather than protecting people who are at the most serious risk from being harmed by influenza, such as elders and young children.
- A commitment to transparency throughout the pandemic influenza planning and response process (p. 3): Language used in explaining reasons for decisions must be clear, the basis for decisions must be open for review, and the process must reflect a respect for persons and involved communities.
- Public engagement and involvement are essential to build public will and trust and should be evidenced throughout the planning and response process (p. 3): The public is treated as a partner with the influenza experts. Vulnerable and marginalized people need to be included in related processes.
- Public health officials have a responsibility to maximize preparedness in order to minimize the need to make allocation decisions later (p. 3): Examples "include shortening the time for virus recognition or vaccine production, increasing the capacity to produce vaccines or antivirals and increasing the supplies of antivirals" (pp. 3–4).
- Sound guidelines should be based on the best available scientific evidence (p. 4): Processes and actions should be evidence based whenever possible. However, some processes and action may need to be based on evidence-informed data, which is a bit less rigorous.
- The pandemic planning process acknowledges the importance of working with and learning from preparedness efforts globally (p. 4): This guideline is not based on merely benefitting U.S. citizens but rather on maximizing the common good of the global community.
- Balancing of individual liberty and community interests (p. 4): During a pandemic, usual individual liberties that are highly valued in our society may need to be suspended. If suspending liberties is necessary, care needs to be taken to use the least

restrictive policies, to ensure "that restrictions are necessary and proportional to the need for protection" (p. 5), and to support people who are affected by the restrictions.

■ Diversity in ethical decision making (p. 5): Historically, groups of people have been abused "in the name of the public good" (p. 5). During pandemic influenza, a variety of public voices must be included in planning and implementation processes.

■ Fair process approach (procedural justice) (p. 5): Procedures must be well designed so that they lead to fair outcomes.

Ethical Reflections

- The people who developed the CDC document about ethical guidelines during an influenza pandemic have proposed that preserving the functioning of society needs to be prioritized above protecting people who are most at risk for developing the flu. How do you interpret this guideline? Do you believe that it is ethical? Why or why not?

- Discuss specific procedures that would be consistent with a "fair process approach" (procedural justice).

- Who (individuals or agencies) should decide about the priorities of distributing scarce resources during a flu pandemic?

- How might governments act in unethical ways during a flu pandemic?

- When are limitations on personal autonomy ethically justified during a flu pandemic?

- If you were a C/PH nurse during the peak of a major flu pandemic would you report to your job at the local health department or stay home with your family? Explain the ethical rationale for your decision. If you worked as an R.N. at a hospital, would you report to work during a flu pandemic? Explain.

- How could a C/PH nurse act as a community advocate during a flu pandemic?

Terrorism and Disasters

The great lesson of September 11 is that we are all connected. Either we are all safe or none of us is safe. Either we are all free of fear or none of us is.

—M. PIPHER, 2002, *THE MIDDLE OF EVERYWHERE*, P. XIII

The terrorist attacks on September 11, 2001, and the anthrax-laced letters that followed this event highlighted the possible dangers of terrorist-related infectious diseases invading society (Farmer, 2001). Farmer proposed that "investing in robust public health infrastructures, and in global health equity in general, remains our best means of being prepared for—and perhaps even preventing—bioterrorism. Indeed, this was the refrain of several of our best public health leaders during the taxing investigations of these [anthrax] attacks" (p. xi).

Ethics-related guidance for C/PH nurses during any type of terrorism attack or before, during, or after natural or human-made disasters can be referred back to a variety of ethical approaches, such as social justice (fair distribution of resources), communitarian ethics (acting to facilitate the common good for communities), utilitarianism (considering actions that produce the greatest good for the greatest number of people), virtue ethics (having a good character and being concerned about the common good), deontology (acting according to one's duty), and ethical principlism (applying rule-based principles). During disasters, public health professionals must make critical decisions about how to triage scarce resources and everyday personal rights—health care, including first aid; food and water; medications and immunizations; warmth and housing; protection from harmful environmental elements; and the individual freedom to travel and mingle with other people. Because of the major impact that public health actions can have on human suffering and well-being, the decisions made by public health professionals during disasters are inherently ethical in nature.

However, there is another important element in ethics and public health care during disaster situations. This element is trust. Members of society expect health care professionals, especially public health professionals, to be trustworthy, as well as competent, while carrying out their roles during disasters. "Public health agencies [and public health professionals] cannot function well in the absence of public trust" (Public Health Leadership Society, 2004, p. 4). People should be able to trust public health professionals to act according to the public's best interest during a disaster. Actions to achieve the common good and good outcomes for the whole community must be balanced with actions directed at caring for the needs of individuals. Each community member has a personal story and each person's life narrative is important. Equanimity—evenness of temperament—is a good virtue for nurses to have during a disaster. Thich Nhat Hanh's story about Vietnamese boat people that was included in Chapter 10 also is very relevant to ethical nursing care during disasters (see Box 10.6 in Chapter 10).

Although standards of nursing practice may need to be altered during a disaster situation, a nurse's ethics should not be compromised during a disaster. At the point of a disaster is not the time for nurses to begin pondering and sorting out their ethical philosophies. The 5 R's Approach to Ethical Nursing Practice provides a pre-event guide for nurses to prepare to act ethically under any sudden and stressful situation, including situations such as those that occur before, during, and after disasters (see Box 11.8).

BOX 11.8: HIGHLIGHTS FROM THE FIELD: THE 5 R's APPROACH TO ETHICAL NURSING PRACTICE

1. Read
Read and learn about ethical philosophies, approaches, and the ANA's *Code of Ethics for Nurses*. Insight and practical wisdom are best developed through effort and concentration.

2. Reflect
Reflect mindfully on one's egocentric attachments—values, intentions, motivations, and attitudes. Members of moral communities are socially engaged and focus on the common good. This includes having good insight regarding life events, cultivating and using practical widsom, and being generous and socially just.

3. Recognize
Recognize ethical bifurcation points, whether they are obvious or indistinct. Because of indifference or avoidance, nurses may miss both small and substantial opportunities to help alleviate human suffering in its different forms.

4. Resolve
Resolve to develop and practice intellectual and moral virtues. Knowing ethical codes, rules, duties and principles means little without being combined with a nurse's good character.

5. Respond
Respond to persons and situations deliberately and habitually with intellectual and moral virtues. Nurses have a choice about their character development and actions.

Intellectual Virtues	Moral Virtues
Insight	Compassion
Practical Wisdom	Loving-Kindness
	Equanimity
	Sympathetic Joy

Insight: awareness and knowledge about universal truths that affect the moral nature of nurses' day-to-day life and work

(continued)

BOX 11.8: HIGHLIGHTS FROM THE FIELD: THE 5 R'S APPROACH TO ETHICAL NURSING PRACTICE (continued)

Practical Wisdom: deliberating about and choosing the right things to do and the right ways to be that lead to good ends

Compassion: the desire to separate other beings from suffering

Loving-Kindness: the desire to bring happiness and well-being to oneself and other beings

Equanimity: an evenness and calmness in one's way of being; balance

Sympathetic Joy: rejoicing in other persons' happiness

Considerations for Practice

- Trying to apply generic algorithms or principles when navigating substantial ethical situations does not adequately allow for variations in life narratives and contexts.
- Living according to a philosophy of ethics already must be a *way of being* for nurses before they encounter disaster situations.

Ethical Reflections

- Nurses are likely to be presented with ethical dilemmas during disaster situations. Review the definition of an ethical dilemma in Chapter 2. Should nurses expect to receive or know clear and certain answers to questions arising from ethically-laden situations during a disaster? Why or why not?
- What can nurses do to best prepare themselves to navigate ethical dilemmas before, during, and after disaster situations? Explain.
- Consider a natural disaster situation such as the one that occurred after Hurricane Katrina. Identify specific opportunities that nurses may have to make ethical decisions in providing disaster care to a community. Include opportunities that are obvious as well as indistinct opportunities.
- Do you believe that public health nurses and acute care nurses face similar or different ethical dilemmas during a disaster? Explain and provide examples.

Genomics

The Institute of Medicine (2003; as cited in ANA, 2007) outlined eight new domains of public health practice. In addition to the content area of ethics, another of the eight domains is genomics. The Human Genome Project (HGP) spanned 13 years and was a joint project overseen by the U.S. Department of Energy (DOE) and the National Institutes of Health (U.S. DOE Office of Science, 2006b). The project was completed in 2003 but a full analysis of the data obtained will require many years of work. The goals of the HGP were to:

- *Identify* all the approximately 20,000-25,000 genes in human DNA
- *Determine* the sequences of the 3 billion chemical base pairs that make up human DNA
- *Store* this information in databases
- *Improve* tools for data analysis
- *Transfer* related technologies to the private sector
- *Address* the ethical, legal, and social issues (ELSI) that may arise from the project (Para 2)

Three to five percent of the HGP budget was allocated to studying ethical, legal, and social issues (ELSI) (U.S. DOE Office of Science, 2006a). Some of the ELSI identified include the fair use of information obtained from genetic testing; the maintenance of informational privacy and confidentiality; stigmatization due to genetic differences among people; a number of reproductive issues, such as the impact of genetic information on reproductive decision making and reproductive rights; clinical issues, such as education and implementation of quality standards; uncertainty in regard to gene testing when multiple genes or gene-environment interactions are involved; considerations of whether behaviors occur according to free will or are determined according to genetic makeup; the safe use of genetically modified foods and microbes; and how property rights should be handled in regard to the commercialization of products. The HGP has opened up a wide array of issues about which all health professionals, including C/PH nurses, will continually need to become more familiar. However, many people in society still are not sure if the HGP has opened a Pandora's box. The following ethical reflections contain some of the questions directly cited from the ELSI study.

————————— Ethical Reflections —————————

Gather reliable data and generate informed positions that answer the following questions. Engage in a debate with your colleagues about differing positions and provide examples.

- Who should have access to personal genetic information, and how will it be used?
- How does personal genetic information affect an individual and society's perceptions of that individual?
- How does genomic information affect members of minority communities?
- What are the larger societal issues raised by new reproductive technologies?
- Should testing be performed when no treatment is available?
- Should parents have the right to have their minor children tested for adult-onset diseases?
- Do people's genes make them behave in a certain way?
- Are genetically modified foods and other products safe for humans and the environment?

C/PH Nursing: Contributing to Building the World

Because C/PH nursing is population focused, C/PH nurses often have opportunities to improve the welfare of many people. C/PH nurses work with members of populations as equal partners and they collaborate with a variety of people to promote and protect the public's health (ANA, 2007). Participating in service learning experiences and adopting a philosophy of servant leadership are two ways to ground nursing practice in the principles of PHN.

Service Learning

Service learning is "academic experiences in which students engage both in social action and in reflection on their experiences in performing that action" (Piliavin, 2003, p. 235). Service learning is ideally suited for supporting the moral development of C/PH nursing students. Kaye (2004) defined service learning as "a teaching method where guided or classroom learning is deepened through service to others in a process that provides structured time for reflection on the service experience and demonstration of the skills and knowledge acquired" (p. 7). Service learning is a means for students and teachers to work with community leaders and agencies in collaboratively identifying and working toward a common good. All participants, including teachers, agency administrators, and staff, learn from the students during their interactions with them while the students benefit from developing an increase in community awareness. In service learning "community develops and builds through interaction, reciprocal relationships, and knowledge of people, places, organizations, governments, and systems" (Kaye, p. 8).

Service is usually focused on direct or indirect services, advocacy, or research (Kaye, 2004). In direct services, person-to-person interactions occur between students and the recipients of the students' work. Direct services may be aimed at students developing a broader awareness of the needs and issues of varying cultures, populations, or age groups while providing a needed service to a population. For example, providing a service to people with AIDS who are living at a specific AIDS hospice, to people who are staying at a particular homeless shelter, or to elderly persons who attend a specific day care center. A whole community or the environment is the focus of indirect service learning interventions, such as activities aimed at helping to organize and implement a community-wide health education program about safe sex or organizing an effort to decrease pollution of a local waterway. Advocacy—which is a key role of C/PH nursing—combined with service learning involves creating and supporting change in communities to benefit people in the community. Advocacy includes grassroots societal and political activism, such as working to educate a city council about the unmet needs of people with AIDS in the city. Service learning provides an excellent opportunity for students to become involved in community research. Students can participate in developing and conducting surveys and gathering, analyzing, and reporting data regarding issues of public health concern.

Students' reflections on service learning experiences are an integral and defining part of service learning. It is in this area that the students' moral imaginations and the development of intelligent habits are cultivated. Reflection helps service learners to consider the "big picture" in working for the good of communities. Reflective experiences can be guided through activities such as journal writing or teacher-led group discussions and processing of experiences. Service learners may benefit from thinking in terms of the intersecting human narratives that exist among themselves, their community collaborators, and the recipients of their services.

Ethical Reflections

- Conduct a literature review about service learning in nursing. Develop suggestions for service learning experiences that focus on each of the following: direct services, indirect services, advocacy, and research.
- Explain why service learning is related to ethics in C/PH nursing.

Servant Leadership

In the late 1960s and early 1970s, Robert Greenleaf (2002) was one of several businesspeople who developed and articulated the concept of servant leadership in management. Greenleaf developed the idea of **servant leadership** after reading the book *The Journey to the East* written by Herman Hesse (1956). Hesse's book relates a story about a servant named Leo who is on a journey to the East with a group of men, members of a mysterious League, who are on a mission to find spiritual renewal. Leo brings the group together as a community with his spirit and songs. When Leo decides to leave the group, the small community becomes dysfunctional and disbands. Later, one of the journeymen discovers that, unknown to the journeymen, Leo was really the head of the League that had sponsored their original journey.

Leo was a noble leader who had chosen the role of a servant, a servant whose leadership was of the utmost importance to the sense of community of the journeying group. Greenleaf (2002) proposed that Hesse's story clearly exemplifies a servant leader through the portrayal of Leo. He suggested that "the great leader is seen as servant first, and that simple fact is the key to his [or her] greatness" (p. 21). In the story, even while Leo was directly in the role of the leader of his League, he viewed himself first and foremost as a servant (see Box 11.9).

Servant leaders who see themselves first as servants, at some later point in time make the choice to lead while serving. People who are more concerned with leading before serving often are motivated by a desire for power or to obtain material possessions, although a strong concurrent secondary motivation to serve is possible. Greenleaf (2002) explained how to distinguish between a servant-first leader and a leader who views service as a secondary or lower priority:

The difference manifests itself in the care taken by the servant-first [leader] to make sure that other people's highest priority needs are being served. The best test, and difficult to administer, is this: Do those served grow as persons? Do they, while being served, become healthier, wiser, freer, more autonomous, more likely themselves to become servants? And, what is the effect on the least privileged in society? Will they benefit or at least not be further deprived? (p. 27)

When thinking about servant leadership, it is important to note that the role of the servant follower is as important as that of the servant leader. If there are no servant followers, or seekers, great leaders are not recognized because there is no one with the awareness to recognize them. "If one is servant, leader or follower, one is always

BOX 11.9: HIGHLIGHTS FROM THE FIELD: THE NATURE OF SERVICE

During a Midwestern storm of rain, hail, lightning, and thunder, my mother stopped at the grocery store and asked me to run in for a loaf of bread. As I prepared to get out of the car, I noticed little Janie running down the street. She wore her usual tattered clothes, and her bald head, the result of some condition unknown to me, was unprotected from the hail. Many of our schoolmates teased her, judging her as inferior because of her poverty and appearance. I jumped out of the car and gave her my raincoat. She put it over her head and continued running. I remember thinking, "I am here to help others." I was ten years old.

Trout, S. S. (1997). *Born to serve: The evolution of the soul through service.* Alexandria, VA: Three Roses Press. (p. 13).

searching, listening, expecting that a better wheel for these times is in the making" (Greenleaf, 2002, p. 24).

Covey (2002) defined servant leadership as being consistent with moral authority and proposed that servant leaders and servant followers are, in reality, both followers. They are both followers because both are following the truth. Moral authority was described in terms of conscience and includes four dimensions:

1. Sacrifice is the heart of moral authority or conscience. Sacrifice involves an elevated recognition of one's small, peaceful inner voice while subduing the selfish voice of one's ego.

2. Being inspired to become involved with a cause that is worth one's commitment to it. A worthy cause inspires people to change their "question from asking what is it we want to what is being asked of us" (p. 7). One's conscience is expanded and becomes a factor of great influence in one's life.

3. The inseparableness of any ends and means. Moral leaders do not use unethical means to reach ends; and as the philosopher Kant advocated for moral behavior, servant leaders always must treat others as ends in themselves, never as a means to an end.

4. The importance of relationships is enlivened through the development of conscience. "Conscience transforms passion into compassion" (Covey, 2002, p. 9). Living according to one's conscience emphasizes the reality of the interdepen-

BOX 11.10 HIGHLIGHTS FROM THE FIELD: "ALL ARE SIGNIFICANT"

During my second year of nursing school, our professor gave us a quiz. I breezed through the questions until I read the last one. "What is the first name of the woman who cleans the school?" Surely this was a joke. I had seen the cleaning woman several times but how would I know her name? I handed in my paper, leaving the last question blank. Before the class ended, one student asked if the last question would count toward our grade. "Absolutely," the professor said. "In your careers, you will meet many people—all are significant. They deserve your attention and care. Even if all you do is smile and say hello." I have never forgotten that lesson. I also learned her name was Dorothy.

Covey, S. (2002). Foreword. In R. K. Greenleaf, *Servant leadership: A journey into the nature of legitimate power and greatness* (25th ed., pp. 1–13). New York: Paulist Press., p. 10.

dence of people and relationships. In relation to this fourth dimension of moral authority, Covey conveyed a story told by a nursing student, JoAnn C. Jones (see Box 11.10).

Ethical Reflections

- Reflect and write a narrative about why you want(ed) to become a nurse.
- Was (is) your primary motivation the desire to be a servant or a leader? Has your perception of the servant/leadership role changed over time? How?
- Consider several different work settings and jobs for C/PH nurses. Describe how you could be a servant leader in each of these settings and jobs.
- Highlights from the Field Box 11.11 contains examples from the ANA's (2001) *Code of Ethics for Nurses with Interpretive Statements*. How are these examples relevant to C/PH nursing?
- What other provisions and statements in the ANA's *Code of Ethics for Nurses* are particularly pertinent to C/PH nursing [see Appendix A]? Discuss these provisions and provide examples of how they apply to nursing practice.

BOX 11.1: HIGHLIGHTS FROM THE FIELD: CODE OF ETHICS FOR NURSES

- Individuals are interdependent members of the community (1.4, p. 9).
- The nurse recognizes that there are situations in which the right to individual self determination may be outweighed or limited by the rights, health and welfare of others, particularly in relation to public health considerations (1.4, p. 9).
- The nurse's primary commitment is to the recipient of nursing and health care services—the patient—whether the recipient is an individual, a family, a group, or a community (2.1, p. 9).
- Nurses, individually and collectively, have a responsibility to be knowledgeable about the health status of the community and existing threats to health and safety (8.2, p. 24).
- Nurses can work individually as citizens or collectively through political action to bring about social change (9.4, p. 25).

Web Ethics

Markkula Center for Applied Ethics: The Common Good
www.scu.edu/ethics/practicing/decision/commongood.html

Science and Environmental Health Network
http://www.sehn.org/about.html

An Inconvenient Truth
http://www.climatecrisis.net/takeaction/

The Luminary Project
http://www.theluminaryproject.org/article.php?list=type&type=3

Bill and Melinda Gates Foundation
www.gatesfoundation.org

HGP Information: Ethical, Legal, and Social Issues
http://www.ornl.gov/sci/techresources/Human_Genome/elsi/elsi.shtml

National Service Learning Clearinghouse
www.servicelearning.org

Greenleaf Center for Servant Leadership
www.greenleaf.org

Summary

Over the centuries there have been amazing strides in public health measures that have improved the well-being of humans. However, members of the global community are still at risk from diseases that are thousands of years old, such as malaria and TB. Also, new environmental toxins, epidemics, and disasters are constantly threatening human health. Health disparities are not limited by geographic boundaries and abound in both rich and poor countries while people are told that health care resources are scarce. All of these issues present important ethical challenges for C/PH nurses, and C/PH nurses have exciting opportunities to be servant leaders at the forefront of working to improve the health of the global community. It is incumbent upon the nursing community to consider and act in response to the words of John Donne: "Any man's death diminishes me, because I am involved in mankind; and therefore never send to know for whom the bell tolls; it tolls for thee."

Key Points

- Members of a community have a shared interest in a common good.
- Communities are moral in nature.
- The epicenter of communitarian ethics is the community rather than the individual perspective of any one person.
- There are a number of ethical theories and approaches that are useful in C/PH nursing. Nurses need to understand different ethical approaches and develop an ethical philosophy before a crisis or stressful situation arises.
- It is a moral choice when people decide how they choose to distribute societal benefits and burdens among the members of communities.
- Health care disparities are often associated with race, ethnicity, and economic status.
- Humans will not achieve true moral progress until people perceive the suffering of others who are not personally known to them as important in their daily lives.
- The human genome project has generated a plethora of ethical questions that will need to be answered by members of the global community
- Servant leaders view themselves as servants first and leaders second.

CASE STUDY: COMMUNITY BUILDING

Imagine that you will be the administrator for a new residential AIDS hospice that will be opened as an agency of Catholic Charities in the midsized conservative southern city where you live. The majority of the money for the hospice is coming from a federal grant, but you will need to raise additional funds in order to provide comprehensive care. The hospice will be located in a house in a mixed residential and business neighborhood, and the location of the hospice is to remain as confidential as possible. The citizens living in the neighborhood are very opposed to having the hospice in their neighborhood. Until now, the board of directors of the local Catholic Charities organization provided oversight of the grant and the plans for the hospice. The plans are to create a partnership with the local AIDS task force to provide community AIDS prevention education. It is now time to turn the hospice project over to you, the RN, hired as administrator.

Case Study Questions

1. You will need a governing body for the hospice. What types of people would you consider and how would you handle the selection process?
2. What types of services would you provide? What ethical issues might affect your decisions about the distribution of resources for the different services? What ethical theories would you use to guide your choices?
3. You may have more applicants for admission to the hospice than you have beds available. What criteria will you use to prioritize admissions to the hospice?
4. How would you recruit the staff and volunteers while trying to maintain confidentiality about the location of the hospice? What ethical issues would you include in your staff and volunteer orientation?
5. What would you do to try to build a sense of community that includes the hospice residents, the hospice staff, and the residents of the neighborhood where the hospice is located? That includes the city? Would building this sense of community be critical to the success of your program? Explain.
6. How might the philosophy of communitarian ethics provide you with guidance in developing the plans for the hospice? How might the use of moral imagination be involved (see Chapter 2)?

References

American Nurses Association. (2001). *Code of ethics for nurses with interpretive statements.* Silver Spring, MD: Author.

American Nurses Association. (2003). *Nursing's social policy statement* (2nd ed.). Silver Spring, MD: Author.

American Nurses Association. (2007). *Public health nursing: Scope and standards of practice.* Silver Spring, MD: Author.

American Public Health Association: Public Health Nursing Section. (2006). Environmental health principles and recommendations for public health nursing, Retrieved August 20, 2007, from http://www.astdn.org/downloadablefiles/Principles%20and%20Recommendations%20Document_4-06.doc

American Public Health Association: Public Health Nursing Section. (2007). Public health nursing. Retrieved August 19, 2007, from http://www.apha.org/membergroups/sections/aphasections/phn/

Beauchamp, D. (1999). Public health as social justice. In D. E. Beauchamp & B. Steinbock (Eds.). *New ethics for the public's health* (101–109). New York: Oxford University Press.

Beauchamp, T. L., & Childress, J. F. (2001). *Principles of biomedical ethics* (5th ed.). New York: Oxford University Press.

Berkowitz, B., Dahl, J., Guirl, K., Kostelecky, B., McNeil, C., & Upenieks, V. (2001). *Public health nursing leadership: A guide to managing the core functions.* Washington, DC: American Nurses Publishing.

British Broadcasting Corporation News. (2006, September 15). WHO backs DDT for malaria control. Retrieved December 26, 2006, from http://news.bbc.co.uk/2/hi/science/nature/5350068.stm

Centers for Disease Control. (2003). Achievements in public health, 1900-1999: Control of infectious diseases. In P. R. Lee & C. L. Estes (Eds.), *The nation's health* (7th ed., pp. 31–37). Boston: Jones and Bartlett.

Centers for Disease Control. (2004). The history of malaria, an ancient disease. Retrieved December 26, 2006, from http://www.cdc.gov/malaria/history/index.htm

Centers for Disease Control. (2006a). Eliminating racial & ethnic health disparities. Retrieved December 23, 2006, from http://www.cdc.gov/omh/AboutUs/disparities.htm#12

Centers for Disease Control. (2006b). Ethical guidelines for pandemic influenza. Retrieved August 20, 2007, from http://www.cdc.gov/od/science/phec/panFlu_Ethic_Guidelines.pdf

Centers for Disease Control. (2007, February 15). Revised recommendations for HIV testing of adults, adolescents, and pregnant women in health-care settings. *Morbidity and Mortality Weekly Report, 55*(RR14), 1–17. Retrieved August 21, 2007, from http://www.cdc.gov/mmwr/preview/mmwrhtml/rr5514a1.htm

Chenneville, T. (2003). HIV, confidentiality, and duty to protect: A decision-making model. In D. N. Bersoff (Ed.), *Ethical conflicts in psychology* (3rd ed., pp. 198–202). Washington, DC: American Psychological Association.

Covey, S. (2002). Foreword. In R. K. Greenleaf, *Servant leadership: A journey into the nature of legitimate power and greatness* (25th ed., pp. 1-13). New York: Paulist Press.

De Mello, A. (1992). *One minute nonsense.* Chicago: Loyola University.

Dempski, K. M. (2006). Clients with AIDS and HIV testing. In S. W. Killion & K. M. Dempski (Eds.), *Quick look nursing: Legal and ethical issues* (pp. 56–57). Sudbury, MA: Jones & Bartlett.

De Saint-Exupery, A. (2002). *A guide for grown-ups: Essential wisdom from the collected works of Antoine De Saint-Exupery*. San Diego, CA: Harcourt.

Donne, J. (1962). Meditation 17. In *Norton Anthology of English Literature* (Vol. 1, 5th ed.). New York: W. W. Norton.

Einstein, A. (1930). *What I believe*. Retrieved August 20, 2007, from http://home.earthlink.net/~johnrpenner/Articles/Einstein3.htmlFarmer, P. (2001). *Infections and inequalities: The modern plagues* (Updated). Berkeley: University of California Press.

Forsey, H. (1993). *Circles of strength: Community alternatives to alienation*. Philadelphia: New Society.

Fry, S. T., & Veatch, R. M. (2006). *Case studies in nursing ethics* (3rd ed.). Sudbury, MA: Jones & Bartlett.

Garrett, L. (2000). *Betrayal of trust: The collapse of global public health*. New York: Hyperion.

Greenleaf, R. (2002). *Servant leadership: A journey into the nature of legitimate power and greatness* (25th ed.) (L. C. Spears, Ed.),. New York: Paulist Press.

Hesse, H. (1956). *The journey to the east*. New York: Picador.

Kaye, C. B. (2004). *The complete guide to service learning: Proven, practical ways to engage students in civic responsibility, academic curriculum, and social action*. Minneapolis, MN: Free Spirit.

Kriebel, D., Tickner, J., & Crumbley, C. (2003). Appropriate science: Evaluating environmental risks for a sustainable world. Retrieved August 21, 2007, from http://www.uml.edu/com/CITA/Kriebel.pdf

Kush, C. (2004). *The one-hour activist: The 15 most powerful actions you can take to fight for the issues and candidates you care about*. San Francisco: Jossey-Bass.

Lobe, J. (2006, September 15). WHO urges DDT for malaria control strategies. *Inter Press Service*. Retrieved December 26, 2006, from http://ipsnews.net/news.asp?idnews=34746

Lundberg, K. (2005). An anthropologist's analysis. In B. C. White & J. A. Zimbelman (Eds.), *Moral dilemmas in community health care: Cases and commentaries* (pp. 152–155). New York: Pearson Education.

MacIntyre, A. (1984). *After virtue: A study of moral theory* (2nd ed.). Notre Dame, IN: University of Notre Dame.

Markel, H. (2004). *When germs travel: Six major epidemics that have invaded America since 1900 and the fears they have unleashed*. New York: Pantheon.

Minkler, M., & Pies, C. (2002). Ethical issues in community organization and community participation. In M. Minkler (Ed.), *Community organizing & community building for health* (pp. 120–138). New Brunswick, NJ: Rutgers University Press.

Nussbaum, M. (2004). Compassion and terror. In L. P. Pojman (Ed.), *The moral life: An introductory reader in ethics and literature* (2nd ed., pp. 937-961). New York: Oxford University.

Pieper, J. (1966). *The four cardinal virtues*. Notre Dame, IN: University of Notre Dame.

Piliavin, J. A. (2003). Doing well by doing good: Benefits for the benefactor. In C. L. M. Keyes & J. Haidt (Eds.), *Flourishing: Positive psychology and the life well-lived* (pp. 227–247). Washington, DC: American Psychological Association.

Pipher, M. (2002). *The middle of everywhere: Helping refugees enter the American community*. Orlando, FL: Harcourt.

Public Health Leadership Society. (2002). *Principles of the ethical practice of public health*. Retrieved July 24, 2006, from http://www.apha.org/codeofethics/ethicsbrochure.pdf

Public Health Leadership Society. (2004). *Skills for the ethical practice of public health*. Retrieved August 21, 2007, from http://209.9.235.208/CMSuploads/EthicalPracticePublicHealth-40199.pdf

Raffensperger, C., & Myers, C. (2001). Ethics for survival. *The Networker, 6*(1). Retrieved August 21, 2007, from http://www.mindfully.org/Sustainability/Ethics-For-Survival.htm

Salamon, J. (2003). *Rambam's ladder: A meditation on generosity and why it is necessary to give.* New York: Workman.

Science and Environmental Health Network. (n.d. a). Precautionary principle: FAQs. Retrieved December 31, 2006, from http://www.sehn.org/ppfaqs.html

Science and Environmental Health Network. (n.d. b). Precautionary principle: Wingspread statement. Retrieved December 31, 2006, from http://www.sehn.org/wing.html

Sherwin, S. (1992). *No longer patient: Feminist ethics & health care.* Philadelphia: Temple University.

Trout, S. S. (1997). *Born to serve: The evolution of the soul through service.* Alexandria, VA: Three Roses Press.

U.S. Department of Energy Office of Science. (2006a). Ethical, legal, and social issues. Retrieved from http://www.ornl.gov/sci/techresources/Human_Genome/elsi/elsi.shtml

U.S. Department of Energy Office of Science. (2006b). Human genome project information. Retrieved from http://www.ornl.gov/sci/techresources/Human_Genome/home.shtml

U.S. Department of Health and Human Services. (2000). *Healthy people 2010: Understanding and improving health* (2nd ed.). Washington, DC: Government Printing Office.

Wheatley, M. (2002). *Turning to one another.* San Francisco: Berrett-Koehler.

Wildes, K. M. (2000). *Moral acquaintances: Methodology in bioethics.* Notre Dame, IN: University of Notre Dame.

World Health Organization. (2002). Training in tropical diseases: Strategic direction for research: Malaria. Retrieved December 26, 2006, from http://www.who.int/tdr/diseases/malaria/files/direction.pdf

World Health Organization. (2005). Ten things you need to know about pandemic influenza. Retrieved December 26, 2006, from http://www.who.int/csr/disease/influenza/pandemic10things/en/index.html

World Health Organization. (2006a). Global AIDS epidemic continues to grow. Retrieved December 26, 2006, from http://www.who.int/hiv/mediacentre/news62/en/index.html

World Health Organization. (2006b). Strategic planning and innovation. Retrieved December 23, 2006, from http://www.who.int/spi/en/

World Health Organization. (2006c). The burden of tuberculosis: Population health burden. Retrieved December 26, 2006, from http://www.who.int/trade/distance_learning/gpgh/gpgh3/en/index4.html

CHAPTER 11 QUESTIONS

1. Most schoolchildren in a group from middle class families have access to health care while a smaller group of children from poor families in the same school have little access to health care. This can best be described as an example of

    a. the difference between a community and a population.

    b. a breach of ethical principlism.

    c. a health care disparity.

    d. the implications of utilitarian ethics.

2. Just generosity is a virtue that can best be described as
   a. fairly distributing resources.
   b. giving and receiving based on need.
   c. donating to good causes.
   d. fairly punishing wrong doers.

3. Mandatory isolation of persons with TB who refuse to take their medications even with DOT is an example of
   a. utilitarian ethics.
   b. deontological ethics.
   c. ethical principlism.
   d. virtue ethics.

4. The key element underlying the precautionary principle is:
   a. Anticipatory action is taken based on scientific proof.
   b. Anticipatory action is taken when scientific certainty is absent.
   c. Anticipatory action is taken based on evidence-based practice.
   d. Anticipatory action is taken based on traditional science.

5. In public health, dilemmas may occur because of the need to consider the rights of individuals as well as the best interests of large groups. This is a conflict between which of the following ethical approaches, respectively?
   a. Utilitarianism and virtue ethics
   b. Principlism and virtue ethics
   c. Utilitarianism and deontology
   d. Deontology and utilitarianism

6. A key activity in protecting the health of the public from environmental harm is
   a. upholding personal rights.
   b. being virtuous.
   c. collaboration.
   d. upholding human dignity.

7. A key element that best describes communities in a moral sense as opposed to populations is
   a. interest in the common good.
   b. interest in community property.
   c. interest in common diseases.
   d. interest in a neighborhood.

8. Voluntary testing for HIV is an ethical issue because
    a. it supports persons' rights.
    b. it is a utilitarian activity.
    c. it is the most virtuous policy.
    d. it involves risks as well as benefits.

9. All of the following are significant ethical issues surrounding the problem of malaria, except
    a. the high incidence of the disease compared with the low cost of prevention and treatment.
    b. the lack of education about the social and economic burdens of the disease.
    c. the high numbers of young children who develop the disease.
    d. the high risk of infection among poor U.S. citizens living in the South.

10. Mr. Samuels is an African American man. One of Mr. Samuel's parents has Huntington's disease. What ethics-related question needs to be considered?
    a. Is it ethical to test for a disease for which there is no curative treatment?
    b. Is Mr. Samuel at greater risk because of his minority status?
    c. Should Mr. Samuel's parents have been better counseled about birth control?
    d. Is Mr. Samuel's wife justified in divorcing him?

CHAPTER 11 ANSWERS

Question 1: The correct answer is C.
Variations in health care access among groups separated by the characteristic of economic status can lead to poor health outcomes. This is called a health disparity.
Choices A, B, and D are incorrect because these choices are unrelated to the question.

Question 2: The correct answer is B.
As a virtue, just generosity means that people give help to other people based on the others' needs without seriously considering what other persons are due or deserve. People with the virtue of just generosity also are willing to receive help from other people.

Choices A, C, and D are incorrect because though fairly distributing resources may be included in just generosity, this answer is not the best description; Choices C and D also might be present in communities that display just generosity, but these choices do not directly define the virtue.

Question 3: The correct answer is A.

The policy to restrict individual persons who refuse treatment for active TB in order to protect groups of people is consistent with utilitarian ethics. Individual liberties are sacrificed for the good of the larger group.

Choices B, C, and D are incorrect because these approaches to ethics do not describe the action proposed.

Question 4: The correct answer is B.

The precautionary principle means that people take action, especially in regard to environmentally related issues, before certain scientific evidence is available. People take action as a "precaution."

Choices A, C, and D are incorrect because the precautionary principle is not consistent with waiting to act until the traditional scientific method produces evidence.

Question 5: The correct answer is D.

Deontology has traditionally been used to support personal autonomy whereas utilitarianism is used to support the good of groups.

Choices A, B, and C are incorrect because these choices do not correctly represent the answer to the question.

Question 6: The correct answer is C.

People and communities must work together to protect the public from environmental harm. Individual efforts alone will not produce the best outcomes.

Choices A, B, and D are incorrect because though these issues may be related to environmental ethics, these choices do not directly address efforts to protect against environmental harm.

Question 7: The correct answer is A.

In communitarian ethics, an essential element of communities is that the members are interested in the whole community's common good.

Choices B, C, and D are incorrect because though these choices represent issues of possible interest to communities, these choices do not provide the best description of the differentiation between communities and populations.

Question 8: The correct answer is D.

Even voluntary testing for HIV has benefits and risks. For example, persons who test positive for HIV may endure emotional suffering, stigmatization, and discrimination.

Choices A, B, and C are incorrect because voluntary testing does support autonomy but does not represent the best answer to this question; voluntary HIV testing is not directly associated with either utilitarian or virtue ethics.

Question 9: The correct answer is D.
People in the southern U.S. are not at high risk for malaria infection.

Choices A, B, and C are incorrect because these choices do represent significant ethical issues surrounding the problem of malaria.

Question 10: The correct answer is A.
One of the ethics-related issues generated by the expansion of the human genome project is that scientists will develop tests to identify diseases for which there is no cure. People may then be burdened with waiting for the inevitable suffering to occur with little hope of physical treatment or emotional relief. People diagnosed with a fatal but untreatable disease may experience problems with insurability, employability, family relationships, and stigmatization.

Choices B, C, and D are incorrect because the issue of minority status does not directly relate to ethics and Huntington's disease; often, persons do not know that they will develop Huntington's disease until after they have had children; the issue of divorce in this case possibly may prompt an ethics-laden debate, but this choice is not the best answer to the question.

Ethical Issues in End-of-Life Nursing Care

Janie B. Butts

A place to stay untouched by death does not exist. It does not exist in space, it does not exist in the ocean, nor if you stay in the middle of a mountain.

—THE BUDDHA

OBJECTIVES

After studying this chapter, the reader should be able to:

1. Discuss the issues surrounding death anxiety and the forces that could prevent an ideal death.
2. Explore the meaning of imaginative dramatic rehearsal in terms of one's own death.
3. Explain the nursing care of suffering patients as it relates to suffering from the perspective of Aristotle's four inseparable parts of the human soul, the ANA *Code of Ethics for Nurses*, and the *ICN Code of Ethics for Nurses*.
4. Compare and contrast the various types of euthanasia.
5. Identify the historical death practices and the issues that led to the President's Commission Uniform Determination of Death Act definition of death in 1981.
6. Differentiate the four conceptions of death that have emerged since the official definition of death in 1981.
7. Contrast whole-brain death and higher-brain death as these conceptions relate to the criteria associated with each of them.
8. Explore the nurse's role in communicating types of advance directives to dying patients and their families, patients not necessarily dying, and the public.
9. Discuss the strengths and weaknesses of each type of advance directive.

10. Explain the types of standards in which proxies or surrogates may participate.
11. Discuss the seven principles for proxy decisions with incompetent patients as they relate to the Terri Schiavo case and name the standard used by the surrogate in this case.
12. Analyze the issues that will emerge in decision making by patients, families, and health team member for a patient whose treatment the physician has judged as medically futile.
13. Describe types of cases or illnesses that a nurse may see in a palliative care situation.
14. Compare the legal and moral differences between a written DNR order and the practice of slow codes.
15. Analyze moral differences from your perspective among the following concepts as they relate to the three highlighted legal cases of Quinlan, Cruzan, and Schiavo: withholding life-sustaining treatment vs. withdrawing life-sustaining treatment; withholding artificial nutrition and hydration vs. withdrawing artificial nutrition and hydration; and letting go vs. killing.
16. Delineate the nurse's role and moral obligations regarding the three conditions of the rule of double effect when caring for a dying patient.
17. Contrast the differences in the nurse's role for terminal sedation, physician-assisted suicide, and relieving pain and suffering with opiates or opiate-synthetic drugs.
18. Identify the nurse's responsibility toward a person who is planning rational suicide.
19. Discuss the rationale for nurses experiencing moral distress and conflicts when caring for dying patients and their families.
20. Delineate the World Health Organization's pain ladder for patients receiving palliative care.
21. Identify the core principles for end-of-life care and relate them to a previous experience with a dying patient or a would-be dying patient.
22. Explore ways in which nurses could give and manage the spiritual care of dying patients and their families.
23. Identify essential aspects from the ANA *Code of Ethics for Nurses with Interpretive Statements* (2001) that is critical for nurses when caring for dying patients and their families.

KEY TERMS

Death anxiety
Suffering

Imaginative dramatic rehearsal
Having suffering

Being suffering

Euthanasia

Passive euthanasia

Nonvoluntary euthanasia

Assisted suicide

Principle of mercy (mercy killing)

Principle of justice

Traditional death

Higher-brain death

Persistent vegetative state

Living will

Durable power of attorney

Substituted judgment standard

Principle of autonomy

Medical futility extended

Do not resuscitate (DNR)

Withholding and withdrawing treatment

Terminal sedation

Rational suicide

Spirituality

Becoming suffering

Active euthanasia

Voluntary euthanasia

Involuntary euthanasia

Suicide

Principle of autonomy

Death

Whole-brain death

Personhood death

Advance directive

Medical care directive

Proxy

Pure autonomy standard

Best interests standard

Palliative care

Right to die and right to refuse treatment

Rule of double effect (RDE)

Physician-assisted suicide

WHO's pain ladder

What Is Death?

Contemporary ethical discussions about death and dying relate to philosophers attempting to answer captivating questions such as "What is a good death?" and "How will we all die?" More recently, the focus of ethicists has been on the challenging issues of readiness to die, acceptance of death, and knowing the right time to die (Battin, 1994; Connelly, 2003; Hester, 2003). Many questions about death are unanswerable, but individuals can develop some sort of subjective notion about the meaning of death. For people to face death more peacefully, they need to come to their own understanding of death and what they think is beyond death, if anything, and develop a personal knowing of death's connection. Nietzsche proposed that everyone needs a philosophy of life in relation to death in his notable quote: "He who has a why to live [for] can bear with almost any how" (as cited in Connelly, p. 51).

The Ideal Death

Andrew Lustig (2003), a philosopher, stated that he has been amazed at how ethicists are engaging in passionate conversations about the meaning of death, yet, Lustig observed, "it seems very hard for each of us to personalize the truth of [our own] mortality. As the title character in the nonfiction bestseller *Tuesdays with Morrie* puts it, 'Everyone knows they're going to die, but nobody believes it'" (Albom, 1997). People "talk death" and romanticize death as if it was something ideal rather than a confrontation with mortality.

People use phrases such as "he passed away" to keep from saying the words "he died" or to avoid facing the reality of death (Spiegel, 1993). The term **death anxiety** indicates a fear of the prospect of dying. Existential philosophers such as Kierkegaard, Heidegger, and Sartre emphasized that it is in facing death and the possibility of nonbeing that a person comes to know oneself best; in other words, a person first has to put death in the proper perspective to attempt to understand any portion of life (as cited in Spiegel, 1993).

Yalom (1980), an existentialist and psychotherapist, stated that individuals avoid facing their own mortality in two ways, or with two defenses. The first defense against death is through immortality projects, where people literally throw themselves into commendable projects, their work, or raising children. People thoroughly and completely engage in these activities and by doing so, they insulate themselves from death. The second defense is through dependence on a rescuer, believing that another person can provide one with a sense of safety or protection from death. Almost all people want to feel some sense of insulation from elements of threat. Death is one of those elements, and dying is a fearful process. Many times patients look to nurses, physicians, and other health care professionals to fulfill a rescuer role.

Spiegel (1993), in his studies about death and dying, consulted several hundred people regarding what they fear most about death. Spiegel summed up the responses of people he interviewed in the following passage:

Strangely enough, it is not being dead; rather, it is the process of dying. Fears of losing control of your body, suffering increasing pain, losing the ability to do things you love to do, being able to make decisions about your medical care, being separated from loved ones: Those are the ways that fears of dying become real. Death is something that pushes the edge of our comprehension. (p. 137)

Death signifies the end to a person's living embodiment. Wanting to die the good death or the ideal death may be everyone's wish at some point in life, but while a person is alive, death often remains a dark secret. Nurses and other health care professionals need to envisage dying as a process that everyone must face, and nurses must serve as an advocate for those who are dying. In an article titled "Inventing the Good Death," Brogan (2006) related the story of how the concept of the modern hospice movement was started in 1967 in London by a nurse, Dame Cicely Saunders, who many regard as the Florence Nightingale of the hospice movement. In Saunders's own words about death and dying, she stated:

I once asked a man who knew he was dying what he needed above all in those who were caring for him. He said, "For someone to look as if they are trying to understand me." I know it is impossible to understand fully another person, but I never forgot that he did not ask for success but only that someone should care enough to try. . . . The suffering of the dying is "total pain" with physical, emotional, spiritual, and social elements. (p. 14)

The suffering man whom Saunders recounted resembles many people's death, meaning that an ideal death does not frequently transpire. Nancy Dubler (as cited in Hester, 2003) presented what she called a "cinematic" myth of the "good American death" when she wrote,

[The good death] includes the patient: lucid, composed, hungering for blissful release—and the family gathers in grief to mourn the passing of a beloved life. The murmurs of sad goodbyes, the cadence of quiet tears shroud the scene in dignity. Unfortunately for many of us, our deaths will not be the spiritual, peaceful "passing" that we might envision or desire. (p. 122)

For most people, death is a mysterious rendezvous to be discovered rather than a comforting scene with the presence of family members and others hovering over them (Hester, 2003). Instead, patients find themselves, if at all conscious, connected to ventilators and other machines, intravenous lines and meters, and receiving many medications. Technology and medicalization have exacerbated the problem of depersonalization. Family members or significant others experience difficulty communicating with their loved one because of physical, technological, and environmental barriers. During this incomprehensible time, the nursing staff could be a patient's most reliable and consistent contact. When decisions about life and end-of-life need to be made, family members are often faced with uncertainty about the kind of treatment their loved one would want in particular circumstances. Even when patients have adequate decision-making capacity, they may want input from family members or significant others in treatment decisions, but family members will often find it difficult to discuss the uncertainties of treatments with their loved one for two reasons.

First, they may have restrictions on their visitation because of inflexible hospital policies. Second, they may feel at a loss to help and, therefore, do not want their loved one to know how they feel.

Whatever death a person is to experience—a good death, an anticipated death, a sudden unexpected death, or a painful, lingering death—most of the time, people do not have a choice of how they will die. Individuals, meanwhile, need to shift the focus from thoughts "that we die" toward "how we die" so that people can place substantial thought on future decisions about end-of-life care and what might be best for them (Hester, 2003, p. 122).

The benefit of persons envisioning an ideal death and reflecting on it from time to time is that the image helps them develop a sense of readiness for a peaceful death. The famous American philosopher John Dewey (as cited in Fesmire, 2003) described a similar moral framework that is based on a person's development of intelligent habits through an imaginative dramatic rehearsal. Dewey discussed dramatic rehearsal in terms of creative dialogue between two or more people in a particular scenario. In applying the **imaginative dramatic rehearsal** to the death process, a person can imagine one's own death by reconstructing the ideal death scenario, during which time individuals imagine the scenario being carried out and, on continued reflection, may later discover a rich meaningful experience through this imagination (Fesmire, 2003; Hester, 2003). Persons who imagine an ideal death may have a greater possibility of finding significance at the end of their lives and then, to some extent, may be able to help shape their dying process (Hester).

The Concept of Human Suffering of Dying Patients

From philosophers, professionals, and researchers to religious leaders, scholars have defined suffering in complex ways, but there is a consensus in the literature that suffering is difficult to condense into one succinct definition probably because of cultural and perceptual variations of human suffering. (See also the discussion of suffering in Chapters 2 and 8.) Human suffering can be connected to many episodes or events, but it has been related with great frequency to dying patients and chronic illness.

Kahn and Steeves (1986) stated that an individual could experience suffering when the being, the self, and existence experience a sense of threat in some way. Similarly, Eric Cassell (2004), Clinical Professor of Public Health in the Weill Medical College of Cornell University and a practicing physician, emphasized that suffering involves the whole person and body but that pain and suffering are separate phenomena. Rodgers and Cowles (1997) conceptualized suffering as "an individualized, subjective, and complex experience that involves the assignment of an intensely negative meaning to an event or a perceived threat" (p. 1048). After several years of studying suffering, Eriksson (1997) defined suffering as a perceived inner experience of something evil that could threaten the whole existence of the being yet is a necessary element of life, as are joy and happiness, and with others showing compassion toward a suffering person one could develop a more meaningful suffering existence.

Stan van Hooft (2000, 2006), Associate Professor of Philosophy at Deakin University in Australia, has been at the forefront of studying the Aristotelian framework of the human soul as a way to explain human suffering. (Refer to Chapter 1 for more information on Aristotle.) Aristotle contended that a soul consists of a being with physical and spiritual interconnections. Aristotle (as cited in van Hooft, 2000) described the being as having four inseparable parts:

1. *Vegetative:* Nonrational biological functions
2. *Appetitive:* Nonrational desires and the striving for attaining desires
3. *Deliberative:* Mostly rational, and reasoned strategic thinking about how to fulfill self goals
4. *Contemplative:* A fully rational soul, the spiritual part, and thinking about the things that are unchangeable, such as laws of nature, math, physics, studying about the meaning of one's existence, and the spiritual soul

Each of these four parts has its own *telos* (meaning purpose or goal), but the overall interconnected and inseparable parts as a whole being have one purpose, which is labeled by Aristotle as achieving eudaimonia (meaning happiness, human fulfillment, and flourishing). If one part cannot reach this would-be goal, the whole being suffers because the mind and body are inseparable insofar as these four parts. The conclusion that van Hooft (2000) made based on his analysis was that suffering is the opposite of happiness and flourishing (or the fulfillment of the *telos*) in that suffering is understood as "the frustration of the *telos* or inherent goals of human existence in its four dimensions" (p. 187).

To differentiate pain from suffering, van Hooft (2000) stated that because pain is a hurtful and unpleasant sensation with a variation of intensities and degrees, pain can frustrate the tendency for a person to achieve a flourishing life and therefore will cause suffering. Pain is a result of a malady (illness, disease, injury) of the vegetative or bodily state, but pain is different from suffering. Pain can steal joy, contentment, and happiness, and when pain is persistent, suffering ensues causing an individual to lose a passion for life. Suffering saturates the whole body in all of its four parts.

Catherine Garrett's (2005) life work on attempting to differentiate pain from suffering is the most interesting, in the opinion of the author of this chapter, of the published work cited and one that serves as the basis for the definition of suffering in this section. Garrett, now retired from the University of Western Sydney, has built on van Hooft's Aristotelian work on suffering. Because of the complexity of suffering, the definition is not a succinct, one-sentence definition. **Suffering** emerges in all beings, including every living thing, and the human capacity to have physical, mental, emotional, social, and spiritual aspects is significant in that if just one part is limited or constrained in any way, the whole being suffers, every aspect.

Garrett (2005) described the suffering person as a tormented being. Though bodily pain can lead to suffering, suffering is a different phenomenon. Humans are not perfect; suffering will inherently be a part of human living, and even though it is not a welcomed part of living, suffering is inevitable. Suffering is as much objective as it is subjective, insofar as the suffering person's symptoms become recognizable signs to others. When the being suffers, as in a dying person, someone suffering a chronic illness such as alcoholism, or a victim of chronic violence, the self is not just thinking or feeling; rather, the self's state becomes evident to others.

In other recent work, Arman and Rehnsfeldt (2003) explored the hidden suffering among breast cancer patients through a qualitative research metasynthesis and concluded that human suffering is an integrated and essential part of health, but can be compatible with health only when the suffering is bearable for the person. (See Box 12.1 for more explanation of this research.) Three patterns emerged in the analysis of the research: (1) having suffering, (2) being suffering, and (3) becoming suffering. Although Arman and Rehnsfeldt's focus for this research was hidden suffering among breast cancer patients, these patterns could be translated to any person facing intense suffering and having to come to terms with death. The Aristotelian framework that Garrett and van Hooft analyzed does not seem to contradict the work of Arman and Rehnsfeldt.

What Responsibility Do Nurses Have Toward Suffering Patients?

How an individual chooses to understand human suffering is a personal comprehension. Nurses need to interpret the suffering of their patients in an attempt to alleviate or minimize pain or distress. There are three official documents highlighting the need for nurses to reduce and alleviate suffering in patients (see Box 12.2).

Cassell (2004) made a connection between human suffering and a person needing compassion. Everything that nurses can know about a patient is discovered by way of data collection from assessments, interviews, and interpersonal interactions. To understand others' suffering, nurses need to have a complete comprehension of patients with a full awareness of various aspects, such as: (1) What makes them the persons

BOX 12.1: HIGHLIGHTS FROM THE FIELD: RESEARCH BRIEF ON HIDDEN SUFFERING

When bearable, suffering can be compared ontologically [nature of being] to the three dimensions of health: health as having or doing, health as being, and health as becoming.

- *For health as having or doing:* **Having suffering** is an awareness of disruption of life, sorrow, trauma, uncertainty, fear, sudden disintegration, and an awareness of death. Alleviation of suffering occurs through a person's actions to improve the solvable problem.
- *For health as being:* **Being suffering** means there is a greater intensity of despair, distrust, hopelessness, and loss of freedom. Alleviation of suffering, though not permanent, is possible through meaningful acts for self.
- *For health as becoming:* **Becoming suffering** means developing deeper feelings of existentialism and spiritual thoughts as people come to terms with suffering and death. Alleviation of suffering is not possible, although people will continue to strive for bearable suffering. The more a person suffers, the more that transformation occurs.

From Arman, M., & Rehnsfeldt, A. (2003). The hidden suffering among breast cancer patients: A qualitative metasynthesis. *Qualitative Health Research, 13*(4), 510–527.

they are? (2) When do these individuals feel whole, threatened, or disconnected? (3) What are their views of the past, future, and the environment surrounding them? (4) What are their aims and goals? and (5) How do they view their purpose in life?

Nurses generally cannot get to a level of knowing their patients to the degree that Cassell indicated, but developing the virtue of compassion is one way to begin the journey of comprehending others' suffering. Correctly interpreting vocalizations of those suffering by observing verbal and facial cues signifies the beginning of involvement by nurses.

Morse, Beres, Spiers, Mayan, and Olson (2003) researched linking verbal and facial cues to suffering by observing and videotaping 19 participants as they told their distressing and agonizing stories. These researchers analyzed transcriptions, performed textual analysis of voice qualities, and then coded the behaviors. Morse and colleagues

> ## BOX 12.2: HIGHLIGHTS FROM THE FIELD: NURSES' MORAL OBLIGATION TOWARD HUMAN SUFFERING
>
> Nursing obligations and responsibilities are commonly published in many official nursing documents. The following documents represent only three of many.
>
> - The ANA *Code of Ethics for Nurses with Interpretive Statements* (2001): "Nurses actively participate in assessing and assuring the responsible and appropriate use of interventions in order to minimize unwarranted treatment and patient suffering" (Provision 1.3, p. 8; see Appendix A).
> - The National Council of State Boards of Nursing *NCLEX-RN Test Plan* (2007): The goal of nursing is "preventing illness; alleviating suffering; protecting, promoting, and restoring health; and promoting dignity in dying" (p. 1).
> - The International Council of Nurses *ICN Code of Ethics for Nurses* (2006): "Nurses have four fundamental responsibilities: to promote health, to prevent illness, to restore health and to alleviate suffering" (p. 1; see Appendix B).

observed for signals of suffering as participants recalled their suffering experience. The data analysis revealed two distinct responses from the interviews:

- *Enduring suffering:* A state of emotional suppression exhibited by blank stares, unfocused gazes, a flat monotone voice, and other expressions as they recalled and would "get through" their stories
- *Emotional suffering:* A state of releasing emotions manifested by crying, grasping a tissue, a cracking voice, and rocking back and forth as patients recalled and relived their suffering experiences

Interestingly, as they told their stories, participants attempted to transition back to a state of enduring suffering after they had entered the state of emotional suffering.

The researchers concluded that responses to basic emotions of suffering produce certain facial cues, which will help nurses to observe the suffering state of patients. This research is mentioned in this chapter because Morse et al.'s (2003) study on the linking of verbal and facial cues to suffering states was the first of its kind. Nurses generally use strategies such as empathy, compassion, and attentive listening to console suffering patients, but there has not been evidence-based research to support that these interventions actually help.

What is more important is that families and patients tend to try not to lose control when coming to terms with ill-fated news or tragic outcomes so as to remain in a state of enduring suffering to prevent transitioning into a state of emotional suffering and release. If a nurse attempted to console a patient by genuinely saying, "This must be difficult for *you!*" the patient may refocus and move into emotional suffering without wanting to do so (p. 12). The issues posed by Morse et al. are related to ways that nurses should therapeutically respond; in other words, do nurses respond with compassion and empathy to facilitate the patient in an enduring state to move toward emotional suffering and release *or* do nurses act in a different way to help facilitate the maintenance of enduring suffering? The researchers have indicated a *sense of urgency* for further research regarding the way that nurses and other caregivers should be responding to patients in enduring suffering and times of crisis, especially with the current emphasis on evidence-based practice in nursing.

Euthanasia

The thought of extended agony and suffering prior to death provokes a sense of dread in most people. Keeping their emotional, financial, and social burdens to a minimum and avoiding suffering are not always possible (Munson, 2004). O'Rourke (2002) noted that most people go to extremes to avoid suffering when he stated, "Suffering in all its forms is an evil, and every reasonable effort should be made to relieve it" (p. 221). However, an untold number of people die every day with tremendous suffering and pain. For more than 90 years, people have debated whether to legalize **euthanasia**, a process often referred to as "mercy killing."

Until his prison sentence and conviction on a second-degree murder charge, Dr. Jack Kevorkian assisted with more than 100 suicides or mercy killings (Public Broadcasting System & WGBH *Frontline*, 1998). From 1990 to 1998, at the request of suffering patients from various parts of the United States, he helped them end their lives. He has been nicknamed "Doctor Death" because of his euthanasia practices. Kevorkian was charged, then later acquitted, on several occasions prior to his conviction for euthanizing Thomas Youk. On November 22, 1998, 15 million viewers of the CBS program *60 Minutes* watched Doctor Death give a lethal injection to Thomas Youk, age 52, who was dying with Lou Gehrig's disease. Once this program aired, strong debates surfaced in the media, health care, political, and legal systems worldwide.

According to Biggar (2006), Kevorkian could die soon from hepatitis C while still in prison. However, Hoffman (2007), an Associated Press writer, stated that he was paroled in June 2007 but still held the belief that people have a right to die and to request death.

Euthanasia, which has come to mean a "good death," has developed a strong appeal in recent years, partly because of the political hubris on the right-to-die issues and the association of these issues with the misery and suffering of dying patients. There are two major types of euthanasia (Munson, 2004). **Active euthanasia** is the intentional and purposeful act of causing the immediate death of another person, such as people with a terminal illness, a painful disease, or who cannot be cured. **Passive euthanasia** is withholding or withdrawing medical treatments or life-sustaining treatments. Another categorization of euthanasia is voluntary or nonvoluntary. **Voluntary euthanasia** occurs when patients with decision-making capacity authorize physicians to take their lives. The voluntary type may include the taking of one's own life with a lethal dose of physician-ordered medication such as in physician-assisted suicide. Oregon's Death with Dignity Act of 1994 is a prime example of physician-assisted suicide based on the voluntary euthanasia principle. **Nonvoluntary euthanasia** occurs when persons *are not able* to express consent to end their lives and are unaware that they are going to be euthanized. For example, a physician could euthanize someone without consent when the person is not able to give consent.

There are other types of euthanasia. One type is **involuntary euthanasia**, where a person's consent may be possible but is not sought, and a physician could euthanize someone without express consent. An example of involuntary euthanasia could be the euthanizing of a death-row inmate. Another type is **assisted suicide**, meaning that an individual, knowing that a patient or person intends to commit suicide, provides the means for that patient to do so. Often the "means" will include some type of lethal medication or street drug. The last type of euthanasia is **suicide**, which means the taking of one's own life.

A vigorous debate continues in the United States about whether there is a real moral difference between active euthanasia, such as the intentional taking of someone's life, and passive euthanasia, such as withholding and withdrawing life-sustaining treatments (Brannigan & Boss, 2001; Jonsen, Veatch, & Walters, 1998). The action versus omission distinction has caused nurses and physicians to mull over the burdensome question: Is there a moral difference between actively killing and letting someone die?

In her book, *The Least Worst Death*, Battin (1994) argued that euthanasia is a morally right and humane act on the grounds of mercy, autonomy, and justice. The **principle of mercy ("mercy killing")** includes two obligations: the duty not to cause further pain and suffering and the duty to act to end existing pain or suffering. The

principle of autonomy involves the thought that health professionals ought to respect a person's right to choose and determine a suitable course of medical treatment. The **principle of justice** in regards to euthanasia decisions is based on how unsalvageable providers of care believe a permanently unconscious person is; in other words, there is moral justification in providers performing euthanasia on patients whom they regard as unsalvageable.

Based on this salvageability/unsalvageability principle, however, a health care provider could justify performing euthanasia on still competent but dying patients if they were regarded as unsalvageable (Battin, 1994). It is in knowing where to draw the line with this principle that providers may face difficult ethical decisions. Because of the legal and moral concerns and the potential for a slippery slope to occur, bioethicists, nurses, and health care providers examine acts of euthanasia with grave caution, especially when the acts may increase the scope and meaning of the principle of unsalvageability (see the Slippery Slope Argument in Chapter 2). There are many opponents presenting convincing viewpoints against the slippery slope euthanasia argument. Battin, in particular, stated:

> But to require the person who chooses to die to stay alive in order to protect those who might unwillingly be killed sometime in the future is to impose an extreme harm—intolerable suffering—on that person, which he or she must bear for the sake of others. [I ask] which is the worse of two evils, death or pain? (p. 119)

Historical Influences on the Definition of Death

There was widespread fear of being buried alive in the 18th and 19th centuries, especially in Europe, because of inadequate methods for detecting when a person was dead. Documented accounts of people being buried alive exist (Bondeson, 2001). Sometimes, when a body was exhumed, claw marks were found on the inside of the coffin lid. Many people had come to believe exaggerated accounts of premature burial. Bondeson based his conclusions on his detailed historical study of the subject.

Nevertheless, and possibly for good reasons, great fear persisted during that era. Out of fear from being buried alive, the great composer Frédéric Chopin left a request in his will to be dissected after his death and before being buried in order to make certain that he was dead (Bondeson, 2001). Even the dying words of George Washington were "Have me decently buried, but do not let my body be put into a vault in less than two days after I am dead" (Australian Museum, 2007, intro.).

When the prevention of premature burials became law, the owners of funeral homes went to the extreme of having their staff monitor dead bodies during the "wait" time. Before the law had taken effect, there were inventions with special devices on the coffins to help the dead, once buried, to communicate with others above the ground. The devices included such things as a rope extending to the surface of the ground with a bell on the other end, a speaking tube to the outer coffin, a shovel, and food and water.

For hundreds of years, when a person became unconscious, physicians or others would palpate for a pulse, listen for breath sounds with their ears, look for condensation on an object when it was held close to the body's nose, and check for fixed and dilated pupils (Mappes & DeGrazia, 2001). Finally, the stethoscope was invented in 1819, which led to reduced fear, because physicians could listen with greater certainty for a heartbeat through a magnified listening device placed on the chest of the body.

A breakthrough in technology occurred at the beginning of the 20th century when Willem Einthoven, a Dutch physician, discovered the existence of electrical properties of the heart with his invention of the first electrocardiograph (EKG) in 1903 (Benjamin, 2003). The EKG provided sensitive information about whether or not the heart was functioning. From the middle of the 19th century to the middle of the 20th century, there seemed to be a consensus about determination of death, meaning that when the heart stopped beating and the person stopped breathing, the person had ceased to exist.

Society began to change its perceptions of death as technology became integrated into medicine. The 1950s and 1960s brought more uncertainty involving death as physicians kept patients alive in the absence of a natural heartbeat. Then, it became apparent that when transplants were being performed in the 1960s and 1970s, a diagnosis of death would not necessarily depend on the absence of a heartbeat and respirations. Rather, in the future, the definition of death would need to include brain death criteria.

In 1968, the members of a Harvard Medical School ad hoc committee first attempted to redefine death in terms not only of heart–lung cessation but also of reliable brain death criteria for respirator-dependent patients with no brain function that the committee members described as patients with irreversible coma (Benjamin, 2003). Back then, this definition led to confusion about the term *brain death* and to a widespread misconception about whether the human organism, the person, was actually dead. Somehow, a misinterpretation of the term *brain death* was accepted. Brain death, which technically means death of the brain, came to mean death of a human organism or person. Because of the way some individuals perceived the meaning of the term *brain death*, they translated the 1968 definition to mean that two kinds of death existed for human organisms: the traditional heart-lung death and now a new kind of death called brain death. Benjamin emphasized that ethicists and physicians had not given sufficient attention to clarifying this term before the article was published in 1968.

The Definition of Death

Ethicists, physicians, and others continued intense debates about death. It was not until 1981 that members of a President's Commission for the Study of Ethical Problems in Medicine and Biomedical and Behavioral Research wrote in the document *Defining Death* that the body was an organism as a whole:

Three organs—the heart, lungs, and brain—assume special significance—because their interrelationship is very close and the irreversible cessation of any one very quickly stops the other two and consequently halts the integrated functioning of the organism as a whole. Because they were easily measured, circulation and respiration were traditionally the basic "vital signs." But breathing and heartbeat are not life itself. They are simply used as signs— as one window for viewing a deeper and more complex reality: a triangle of interrelated systems with the brain at its apex. (President's Commission, 1981, p. 33; as cited in Benjamin, 2003, p. 198)

The commission members sanctioned a definition of death in 1981 in the same document and recommended its adoption by all states (Mappes & DeGrazia, 2001; Youngner & Arnold, 2001). See Box 12.3 for the definition of death according to the Uniform Determination of Death Act of 1981 (UDDA). Debates continue to occur concerning the question of which criteria belong in the definition of death and, more specifically, death of the brain. Since this 1981 definition was adopted, criteria for death of the brain have been adopted by almost every state.

Veatch (2003) has extended the debate on the definition of death by posing an intriguing question regarding the loss of full moral standing for human beings. (See also the discussion of full moral standing in Chapter 5.) This statement triggers the question as to when humans should be treated as full members of the human community. Almost every person has reconciled the thought insofar as some persons have full moral standing and others do not, but there is continued controversy about when full moral standing ceases to exist and what characteristics qualify the cessation of full moral standing. Losing full moral standing is equivalent to ceasing to exist. Various groups have proposed and debated four different conceptions of death since the UDDA definition in 1981 (see Box 12.4).

With whole-brain death, the patient may survive physically for an indeterminate duration with a mechanical ventilator. Some patients may seemingly have complete loss of brain function only to have the electrical activity of the brain reappear later, even if

BOX 12.3: HIGHLIGHTS FROM THE FIELD: DEATH DEFINED IN 1981

The members of the President's Commission defined **death** in accordance with accepted medical standards set forth in the UDDA. A person who is dead is one who has sustained either:

- Irreversible cessation of circulatory and respiratory functions

  or

- Irreversible cessation of all functions of the entire brain, including the brain stem. . . .

From President's Commission for the Study of Ethical Problems in Medicine and Biomedical and Behavioral Research. (1981). *Defining death: Medical, legal, & ethical issues in the determination of death.* Washington, DC: Government Printing Office, p. 73; as cited in Mappes, T. A., & DeGrazia, D. (2001). *Biomedical ethics* (5th ed.). Boston: McGraw-Hill, p. 318.

minimal, which makes the UDDA whole-brain death criteria difficult to use for pronouncing a person dead (Munson, 2004). The peculiarity of such an event is as noted by Veatch (2003): "A brain-dead patient on a ventilator does, of course, make for an unusual corpse. On the ventilator, he is respiring and his heart is beating. But if his whole brain is dead, the law in most jurisdictions says that the patient is deceased" (p. 38).

At the point when the person has met brain death UDDA criteria and therefore is pronounced dead, mechanical ventilation and medical treatment can be discontinued (as cited in Benjamin, 2003). An electroencephalogram (EEG) is a meter device used to measure the electrical activity of the brain (Munson, 2004). If a person is on life-sustaining support when in the process of being pronounced dead, such as in whole-brain death, an EEG is needed in addition to the physician's establishing absence of heartbeat and respirations. The following criteria are required to establish whole-brain death (Mappes & DeGrazia, 2001):

- Flat EEG with other tests that document the absence of cerebral blood flow
- Fixed and dilated pupils
- Inability to breathe without mechanical support
- Absent brain stem reflexes

BOX 12.4: HIGHLIGHTS FROM THE FIELD: FOUR CONCEPTIONS OF DEATH SINCE 1981

- *Traditional death:* A person is dead by cardiopulmonary criteria when the cessation of breathing and heartbeat is irreversible [known as cardiopulmonary death].
- *Whole-brain death:* Death is regarded as the irreversible cessation of all brain functions, with no electrical activity in the brain, and even the brain stem is not functioning [death of the brain].
- *Higher-brain death:* Death is considered to involve the permanent loss of consciousness—someone in an irreversible coma would be considered dead, even though the brain stem continued to regulate breathing and heartbeat [persistent vegetative state].
- *Personhood death:* Death occurs when an individual ceases to be a person. This may mean loss of features that are essential to personal identity or for being a person.

Munson, R. (2004). *Intervention and reflection: Basic issues in medical ethics* (7th ed.). Victoria, Australia: Wadsworth-Thomson, pp. 692–693.

Usually, two EEGs with no brain activity, 24 hours apart, are performed on patients before physicians can disconnect them from life-sustaining support. Physicians and nurses must also make certain that loss of brain function is not due to mind-altering medications, hypoglycemia, or hyponatremia. It should be noted that every single neuron must be dead, along with a flat EEG, to meet the criteria for the definition of whole-brain death.

With higher-brain death, or loss of higher-brain function, the patient lives in a **persistent vegetative state** indefinitely but without the need for mechanical ventilation. A person with higher-brain death may have some functions permanently lost but other functions not lost, which has been the cause of enormous dispute. Even very minimal brain functioning, such as limited reflexes in the brain stem, is cause for a patient to be diagnosed with higher-brain death or being in a persistent vegetative state (Veatch, 2003). It is because of these situations that questions exist regarding whether a person should be treated as one who has full moral standing in the human community. Society, physicians, and nurses have had difficulty defining death by the

UDDA definition, which includes the traditional and whole-brain concepts, but the greatest difficulty has been when they have tried to incorporate the concepts of higher-brain and personhood death (Munson, 2004). No definite criteria for either of these concepts—higher-brain or personhood—have been established for defining death. The controversy continues. Meanwhile, Benjamin (2003) posed this question for people to consider: "Exactly what is it that ceases to exist when we say someone like you or me is dead?" (p. 197). Benjamin and Veatch affirmed that there will be no answers to questions like this one until ethicists and others can come to some sort of consensus about what life is, when life begins, when life ends, and then, who does and does not have full moral standing.

Advance Directives

An **advance directive** is "a written expression of a person's wishes about medical care, especially care during a terminal or critical illness" (Veatch, 2003, p. 119). When individuals lose control over their lives, they may also lose their decision-making capacity, and advance directives become instructions about their future health care for others to follow. Advance directives can be self-written instructions or prepared by someone else as instructed by the patient. Under the federal Patient Self-Determination Act of 1990, states, under mandated authority, have developed state laws to protect the rights of individuals making decisions about end-of-life and medical care. (See Appendix D for an example of a complete legal packet for a health care advance directive.) Critical issues that need to be addressed in any advance directive include specific treatments to be refused or that are desired; the time the directive needs to take effect; specific hospitals and physicians to be used; what lawyer, if any, should be consulted; and specific other consultations, such as an ethics team, a chaplain, or a neighbor. There are three types of advance directives: living will, medical care directive, and durable power of attorney.

A **living will** is a formal legal document that provides written directions concerning what medical care is to be provided in specific circumstances (Devettere, 2000). The living will gained recognition in the 1960s, but the Karen Ann Quinlan case in the 1970s brought public attention to the living will and subsequently prompted legalization of the document. Although at the time living wills were a good beginning, today they are not completely adequate. Problems can arise when living wills consist of vague language, contain only instructions for unwanted treatments, and lack a description of legal penalties for those people who choose to ignore the directives of living wills, and when they are legally questionable as to their authenticity.

A **medical care directive** is not a formal legal document but provides specific written instructions to the physician concerning the type of care and treatments that individuals want to receive if they become incapacitated. The biggest advantage to medical care directives is that physicians use them as a guide to know what incapacitated patients want in terms of specific health care treatments. Convinced that medical care directives are only extended informed consents, attorneys believe that medical care directives are only a minimal improvement over living wills. Other weaknesses of medical care directives are that people cannot possibly anticipate every medical problem that may occur in their future. People change over time and may change their mind about future wishes even after they have delineated the instructions for their medical care directive.

The **durable power of attorney** is a legal written directive in which a designated person can make either general or specific health care and medical decisions for a patient. This durable power of attorney has the most strength for facilitating health care decisions. However, even with a power of attorney, families and health care professionals may experience fear about making the wrong decisions regarding an incapacitated patient (Beauchamp & Childress, 2001).

In addition to the weaknesses previously discussed about advance directives, other weaknesses that may present problems include the fact that very few people ever complete an advance directive, a proxy may be unavailable for decision making, and health care professionals cannot overturn advance directives in the event that a decision needs to be made in the best interest of a patient. The existence of advance directives can be a source of comfort for patients and families as long as they realize their limitations and scope. Ensuring the validity of the advance directive, realizing the importance of preserving patients from unwanted intrusive interventions, and respecting the possibility that patients may change their minds about their expressed written wishes are several ways that nurses must demonstrate benevolence toward patients and their families.

Deciding for Others

When patients can no longer make competent decisions, families may experience problems in trying to determine a progressive right course of action. The ideal situation is for patients to be autonomous decision makers, but when autonomy is no longer possible, decision making falls to a proxy (Beauchamp & Childress, 2001). The **proxy** is an individual who acts on behalf of a patient and either is chosen by the patient, such as a family member; is court appointed; or has other authority to make decisions. Family members serving as proxies are generally referred to as surrogates.

Decisions about treatment options and motives for decisions may be complex and destructive. Before the proxy makes any decisions, there needs to be appropriate dialogue among the physicians, the nurses, and the proxy (Emanuel, Danis, Pearlman, & Singer, 1995). Proxies may not be able to distinguish between their own emotions and concerns for patients or they may have monetary motives for making certain decisions. It is the responsibility of nurses and physicians to be observant for these kinds of motives or concerns and then to look for therapeutic ways to deliberate with the proxy. There are three types of proxy decision making (Beauchamp & Childress, 2001; Veatch, 2003). Box 12.5 contains seven principles called pillars that form the foundation for proxies to decide to forgo life-sustaining treatment on behalf of incompetent patients. These seven principles derived from the issues surrounding the 1970s case of Karen Ann Quinlan and her family (discussed later in this chapter). As Olick (2001) stated, "In many respects, [these principles] may be said to be a part of the legacy of Karen Ann Quinlan and her family" (p. 30). Of interest too is the influence that these principles had recently on the Terri Schiavo case and her family. (The Schiavo case is discussed later in this chapter.)

The **substituted judgment standard** is used to guide medical decisions that involve formerly competent patients who no longer have any decision-making capacity. This standard is based on the assumption that incompetent patients have the exact same rights as competent patients to make judgments about their health care (Buchanan & Brock, 1990). Proxies make medical treatment decisions based on what the surrogates believe the patients would have decided were the patients still competent and able to express their wishes. In making decisions, the proxies use their understanding of the patients' previous overt or implied expressions of their beliefs and values (Veatch, 2003). Before losing competency, the patient could have either explicitly informed the proxy of treatment wishes by oral or written instruction or implicitly made treatment wishes clear through informal conversations with the proxy.

When more than one sibling is involved in the decisions regarding the care of a dying parent, many times misunderstandings occur, and angry feelings over practical, legal, and financial matters become apparent. The siblings will be affected uniquely by their parent's death, depending on several factors: the type of relationship that exists between each sibling and the parent, if and how each sibling has experienced death in the past, each sibling's present life situation and stressors, their past grudges toward siblings, and current sibling relationships. One sibling usually takes charge or the siblings give one sibling the label of speaker for the group. Even when one is empowered, however, the others usually desire an equal voice in the decision-making process. This may be a frustrating process for everyone if the siblings cannot come to a decision.

BOX 12.5: HIGHLIGHTS FROM THE FIELD: SEVEN PRINCIPLES FOR PROXY DECISIONS WITH INCOMPETENT PATIENTS

1. Competent patients have an autonomy-based right, recognized under the Constitution and common law, to refuse treatment, including life-sustaining treatment. Life-sustaining treatment includes artificially provided nutrition and hydration.
2. Incompetent patients have the same panoply [full array] of rights as competent patients, although the manner in which those rights are exercised is different.
3. No right is absolute, but instances in which a patient's right to refuse life support is outweighed by societal interests are rare.
4. Withholding and withdrawing treatment from a terminally ill or permanently unconscious patient allows a natural dying process to take its course. It does not constitute killing or assisted suicide.
5. In making decisions for incompetent patients, surrogate decision makers should seek first and foremost to follow a subjective standard of implementing the patient's wishes. When this test proves inadequate, a best interests standard may be applied.
6. In ascertaining an incompetent patient's wishes, the proxy, family, and physician should rely on a patient's advance directive if one has been issued.
7. A local process of review in the clinical setting should be employed to facilitate resolution of disagreements. Recourse to the courts should be rare.

Olick, R. S. (2001). *Taking advance directives seriously: Prospective autonomy and decisions near the end of life.* Washington, DC: Georgetown University Press, p. 30.

Dialogue is important so that all involved can come to an understanding and avoid further misunderstandings and pain.

The **pure autonomy standard** is based on a decision that was made by an autonomous patient while competent but later drifts to incompetency. In this particular case, the decision is upheld most of the time based on the **principle of autonomy extended** (Veatch, 2003). The **best interests standard** is an evaluation of what is good for an incompetent patient in particular health care situations when the patient has probably never been competent, for example, an infant or mentally retarded adult. The proxy attempts to decide what is best for the incompetent patient based on the patient's dignity and worth as a human being without taking into consideration the patient's concept of what is good or bad. The proxy will have no evidence or basis for determining the incompetent patient's desires or what is "best" for that patient but the proxy evaluates benefits and burdens for available treatment options. Because the best interests standard is patient-centered, the proxy must make decisions based on current and future interests (Buchanan & Brock, 1990). These decisions inevitably involve muddy, subjective quality of life judgments such as appraising the incompetent patient's simple life pleasures and contentment, sense of social worth of that patient, degree of pain and suffering experienced, and treatment benefits and costs.

Ethical Reflections

The ANA (2001) *Code of Ethics for Nurses with Interpretive Statements* (see Appendix A), Provision 1.4 delineates the nurse's moral obligation to respect human dignity and recognize certain patient rights, especially that of patient self-determination. Explore Kant's perspective on human dignity and self-determination. Think of strategies that you would use to respect self-determination when caring for an incompetent person.

Medical Futility

Humpty Dumpty sat on a wall,
Humpty Dumpty had a great fall;
All the King's horses,
And all the King's men,
Could not put Humpty Dumpty together again.

—Lewis Carroll, 1872,
Adventures of Alice in Wonderland and Through the Looking Glass

The writer of this chapter has posed an analogy between the meaning of medical futility and that of the life of Humpty Dumpty and his broken body after the fall—"All the King's horses and all the King's men could not put Humpty Dumpty together again" (see Figure 12.1). The term *futile* represents pointless or meaningless events or objects (O'Rourke, 2002). **Medical futility** is defined as "the unacceptably low chance of achieving a therapeutic benefit for the patient" (Schneiderman, 1994, Para 10).

Figure 12.1 Humpty Dumpty Cartoon

Source: Andy Marlette Cartoons.

In a recent presentation, the writer of this chapter posed the question: "Futility: Is the concept too heavy for the moral ground?" Questions asked of the audience regarding the heaviness of futility related to the moral ground were:

- What is at stake?
- What weight does the term *futility* carry?
- Is the meaning and weight of the term *futility* appreciated from the broader dominion of bioethics?
- What are health care professionals' ethical obligations insofar as thinking that a medical intervention is clearly futile?
- Who makes the final decision—who has the power?
- How can hospitals and other health care agencies incorporate a reasonable, fair, objective, and clear policy on futility?

Schneiderman (1994) linked his definition of medical futility to the whole person, the wholeness similar to the way that Aristotle spoke of a human being with four inseparable parts. In other words, a suffering person will seek a cure, healing, or care from a provider to become as whole as possible again. In weighing the concept of futility, the nurse must understand that the suffering-healing-provider relationship is integral to the health process and the goals of medicine and nursing. The provider of care is responsible for administering medical treatments and interventions that will benefit the patient and not just have a mere effect on some part of the body or an organ. Integrated throughout this process is the necessity of the patient comprehending and appreciating the benefits of medical treatment. To comprehend these benefits, the person must be conscious at least partially. Patients who are in a persistent vegetative state cannot possibly appreciate the beneficiary effects of the treatment. (See the Definition of Death section in this chapter.) The mere effect is of no benefit if that effect does not help a patient to achieve some degree of life goals or human fulfillment, or the type of *telos* that Aristotle emphasized.

Medical futility goes back in history as long as can be remembered, and in ancient Greek times there was an acceptance of physicians refusing to treat people who were overwrought with disease. The futility movement became more important in the 1970s when medical technology brought about extraordinary life support measures. As physicians began asking the questions "What is a good death?" and "When do we let go?" medical futility emerged as an important concept. Throughout the 1970s and 1980s, philosophers and physicians strongly debated the concept of futility in an effort to define the term and create guidelines for putting it into practice. In the 1990s, definitions began to shift from the theme of blaming providers of care for failures to more quantitative and qualitative values insofar as treatments indicating low probabilities of benefits in the past.

There have been landmark cases of legal medical futility, including (1) the case of Helga Wanglie, (2) *In the Matter of Baby K*, and (3) *Gilgunn v. Massachusetts General Hospital*. Box 12.6 contains a brief highlight of these three cases.

Health care professionals and most other people have accepted and ethically justified withholding and withdrawing treatments deemed as futile or extraordinary. In *Schindler and Schiavo v. Michael Schiavo*, Terri's case was not about medical futility; rather, it was about Michael's legal, not ethical, responsibility of carrying out Terri's express and previous verbal wishes of not wanting to stay alive in such circumstances (discussed later in this chapter). However, Terri Schiavo, with all evidential information set forth by the physician who performed the autopsy, met the legal definition of persistent vegetative state and therefore was a futile case regarding treatment, even though the case was not about futility in itself.

Box 12.6: Highlights From the Field: Landmark Legal Cases Involving Medical Futility Decisions

1988: The Case of Helga Wanglie
An elderly woman, age 85 at that time, fractured her hip when she slipped on a rug and then developed severe ventilator-dependent pneumonia. She was later diagnosed with persistent vegetative state (PVS, or higher-brain death) secondary to hypoxic-ischemic neuropathy and was ventilator dependent secondary to chronic lung disease. (Patients with PVS do not require mechanical ventilation because the brain stem is intact. Her dependency on the ventilator related strictly to her chronic lung disease.) Physicians at two facilities agreed that treatment would be futile, but the family members wanted her to be treated and kept alive as long as possible. They believed the physicians were "playing God" but did agree to a DNR physician order with much trepidation. After an intense legal battle, the court on July 1, 1991, authorized Mr. Wanglie, her husband, to be the surrogate decision maker for Ms. Wanglie. However, on July 4, 1991, only 3 days after the final court decision, Ms. Wanglie died.

1993: *In the Matter of Baby K* (see more detail in Chapter 6)
In 1992, Baby K was born with anencephaly, meaning with a brain stem but with no capacity for a conscious life, and statistically was predicted not to be able to survive more than a few days to months. Physicians and ethics committee members argued that it would be futile to keep Baby K alive on ventilator support but the mother insisted that Baby K be kept alive because she believed that all human life is precious and is to be preserved. The federal court supported the mother's claim only if someone would assume the amount of the mother's bills for care of Baby K. The mother found that monetary support, and Baby K lived for 2 years in a nursing home on ventilator support.

1995: *Gilgunn v. Massachusetts General Hospital*
In an rare early known case of a court's supporting a physician's claim of medical futility, the jury, *after the fact*, found that cardiopulmonary resuscitation need not be provided to a patient dying with multiple organ-system failure, as in the case of Ms. Gilgunn, age 71, who was comatose. The family had sought treatment but the physician objected. The jury's decision was the result of a retrospective evaluation of the medical decision. The jury's decision for stopping futile treatment was unique at that time.

When a health care provider cannot have reasonable hope that a treatment will benefit a terminally ill person, the medical treatment is considered futile care. Treatments often considered medically futile include cardiopulmonary resuscitation (CPR), medications, mechanical ventilation, artificial feeding and fluids, hemodialysis, chemotherapy, and other life-sustaining technologies. When proxies are the spokespersons for patients, one of the nurse's responsibilities is to make sure that communication remains open between the health care team and the decision maker for the family. Everyone needs to have a chance to express feelings and concerns about treatment options viewed as medically futile (Ladd, Pasquerella, & Smith, 2002).

Complete black and white boundaries do not exist regarding medical futility because there are always questionable gray areas, and even Humpty Dumpty's case was questionable. Remember that it was all the King's horses and all the King's men who could not put Humpty Dumpty together again. However, no men or horses from another King's court tried to put Humpty Dumpty together again such as what occurs in real medical futility cases in which a second opinion is an essential component in declaring medical futility.

Grayness will always exist because health care providers and other professionals attempt to embrace the patient's hope and consider the patient's values and feelings, even though the patient may not cognitively have feelings. At the same time, however, providers of care acknowledge that all human beings have limits. By the sheer fact that the human component exists on both sides of the futility-value issue, there will always be gray areas that blur the boundaries. Patients, families, judges, patient advocacy groups, the media, socio-politicos, and the public will challenge these gray boundaries time after time.

Ethical Reflections

Questions to ponder as you develop your beliefs and opinions on the medical futility of a patient such as one in the last stages of metastasized cancer:

- What ethical theory, approach, or principle provides the rationale for your beliefs on autonomy and medical futility? Explain.
- How far does one go with patient autonomy?
- Do you believe that patient autonomy should have limits?
- Should patient autonomy (and surrogate autonomy) be unlimited no matter what the physicians believes should and should not be done?

- Would the health care system's financial burden be a factor for setting limits on patient autonomy (and surrogate autonomy) in your personal opinion or as a societal stance?
- Do patients or families have a moral right to insist on medical treatment that two or more physicians and hospitals have deemed futile? Give your rationale based on your ethical theory, approach, or principle.
- Do providers of care have a moral duty to provide medically futile treatment at the family's request, just because the family wants it?

Palliative Care

Palliative care consists of comfort care measures that patients may request instead of aggressive medical treatments when their condition is terminal. Nurses are probably the most active of all the health care professionals in meeting palliative needs of dying patients. Palliative care has become an organized movement through official associations and organizations since the 1990s. The World Health Organization (WHO, 2007a) has defined palliative care as

an approach that improves the quality of life of patients and their families facing the problems associated with life-threatening illness, through the prevention and relief of suffering by means of early identification and impeccable assessment and treatment of pain and other problems, physical, psychosocial and spiritual. (Para 1)

Understanding what quality of life means to the dying patient is an important part of end-of-life care for nurses, and no matter what stage of dying the patient is experiencing, the main goals of palliative care are to prevent and relieve suffering and to allow for the best care possible for patients and families.

When nurses provide palliative care, they do not hasten or prolong death for these patients; rather, they try to provide patients with relief from pain and suffering and help them maintain dignity in the dying experience. Palliative treatment may include a patient's and family's choice to forego, to withhold, or to withdraw treatment. Some patients will have a **do not resuscitate (DNR)** order, which is a written physician's order placed in a patient's chart, meaning that hospital personnel are not to carry out any type of CPR or other resuscitation measures. Each hospital and agency has specific policies and procedures for how a DNR order is to be written and followed. A critical ethical violation to informed consent may occur if a physician writes a DNR order on a patient's record without discussing the order and decision with the patient, family members, or proxy (O'Rourke, 2002). A DNR physician order needs to be justified by one of three reasons: no medical benefit can come from CPR, a person has a very poor quality of life before CPR, and a person's life after CPR is anticipated to be very poor (Mappes & DeGrazia, 2001).

Unofficial—and unauthorized—"slow codes" have been practiced and can be described as "going through the motions" or as giving half-hearted CPR to a patient whose condition has been deemed futile. At one time, nurses initiated slow codes when a physician had not yet written the DNR order of a terminally ill patient. However, a slow code is an unethical and illegal practice, and physicians and nurses should never initiate them. Slow codes are not recognized as a legal procedure.

The Right to Die and the Right to Refuse Treatment

The **right to die and right to refuse treatment** is a patient's autonomy over the dying process insofar as well-informed patients with decision-making capacity have an autonomous right to refuse and forego recommended treatments. (See more about autonomy and the patient's self-determination in Chapter 2.) Most of the time there are no ethical or legal ramifications if a person decides to forego treatments. The courts uphold the right of competent patients to refuse treatment (Jonsen, Siegler, & Winslade, 2006; Mappes & DeGrazia, 2001). Nevertheless, health care professionals need to make certain that the patient's decision is truly autonomous and not coerced. However, health care professionals may find it very difficult to accept a competent patient's decision to forego treatment.

Sometimes, in a patient's mind the burdens of medical treatments outweigh the benefits (O'Rourke, 2002). Perceived burden is a concern for nurses, physicians, and patients because physical pain and emotional suffering from treatments or the prolongation and dread of carrying out treatments may be too much to bear. Other views of burden consist of the economic, social, and spiritual burdens on a patient and family. Whether at the end of life or not, adult autonomous patients with competent decision-making capacity may refuse medical treatments at any time in life and may base their refusal on religious or cultural beliefs.

Withholding and Withdrawing Life-Sustaining Treatment

Withholding and withdrawing treatment is the foregoing of life-sustaining treatment that the patient does not desire because of a perceived disproportionate burden on the patient or family members or for other reasons. Notable legal decisions led to many questions regarding the right to die and the right to withhold and withdraw life-sustaining treatments. (See more about autonomy and patient self-determination in Chapter 2.) Specifically, there are three landmark legal cases about withholding and withdrawing treatments (Brannigan & Boss, 2001; Jonsen et al., 1998; U.S. District Court for the Middle District of Florida Tampa Division, 2005).

The case of Karen Ann Quinlan in 1975 led to her parents receiving the right to have Karen Ann's mechanical ventilator discontinued (In Supreme Court of New Jersey, 1976; Jonsen et al., 1998). Karen Ann, who was age 17, attended a party and ingested barbiturates and alcohol then lapsed into a coma. She was placed on a ventilator, and consequently her parents were involved in legal battles for several years to have Karen Ann removed from the ventilator. Finally, the U.S. Supreme Court district of New Jersey ordered the physicians to unplug the ventilator. Once unplugged, Karen Ann breathed without the help of the ventilator and continued living for 10 years. Her death was a result of pneumonia and its complications. The legacy of Quinlan's case included: (1) contributing to the definition of the term persistent vegetative state; (2) setting precedence for parents (or legal guardian) to have a right to choose; and (3) formation of ethics committees in most health care settings, and the creation and implementation of the advance directive.

Nancy Cruzan, age 25, was in a motor vehicle accident in 1983 when she sustained severe injuries that led to complete loss of consciousness and later persistent vegetative state with continuous artificial nutrition and hydration. Nancy's parents and co-guardians filed several cases to have her feeding tube removed on the basis that there was no chance for a return of cognitive capacity. The courts denied each case. Finally, after almost 8 years, the Supreme Court of Missouri granted the wishes for the discontinuance of her feeding tube. Nancy died on December 26, 1990, only 3 days after the court's final decision. The judge based the decision on a previous comment by Nancy, who had stated to the housekeeper that she would not want to live in that condition.

Of particular interest is Nancy Cruzan's grave marker. The family members, adapting their idea from a political cartoon about the case, had three dates etched on the grave marker; one date reflects her birth, one reflects her "death" at the time of the accident, and one reflects her actual physical death (Colby, 2004). The etching on the grave marker shows

Born July 20, 1957
Departed January 11, 1983
At Peace December 26, 1990

The grave marker is slightly confusing based on the meanings of the terms persistent vegetative state and brain death. Nancy's state of persistent vegetative state never equated to the definition of brain death, as the grave marker implies.

At the ruling of Nancy Cruzan, the judges of the Supreme Court of Missouri established three conditions for withdrawing treatments, including artificial nutrition and hydration: (1) the patient has a right to refuse medical treatment; (2) artificial feeding constitutes medical treatment; and (3) when the patient is mentally incompetent, each state must document clear and convincing evidence that the patient's desires had been for discontinuance of medical treatment (In Supreme Court of Missouri, 1990; Jonsen et al., 1998).

The third case is a more recent one: Terri Schiavo, on March 21, 2005 (refer to Box 12.7 for a synopsis of the case). There was a total of 21 legal suits, but the last few cases involved her husband Michael's request to have her feeding tube discontinued, which would stop the artificial nutrition and hydration. Terri's parents fought this request. By Florida law Michael Schiavo as a spouse and guardian had a legal right to serve as a surrogate decision maker for Terri Schiavo. Substituted judgment became the ethical and legal standard, with guardianship as the focal point, and a critical factor in decision making regarding Terri Schiavo's care and outcome in light of no advance directive. Surrogates must make unbiased substituted judgments based on an understanding of what patients would decide for themselves, and not the values of the surrogate. As the reader will see in the Box 12.7, the court obtained documented evidence from Michael Schiavo and other people that Terri had stated she did not want to live in a condition in which she would be a burden to anyone else. This evidence served as the basis for many of the court denials to the Schindlers.

Nurses need to give compassionate and excellent care to patients. No matter what the decision will be, family members and patients need to feel a sense of confidence that nurses will maintain moral sensitivity with a course of right action. In the *Code of Ethics for Nurses with Interpretive Statements*, Provision 1.3, the ANA (2001) has taken the position that nurses ethically support the provision of compassionate and dignified end-of-life care as long as nurses do not have the sole intention of ending a person's life. A special statement concerning the Terri Schiavo case was released to the press by the ANA on March 23, 2005, that upheld the decision for the right of the patient or surrogate to choose foregoing artificial nutrition and hydration. (Refer to this press release in Box 12.8.) The ANA updated its position statement on foregoing nutrition and hydration as of 2005, but this newer version is pending, and the 1992 position is the only one available. In the 1992 version the ANA included the statement that the patient or surrogates, along with guidance from the health care team, should make the

BOX 12.7: HIGHLIGHTS FROM THE FIELD: FACTS IN THE THERESA "TERRI" MARIE SCHIAVO CASE

In Theresa Marie Schindler Schiavo and Robert *ex relatione* [on behalf of] Mary Schindler (plaintiffs) v. Michael Schiavo, Judge George W. Greer, and The Hospice of the Florida SunCoast, Inc. (defendants) [Civ. Act. No. 8:05-CV-530-T-27TBM]

Major Final Court Rulings

March 21, 2005—A federal court order denied the injunction relief sought by the Schindlers, and the court refused to compel Theresa Schiavo to undergo surgery for re-insertion of the feeding tube.

March 24, 2005—The second federal court denied a motion by the Schindlers for a temporary restraining order against Michael Schiavo and the hospice regarding an alleged violation of Terri's right to artificial nutrition and hydration based on the Americans with Disabilities Act (ADA). The courts ruled that Terri's rights based on the ADA were not violated.

March 24, 2005—The U.S. Supreme Court denied the application by the Schindlers for a stay of enforcement of the Florida judgment.

March 25, 2005—The U.S. Court of Appeals 11th Court District denied an appeal by the Schindlers for a rehearing.

History and Facts of the Case

In 1990 Terri Schiavo's husband, Michael, found Terri unresponsive in the couple's home. Florida physicians affirmed that Terri, at age 26, had experienced prolonged cerebral hypoxia after an acute cardiac arrest. Physicians determined that a severely low potassium level, which was secondary to an eating disorder, brought on her cardiac arrest. Her condition was determined to be consistent with the diagnosis of persistent vegetative state because of the brain insult. In a 1992 medical malpractice suit against her fertility obstetrician, Terri Schiavo was awarded $750,000, which was placed in a trust fund for her future medical care. Michael Schiavo was awarded $300,000 (Cerminara & Goodman, 2005). In 1992, the Schindlers (Terri's parents) and Michael became alienated over the management of Terri's therapy and the awarded money to the Schiavos. In February 1993, the

(continued)

BOX 12.7: HIGHLIGHTS FROM THE FIELD: FACTS IN THE THERESA "TERRI" MARIE SCHIAVO CASE (continued)

Schindlers unsuccessfully demanded a share of Michael's money from the malpractice settlement.

The first lawsuit filed toward a family member was initiated in 1993 by the Schindlers in an attempt to have Michael removed as Terri's guardian, but the judge dismissed the case. Rehabilitation efforts continued for several years without success. Michael first petitioned the court in 1998 to have Terri's feeding tube removed and artificial nutrition and hydration discontinued, which was vehemently opposed by the Schindlers. Michael testified that before her 1990 event Terri told him, "If I ever have to be a burden to anybody, I don't want to live like that" (Lynne, 2005). There is court-documented testimony that Terri made similar statements about her wishes to other people. Judge Greer at the 6th Judicial Circuit Court in Clearwater, Florida, avowed that there was clear and convincing evidence of Terri's wishes.

From 1993 to 2005, there were 21 lawsuits and appeals. The majority of the lawsuits were filed after 1998, and most of them upheld Michael's initial contention that he was attempting to carry out Terri's wishes. During the appeals, Terri's feeding tube was removed on three occasions; on the first two occasions, the feeding tube was reinserted and artificial nutrition and hydration was resumed.

Thirteen days after the third and final removal of her feeding tube, Terri died on March 31, 2005, at the age of 41. The ethics and legality of removing the feeding tube were scrutinized until her death through lawsuits, political and media statements, actions of the U.S. Congress, and pleas from high-ranking public figures, such as Pope John Paul II.

From Cerminara, K., & Goodman, K. (2005). Key events in the case of Theresa Marie Schiavo. University of Miami Ethics. Retrieved April 20, 2007, from http://www6.miami.edu/ethics2/schiavo/timeline.htm; Lynne, D. (2005). Life and death tug of war—The whole Terri Schiavo story: 15-year saga of brain-injured woman no clear-cut, right-to-die case. *WorldNetDaily.* Retrieved April 20, 2007, from http://www.worldnetdaily.com/news/article.asp?ARTICLE_ID=43463

decision regarding withholding artificial nutrition and hydration, and if discontinued the nurse will continue to provide competent care even without artificial nutrition and hydration. This ANA (1992) position statement includes a clear distinction between regular food and water and artificial nutrition and hydration:

Artificial nutrition and hydration should be distinguished from the provision of food and water. Food and water provided to patients by mouth is the usual means of providing nutrition to patients. There are, however, situations in which nutrition can only be provided by artificial means. The provision of nourishment and hydration by artificial means (i.e., through tubes inserted into the stomach, intestine, or blood vessel) is qualitatively different from merely assisting with feeding. . . . Like all other interventions, artificially provided hydration and nutrition may or may not be justified. It should be instituted or foregone only after a process of reasoned decision [can be made that] focused upon estimates of benefits and burdens to the patient. (Para 2 & 4)

Alleviation of Pain and Suffering in the Dying Patient

Attempting to relieve pain and suffering is a primary responsibility for nurses and providers of care, which makes the whole arena of palliative care an ethical concern. Patients fear the consequences of disease; that is, they fear pain, suffering, and the process of dying. Patients mostly fear unnecessary suffering. Most of the time, it is the nurse who administers the pain medication and evaluates a patient's condition between and during pain injections. (See The Concept of Human Suffering of Dying Patients and Cultivating the Nursing Care sections in this chapter.)

Rule of Double Effect

According to Cavanaugh (2006), the **rule of double effect (RDE)** is based on an individual's reasoning that an act causing good and evil is permitted when the act meets the following conditions:

1. The act considered independently of its evil effect is not in itself wrong.
2. The agent intends the good and does not intend the evil either as an end or as a means.
3. The agent has proportionately grave reasons for acting, addressing his relevant obligations, comparing the consequences, and, considering the necessity of the evil, exercising due care to eliminate or mitigate it. (p. 36)

BOX 12.8: HIGHLIGHTS FROM THE FIELD: PARTIAL STATEMENTS

ANA's Press Release on March 23, 2005, on the Terri Schiavo Case

[The] . . . ANA has consistently upheld the right of patients, or if the patient is incapacitated, the right of the designated surrogate, to decide whether to submit to or continue medical treatment.

As nurses, we are ethically bound to assist our patients in maintaining control over their lives and to help them preserve their dignity. The ANA believes that it is the responsibility of nurses to facilitate informed decision-making for patients and families who are making choices about end-of-life care. The *Code of Ethics for Nurses* specifically outlines the nurse's obligation to protect the patient's right to self-determination and the role of a designated surrogate in situations where the patient lacks capacity. In this case, Terri Schiavo's physicians, over many years, have declared her to be in a "persistent vegetative state." Furthermore, there is evidence that Terri Schiavo expressed her wishes not to have her life artificially maintained under such circumstances. ANA believes the Congress and the president have acted inappropriately in this case. It is unfortunate that Terri Schiavo has now become the symbol of so many political agendas.

The positive outcome from this case is that it raises the public's awareness of the importance of discussing end-of-life issues with family members and underscores how an advance directive, a living will and/or durable power of attorney for health care, clarifies and provides evidence of the wishes of an individual regarding end-of-life decisions. . . .

Chosen statements from this press release were quoted from ANA (2005, March 23). ANA statement on the Terri Schiavo case. Statement attributed to B. Blakeney, ANA President. Retrieved April 20, 2007, from http://nursingworld.org/pressrel/2005/pr0323.htm

Some historians of philosophy and ethics have attributed the double-effect reasoning to St. Thomas Aquinas's writing about a person's self-defense in a homicide, and other historians have not. Today's double-effect reasoning is inclusive of actions that could cause harm, which is a foreseen but inevitable outcome. The use of the double-effect reasoning is an area of substantial concern when the health care professional sees some good in the action but also foresees with certainty that there will be bad in the action. Refer to Box 12.9 for an examination of an instance of each designated condition of the RDE.

The use of opiate or opiate-synthetic analgesics is a frequent source for the application of the RDE. Many bioethicists (e.g., Fohr, 1998; Marker, 2004) are convinced that opiates and other medications play only a minimal role in hastening death, even unintended death of patients. Instead, Fohr has emphasized that because of this "drug myth" regarding the RDE in terms of end-of-life issues, physical pain and suffering are vastly undertreated.

Even so, when the rule is applied, nurses need to be aware that the hastening of death must be a possible foreseen inevitable but unintended effect. In Provision 1.3 of the *Code of Ethics for Nurses with Interpretive Statements*, the ANA (2001) supports nurses in their attempts to relieve patients' pain, "even when those interventions entail risks of hastening death" (p. 8). Nurses may have conflicting moral values concerning the use of high doses of opiate-containing drugs, such as morphine sulfate or

BOX 12.9: HIGHLIGHTS FROM THE FIELD: EXAMPLES OF DOUBLE-EFFECT REASONING CONDITIONS

Condition 1:
An example of the first condition of the rule of RDE is applied when a nurse administers a medication that is, "apart from circumstances and intent, neither good [n]or bad" (Jonsen et al., 2006, p. 129).

Condition 2:
The second condition involves the *intention* of a nurse or physician. An example could be a nurse's intent is to relieve pain by administering a medication but not for the patient to be compromised in any way.

Condition 3:
The third condition, said another way, is that the bad effect cannot be the means to the intended good effect; for instance, a nurse cannot administer an opiate-containing or other type medication to produce the harmful bad effect, such as respiration cessation, in order to achieve the intended good effect, which in this case is pain relief.

even opiate-synthetic medications. In times when nurses feel uncomfortable, they need to explore their attitudes and opinions with their supervisor and, when appropriate, in clinical team meetings. Individually evaluating each patient and circumstance is essential.

Terminal Sedation

Terminal sedation (TS) is a phrase that did not appear in the literature until the 1990s, but even today, there is no clear consensus regarding its meaning (Marker, 2004). Whether or not physicians and nurses should use TS as a palliative treatment remains unanswered. McStay (2003) stated, "In 1997, the U.S. Supreme Court [Judges O'Connor, Ginsberg, &, in part, Breyer] tacitly endorsed terminal sedation as an alternative to physician-assisted suicide thus intensifying the 'right to die' controversy" (p. 45). TS remains ethically controversial because of the perception of its being a "last option" alternative and a compromise for physician-assisted suicide, but it seems to be moving toward a social and an ethical acceptance (McStay; Quill, 2001). Quill defined terminal sedation as "when a suffering patient is sedated to unconsciousness, usually through the ongoing administration of barbiturates or benzodiazepines. The patient then dies of dehydration, starvation, or some other intervening complication, as all other life-sustaining interventions are withheld" (p. 181).

When the word *terminal* is used, there is an understanding among the health care team and family members that the outcome, and possibly a desired outcome, is death (Sugarman, 2000). TS has been used in three situations: to provide relief of physical pain, to produce unconsciousness before withdrawing artificial food and fluids, and to relieve suffering (McStay, 2003). The practices of producing unconsciousness and withholding or withdrawing artificial food and fluids lead to an unresolved question of whether these two practices occur as a single action. Nurses must evaluate the moral, ethical, and legal implications of these practices, especially as a single action, and then understand the underlying principles for the practices.

The ANA (2001) did not directly address TS in the *Code of Ethics for Nurses with Interpretive Statements*, but did address nurses' obligations to give compassionate care at the end of life. According to the code, nurses are not to have the sole intent of ending a person's life. Nurses need to evaluate the intentions of physicians' orders to the extent possible and the intentions of their own actions when giving care to patients in questionable TS situations. Understanding the moral and ethical implications will guide nurses in their individualized direction. The judges of the U.S. Supreme Court may have tacitly endorsed TS, but there is a question as to its legal acceptance, and great controversy continues over whether TS is a euthanasia practice.

Physician-Assisted Suicide

Society has reacted with everything from moral outrage to social acceptance with regard to physician-assisted suicide. Sugarman (2000) defined **physician-assisted suicide** as "the act of providing a lethal dose of medication for the patient to self-administer" (p. 213). However according to Kopala and Kennedy (1998), the act must meet three conditions in accordance with the ANA insofar as calling the act physician-assisted suicide:

1. You (the nurse) must know the person intends to end his or her life.
2. You (the nurse) must make the means to commit suicide available to the person.
3. The person must then end his or her own life. (p. 19)

The only state in the United States to legally allow physician-assisted suicide today is Oregon, which passed the Death with Dignity Act in 1994. With certain restrictions, patients who are near death may obtain prescriptions to end their lives in a dignified way (Ladd et al., 2002).

During a 20-year dispute over euthanasia practices, under certain guidelines, physicians could practice euthanasia in the Netherlands. In February 2002, the Dutch passed a law that permitted voluntary euthanasia and physician-assisted suicide. In the discussions of euthanasia in the United States, the scope has been limited to only physician-assisted suicide, whereas in the Netherlands, the discussion has a much wider perspective.

Special guidelines relating to the Death with Dignity Act in Oregon were written in 1995 by the Oregon Nurses Association for nurses who care for patients who choose physician-assisted suicide (as cited in Ladd et al., 2002; Kopala & Kennedy, 1998). The guidelines include maintaining support, comfort, and confidentiality; discussing end-of-life options with the patient and family; and being present for the patient's self-administration of medications and during the death. Nurses may not inject the medications themselves, breach confidentiality, subject others to any type of judgmental comments or statements about the patient, or refuse to provide care to the patient. It is critical to note that the ANA (2001), in the *Code of Ethics for Nurses with Interpretive Statements*, plainly stated that nurses are not to act with the sole intent of ending a person's life.

Rational Suicide

The idea of saving people vs. allowing people to die or commit suicide is at the very essence of one of the most debated and controversial dilemmas today. As long as there is difficulty in determining rationality in suicide, this controversy will remain. Moral progress in nursing necessitates that nurses ponder these ethical uncertainties . . . with patients who are contemplating rational suicide. Meanwhile, nurses should never be caught off-guard in relation to the ethical and political changes in health care for fear of losing their power and voice.

—RICH & BUTTS, *JOURNAL OF ADVANCED NURSING*, 2004, P. 277

Rational suicide is a self-slaying based on reasoned choice and categorized as voluntary active euthanasia. Siegel (1986) stated that the person who is contemplating rational suicide has a realistic assessment of life circumstances, is free from severe emotional distress, and has a motivation that would seem understandable to most uninvolved people in the person's community.

To morally accept a person's act of committing rational suicide seems outrageous to most people, and the very thought of it weighs heavily on their hearts, even today. No matter what people think morally about suicide, an enormous public health crisis exists because worldwide an estimated 1 million suicides occur every year, or 1 every 40 seconds (WHO, 2005). In the United States, there were more than 30,000 suicides in 2001 (Centers for Disease Control [CDC], 2006).

Should people criticize others for making a choice of rational suicide? More and more people view rational suicide as a rational alternative to life, especially when faced with unbearable pain, suffering, or loneliness (O'Rourke, 2002). However, the terms *rational* and *suicide* seem to contradict each other (Engelhart, 1986; Finnerty, 1987). David Peretz (as cited in O'Rourke, 2002), a noted psychiatrist and suicidologist, gave his interpretation of why rational suicides seem to be occurring and more accepted in society when he stated:

Under the unprecedented stress of recent decades, denial mechanisms are breaking down and we have become increasingly vulnerable to the threats of intensely painful feelings of anxiety, fear, panic, rage, guilt, shame, grief, longing and helplessness. In order to avoid being overwhelmed, we seek new ways to adapt. . . . I believe that the growing concern with a good death, death with dignity and the right-to-die reflect this search—If our deepest known fear is of being destroyed, and we cannot deal with that fear, we take refuge in planning death and rational suicide. We find comfort in the illusion, "It will not be done to me—I will do it myself." (pp. 206–207)

Peretz believes that this motivation is unethical, dangerous, and harmful because it leads a person to a false sense of omnipotence. Two other elements may contribute to rational suicide but are also unrealistic and unethical, according to Peretz (as cited in O'Rourke, 2002). One element is that people who are advocates of rational suicide believe strongly that personal autonomy is the goal of human life, and therefore, if a person cannot have complete personal autonomy, life is not worth living. The other element is an act of self-destruction, which has a potential to mythologize rational suicide. Peretz stated that by mythologizing an object, it is given false power. Advocates of rational suicide promote self-destruction as a way to realize a false sense of freedom from serious human problems, such as physical suffering, loneliness, or frailty.

For nurses to endorse any suicide seems contradictory to good practice, because traditionally nurses and mental health professionals have intervened to prevent suicide. Many times cultural, religious, and personal beliefs guide nurses in how they respond to patients who are thinking about suicide. Does a nurse have a right to try to stop a person from committing rational suicide; in other words, to act in the best interest of a patient? Or is a nurse supposed to support a person's autonomous decision to commit rational suicide, even when that decision is morally and religiously incompatible with the nurse's perspective? If the nurse knows of the plan for rational suicide, would care toward that patient be obligatory? In other words, would nurses be obligated to render care despite their own value conflicts? What actions could the nurse take at this point?

According to Rich and Butts (2004), no clear answers exist to this ethical dilemma but interventions become unique to each situation. Interventions may include everything from providing information regarding the Hemlock Society to answering questions about lethal injections. Nurses need to consider autonomy and beneficence when deciding on interventions for persons who are planning rational suicide. Nurses are closely involved with more end-of-life ethics as the issue of voluntary active euthanasia is becoming increasingly prevalent.

Uncertain Moral Ground for Nurses

Nurses first must sort out their own feelings about euthanasia and dying before they provide appropriate moral guidance and direction to patients and families. The sights, sounds, and smells of death can be an emotionally draining experience for nurses. At the same time, nurses must meet the needs of patients and families. Every day nurses face disturbing moral conflicts and distress, such as whether they should keep giving a continuous morphine sulfate infusion to a dying patient for comfort in light of the risk of depressed respirations or whether they should assist in withdrawing or withholding artificial nutrition and fluids or other life-sustaining interventions. When nurses experience personal value and professional moral suffering and distress, they may find themselves on uncertain moral ground.

NANDA International (2007) accepted and published a new nursing diagnosis *Moral Distress* and a revision to the nursing diagnosis *Decisional Conflict* to include ethical issues. Kopala and Burkhart proposed this information in their article in 2005. Kopala and Burkhart proposed this information as part of the taxonomy because NANDA had not provided a standardized method for nurses to document and express the interventions and rationales for ethical issues or moral distress. (See Chapter 2 for more detailed information on these topics.) These authors made a case that many interventions exist within the Nursing Interventions Classification (NIC) that nurses can implement regarding ethical issues and moral distress (Dochterman & Bulechek, 2004). Nursing Outcomes Classification (NOC) is a universal system of labeled outcomes that nurses strive to achieve in particular diagnoses and interventions (Moorhead, Johnson, & Maas, 2004). Nurses can use NOC outcomes to complement NANDA and NIC.

The NANDA diagnosis *Moral Distress* and ethical issues added under the diagnosis *Decisional Conflict* will be ideal for use by nurses caring for terminally ill or dying patients. With the emphasis on evidence-based practice today, nursing researchers and clinicians can begin to collect data and document effectiveness of these new topics, not only with terminally ill patients but in all patient situations. The substance involved in decision making of ethical issues and the experience of moral distress needs documenting so as not to lose the richness of the narratives and the degree to which these diagnoses are used.

Barbara Couden (2002), a registered nurse, wrote a beautiful and poignant description of her emotional experiences with loss and death in intensive care. She stated that at times she just wanted to run (see Box 12.10). She portrayed her experiences of physical and emotional exhaustion; periods of fatigue, guilt, and sometimes relief when death finally came; the smell of death on her clothes and wetness on her face from crying families pressing against her face; tearfulness and sadness; and her own intense feelings of grief and loss. Couden experienced immeasurable unexpressed grief and unresolved personal losses, along with the losses of her patients, until she had no emotions left to express toward her patients and no energy left to spend on them.

BOX 12.10: HIGHLIGHTS FROM THE FIELD: *SOMETIMES I WANT TO RUN*

From the words of Barbara A. Couden . . .

Sometimes I want to run. It's work not to recoil from the rawness of life in those rooms. It is probably easier to behave as a starchy, mechanical nurse who staves off discomfort with a cheerful cliché. However, people deserve to experience hospitalization, grief, or even dying at its very best. To provide less isn't care at all. So I give my open heart and plunge into their circumstances, even though really I'm no one special to them—just there by default. In return, they honor me with the privilege of sharing their pain, struggle, and the richness of life, death, and love. In some way, we each live on in the other's memory: endeared by shared suffering, strivings to nurture hope, and our individual attempts to love. So there are nights that I reflect on my heartfelt efforts, smell death on my clothes, and feel dampness where the tears of grieving loved ones have pressed against my face. Sometimes it seems that my role as a nurse is to absorb the feelings of others: pain, sadness, and loss. I'm sitting up in bed tonight, waiting for mine to dissipate.

Quote from Couden, B. A. (2002). "Sometimes I want to run": A nurse reflects on loss in the intensive care unit. *Journal of Loss and Trauma, 7*(1), pp. 41–42.

After she sought ways to deal with her crisis, she discovered three important aspects of her emotional work. First, she has had to face her own grief and loss, which includes continuous expressions of loss through tears and discussions. Second, she had to find ways to deal with her own intense feelings of grief and loss before she "could dare to give them [her feelings] utterance" (p. 42). She cries and expresses her own grief with patients and, as she does, the environment becomes a unique environment for her and her patients as they exchange their emotions. She finds ways to pamper herself. Her third aspect of emotional work involves her mannerisms toward patients and feeling good about the way she responds to her patients. Couden confirmed her feelings about the way she responds to her patients when she saw her therapist emotionally moved by her own stories.

Relationships with patients are at the heart of nursing ethics. Wright (2006) emphasized that nursing at its best is good for the souls of the patient and nurse, and stated, "For the heart is the seat of the soul, and when we nurse another, we nurse a soul too. Soulful work requires soulful individuals and communities" (p. 23). Without this soulful work, patients will feel disconnected. Maeve (1998) stated that relationships can become quite complex because of the accompanied interrelational experiences and emotions.

Most nurses share in patients' emotional experiences of pain, suffering, and joy and do not just give superficial care and then forget about it. The care that nurses provide to their dying patients becomes an essential component of their own lives, and the stories that they remember about their patients become interwoven into their own life stories. Maeve (1998) studied nine nurses who worked with suffering and dying patients. As Maeve listened to the nurses' stories, she realized that moral issues about practice and relationships were dominant where suffering and dying patients were concerned.

Three major themes were identified from the study (Maeve, 1998). One was "tempering involvement," which meant that nurses had a dilemma or conflict about becoming involved: how much involvement, setting limits, setting boundaries to distinguish their lives from their patients' lives, and becoming embodied, such as when nurses may actually live in the experience with their patients (p. 1138). The second theme was "doing the right thing/the good thing," which involved education, experience, courage, moral dilemmas, and past regrets for a few of their performances or decisions with patients (p. 1139). "Cleaning up" was the third theme that emerged, and this theme marked the end of the involvement with the patient (p. 1140). During this time, the nurse needs to reflect on experiences and clean up grief.

In one Japanese study of 160 nurses, Konishi, Davis, and Aiba (2002) studied withdrawal of artificial food and fluid from terminally ill patients. The majority of the nurses supported this act only under two conditions: if the patient requested withdrawal of artificial food and fluids and if the act relieved the patient's suffering. Nurses agreed that comfort for the patient was of great concern. One nurse in the study stated: "[Artificial food and fluid] AFF only prolongs the patient's suffering. When withdrawn, the patient showed peace on the face. I have seen such patients so many times" (Konishi et al., p. 14). In the same study, another nurse who was experiencing moral conflict with a decision to withdraw artificial food and fluid stated: "Withdrawal is killing and cruel. I feel guilty" (Konishi et al., p. 14).

Other end-of-life issues may be reasons for moral conflicts, as well. Georges and Grypdonck (2002) conducted a literature review on the topic of ethical issues in terms of how nurses perceive their care to dying patients. There has been a deficiency of systematic research on this topic specific to nurses' moral conflicts and distress. However, Georges and Grypdonck outlined some of the moral dilemmas that nurses perceive as particularly critical to end-of-life care. Some of the moral problems of nurses found in the literature were:

- Communicating truthfully with patients about death because they were fearful of destroying all hope in the patient and family
- Managing pain symptoms because of fear of hastening death
- Feeling forced to collaborate with other health team members about medical treatments that in the nurses' opinion are futile or too burdensome
- Feeling insecure and not adequately informed about reasons for treatment
- Trying to maintain their own moral integrity throughout relationships with patients, families, and co-workers because of feeling that they are forced to betray their own moral values

Although a nurse has an obligation to provide compassionate and palliative care, the nurse has a right to withdraw from treating and caring for a dying patient as long as another nurse has assumed that care. When care is such that the nurse perceives it as violating personal and professional morality and values, the professional nurse must pursue alternative approaches to care.

Cultivating the Nursing Care

Nursing care for dying patients needs to be cultivated over time. New nurses and nurses not routinely caring for dying patients are not automatically skilled in this type of care. Nurses must acquire expertise and skills in end-of-life care as any other area of practice. Compassion and genuine care are critical components to end-of-life nursing care.

The Compassionate Nurse with a Dying Patient

Nurses find themselves on uncertain moral ground when attempting to sustain dying patients, but they must be honest with patients and give sufficient information concerning advance directives and medical treatment options. However, the most important aspect is to offer support to dying patients by relating to their fear of death and by alleviating pain and suffering. Family members need to support their loved one and often learn support strategies from talking with nurses and observing how nurses interact with the patient. When dying patients experience the compassionate acts of nurses and family members, death can be a positive experience for them. Nurses must remember that the little things are what make a big difference in the care of dying patients. Medical treatments aimed at relieving pain and suffering can coexist with palliative care, and nurses' compassionate acts are essential to this cohesive coexistence (Ciccarello, 2003). One particular compassionate act is for nurses to teach individuals and patients in community and hospital settings about treatment decisions at the end of life, such as life-sustaining treatments and palliative care with symptom management. Nurses can teach patients about advance directives and surrogate decision making. The case of Terri Schiavo could possibly have a positive influence on people's need for understanding and having advance directives. Refer to Box 12.11 for the essential aspects from the ANA *Code of Ethics for Nurses with Interpretive Statements* that nurses need to consider when caring for dying patients and their families.

Physical and Emotional Pain Management

Understanding and actually upholding aggressive pain management precepts may be the most challenging moral dilemma that nurses face when caring for dying patients. The lack of understanding regarding the issues and fears of patient addiction or death causes nurses and physicians to undertreat pain and suffering in many cases. Miller, Miller, and Jolley (2001) emphasized the importance for nurses to apply three basic precepts when controlling pain: (1) nurses and physicians need to follow the WHO's "pain ladder" protocol for palliative pain management (see next section); (2) nurses and physicians need to treat pain early because once out of control, pain is more difficult to treat; and (3) nurses and physicians need to explain to terminally ill patients that addiction should not be feared and dying patients rarely develop an addiction to properly administered pain medications.

Types of Pain

Miller et al. (2001) have described two major types of pain: nociceptive and neuropathic. Nociceptive pain involving tissue damage occurs with two types of pain: somatic (musculoskeletal pain) and visceral (organ pain—the most common type of pain). Once nurses have performed a thorough pain assessment, the **WHO's pain ladder** (2007b) is an excellent approach for providers of care. (See the Web Ethics box in this chapter for Web site information and an excellent diagram of the ladder approach.) The WHO's pain ladder is a step-by-step approach to managing pain with palliative care of patients. At the first sign of a patient's pain, as a first step, nurses should administer oral nonopiate medications, given that a primary provider has ordered pain relievers. The next progressive step involves use of mild opiates such as codeine. Then the last step involves use of strong opiates such as morphine sulfate.

Nurses and physicians can use a variety of other pain medications for neuropathic pain, which is pain described as either dysesthesias (burning or electrical sensations) or lancinating pain (shooting, stabbing, or knifelike pain) (Miller et al., 2001). Pain medications and treatment options for these types of pain include antidepressants, anticonvulsants, sedatives, nerve blocks, epidural catheters, and others.

Because pain and symptom control are complex and ethically challenging areas that nurses face in the care of dying patients, nurses need to recognize and evaluate their own moral conflicts and the impact of these conflicts on the care of their patients. A major ethical issue that nurses must evaluate is their giving high-dose pain medication to dying patients to alleviate suffering when the medication could unintentionally hasten death. Nurses need to be aware of the moral conflicts that patients and family members experience when it comes to the impact of the relief of pain and suffering during end times. Sharing in each patient's experience of pain and emotional suffering will provide a better experience for nurses and their patients during the death process.

Core Principles for End-of-Life Care

Benner, Kerchner, Corless, and Davies (2003) delineated core principles for end-of-life nursing care, which are based on a central thought of "death as a human passage" (p. 558). The core ethical principles reflect a summary of the work of Benner et al. on the Expert Panel on End-of-Life Care at the American Academy of Nursing. The group's core principles are ethical approaches that nurses can apply when caring for dying patients. The core principles are as follows:

- Because death is an essential human passage, nurses must acknowledge and respect the passage. Nurses, significant others, and patients themselves have an impact on how that passage occurs.
- Always consider if patients actually desire an optimal level of pain management and sedation to relieve pain and suffering and respect their wishes. Patients may wish for a balance between alertness and level of comfort so that they can chat and feel the presence of others.
- Palliative care should be comprehensive and flexible for pain and symptom management. Nurses should provide treatments to enhance quality of life.
- Avoid offering treatment options or any other options that are unrealistic. Dying patients are very limited as to their choices and options and do not need to be offered treatment options that do not have any beneficial effects.

- Be respectful of the time that patients and family members need for coming to terms with the realization of death. Each person and family member is unique.
- Be respectful of time that is needed for family members or significant others to grieve, to come to terms with their loved one's death, and for their own spiritual practices.
- Give attentive end-of-life care to dying patients so that the ones who are grieving can witness the nurse's impact on the facilitation of human passage. The sight of well-cared-for dying loved ones promotes emotional and physical well-being among the grieving family members and significant others.
- Avoid universal prescriptions and expectations for dying patients. Every death and death narrative is unique.

Spiegel (1993) captured the importance of following these core principles in end-of-life care. The following passage describes how people feel about unfinished business and caring for one another during the dying process.

There is such an absoluteness to death. Harsh words cannot be taken back. Promises unfulfilled can never be completed. One cannot even say goodbye. Facing the absoluteness of death can be a tremendous stimulus to life. If it is important, do it now. . . . Say what you mean to say. Settle old grievances. Accomplish what needs doing, sooner rather than later. . . . Death is so overwhelming that it is rather humbling. There seems to be so little one can do about it. Strangely enough, we always resort to the same comfort: our sense of caring about one another. In some sense, we huddle together. Our bond of caring forms a kind of talisman against the power of death. Although, ultimately, each of us has to face death alone, it is a tremendous relief to do some of the work with someone else. A good hug or some shared tears may not save a life, but it will make you feel more alive. (pp. 144–145)

Spiritual Considerations

Spirituality is one of the most important aspects of end-of-life nursing care, but often nurses feel helpless when it comes to providing the right type of spiritual care for their patients. Meaningful experiences, especially during end-of-life times, are important for nurses in their care of patients because nurses feel that they touch patients' lives in some way through generous or compassionate acts. One such way may be the facilitation of spirituality. Spirituality has become more essential to nursing care since it has been included in the definition of palliative care, yet many people in the United States and Europe fall outside of a faith or religious network (Walter, 2003). Most Americans believe that end-of-life spiritual care is an important part of the dying process, and at the same time, they believe that nurses and others do not effectively provide spiritual care.

Today, the Joint Commission on Accreditation of Healthcare Organizations (JCAHO, 2007) mandates that a spiritual assessment be conducted for each hospitalized patient. Furthermore, in the International Council of Nurses (ICN, 2006) *Code of Ethics for Nurses*, Element 1, and the ANA (2001) *Code of Ethics for Nurses with Interpretative Statements*, Provision 1.3, phrases are included relating to the importance of nurses' promoting an environment that enables patient spirituality.

In her book, *Spiritual Care: Nursing Theory, Research, and Practice*, Taylor (2002) explored spirituality in nursing and portrayed spirituality as a deeply personal and integral part of a person's life. Several definitions of spirituality exist in nursing (see, e.g., Dossey & Guzzetta, 2000; as cited in Taylor, 2002; Narayanasamy, 1999). Spirituality as defined by Dossey and Guzzetta is "a unifying force of a person; the essence of being that permeates all of life and is manifested in one's being, knowing, and doing; the interconnectedness with self, others, nature, and God/Life Force/Absolute/Transcendent" (p. 7).

In a notable study, Stephenson and Draucker (2003) explored spirituality by conducting interviews with hospice patients. Participants in the study identified what they thought were characteristics that health care workers should display in spiritual care. They identified these characteristics as "good" qualities of humankind, which are "being kind, living the life of a good Christian, living the Golden Rule, and being attentive to those in need" (p. 57). Stephenson and Draucker concluded that intently listening to patients' stories and displaying the good qualities of humankind are ways that nurses and other health care professionals need to approach spiritual care with dying patients.

The studies of Taylor (2003) and Stephenson and Draucker (2003) have a few similarities in their findings about the spiritual needs of dying patients. Taylor studied the expectations of patients and family members regarding spiritual needs and care from nurses. An in-depth tape-recorded interview was conducted with 28 adult patients with cancer and their family caregivers. Six categories, and consequently specific nursing interventions, are listed in the priority of responses; they are "kindness and respect," "talking and listening," "prayer," "connecting," "quality temporal nursing care," and "mobilizing religious or spiritual resources" (Taylor, p. 588).

The category with the most responses was kindness and respect, and a few responses regarding this theme included "just be nice," "giving loving care," and "a smile does a lot" (Taylor, 2003, pp. 587–588). For the next category, talking and listening, the responses varied widely because some patients enjoyed the superficial chatter, whereas others, especially African Americans, were pleased about nurses sharing their own deep religious experiences as comforting measures. Another category, prayer and the nurse's offering to pray with patients, varied widely in responses according to individualized beliefs. The category of connecting relates to certain characteristics, such as nurses being authentic and genuine, having physical presence, and having symmetry with patients. Symmetry with patients means that patients want to have a sense of working with nurses in a notion of friendship. Giving quality temporal nursing care, another category, relates to the mechanisms that support the spirit of the person, such as keeping the room clean and not allowing the patient to suffer. The last category is mobilizing religious or spiritual resources. Nurses can facilitate mobilization by consulting chaplains, having Bibles in the room, and having other religious materials available as needed.

There are no completely "right" ways to help a person die because dying processes are individual experiences (Benner et al., 2003). Nursing care depends on each situation. Stories told by family members and dying patients are particularly significant to the understanding of death and are central to paying proper tribute to human passage. As Benner et al. pointed out, "death forever changes the world of those who experience the loss of the person dying" (p. 558). The involvement of nurses in decisions about death becomes more complex every day as more technology emerges in the dying process. Family members and patients must be involved with all ethical decisions.

Web Ethics

Organizations to Help Patients and Families

End of Life Compassion and Choices
    http://www.compassionandchoices.org/aboutus/themovement.php

Caring Connections
    http://www.caringinfo.org

Spiritual Care Program
    http://spcare.org

Organizations for Nurses

National Hospice and Palliative Care Organization
    http://www.nhpco.org

End-of-Life Care
    http://www.aacn.nche.edu/elnec

Hospice and Palliative Nurses Association
    http://www.hpna.org

WHO's Pain Ladder
    http://www.who.int/cancer/palliative/painladder/en/

Summary

In this chapter, the author discussed the ethical approaches to end-of-life nursing care. Numerous terms were defined and concepts were explained.

The first major section of the chapter offers a detailed discussion of the questions "What is death?" and "Can a person expect an ideal or good death?" The concepts of death anxiety and the imaginative dramatic rehearsal were introduced in this section. In this same section, the author details the concept of human suffering as it relates to dying patients and their families. Suffering is defined as something that emerges in all human beings and every living thing, and because of the multi-dimensional aspects of humans, suffering affects every part of people's lives—physical, mental, emotional, social, and spiritual. In this section, the author highlighted the moral obligation that nurses have regarding the relief and prevention of human suffering in dying patients.

Continuing in that same section is the introduction of euthanasia with definitions of each type of euthanasia—active euthanasia, passive euthanasia, voluntary euthanasia, nonvoluntary euthanasia, involuntary euthanasia, assisted suicide, and suicide. The UDDA (President's Commission..., 1981) definition of death is the "irreversible cessation of circulatory and respiratory functions *or* irreversible cessation of all functions of the entire brain, including the brain stem" (p. 73). Four conceptions of death emerged after the 1981 definition of death: traditional death, whole-brain death, higher-brain death, and personhood death.

The next major section consists of a presentation of each type of advance directive: living will, medical care directive, and durable power of attorney. Following advance directives is another major section on deciding for others, which consists of the perspective of the proxy in the case of an incompetent patient. The standards used in deciding for others include the substituted judgment standard, pure autonomy standard, principle of autonomy extended, and best interest standard.

The next major section is on medical futility and issues involved with patients whose physicians have deemed treatments as futile. The author offers questions for the reader to ponder, such as, "How far does one go with patient autonomy?" and "Would the health care system's financial burden be a factor for setting limits on patient autonomy (and surrogate autonomy) in your personal opinion or as a societal stance?"

In the next major section, the author defined palliative care according to the World Health Organization's definition. Included in this section are concepts such as a contrast between full codes, called DNR codes, and "slow codes," a phenomenon not recognized as legal; the right to die and the right to refuse treatment; withholding and withdrawing life-sustaining treatment; alleviation of pain and suffering in dying patients; and the rule of double effect. Highlighted in the section is a presentation of three landmark cases—Karen Ann Quinlan, Nancy Cruzan, and Terri Schiavo—that brought recognition to the concept of patient (or surrogate) self-determination as related to withholding and withdrawing life-sustaining treatment such as artificial nutrition and hydration and mechanical ventilation.

The next three major sections include discussions of terminal sedation, physician-assisted suicide, and rational suicide. Uncertain moral ground for nurses is the next big section; the author discussed the moral conflicts and distress that nurses experience when making ethical decisions that affect others' lives.

The last major section is cultivating the nursing care. Included in this section is a highlight of the compassionate nurse with a dying patient, and subsections regarding physical and emotional pain management, types of pain, and the WHO's pain ladder; core principles for the end-of-life care as created by Benner, Kerchner, Corless, and Davies in 2003; and spiritual considerations. At the closing of the nursing care section is a presentation of essential aspects of the ANA *Code of Ethics for Nurses with Interpretive Statements* (2001) that relate to care of dying patients and their families. Key concepts of nursing care at the end of life include:

- Nurses need to recognize and evaluate their own moral conflicts and come to recognize their own mortality before they can give genuine end-of-life care.
- Death and dying can have positive aspects for patients and families, especially if nurses give compassionate care by offering little ways to assist patients and showing genuine concern.
- Compassionate nursing care is aimed at relieving pain and suffering when patients and family members are in agreement.
- Nurses need to realize that they are obligated to provide pain management (coordinated with desires of family members and the patient) and alleviate suffering in dying patients even when giving that medication may cause death. This concept is called the rule of double effect.
- Nurses must give spiritual care to dying patients by performing spiritual assessments and appropriate interventions. Giving spiritual care is a standard designated by the Joint Commission on Accreditation of Healthcare Organizations.

CASE STUDY: END OF LIFE WITH MARY LOU WARNING

Tom Warning, the oldest son, took his mother, Mary Lou Warning, a 73-year-old widow, to the emergency department (ED) after he found her disoriented and confused. He was going to her house to take her refilled prescriptions on his way home from work. The ED physician and her primary provider agreed that they could not rule out a stroke and therefore wanted to admit her for "observation only." Tom thought, "This seems minor enough!" Tom went home to rest for the night once he signed the papers for his mother's admission. She went to a regular room. During the night, alone in her room, her stroke extended, and, when the registered nurse made one of her visits, she found Ms. Warning breathing but unresponsive to commands and pain. She immediately called the ED physician to check her and asked another nurse to call her primary physician and her son. Ms. Warning had five sons and one daughter, all of whom lived out of town except for Tom.

An occlusive stroke was the diagnosis after CT and MRI scans. Treatment was probably not going to be helpful because of the degree of damage. The ED and primary physicians prepared to send her to the intensive care unit (ICU) and prepared themselves for how they were going to approach Tom. The primary physician informed Tom that she might not live, but, if she did, he and his siblings had to make some decisions about whether or not they wanted her to be on a mechanical ventilator, if it came to that decision. He also told Tom that currently she was in an unconscious state, which could mean an indefinite existence, and they needed to think about what types of treatment, if any, they wanted for her. The physician thoroughly explained the treatment options and the siblings' options to withdraw or withhold treatment for their mother. He explained to Tom that her prognosis was poor and that, if she lived, she probably would never regain consciousness.

Meanwhile, Tom frantically called all of his siblings to tell them to "come fast" and that decisions needed to be made "now" regarding their mother's end-of-life care. Tom was pacing back and forth with distress and fear because no one in his family had ever discussed these issues among themselves or with his mother. When all of the siblings arrived the next day, they made a decision for the physician to withdraw all medications and intravenous fluids and requested no treatments of any kind. The physician wrote a DNR order on Ms. Warning's chart.

(continues)

CASE STUDY: END OF LIFE WITH MARY LOU WARNING (continued)

Case Study Questions

Apply a nursing theory, approach, or principle to justify your answers and decisions in this case study.

1. You are the nurse who is caring for Ms. Warning in the ICU. Before bedtime, you keep a daily journal of all of your experiences. The day you had to discontinue all of her treatments, you went home to reflect and write down the day's event and your feelings in an effort to express pent-up emotions concerning the day. Imagine becoming part of this experience, then dramatically rehearse this whole event as if you were that nurse, experiencing the event, seeing the sights and sounds, and feeling the intense emotions. Please complete this journaling process as an exercise.

2. What is the role that medical futility plays in this situation and in the family's decision?

3. The primary physician mentioned to Tom that Ms. Warning could need a mechanical ventilator at some point. Clarify this statement by explaining the difference in the levels of care (nonmechanical ventilation care and mechanical ventilation dependent care) and the significance of brain death. Discuss nursing ethical implications involved with each level.

4. What ethical role could you as a nurse take to help support Tom and his siblings?

5. How could an advance directive have helped Tom's distressed state of mind when the physician presented him with "options"? Which one of the advance directives would have been the most suitable in Ms. Warning's case? Please explain.

6. What type of nursing care does Ms. Warning need to receive? In answering this question, explore the ethical issues that you as a nurse must face. Please explain your answer.

7. In Ms. Warning's case, the siblings came to a unified decision. However, if the siblings had not come to a consensus about a course of action for their mother, there could have been disagreement and arguing between them. Consider the

(continues)

CASE STUDY: END OF LIFE WITH MARY LOU WARNING (continued)

nature of "equal voice" for each of the siblings when discussing how they might view the equality of their input compared with the other siblings. If they could agree on one spokesperson for them, what approach might they take to channel their equal voice to one sibling spokesperson? Do you think the siblings would consider appointing the eldest son, Tom, to be the spokesperson to represent them? Please discuss this issue.

8. Which principle serves as the basis for surrogate decision making in Ms. Warning's case? Please define this principle and discuss why this particular principle is best for this particular patient.

References

Albom, M. (1997). *Tuesdays with Morrie: An old man, a young man, and life's greatest lesson.* New York: Random House—Broadway Books.

American Nurses Association. (1992). Ethics and human rights position statements: Foregoing nutrition and hydration. Retrieved April 20, 2007, from http://nursingworld.org/readroom/position/ethics/etnutr.htm

American Nurses Association. (2001). *Code of ethics for nurses with interpretive statements.* Silver Spring, MD: Author.

American Nurses Association. (2005). ANA statement on the Terri Schiavo case. Statement attributed to Barbara A. Blakeney, MSN, RN, President. Retrieved April 20, 2007, from http://nursingworld.org/pressrel/2005/pr0323.htm

Arman, M., & Rehnsfeldt, A. (2003). The hidden suffering among breast cancer patients: A qualitative metasynthesis. *Qualitative Health Research, 13*(4), 510–527.

Australian Museum. (2007). Death: The last taboo. What is death? Retrieved April 10, 2007, from http://deathonline.net/what_is/

Battin, M. P. (1994). *The least worst death: Essays in bioethics on the end of life.* New York: Oxford University Press.

Beauchamp, T. L., & Childress, J. F. (2001). *Principles of biomedical ethics* (5th ed.). New York: Oxford University Press.

Benjamin, M. (2003). Pragmatism and the determination of death. In G. McGee (Ed.), *Pragmatic bioethics* (2nd ed., pp. 193-206). London: Bradford Book, MIT.

Benner, P., Kerchner, S., Corless, I. B., & Davies, B. (2003). Attending death as a human passage: Core nursing principles for end-of-life care. *American Journal of Critical Care, 12*(6), 558–561.

Biggar, N. (2006, September 9). Death and the doctor. *Irish Times* (Dublin), Weekend section, p. 13. Retrieved April 10, 2007, from ProQuest database.

Bondeson, J. (2001). *Buried alive: The terrifying history of our most primal fear.* New York: W. W. Norton.

Brannigan, M. C., & Boss, J. A. (2001). *Healthcare ethics in a diverse society.* Mountain View, CA: Mayfield.

Brogan, G. (2006). Inventing the good death. *Registered Nurse: Journal of Patient Advocacy, 102*(7), 10–14.

Buchanan, A. E., & Brock, D. W. (1990). *Deciding for others: The ethics of surrogate decision making.* New York: Cambridge University Press.

Cassell, E. J. (2004). *The nature of suffering and the goals of medicine* (2nd ed.). New York: Oxford University Press.

Cavanaugh, T. A. (2006). *Double-effect reasoning: Doing good and avoiding evil.* Oxford, UK: Clarendon Press.

Centers for Disease Control and Prevention. (2006). National Center for Injury Prevention and Control. Suicide: Fact sheet. Suicide in the United States. Retrieved April 10, 2007, from http://www.cdc.gov/ncipc/factsheets/suifacts.htm

Cerminara, K., & Goodman, K. (2005). Key events in the case of Theresa Marie Schiavo. University of Miami Ethics. Retrieved April 20, 2007, from http://www6.miami.edu/ethics2/schiavo/timeline.htm

Ciccarello, G. P. (2003). Strategies to improve end-of-life care in the intensive care unit. *Dimensions of Critical Care Nursing, 22*(5), 216–222.

Colby, B. (2004). The legacy of Nancy Cruzan. Retrieved August 11, 2007, from the University of Virginia Web site at http://www.healthsystem.virginia.edu/internet/him/nancycruzan.cfm

Connelly, R. (2003). Living with death: The meaning of acceptance. *Journal of Humanistic Psychology, 43*(1), 45–63.

Couden, B. A. (2002). "Sometimes I want to run": A nurse reflects on loss in the intensive care unit. *Journal of Loss and Trauma, 7*(1), 35–45.

Devettere, R. J. (2000). *Practical decision making in health care ethics: Cases and concepts* (2nd ed.). Washington, DC: Georgetown University Press.

Dochterman, J., & Bulechek, G. (2004). The nursing interventions classification (NIC). St. Louis, MO: Mosby.

Dossey, B. M., & Guzzetta, C. E. (2000). Holistic nursing practice. In B. M. Dossey, L. Keegan, & C. E. Guzzetta (Eds.), *Holistic nursing: A handbook for practice* (3rd ed., pp. 5–26). Rockville, MD: Aspen.

Emanuel, L. A., Danis, M., Pearlman, R. A., & Singer, P. A. (1995). Advance care planning as a process: Structuring the discussions in practice. *American Geriatrics Society, 43,* 440–446.

Engelhardt, H. T. (1986). Suicide in the cancer patient. *Cancer, 36*(2), 105–109.

Eriksson, K. (1997). Understanding the world of the patient, the suffering human being: The new clinical paradigm from nursing to caring. *Advanced Practice Nursing Quarterly, 3*(1), 8–13.

Fesmire, S. (2003). *John Dewey and moral imagination.* Bloomington: Indiana University Press.

Finnerty, J. L. (1987). Ethics in rational suicide. *Critical Care Nursing Quarterly, 10*(2), 86–90.

Fohr, S. A. (1998). The double effect of pain medication: Separating myth from reality. *Journal of Palliative Medicine, 1,* 315–328.

Garrett, C. (2005). *Gut feelings: Chronic illness and the search for healing.* (At the Interface/Probing the Boundaries series, Vol. 16). Amsterdam: Rodopi.

Georges, J. J., & Grypdonck, M. (2002). Moral problems experienced by nurses when caring for terminally ill people: A literature review. *Nursing Ethics, 9*(2), 155–178.

Hester, D. M. (2003). Significance at the end of life. In G. McGee (Ed.), *Pragmatic bioethics* (2nd ed., pp. 121-136). London: Bradford Book, MIT.

Hoffman, K. B. (2007, June 1). Kevorkian news. Kevorkian out of prison after 8 years. *The Associated Press*. Retrieved August 11, 2007, from http://www.fansoffieger.com/kevonews.htm

International Council of Nurses. (2006). *The ICN code of ethics for nurses*. Geneva: Author. Retrieved April 10, 2007, from http://www.icn.ch/icncode.pdf

Joint Commission on Accreditation of Healthcare Organizations. (2007, May). The Joint Commission 2007 requirements related to the provision of culturally and linguistically appropriate health care. Retrieved August 11, 2007, from http://www.jointcommission.org/NR/rdonlyres/1401C2EF-62F0-4715-B28A-7CE7F0F20E2D/0/hlc_jc_stds.pdf

Jonsen, A. R., Siegler, M., & Winslade, W. J. (2006). *Clinical ethics* (6th ed.). New York: McGraw-Hill.

Jonsen, A. R., Veatch, R. M., & Walters, L. (1998). *Source book in bioethics*. Washington, DC: Georgetown University Press.

Kahn, D. L., & Steeves, R. H. (1986). The experience of suffering: Conceptual clarification and theoretical definition. *Journal of Advanced Nursing, 11*, 623–631.

Konishi, E., Davis, A. J., & Aiba, T. (2002). The ethics of withdrawing artificial food and fluid from terminally ill patients: An end-of-life dilemma for Japanese nurses and families. *Nursing Ethics, 9*(1), 7–19.

Kopala, B., & Burkhart, L. (2005). Ethical dilemma and moral distress: Proposed new NANDA diagnoses. *International Journal of Nursing Technologies and Classifications, 16*(1), 3–13.

Kopala, B., & Kennedy, S. L. (1998). Requests for assisted suicide: A nursing issue. *Nursing Ethics, 5*(1), 16–26.

Ladd, R. E., Pasquerella, L., & Smith, S. (2002). *Ethical issues in home health care*. Springfield, IL: Charles C. Thomas.

Lustig, A. (2003). End-of-life decisions: Does faith make a difference? *Commonweal, 130*(10), 7.

Lynne, D. (2005). Life and death tug of war—The whole Terri Schiavo story: 15-year saga of brain-injured woman no clear-cut, right-to-die case. *WorldNetDaily*. Retrieved April 20, 2007, from http://www.worldnetdaily.com/news/article.asp?ARTICLE_ID=43463

Maeve, M. K. (1998). Weaving a fabric or moral meaning: How nurses live with suffering and death. *Journal of Advanced Nursing, 27*, 1136–1142.

Mappes, T. A., & DeGrazia, D. (2001). *Biomedical ethics* (5th ed.). Boston: McGraw-Hill.

Marker, R. L. (2004). International Task Force on Euthanasia and Assisted Suicide. Assisted suicide: The continuing debate. Retrieved April 10, 2007, from http://www.internationaltaskforce.org/cd.htm

McStay, R. (2003). Terminal sedation: Palliative care for intractable pain, post Glucksberg and Quill. *American Journal of Law and Medicine, 29*, 45–76.

Miller, K. E., Miller, M. M., & Jolley, M. R. (2001). Challenges in pain management at the end of life. *American Family Physician, 64*(7), 1227–1234.

Moorhead, S., Johnson, M., & Maas, M. (2004). *The nursing outcomes classification (NOC)*. St. Louis, MO: Mosby.

Morse, J. A., Beres, M. A., Spiers, J. A., Mayan, M., & Olson, K. (2003). Identifying signals of suffering by linking verbal and facial cues. *Qualitative Health Research, 13*(8), 1063–1077.

Munson, R. (2004). *Intervention and reflection: Basic issues in medical ethics* (7th ed.). Victoria, Australia: Wadsworth-Thomson.

NANDA International. (2007). *Nursing diagnoses: Definitions and classification 2007–2008* (7th ed.). Philadelphia: Author.

Narayanasamy, A. (1999). ASSET: A model for actioning spirituality and spiritual care education and training in nursing. *Nurse Education Today, 19*, 274–285.

National Council of State Boards of Nursing. (2007). *NCLEX-RN examination: Test plan for the National Council Licensure Examination for Registered Nurses.* Chicago: Author.

Olick, R. S. (2001). *Taking advance directives seriously: Prospective autonomy and decisions near the end of life.* Washington, DC: Georgetown University Press.

O'Rourke, K. (2002). *A primer for health care ethics: Essays for a pluralistic society* (2nd ed.). Washington, DC: Georgetown University Press.

President's Commission for the Study of Ethical Problems in Medicine and Biomedical and Behavioral Research. (1981, July). *Defining death: Medical, legal, and ethical issues in the determination of death.* Washington, DC: Government Printing Office.

Public Broadcasting System & WGBH/*Frontline*. (1998). The Kevorkian verdict: The chronology of Dr. Jack Kevorkian's life and assisted suicide campaign. Retrieved April 10, 2007, from http://www.pbs.org/wgbh/pages/frontline/kevorkian/chronology.html

Quill, T. E. (2001). *Caring for patients at the end of life: Facing an uncertain future together.* New York: Oxford University.

Rich, K. L., & Butts, J. B. (2004). Rational suicide: Uncertain moral ground. *Journal of Advanced Nursing, 46*(3), 270–283.

Rodgers, B. L., & Cowles, K. V. (1997). A conceptual foundation for human suffering in nursing care and research. *Journal of Advanced Nursing, 25*, 1048–1053.

Schneiderman, L. J. (1994). Medical futility and aging: Ethical implications. *Generations, 18*(4), 61–64.

Siegel, K. (1986). Psychosocial aspects of rational suicide. *American Journal of Psychotherapy, 40*(3), 405–418.

Spiegel, D. (1993). *Detoxifying dying. Living beyond limits: New hope and help for facing life-threatening illness.* New York: Random House, Times Books.

Stephenson, P. L., & Draucker, C. B. (2003). The experience of spirituality in the lives of hospice patients. *Journal of Hospice and Palliative Nursing, 5*(1), 51–58.

Sugarman, J. (2000). *20 common problems: Ethics in primary care.* New York: McGraw-Hill.

Supreme Court of Missouri. (1990). Cruzan by Cruzan v. Missouri Department of Health [497 U.S. 261]. Reprinted and summarized (n.d.) by Cornell University Law School. Retrieved August 11, 2007, from the Cornell University Law School Web site at http://www.law.cornell.edu/supct/html/historics/USSC_CR_0497_0261_ZS.html

Supreme Court of New Jersey. (1976). In re Quinlan—In the matter of Karen Ann Quinlan, an alleged incompetent [70 N.J. 10; 355 A.2d 647; 1976 N.J. LEXIS 181; 79 A.L.R.3d205]. Lexus-Nexus, a division of Elsevier Reed. Reprinted 1999 by The University of Wisconsin. Retrieved August 11, 2007, from http://philosophy.wisc.edu/streiffer/BioandLawF99Folder/Readings/In_re_Quinlan.pdf

Taylor, E. J. (2002). *Spiritual care: Nursing theory, research, and practice.* Upper Saddle River, NJ: Prentice Hall.

Taylor, E. J. (2003). Nurses caring for the spirit: Patients with cancer and family caregiver expectations. *Oncology Nursing Forum, 30*(4), 585–590.

U.S. District Court for the Middle District of Florida Tampa Division. (2005, March 21). *Theresa Marie Schindler Schiavo and ex relatione Robert Schlinder and Mary Schindler (plaintiffs) v. Michael Schiavo, Judge George W. Greer, and The Hospice of the Florida Suncoast, Inc. (defendants).*

(Civ. Act. No. 8:05-CV-530-T-27TBM). Retrieved April 20, 2007, from http://fl1.findlaw.com/news.findlaw.com/hdocs/docs/schiavo/hus32105opp.pdf

van Hooft, S. (2000). The suffering body. *Health, 4*(2), 179–195.

van Hooft, S. (2006). *Caring about health* (Ashgate Studies in Applied Ethics series). Burlington, VT: Ashgate.

Veatch, R. M. (2003). *The basics of bioethics* (2nd ed.). Upper Saddle River, NJ: Prentice Hall.

Walter, T. (2003). Historical and cultural variants on the good death. *British Medical Journal, 327*, 218–220.

World Health Organization. (2005). Suicides on the rise: World mental health day 10 October. Retrieved April 10, 2007, from http://www.wpro.who.int/media_centre/press_releases/pr_20011009.htm

World Health Organization. (2007a). WHO definition of palliative care. Retrieved April 10, 1007, from http://www.who.int/cancer/palliative/definition/en/print.html

World Health Organization. (2007b). WHO's pain ladder. Retrieved April 10, 2007, from http://www.who.int/cancer/palliative/painladder/en/

Wright, S. (2006). The heart of nursing. *Nursing Standard, 20*(47), 20–23.

Yalom, I. D. (1980). *Existential psychotherapy.* New York. Basic.

Youngner, S. J., & Arnold, R. M. (2001). Philosophical debates about the definition of death: Who cares? *Journal of Medicine and Philosophy, 26*(5), 527–537.

CHAPTER 12 QUESTIONS

1. How would the nurse, based on Aristotle's and others' views, differentiate human suffering from pain?
   a. Suffering and pain are subjective symptoms only, and therefore nurses cannot judge the difference between the two concepts.
   b. Suffering involves having suffering, being suffering, and becoming suffering and pain involves only a subjective statement of what the patient says that it is.
   c. Pain affects the biological aspect of a human, which in turn could affect the human fulfillment or capacity, and suffering is as objective as it is subjective and affects every aspect of the being.
   d. Pain steals joy, contentment, and happiness from a rational person and suffering does not.

2. All of the following items generally indicate desires by dying patients *except:*
   a. to be cared for by a competent nurse.
   b. to have pain and suffering relieved as much as possible.
   c. to have a provider of care who makes all decisions regarding treatment and care.
   d. to have decision making using a collaborative approach with the family and health care team.

3. The proxy or surrogate is one who has the power to make health care decisions and consent to or refuse treatments for the dying patient *except* when:
   a. the provider assigned a surrogate family member.
   b. the patient is incompetent and needs someone to step in for decision making.
   c. the patient has asked a family member to be the surrogate.
   d. a court has appointed a proxy to make decisions.

4. Which one of the following items is correct regarding palliative care and treatment?
   a. Nurses need to be cautious of opiates and opiate-synthetic medications because of the addictive effects and respiratory depression that occurs with their use on dying and suffering patients.
   b. Nurses do not need to treat pain with opiates until patients have adequately explained why they need the medication.
   c. The WHO's pain ladder is a good way to manage pain in a step-by-step approach, but it is too rigid to be effective.
   d. Consider first whether the patient desires pain management or sedation to relieve pain.

5. Dr. Kevorkian, also known as Doctor Death, primarily carried out euthanasia for several years in the United States by applying:
   a. the principle of physician-assisted suicide at all times.
   b. a variation of principles including voluntary euthanasia, nonvoluntary euthanasia, and active euthanasia practices.
   c. only the principle of nonvoluntary euthanasia.
   d. the principles of passive euthanasia and mercy.

6. What standard served primarily as the basis for all of the courts' rulings in the Schiavo case?
   a. Principle of autonomy extended.
   b. Substituted judgment standard.
   c. Best interests standard.
   d. Medical futility standard.

7. Which one of the following practice situations would cause the most moral distress for the nurse?
   a. Giving the dying patient opiates for pain and suffering relief, but about 30 minutes later the patient's respirations stopped and the patient passed away.

    b. Not resuscitating a patient with a DNR order.

    c. Discontinuing artificial nutrition and hydration when the patient had not left an advance directive.

    d. "Unplugging" the mechanical ventilator with the stipulation that family members requested this procedure based on an advance directive and the patient had a completely flat EEG two different times within a 24-hour period.

CHAPTER 12 ANSWERS

1. c
2. c
3. a
4. d
5. b
6. b
7. c

Code of Ethics for Nurses with Interpretive Statements

Preface

Ethics is an integral part of the foundation of nursing. Nursing has a distinguished history of concern for the welfare of the sick, injured and vulnerable and for social justice. This concern is embodied in the provision of nursing care to individuals and the community. Nursing encompasses the prevention of illness, the alleviation of suffering, and the protection, promotion and restoration of health in the care of individuals, families, groups and communities. Nurses act to change those aspects of social structures that detract from health and well-being. Individuals who become nurses are expected not only to adhere to the ideals and moral norms of the profession but also to embrace them as a part of what it means to be a nurse. The ethical tradition of nursing is self-reflective, enduring, and distinctive. A code of ethics makes explicit the primary goals, values, and obligations of the profession.

The Code of Ethics for Nurses serves the following purposes:

- It is a succinct statement of the ethical obligations and duties of every individual who enters the nursing profession.
- It is the profession's nonnegotiable ethical standard.
- It is an expression of nursing's own understanding of its commitment to society.

There are numerous approaches for addressing ethics; these include adopting or ascribing to ethical theories, including humanist, feminist, and social ethics, adhering to ethical principles, and cultivating virtues. The Code of Ethics for Nurses reflects all of these approaches. The words "ethical" and "moral" are used throughout the Code of Ethics. "Ethical" is used to refer to reasons for decisions about how one ought to act, using the above mentioned approaches. In general, the word "moral" overlaps with "ethical" but is more aligned with personal belief and cultural values. Statements that describe activities and attributes of nurses in this Code of Ethics are to be understood as normative or prescriptive statements expressing expectations of ethical behavior.

The Code of Ethics uses the term *patient* to refer to recipients of nursing care. The derivation of this word refers to "one who suffers," reflecting a universal aspect of human existence. Nevertheless, it is recognized that nurses also provide services to those seeking health as well as those responding to illness, to students and to staff, in health care facilities as well as in communities. Similarly, the term *practice* refers to the actions of the nurse in whatever role the nurse fulfills, including direct patient care provider, educator, administrator, researcher, policy developer, or other. Thus, the values and obligations expressed in this Code of Ethics applies to nurses in all roles and settings.

The Code of Ethics for Nurses is a dynamic document. As nursing and its social context change, changes to the Code of Ethics are also necessary. The Code of Ethics consists of two components: the provisions and the accompanying interpretive statements. There are nine provisions. The first three describe the most fundamental values and commitments of the nurse; the next three address boundaries of duty and loyalty, and the last three address aspects of duties beyond individual patient encounters. For each provision, there are interpretive statements that provide greater specificity for practice and are responsive to the contemporary context of nursing. Consequently, the interpetive statements are subject to more frequent revision than are the provisions. Additional ethical guidance and detail can be found in ANA or constituent member association position statements that address clinical, research, administrative, educational or public policy issues.

Code of Ethics for Nurses with Interpretive Statements provides a framework for nurses to use in ethical analysis and decision-making. The Code of Ethics establishes the ethical standard for the profession. It is not negotiable in any setting nor is it subject to revision or amendment except by formal process of the House of Delegates of the ANA. The Code of Ethics for Nurses is a reflection of the proud ethical heritage of nursing, a guide for nurses now and in the future.

Code of Ethics for Nurses with Interpretive Statements

1 The nurse, in all professional relationships, practices with compassion and respect for the inherent dignity, worth and uniqueness of every individual, unrestricted by considerations of social or economic status, personal attributes, or the nature of health problems.

1.1 Respect for human dignity

A fundamental principle that underlies all nursing practice is respect for the inherent worth, dignity, and human rights of every individual. Nurses take into account the needs and values of all persons in all professional relationships.

1.2 Relationships to patients

The need for health care is universal, transcending all individual differences. The nurse establishes relationships and delivers nursing services with respect for human needs and values, and without prejudice. An individual's lifestyle, value system and religious beliefs should be considered in planning health care with and for each patient. Such consideration does not suggest that the nurse necessarily agrees with or condones certain individual choices, but that the nurse respects the patient as a person.

1.3 The nature of health problems

The nurse respects the worth, dignity and rights of all human beings irrespective of the nature of the health problem. The worth of the person is not affected by disease, disability, functional status, or proximity to death. This respect extends to all who require the services of the nurse for the promotion of health, the prevention of illness, the restoration of health, the alleviation of suffering, and the provision of supportive care to those who are dying.

The measures nurses take to care for the patient enable the patient to live with as much physical, emotional, social, and spiritual well-being as possible. Nursing care aims to maximize the values that the patient has treasured in life and extends supportive care to the family and significant others. Nursing care is directed toward meeting the comprehensive needs of patients and their families across the continuum of care. This is particularly vital in the care of patients and their families at the end of life to prevent and relieve the cascade of symptoms and suffering that are commonly associated with dying.

Nurses are leaders and vigilant advocates for the delivery of dignified and humane care. Nurses actively participate in assessing and assuring the responsible and appropriate use of interventions in order to minimize unwarranted or unwanted treatment and patient suffering. The acceptability and importance of carefully considered decisions regarding resuscitation status, withholding and withdrawing life-sustaining therapies, forgoing medically provided nutrition and hydration, aggressive pain and symptom management and advance directives are increasingly evident. The nurse should provide interventions to relieve pain and other symptoms in the dying patient even when those interventions entail risks of hastening death. However, nurses may not act with the sole intent of ending a patient's life even though such action may be motivated by compassion, respect for autonomy and quality of life considerations. Nurses have invaluable experience, knowledge, and insight into care at the end of life and should be actively involved in related research, education, practice, and policy development.

1.4 The right to self-determination

Respect for human dignity requires the recognition of specific patient rights, particularly, the right of self-determination. Self-determination, also known as autonomy, is the philosophical basis for informed consent in health care. Patients have the moral and legal right to determine what will be done with their own person; to be given accurate, complete, and understandable information in a manner that facilitates an informed judgment; to be assisted with weighing the benefits, burdens, and available options in their treatment, including the choice of no treatment; to accept, refuse, or terminate treatment without deceit, undue influence, duress, coercion or penalty; and to be given necessary support throughout the decision-making and treatment process. Such support would include the opportunity to make decisions with family and significant others and the provision of advice and support from knowledgeable nurses and other health professionals. Patients should be involved in planning their own health care to the extent they are able and choose to participate.

Each nurse has an obligation to be knowledgeable about the moral and legal rights of all patients to self-determination. The nurse preserves, protects, and supports those interests by assessing the patient's comprehension of both the information presented and the implications of decisions. In situations in which the patient lacks the capacity to make a decision, a designated surrogate decision-maker should be consulted. The role of the surrogate is to make decisions as the patient would, based upon the patient's previously expressed wishes and known values. In the absence of a designated surrogate decision-maker, decisions should be made in the best interests of the patient, considering the patient's personal values to the extent that they are known. The nurse supports patient self-determination by participating in discussions with surrogates, providing guidance and referral to other resources as necessary, and identifying and addressing problems in the decision-making process. Support of autonomy in the broadest sense also includes recognition that people of some cultures place less weight on individualism and choose to defer to family or community values in decision making. Respect not just for the specific decision but also for the patient's method of decision making is consistent with the principle of autonomy.

Individuals are interdependent members of the community. The nurse recognizes that there are situations in which the right to individual self-determination may be outweighed or limited by the rights, health and welfare of others, particularly in relation to public health considerations. Nonetheless, limitation of individual rights must always be considered a serious deviation from the standard of care, justified only when there are no less restrictive means available to preserve the rights of others and the demands of justice.

1.5 Relationships with colleagues and others

The principle of respect for persons extends to all individuals with whom the nurse interacts. The nurse maintains compassionate and caring relationships with colleagues and others with a commitment to the fair treatment of individuals, to integrity-preserving compromise, and to resolving conflict. Nurses function in many roles, including direct care provider, administrator, educator, researcher and consultant. In each of these roles, the nurse treats colleagues, employees, assistants, and students with respect and compassion. This standard of conduct precludes any and all prejudicial actions, any form of harassment or threatening behavior, or disregard for the effect of one's actions on others. The nurse values the distinctive contribution of individuals or groups, and collaborates to meet the shared goal of providing quality health services.

2 The nurse's primary commitment is to the patient, whether an individual, family, group or community.

2.1 Primacy of the patient's interests

The nurse's primary commitment is to the recipient of nursing and health care services—the patient—whether the recipient is an individual, a family, a group, or a community. Nursing holds a fundamental commitment to the uniqueness of the individual patient; therefore, any plan of care must reflect that uniqueness. The nurse strives to provide patients with opportunities to participate in planning care, assures that patients find the plans acceptable and supports the implementation of the plan.

Addressing patient interests requires recognition of the patient's place in the family or other networks of relationship. When the patient's wishes are in conflict with others, the nurse seeks to help resolve the conflict. Where conflict persists, the nurse's commitment remains to the identified patient.

2.2 Conflict of interest for nurses

Nurses are frequently put in situations of conflict arising from competing loyalties in the workplace, including situations of conflicting expectations from patients, families, physicians, colleagues, and in many cases, health care organizations and health plans. Nurses must examine the conflicts arising between their own personal and professional values, the values and interests of others who are also responsible for patient care and health care decisions, as well as those of patients. Nurses strive to resolve such conflicts in ways that ensure patient safety, guard the patient's best interests and preserve the professional integrity of the nurse.

Situations created by changes in health care financing and delivery systems, such as incentive systems to decrease spending, pose new possibilities of conflict between economic self-interest and professional integrity. Bonuses, sanctions, and incentives tied to financial targets are examples of features of health care systems that may present such conflict. Conflicts of interest may arise in any domain of nursing activity including clinical practice, administration, education or research. Advance practice nurses who bill directly for services and nursing executives with budgetary responsibilities must be especially cognizant of the potential for conflicts of interest. Nurses should disclose to all relevant parties (e.g., patients, employers, colleagues) any perceived or actual conflict of interest and in some situations should withdraw from further participation. Nurses in all roles must seek to ensure that employment arrangements are just and fair and do not create an unreasonable conflict between patient care and direct personal gain.

2.3 Collaboration

Collaboration is not just cooperation, but it is the concerted effort of individuals and groups to attain a shared goal. In health care, that goal is to address the health needs of the patient and the public. The complexity of health care delivery systems requires a multi-disciplinary approach to the delivery of services that has the strong support and active participation of all the health professions. Within this context, nursing's unique contribution, scope of practice, and relationship with other health professions needs to be clearly articulated, represented and preserved. By its very nature, collaboration requires mutual trust, recognition, and respect among the health care team, shared decision making about patient care, and open dialogue among all parties who have an interest in and a concern for health outcomes. Nurses should work to assure that the relevant parties are involved and have a voice in decision-making about patient care issues. Nurses should see that the questions that need to be addressed are asked and that the information needed for informed decision-making is available and provided. Nurses should actively promote the collaborative multi-disciplinary planning required to ensure the availability and accessibility of quality health services to all persons who have needs for health care.

Intra-professional collaboration within nursing is fundamental to effectively addressing the health needs of patients and the public. Nurses engaged in non-clinical roles, such as administration or research, while not providing direct care, nonetheless are collaborating in the provision of care through their influence and direction of those who do. Effective nursing care is accomplished through the interdependence of nurses in differing roles—those who teach the needed skills, set standards, manage the environment of care, or expand the boundaries of knowledge used by the profession. In this sense, nurses in all roles share a responsibility for the outcomes of nursing care.

2.4 Professional boundaries

When acting within one's role of a professional, the nurse recognizes and maintains boundaries that establish appropriate limits to relationships. While the nature of nursing work has an inherently personal component, nurse-patient relationships and nurse-colleague relationships have, as their foundation, the purpose of preventing illness, alleviating suffering, and protecting, promoting, and restoring the health of patients. In this way, nurse-patient and nurse-colleague relationships differ from those that are purely personal and unstructured, such as friendship. The intimate nature of nursing care, the involvement of nurses in important and sometimes highly stressful life events, and the mutual dependence of colleagues working in close concert all present the potential for blurring of limits to professional relationships. Maintaining authenticity and expressing oneself as an individual, while remaining within the bounds established by the purpose of the relationship, can be especially difficult in prolonged or long-term relationships. In all encounters, nurses are responsible for retaining their professional boundaries. When these boundaries are jeopardized, the nurse should seek assistance from peers or supervisors or take appropriate steps to remove her/himself from the situation.

3 The nurse promotes, advocates for, and strives to protect the health, safety, and rights of the patient.

3.1 Privacy

The nurse safeguards the patient's right to privacy. The need for health care does not justify unwanted intrusion into the patient's life. The nurse advocates for an environment that provides for sufficient physical privacy, including auditory privacy for discussions of a personal nature and policies and practices that protect the confidentiality of information.

3.2 Confidentiality

Associated with the right to privacy, the nurse has a duty to maintain confidentiality of all patient information. The patient's well-being could be jeopardized and the fundamental trust between patient and nurse destroyed by unnecessary access to data or by the inappropriate disclosure of identifiable patient information. The rights, well-being, and safety of the individual patient should be the primary factors in arriving at any professional judgment concerning the disposition of confidential information received from or about the patient, whether oral, written or electronic. The standard of nursing practice and the nurse's responsibility to provide quality care require that relevant data be shared with those members of the health care team who have a need to know. Only information pertinent to a patient's treatment and welfare is disclosed, and only to those directly involved with the patient's care. Duties of confidentiality, however, are not absolute and may need to be modified in order to protect the patient, other innocent parties, and in circumstances of mandatory disclosure for public health reasons.

Information used for purposes of peer review, third-party payments, and other quality improvement or risk management mechanisms may be disclosed only under defined policies, mandates, or protocols. These written guidelines must assure that the rights, well-being, and safety of the patient are protected. In general, only that information directly relevant to the task or specific responsibility should be disclosed. When using electronic communications, special effort should be made to maintain data security.

3.3 Protection of participants in research

Stemming from the right to self-determination, each individual has the right to choose whether or not to participate in research. It is imperative that the patient or legally authorized surrogate receive sufficient information that is material to an informed decision, to comprehend that information, and to know how to discontinue participation in research without penalty. Necessary information to achieve an adequately informed consent includes the nature of participation, potential harms and benefits, and available alternatives to taking part in the research. Additionally, the patient should be informed of how the data will be protected. The patient has the right to refuse to participate in research or to withdraw at any time without fear of adverse consequences or reprisal.

Research should be conducted and directed only by qualified persons. Prior to implementation, all research should be approved by a qualified review board to ensure patient protection and the ethical integrity of the research. Nurses should be cognizant of the special concerns raised by research involving vulnerable groups, including children, prisoners, students, the elderly, and the poor. The nurse who participates in research in any capacity should be fully informed about both the subject's and the nurse's rights and obligations in the particular research study and in research in general. Nurses have the duty to question and, if necessary, to report and to refuse to participate in research they deem morally objectionable.

3.4 Standards and review mechanisms

Nursing is responsible and accountable for assuring that only those individuals who have demonstrated the knowledge, skill, practice experiences, commitment, and integrity essential to professional practice are allowed to enter into and continue to practice within the profession. Nurse educators have a responsibility to ensure that basic competencies are achieved and to promote a commitment to professional practice prior to entry of an individual into practice. Nurse administrators are responsible for assuring that the knowledge and skills of each nurse in the workplace are assessed prior to the assignment of responsibilities requiring preparation beyond basic academic programs.

The nurse has a responsibility to implement and maintain standards of professional nursing practice. The nurse should participate in planning, establishing, implementing, and evaluating review mechanisms designed to safeguard patients and nurses, such as peer review processes or committees, credentialing processes, quality improvement initiatives, and ethics committees. Nurse administrators must ensure that nurses have access to and inclusion on institutional ethics committees. Nurses must bring forward difficult issues related to patient care and/or institutional constraints upon ethical practice for discussion and review. The nurse acts to promote inclusion of appropriate others in all deliberations related to patient care.

Nurses should also be active participants in the development of policies and review mechanisms designed to promote patient safety, reduce the likelihood of errors, and address both environmental system factors and human factors that present increased risk to patients. In addition, when errors do occur, nurses are expected to follow institutional guidelines in reporting errors committed or observed to the appropriate supervisory personnel and for assuring responsible disclosure of errors to patients. Under no circumstances should the nurse participate in, or condone through silence, either an attempt to hide an error or a punitive response that serves only to fix blame rather than correct the conditions that led to the error.

3.5 Acting on questionable practice

The nurse's primary commitment is to the health, well-being, and safety of the patient across the life span and in all settings in which health care needs are addressed. As an advocate for the patient, the nurse must be alert to and take appropriate action regarding any instances of incompetent, unethical, illegal, or impaired practice by any member of the health care team or the health care system or any action on the part of others that places the rights or best interests of the patient in jeopardy. To function effectively in this role, nurses must be knowledgeable about the Code of Ethics, standards of practice of the profession, relevant federal, state and local laws and regulations, and the employing organization's policies and procedures.

When the nurse is aware of inappropriate or questionable practice in the provision or denial of health care, concern should be expressed to the person carrying out the questionable practice. Attention should be called to the possible detrimental effect upon the patient's well-being or best interests as well as the integrity of nursing practice. When factors in the health care delivery system or health care organization threaten the welfare of the patient, similar action should be directed to the responsible administrator. If indicated, the problem should be reported to an appropriate higher authority within the institution or agency, or to an appropriate external authority.

There should be established processes for reporting and handling incompetent, unethical, illegal, or impaired practice within the employment settings so that such reporting can go through official channels, thereby reducing the risk of reprisal against the reporting nurse. All nurses have a responsibility to assist those who identify potentially questionable practice. State nurses associations should be prepared to provide assistance and support in the development and evaluation of such processes and reporting procedures. When incompetent, unethical, illegal or impaired practice is not corrected within the employment setting and continues to jeopardize patient well-being and safety, the problem should be reported to other appropriate authorities such as practice committees of the pertinent professional organizations, the legally constituted bodies concerned with licensing of specific categories of health workers and professional practitioners, or the regulatory agencies concerned with evaluating standards of practice. Some situations may warrant the concern and involvement of all such groups. Accurate reporting and factual documentation, and not merely opinion, undergird all such responsible actions. When a nurse chooses to engage in the act of responsible reporting about situations that are perceived as unethical, incompetent, illegal or impaired, the professional organization has a responsibility to provide the nurse with support and assistance and to protect the practice of those nurses who choose to voice their concerns. Reporting unethical, illegal, incompetent, or impaired practices, even when done appropriately, may present substantial risks to the nurse; nevertheless, such risks do not eliminate the obligation to address serious threats to patient safety.

3.6 Addressing impaired practice

Nurses must be vigilant to protect the patient, the public and the profession from potential harm when a colleague's practice, in any setting, appears to be impaired. The nurse extends compassion and caring to colleagues who are in recovery from illness or when illness interferes with job performance. In a situation where a nurse suspects another's practice may be impaired, the nurse's duty is to take action designed both to protect patients and to assure that the impaired individual receives assistance in regaining optimal function. Such action should usually begin with consulting supervisory personnel and may also include confronting the individual in a supportive manner and with the assistance of others or helping the individual to access appropriate resources. Nurses are encouraged to follow guidelines outlined by the profession and policies of the employing organization to assist colleagues whose job performance may be adversely affected by mental or physical illness or by personal circumstances. Nurses in all roles should advocate for colleagues whose job performance may be impaired to ensure that they receive appropriate assistance, treatment and access to fair institutional and legal processes. This includes supporting the return to practice of the individual who has sought assistance and is ready to resume professional duties.

If impaired practice poses a threat or danger to self or others, regardless of whether the individual has sought help, the nurse must take action to report the individual to persons authorized to address the problem. Nurses who advocate for others whose job performance creates a risk for harm should be protected from negative consequences. Advocacy may be a difficult process and the nurse is advised to follow workplace policies. If workplace policies do not exist or are inappropriate—that is, they deny the nurse in question access to due legal process or demand resignation—the reporting nurse may obtain guidance from the professional association, state peer assistance programs, employee assistance program or a similar resource.

4 *The nurse is responsible and accountable for individual nursing practice and determines the appropriate delegation of tasks consistent with the nurse's obligation to provide optimum patient care.*

4.1 Acceptance of accountability and responsibility

Individual registered nurses bear primary responsibility for the nursing care that their patients receive and are individually accountable for their own practice. Nursing practice includes direct care activities, acts of delegation, and other responsibilities such as teaching, research, and administration. In each instance the nurse retains accountability and responsibility for the quality of practice and for confirmity with standards of care.

Nurses are faced with decisions in the context of the increased complexity and changing patterns in the delivery of health care. As the scope of nursing practice changes, the nurse must exercise judgment in accepting responsibilities, seeking consultation, and assigning activities to others who carry out nursing care. For example, some advanced practice nurses have the authority to issue prescription and treatment orders to be carried out by other nurses. These acts are not acts of delegation. Both the advanced practice nurse issuing the order and the nurse accepting the order are responsible for the judgments made and accountable for the actions taken.

4.2 Accountability for nursing judgment and action

Accountability means to be answerable to oneself and others for one's own actions. In order to be accountable, nurses act under a code of ethical conduct that is grounded in the moral principles of fidelity and respect for the dignity, worth, and self-determination of patients. Nurses are accountable for judgments made and actions taken in the course of nursing practice, irrespective of health care organizations' policies or providers' directives.

4.3 Responsibility for nursing judgment and action

Responsibility refers to the specific accountability or liability associated with the performance of duties of a particular role. Nurses accept or reject specific role demands based upon their education, knowledge, competence, and extent of experience. Nurses in administration, education and research also have obligations to the recipients of nursing care. Although nurses in administration, education and research have relationships with patients that are less direct, in assuming the responsibilities of a particular role, they share responsibility for the care provided by those whom they supervise and instruct. The nurse must not engage in practices prohibited by law or delegate activities to others that are prohibited by the practice acts of other health care providers.

Individual nurses are responsible for assessing his or her own competence. When the needs of the patient are beyond the qualifications and competencies of the nurse, consultation and collaboration must be sought from qualified nurses, other health professionals, or other appropriate sources. Educational resources should be sought by nurses and provided by institutions to maintain and advance the competence of nurses. Nurse educators act in collaboration with their students to assess the learning needs of the student, the effectiveness of the teaching program, the identification and utilization of appropriate resources, and the support needed for the learning process.

4.4 Delegation of nursing activities

Since the nurse is accountable for the quality of nursing care given to patients, nurses are accountable for the assignment of nursing responsibilities to other nurses and the delegation of nursing care activities to other health care workers. While delegation and assignment are used here in a generic moral sense, it is understood that individual states may have a particular legal definition of these terms.

The nurse must make reasonable efforts to assess individual competency when assigning selected components of nursing care to other health care workers. This assessment involves evaluating the knowledge, skills, and experience of the individual to whom the care is assigned, the complexity of the assigned tasks, and the health status of the patient. The nurse is also responsible for monitoring the activities of these individuals and evaluating the quality of the care provided. Nurses may not delegate responsibilities such as assessment and evaluation; they may delegate tasks. The nurse must not knowingly assign or delegate to any member of the nursing team a task for which that person is not prepared or qualified. Employer policies or directives do not relieve the nurse of responsibility for making judgments about the delegation and assignment of nursing care tasks.

Nurses functioning in management or administrative roles have a particular responsibility to provide an environment that supports and facilitates appropriate assignment and delegation. This includes providing appropriate orientation to staff, assisting less experienced nurses in developing necessary skills and competencies, and establishing policies and procedures that protect both the patient and nurse from the inappropriate assignment or delegation of nursing responsibilities, activities, or tasks.

Nurses functioning in educator or preceptor roles may have less direct relationships with patients. However, through assignment of nursing care activities to learners they share responsibility and accountability for the care provided. It is imperative that the knowledge and skills of the learner be sufficient to provide the assigned nursing care and that appropriate supervision be provided to protect both the patient and the learner.

5 *The nurse owes the same duties to self as to others, including the responsibility to preserve integrity and safety, to maintain competence, and to continue personal and professional growth.*

5.1 Moral self-respect

Moral respect accords moral worth and dignity to all human beings irrespective of their personal attributes or life situation. Such respect extends to oneself as well; the same duties that we owe to others we owe to ourselves. Self-regarding duties refer to a realm of duties that primarily concern oneself and include professional growth and maintenance of competence, preservation of wholeness of character, and personal integrity.

5.2 Professional growth and maintenance of competence

Though it has consequences for others, maintenance of competence and ongoing professional growth involves the control of one's own conduct in a way that is primarily self-regarding. Competence affects one's self-respect, self-esteem, professional status, and the meaningfulness of work. In all nursing roles, evaluation of one's own performance, coupled with peer review, is a means by which nursing practice can be held to the highest standards. Each nurse is responsible for participating in the development of criteria for evaluation of practice and for using those criteria in peer and self-assessment.

Continual professional growth, particularly in knowledge and skill, requires a commitment to lifelong learning. Such learning includes, but is not limited to, continuing education, networking with professional colleagues, self-study, professional reading, certification, and seeking advanced degrees. Nurses are required to have knowledge relevant to the current scope and standards of nursing practice, changing issues, concerns, controversies, and ethics. Where the care required is outside the competencies of the individual nurse, consultation should be sought or the patient should be referred to others for appropriate care.

5.3 Wholeness of character

Nurses have both personal and professional identities that are neither entirely separate, nor entirely merged, but are integrated. In the process of becoming a professional, the nurse embraces the values of the profession, integrating them with personal values. Duties to self involve an authentic expression of one's own moral point-of-view in practice. Sound ethical decision making requires the respectful and open exchange of views between and among all individuals with relevant interests. In a community or moral discourse, no one person's view should automatically take precedence over that of another. Thus the nurse has a responsibility to express moral perspectives, even when they differ from those of others, and even when they might not prevail.

This wholeness of character encompasses relationships with patients. In situations where the patient requests a personal opinion from the nurse, the nurse is generally free to express an informed personal opinion as long as this preserves the voluntariness of the patient and maintains appropriate professional and moral boundaries. It is essential to be aware of the potential for undue influence attached to the nurse's professional role. Assisting patients to clarify their own values in reaching informed decisions may be helpful in avoiding unintended persuasion. In situations where nurses' responsibilities include care for those whose personal attributes, condition, lifestyle, or situation is stigmatized by the community and are personally unacceptable, the nurse still renders respectful and skilled care.

5.4 Preservation of integrity

Integrity is an aspect of wholeness of character and is primarily a self-concern of the individual nurse. An economically constrained health care environment presents the nurse with particularly troubling threats to integrity. Threats to integrity may include a request to deceive a patient, to withhold information, or to falsify records, as well as verbal abuse from patients or coworkers. Threats to integrity may also include an expectation that the nurse will act in a way that is inconsistent with the values or ethics of the profession, or more specifically a request that is in direct violation of the Code of Ethics. Nurses have a duty to remain consistent with both their personal and professional values and to accept compromise only to the degree that it remains an integrity-preserving compromise. An integrity-preserving compromise does not jeopardize the dignity or well-being of the nurse or others. Integrity-preserving compromise can be difficult to achieve, but is more likely to be accomplished in situations where there is an open forum for moral discourse and an atmosphere of mutal respect and regard.

Where nurses are placed in situations of compromise that exceed acceptable moral limits or involve violations of the moral standards of the profession, whether in direct patient care or in any other forms of nursing practice, they may express their conscientious objection to participation. Where a particular treatment, intervention, activity, or practice is morally objectionable to the nurse, whether intrinsically so or because it is inappropriate for the specific patient, or where it may jeopardize both patients and nursing practice, the nurse is justified in refusing to participate on moral grounds. Such grounds exclude personal preference, prejudice, convenience or arbitrariness. Conscientious objection may not insulate the nurse against formal or informal penalty. The nurse who decides not to take part because of conscientious objection must communicate this decision in appropriate ways. Whenever possible, such a refusal should be made known in advance and in time for alternate arrangements to be made for patient care. The nurse is obliged to provide for the patient's safety, to avoid abandonment, and to withdraw only when assured that alternative sources of nursing care are available to the patient.

Where patterns of institutional behavior or professional practice compromise the integrity of all its nurses, nurses should express their concern or conscientious objection collectively to the appropriate body or committee. In addition, they should express their concern, resist, and seek to bring about a change in those persistent activities or expectations in the practice setting that are morally objectionable to nurses and jeopardize either patient or nurse well being.

6 *The nurse participates in establishing, maintaining and improving health care environments and conditions of employment conducive to the provision of quality health care and consistent with the values of the profession through individual and collective action.*

6.1 Influence of the environment on moral virtues and values

Virtues are habits of character that predispose persons to meet their moral obligations; that is, to do what is right. Excellences are habits of character that predispose a person to do a particular job or task well. Virtues such as wisdom, honesty, and courage are habits or attributes of the morally good person. Excellences such as compassion, patience, and skill are habits of character of the morally good nurse. For the nurse, virtues and excellences are those habits that affirm and promote the values of human dignity, well-being, respect, health, independence, and other values central to nursing. Both virtues and excellences, as aspects of moral character, can be either nurtured by the environment in which the nurse practices or they can be diminished or thwarted. All nurses have a responsibility to create, maintain, and contribute to environments that support the growth of virtues and excellences and enable nurses to fulfill their ethical obligations.

6.2 Influence of the environment on ethical obligations

All nurses, regardless of role, have a responsibility to create, maintain, and contribute to environments of practice that support nurses in fulfilling their ethical obligations. Environments of practice include observable features, such as working conditions, and written policies and procedures setting out expectations for nurses, as well as less tangible characteristics such as informal peer norms. Organizational structures, role descriptions, health and safety initiatives, grievance mechanisms, ethics committees, compensation systems, and disciplinary procedures all contribute to environments that can either present barriers or foster ethical practice and professional fulfillment. Environments in which employees are provided fair hearing of grievances, are supported in practicing according to standards of care, and are justly treated allow the realization of the values of the profession and are consistent with sound nursing practice.

6.3 Responsibility for the health care environment

The nurse is responsible for contributing to a moral environment that encourages respectful interactions with colleagues, support of peers, and identification of issues that need to be addressed. Nurse administrators have a particular responsibility to assure that employees are treated fairly and that nurses are involved in decisions related to their practice and working conditions. Acquiescing and accepting unsafe or inappropriate practices, even if the individual does not participate in the specific practice, is equivalent to condoning unsafe practice. Nurses should not remain employed in facilities that routinely violate patient rights or require nurses to severely and repeatedly compromise standards of practice or personal morality.

As with concerns about patient care, nurses should address concerns about the health care environment through appropriate channels. Organizational changes are difficult to accomplish and may require persistent efforts over time. Toward this end, nurses may participate in collective action such as collective bargaining or workplace advocacy, preferably through a professional association such as the state nurses association, in order to address the terms and conditions of employment. Agreements reached through such action must be consistent with the profession's standards of practice, the state law regulating practice, and the Code of Ethics for Nursing. Conditions of employment must contribute to the moral environment, the provision of quality patient care, and professional satisfaction for nurses.

The professional association also serves as an advocate for the nurse by seeking to secure just compensation and humane working conditions for nurses. To accomplish this, the professional association may engage in collective bargaining on behalf of nurses. While seeking to assure just economic and general welfare for nurses, collective bargaining, nonetheless, seeks to keep the interests of both nurses and patients in balance.

7 *The nurse participates in the advancement of the profession through contributions to practice, education, administration, and knowledge development.*

7.1 Advancing the profession through active involvement in nursing and in health care policy

Nurses should advance their profession by contributing in some way to the leadership, activities, and the viability of their professional organizations. Nurses can also advance the profession by serving in leadership or mentorship roles or on committees within their places of employment. Nurses who are self-employed can advance the profession by serving as role models for professional integrity. Nurses can also advance the profession through participation in civic activities related to health care or through local, state, national, or international initiatives. Nurse educators have a specific responsibility to enhance students' commitment to professional and civic values. Nurse administrators have a responsibility to foster an employment environment that facilitates nurses' ethical integrity and professionalism, and nurse researchers are responsible for active contribution to the body of knowledge supporting and advancing nursing practice.

7.2 Advancing the profession by developing, maintaining, and implementing professional standards in clinical, administrative, and educational practice

Standards and guidelines reflect the practice of nursing grounded in ethical commitments and a body of knowledge. Professional standards and guidelines for nurses must be developed by nurses and reflect nursing's responsibility to society. It is the responsibility of nurses to identify their own scope of practice as permitted by professional practice standards and guidelines, by state and federal laws, by relevant societal values, and by the Code of Ethics.

The nurse as administrator or manager must establish, maintain, and promote conditions of employment that enable nurses within that organization or community setting to practice in accord with accepted standards of nursing practice and provide a nursing and health care work environment that meets the standards and guidelines of nursing practice. Professional autonomy and self-regulation in the control of conditions of practice are necessary for implementing nursing standards and guidelines and assuring quality care for those whom nursing serves.

The nurse educator is responsible for promoting and maintaining optimum standards of both nursing education and of nursing practice in any settings where planned learning activities occur. Nurse educators must also ensure that only those students who possess knowledge, skills and the competencies that are essential to nursing graduate from their nursing programs.

7.3 Advancing the profession through knowledge development, dissemination, and application to practice

The nursing profession should engage in scholarly inquiry to identify, evaluate, refine, and expand the body of knowledge that forms the foundation of its discipline and practice. In addition, nursing knowledge is derived from the sciences and from the humanities. Ongoing scholarly activities are essential to fulfilling a profession's obligations to society. All nurses working alone or in collaboration with others can participate in the advancement of the profession through the development, evaluation, dissemination, and application of knowledge in practice. However, an organizational climate and infrastructure conducive to scholarly inquiry must be valued and implemented for this to occur.

8 *The nurse collaborates with other health professionals and the public in promoting community, national, and international efforts to meet health needs.*

8.1 Health needs and concerns

The nursing profession is committed to promoting the health, welfare, and safety of all people. The nurse has a responsibility to be aware not only of specific health needs of individual patients, but also of broader health concerns such as world hunger, environmental pollution, lack of access to health care, violation of human rights, and inequitable distribution of nursing and health care resources. The availability and accessibility of high-quality health services to all people require both inter-disciplinary planning and collaborative partnerships among health professionals and others at the community, national, and international levels.

8.2 Responsibilities to the public

Nurses, individually and collectively, have a responsibility to be knowledgeable about the health status of the community and existing threats to health and safety. Through support of and participation in community organizations and groups, the nurse assists in efforts to educate the public, facilitates informed choice, identifies conditions and circumstances that contribute to illness, injury and disease, fosters healthy life styles, and participates in institutional and legislative efforts to promote health and meet national health objectives. In addition, the nurse supports initiatives to address barriers to health, such as poverty, homelessness, unsafe living conditions, abuse and violence, and lack of access to health services.

The nurse also recognizes that health care is provided to culturally diverse populations in this country and in all parts of the world. In providing care, the nurse should avoid imposition of the nurse's cultural values upon others. The nurse should affirm human dignity and show respect for the values and practices associated with different cultures and use approaches to care that reflect awareness and sensitivity.

9 *The profession of nursing, as represented by associations and their members, is responsible for articulating nursing values, for maintaining the integrity of the profession and its practice, and for shaping social policy.*

9.1 Assertion of values

It is the responsibility of a professional association to communicate and affirm the values of the profession to its members. It is essential that the professional organization encourages discourse that supports critical self-reflection and evaluation within the profession. The organization also communicates to the public the values that nursing considers central to social change that will enhance health.

9.2 The profession carries out its collective responsibility through professional associations

The nursing profession continues to develop ways to clarify nursing's accountability to society. The contract between the profession and society is made explicit through such mechanisms as (a) The Code of Ethics for Nurses, (b) the standards of nursing practice, (c) the ongoing development of nursing knowledge derived from nursing theory, scholarship, and research in order to guide nursing actions, (d) educational requirements for practice, (e) certification, and (f) mechanisms for evaluating the effectiveness of professional nursing actions,

9.3 Intraprofessional integrity

A professional association is responsible for expressing the values and ethics of the profession and also for encouraging the professional organization and its members to function in accord with those values and ethics, Thus, one of its fundamental responsibilities is to promote awareness of and adherence to the Code of Ethics and to critique the activities and ends of the professional association itself. Values and ethics influence the power structures of the association in guiding, correcting, and directing its activities. Legitimate concerns for the self-interest of the association and the profession are balanced by a commitment to the social goods that are sought. Through critical self-reflection and self-evaluation, associations must foster change within themselves, seeking to move the professional community towards its stated ideals.

9.4 Social reform

Nurses can work individually as citizens or collectively through political action to bring about social change. It is the responsibility of a professional nursing association to speak for nurses collectively in shaping and reshaping health care within our nation, specifically in areas of health care policy and legislation that affect accessibility, quality, and the cost of health care, Here, the professional association maintains vigilance and takes action to influence legislators, reimbursement agencies, nursing organizations, and other health professions, In these activities, health is understood as being broader than delivery and reimbursement systems, but extending to health-related sociocultural issues such as violation of human rights, homelessness, hunger, violence and the stigma of illness.

The ICN Code of Ethics for Nurses

The ICN Code of Ethics for Nurses

An international code of ethics for nurses was first adopted by the International Council of Nurses (ICN) in 1953. It has been revised and reaffirmed at various times since, most recently with this review and revision completed in 2005.

Preamble

Nurses have four fundamental responsibilities: to promote health, to prevent illness, to restore health and to alleviate suffering. The need for nursing is universal.

Inherent in nursing is respect for human rights, including cultural rights, the right to life and choice, to dignity and to be treated with respect. Nursing care is respectful of and unrestricted by considerations of age, colour, creed, culture, disability or illness, gender, sexual orientation, nationality, politics, race or social status. Nurses render health services to the individual, the family and the community and co-ordinate their services with those of related groups.

Copyright © 2006 by ICN—International Council of Nurses, 3, place Jean-Marteau, 1201 Geneva (Switzerland) ISBN: 92-95040-41-4 Printing: Imprimerie Fornara

The ICN Code

The *ICN Code of Ethics for Nurses* has four principal elements that outline the standards of ethical conduct.

Elements of the Code

1. Nurses and People

The nurse's primary professional responsibility is to people requiring nursing care.
In providing care, the nurse promotes an environment in which the human rights, values, customs and spiritual beliefs of the individual, family and community are respected.

The nurse ensures that the individual receives sufficient information on which to base consent for care and related treatment.

The nurse holds in confidence personal information and uses judgement in sharing this information.

The nurse shares with society the responsibility for initiating and supporting action to meet the health and social needs of the public, in particular those of vulnerable populations.

The nurse also shares responsibility to sustain and protect the natural environment from depletion, pollution, degradation and destruction.

2. Nurses and Practice

The nurse carries personal responsibility and accountability for nursing practice, and for maintaining competence by continual learning.

The nurse maintains a standard of personal health such that the ability to provide care is not compromised.

The nurse uses judgement regarding individual competence when accepting and delegating responsibility.

The nurse at all times maintains standards of personal conduct which reflect well on the profession and enhance public confidence.

The nurse, in providing care, ensures that use of technology and scientific advances are compatible with the safety, dignity and rights of people.

3. Nurses and the Profession

The nurse assumes the major role in determining and implementing acceptable standards of clinical nursing practice, management, research and education.

The nurse is active in developing a core of research-based professional knowledge.

The nurse, acting through the professional organisation, participates in creating and maintaining safe, equitable social and economic working conditions in nursing.

4. Nurses and Co-workers

The nurse sustains a co-operative relationship with co-workers in nursing and other fields.

The nurse takes appropriate action to safeguard individuals, families and communities when their health is endangered by a coworker or any other person.

Suggestions for Use of the *ICN Code of Ethics for Nurses*

The *ICN Code of Ethics for Nurses* is a guide for action based on social values and needs. It will have meaning only as a living document if applied to the realities of nursing and health care in a changing society.

To achieve its purpose the *Code* must be understood, internalised and used by nurses in all aspects of their work. It must be available to students and nurses throughout their study and work lives.

Applying the Elements of the *ICN Code of Ethics for Nurses*

The four elements of the *ICN Code of Ethics for Nurses*: nurses and people, nurses and practice, nurses and the profession, and nurses and co-workers, give a framework for the standards of conduct. The following chart will assist nurses to translate the standards into action. Nurses and nursing students can therefore:

- Study the standards under each element of the *Code*.
- Reflect on what each standard means to you. Think about how you can apply ethics in your nursing domain: practice, education, research or management.
- Discuss the *Code* with co-workers and others.
- Use a specific example from experience to identify ethical dilemmas and standards of conduct as outlined in the *Code*. Identify how you would resolve the dilemmas.
- Work in groups to clarify ethical decision making and reach a consensus on standards of ethical conduct.

■ Collaborate with your national nurses' association, co-workers, and others in the continuous application of ethical standards in nursing practice, education, management and research.

ELEMENT OF THE CODE # 1: NURSES AND PEOPLE

Practitioners and Managers

Provide care that respects human rights and is sensitive to the values, customs and beliefs of all people.

Provide continuing education in ethical issues.

Provide sufficient information to permit informed consent and the right to choose or refuse treatment.

Use recording and information management systems that ensure confidentiality.

Develop and monitor environmental safety in the workplace.

Educators and Researchers

In curriculum include references to human rights, equity, justice, solidarity as the basis for access to care.

Provide teaching and learning opportunities for ethical issues and decision making.

Provide teaching/learning opportunities related to informed consent.

Introduce into curriculum concepts of privacy and confidentiality.

Sensitise students to the importance of social action in current concerns.

National Nurses' Associations

Develop position statements and guidelines that support human rights and ethical standards.

Lobby for involvement of nurses in ethics review committees.

Provide guidelines, position statements and continuing education related to informed consent.

Incorporate issues of confidentiality and privacy into a national code of ethics for nurses.

Advocate for safe and healthy environment.

ELEMENT OF THE CODE # 2: NURSES AND PRACTICE

Practitioners and Managers

Establish standards of care and a work setting that promotes safety and quality care.

Establish systems for professional appraisal, continuing education and systematic renewal of licensure to practice.

Monitor and promote the personal health of nursing staff in relation to their competence for practice.

Educators and Researchers

Provide teaching/learning opportunities that foster life long learning and competence for practice.

Conduct and disseminate research that shows links between continual learning and competence to practice.

Promote the importance of personal health and illustrate its relation to other values.

National Nurses' Associations

Provide access to continuing education, through journals, conferences, distance education, etc.

Lobby to ensure continuing education opportunities and quality care standards.

Promote healthy lifestyles for nursing professionals.

Lobby for healthy workplaces and services for nurses.

ELEMENT OF THE CODE # 3: NURSES AND THE PROFESSION

Practitioners and Managers

Set standards for nursing practice, research, education and management.

Foster workplace support of the conduct, dissemination and utilisation of research related to nursing and health.

Promote participation in national nurses' associations so as to create favourable socio-economic conditions for nurses.

Educators and Researchers

Provide teaching/learning opportunities in setting standards for nursing practice, research, education and management.

Conduct, disseminate and utilise research to advance the nursing profession.

Sensitise learners to the importance of professional nursing associations.

National Nurses' Associations

Collaborate with others to set standards for nursing education, practice, research and management.

Develop position statements, guidelines and standards related to nursing research.

Lobby for fair social and economic working conditions in nursing. Develop position statements and guidelines in workplace issues.

ELEMENT OF THE CODE #4: NURSES AND CO-WORKERS

Practitioners and Managers

Create awareness of specific and overlapping functions and the potential for interdisciplinary tensions.

Develop workplace systems that support common professional ethical values and behaviour.

Develop mechanisms to safeguard the individual, family or community when their care is endangered by health care personnel.

Educators and Researchers

Develop understanding of the roles of other workers.

Communicate nursing ethics to other professions.

Instill in learners the need to safeguard the individual, family or community when care is endangered by health care personnel.

National Nurses' Associations

Stimulate co-operation with other related disciplines.

Develop awareness of ethical issues of other professions.

Provide guidelines, position statements and discussion fora related to safeguarding people when their care is endangered by health care personnel.

Dissemination of the *ICN Code of Ethics for Nurses*

To be effective the *ICN Code of Ethics for Nurses* must be familiar to nurses. We encourage you to help with its dissemination to schools of nursing, practising nurses, the nursing press and other mass media. The Code should also be disseminated to other health professions, the general public, consumer and policy-making groups, human rights organisations and employers of nurses.

Glossary of Terms Used in the *ICN Code of Ethics for Nurses*

Co-worker   Other nurses and other health and non-health related workers and professionals.

Co-operative relationships   A professional relationship based on collegial and reciprocal actions, and behaviour that aim to achieve certain goals.

Family   A social unit composed of members connected through blood, kinship, emotional or legal relationships.

Nurse shares with society   A nurse, as a health professional and a citizen, initiates and supports appropriate action to meet the health and social needs of the public.

Personal health   Mental, physical, social and spiritual wellbeing of the nurse.

Personal information   Information obtained during professional contact that is private to an individual or family, and which, when disclosed, may violate the right to privacy, cause inconvenience, embarrassment, or harm to the individual or family.

Related groups   Other nurses, health care workers or other professionals providing service to an individual, family or community and working toward desired goals.

International Council of Nurses
3, place Jean-Marteau
1201 Geneva, Switzerland
Tel. +41 (22) 908 01 00
Fax +41 (22) 908 01 01
email: icn@icn.ch
Web site: www.icn.ch
• CONSEIL INTERNATIONAL DES INFIRMIÈRES • CONSEJO INTERNACIONAL DE ENFERMERAS • INTERNATIONAL COUNCIL OF NURSES

American Hospital Association Management Advisory

A Patient's Bill of Rights

A Patient's Bill of Rights was first adopted by the American Hospital Association in 1973. This revision was approved by the AHA Board of Trustees on October 21, 1992.

Introduction

Effective health care requires collaboration between patients and physicians and other health care professionals. Open and honest communication, respect for personal and professional values, and sensitivity to differences are integral to optimal patient care. As the setting for the provision of health services, hospitals must provide a foundation for understanding and respecting the rights and responsibilities of patients, their families, physicians, and other caregivers. Hospitals must ensure a health care ethic that respects the role of patients in decision making about treatment choices and other aspects of their care. Hospitals must be sensitive to cultural, racial, linguistic, religious, age, gender, and other differences as well as the needs of persons with disabilities.

The American Hospital Association presents A Patient's Bill of Rights with the expectation that it will contribute to more effective patient care and be supported by the hospital on behalf of the institution, its medical staff, employees, and patients. The American Hospital Association encourages health care institutions to tailor this bill of rights to their patient community by translating and/or simplifying the language of this bill of rights as may be necessary to ensure that patients and their families understand their rights and responsibilities.

Bill of Rights

These rights can be exercised on the patient's behalf by a designated surrogate or proxy decision maker if the patient lacks decision-making capacity, is legally incompetent, or is a minor.

1. The patient has the right to considerate and respectful care.

2. The patient has the right to and is encouraged to obtain from physicians and other direct caregivers relevant, current, and understandable information concerning diagnosis, treatment, and prognosis.

   Except in emergencies when the patient lacks decision-making capacity and the need for treatment is urgent, the patient is entitled to the opportunity to discuss and request information related to the specific procedures and/or treatments, the risks involved, the possible length of recuperation, and the medically reasonable alternatives and their accompanying risks and benefits.

   Patients have the right to know the identity of physicians, nurses, and others involved in their care, as well as when those involved are students, residents, or other trainees. The patient also has the right to know the immediate and long-term financial implications of treatment choices, insofar as they are known.

3. The patient has the right to make decisions about the plan of care prior to and during the course of treatment and to refuse a recommended treatment or plan of care to the extent permitted by law and hospital policy and to be informed of the medical consequences of this action. In case of such refusal, the patient is entitled to other appropriate care and services that the hospital provides or transfer to another hospital. The hospital should notify patients of any policy that might affect patient choice within the institution.

4. The patient has the right to have an advance directive (such as a living will, health care proxy, or durable power of attorney for health care) concerning treatment or designating a surrogate decision maker with the expectation that the hospital will honor the intent of that directive to the extent permitted by law and hospital policy.

   Health care institutions must advise patients of their rights under state law and hospital policy to make informed medical choices, ask if the patient has an advance directive, and include that information in patient records. The patient has the right to timely information about hospital policy that may limit its ability to implement fully a legally valid advance directive.

5. The patient has the right to every consideration of privacy. Case discussion, consultation, examination, and treatment should be conducted so as to protect each patient's privacy.

6. The patient has the right to expect that all communications and records pertaining to his/her care will be treated as confidential by the hospital, except in cases such as suspected abuse and public health hazards when reporting is permitted or required by law. The patient has the right to expect that the hospital will emphasize the confidentiality of this information when it releases it to any other parties entitled to review information in these records.

7. The patient has the right to review the records pertaining to his/her medical care and to have the information explained or interpreted as necessary, except when restricted by law.

8. The patient has the right to expect that, within its capacity and policies, a hospital will make reasonable response to the request of a patient for appropriate and medically indicated care and services. The hospital must provide evaluation, service, and/or referral as indicated by the urgency of the case. When medically appropriate and legally permissible, or when a patient has so requested, a patient may be transferred to another facility. The institution to which the patient is to be transferred must first have accepted the patient for transfer. The patient must also have the benefit of complete information and explanation concerning the need for, risks, benefits, and alternatives to such a transfer.

9. The patient has the right to ask and be informed of the existence of business relationships among the hospital, educational institutions, other health care providers, or payers that may influence the patient's treatment and care.

10. The patient has the right to consent to or decline to participate in proposed research studies or human experimentation affecting care and treatment or requiring direct patient involvement, and to have those studies fully explained prior to consent. A patient who declines to participate in research or experimentation is entitled to the most effective care that the hospital can otherwise provide.

11. The patient has the right to expect reasonable continuity of care when appropriate and to be informed by physicians and other caregivers of available and realistic patient care options when hospital care is no longer appropriate.

12. The patient has the right to be informed of hospital policies and practices that relate to patient care, treatment, and responsibilities. The patient has the right to be informed of available resources for resolving disputes, grievances, and conflicts, such as ethics committees, patient representatives, or other mechanisms available in the institution. The patient has the right to be informed of the hospital's charges for services and available payment methods.

The collaborative nature of health care requires that patients, or their families/surrogates, participate in their care. The effectiveness of care and patient satisfaction with the course of treatment depend, in part, on the patient fulfilling certain responsibilities. Patients are responsible for providing information about past illnesses, hospitalizations, medications, and other matters related to health status. To participate effectively in decision making, patients must be encouraged to take responsibility for requesting additional information or clarification about their health status or treatment when they do not fully understand information and instructions. Patients are also responsible for ensuring that the health care institution has a copy of their written advance directive if they have one. Patients are responsible for informing their physicians and other caregivers if they anticipate problems in following prescribed treatment.

Patients should also be aware of the hospital's obligation to be reasonably efficient and equitable in providing care to other patients and the community. The hospital's rules and regulations are designed to help the hospital meet this obligation. Patients and their families are responsible for making reasonable accommodations to the needs of the hospital, other patients, medical staff, and hospital employees. Patients are responsible for providing necessary information for insurance claims and for working with the hospital to make payment arrangements, when necessary.

A person's health depends on much more than health care services. Patients are responsible for recognizing the impact of their life-style on their personal health.

Conclusion

Hospitals have many functions to perform, including the enhancement of health status, health promotion, and the prevention and treatment of injury and disease; the immediate and ongoing care and rehabilitation of patients; the education of health professionals, patients, and the community; and research. All these activities must be conducted with an overriding concern for the values and dignity of patients.

Patient Self-Determination Act

Mississippi Advance Health-Care Directive

Introduction

You have the right to make health care decisions, including decisions about nursing home care, for yourself. Under the law, a patient must consent to any treatment or care received. Generally, if you are a competent adult, you can give this consent for yourself. For you to give this consent, you should be told what the recommended procedure is, why it is recommended, what risks are involved with the procedure, and what the alternatives are.

If you are not able to make your own health care decisions, your advance directives can be used. An "advance directive" can be an Individual Instruction or a Power of Attorney for Health Care.

An "Individual Instruction" is a directive concerning a health care decision. An Individual Instruction can be written or oral. No specific format is required for Individual Instructions.

A "Power of Attorney for Health Care" ("PAHC") is a document through which you designate someone as your agent to make health care decisions for you if you are unable to make such decisions. The PAHC comes into play when you cannot make a health care decision, either because of a permanent or temporary illness or injury. The PAHC must specifically authorize your agent to make health care decisions for you and must contain the standard language set out in the law. This language is included in the form of the PAHC contained in the Form section at the back of this document. Otherwise, the PAHC can contain any instructions which you wish.

If you are unable to make a decision and have not given or prepared individual instructions or a PAHC, you may designate an adult of your choice, called a surrogate, to make health care decisions for you. If you do not appoint a surrogate, the members of your family may make decisions for you.

The law on making health care decisions and advance directives is discussed in this [document] in detail.

Please read the entire document.

Your Right Under Mississippi Law to Make Decisions Concerning Health Care

The Patient Self-Determination Act of 1990 (The "PSDA") is a federal law which imposes on the state and providers of health care—such as hospitals, nursing homes, hospices, home health agencies, and prepaid health care organizations—certain requirements concerning advance directives and an individual's rights under state law to make decisions concerning medical care. This [document] will discuss your rights under state law to make health care decisions and set out a description of the Mississippi law on advance directives.

- **What Are My Rights to Accept or Refuse Treatment or Care?**
  In general, you have the right to make health care decisions, including decisions about nursing home care, for yourself if you are 18 or older and are competent.

- **What Information Must I Be Told to Give My Consent?**
  The physician should explain to you the pertinent facts about your illness and the nature of the treatment in nontechnical terms which are understandable to you.

  The physician also should explain to you why the proposed treatment is recommended.

  The physician should inform you of all reasonable risks and material consequences or "side effects" associated with the proposed treatment.

  Finally, the physician must tell you about any other types of treatment which you could undergo instead. The nature, purpose, and reasonable risks and consequences of these treatments should be explained to you.

  With this information, you can then make your health care decision.

■ **What If I Am Unable to Make These Decisions?**

If you cannot make a health care decision because of incapacity, your advance directive, such as an Individual Instruction or Power of Attorney for Health Care, can be used. If you have not signed an advance directive, you may designate an adult of your choice, called a surrogate, to make the decision. If you do not have an advance directive and you have not designated a surrogate, a family member may make the decision for you. If you do not have an advance directive, have not designated a surrogate, and do not have a family member available to make a health care decision for you, then an adult who shows care and concern and who is familiar with your values may make health care decisions for you. If you do not have advance directives and do not have anyone to make health care decisions for you, then a court might have to make the decision for you.

■ **What Is an Advance Directive?**

The PSDA defines an "advance directive" as a written instruction, such as an Individual Instruction or Power of Attorney for Health Care, recognized under State law and relating to the provision of health care when the individual is incapacitated. Two types of advance directives are statutorily recognized in Mississippi: Individual Instruction and Power of Attorney for Health Care.

Individual Instruction

■ **What Is an Individual Instruction?**

An Individual Instruction means an individual's direction concerning a health care decision for the individual. The instruction may be oral or written. The instruction may be limited to take effect only if a specified condition arises.

■ **What Must the Individual Instruction Say?**

Mississippi law does not prescribe any particular format for individual instructions. However, the law does specify an acceptable format for those instructions which deal with End-of-Life Decisions, Artificial Nutrition and Hydration, and Relief from Pain. This form is Part 2 of the form at the back of this document.

■ **Where Should I Keep My Individual Instruction?**

You should provide a copy of your Individual Instruction to anyone you designate to make health care decisions for you and to your health care provider. Your Individual Instruction should not be filed with the Mississippi Department of Health.

■ **How Can My Individual Instruction Be Revoked?**

The Individual Instruction is valid until revoked. You may revoke an Individual Instruction in any manner that indicates an intent to revoke.

■ **Will My Individual Instruction Be Followed?**

Your Individual Instruction must be honored by your agent, family, surrogate or health care provider.

For reasons of conscience, a physician, hospital, nursing home or other provider has the right to refuse to follow your Individual Instruction; but a provider not honoring your Individual Instruction must cooperate in your transfer to another provider who will follow your Individual Instruction.

Upon admission, you should receive a copy of the facility's policies concerning advance directives. You should review these policies and determine whether the facility will follow your Individual Instruction.

■ **Should I Give My Physician a Copy of My Individual Instruction?**

Yes. If you have a written Individual Instruction, you should give a copy to the physician who has primary responsibility for your health care. A copy also should be given to any other provider, such as a hospital, home health agency, or nursing home, from which you are receiving care.

Power of Attorney for Health Care

■ **What Is a Power of Attorney for Health Care?**

You may designate an individual or agent to make health care decisions for you if you are unable to make such a decision because of a permanent or temporary illness or injury. The document authorizing this action is the Power of Attorney for Health Care (PAHC).

■ **What Must the PAHC Contain?**

The PAHC must be properly witnessed, must specifically authorize your agent to make health care decisions for you, and must contain the standard language set out in the law. This language is included in the form of PAHC contained in the Form section at the back of this document.

Otherwise, the PAHC can contain any instructions which you wish.

- **What Should I Do with the PAHC?**
  The PAHC does not need to be filed with the Mississippi Department of Health or any court. You should keep the PAHC for yourself and give a copy to the agent you named in the PAHC.

  A copy should also be given to your physician to make a part of your medical records. You should also give a copy to any other provider from which you are receiving care, such as a nursing home, hospital, or a home health agency. You might also want to provide a copy to your clergy, family members, and friends who are not named in the documents.

- **Who Will Decide that I Cannot Act and My Agent Should Act for Me?**
  Unless otherwise specified in the PAHC, the physician designated by you or your agent to have primary responsibility for your health care will make this determination. In making this determination, your physician will act in accordance with "generally accepted health care standards."

- **Who Can Act as My Agent?**
  Unless related to you by blood, marriage, or adoption, your agent may not be an owner, operator, or employee of a residential long term care institution at which you are receiving care. Otherwise, any person, such as a family member or a friend, may act as the agent. The agent does not need to be a lawyer.

- **What Are the Powers of My Agent?**
  Your agent has whatever power you give in the PAHC to make health care decisions for you. "Making health care decisions" means a decision regarding your health care, including the selection and discharge of health care providers and institutions; approval and disapproval of diagnostic tests, surgical procedures, medications, and orders not to resuscitate; and direction to provide, withhold, or withdrew artificial nutrition and hydration.

- **Are There Limitations on the Power of My Agent?**
  Your agent has a duty to act according to what you put in the PAHC or as you otherwise have made known to him or her. If your desires are unknown, he or she must act in your best interest. Your agent cannot make a particular health care decision for you if you are able to make that decision.

- **What If Someone Other than the Agent Wants to Make Health Care Decisions for Me?**
  Unless the PAHC says otherwise, your agent has priority over any other person to act for you.

- **Will a Health Care Provider Recognize My Agent's Authority?**
  In general, yes.

  Upon admission, you should receive a copy of the facility's policies on advance directives. You should review these policies and determine whether the facility will follow your PAHC.

- **Can My PAHC Be Changed?**
  You can change your agent by a signed writing, or you can revoke the authority for your agent to make decisions by personally informing your primary physician or the health care provider who has undertaken primary responsibility for your health care.

General

- **What If I Have an Individual Instructions or PAHC I Signed When Living in Another State?**
  To be binding, these documents must meet Mississippi law. Many out-of-state documents will not meet these requirements. The safest route is to execute new documents following the Mississippi statute.

- **Do I Need Both an Individual Instruction and PAHC?**
  No. You may include Individual Instructions in your PAHC.

- **What Other Documents Should Be Considered?**
  Individual Instructions and PAHC are the only documents recognized in Mississippi by statute. However, depending upon particular circumstances, the state may recognize other health care directives or indications of your desires concerning health care. You also should discuss these options with your lawyer.

- **Can I Let My Family Make These Decisions?**
  Members of your family may make decisions for you if you are unable to do so and have not left Individual Instructions or PAHC. Family members, however, might disagree among themselves or with the physician. In such instances, Individual Instructions or PAHC can help to clarify the decisions and who can make them.

- **When Will a Court Make This Decision?**
  As a last resort, if someone authorized to consent for you has refused or declined to do so and no other person known to be available is authorized to consent, a court may order treatment for you if you are not able to do so.

Advance Health Care Directive

Explanation

You have the right to give instructions about your own health care. You also have the right to name someone else to make health care decisions for you. This form lets you do either or both of these things. It also lets you express your wishes regarding the designation of your primary physician. If you use this form, you may complete or modify all or any part of it. You are free to use a different form.

Part 1 of this form is a power of attorney for health care. Part 1 lets you name another individual as agent to make health care decisions for you if you become incapable of making your own decisions or if you want someone else to make those decisions for you now, even though you are still capable. You may name an alternate agent to act for you if your first choice is not willing, able, or reasonably available to make decisions for you. Unless related to you, your agent may not be an owner, operator, or employee of a residential long term health care institution at which you are receiving care.

Unless the form you sign limits the authority of your agent, your agent may make all health care decisions for you. This form has a place for you to limit the authority of your agent. You need not limit the authority of your agent if you wish to rely on your agent for all health care decisions that may have to be made. If you choose not to limit the authority of your agent, your agent will have the right to:

- Consent or refuse consent to any care, treatment, service, or procedure to maintain, diagnose, or otherwise affect a physical or mental condition;
- Select or discharge health care providers and institutions;
- Approve or disapprove diagnostic tests, surgical procedures, programs of medication, and orders not to resuscitate; and
- Direct the provision, withholding, or withdrawal of artificial nutrition and hydration and all other forms of health care.

Part 2 of this form lets you give specific instructions about any aspect of your health care. Choices are provided for you to express your wishes regarding the provision, withholding, or withdrawal of treatment to keep you alive, including the provision of artificial nutrition and hydration, as well as the provision of pain relief. Space is provided for you to add to the choices you have made or for you to write out any additional wishes.

Part 3 of this form lets you designate a physician to have primary responsibility for your health care.

Part 4 of this form lets you authorize the donation of your organs at your death, and declares that this decision will supersede any decision by a member of your family.

After completing this form, sign and date the form at the end and have the form witnessed by one of the two alternative methods listed below. Give a copy of the signed and completed form to your physician, to any other health care providers you may have, to any health care institution at which you are receiving care, and to any health care agents you have named. You should talk to the person you have named as agent to make sure that he or she understands your wishes and is willing to take the responsibility.

You have the right to revoke this advance health care directive or replace this form at any time.

Part 1

Power of Attorney for Health Care

(1) *Designation of Agent:* I designate the following individual as my agent to make health care decisions for me.

(Name of individual you choose as agent)

(Address) (City) (State) (Zip code)

(Home phone) (Work phone)

Optional: If I revoke my agent's authority or if my agent is not willing, able or reasonably available to make a health care decision for me, I designate as my first alternate agent:

(Name of individual you choose as first alternate agent)

(Address) (City) (State) (Zip code)

(Home phone) (Work phone)

Optional: If I revoke the authority of my agent and first alternate or if neither is willing, able or reasonably available to make a health care decision for me, I designate as my second alternate agent:

_____

(Name of individual you choose as second alternate agent)

_____

(Address) (City) (State) (Zip code)

_____

(Home phone) (Work phone)

(2) *Agent's Authority*: My agent is authorized to make all health care decisions for me, including decisions to provide, withhold, or withdraw artificial nutrition and hydration and all other forms of health care to keep me alive, except as I state here:

_____

_____

_____

(add additional sheets if needed)

(3) *When Agent's Authority Becomes Effective*: My agent's authority becomes effective when my primary physician determines that I am unable to make my own health care decisions unless I mark the following box. If I mark this box [ ], my agent's authority to make health care decisions for me takes effect immediately.

(4) *Agent's Obligation*: My agent shall make health care decisions for me in accordance with this Power of Attorney for Health Care, any instructions I give in Part 2 of this form, and my other wishes to the extent known to my agent. To the extent my wishes are unknown, my agent shall make health care decisions for me in accordance with what my agent determines to be in my best interest. In determining my best interest, my agent shall consider my personal values to the extent known to my agent.

(5) *Nomination of Guardian*: If a guardian of my person needs to be appointed for me by a court, I nominate the agent designated in this form. If that agent is not willing, able, or reasonably available to act as guardian, I nominate the alternate agents whom I have named, in the order designated.

Part 2

Instructions for Health Care

If you are satisfied to allow your agent to determine what is best for you in making end-of-life decisions, you need not fill out this part of the form. If you do fill out this part of the form, you may strike any wording you do not want.

(6) *End-of-life Decisions*: I direct that my health care providers and others involved in my care provide, withhold, or withdraw treatment in accordance with the choice I have marked below:

[ ] (a) Choice Not To Prolong Life

I do not want my life to be prolonged if (i) I have an incurable and irreversible condition that will result in my death within a relatively short time, (ii) I become unconscious and, to a reasonable degree of medical certainty, I will not regain consciousness, or (iii) the likely risks and burdens of treatment would outweigh the expected benefits, or

[ ] (b) Choice to Prolong Life

I want my life to be prolonged as long as possible within the limits of generally accepted health care standards.

(7) *Artificial Nutrition and Hydration*: Artificial nutrition and hydration must be provided, withheld or withdrawn in accordance with the choice I have made in paragraph (6) unless I mark the following box. If I mark this box [ ], artificial nutrition and hydration must be provided regardless of my condition and regardless of the choice I have made in paragraph (6).

(8) *Relief from Pain:* Except as I state in the following space, I direct that treatment for alleviation of pain or discomfort be provided at all times, even if it hastens my death:

_____

_____

(9) *Other Wishes:* (If you do not agree with any of the optional choices above and wish to write your own, or if you wish to add to the instructions you have given above, you may do so here.):

I direct that:

_____

_____

_____

(Add any additional sheets if needed.)

Part 3

Primary Physician

(Optional)

(10) *I designate the following physician as my primary physician:*

_____
(Name of physician)

_____
(Address) (City) (State) (Zip code)

_____
(Phone) (Phone)

Optional: If the physician I have designated above is not willing or reasonably available to act as my primary physician, I designate the following physician as my primary physician:

_____
(Name of physician)

_____
(Address) (City) (State) (Zip code)

_____
(Phone) (Phone)

(11) *Effect of Copy*: A copy of this form has the same effect as the original.

(12) *Signatures:* Sign and date the form here:

_____ _____

(Date) (Sign your name)

_____ _____

(Address) (Print your name)

_____

(City) (State)

Part 4

Certificate of Authorization for Organ Donation

(Optional)

I, the undersigned, this _____day of _____, 20__, desire that my
_____organ(s) be made available after my demise
for:

(a) Any licensed hospital, surgeon or physician, for medical education, research, advancement of medical science, therapy or transplantation to individuals;

(b) Any accredited medical school, college or university engaged in medical education or research, for therapy, educational research or medical science purposes or any accredited school or mortuary science;

(c) Any person operating a bank or storage facility for blood, arteries, eyes, pituitaries, or other human parts, for use in medical education, research, therapy or transplantation to individuals;

(d) The donee specified below, for therapy or transplantation needed by him or her, do donate my _____ for that purpose to _____
(name) at _____
(address).

I authorize a licensed physician or surgeon to remove and preserve for use my
_____ for that purpose.

I specifically provide that this declaration shall supersede and take precedence over any decision by my family to the contrary.

Witnessed this _____ day of_____, 20_____.

_____
(donor)

_____
(address)

_____
(telephone)

_____
(witness)

_____
(witness)

(13) *Witnesses*: This Power of Attorney will not be valid for making health care decisions unless it is either (a) signed by two (2) qualified adult witnesses who are personally known to you and who are present when you sign or acknowledge your signature; or (b) acknowledged before a notary public in the state.

Alternative No. 1

Witness:

I declare under penalty of perjury pursuant to Section 97-9-61, Mississippi Code of 1972, that the principal is personally known to me, that the principal signed or acknowledged this Power of Attorney in my presence, that the principal appears to be of sound mind and under no duress, fraud or undue influence, that I am not the person appointed as agent by this document, and that I am not a health care provider, nor an employee of a health care provider or facility. I am not related to the principal by blood, marriage or adoption, and to the best of my knowledge, I am not entitled to any part of the estate of the principal upon the death of the principal under a will now existing or by operation of law.

_____
(Signature of witness) (Date)

_____
(Printed name of witness)

_____
(Street address City State Zip code)

Witness:

I declare under penalty of perjury pursuant to Section 97-9-61, Mississippi Code of 1972, that the principal is personally known to me, that the principal signed or acknowledged this Power of Attorney in my presence, that the principal appears to be of sound mind and under no duress, fraud or undue influence, that I am not the person appointed as agent by this document, and that I am not a health care provider, nor an employee of a health care provider or facility.

_____
(Signature of witness) (Date)

_____
(Printed name of witness) (Date)

_____
(Street address City State Zip code)

Alternative No. 2

State of_____

County of _____

On this the _____day of _____, in the year___, before me, _____ (insert name of notary public) appeared _____, personally known to me (or proved to me on the basis of satisfactory evidence) to be the person whose name is subscribed to this instrument, and acknowledged that he or she executed it. I declare under the penalty of perjury that the person whose name is subscribed to this instrument appears to be of sound mind and under no duress, fraud or undue influence.

Notary Seal:

_____
(Signature of Notary Public)

Index